PENGUIN BOOKS
REVENGE AND RECONCILIATION

Rajmohan Gandhi, born in 1935, has written, among other works, *Rajaji: A Life* (Penguin), *The Good Boatman: A Portrait of Gandhi* (Viking/Penguin), *Understanding the Muslim Mind* (Penguin) and *Patel: A Life*.

Currently, he is a professor with the Centre for Policy Research, New Delhi.

Revenge and Reconciliation
Understanding South Asian History

RAJMOHAN GANDHI

PENGUIN BOOKS

Penguin Books India (P) Ltd., 11 Community Centre, Panchsheel Park, New Delhi 110 017, India
Penguin Books Ltd., 27 Wrights Lane, London W8 5TZ, UK
Penguin Putnam Inc., 375 Hudson Street, New York, NY 10014, USA
Penguin Books Australia Ltd., Ringwood, Victoria, Australia
Penguin Books Canada Ltd., 10 Alcorn Avenue, Suite 300, Toronto, Ontario, MAV 3B2, Canada
Penguin Books (NZ) Ltd., Cnr Rosedale and Airborne Roads, Albany, Auckland, New Zealand

First published by Penguin Books India 1999

Under the auspices of the Centre for Policy Research, New Delhi
With support from the Friedrich Naumann Stiftung

Copyright © Rajmohan Gandhi 1999

10 9 8 7 6 5 4 3

Typeset in *Garamond* by SÜRYA, New Delhi
Printed at Chaman Enterprises, New Delhi

To South Asia's abruptly orphaned children and violently bereaved women and men.
To the memory of Eqbal Ahmad, 1933-99, foe of injustice, reconciler, and friend.

Contents

Contents

Preface

THOUGH I HAVE written biographies of influential figures in modern South Asia and taught modern Indian history for short terms, I do not see myself as a professional historian. If I have nonetheless ventured into the domain of historians, it is because the South Asian violence around me has impelled me to search for its historical roots. I have been driven, too, to search for reasons in history that have restrained feuding in the past and the present, for around me I have often also felt the magnanimity of accommodating or forgiving South Asians.

These urges to look for the springs of revenge and reconciliation were joined in my mind by other related questions about our past. For instance, does the Gita prescribe war? Does the Mahabharata constitute, as tradition holds, a Dharmashastra, a science of righteousness? Why did Buddhism and Jainism meet with comparative failure in India? If there are central impulses in Indian history, what are they?

What are the historical truths about castes and relations among them? What does history say about Hindus, Muslims and Sikhs and relations among them? About the impact, positive and negative, of British rule? About the impact of Gandhi? Of Nehru and Indira? Of Jinnah, Bhutto, Mujib, Pakistan's Zia and the Zia of Bangladesh, the Bandaranaikes and their rivals in Sri Lanka? Of the militants in the Punjab, Kashmir and the Northeast (India's and Sri Lanka's)? Again, why were South Asians seemingly lukewarm about the fiftieth year of independence?

Each question of this sort could warrant a separate book, if not more than one, but there was also a case, it seemed to me, for a simpler and a bolder study, one that would roam the large forest of Indian and South Asian history, including some of its trickiest branches, but armed with a compass of Revenge and Reconciliation.

I wanted to test a hypothesis that such a compass might contribute a little to an understanding of India's (and South Asia's) famed complexities—'Anything said about India is true, and so is its opposite'—and of India's historical conflicts.

In opting against a narrower and possibly over-prudent focus, I was also influenced by the need, at the end of our century, for a broad appraisal of South Asia's past and present, to supplement, God willing, what is being gained from close studies of fragments.

If the approach chosen has restricted the attention given to some of the issues listed above, it has also perhaps revealed a few of them in fresh colours. I would like to think that this study offers some new insights, but it does not unearth new facts. It seeks to read known 'facts' of South Asian history—episodes, beliefs, myths—in a different light, and from an underused angle.

This was not conceived as a feel-good book, though it contains items that will lend pride. I realize that its reading of some of our history's wellsprings may in places cause disappointment or even pain, a possibility that distresses me. I console myself with the thought that frankness is indispensable at the ending of a millennium.

*

As was the case with *The Good Boatman: A Portrait of Gandhi* (Viking 1995), this study is the outcome of a project of the Centre for Policy Research (CPR), New Delhi, with which I have been associated from the summer of 1992. I can never be grateful enough for CPR's facilities, opportunities and atmosphere. To CPR's President, Dr V.A. Pai Panandiker, I owe a large debt of gratitude; discussions over the last seven years with him and other scholars on the CPR Faculty, on the themes of this study and on other topics, have been of considerable profit to me.

The views expressed in this study are, however, mine, and not necessarily CPR's. I would also like to express my warm gratitude to Frederich Naumann Stiftung, New Delhi, which made a generous contribution to CPR towards this project.

Engaged by CPR to assist me with research, Rakesh Chaubey plied me with reams of material and also with valuable leads. His labours have been of considerable help in the creation of this book.

As always, my wife Usha has shared in this effort with research, faith and encouragement.

My biggest debts, however, are to the large number of authors, ancient and modern, living and dead, Indian and non-Indian, referred to in the text, who took me closer to South Asia's story, or to ideas that helped illumine that story. Their pages frequently instructed or moved me; their research supplied the bulk of this book's substance. If the pile I have made is ungainly or unstable, the stones borrowed from others cannot be to blame. But theirs is the credit if the pile 'says something.' I merely put the stones on top of one another, as a boy playing pitthoo might.

New Delhi, June 1999   **Rajmohan Gandhi**

Introduction

THIS STUDY IS the outcome of a recognition and an inquiry. The recognition, overdue as a century ends, is of the violence in India's past and present, and the inquiry is about the comparative strengths, in India's and South Asia's history, of the threads of revenge and reconciliation.

RECOGNITION

> Our motherland is calling for blood and we shall satiate the thirst of our mother with blood.[1]

So said Master Tara Singh, the chief of the Akali Dal, on 3 March 1947, six months before India's independence and Pakistan's creation. But India's earth seems to have demanded blood for a long time. A brief look at two spots, Delhi and Kurukshetra, can give a feel of the depth of violence in India's history.

Delhi

Not to reflect on history is hard if you happen to sit on a stand on the ramparts of Delhi's Red Fort on independence day, face a large crowd gathered on the grounds below you, and face also the city that Shah Jahan had recreated in the seventeenth century. It is harder if the independence day is the fiftieth.

On that day, 15 August 1997, I was thus sitting and musing, having been invited, for no fault of mine, to join the privileged ranks on the stand at the Red Fort heights. There were more than fifteen minutes before Prime Minister Inder Kumar Gujral would join us, unfurl the flag, and deliver the independence day speech, following an unbroken tradition started on 15 August 1947 by Prime Minister Jawaharlal Nehru.

Shah Jahan had built the fort where I sat, as well as the great mosque that stood on the horizon on my left, and also, right ahead of me, the Chandni Chowk, the street of rich shops that looked like an arrow shot from the middle of the Fort into the city.

But my eyes rested on the Sisganj Gurdwara, which rose, beyond the assembled crowd, on one side of Chandni Chowk. Sisganj Gurdwara, I knew, marked the spot where in 1675, i.e., 322 years earlier, Guru Tegh Bahadur, the ninth Guru of the Sikhs, had been executed.

Seated in a yoga posture, unarmed and showing no interest in fighting or pleading for his life, Guru Tegh Bahadur, I had read, was calm as he awaited the death blow. Peace had reigned on his face.

The imperial executioner swung his sword and swept off the Guru's head.

He was killed, I reminded myself that 15 August morning, almost exactly the way Drona had been killed in the Mahabharata. It was a thought that had often occurred to me.

For a while my mind went to a predecessor of Guru Tegh Bahadur, the fifth Guru, Arjan Dev, who, during the reign of Aurangzeb's grandfather, Emperor Jahangir, was killed in Lahore in 1606 on charges of blasphemy and high treason; to Guru Tegh Bahadur's young grandsons, the sons of Guru Gobind Singh, who were buried alive in Sirhind; and to Guru Gobind Singh's death by stabbing in Nanded, in Maratha country, in 1708.

I thought of Babur, the ancestor of the fort's builder, of the Central Asian Muslims who had captured Delhi before Babur, and of Prithviraj Chauhan, who had ruled over Delhi ahead of any of these.

However, it was to the Gurdwara in front of me and to the city of Delhi that my thoughts returned. *This city has seen blood*, I reminded myself. We are celebrating fifty years of independence, the PM will soon pour out his thoughts on the topic, but have we confronted the history, the blood-soaked history, of where we are sitting?

Delhi's history is crammed with dynasties. Its geographical location offered scope for rulers to control the subcontinent's east, west and south, and, at the same time, keep a fairly close eye on the passes in the northwest that external invaders had used. However, while it seemed ideal for ruling over and defending India, Delhi was also severely exposed, and especially vulnerable if attacked from several sides. So dynasties fell in Delhi as easily as they rose.

Though flattered, cursed, analysed and described over the centuries, and in recent times the subject of a television serial, the city remains to be properly understood. Perhaps we cannot understand Delhi without acknowledging the wounds to its soul—wounds caused by the sequence of killings on the soil of Delhi.

Whether some part of the Mahabharata bloodshed, or the bloodshed that inspired the Mahabharata story, took place in Delhi when the city was called Indraprastha may be a matter for conjecture.

All we seem to know is that the city of Indraprastha figures in the epic, as having been built by the Pandavas after a previous town, Khandavaprastha, had been burnt down by a forest fire, and that painted grey pottery of about tenth century BC—when, according to some, the Mahabharata war was fought—has been found in Indraprastha, the site of the Purana Qila.[2] A village called Inderpat, overlapping the grounds of the Purana Qila, existed until the beginning of this century.

*

But the following (illustrative) list of events in Delhi is indisputably historical:

1192 or 1193: Representing Shiabuddin Ghauri (Muhammad of Ghaur), Qutb-ud-din Aibak takes over Qila Rai Pithora, the fort of Prithviraj Chauhan, starting Muslim control over Delhi.

December 1398: Timur, son of the Central Asian steppes, sacks Delhi during Tughluq rule, kills a massive number of Delhiites and takes about 1,00,000 into slavery. 'For two months not a bird moved a wing in Delhi,'[3] and the 200-year-old 'Delhi Sultanate' of Turkic-Afghan Muslims enters its long period of decline.

1526: Having defeated Ibrahim Lodi in Panipat, Babur occupies Delhi and launches the Mughal dynasty.

1658: Aurangzeb orders the execution in the city of his older brother Dara Shukoh and of Dara's son.

1675: Execution at Chandni Chowk of Guru Tegh Bahadur.

Aurangzeb, son and successor to Shah Jahan, had authorized the sentence, and, prior to that, the Guru's arrest. The Guru had been moved by the coercion faced by Brahmins in Kashmir, who informed him through a deputation that the janeu, their sacred thread, was being snatched off their bodies, and they were being pressurized to accept Islam.

Aurangzeb thought he could keep his large empire together through zeal and firmness, which would appeal to the orthodox Sunnis influential in the Mughal establishment.

Though Guru Tegh Bahadur had assisted the Mughals in Assam,[4] he knew that his growing following was seen as potentially rebellious, and that he would risk death if he asked Delhi about the Brahmins of Kashmir.

Yet he chose to proceed to Delhi. On his way to the capital, he was arrested. Three of his followers, Mati Das, Dyal Das and Sati Das, were cruelly killed before Guru Tegh Bahadur's eyes. Then, on 11 November 1675, the Guru was brought to the Chandni Chowk spot and given a last chance to save his life by accepting Islam. He rejected the option. According to one author, Harbans Singh:

> Guru Tegh Bahadur allowed himself to be beheaded without uttering a groan. He remained wholly composed in face of the executioner's blow . . . There was no rancour or ill will towards anyone in the Guru's heart.[5]

Disregarding any fear of the Empire's officers, a few Mazhabi Sikhs, formerly Hindus of the Chuhra or sweeper caste, managed to secure the Guru's severed head and deliver it for honourable cremation to his son, Guru Gobind Singh.[6]

Pointing out that Guru Nanak, the first Sikh Guru, had declined the janeu that a Brahmin priest had brought for him, saying that he preferred a janeu of the spirit, or one made of compassion, self-control and truth, Harbans Singh adds that Guru Tegh Bahadur had nonetheless stood up 'for the rights of others.' He had sacrificed his 'life to secure [for others] the freedom of conscience.'[7]

According to Harbans Singh, the Guru's 'martyrdom was a superb act of self-giving . . . In the political milieu of that time, it was an act of extreme courage . . . [Through it] a new impulse of chivalry arose. Men felt stirred by a sense of fearlessness.'

The author then quotes another historian on a consequence of the Guru's execution: 'The whole Punjab began to burn with indignation and revenge.'[8]

Aurangzeb died in 1707. Guru Gobind Singh, son of Guru Tegh Bahadur and the last Sikh Guru, died in 1708, after being stabbed by a man allegedly connected with the Mughal governor of Sirhind.

> 1716: Banda Bahadur Singh is captured by Mughal forces, brought to Delhi, and executed with his followers. Armed Sikhs led by Banda had attacked and killed numerous Muslims in the Punjab including Wazir Khan, the Mughal governor of Sirhind responsible for the death of Guru Gobind Singh's sons.

1739: Defeating Mughal forces, the Persian, Nadir Shah, sacks Delhi following a report of the murder of Persian soldiers in Delhi's alleys.

'The streets were strewn with corpses like a garden with dead leaves. The city was reduced to ashes and looked like a burnt plain.'⁹

1756: Ahmed Shah Abdali overruns Delhi, killing many and triggering a twenty-year period of anarchy. Mughal Empire on its last legs.

1787: Brutalities by Ghulam Qadir Khan, the Rohilla chief, including the blinding of Emperor Shah Alam.

1803: Led by Lord Lake, the British take Delhi, defeating the French-trained Maratha forces who were controlling the capital. Shah Alam II, Delhi's Mughal 'ruler' who had been in alliance with the Marathas, places himself under British protection.

1857: After Delhi is taken over by Indian sepoys rebelling against their British officers, and Bahadur Shah Zafar, the last Mughal, hitherto reigning on British sufferance, agrees to lead the rebels as the emperor of Hindustan, the killing in May of all Britons and Indian Christians in the city, some of whom were imprisoned in the Red Fort before being killed; and in September, after the British, supported by the Sikhs, recapture Delhi, a general massacre of all who were seen as linked to the rebels.

History thus used Nadir Shah of Persia to decimate Mughal rule and, later, the British to eliminate it. Some young Mughal princes were among those killed by the British Empire's avenging forces. In this act the Sikhs saw retribution, even if belated, for the killing of Guru Tegh Bahadur.

All the city people found within the walls when our troops entered were bayoneted on the spot; and the number was considerable, as you may suppose when I tell you that in some houses forty or fifty people were hiding. —British official in 1857.¹⁰

In the name of outraged humanity, in memory of innocent

blood ruthlessly shed and in acknowledgement of the first
signal vengeance inflicted on the foulest treason, the
Governor-General-in-Council records his gratitude to Major-
General Wilson and the brave army of Delhi.
—Lord Canning, 1857.[11]

Thus the Empire's Governor-General, at other times accused by the
Calcutta British of softness towards the rebels, here flaunts the
'vengeance.'

The deaths and destruction ordered in reprisal changed Delhi's
face. 'When the dust of the demolitions had settled down, the people
of Delhi rubbed their tired eyes and looked in vain for their familiar
landmarks.'[12] 'By God, it is not a city,' Ghalib wrote. But the poet
also said:

We had only one thing left—/ The wish to reconstruct the
city/ Everything else was plundered.[13]

1926: Swami Shraddhanand, who in 1919 had been invited
to speak at Jama Masjid, is stabbed to death by a Muslim.

September 1947: Hundreds, possibly thousands, of Muslims
are killed in Delhi in post-Partition riots. On 5 September,
Muslim students are separated from non-Muslim pupils
during an examination in a Karol Bagh school and killed.[14]
By the end of October, only one-and-a-half lakh out of five
lakh Delhi Muslims remain in the city, most of the others
having fled to Pakistan; and half a million Hindu and Sikh
refugees arrive from Pakistan.[15]

1948: On 30 January, while walking towards his prayer-site
in Birla House, Mahatma Gandhi is killed by a man who
first bowed before him and then, when Gandhi's hands had
come together in a gesture of greeting and prayer, fired his
bullets into the old man's open chest. Gandhi falls with the
word 'Rama' on his lips.

1984: Indira Gandhi's assassination by Sikh members of her
bodyguard—a revenge for her government's June 1984 assault
on Amritsar's Golden Temple; in retaliation, the killing of
thousands of Sikhs, and a second uprooting for many Sikhs
uprooted during the 1947 Partition.

*

What was expressed by Khwaja Altaf Husain 'Hali' after the 1857 reprisals has since been felt by others:-

> Dear God I beseech you,/ Speak not of the Delhi that is no more/ I cannot bear to listen to the sad story of this city.[16]

So Delhi is a city of blood, of killing streets. It is a city where the spirits of many of the killed cry out for vengeance, and perhaps the spirits of some killers cry out in guilt or remorse. No wonder some feel Delhi to be a tortured city. When an inhabitant described Delhi to him as a city of djinns, William Dalrymple felt he had found a key for unlocking its mystery, as well as a title for his successful 1993 book.

Others, too, have noted Delhi's violent past. In his novel, *Twilight in Delhi*, Ahmed Ali writes:

> [Delhi] was built after the great battle of Mahabharat by Raja Yudhishtra (*sic*) . . . Destruction is in its foundations and blood is in its soil. It has seen the fall of many a glorious kingdom, and listened to the groans of birth. It is the symbol of Life and Death, *and revenge is its nature*.[17]

*

Mercifully, Delhi's past also includes 'physicians-healers of the soul and quickeners of the spirit' like Khwaja Qutb-ud-din (12th/13th C.) and Nizamuddin Auliya (13th/14th C.), who taught the love of God and of humans and won Hindu as well as Muslim disciples.

It includes, as we have seen, Guru Tegh Bahadur, who in 1675 offered his head 'with no rancour or ill will towards anyone' but refused to yield his faith.[18]

Also belonging to that past is Prince Dara Shukoh, who befriended the Muslim or Hindu poor of the city, Sufis, Hindu philosophers and Christian priests before his younger brother Aurangzeb had him killed in 1658.

Then, during British rule, there were White men like Charles Freer Andrews who dissociated themselves from the Raj and fought for the rights of Indians, especially the humble and the outcast; and even a Viceroy, Lord Irwin, who in the teeth of opposition from imperialist diehards in London signed in 1931 a pact with the Empire's chief rebel, Gandhi.

Spending the last five months of his life in Delhi, Gandhi too is part of the city's story. Delhi, Gandhi said, was not only a capital over the ages; it was 'the heart of India' and would 'decide the destiny of the whole country.'[19] After visiting Muslim refugees crammed in Delhi's Purana Qila or Old Fort, Gandhi said on 13 September 1947:-

> It is said that in the Mahabharata period the Pandavas used to stay in this Purana Qila. Whether you call it Indraprastha or Delhi, the Hindus and Muslims have grown here together. It was the capital of the Mughals. Now it is the capital of India. The Mughals came from outside [but] identified themselves with the manners and customs of Delhi. In such a Delhi of yours the Hindus and Muslims used to live together peacefully . . . They would fight for a time and then be united again . . . This is your Delhi.[20]

Gandhi repeated the thought in January 1948, two weeks before he was killed:

> Delhi has always been the capital. It is this city which was Indraprastha, which was Hastinapur. It is the heart of India. It would be the limit of foolishness to regard it as belonging only to the Hindus or the Sikhs . . . All Hindus, Muslims, Sikhs, Parsis, Christians and Jews who people this country from Kanyakumari to Kashmir and from Karachi to Dibrugarh in Assam . . . have an equal right to it.[21]

In the first two decades of independence, Delhi under Jawaharlal Nehru and, for a short time, Lal Bahadur Shastri was the seat of an Indian government that by and large was magnanimous towards erstwhile foes and tolerant towards current opponents.

We know too that in the terrible massacres of 1857, 1947 and 1984 (and, it is more than likely, during earlier carnages as well) some inhabitants of Delhi daringly and resourcefully saved targeted lives. Any acknowledgement of Delhi's violent past must then include a recognition of agents of reconciliation or accommodation.

*

Kurukshetra

As instructive, perhaps, as an overview of Delhi's past is a glance at the story of a region north and northwest of Delhi—Kurukshetra, now part of Haryana and before 1966 of the larger state of East

Punjab. About the Punjab as a whole, distributed since 1947 between India and Pakistan, a British historian has written:-

> The great Aryan and Scythian swarms which in successive waves of migration left their arid plateaus for the fruitful plains of India, the conquering armies of Alexander, the peaceful Chinese pilgrims in search of the sacred scriptures of their faith, the Muhammadan invaders who came to found one of the greatest Muhammadan Empires the world has ever seen, the devastating hordes led successively by Mahmud, Tamerlane, Nadir Shah and Ahmed Shah, the armies of Baber and Humayun—all alike entered India across the wide plains of the five rivers from which the Province takes its name.

The same historian, Hugh Trevaskis, writing in 1928, has this to say about the struggles in Kurukshetra and its East Punjab surroundings:

> The great central watershed between the basins of the Indus and the Ganges which constitutes the eastern portion of the Punjab has repeatedly been the battlefield of India. It was in prehistoric times the scene of that conflict which, described in the Mahabharata, forms the main incident of one of the oldest epics in existence; while in later days it witnessed the struggles which first gave India to the Muhammadans, which in turn transferred the Empire of Hindustan from the Lodi to the Mogul dynasty and from the Moguls to the Mahrattas, which shook the power of the Mahrattas at Panipat, which finally crushed it at Delhi and made the British masters of Northern India, and which saved the British Empire in India from the terrible outbreak of 1857.[22]

Any 'proof' that the Mahabharata war never occurred in history— that it was only the creation of a master poet—would make no difference to the influence of the Mahabharata on the Indian mind and heart, or the influence of Kurukshetra on Indian history.

In the epic, the Pandavas, aided by Krishna, defeat the Kauravas on the Kurukshetra battlefield. In the process a great carnage occurs. But the epic also tells us that blood had flowed in Kurukshetra long before the Mahabharata war.

The Mahabharata says in its opening volume, the Adi Parva, that at the meeting point of the Treta and Dwapara ages—that is, long before the Kurukshetra battle—Parasurama, an axe-wielding Brahmin hero, had filled five ponds in Kurukshetra with the blood of the Kshatriya race, because that race's forebears had tormented his ancestors.

From the hermitage of Parasurama's father Jamadagni, a Kshatriya king called Kartavirya had stolen a prized cow. Parasurama killed the thief and recovered the cow. Kartavirya's sons killed Jamadagni in revenge, whereupon Parasurama vowed to rid the earth of Kshatriya blood. In some accounts, he clears the earth of Kshatriyas twenty-one times.

'Pleased beyond description with this deed of their offspring,' the forefathers pronounced a boon that turned the ponds of blood into beautiful lakes of water.

Parasurama is also projected as the sixth avatar or incarnation of God Vishnu, the immediate predecessor of Rama, God's seventh incarnation, and Krishna, the eighth. What are we to make of a view of creation and history that can regard 'the brutish, violent, uncivilised' Parasurama, to quote Radhakrishnan's description, as God's incarnation?[23]

Perhaps, as Radhakrishnan seems to suggest, the supposed avatars— the fish, the tortoise, the boar, the man-lion, and Vamana the dwarf precede Parasurama in the series—should be seen as 'stages in the evolution on earth.' Following Krishna, who is fully implicated in the Mahabharata war, the ninth avatar is Buddha, 'who, full of compassion, works for the redemption of mankind,'[24] presumably marking a further advance in evolution.

But if Parasurama is spectacularly blessed and rewarded in the Mahabharata, let us also note the story from the Vamana Purana that Kuru, the king and farmer who founded Kurukshetra, claimed that kshama—forgiveness—was one of the eight virtues he was cultivating in the fields of Kurukshetra. (The other seven were truth, austerity, compassion, cleanliness, charity, composure and chastity.)[25]

Scholars tell us that the Puranas, including, presumably, the Vamana Purana, were written many centuries after the Mahabharata, perhaps between the third and the sixth centuries AD. If so, we have to ask why the author or compiler of the Vamana Purana inserted forgiveness as a quality that Kuru, the ancestor of the Kauravas and the Pandavas, was cultivating. Was the Vamana Purana compiler reacting to the Mahabharata's bloodletting and revenge? Did he miss in the epic the element of forgiveness, and wish to recreate the story?

Whether or not his fame can be ascribed to Kuru's toil, the

seventh century Hindu-Buddhist king Harshavardhana is associated with Kurukshetra—Thanesar (Thanesvar) in the heart of Kurukshetra was one of his two capitals, Kanauj being the other.

Kuru's toil was no doubt successful in one respect. Kurukshetra, all of Haryana, and all of the Punjab, including the Pakistani portion, learned to produce great quantities of grain—and milk, and fruit, and vegetables.

But the growth of forgiveness and compassion was not to prove easy in Kurukshetra. If we accept the boundaries of Kurukshetra provided by scholars,[26] then in addition to the Mahabharata war the following were some of the events that also took place in Kurukshetra or on its edge in Panipat:

> The battle of 1191 in Tarain near Thanesar in which Prithviraj Chauhan III defeated the Turk, Muhammad, who hailed from Ghaur in modern Afghanistan.

> In 1192, another battle in Tarain between Prithviraj III and Muhammad, this time resulting in the Turk's victory and the execution of Prithviraj. 'For miles the stricken field was bestrewn with castaway flags and spears and shields, and heaped bows and jewelled swords.'[27]

> In 1398, Timur's attack on the town of Kaithal and on Kurukshetra villages en route to Panipat and Delhi.

> In 1526, the first battle of Panipat, sixty miles north of Delhi, in which Babur, a descendant of Timur, marching from the northwest with an army of 8,000 men, defeated Ibrahim Lodi, the Afghan ruler of Delhi, who had 50,000 men and 8,000 elephants. Some 20,000 died, including Ibrahim.

> In 1556, the second battle of Panipat, when Babur's grandson Akbar defeated Hemu, the Hindu minister of the Afghan claimant to the throne of Delhi. Again there were huge casualties: 'A minaret of the heads of the slain was erected to mark the victory.'[28]

> In 1760-61, the third battle of Panipat, a face-off between the invading Afghan, Ahmed Shah Abdali, and the Marathas, who were protecting the Mughal throne in Delhi. The Sikhs, by now a major force, watched the battle from the

sidelines. The Marathas lost, but the Afghans did not stay to
rule Delhi. The net result of Panipat III was to create
opportunities for the Sikhs and the British.

In 1947, post-Partition killings of tens of thousands in both
parts of the Punjab, including in Panipat/Kurukshetra.

*

Yet faith in Kurukshetra, where took place, Hindus believe, the
Krishna-Arjuna dialogue of the Bhagavad Gita, has never died.
Accompanying Mahmud of Ghazni in the eleventh century, the
scholar Alberuni saw that Hindus thronged to bathe in the waters at
Thanesar.[29] Sikh Gurus and Sufi saints halted at Thanesar, where a
notable specimen of Mughal architecture, the tomb of Sheikh Chehli,
an Iranian sufi who came during Shah Jahan's reign, continues to
attract visitors.

Despite the violence it has seen, Hindu pilgrims think of
Kurukshetra as Karmakshetra, Tapakshetra and Dharmakshetra—a
blessed site for duties, austerities and rituals.

This calls for sober reflection. Putting aside its history of
carnage, we venerate Kurukshetra for its believed religious significance.
When we touch its soil or cleanse ourselves with its waters, we are
unmindful of the corpses and bloodstreams that over centuries
helped create that earth and water.

Standing with closed eyes on Kurukshetra's soil, we hear what
we want to. Perhaps we hear the Gita's cadences. Yet we are deaf to
the groans and wailings let out in Kurukshetra, a chain of pain that
probably began before Parasurama and has continued ever since. In
Kurukshetra we petition for good fortune for ourselves and for loved
ones. Perhaps, in the spirit of some of Kurukshetra's rousing battles,
we invoke defeat or worse on our enemies. But we do not allow
Kurukshetra's sanguinary past to disturb our souls, nor do we seek
a healing of its hurts through the ages.

*

The Prithviraj-Ghauri clashes have figured twice, under both Delhi
and Kurukshetra, in our quick glimpse. In 1998 these clashes were
widely recalled on the subcontinent because Pakistan had given the
designation Ghori or Ghauri to a missile that it claimed to have
developed in the first quarter of that year.

Shortly after the missile's launch, the well-known Pakistani commentator, Eqbal Ahmad, told me that its name was a response to the Indian missile Prithvi, which was supposed by some in the Pakistani establishment to have been named after Prithviraj Chauhan. Pakistan's next missile, the Press speculated, might be called Ghazni or Ghaznavi, after Mahmud of Ghazni, Ghauri's predecessor in vandalizing India and its temples.

'Prithvi ("Earth") was an obvious name for an Indian ground-to-ground missile,' a defence specialist told me in New Delhi. However, once Pakistan had placed the missile race squarely in the column of history, Indians seemed more than willing to discuss the past. An article in the *Indian Express*[30] claimed that while Prithviraj might have been defeated through treachery in the second battle of Tarain, he did not die there. Blinded, captured, and removed to Afghanistan, Prithviraj—so the article suggested—managed to kill Ghauri in the town of Ghazni through a clever stratagem. That according to most histories Ghauri was killed elsewhere by a member of the Ghakkar tribe in revenge for Ghauri's attacks seemed of no relevance to the writer.

The naming of the Pakistani missile and the ensuing discussion threw light on how the subcontinent uses or sees the past. One side thought nothing of using a historical name that was bound to give offence—and elicited a response in which the past was rewritten. It almost seemed as though the 'historical' discussion would elbow out debate on the implications of a subcontinental missile race.

While its wounds are unacknowledged, its facts unaccepted and its lessons unlearnt, the past occupies our present and unsettles it, a realization made more disquieting by the nuclear tests conducted by India and Pakistan in May 1998.

INQUIRY

In this study we will revisit India's and South Asia's past, looking out in particular for the strands of revenge and reconciliation. While there have been several portrayals of South Asia as a region steeped in violence, sufficient attention has not been given to the history and continuing culture of settling scores, or to the fact that over time triumphs and defeats in the region have led not to stable treaties or settlements but to oaths of revenge and preparations for new rounds of battle.

Some harbour a continuing belief in the essentially pacific nature of the Indian subcontinent. Their faith has withstood past and

contemporary explosions of violence. Possibly this study's facts will
help in disturbing that impressive belief. However, the focus of this
study is revenge and its opposites, rather than violence versus
nonviolence.

'*Is Ashwatthama dead?*' In alarm and disbelief, this, as most
Hindus know, is the question that Ashwatthama's father, Drona,
asked when, on the Kurukshetra battlefield, he heard a shout that the
son on whom he doted had perished. In fact Ashwatthama was not
dead; he lived on to become revenge's personification. In repeating
Drona's question and making it our inquiry, we ask how revenge
fares in India and South Asia.

Were I gifted with the necessary art, I would paint Ashwatthama
in his evidently endless wanderings. He is the world's oldest and
most exhausted man. Towards the end of the Mahabharata, say about
two or three thousand years ago, Krishna cursed him with immortality
for killing Draupadi's sons, brothers and nephews in the dark of the
night: 'For ever you will wander this earth alone, without a single
companion, without a loving word from anyone.'

Ever since then, we are told, Ashwatthama has been trudging the
mountains and deserts of this world, unable to die. The sores and
deformities of age grow by the hour on his limbs, torso, and face; he
is the world's most hideous man as well (among other things, there
is a strange hole in his forehead), but his torment cannot end. He
seems to know no sleep nor any slide into an all-forgetting coma—
there seems to be no record of Krishna, lord of all the worlds,
instructing an occasional respite from his curse on Ashwatthama.

Nights bring Ashwatthama no rest, and the thought of morning
no hope. Yet, despite Krishna and the might of his curse, there is
perhaps some light in Ashwatthama's bleak life, something that
always seems to act like a tonic on him. For he is sought out by the
spirits of men and women who are thirsty for revenge, or dissatisfied
with the degree in which they have exacted it.

Tracking him down in his wilderness, these spirits hover around
him in hopes of encouragement, and also to offer praise. Perhaps
they try to remove stones from his path, or they flap and flutter
beside his thorny bed, seeking somehow to inform him of their
presence and even to soothe his agonies, or to assure him that he
continues to provide inspiration, and to promise that they would
keep revenge alive in the world.

They cannot hold Ashwatthama's hands, and he cannot pat their
backs. But he seems aware of their presence when they arrive—he

senses some sympathy stirring in the air around him.

Daily, hourly, minute-by-minute, he confronts Krishna's curse with his cause, propped up by unseen yet unmistakable intimations of support from visiting spirits. His cause continues to flourish, they want to say; people of many a skin, tongue and belief are enlisting.

Each visit of this kind appears to cheer him up—even as, after the Kurukshetra battle, Ashwatthama himself had revived the spirits of the dying Duryodhana as he lay on the ground, his thighs smashed by his Pandava cousin Bhima. Ashwatthama took Duryodhana's hands in his and promised that before the night was over he would avenge on the sleeping children of the Pandavas the treacherous defeat that the supposedly fair-minded Pandavas had inflicted on Duryodhana and his Kaurava hosts, the epic's 'bad' faction.

Loyalty to his prince was not Ashwatthama's sole motive. Revenge was driving him. His dearly beloved father, Drona, the apparently invincible commander of the Kaurava army, had been disarmed, paralysed, and decapitated by the Pandavas following a dishonorable stratagem on their part.

For the sake of those not knowing it, let me summarize the famous story. On the fourteenth day of the Kurukshetra war, Drona, leading the Kauravas, seemed set to carry all before him. Thousands fell to his arrows and javelins, including an old and influential enemy, Drupada, whom Drona had always hoped to humble. Drupada's daughter, Draupadi, was the wife of the five Pandava brothers; his son Dhrishtadyumna commanded the Pandava forces. Also killed by Drona on this day were three of Drupada's grandsons.

Though an old Brahmin, Drona was unrivalled in the skills of warfare, which he had taught to both the Pandavas and the Kauravas. The Pandava hero Arjuna was in fact his favourite pupil, alongside his son Ashwatthama, but loyalty to Dhritarashtra, the Kauravas' father, had obliged Drona to side with the Kauravas.

Watching Drona's all-conquering role, Krishna, aiding the Pandavas as Arjuna's charioteer, said:

> O Arjuna, no one who fights according to strict rules of war can defeat this Drona. We cannot cope with him unless dharma is discarded. There is but one thing that will make him desist from fighting. If he hears that Ashwatthama is dead, Drona will lose all interest in life and throw down his weapons. Someone must therefore tell him that Ashwatthama has been slain.

Only a few days previously, Ashwatthama and Drona had joined other Kaurava stalwarts in killing Arjuna's teenage son Abhimanyu. Even so, Arjuna shrank in horror at Krishna's proposal of deceit against a revered guru. However, Yudhishthira, the Pandavas' eldest brother and chief, who was celebrated for his truthfulness, offered to play the mean role. 'I shall bear the sin,' Yudhishthira said.

An elaborate charade was enacted. Bhima, strongest of the Pandava brothers, lifted his iron mace, brought it down on the head of a huge elephant called Ashwatthama, killed it, walked towards Drona, and roared, 'I have killed Ashwatthama.' Because he felt ashamed, he roared the louder.

Though shaken, Drona wondered whether Bhima was speaking the truth about his son. Certain that Yudhishthira would not lie even for the kingship of the three worlds, Drona asked him, 'Is it true that Ashwatthama has been slain?' 'If Yudhishthira fails us now,' Krishna remarked to Arjuna, 'we are lost.' Krishna was aware that Drona possessed the Brahmastra, a weapon of unquenchable potency, and had come close to using it.

But Yudhishthira had hardened himself. 'Yes, it is true that Ashwatthama has been killed,' he replied. Then, as shame pierced his heart, he added words in a low and tremulous voice that were drowned in the din and never reached Drona—'I mean Ashwatthama the elephant.'

Vyasa, the author of the Mahabharata, writes that when these remarks escaped Yudhishthira's lips, his chariot's wheels, hitherto moving four inches above the ground because of his integrity, came down and hit the earth.

But Yudhishthira's words had done their work. The will to live and fight left Drona. As he seemed to collapse, Bhima taunted him: 'You Brahmins teach that non-killing is the highest dharma, but you are a Brahmin only by birth. By profession you are a butcher. For money's sake you have shamelessly adopted the profession of killing and brought ruin to us princes.'

At this Drona threw his weapons away and sat down on the floor of his chariot in a yoga posture, his legs crossed, eyes closed, and soul praying. Seeing Drona unarmed and unprepared for battle, Dhrishtadyumna, who had scores to settle, climbed onto the chariot with drawn sword and swept off the old warrior's head, even though Arjuna had cried out that he should capture Drona alive and not kill him.

Some days later, after he had found out how his father had been killed and learnt also of the less than noble manner in which the Pandavas had defeated Duryodhana, Ashwatthama went to the fallen but still living Kaurava chief and vowed revenge. Thereafter, enlisting two surviving Kaurava warriors, Kripacharya and Kritavarma, Ashwatthama set off in the dark for the Pandava camp, where, violating every canon of war, he first killed the sleeping Dhrishtadyumna, and then, one by one, in their sleep, all his sons and brothers and also all the sons of his sister Draupadi. The three attackers then set fire to the Pandava tents. As awakened Pandava soldiers tried to flee, they were slaughtered.

'It's done!' a panting Ashwatthama told Duryodhana before the Kaurava chief breathed his last.

Draupadi now asked her husbands to produce Ashwatthama's head, and also a shining jewel embedded in the forehead that was the source of Ashwatthama's strength. If they did not, she would die, Draupadi vowed.

Accompanied by Krishna, the Pandava brothers went in search of Ashwatthama. Eventually they found him on the bank of the Ganga, hiding behind Vyasa. (The author of the Mahabharata, who off and on puts himself on stage, takes a special interest in Ashwatthama.) Plucking a blade of grass, an evil-looking Ashwatthama charged it with the mantra of destruction, and launched it, saying, 'May this destroy the Pandava race.'

The missile went straight to the womb of Uttara, the wife of Abhimanyu, who was carrying his child—the last hope for continuing the Pandava line—but Krishna nullified the weapon and saved the child Parikshit, who was crowned king when, some years later, the Pandavas retired to the forest. Krishna also ordered Ashwatthama to remove the jewel from his forehead and give it to the Pandavas. Then Krishna condemned Ashwatthama to an unceasing life of solitude, wandering and ignominy.

> Receiving the gem, and hearing that Ashwatthama was deprived of his weapons and left to roam the earth, Draupadi forgave him as the son of the preceptor, Drona, and gave up her vow.[31]

Though Ashwatthama is revenge's personification, we should mark that almost everyone in the Mahabharata is driven by revenge. We have already seen, for instance, that Draupadi, Dhrishtadyumna and Drona are. 'A Story of Revenge' would in fact be an appropriate subtitle for Vyasa's classic. (At least one version of the Mahabharata, in Marathi, is entitled 'Revenge.')

*

Soon we will study in greater detail the place of revenge in the Mahabharata, and also what, in contrast, the Buddha offered to India, but here let us note the relevance for our times of the question, 'Is Ashwatthama dead?' In several parts of our world, whether or not revenge is alive might determine whether some lives are going to be destroyed or preserved.

If Ashwatthama is alive and kicking, killings may any day occur between Hutus and Tutsis in Africa, or Catholics and Protestants in Ireland, or Shias and Sunnis in Pakistan, or Tamils and Sinhalese in Sri Lanka, or Tangkhuls and Kukis in Manipur, or Jats and Jatavs in western U.P., or Bhumihars and Dalits in Bihar, to mention only some running vendettas.

A seed for this book was sown in my mind by the Mahabharata scenes on TV, presented first in the late 1980s. Episode after episode seemed to end with a hero or heroine vowing revenge, not merely as an immediate reaction to a horrible event, but as a well-considered, sacred and clearly spelt-out duty. A suitably gruesome manner of destroying the guilty person, and perhaps some others, was often part of a pledge; frequently, another part invoked suffering on the oath-taker's ancestors and progeny if the oath remained unfulfilled.

That in each instance the revenge seemed to be fully deserved did not suffice to calm my mind. I marked, too, that the often cruel revenge scenes riveted, and at times thrilled, audiences.

More disturbingly, real life in India and South Asia seemed no different. In 1984, Indira Gandhi was killed by some of her guards in revenge for Operation Bluestar, which had been carried out four months earlier; to avenge Mrs Gandhi's death, within days thousands of Sikhs were killed, in many cases burnt alive.

Seven years later, Indira's son Rajiv was blown to bits in an apparent 'reply' to what, under his Premiership, the Indian armed forces had supposedly done in Sri Lanka.

Eighteen months later, in December 1992, Ayodhya's Babri Masjid was demolished by a mob in revenge for what the invader/ruler Babur had allegedly done 464 years earlier.

Leaders of the government of Uttar Pradesh, the state where

Ayodhya lies, sat among the mob, as did national leaders of the political party to which the U.P. government gave allegiance. Large numbers of policemen were also present. But no one who was there seemed to try to prevent the destruction.

In the excitement of successful, even if long-delayed, revenge, a number of poor Muslims in Ayodhya were also killed.

In the following weeks, hundreds perished in riots or in police firing in Mumbai; a large majority were Muslims. The serial bomb blasts set off in Mumbai in revenge also took several hundred— mostly Hindu—lives. By this time a number of Hindu temples in Pakistan and Bangladesh had been destroyed.

*

The foregoing indicates this study's impulse and thrust. Its material is organized as follows. The opening chapter focuses on the Mahabharata, which is seen as embodying and also constantly recharging the currents of revenge, and on interpretations of the Gita. The second chapter starts with the injection by the Buddha of an alternative idea into the Indian bloodstream, and enquires whether the clash between the ideas of the Mahabharata and the Buddha may not constitute a theoretical context for a reading of Indian history.

This second chapter also views Vardhamana Mahavira, Asoka, Dutugemunu of Sri Lanka, the Guptas and Harsha. Islam's burst into India, the evolution of India's response to Islam and its often destructive standard-bearers, Akbar's attempts at accommodation, and, before him, the initiatives of Kabir and Guru Nanak constitute chapter three.

Mughal-Sikh and Maratha-Muslim relations are seen in the fourth chapter in the light of the aforementioned clash of ideas. Chapters five, six and seven deal with the British entry and conquest and the reactions these evoked, including the 1857 rebellion. Chapter eight examines the unexpected turn given to events by Gandhi, while the ninth looks at 1947's wounds and asks why Partition occurred.

The times of Nehru and Shastri are studied in chapter ten, and chapter eleven, this book's longest, considers the post-independence history of India, Pakistan, Bangladesh and Sri Lanka. Concluding thoughts are offered in chapter twelve.

This study's limited focus—the questions it addresses or ignores, the parts of India/South Asia and portions of history it looks at or leaves out—can justly be ascribed to the writer's inclinations and circumstances. All history surely is selective, the selection being governed as much by a student's sense of the comparative significance of questions as by life's accidents bringing the writer face to face with some questions from the past, thereby also, no doubt, removing other items from his or her gaze. For any disappointments caused by the selection for these pages, apologies are sincerely offered.

1

The Mahabharata Legacy, and the Gita's Intent

This precious work (the Mahabharata) has been preserved with infinite trouble, and cherished with deepest love and reverence by [our] ancestors for at least twenty centuries, if not more, and handed down to us as a great legacy.[1]

WE WILL ENTER the question of the Mahabharata's legacy by recalling that violence versus nonviolence was a major question during India's freedom struggle, and that a key item in the debate was whether or not violence was sanctioned by the Gita, to some the spiritual or ethical heart of the Mahabharata and to others an interpolation. As far as violence is concerned, today—in 1999—there seems to be no argument: whether out on the street or on the small screen inside the home, it dominates—not merely violence in self-defence but violence in revenge, or for power, or for a thrill, or in the name of justice.

But domination does not necessarily mean wisdom, or even the last word, and so we will touch on this debate regarding violence and the message of the Gita. Before that, however, we will ask whether there is such a thing as a message of the Mahabharata as a whole.

According to a popular view, the Mahabharata, like the Ramayana, revolves around a struggle between good and evil forces; that as in the Ramayana the evil Rakshasas led by Ravana are defeated by Rama, so in the Mahabharata the 'good' Pandavas manage, after tribulations and the Kurukshetra war, to vanquish the 'bad' Kauravas. In this simple yet contested picture, the message of the Mahabharata is that good struggles but in the end triumphs. Opponents of the view point out that the war in the Mahabharata is between cousins—between, one might say, brothers—, whereas the Ramayana separates demons from humans.

Another view is that the Gita is not only an integral part of the Mahabharata; it is the essence of the epic. In other words, the

philosophy offered by the eighteen short chapters of the Gita is also
the message left by the long tale of the epic. The illustrious scholar,
V.S. Sukthankar (d.1942), 'whose claims to speak . . . on the great
epic were, perhaps, better than those of any of his contemporaries,'[2]
and who wrote the words with which this chapter begins, favoured
this conclusion. In his judgment,

> The Gita is in fact the heart's heart of the Mahabharata . . .
> and the Mahabharata is a sort of a necessary commentary on
> the Gita.[3]

Ostensibly a story of a great war, the epic, said Sukthankar, conveyed
the Gita's ethical and metaphysical message 'in a very audible
undertone.'[4] To consider this significant claim, let us first look at
summaries of the Gita's message offered in recent times by five of its
well-known students and devotees.

Annie Besant: 'That the spiritual man need not be a recluse, that
union with the divine Life may be achieved and maintained in the
midst of wordly affairs, that the obstacles to the union lie not outside
us but within us—such is the central lesson of the Bhagavad Gita.'[5]

Bal Gangadhar Tilak: 'Karma-Yoga (the way of action) fused
with Spiritual Knowledge and Devotion is the true purpose of the
Gita . . . It has also been maintained in the Gita that Karma-Yoga is
superior to the path of renunciation.'[6]

Mohandas Karamchand Gandhi: 'How can the body be made the
temple of God? . . . The Gita has answered the question in decisive
language: "By desireless action; by renouncing fruits of action; by
dedicating all activities to God, i.e., by surrendering oneself to Him
body and soul." '[7]

Vinoba Bhave: 'I have called the Gita the *Samyayoga*, the yoga of
equanimity, because the word *samya*, equanimity, lies at the very
basis of its teaching. The thing to be attained is equanimity.'[8]

C. Rajagopalachari: '[The Gita offers] the gospel of devotion to
duty, without attachment or desire of reward.'[9]

Though these statements are far from being identical, they do
not contradict one another. Does the Mahabharata leave us with a
thought similar to any of these? Statements of scholars that they have
caught undertones of such a thought from the epic, or evidence that
here and there the text spells it out, would not suffice. What we have
to ask is whether the dominant thought left by the epic on the
average person's mind is that the spiritual man need not be a recluse

and can (or, in Tilak's reading, should) be an activist, or that union with the divine is possible through selfless action, or devotion, or knowledge.

Thus put, the question is answered without difficulty. This is not above all how readers, listeners, or viewers remember the Mahabharata. Sukthankar indeed claimed that the simple 'believing Indian' discounted 'the martial aspect' and grasped the epic's deeper message by some 'automatic mental adjustment' not available to the intellectual Indian or the average foreigner.[10] He also picturesquely warned against

> the habit of reading our ancient books through the spectacles balanced on our noses by our western gurus.[11]

Yet Sukthankar's comments preceded the Mahabharata teleserial by four decades, and it is doubtful that any observer of the 1980s or 1990s would have found that the average Indian, unable to absorb the whole of the vast epic but exposed to popular selections or abridgments, connected the Mahabharata above all to duty without hopes of reward. In fact we may wonder similarly about the common Indian of earlier periods. That is, we could ask whether a celebrated scholar like Sukthankar is not reading the ancient book through spectacles that conceal the fiery, the vengeful and the ignoble, elements likely in all epochs to arrest the popular mind.

*

Perhaps one way of discovering how people remember the Mahabharata is to ask who they think of as its most compelling character. Six people asked may well give six different answers: Krishna, Arjuna, Karna, Draupadi, Yudhishthira or Bhishma.

Popular India clearly chooses one of the first three named. Parents who name their children Krishna, Arjuna or Karna easily outnumber those who call their children Draupadi, or Yudhishthira or Bhishma. Of the first three, Krishna is a god's name, or a name for Almighty God (there is, of course, a difference between the two). Since the name of God is hard to give to one's child, parents call their son or daughter Krishna Kumar or Kumari, i.e. a child of God, or qualify it by adding a word like Das, Lal, Prasad, Chandra, Datta or Kant. In this way they can address their son or daughter as God's servant, loved one, blessing, reflection, gift or lover, rather than as God.

India may contain as many, or more, Krishnas, or Krishans, Krishnans or Kishens (with a suffix or prefix added), as Arjunas and Karnas (or Arjuns, Arjans, and Karans), but if asked to select the Mahabharata's hero a number of Indians might well choose Arjuna or Karna over Krishna. Not that they think Arjuna or Karna greater than Krishna, erring man greater than a powerful god, but they may regard Arjuna or Karna as a personality more attractive or interesting than Krishna.

Because of his divine power, Krishna is predictable. From any clash, trial, dilemma or trap, Krishna is bound to emerge with success. The same cannot be said of Arjuna, and even less of Karna. These two are subject to twists of circumstance or fortune; though always heroic in battle, they are never certain to win. We may bend our knees before Krishna, but are likely to prefer Arjuna or Karna for company, and pick one of them as the epic's star character.

Between the two, many would choose Karna despite his being on the 'wrong,' and eventually losing, side at Kurukshetra, that of the Kauravas. Karna is the wronged hero, wronged by teachers, brothers and mother, more wronged and more heroic than other wronged heroes. Inevitably we are drawn to him.

Others, however, far fewer no doubt, might pick Yudhishthira, for he reveals the dilemmas, fallibility and integrity of the noble and the responsible. Not for Yudhishthira the luxury of attractive indiscretion or bold couldn't-care-lessness. With him the buck stopped. While shamefully reckless on one crucial peacetime occasion, and shockingly hard-hearted at another decisive wartime moment, he is memorably compassionate at the end of the story.

Draupadi, wife to Yudhishthira, Arjuna and his brothers, and the woman Karna had wanted for himself, causes bends in the Mahabharata's course by the firmness, not to say toughness, that is allied to her beauty. Her spirit sees her through every devastating tragedy, and she is intellectually devastating in the scene of her humiliation.

To a Bhishma lying on a bed of arrows towards the end of the epic, Krishna says, 'You are the greatest hero.' For one thing, Bhishma stands on a summit of self-denial. Learning of his royal father's infatuation for a young woman who wants succession reserved for her offspring, Bhishma not only forswears his claim to the throne; pledging lifelong celibacy, he also shuts out the possibility of any son of his claiming the throne in the future.

Unconquerable in battle and unshakeable in loyalty, Bhishma

loves the Pandavas but fights for the Kauravas whose salt he has eaten. Among the many students of the Mahabharata who have fallen for Bhishma is Annie Besant, who in her condensation of the Mahabharata calls Bhishma 'the greatest and most heroic figure in this story.'[12]

The Krishna of the Mahabharata is radiant, resourceful, eloquent. He is a human who knows he is all-powerful. His friends the Pandavas, and men like Bhishma, know it too.

This Krishna is capable of 'infinite pity.' When, for instance, Kunti, the mother of the Pandavas, had to tell her sons after the war that Karna, whom they had killed, was her eldest child though not the son of their father, and thus their half-brother, she felt strengthened by the compassion for her that she saw in the eyes of Krishna, who was present.

Krishna, the giver of boons, is however also subject to curses and in the end dies of a curse pronounced by Gandhari, the mother of the Kauravas killed with Krishna's aid. Said Gandhari to Krishna, just before uttering her curse:

> The Pandavas and Kauravas are all dead
> Why did you allow this?
> O Krishna, you could have stopped the war.
> You had the tongue, you had the power.[13]

Gandhari does not quite say, you were God, and yet you allowed it. Except in the Gita interlude (or interpolation) and other occasional passages, the Mahabharata's Krishna seems more an extraordinarily brilliant and astute man than God.

Vyasa, the author, has other characters in the Mahabharata also voicing to Krishna the complaint made by Gandhari. Thus Krishna's old Brahmana friend Utanga tells him after the war, with eyes red with indignation, at the destruction of life:-

> Vasudeva (Krishna), were you there standing by and did you
> let all this happen? You have indeed failed in your duty.[14]

In one of his own appearances in the epic, Vyasa says to Arjuna after Krishna's death: 'Krishna could have prevented it (the chain of massacres), but he allowed it to happen.'[15] The life-loving poet seems to chastise the god of duty who prescribed to Kshatriyas their duty to kill, and wonders why he refused to be the God of Compassion.

With interventions of this kind, and with his gift to a hundred succeeding generations of a wealth of haunting characters, Vyasa himself also qualifies for selection as the Mahabharata's most interesting figure.

That Vyasa sires the oldest people as the Mahabharata starts, and converses with characters at the end of the war, are interesting facts that perhaps confirm his authorship of the epic. He, ageless, is there at the beginning and the end of the story; he starts it and concludes it. It is his creation, and his genius is proved by the fact that in the popular imagination the created have eclipsed the creator.

More than the principal characters, and more than the reader dazzled by the principal characters, Vyasa is aware of their limitations and of what perhaps is needed to overcome these—compassion and forgiveness. Some would therefore pick Vyasa as the true hero of the epic.

Bhima, the strong Pandava with unexpected sensitivities, and Vidura, the half-caste half-brother of the fathers of the Pandavas and the Kauravas—seen by some critics as Yudhishthira's true father[16]—are also figures that readers might 'vote' for.

Where opinions diverge on the epic's key character, they must also diverge on its message. Or perhaps the epic has no message, not, at any rate, one that its author had in mind. Perhaps, as suggested by the old, even ancient, view that the Mahabharata, apart from being a dharmasastra, is an itihaasa—a history—, Vyasa was only relating events, or a story inspired by events he had seen or gathered, in which case any message from the epic would be no more, and no less, than the meaning of the events that had occurred. Says *The Gazetteer of India*:

> [S]cholars agree that the basis of the epic story has a
> foundation in facts. It is of inestimable worth for
> reconstructing the social and cultural history of the period.[17]

Yet a creation may make an impact other than what its author had in mind, and the message of the Mahabharata for 'us' may depend partly on what we want to see in it, and partly on what from the vast epic we focus on, on where we start and where we end.

*

'*An unending shower of the arrows of revenge.*'[18] In the introduction we referred to the Mahabharata as a story of revenge. A number of parallel or intersecting feuds add up to the Mahabharata before destroying almost all its characters.

The jealousy and hate of the Kauravas led by Duryodhana for their Pandava cousins, the revenge the Pandavas exact after their pleas for bare justice are dismissed, and the rivalry between Arjuna and Karna are key strands of the epic's story. But other rivalries and hates seem almost as crucial to it.

For one, there is Drona's feud with Drupada, which, as we saw in the opening chapter, was carried forward by Drona's son Ashwatthama to the sons and grandsons of Drupada. The feud started when, on the strength of a promise received from Drupada in boyhood, Drona, a poor Brahmana skilled in archery, went to Drupada, now king of the Panchalas, and asked for the king's hospitality. It was his child Ashwatthama's cry for milk he could not afford that had taken Drona to his old friend. Replied Drupada in open court:

> Don't you know that friendship is possible only between equals? Only two poor men, or two rich men, can be friends. Go away from here, and do not return to pester me with a tale of an imaginary promise made long ago.

'The insulted Brahmana stood silent for a few moments . . . and decided his future course of action: Revenge.'[19] He would train Kshatriya youths in archery and through them destroy Drupada. The chance to begin acting on his resolve came to Drona when Bhishma, guardian of the Kaurava and Pandava boys and looking for someone to guide them in archery, engaged Drona. Arjuna and his own son Ashwatthama, in that order, became Drona's best pupils.

Another incident involving Drona reveals Vyasa's frankness about the high-low relationship in ancient India. Ekalavya, a young tribal anxious to learn archery, begs Drona to be his guru. For caste and class reasons Drona declines. Practising by himself and drawing inspiration from a clay statue of Drona, Ekalavya acquires great skill, a fact accidentally discovered by the Pandavas.

At their instance, and in order to eliminate rivalry to Arjuna in archery, Drona asks Ekalavya for a cruel guru dakshina, the present owed to a teacher—the thumb of his right hand! Ekalavya cuts it off and gives it to his 'teacher,' and loses half his art.

Vyasa might not have guessed that in course of time his Ekalavya would become a powerful symbol for struggles against ethnic injustices. Writes Waman Nimbalkar:

> Taking in one hand the sun, in the other the moon,/ I am

conscious of my resolve,/ the worth of the blood of
Ekalavya's broken finger.[20]

On occasion the symbol is blamed for not revolting, as in these lines
of Shashikant Hingonekar:

If you had kept your thumb/ History would have happened
somehow differently./ But . . . you gave your thumb/ And
history also became theirs . . ./ Forgive me, Ekalavya, I
won't be fooled now/ by their sweet words./ My thumb
will never be broken.[21]

As for Bhishma, we should also note the wrath he had sparked in
Amba, a princess of Kashi. Amba had been on the verge of marrying
another prince when Bhishma abducted her on behalf of his half-
brother Vichitravirya, but Vichitravirya died, and the other prince
was unwilling to accept the compromised Amba. She was certain that
Bhishma was now honour-bound to marry her, but he reiterated his
vow of celibacy, and Amba was incensed. 'In her heart there was
place for only one emotion: hatred for Bhishma. Her only desire was
to see him dead.'[22]

Penances enabled Amba first to be reborn as a princess in
Drupada's family, and then to change her sex. As Shikhandin she (he)
would be instrumental in Bhishma's fall and death in the Kurukshetra
war.

Karna and Bhishma, the Kauravas' finest warriors, cannot get
along with each other—envy is at work—, and when Duryodhana
asks Bhishma to lead his forces in the war, Bhishma lays down a
condition: Karna should stay off the battle as long as Bhishma is
alive. The Bhishma-Karna enmity however ends when Bhishma falls
and a reconciling dialogue takes place during Karna's visit to the old
warrior stretched out on his bed of arrows.

Some of the epic's most passionate calls for battle and revenge
come from Kunti and Draupadi. When Krishna reports to Kunti his
failure in negotiating a peace with the Kauravas and asks for a
message for her sons, the Pandavas, Kunti says:-

The time has come for that for which a Kshatriya woman
brings forth sons. Tell my sons that they are the sons of
Kunti; that I expect them to behave as Kshatriyas.[23]

A Kshatriya woman brings forth sons to be sacrificed in war.

Draupadi had not liked the negotiations, and had been particularly agitated when, on the eve of Krishna's talks with the Kauravas and their father, Dhritarashtra, Bhima—to the surprise of several—had expressed himself in favour of a peaceful settlement. 'Let us be gentle first, we shall fight only in the last resort,' Bhima had said.[24]

At this Draupadi recalled the occasion when Duryodhana had made lewd gestures towards her in the presence of her husbands, and—while she was in her period and wearing only a single cloth—Duryodhana's brother Duhshasana had dragged her by the hair. To Krishna she said (P. Lal's translation):

> I will never know peace till the arm of Duhshasana is severed from his body and smashed. Thirteen years I have waited for that day, thirteen years I have nourished revenge in my heart. And now Bhima is suddenly become moral, and my heart breaks.[25]

Draupadi adds (Rajagopalachari's version):

> Look at these tresses of mine and do what honour requires. There can be no peace with honour. Even if Arjuna and Bhima are against war, my father, old though he is, will go to battle, supported by my children.

If my husbands will not fight, my father and my sons will, Draupadi says, and sobs. Krishna assures Draupadi that her fear that peace was round the corner was baseless:

> Weep not. Dhritarashtra's sons will not listen to my words of peace. They are going to fall and their bodies will be food for wild dogs and jackals . . . The insult to you will be fully avenged.[26]

Earlier, when the Pandavas were in the forest and Krishna had joined them, Draupadi had similarly challenged Krishna (Lal):

> They dragged me, the sister of Dhrishtadyumna, the wife of the Pandavas, during my period, stained with blood, dressed in a single cloth—they dragged me in front of all the kings— and the sons of Dhritarashtra laughed at me! They wanted to make me their slave by force! And my husbands sat through it, unmoving! . . . Shame on Arjuna's magic bow, which slept while I was dragged! . . . Shame on Bhima's strength! Poison he could drink, serpents he could kill,

Kunti he could save from [flames], but me he could not protect!

I have neither husbands, nor sons, nor friends, nor father. I do not even have you, O Krishna, for you also are silent.

Replied Krishna:

Just as you weep now, fair lady, so will weep the wives of those who made you angry, when they see their husbands dead, pierced with arrows. I will do all I can for the Pandavas—I give you my word.[27]

In that scene of her humiliation, the gambling duel where, after losing his brothers and himself, Yudhishthira had also staked and lost Draupadi to the Kauravas, she had silenced every elder present with her argument:

When my husband Yudhishthira lost himself and became a slave, he no longer owned anything, not even me. He had no right, moral or legal, to stake me. I am not lawfully made over to the Kauravas.

Duhshasana tried to ridicule the reasoning, and most of his brothers cheered him, but there was one brother, Vikarna, who dissented (Subramaniam version):

We all deserve to be sent to hell . . . All these righteous men here, Bhishma, Drona, Dhritarashtra and the rest, did not question Yudhishthira when he staked Draupadi . . . But in my opinion, Draupadi has not been lost. Yudhishthira had no right to stake her. She is the wife of all the Pandava brothers, not his alone. How could he stake her without the consent of his brothers?[28]

Karna led the shouting that dismissed Vikarna's plea for compassion and justice, and the scene of Draupadi's molestation was enacted, whereupon Bhima took a fearsome oath. He declared that he would smash Duryodhana's thighs, rend Duhshasana's breast, and drink his blood. 'May I never go to the blest abode of my ancestors if I do not,' Bhima said. Shortly afterwards, Krishna too promised Draupadi that she would be amply avenged.

Eventually, the oaths were fully redeemed. Indeed, as Bhima fulfilled his fierce vow, Draupadi herself dipped her tresses in

Duhshasana's blood. Lal, the dedicated Mahabharata scholar, sees in Draupadi's 'startling action . . . a symbolic gesture of appropriate redemptive revenge,' and adds, 'Call it karma, or poetic justice, what you will—it makes good epic sense.'[29]

After Ashwatthama is forced by Krishna to part with his potent gem and banished, and the stone is handed to Draupadi, she says, 'Revenge was all that I wanted. Let Yudhisthira wear the gem on his head.'[30]

Before Gandhari's curse on Krishna took effect, Krishna's clansmen had destroyed themselves, wiping out their race from the earth, in an orgy of temper, drunkenness, boastfulness and violence during which blades of grass turned into lances that the clansmen used on one another. Vyasa seems to suggest that the seed of revenge produced the crop of unrelieved slaughter.

Greater distress was to follow. Arjuna, who had married Krishna's sister Subhadra, escorted the women, children and elderly members of Krishna's clan towards Indraprastha, the capital of the 'victorious' Pandavas, but hunters obstructing the trek carried off many women in Arjuna's care, some of whom went willingly with the hunters. In this trial, Arjuna's famed bow Gandiva, which was supposed to be unfailing and invincible, let him down. Arjuna's pride in his Gandiva was total—for denigrating it, Yudhishthira had once been nearly killed by Arjuna. We can see the Gandiva's failure at a critical moment as Vyasa's smile at the warrior's pride in his weapon.

*

As striking as the epic's revenge demands is its recognition, in numerous passages, of the need for forgiveness. However, again and again in the story, the hand of fate—or human nature—tips the scale in favour of revenge.

Soon after the dice game that resulted in the Pandavas' slavery and Draupadi's humiliation, she managed, thanks to omens that frightened Dhritarashtra, to secure her husbands' freedom, which however proved short-lived. When she had won it, Karna commented, 'Draupadi has rowed the drowning Pandavas to safety.'

Stung by the implied taunt, 'Bhima looked around fiercely,' but Arjuna calmed him, saying:

> Good men remember good, and forgive wrong. Revenge does not go with self-respect.[31]

Yudhishthira backed Arjuna, whose remark, we may note, seems to advocate forgetting as well as forgiving. Soon, however, the Pandavas were trapped again, and obliged to retire to the forest, where the conversation quoted above between Draupadi and Krishna took place.

Shortly afterwards, Draupadi repeated her demand for revenge, this time to Yudhishthira (Lal):

> Are you not moved to anger . . .? Has all feeling deserted you? Are you a Kshatriya or not? Is a Kshatriya ever expected to forgive his enemies? Kill them. Do it now! This isn't the time for forgiveness . . . You have been soft for too long; learn to be fierce now.

Yudhishthira's reply, taken here from Lal's translation, is a passionate defence of forgiveness:

> Draupadi, my beautiful wife . . .
> How will the world run
> If bitterness rewards bitterness,
> Injury is returned for injury, hate for hate,
> If fathers suspect sons, sons suspect fathers,
> If trust disappears between husband and wife?

Adding that forgiveness was the only virtue, that it was sacrifice, the Vedas, and 'our tradition,' that it was Brahma, truth, penance, holiness, and it held the world together, Yudhishthira concluded: 'Do not argue me away from forgiveness, my wife.'[32]

Stirred by this dialogue, and describing its Draupadi as 'this feminine apostle of violence,' Sukthankar would like us to treat Yudhishthira's words as 'the substance of the entire ethical teaching of the epic.'[33]

When a huge snake—in a previous life Nahusha, a Kshatriya king, but cursed to his present state by Brahmins he had insulted—, held Bhima in a tight grip in the forest, Yudhishthira rescued his brother by answering questions to the snake's satisfaction. One of Yudhishthira's answers was that character and not birth determined one's caste. On his part, Nahusha praised charity, nonviolence, gentleness and truth to Yudhishthira.

After the Kurukshetra war, when the blind Dhritarashtra, who had lost all his sons, was, in his wrath, about to crush Bhima to death in an 'embrace,' Krishna had the presence of mind to substitute an iron image for Bhima. This figure was pulverized by Dhritarashtra, who apologized for having killed Bhima.

Explaining that only an object of metal had been destroyed, Krishna said to Dhritarashtra:

> How would killing Bhima have helped you? Would it have restored your sons to life?[34]

This of course was a question that Krishna could have asked, but did not ask, before and after the epic's numerous revenge killings.

Dhritarashtra's wife Gandhari was, as we have seen, as embittered as her husband. To pacify her, Vyasa makes one of his appearances. He tells Gandhari:

> This is the time for forgiveness. Cast off anger, Gandhari. Cultivate the art of peace.[35]

Vyasa, who more than anyone else knows the Mahabharata tragedy— he has seen, created or reenacted it—, *he* is alive to the need for forgiveness. The forgiveness he seeks seems to be pure, whereas the forgiveness that others on occasion ask for, including Krishna, resembles a give-and-take within divided Pandava ranks, designed to strengthen them against the Kauravas.

Some contrition can be detected in Bhima's explanation to Gandhari of his departure from the code of battle to kill her son Duryodhana and of his drinking of Duhshasana's blood:

> Right or wrong, I did what I did because I was afraid. I did it to save my own skin. Forgive me. No one could defeat your son in a fair duel . . .

> It is immoral to drink the blood of a stranger, even more immoral to drink one's own blood—one's brother is oneself. But listen to me, mother, and believe when I say that the blood never went beyond my lips and teeth. Karna was witness to it . . . If I had failed to keep my vow, I would have lost my Kshatriya honour.[36]

Draupadi's 'forgiveness' of Ashwatthama, seen by us in the Introduction, was not a prelude to reconciliation. But it enabled her to live on—she gave up her vow to die.

Forgiveness is also extolled in a story that Bhishma relates from his couch of arrows to Yudhishthira. It is the story of Gautami, an old lady whose son was killed by a snake. Gautami says to the fowler who wishes to kill the snake: 'Release him. Killing him won't revive my son.' Arjunaka, the fowler: ' An enemy deserves to be killed. Killing an enemy brings merit.' Gautami: 'Forgiving an enemy brings more merit.'[37]

But at the end of this story, karma or fate is blamed for all deaths, and resignation before fate, whether that fate is a son's death or a carnage, is the note one is left with, rather than forgiveness.

The sage Brihaspati, who comes to Bhishma's 'bedside' after the end of the war, makes two interesting pronouncements in the hearing of Yudhishthira and his brothers: 'Nothing is more virtuous than compassion,' and 'Never should a man do to another what he would not want another to do to him.' Then he ascends the sky above the bed of arrows. Bhishma now tells Yudhishthira, 'Nothing is greater than Ahimsa.'[38]

Yudhishthira, at different stages in the epic, and occasionally Arjuna too, as when, at the start of the Gita, he questions before Krishna the rightness of killing his teachers, elders and cousins, seem to go beyond caste duty and fate, and to reflect on what is right or wrong for them as human beings. As one scholar puts it, during such moments Yudhishthira and Arjuna are 'self-reflexive' and 'humanistic.' Confronting their dilemmas, guilt and remorse, they seem reluctant, at such times, to blame fate, or to accept caste imperatives unquestioningly.[39]

One such moment occurred during the war when, to save his close friend Satyaki, Arjuna, standing behind the Kaurava stalwart Bhurishravas, shot an arrow at Bhurishravas, violating the code of chivalry. Bhurishravas, who lost an arm to Arjuna's arrow, turned round and said:

> Son of Kunti! I had not expected this of you! I was engaged in conflict with someone else and you have attacked me without notice.

Arjuna's reply contained an unusual sentence:

> Don't blame me; if you like, let us all blame the violence which governs Kshatriya life.[40]

However, right after this intriguing reflection by Arjuna, the friend rescued by him, Satyaki, swung a sword that removed the head of Bhurishravas, who by this time was seated in a yoga posture and meditating—a killing resembling the death of Drona and, in 1675, the execution of Guru Tegh Bahadur.

A picture of remorse, acceptance and reconciliation emerges once during Arjuna's victory ride after the Kurukshetra victory. Entering the Saindhava (Sindh) country, Arjuna is met outside her palace by Duhshala, the sister of Duryodhana. Duhshala had been married to Jayadratha, the Kaurava warrior killed (not very fairly) by Arjuna at Kurukshetra.

Arjuna asks, 'Where is Suratha?' Suratha was her son. 'Dead,' Duhshala replies. 'He died of a broken heart, for he knew that you had killed his father. I now bring you his son, and I seek your protection.' Proceeds Vyasa:

> Arjuna stared at the ground. Great sorrow afflicted him. 'I am your sister,' Duhshala said. 'You will not refuse me. As Parikshit is to your son Abhimanyu, this boy is to my son Suratha. I have come to plead for the lives of my people.'

Adds Vyasa:

> Arjuna embraced Duhshala, and asked her to return to her palace. Then he made peace with the Saindhavas.[41]

In this Arjuna-Duhshala encounter, Vyasa has given us a powerful scene. As one commentator puts it, 'The great poet, who does not minimize his words on many other occasions, does not dare to say more here.'[42]

In this encounter no verbal apology was offered by either side, but, apart from the picture of remorse in Arjuna for the past, there was also, in him as well as Duhshala, a practical concern for the future.

Arjuna's victory ride, the Ashwamedha, was supposed to demonstrate Pandava supremacy across India's vast spaces. But a mongoose, shining with gold on one side, puts the Pandavas in their place by declaring before a distinguished assembly that a country-wide Ashwamedha, for all its pomp, earned less merit than a single act of hospitality that a starving family had shown to a poor guest. 'I rolled with joy on the ground where this family lived,' the mongoose said. 'Some of the flour they had poured out for their guest had fallen there. It made half of me golden.'

The epic's most memorable reconciliation scene takes place one morning after the war when Vyasa takes Kurukshetra's survivors, Draupadi and the Pandava brothers, their mother Kunti, and the parents of the Kauravas, all grieving for the dead heroes, to the banks of the river Bhagirathi.

'I shall dispel your grief,' Vyasa tells them. 'At night I will give you a vision of the dead heroes.' The survivors' sorrow was such that the hours until sundown felt like a whole year. Then, after a roar heard in the waters, the dead emerged, led by Bhishma and Drona. Drupada and Draupadi's sons, Abhimanyu, Karna and Duryodhana, Gandhari's other sons, all returned. In Lal's rendering:-

> Cleansed of hate and jealousy
> Son met father and mother, wife met husband,
> Friend greeted friend.
> The Pandavas met Karna,
> And embraced him.
> A scene of reconciliation:
> No grief, no fear, no suspicion, no reproach,
> Nothing but the meeting of loving minds.[43]

Before morning, the reunion was over. Dismissed by Vyasa, all vanished, chariots and warriors plunging into the Bhagirathi.

It is a powerful scene, perhaps a glimpse, in a vision, of what God desires for all warring groups. In the Mahabharata, revenge is a fact, reconciliation a fancy; forgiveness is preached, vengeance practised; healing is conceived, injury executed. India would wait some centuries after the Mahabharata for a demonstration that reconciliation was possible on the ground, in daylight, and among the living, a demonstration provided by one who was strong, had been cruel, and repented: Asoka.

However, as has been indicated even in this short summary, the epic makes occasional departures from its apparent note of the unavoidable triumph of pride, envy, greed and hate in the human heart. One such departure is the scene at the epic's end where Yudhishthira, now the sole survivor—Draupadi and his brothers having also died—, refuses to abandon a faithful dog accompanying him, even when told that if he lets go of the dog, a chariot would at once fly him to heaven and its joys.

This scene is soon matched by the account of Yudhishthira's choice of a horrid hell, where he finds his brothers, over a comfortable heaven which can be his if he ignores his brothers' fate. Much earlier, in another test, when it seemed that Yudhishthira must lose all his brothers save one and was given the choice of naming the one who should survive along with him, he named not the seemingly priceless Arjuna or Bhima but Nakula.

This Yudhishthira did because while he, Bhima and Arjuna were born to Kunti, their father Pandu's first wife, Nakula and Sahadeva, the fifth brother, were the children of Pandu's second wife Madri, who had thrown herself on her husband's funeral pyre. 'Let a son of Madri be among the two living,' Yudhishthira decided.

In such all-too-rare scenes in the epic, compassion for others triumphs over self.

*

Before concluding this attempt to describe the Mahabharata's message, let us turn, as promised, to the message of the Gita.

We started this chapter with statements about the Gita from five individuals who loved it and had studied it. The statements appear strangely unconnected with the setting of the Kurukshetra battle in which the Gita emerges in the epic.

Let us recall the scene. All negotiations failing, a battle is called. Duryodhana, who is given the choice of Krishna or Krishna's huge armies, picks the latter. Arjuna, on the Pandavas' behalf, delightedly takes Krishna, who serves as Arjuna's charioteer.

Seeing men arrayed on both sides for mutual slaughter, 'seeing uncles and grandfathers, teachers, cousins, sons, comrades, fathers-in-law and benefactors also in both armies, deeply moved to pity,' Arjuna says in sadness to Krishna (Chapter One):-

> My limbs fail and my mouth is parched, my body quivers, and my hair stands on end, the Gandiva (Arjuna's bow blessed with supernatural powers) slips from my hand, and my skin burns all over; I am unable to stand, my mind is whirling . . . Nor do I see any advantage from slaying kinsmen in battle . . .
>
> In committing a great sin are we engaged, we who are endeavouring to kill our kindred from greed of the pleasures of kingship.[44]

After this appealing hesitation against slaughter come six verses that have to be regarded as a letdown, for in these verses Arjuna suggests that slaughter will produce innumerable widows who will become unchaste; races and castes will mix; the offspring being impure, Brahmins will abstain from ceremonies for deceased ancestors, who will fall from blessedness. Arjuna's concern over bloodshed is overtaken by a less agreeable anxiety about the mixing of castes and pollution of ritual.

Accusing Arjuna of impotence and faint-heartedness, Krishna explains at the start of Chapter Two that the soul in Arjuna or the Kauravas can never die, that in truth therefore there is no slayer and none slain. Seemingly there is death, but since that overtakes even those not engaged in war, Arjuna should not be troubled by the prospect of killing.

Furthermore, it is the Kshatriya dharma or duty to fight, and if Arjuna did not, he would incur both sin and dishonour. The generals on both sides would think that he had fled from the battle in fear. Adds Krishna (2:37):

> Slain, thou wilt obtain heaven; victorious, thou wilt enjoy
> the earth. Therefore stand up, O son of Kunti, resolute to
> fight.[45]

As a final argument, Krishna says that Arjuna can fight not for pleasure, gain or victory, but merely as duty, and thus incur no sin. (2:38)

The Gita's references to the Kurukshetra battle end with this. From here—midway in Chapter Two—to the Gita's close at the end of Chapter Eighteen, Krishna discourses on the secret of a detached yet active life. The marks of the stable-minded man, the virtue of duty done without concern for its fruits, and different paths taking humans to the divine are among his subjects. For most of the Gita, Krishna is a teacher of right living.

However, at one stage in Chapter Eleven, Krishna reveals himself as the Supreme Being in his dazzling omnipotent form; and in the concluding chapter he says, 'Abandoning everything come unto Me alone for shelter; sorrow not, I will liberate thee from all sins.' Responds Arjuna:-

> Destroyed is my delusion, I have gained knowledge through
> Thy grace. My doubts have fled. I will do according to Thy
> word. (18:73)

But he does not explicitly refer to the battle.

*

The battlefield setting at the Gita's start and Krishna's words about victory or heaven seem to support a reading of the Gita as Krishna's call to warriors to battle. And Arjuna's opening lines seem to justify Lal's memorable description of him as 'the world's first pacifist, a conscientiously objecting, bravely quaking and Quaker Hindu.'[46]

Challenging this reading, Gandhi made several arguments. Thus he questioned the naturalness of holding a great war in abeyance while one key warrior engages in a long ethico-religious conversation with his charioteer. Gandhi claimed that the Gita did not seem a natural fit at the start of the Kurukshetra war.

Secondly, said Gandhi, in the Gita text given to us Arjuna was not arguing against war or killing; he was only objecting to killing relatives. Arjuna, Gandhi correctly points out, had previously fought several wars. Expanding this argument, Gandhi's close associate and Gita scholar Vinoba Bhave says that Arjuna's seeming objection to war reminded him of a judge who had given several death sentences but who started questioning capital punishment when his son was accused of murder.

Vinoba Bhave makes an additional point along these lines. Is it reasonable to suppose, he asks, that the only faint-hearted person at the start of battle was the peerless warrior Arjuna? That all his countless soldiers were ready to kill and be killed but Arjuna alone, their leader, quailed?

Thirdly, Gandhi contended that since the Gita took a consistent position against anger—for instance, in the last verse of Chapter Ten, Krishna tells Arjuna, 'He who is without hatred of any being comes to me'—, and since it did not seem possible to kill without anger, the Gita cannot be on the side of killing. In the Mahabharata war, Gandhi points out, Arjuna is portrayed as shooting arrows with 'eyes red with anger.' To Gandhi this was contrary to the Gita's advice.

Fourthly, said Gandhi, though in Chapter One and in the first half of Chapter Two the Gita referred to fighting, everywhere else it was a treatise on self-control and union with the divine; no one could call it a course-book on warfare or military strategy.

Finally, Gandhi argued that if the Gita was an integral part of the Mahabharata, its message could not be different from the message of the epic. To Gandhi the message of the epic is the folly of war. Stressing that resentments from the Mahabharata war finally destroyed almost everybody, including Krishna and his clansmen, and left the world a virtual void, Gandhi reads the Mahabharata as a lesson that violence and revenge lead inexorably to a desert—a moral, emotional, and physical desert.

If this is what the Mahabharata teaches, asks Gandhi, how can the Gita, its 'integral part,' teach its opposite, the duty to kill?

To an extent, the question seems to hang on the Gita's internal unity, on whether the opening one-and-a-half chapters blend harmoniously with the remaining sixteen-and-a-half chapters, or are unnaturally tied together. That there is a jump in the Gita between its war-related start and its general teaching comes across vividly in Vinoba Bhave's recollection of his attempt as a boy to read the Gita:

> [T]here was a copy of *Jnaneshwari* (Jnanadeva's thirteenth-century Marathi version of the Gita) in the house. I took it up and read the first chapter. There was a tremendous description of imminent war—the conches blew, the earth trembled . . . Now, I thought happily, there will be something really worthwhile. But when I read on I was bitterly disappointed—the wretched Arjuna had cooled off! Then in the second chapter the Lord rebuked him, rebuked him so severely that my hopes began to revive; now, I thought, the battle will begin! But what followed was an exposition of philosophy; it was too deep for me and I gave it up.[47]

Gandhi solves his Gita 'problem' by seeing its opening verses as an allegory. He claims that the Gita's Kurukshetra is the human soul where good fights evil.

> Even in 1888-89, when I first became acquainted with the Gita, I felt that it was not a historical work, but that, under the guise of physical warfare, it described the duel that perpetually went on in the hearts of mankind.[48]

On his part, Lal, as we have noted, sees the war as a real one and the Gita's Arjuna as the world's first pacifist. However, anxious to win India to nonviolence, Gandhi is unwilling to be content only with Arjuna's support, or to concede Krishna to political opponents believing in violence.

Lal, on the other hand, appears to see both the Gita and the Mahabharata as a contest between a peace-loving Arjuna and Krishna the enthusiast for war, and to claim that the Mahabharata's end—the unsparing carnage—vindicates Arjuna.

Gandhi's argument about the Gita not fitting into the scheme of the epic's story applies only to its longer, ethico-religious portion. The events in the opening one-and-a-half chapters form a natural part of the developing plot of the Mahabharata. The Arjuna hesitating to fight appears several times in the epic, and it is not strange to find him thus at the start of the Kurukshetra war. Not so strangely, Krishna succeeds in persuading him to fight.

On the other hand, it is not hard to concede the longer portion as an interpolation. (Some scholars see it as a post-Buddhist adaptation of key Buddhist ideas.[49]) And if we regard this longer portion as the Gita, then we can certainly agree with Gandhi that the Krishna in it issues no call for war.[50] Not only that, in Chapter Sixteen, verses 2 and 3, Krishna describes Ahimsa or Nonviolence, Peacefulness, Forgiveness and Compassion as divine qualities. Earlier, too, in Chapter Ten, verse 5, Ahimsa is eulogized.

If this major portion of the Gita were indeed an interpolation, it would be similar to numerous other interpolations that in different places break the epic's flow. We can look at an explanation of these interpolations:

> The Mahabharata was composed many thousand years ago. But generations of gifted reciters have added to Vyasa's original a great mass of material. All the floating literature that was thought to be worth preserving, historical, geographical, legendary, political, theological and philosophical, of nearly thirty centuries, found a place in it. In those days, when there was no printing, interpolation in a recognized classic seemed to correspond to inclusion in the national library.[51]

Sukthankar disagreed with the interpolation theory. To him the Gita and the Mahabharata as a whole, while using the imagery of war and 'the background of generalized history,' hint at the 'psychological conflict within man of the good and evil propensities.' Symbolizing powerlust, Duryodhana (adds Sukthankar) chose Krishna's armies, for they represented power, while Arjuna, symbolizing decency, chose Krishna, the man who was God.

The rider Arjuna is in reality the human soul, and Krishna the charioteer is the divine guide. Pointing out that the Gita calls the body 'kshetra' or the field (13:1), Sukthankar holds, in an opinion similar to Gandhi's, that Kurukshetra is actually 'the battlefield of the different emotions and passions in the heart of man.'[52]

*

More important, perhaps, than any 'real' or 'true' meaning of the

Gita is what contemporary Hindus believe its meaning to be. Many Hindus display in their homes a painting or sculpture of Krishna counselling Arjuna in a war chariot. That to them is the historical Gita—the divine song that restored Arjuna's courage, his manliness, his Kshatriya duty to fight in Kurukshetra.

But when it comes to the Gita as a guide to daily life, most Hindus are likely to ignore the battlefield and to say that the Gita asks human beings to do what they must, and to leave results in God's hands, or to Fate.

This meaning is amplified in 'Gita-Saar' ('Gita-Essence'), a one-page Hindi text often seen in north and central India on the sides of three-wheeler taxi-cabs or stuck on office walls or desks. No doubt distributed in other ways as well, 'Gita-Saar' comes as a free enclosure with a popular brand of incense. It can be translated as follows:

*Why do you worry in vain? Whom are you foolishly afraid of? Who can kill you? The soul is not born; neither does it die.

*What happened was for the best; what is happening is for the best; what will happen will also be for the best. Do not regret the past or be anxious for the future. As for the present, it moves on.

*What has been taken from you that you cry? What did you bring that you have lost? What did you create that has been destroyed? You brought nothing with you; your giving and receiving is here; it is from God and to God. You came empty-handed and that is how you will go. What you have belonged to another yesterday. Day after tomorrow it will belong to another. Thinking it is yours you feel happy—that is the source of your sorrows.

*Change is the law of the world. That which you think to be death is life. One moment you are the master of millions. The next moment you are reduced to poverty. Wipe out mine-thine, high-low, ours-theirs from your mind, banish it from your thoughts. Then all is yours and you are everyone's.

*This body is not yours; neither do you belong to this body. It is made of fire, water, air, earth, and sky, and there it will vanish. But the soul is firm. So what are you?

*Offer yourself to God, the strongest rock. Whoever knows of its support is freed forever from fear, anxiety, and grief.

* Keep offering whatever you do to God. So doing you will always experience the joy of deliverance.

In the Gita, Krishna speaks to Arjuna; in the 'essence' a modern and anonymous distiller of the Gita speaks to the reader. Relating sentences from this 'essence' to specific verses in the Gita can be a difficult exercise. Phrases such as 'change is the law of the world,' 'high-low' or 'ours-theirs' are not to be found in the Gita. Yet a student scanning the scripture can glimpse a basis for Gita-Saar's sentences. It is noteworthy that Gita-Saar makes no reference to war.

Reprinted recently for the thirty-eighth time and providing a verse-by-verse, word for word translation in Hindi, the *Shrimadbhagavadgita* published by the long-established Gita Press of Gorakhpur in eastern U.P. also sees the Gita outside its battlefield setting. A concluding chapter calls the Gita 'a wonderful, influential scripture that lifts man from the nadir to the summit,' assures non-Hindus and non-Indians that they can profit from it as much as Hindus and Indians, and adds:

> Let a man lost in anxiety, doubt or sorrow, and unable to see his way, turn to the Gita's verses, to their meaning and spirit; he will be freed from his burden and find contentment and peace.[53]

Like the unknown composer of Gita-Saar, the anonymous scholar providing the complete Hindi translation also sees the Gita as a guide, a balm, a staff or a lamp for human beings, rather than as a call to arms.

*

Differing in their reading of the Gita, Gandhi, Sukthankar and Lal seem to agree on the meaning of the Mahabharata. Says Lal:

> [The Mahabharata] is our Doomsday Epic, a grand tale of a pyrrhic victory. It ends with the Pandavas leaving Hastinapura with the taste of ashy triumph still in their mouths. What is the point of ruling when eighteen akshauhinis (one akshauhini = several divisions) of soldiers have been slaughtered and almost everyone you know is dead or dying? . . .

But Doomsday Epic should not be mistaken to mean Despair
Epic . . . To know all is to transcend all, to forgive all;
perhaps; one cannot be very sure; 'all' is too much and
forgiveness very difficult. But even the glimpse of totality
that Vyasa provides is an experience that suffices by helping
to minimise the malice we feel towards our enemies, soften
the contempt we have for the fanatic and the stupid . . .

╱Krishna does win the first round—he is able to get Arjuna to
fight and kill—but the end of the Mahabharata underlines
the futility of revengeful warfàre and restores the validity of
Arjuna's 'compassion.' Such is the essential structure and
message of India's Doomsday Epic: Without compassion all
is lost.[54]

To Sukthankar, 'the central theme of the poem is . . . the tragedy of
a futile and terrible war of annihilation.'[55] Gandhi, whose study of
the Mahabharata included 163 days given to it in prison in
1922-4,[56] wrote:

The author of the Mahabharata has not established the
necessity of physical warfare; on the contrary, he has proved
its futility. He has made the victors shed tears of sorrow and
repentance and has left them nothing but a legacy of miseries.[57]

Others draw similar conclusions. To Rajagopalachari, the Mahabharata
'drives home—as nothing else does—the vanity of ambition and the
evil and futility of ambition and hatred.'[58] To Kamala Subramaniam
'the Mahabharata is like a Greek tragedy.'[59] According to S.P. Dubey,
'the Mahabharata teaches us that the real conquest is not achieved in
the battlefield. There is a battle going on within man on his own
lower nature, and it must be won.'[60]

    Eleven centuries earlier, a Kashmiri literary critic,
Anandavardhana, argued that the 'meaning of the poem is *vairagya*,
profound disenchantment with the world.'[61]

    In his famous lament at the end of his epic, Vyasa says that
though he raises his arms and shouts that Artha and Kama, wealth
and pleasure, come from Dharma, no one listens. Translating Dharma
here as compassion—rather than as duty, which is how Dharma is
often regarded in the Mahabharata, including the Gita—, Lal gives his
interpretation of the lament:-

In compassion lies the meaning of life, and because both the

Kauravas and Pandavas lacked such compassion they destroyed themselves.[62]

Noting that Vyasa 'does not pause to ask why no one listens,' Lal wonders whether the answer might not lie in the fact 'that such dharmic compassion is very difficult, almost impossible for the common man to achieve.'

He may well be right. Yet in that case Lal would seem to be contradicting his own earlier statement that the Mahabharata 'should not be mistaken to mean Despair Epic.' Also, he would be discounting the capacity of ordinary human beings, especially when aided by God, to show compassion and forgiveness, a capacity that seems to be shown in age after age, including our own.

*

Here I may be allowed to refer to a remark a Japanese graduate student of mine made in the spring of 1997, during a study of the Mahabharata. With a frankness of the kind that the Japanese usually do not allow themselves, he blurted out, referring to the characters in the Mahabharata, 'But they are so weak!'

That many in the Mahabharata cast were angry, vengeful and violent, I well knew; who did not? But *weak*? Though that word had not earlier occurred to me in connection with the epic's characters, I felt unable to quite dismiss it. And I was less able to do so when, in answer to a question, the student explained his remark: 'They have no self-control.'

Re-reading the epic with the comment in mind, I felt I could often agree with it. Take, for instance, the discussion in the Pandava camp following Drona's death (Subramaniam).

> The roars and trumpets of Ashwatthama's counter-attack sounded frightening to the Pandavas. Arjuna blamed Yudhishthira and Dhrishtadyumna for the dishonest and unlawful way in which Drona had been killed, whereupon Bhima defended Yudhishthira, and Dhrishtadyumna criticized Arjuna for the subterfuges he had used against some of his Kaurava adversaries.

> At this Satyaki, who had a close bond with Arjuna, rose and shouted at Dhrishtadyumna: 'Do not dare to speak a word about Arjuna. If you do, I will split your head with this mace of mine.' Dhrishtadyumna 'laughed loud and long at

the words of Satyaki,' answered him with a list of Satyaki's
offences, including the beheading of Bhurishravas while the
latter was in yoga, and said, 'Come, let me see you break my
head.'

Satyaki rushed at Dhrishtadyumna (who, let us recall, was
the commander-in-chief of the Pandava forces) and was
about to smash his head when Bhima and Sahadeva grabbed
hold of him and pacified the two angry men. 'Krishna and
Sahadeva joined in the entreaties, and peace was brought
about with the greatest difficulty.'[63]

No doubt, as Lal points out, compassion is difficult, but is immaturity
as normal as suggested by the scene we have just looked at? Is
restraint in face of provocative remarks unthinkable? Even when a
great attack by the enemy is imminent?

If the questions can legitimately be answered negatively, then it
may also be permissible to ask whether perhaps the great Vyasa has
not conceded too much to weaknesses in human nature, and too
little to the capacity of men and women to rise above them.

Not that it is an ignoble society that he portrays. By the end of
the epic, his characters violate almost every item in their code of
chivalry, yet the code exists, and it is an impressive one, the more so
when one considers its ancient date.

Not to shoot from the rear, not to attack one engaged against
another foe, to spare women, children and the old, to withdraw from
the battlefield at sundown—these were only some of the norms to
which Vyasa's characters subscribed. And while violations occurred,
they were also censured.

A few codes remain unbroken. Thus the unity of the five
Pandava brothers survives despite every trial or twist of fate, as
indeed does the unity of the hundred Kaurava brothers. Considering
the history of fratricide in India and elsewhere, this is no mean feat
on the part of Vyasa's characters.

Nonetheless we must ask whether Vyasa quite satisfies us by
treating revenge as fact while regarding reconciliation, accommodation
and even acceptance as fancies, except in the rarest of rare cases.

Justice in the epic seems to belong to the Pandavas. They fulfil
their extraordinarily tough part of an agreement made with the
Kauravas, who, however, resolutely refuse to implement their half of
the deal. Their rampant envy and greed deprive the Kauravas of

escape-doors, and war becomes inevitable.

Yet equalling or even exceeding the Pandava thirst for justice is their desire for revenge. As for the Kauravas, they seek neither justice nor reconciliation but the elimination of the Pandavas.

In that famous and moving scene after the dice game, Draupadi finds herself totally helpless before a set of greedy, lustful men. Won and in effect fettered by the Kauravas, her powerful husbands are present but can only watch her misery as Duhshasana pulls at her single garment. In her isolation she cries out to God and her honour is saved; the garment is endlessly lengthened. It is Duhshasana's turn to feel defeated.

God—Krishna—protects Draupadi's honour, but can He not also protect lives and prevent bloodshed by quenching revenge? We saw that Gandhari asks the question in the epic. Yet Vyasa will not go beyond recording the question. No character of his cries out for such an intervention the way Draupadi burned and prayed for the protection of her honour.

In the epic, is reconciliation anyone's, even Krishna's, aim? Vidura's, perhaps, though he is really partial to the Pandavas and even possibly Yudhishthira's undisclosed father. Justice, revenge, war and even negotiation, all these are superbly delineated in the Mahabharata, but reconciliation is not, even though Vyasa sees its need. Though sometimes referred to, and once, as we saw, magnificently portrayed in a vision, no character embodies or even seriously attempts reconciliation.

Krishna does not ask the Pandava brothers or anyone else to cultivate forgiveness. True, he mentions it in the Gita as a divine quality, and we also saw Yudhishthira extolling it in fine language. But the epic supplies few instances of someone actually struggling with an impulse to forgive, or praying for the ability to forgive. With trembling hands Arjuna wonders whether or not he should fight, yet no warrior on either side trembles about forgiving, or not forgiving, an injurer.

'I want to forgive, but the hurt is too deep, and forgiveness too hard, help me O Krishna.' Such a plea we do not hear, and Krishna does not encourage. Again, seldom is a blow from a warrior restrained by his pity, or followed by remorse. Cries for mercy—'Spare me!'— can be found in the epic, but not pleas for forgiveness for injury caused. This hardness is joined by a blindness—no character seems able to glimpse something of his nature in the enemy, or of the enemy's nature in himself.

Perhaps Vyasa was only portraying history, and could not create a reconciling character or attempt that did not exist. If so, his pessimism was only faithfulness to the facts as he saw them. And perhaps, as Lal and others have suggested, we can detect a message of compassion in the fumes of the epic's vast tragedy.

However, the fact remains that thanks to his genius and the power of his Mahabharata, Vyasa has bequeathed to Indian centuries that followed him a sense that tempests of hate, war, and revenge must follow one another in an unending sequence—that Ashwatthama can never die, or even sleep.

No wonder there has been a tradition that while the Mahabharata may be respected as the fifth Veda, a Dharmashastra as well as an Itihaasa, it should be approached warily. One version of the tradition even discourages householders from keeping a copy of the Mahabharata at home.

*

Revenge and cruelty also mark Homer's Iliad, which was probably written around 1000 BC, i.e. at about the time of the War that the Mahabharata describes. When Achilles' dear friend Patroclus is killed by Hector, Achilles swears: 'I will no longer live among men if I do not make Hector pay with his death for Patroclus dead.' The oath is fearsomely redeemed:

> On came Achilles, glorious as the sun when he rises. Beside him was Athena (the goddess Minerva), but Hector was alone . . . [He] turned and fled. Three times around the wall of Troy pursued and pursuer ran with flying feet . . . Athena had tricked him and there was no way of escape . . .

> Achilles had a spear, the one Athena had recovered for him. Before Hector could approach, he who knew well that armour [worn] by Hector aimed at an opening near the throat, and drove the spearpoint in. Hector fell, dying at last. With his last breath he prayed, 'Give back my body to my father and my mother.' 'No prayers from you to me, you dog,' Achilles answered. 'I would that I could make myself devour raw your flesh for the evil you have brought upon me.' Then Hector's soul flew forth from his body and was gone to Hades . . .

> Achilles stripped the bloody armour from the corpse while

the Greeks ran up to wonder how tall he was as he lay there and how noble to look upon. But . . . Achilles pierced the feet of the dead man and fastened them with thongs to the back of his chariot, letting the head trail. Then he lashed his horses and round and round the walls of Troy he dragged all that was left of glorious Hector.

At last when his fierce soul was satisfied with vengeance he stood beside the body of Patroclus and said, 'Hear me even in the house of Hades. I have dragged Hector behind my chariot and I will give him to the dogs to devour . . .'[64]

Wanting his son's body, Hector's old father Priam, guided by the god Zeus, goes to Achilles with gifts and 'stretches out [his] hand to the slayer of his son.' Appeased and moved, Achilles says to Priam: 'Sit by me here, and let our sorrow lie in our hearts. Evil is all men's lot, but yet we must keep courage.' . . . Then Priam brought Hector home, and after nine days' lamentation there was a stately funeral.[65]

In this story, as in the Mahabharata, we witness trickery by a divine person (a goddess in this case), a chariot, a god[dess] and a warrior together, and a terrible revenge, all reminding us of Bhima and Duhshasana/Duryodhana, and of Krishna/Arjuna versus Karna. Also, the Bhima-Gandhari conversation we have seen is suggestive of the Priam-Achilles conversation. Again, the suspense before the funeral of Hector reminds us of a Mahabharata discussion before last rites for the Kauravas were allowed by Bhima. In both cases the dead were finally honoured, even if the living had been cruelly killed.

Yet the Iliad underwent changes not paralleled in the Mahabharata's case. Thus in the hands of Ovid, the Latin poet writing a thousand years later after Homer, 'the stories which were factual truth and solemn truth to the early Greek poets . . . and vehicles of deep religious truth to the Greek tragedians, [became] idle tales, sometimes witty and diverting . . .'[66] A similar change in attitudes to the Mahabharata has not occurred in India. Despite the passage of centuries, the epic's tales remain solemn, grave and grim.

We may note the irony that while in the Greek epics 'the Hellenic race was marked off from the barbarian as more keen-witted and more free from nonsense,'[67] in the Mahabharata it is the Greeks who are referred to as the Mlecchas or barbarians.

*

We will conclude this chapter with a glance at the relationship between the epic and India. The late V.S. Sukthankar had said:

> The Mahabharata is the content of our collective unconscious
> . . . It refuses to be discarded. We must therefore grasp this
> great book with both hands and face it squarely. Then we
> shall recognise that it is our past which has prolonged itself
> into the present. We are it: I mean the real We.[68]

In Lal's view, 'Vyasa's epic is a mirror in which the Indian sees
himself undeceived.' Also, 'the theme of this epic is the history of
India.'[69]

According to Rajagopalachari, 'The Mahabharata discloses a . . .
civilisation and a . . . society which, though of an older world,
strangely resembles the India of our own times, with the same values
and ideals.'[70]

Every bloody event, war, act of revenge or victory by treachery
witnessed on Indian soil subsequent to the epic seems to bear some
resemblance to a scene from it. As Sukthankar put it, the past appears
to have thrust itself into the present.

The carnage in the battles of Tarain, where Prithviraj fought
Ghauri, or in the three battles of Panipat, not only bore a similarity
to the Kurukshetra bloodshed but took place on the same tract north
of Delhi.

Some conflicts of Indian history such as the Muslim-Sikh clashes
of the seventeenth and eighteenth centuries (which found echoes also
in the nineteenth and twentieth centuries) and the Maratha-Mughal
and the Maratha-Afghan tussles in the seventeenth and eighteenth
centuries displayed elements that were central to the Mahabharata—
cruelty, revenge and recrimination regarding foul play.

Apart from the similarity, previously noted, in the killings of
Drona and Guru Tegh Bahadur, we can also observe that words
expressed by the Guru on forgiveness resemble the words, quoted
earlier, that Yudhishthira had addressed to Draupadi on the same
subject. Said the Guru:

> Forgiveness is the austerity most meritorious; forgiveness is
> the best of charities. It is equivalent to all the pilgrimages
> and ablutions. In forgiveness lies liberation. No other virtue
> parallels forgiveness.

Yet Guru Tegh Bahadur seemed to go beyond the Mahabharata in
demonstrating forgiveness in his life. When an attempt on the Guru's

life by his nephew Dhir Mall, who aspired to the throne of the Guru, failed, the Guru's reply was: 'Blessed be Dhir Mall, blessed be he.' When a follower of the Guru plundered Dhir Mall, the Guru had all his possessions returned.[71]

Perhaps no historical event recalls the epic to mind more than the 1857 Rebellion and the British empire's reply to it. If some other clashes do not suggest the same degree of similarity with the Mahabharata, the reason may partly lie in our lack of detailed knowledge about them. Like the Mahabharata, but unlike many other conflicts, the 1857 Rebellion is voluminously recorded.

Loyalty to those who had provided shelter or position was an issue both in the Mahabharata and in 1857. Despite strong pulls, Bhishma, Drona, and Karna remained with the Kauravas for the sake of loyalty.

When Kunti, Karna's mother, strove to win him to the Pandava side, Karna recalled the kingship of Anga given to him by Duryodhana, and added:

> There are men who accept food and shelter, but turn into scoundrels when the time for repayment comes. They betray the bread of their masters, they deceive the rajas they once served. For such rascals, there is neither this world nor the next. I have chosen the side of Duryodhana . . . I will not play false . . . How can I desert them?[72]

For the same reason, some Indians continued to serve the British in 1857 even after a widespread mutiny had broken out, while after their defeat some of the rebels felt that their disloyalty may have helped cause it. A group of sepoys are quoted as having said:

> Sahib, it has been all the work of fate. After what we had done, we never could fight. No matter whether your troops were black or white, native or European, we could not fight; *our salt choked us.*[73]

Trapped in the Lucknow Residency, British officers, we learn, sent spies out in 1857 with messages written in Greek: even if seized, the messages were likely to remain ununderstood. In identical fashion, when in the presence of Duryodhana's spies Vidura wanted to convey a private message to Yudhishthira, he 'whispered it,' Vyasa tells us, 'in the little-known dialect of the Mlecchas.'[74] The derogatory term Mleccha could refer to outcastes or to aliens; here a foreign language was meant.

It was Ashwatthama's attack on the sleeping children in the Pandava tents that had incurred Krishna's deepest wrath in the Mahabharata. 'Because you kill children,' Krishna told him, 'your punishment will be this—you will wander for three thousand years on the face of this earth.'[75] Likewise, it was the killing of British children in Delhi, Kanpur and elsewhere that in 1857 roused the extreme hostility of Britain.

The rebels, an enraged missionary wrote, had 'imbrued their hands in the innocent blood of women and children . . . and that very blood was appealing to heaven for vengeance.'[76] After the British recaptured Kanpur, they had found evidence, 'tresses and plaits of hair,' that women and children or their bodies had been dragged—a merger of the epic's scenes of Draupadi's humiliation by Duhshasana and Ashwatthama's attack on the Pandava children.

Then Neill, leader of the British force in Kanpur, ordered his notorious punishment, which we can see as a modified version of Bhima's revenge with Duhshasana's blood, with the difference that under Neill's 1857 orders the captured rebel was forced, before being hanged, to lick a square foot of dried British blood, instead of the British drinking the Indian enemy's blood.[77]

In the Mahabharata, Bhima kills the terrorizing king of Magadha, Jarasandha, by catching his two legs and splitting his body into two. There is a record of an 1857 incident where Indians on the British side killed a captured rebel in identical fashion.

Detailed in several accounts, the sack of Lucknow after its capture by the British in 1858—the revelry, loot, plunder, and excitement—seems not very different from the end-Mahabharata scenes of the Yadavas of Dwarka.

> The Yadavas went to the beach for a picnic and spent the whole day in dance and drink and revelry . . . At first merry, then pugnacious, they began to talk without restraint, raking up old offences and quarrelling with one another.[78]

Even more than events, a value exalted by some protagonists on the real stage of Indian history reminds us of the message of the Gita. We have seen how some Gita students, including those fighting for India's independence from the British, picked out its emphasis on duty performed without concern for results. In the 1820s, Sir Thomas Munro, who served the British Raj in several offices including as the governor of Madras, gave the following advice to the Court of

Directors of the East India Company in London:

> Your rule is alien and it can never be popular. You have
> much to bring to your subjects but you cannot look for
> more than passive gratitude. You are not here to turn India
> into England or Scotland. Work through, not in spite of,
> native systems and native ways, and with a prejudice in their
> favour rather than against them; and when in the fulness of
> time your subjects can frame and maintain a worthy
> Government for themselves, get out and take *the sense of
> having done your duty as the chief reward of your exertions.*[79]

When Henry Lawrence, Lieutenant-Governor of the North-West
Province (soon to become part, along with Awadh, of the United
Provinces) was critically injured during the Lucknow siege in 1857,
he dictated his own epitaph: 'Put on my tomb only this—"Here lies
Henry Lawrence who *tried to do his duty.* May God have mercy on
him." '[80]

As one writer puts it, 'A number of generals at the time of the
Mutiny were old, infirm and gout-ridden, but as there was no
compulsory retirement they *generalled on until they died.*'[81]

So the Gita's central precept, Duty, was religiously followed by
the Raj—an ever-relevant and seemingly satisfying norm, yet
insufficient to cut the chain of revenge.

In fact many a political act in modern India, irrespective of who
it involved, white or brown, Christians, Muslims, Hindus or Sikhs,
seemed directly or indirectly to recall a Mahabharata scene.

Thus Jallianwala (1919), a mass killing that gave the mass no
opening to escape, could have come straight out of the Mahabharata;
and the 1922 mowing down of policemen fleeing from the burning
police post in Chauri Chaura was reminiscent of the slaughter by
Ashwatthama, Kripacharya and Kritavarma of Pandava soldiers
running from their burning tents.

In less dramatic ways also the Mahabharata and 'real' history can
match each other. Thus in one of the epic's post-war scenes,
Yudhishthira assures Vidura that Dhritarashtra can have the money
he had requested for a shraddha ceremony for the Kaurava dead—for
Bhishma, Drona, Jayadratha and the hundred sons. When Vidura
wonders whether Bhima would not object to this expenditure on
rites for the enemy, Yudhishthira says, 'Bhima will agree, whether he
likes it or not.'

This reminded me of something I had come across while

researching for my biography of Sardar Vallabhbhai Patel: Gandhi's confidence that Patel, his 'tough' associate, 'my younger brother', as Gandhi sometimes called him, would agree to a step contemplated, e.g. a gesture towards Jinnah or the Muslim League. 'Whether he likes it or not, the Sardar will agree,' Gandhi would claim, and be proved right.

Outside India as well, the war of the Mahabharata was at least faintly reproduced in the Crusades, which even had a Krishna of their own. In the Crusades, Christ (or at least the figure of Christ) supported one side, like Krishna in the Mahabharata, rather than remaining neutral. They have left a legacy of revenge, rather like the note left by the Mahabharata war.

*

'What is in this work may be found elsewhere, but what is not in this work is to be found nowhere,' claims the Mahabharata.[82] An empty boast? Even our quick glance indicates the epic's breadth and depth, and shows reflections of the epic's patterns in Indian history; we mark the truth in Sukthankar's comment that the Mahabharata is our past thrusting itself into the present—that we were, are, and possibly will be the Mahabharata.

Yet this truth is not wholly comforting. That the epic, emerging from a history of our past, is continually recreated on Indian soil can of course only be true in spirit; the epic cannot recreate itself literally. Yet even in spirit an inescapable continual recreation of the Mahabharata, while an extraordinary tribute to the epic's grasp of human nature and of some forces of history, would also be an extraordinary condemnation of the Indian people's maturity and common sense levels.

Proud as we are of the epic's codes of chivalry, we cannot be proud, I suggest in all humility, of the story, or history, it reveals. In particular, we cannot be proud of the epic's acquiescence in the triumph of revenge over reconciliation. I suggest, further, that we cannot be glad that the epic is reproduced in varied forms in our history.

When Lal calls the epic 'a mirror in which the Indian sees himself undeceived,' I infer that the Mahabharata enables human beings (not Indians alone) to see the pride, revenge, and treachery of which they are capable. When he adds that 'the theme of this epic is the history of India,' I say yes, but sadly, and I am unable to say, 'So be it.'

Part of me filled with pride at the range and power of 'my' Mahabharata, as every Indian can think of the epic, another part of me sorrows for the pain that pride, revenge and treachery have brought to India. I suggest, deferentially again, that a continual recreation of the epic, a continual prolongation of the past into the present, is the opposite of what we should be hoping for.

To me this sentence from that noble scholar of the epic, Sukthankar, is significant:

> We must therefore grasp this great book with both hands
> and face it squarely.

Not only must we, with all hands, grasp this great book—this powerful vehicle careering down the slopes of India's history; we must stop it in its tracks, and control and use it for India's peace and joy.

Today the Mahabharata overawes and overwhelms us. 'We are it'—but also stared down by It. In the relationship between India and the Mahabharata, the former seems the weaker party!

Rightly does Lal say that 'the quality of [a] person's Indianness' is determined by the 'degree, range and subtlety' of his or her exposure to the Ramayana and the Mahabharata.[83] Yet joy in Indianness or being Indian may also depend on our ability to grasp and stop the Mahabharata with our hands, and see it squarely.

As we have found even in this short survey, clues for this crucial exercise are contained in the epic itself. As one of the greatest of the epic's modern scholars, Lal, says:

> The essential Mahabharata is whatever [in the epic] is relevant
> to us in the second half of the twentieth century; . . .
> whatever we would like to see passed on to our children so
> that they get clearer insights and perspectives into the
> intricate business of living . . .[84]

If, facing the Mahabharata squarely and rejecting the pride and revenge that triumph in it, we learn what may be 'essential' to it— the (unimplemented) reconciliation it envisions and the (undemonstrated) forgiveness it prescribes—, then future generations might speak of the Mahabharata's blessing and not of its curse.

Vyasa says towards the end of the Mahabharata: 'The intelligent interpreter of this great epic is cleansed of all impurities.'[85] To see our history with the aid of the Mahabharata, and to seek humbly to interpret the Mahabharata wisely, is therefore not only a permissible duty; it is a prescribed duty.

2

A Dissenting Tradition,
or the Second Thread

BORN IN THE fifth or sixth century BC, Siddhartha Gautama, who became the Buddha or the Enlightened One, was the son of the chief of the Kshatriya clan that dominated the Sakya republic straddling the modern borders of Nepal, eastern U.P. and north Bihar. South of the Sakyas lay the kingdom of Magadha, ruled by Bimbisara, perhaps the first significant king recorded by Indian history. An energetic ruler who contracted marriage alliances with neighbouring princes, Bimbisara raised an efficient bureaucracy, built roads, conquered Anga on the edge of modern Bengal, and controlled trade along the Ganga.

The land was rich, yielding revenue to farmers and to the king. The Ganga and the new roads made trade rewarding. Towns were emerging along the great river, and across a fair part of North India tribal society was giving way either to new kingdoms such as Magadha, or to republics, which tended to occupy the Himalayan foothills. It was an age of change.

Seven years before the Buddha's death, Bimbisara was killed by his son Ajatashatru, who was succeeded by five kings each of whom had killed his father and seized the throne. It was in such a context of ambition, greed and parricide that the Buddha's message of compassion, ahimsa or nonviolence, and renunciation of desire was delivered.

Troubled by the suffering he saw around him, the young Siddhartha first sought a remedy in asceticism. The serene face of an ascetic had impressed him, and he left his beautiful wife and infant son to search for 'the truth.' After several years of wandering, austerities and reflection, he received, in Gaya in Bihar, the enlightenment that desires produced suffering, and that renunciation of desires was possible, not through extreme austerities but through understanding and disciplining one's changing and transient self. Said the Buddha:

'He insulted me, he struck me
He defeated me, he robbed me!'
Those who harbour such thoughts
Are never appeased in their hatred . . .
But those who do not harbour them
Are quickly appeased.

Never in the world is hate
Appeased by hatred;
It is only appeased by love—
This is the eternal law.

Victory (conquest) breeds hatred
For the defeated lie down in sorrow.
Above victory or defeat
The calm man dwells in peace.[1]

Another Buddhist text states:

The monk Gautama has given up injury to life . . .; he has
laid aside the cudgel and the sword, and he lives modestly,
full of mercy, desiring in compassion the welfare of all
things living . . .

He has given up false speech, he has lost all inclination to it.
He speaks the truth, he keeps faith, . . . he does not break
his word to the world.[2]

Elsewhere the Buddha said that even if 'carved limb from limb with
a double-handed saw,' his true disciple should not entertain hate.[3]

The contrast that these verses and texts provide to the
Mahabharata's oaths of vengeance is complete. While 'Conquer
yourself' was 'the demand that Buddhism had taught the Indian
people to make of manly men,'[4] many of the Mahabharata's heroes,
we saw, were disinclined to check themselves.

We should note, too, that while orthodoxy stressed caste duty—
the duty of a Brahmin, or a Kshatriya, or a Vaishya or a Shudra—
the Buddha addressed each person as an individual rather than as a
member of a caste. Without revolting against caste, the Buddha
disregarded it. Also, he privileged individual judgment. Before dying,
he left a message for all his disciples through one of them:

So, Ananda, you must be your own lamps, be your own
refuges . . . Hold firm to the truth as a lamp and as a refuge.[5]

For merit or reward, and also for propitiating nature, orthodoxy prescribed ceremonies of sacrifice, with Brahmin priests chanting verses from the Vedas, and animals being slaughtered. The Buddha declared that such ceremonies were unnecessary, and he saw cruelty in animal sacrifices.

Mingling with sinners, outcastes and prostitutes and using, in his speech, the Magadhi of his area rather than Sanskrit, the language of the elect, the Buddha held a special appeal for the socially downtrodden. These included the farmers and traders of the Vaishya caste, who though often well-off were denied social status, the Shudras, and women. In the Brahmanical system, the latter two categories, deemed of low status, were barred from learning the Vedic verses. Women and Shudras were thus inclined to think favourably of someone who questioned the value of reciting the verses.

While opposing the Brahmanical system, the Buddha took care not to turn Brahmin or Brahman into a pejorative phrase. Holding that anyone, irrespective of birth, could acquire spiritual merit and become a Brahmin, the Buddha seems to have asserted that he himself had become one.[6]

Though advocating renunciation of desire and giving rise to associations of celibate monks and nuns, Buddhism had a vision for worldly life and society as well. Among other things it envisaged a king—a chakravarti (cakkavatti in Pali)—who maintained order and justice, and was the counterpart in the social world of the spiritual world's Enlightened One. But in the Buddhist perspective the king had no divine right, and the throne he was able to occupy obliged him to look after his subjects—a perspective that has been termed 'one of the world's oldest versions of the contractual theory of the state.'[7]

The Buddha also seemed to imply a connection between renunciation and reconciliation. Where revenge is renounced, the link is obvious, but even where other desires are renounced, and even when, as happened with the Buddha himself and with the monks who emerged as a result of his teaching, the family is 'renounced,' human beings outside the family—more numerous than the family—may obtain the renouncer's attention. A renouncing king may thus prove to be a reconciling king.

The influence of Siddhartha Gautama, the scion of the Sakya clan and thus also known as Sakyamuni, would in time reach the ends of the earth. In countries as populous as China and Japan and in Korea and Vietnam, Buddhism would claim more adherents than any other faith, and Thailand, Burma, Sri Lanka, Tibet, Cambodia, and Laos would call themselves Buddhist lands. In the twentieth century many in the West would seek solace in Buddhism, and towards the century's end Asia would contain nearly 750 million Buddhists.[8]

After initially embracing the Buddha's message as a doctrine and a faith, India chose to incorporate and even to dissolve Buddhism in Hindu orthodoxy, which however was modified by some of Buddhism's insights. Buddhist manifestations that survived Hindu absorption—monasteries, universities and Buddhist images—were destroyed by Muslim rulers who occupied northern India from the end of the twelfth century. Schisms and sects would divide Buddhists in many countries; societies calling themselves Buddhist would at times practise revenge and oppression; and in India Buddhism, and a sister heterodoxy, Jainism, would on occasion be reduced to a question of diet. Yet a standard had been raised from Indian soil that would remain an alternative to revenge and powerlust.

*

Scholars have linked Buddhism to India's Sramana or Samana tradition, which is seen as having a pre-Vedic and pre-Aryan origin. Wandering free of family ties, living by alms, thinking for themselves, and often rejecting the cosmic or nature gods praised in the verses of the Vedas, the Sramanas belonged to a variety of schools. One comprised the severely austere Ajivikas, who often fasted or went naked but believed that humans could not influence their future lives, another the Materialists (the Charvakas), who denied a future life and thought that death extinguished everything forever, and a third, the Skeptics, who asserted that truths of life and afterlife were beyond knowledge.

Though he had become a Sramana himself, the Buddha opposed the views of the extreme ascetics as sharply as he opposed Brahmin orthodoxy. Two of his chief disciples were Skeptics to begin with, and the Buddha agreed with the Materialists that experience was the source of knowledge.[9]

Vardhamana Mahavira

Another follower of the Sramana tradition who would go down in history and whose influence would last was Vardhamana, or Mahavira, the Great Hero, the founder, as some think, of the Jaina view of life.

Others regard him as the twenty-fourth and last propounder of the Jaina religion. A contemporary of Siddhartha Gautama, Vardhamana too was a Kshatriya emerging from the republics of the Himalayan foothills to the north of Bihar. His father was a clan chief, and his mother a sister of the chief of the bigger Lichavi clan. At thirty, Vardhamana too left home in search of truth or salvation; after twelve years as an ascetic wanderer across the Ganga valley he also found Enlightenment; and ahimsa was a value that Mahavira also stressed.

The string of similarities would suggest that Siddhartha and Vardhamana were two names for the same person, but there seems to be enough historical evidence to show their separate identities, and dissent from some Jaina views is carefully spelt out in ancient Buddhist texts.

Both Mahavira and the Buddha disagreed with the fatalism of the Ajivikas, but the Buddha seems to have regarded as too extreme the asceticism of Mahavira,[10] whose death at the age of seventy-two, in a village near modern Patna, is said to have followed a self-imposed fast.

Perfection in self-control was a Jaina goal; the term Jaina or Jain comes from Jina, a spiritual conqueror or victor. Some Jaina texts can, not very appealingly, suggest (as can some Buddhist texts) that violence to others is 'to be avoided not so much because it harms other beings as because it harms the individual who commits it,' or that 'the chief reason for doing good is the furtherance of one's own spiritual ends.'[11] Also, the emphasis given in some Jaina traditions to avoiding injury to insects can seem disproportionate.

The strength of Jainism lay in two remarkable philosophical concepts, syadavada, the doctrine of 'perhaps' or 'maybe,' and anekantavada, the doctrine of the many-sidedness of truth. These ideas were powerful obstacles to any march of intolerance or arrogant self-righteousness, usual companions of revenge.

Equally significant is a trinity of values often stressed in Jainism, maitri (friendliness), kshama (forgiveness), and abhaya (fearlessness), although the context or period in which these values became important to Jainism does not seem to be clear. At the end of the Jaina year, a Jaina, whether a monk or a layperson, is expected to confess sins, repay debts, and ask forgiveness of neighbours for hurts caused. Jaina scholars trace back the word kshama to a BC time, but the annual forgiveness ceremony seems to have started in the nineteenth century.[12]

A THEORETICAL DISCUSSION

In a book edited by him, *Orthodoxy, Heterodoxy and Dissent in India*, S.N. Eisenstadt reminds us that

> Max Weber in his classic essays on the comparative sociology of religions . . . was one of the first to stress the role played by dissent and heterodoxy. [This role determined] how different civilizations varied in the dynamics of their innovative capacity.

For Europe, Weber identified the Protestant ethic, or the work ethic, the Wirtschaftsethik, as a key fruit of Protestant dissent. According to Eisenstadt, an ethic 'can be viewed as a kind of code, a general orientation or deep structure which programs or regulates the social organization of any given society.'[13]

In our look at Indian history, we will keep in mind this Weberian hypothesis regarding orthodoxy and dissent. Though proof may be lacking that the Mahabharata describes historical events, we will treat the epic as the Indian orthodoxy. And we will regard as the 'message' of this orthodoxy not what some readers of the Mahabharata including Gandhi and Lal have culled from its ending, or what its creator, Vyasa, might have wished to convey, namely the *folly* of revenge, but what has pervaded most of the epic and gripped its readers, listeners and viewers—the *appeal* of revenge.

As the fount and start of the Indian heterodoxy, we shall take the Buddha. Looking at the contest over time between the lure of revenge and the call of those who in spirit if not always in form were the Buddha's followers or successors, we may perhaps, in accordance with the hypothesis, obtain a useful angle on the dynamics of Indian civilization.[14]

Our characterization of orthodoxy and dissent in India differs from the conventional, which regards the Vedic or Brahmanical system as the Indian orthodoxy, and the religions of Buddhism and Jainism as the heterodoxy. Thus one of those who sharply differentiated Buddhist India from what he saw as Brahmanic India was Ambedkar. He wrote:

> It must be recognized that there never has been a common Indian culture . . . It must be recognized that the history of India before the Muslim invasions is the history of a mortal conflict between Brahmanism and Buddhism.[15]

However, while Ambedkar spoke of Brahmanism and Buddhism, and others have underlined the heterodox dissent from the Brahmin-privileging Vedas, we will contrast (the Mahabharata's) revenge with (the Buddha's) reconciliation.

As we look at this contrast and contest between the legacies of the Mahabharata and the Buddha, we will try to see whether, or to what extent, this heterodoxy or dissent in India produced an ethic or culture opposed to that of revenge and comparable in influence to the work ethic that Weber detected in Europe. In particular, we will examine the hospitality that Indian soil has offered to reconciliation, or to its lesser sisters, accommodation and acceptance. As we shall see, all three may be regarded as issuing from, or closely allied to, the Buddha's message.

In line with Eisenstadt's definition of a national or civilizational ethic, our study would ask if there are grounds in India's history and contemporary life for believing that reconciliation rather than revenge can become a code, orientation, or basic impulse in Indian and South Asian society. If, for example, some like Asoka, Akbar, Kabir, Guru Nanak and Gandhi are found to belong to a line, started by the Buddha, of those dissenting from the Mahabharata's orthodoxy of revenge, it would also be necessary to ask questions about the strength and longevity of their influence.

There is an obvious objection to our approach. While there seems to be general agreement that the Great War which is the subject matter of the Mahabharata may have taken place several hundred or even a thousand years before the Buddha (who died circa 483 BC[16]), it is by no means universally accepted that the epic was composed before the Buddha's time. Thus, *The Gazetteer of India* holds that 'the epic attained its present shape in a hundred thousand verses . . . over the long stretch of years between the 4th century BC and the 4th century AD'.[17]

Then there is the view that portions of the Mahabharata, including the Bhagavad Gita and parts of the Shanti Parva devoted to ethical and philosophical teaching, indirectly refer to, and indeed refute, aspects of Buddhist doctrines. For instance, it is held that the Gita's defence of action, while coupled with the advice of unconcern with the fruits of action, was a reply to the withdrawal from the world supposedly recommended by Buddhism.

Given this view of what came first and who was answering whom, is it logical to describe the Buddha as dissenting from the Mahabharata? Well, yes, provided we can suppose that the doctrines, histories and legends of revenge and counter-revenge that found expression in epic form after the Buddha's death enjoyed currency in his lifetime, or earlier.

That this was so seems generally accepted.[18] If, in all probability, the legends and histories of the Great War were part of the collective memory during the lifetime of the Buddha—the epic refers to kings from Magadha and Anga, lands with which the Buddha was deeply involved—, we can also assume that the future Mahabharata's themes of powerlust, pride and revenge were already in the public mind.

Writes Sarvepalli Radhakrishnan, the philosopher who was India's President from 1962 to 1967:

> We do not know exactly when the Mahabharata was composed. We may be pretty certain that about the time of the rise of Buddhism the Mahabharata was known . . . The Mahabharata was well established about the time of Buddha.[19]

But he adds:

> The Mahabharata is sometimes called the fifth Veda . . . The Buddhist scriptures were thrown open to all, while the sacred books of the Brahmins were confined to the three higher classes. Hence the necessity for a fifth Veda open to all.[20]

Taken together, the two quotes imply that while the Mahabharata was 'known' and even 'established' during the Buddha's time, the epic was presented to the public after Buddhist scriptures had been thrown open. The epic might not have been composed by the time of the Buddha, but revenge had found a home in India and in Indian history. We can assume that it was seen as a normal and unavoidable human response, and for Kshatriyas a required response, a sign of their manhood and authenticity.

The Buddha had challenged this thinking, and he had also undermined the privileged status of the Brahmins. In reply, the 'well-established' epic was 'presented' to the public.

It will be noticed that we do not regard the Mahabharata's revenge as a recent distillation, interpretation or construct. Our assumption is that revenge was always associated with the epic. We believe, further, that throughout Indian history rulers and political leaders wishing to mobilize a clan, a caste or an ethnic or sectarian group for revenge would have found encouragement, stimulus or justification in the Mahabharata. It is submitted that these are reasonable assumptions.[21]

With the Buddha's message a second thread entered the Indian story. Compassion was presented as an alternative to revenge. That the Buddha was a Kshatriya made his dissenting doctrine of compassion more interesting. In the pages that follow, we will attempt to understand the subsequent history of India against the background of a continuing clash between (the Mahabharata's) revenge and (the Buddha's) reconciliation.

*

The revenge-reconciliation dialectic is of course only one of several ways in which some meaning in Indian/South Asian history may be sought. We could have tried to extend the discussion of the *Sramanical/ Brahmanical dialectic*, contrasting the tradition of the ascetic interested in transcendental rather than worldly goals with the tradition of the priest who blesses secular activities and is indispensable for legitimizing them, and who may also exercise varying degrees of control.[22]

Early in the fourth century BC, Megasthenes had observed Sramanas and Brahmins in Mauryan India; they and their descendants, theological or political, have played crucial roles ever since. Buddhism and Jainism are usually seen as Sramanical, and popular Hinduism as Brahmanical; it can be instructive to study, over a period, the conflicts and compromises between the two tendencies.

We have noted that the Sramanical has been identified with what is perceived as the pre-Aryan Indus Valley civilization, while the Brahmanical is linked to 'the Aryan migrants who came to India sometime later in the course of prehistory.'[23] One problem with this perspective is that controversies about the origins of the Aryans, the identity of the members of the Indus Valley civilization, and the origins and identities of others inhabiting South Asia in prehistory are far from being resolved.

These controversies, and the sharp disagreements about who at the dawn of history was indigenous to the subcontinent and who an outsider, also complicate any attempt to study Indian history *as an evolving conflict between races.* On the other hand, looking at the past with Marxian and neo-Marxian postulates of *a succession of struggles between haves and have-nots* is unlikely to be a fresh exercise. One reason for proceeding along *rejection/accommodation* is that it is a road less travelled.

Allied values. It may be useful to look at some siblings of revenge and reconciliation. We will find, as this narrative proceeds, that the latter has several brothers or sisters: forgiveness, accommodation, acceptance, adjustment, innovation, compromise, coalition, teamwork, flexibility, trust, concern with the present and the future, redress, restitution, submission to the rule of law, and more.

To forgive is not necessarily to forget or to disregard an enemy's offences. An American scholar, Donald Shriver, argues that 'forgiveness begins with a remembering and a moral judgment of wrong, injustice, and injury.' According to Shriver, forgiveness in a political context is an act that joins moral truth (or moral judgment, plus memory of wrong), forbearance from vengeance, empathy (for the enemy's humanity, which is different from sympathy for the enemy's aims), and commitment to repair a fractured human relationship.[24]

Revenge's siblings include rejection, take it or leave it, all or nothing, now or never, one-sided and emotional recollections of the past, rigidity, powerlust, going-it-alone, dismissal, exclusion, rebuff, repudiation, suspicion, distrust, elimination, and submission to an individual's wishes.

'Revenge . . . was held of more account than self-preservation.' Writing in the fifth century BC, Thucydides might have been commenting on the Mahabharata's Great War, but in fact he was referring to the consequences of the Peloponnesian War.

Siblings of revenge differ in meaning or emphasis. Shriver has tried to spell out the different implications of some of them. In his table, terror means that for damage to one of our eyes, we put out all the eyes we wish. Some of his other equations are as follows:

Vindictiveness: two or more eyes for one.

Retaliation: eye for eye, tooth for tooth, *and no more.*

Punishment (though often a sibling of revenge or retribution, it may at times signify justice): for your hurt we will hurt you, but in more humane ways. Our punishment must reassert the norms you have defiled.[25]

There are values that would seem to lie outside the two columns, e.g. honour, justice, courage, equality, autonomy, independence, self-respect, self-defence, deterrence, dignity and strength—values that we might, in a very broad sense, describe as justice and its siblings. An apparent seeker after revenge might also, or perhaps primarily, be striving for some of these goals; or honour, justice or independence might merely be a mask for vengeance.

> He has no regard for due process of law, justice or democracy. Tolerance is non-existent in his dictionary.

So former Premier Benazir Bhutto of Pakistan was quoted as having commented in Washington on Premier Nawaz Sharif. (*The Pioneer*, 11.5.98.) In this remark, Benazir Bhutto places law, justice, democracy and tolerance in one camp, in the camp, we can almost say, of reconciliation—and Premier Nawaz Sharif in the opposite camp of revenge. Premier Sharif might agree with the first equation, and substitute Benazir Bhutto's name for his in the second.

Retribution is a word hovering between revenge and justice. What some label revenge will to others seem well-earned retribution. In a 1998 book on women in India's Partition, *Borders and Boundaries*, edited by Ritu Menon and Kamla Bhasin, profoundly shaking incidents of marking and physically stigmatizing women—branding, tattooing, and worse—are described. The 'field' is conquered, and the conquest is forever proclaimed by the insignia of the victor.

In such a case, punishment, including violent punishment, of the men who committed the crime would be deemed justice—maybe insufficient or useless justice, yet justice nonetheless—by most persons. Some might view violence against men with blood ties or other links to the criminals but with no role in the crime as also natural in the circumstances, as inescapable retribution; to others such violence might seem like revenge. Similar violence against women associated with the male perpetrators of the crime would, however, be generally seen as revenge.

An instance of the kind we have just viewed shows us how inadequate, indeed poor, concepts of reconciliation and justice can suddenly become. Dare a scholar offer a 'lesson' from history to the victims of such atrocities? Can a sage provide wisdom to them, a judge justice, or a ruler relief? They *will* look for retribution or revenge, and possibly invite a fresh round of the same, unless by some heavenly gift they find healing.

That reconciliation without justice would be unreal or short-lived is obvious; frequently control or domination has been sought, or sought to be prolonged, in the name of reconciliation. In other words, accommodation can be real or bogus. There may be accommodation in order to overcome, a 'synthesis' intended to kill, a swallowing up in the name of inclusion.

It is equally obvious that a state of justice would be temporary and unstable if those compelled to render justice remain unreconciled— if little is done to assuage wounds to self-respect or feelings of humiliation.

On the other hand, as Aeschylus suggested centuries ago, revenge might be tamed by institutions of justice. If an agency of the state brings oppressors to justice, victims might relinquish revenge. It can be argued, therefore, that studying *a triangular relationship involving revenge, reconciliation and justice*, might be more valuable than a focus confined to the first two.

My defence of the latter focus is that justice demands its fleeting consignment to the wings. Towards justice, often occupying the centre of the stage, scholars in India and the world as a whole have gravitated with an eagerness not shown for revenge or reconciliation; compared with justice, the other two are Cinderellas, calling out for notice. That despite this concentration of attention justice is often absent from real life may suggest that much also hinges on other factors, e.g. accommodation and reconciliation. In any case, the crucial significance of justice and its siblings will unfold at every stage of our discussion.

I should here refer to Simon Wiesenthal's *The Sunflower*. A classic study of the conflict between justice and forgiveness, *The Sunflower* is born of the Holocaust, of which Wiesenthal by turns became victim, recorder, avenger and scholar. Recalling in the book an incident when as a prisoner he had *both withheld and offered compassion* to a dying SS man who, confessing horrible brutalities to Wiesenthal, pleaded for forgiveness from a Jew—any Jew—, Wiesenthal sparked off a rich and continuing debate on the possibilities and hazards of forgiveness. Reflected in successive editions of *The Sunflower*, the debate has had Jewish, Christian and Buddhist participants but not, interestingly enough, Hindu or Muslim ones.

More than one contributor to the debate underlined the SS man's inability to think of a Jew as an individual, an inability basic to the Nazi mindset. Thus Rodger Kamenetz points out that Wiesenthal was 'not addressed as a person, . . . not as *a* Jew, a Jewish person, as an individual, with a life, a history, a heartbreak of [his] own, but merely as *Jew*. For [the SS man's] purposes, any Jew would do.'[26] The insight recalls an item we had noted in the Buddha's teaching—his shift of focus from a member of a caste, a (any) Brahmin, Kshatriya, Shudra or untouchable, to the person, unique and distinct.

In a searing intervention in *The Sunflower*, the novelist Cynthia Ozick writes that 'so-called vengeance' is only 'justice in apposite dress.' Moreover, 'fired by the furnaces of pity, . . . vengeance, only vengeance, knows pity for the victim.' On the other hand,

> Forgiveness is pitiless. It forgets the victim. It negates the right of the victim to his own life. It blurs over suffering and death. It drowns the past. It cultivates sensitiveness toward the murderer at the price of insensitiveness toward the victim.[27]

Ozick's justified hostility against cheap forgiveness, expressed in the Holocaust's context, supplies powerfully plausible words to anyone anywhere who believes in revenge or hopes to profit from it. All the same, in our survey we will do well to remember *The Sunflower*'s warning against easy forgiveness, even as we bear in mind another comment in *The Sunflower*, this time from the French writer, Manes Sperber:

> The surest and most lasting . . . reconciliation is when the descendants of evildoers and those of the victims bind themselves into a collective and unbreakable unity—into a family, a tribe, a people, a nation . . . The existence of nations depends on forgetting. Each nation represents the amalgamation of tribes who for many years, and possibly for hundreds of years, had inflicted the worst sufferings and griefs on each other.[28]

We will end this brief theoretical discussion by quoting a similar opinion of the Jewish political philosopher, Hannah Arendt. Asking, 'How do societies get over the evils in their pasts, and how do they change for the better?' Arendt answers that they do so in two ways. One, by forgiveness. Two, by mutual commitment or treaty.[29]

Innovation and survival have traditionally been seen as history's main motors. But reconciliation is an innovation each time it occurs and may at times be the sole route to survival.

*

Asoka: The emperor who sought to practise and spread the Buddha's message grew up in the exciting atmosphere of conquest. His grandfather Chandragupta Maurya, the founder of the Magadha-based Maurya dynasty, while described variously as a Shudra, Kshatriya, or Vaishya, may have belonged to a merchant community residing in the subcontinent's northwestern region. Taxila, now in Pakistan, was the capital of this province, which at the time was under the control of Greeks left behind by Alexander's forays.

Known to classical Greece as Sandrocottus, and described by the Greeks as being of humble origin, Chandragupta had the counsel of the shrewd Kautilya, or Vishnugupta or Chanakya, associated with the famous treatise on economics, diplomacy and national security, *Arthasastra*. It is not certain, nor very important, whether Kautilya, a Brahmin, was himself the Vishnugupta who authored the *Arthasastra*, or merely supplied the views later embodied within the *Arthasastra*'s covers. Realpolitik is exalted, and its maxims spelt out, in *Arthasastra*.

With Kautilya's help, Chandragupta expelled the Greeks from India's northwest and also seized—in India's east—the kingdom of Magadha from the Nanda dynasty, which had replaced the descendants of Bimbisara. A long-nursed desire in Kautilya to avenge an insult from the Nanda ruler is said to have fuelled this seizure. Ascending the Magadha throne around 321 BC, Chandragupta ruled over much of northern and central India.

A story that Chandragupta and Alexander met each other is thought fanciful by most scholars, but there seems agreement about Chandragupta's treaty with the Greek general Seleucus Nikator, which earned him three provinces roughly comprising Kabul, Kandahar and Herat in modern Afghanistan.

In addition, it seems, Chandragupta may have married a Greek woman, perhaps Seleucus's daughter, which would allow for the possibility of Greek blood in his grandson Asoka. Another suggestion is that Chandragupta accepted a Greek noblewoman as a wife for his son Bindusara, so that Asoka, Bindusara's son, may have had a Greek mother. However, all we can be certain of is that numerous foreigners resided in Chandragupta's capital, Pataliputra, close to the site of today's Patna, and that among them was a Greek ambassador, Megasthenes, who left behind his impressions of Pataliputra, its social and political life, and its administration.

Asoka's mind was influenced, and heart fanned, by his boyhood in the battlefronts in the northwest, his grandfather's seizure of the Magadha kingdom and consequent glory, Kautilya's strategies and stratagems, and the presence of Greeks in his grandfather's court and probably of Greek women in the imperial harem.

Jewelled thrones, perfumed women, sharp swords, enemies outwitted or on their knees—we may assume that such images filled young Asoka's thoughts and dreams while his grandfather, the emperor, grew old and became, it would appear, a wandering Jaina ascetic. Chandragupta was succeeded by Bindusara. After Bindusara's death, Asoka, who though not the crown prince was as tough as he was ambitious, eliminated all rivals, killing several brothers including the eldest, and grabbed the imperial throne.

Earlier, as Viceroy at Taxila in the northwest and at Ujjain in central India, Asoka had had two important apprenticeships. At Taxila he quelled a dangerous rebellion, and during his Ujjain posting he appears to have fallen in love with the beautiful Devi, daughter of a merchant in Vidisha. No marriage seems to have been recorded, but Mahinda and Sanghamitta, two children born to Asoka and Devi, feature in accounts of the spread of Buddhism in Sri Lanka and elsewhere in Asia.

Firm, fierce even, in consolidating and extending the empire he had secured, Asoka was in particular anxious to conquer Kalinga, a rich state lying southeast of Magadha that hindered access both to the subcontinent's southern segment and to the sea washing the east coast. This desire was fulfilled but what followed was different from what Asoka, the people of Kalinga, or anyone else might have expected.

*

Mauryan kings including Asoka are listed in the Puranas dating from the fourth century AD. Asoka is described in the Sri Lankan Buddhist chronicles, the Dipavamsa, compiled by monks between the third century BC and the fourth century AD, and the Mahavamsa, apparently prepared in the fourth century AD, the Divyavadana, a collection of legends preserved in Tibetan and Chinese Buddhist sources, and in the history of Tibet written in the late sixteenth century by Taranatha. In Kalhana's *Rajatarangini*, a twelfth-century text on the kings of Kashmir, Asoka is referred to as the founder of Srinagari, Kashmir's capital, and as 'that king who had extinguished sin and accepted the teaching of Buddha.'[30]

But our knowledge of his life and times owes much to the European scholar Prinsep, who decoded the script of common texts found on rocks and pillars in different parts of India and found that they referred to someone called Piyadassi, a Prakrit word meaning one of friendly appearance. In 1837 Prinsep was informed by scholars examining Sri Lanka's Buddhist chronicles that the Dipavamsa and the Mahavamsa gave the title Piyadassi to Asoka, and the connection of the rocks and pillars with Asoka was discovered. The discovery unleashed a flood of new material about Asoka and the India of his times, not least because the texts contained dates and other details.

For centuries, rocks and pillars containing these texts had been noticed, including by the Chinese travellers Fa-hien and Hsuan Tsang in the fourth and seventh centuries, respectively, who referred to them in their journals, and by some Muslim rulers in North India who, sensing yet not comprehending their value, even had some pillars moved from their locations. Thus in the fourteenth century Firoz Shah Tughluq brought pillars from Meerut and Topra to Delhi, and later the Mughal emperor, Jahangir, had a pillar shifted from Kosambi to Allahabad.

But what the texts said, and who they referred to, was not known until 1837. The world found significance, and India felt pride, in the deciphered meaning of the texts. Yet there is meaning also in the fact that, notwithstanding the presence for centuries of intriguing texts on rocks and pillars in dozens of far apart places, India had largely forgotten Asoka, his deeds and his words, until European scholars put two and two together.

*

Asoka's engraved texts are divided into (a) the Major Rock Edicts, (b) the Minor Rock Inscriptions and (c) the Pillar Edicts. It is the 13th Major Rock Edict that tells us about Asoka's conquest of Kalinga, in its boundaries an area not differing greatly from modern Orissa. It says:

> When he had been consecrated eight years, Devanampiya ('the Beloved of the Gods'), the king Piyadassi, conquered Kalinga. A hundred and fifty thousand people were deported, a hundred thousand were killed and many times that number perished . . .
>
> On conquering Kalinga Devanampiya felt remorse, for when an independent country is conquered the slaughter, death, and deportation of people is extremely grievous to [him] . . . What is even more deplorable to [him] is that those who

dwell there . . . all suffer violence, murder and separation
from their loved ones . . .

This participation of all men in suffering weighs heavily on
the mind of Devanampiya . . . Today if a hundredth or
thousandth part of those people who were killed or died or
deported when Kalinga was annexed were to suffer similarly,
it would weigh heavily on the mind of the Beloved of the
Gods . . .

Devanampiya believes that one who does wrong should be
forgiven as far as it is possible to forgive him. And the
Beloved of the Gods conciliates the forest tribes of his
empire, but he warns them that he has power even in his
remorse . .

The Beloved of the Gods considers victory by Dhamma to
be the foremost victory . . .[31]

The historian Romila Thapar, whose scholarly studies have made
Asoka comprehensible to two generations of students, cautions us
against thinking of Asoka 'as an extremely wicked man suddenly
converted to a life of piety,' or as a dogmatic 'Hindu' suddenly
converted into a 'Buddhist.' Though after Kalinga Asoka clearly
became a follower of the Buddha and a benefactor of monks, the
cleavage between a Hindu and a Buddhist, or between a Buddhist and
a Jaina, was not necessarily sharp or even clear in his time.

Thapar also stresses that the wording of the 13th Edict discloses
'not the regret of a man moved by a passing emotion but the
meaningful contrition of a man who is consciously aware of the
sorrow he had caused.'[32]

Again, she asks us not to forget the down-to-earth Asoka who,
among other things, ensures that this 13th Edict is left out of the
texts engraved on the rocks in Kalinga—in Dhauli and Jaugada. He
knows that if they serve as a reminder of his attack on Kalinga, even
words of contrition might arouse disruptive emotions in the Kalingans.
So in Dhauli and Jaugada a special edict replaces the 13th Edict.
Among other things, this substituted edict says:

All men are my children . . . If the unconquered peoples on
my borders ask what is my will, they should be made to
understand that this is my will with regard to them—'The

king desires that they should have no trouble on his account, should trust in him, and should have in their dealings with him only happiness and no sorrow. They should understand that the king will forgive them as they can be forgiven . . . His officers shall at all times attend to the conciliation of the people of the frontiers.''[33]

As Thapar helps us to see, Asoka's change after Kalinga is not instantaneous (the text of the 13th Edict makes it clear that it was composed a while after the conquest, not quite on its morrow), nor does it swing Asoka from an extreme of evil to an extreme of good, or turn him from one with a hard heart to a man with a soft head.

Still, the change was remarkable, especially when set against Asoka's goals before Kalinga, or against battles in the Mahabharata. After Kalinga, Asoka is as concerned with the non-combatants killed or hurt by the war as the combatants; he does not divide the casualties into 'ours' and 'theirs'; the blood and tears shed by others affect Asoka more than the fulfilment of his long-cherished ambition.

In the Mahabharata we seldom hear of the ordinary man or woman, the one not engaged in the War. We don't even hear of the foot soldier, except when the killing of five or seven or ten thousand is announced. The epic is a story of heroes in their dramatic moments when they avenge wounds and redeem oaths. In contrast, Asoka's 13th Edict portrays the lingering pain and lasting grief of ordinary men and women trapped in clashes between ambitious men.

In the epic the past is constantly triumphing—an old curse takes effect, an old ambition is fulfilled, an old humiliation avenged. In the Edict the needle points to present suffering, and hints that compassion and reconciliation may lead to a better future.

*

From the edicts, we can mark several other features distinguishing the new Asoka:

> He affirms that the respect, goodwill, and friendship of neighbours, which Dhamma or virtue can gain, were the true source of his security and defence, not conquest and occupation. In the 13th Edict he claims that the Cholas and Pandyas ruling South India, the ruler of Sri Lanka, and, to his West, the Greek kings of five states have acknowledged Asoka's conquest by Dhamma.

Though stressing goodwill as against the sword, a sword lay not too far behind Asoka's goodwill, even after Kalinga. As the 'warning' to 'forest tribes' reveals, Asoka did not become a pacifist in any extreme or doctrinaire sense. However, there is evidence—e.g. his emphasis on conciliation—that after Kalinga he sought cooperation and respect rather than fear from those close to his empire's borders.

The 4th Major Rock Edict claims that 'the sound of the drum has become the sound of Dhamma.' Asoka wanted to issue a call to Dhamma—'abstention from killing and non-injury to living beings'— rather than a call to battle, to foster goodwill rather than the militarist spirit.

Apparently he succeeded to some extent. There was warmth for Asoka in Sri Lanka, which, thanks to his son Mahinda and other emissaries and missionaries from India, became Buddhist, and where the king, Tissa, seemed to admire Asoka and to model himself on him, taking, like Asoka, the royal name Devanampiya. However, Sri Lanka remained independent of Asoka's empire.

Lying much closer to the empire, South India, which did not become Buddhist, acknowledged Asoka's nominal suzerainty, but there is little evidence of fear, resentment or enmity in South India towards Asoka or his empire. Something of the goodwill Asoka hoped to convey to neighbours did seem to get across.[34]

The 2nd Major Rock Edict speaks of the Asokan empire's medical services—for humans and animals both—being extended to 'lands on its frontiers, those of the Cholas, Pandyas, Satyaputras, Keralaputras, and as far as Sri Lanka, and of the Greek king named Antiochus and of those kings who are neighbours of Antiochus.'

That the king existed for the people, not vice versa, is the message of the 6th Major Rock Edict:

> At all times, whether I am eating, or am in the women's apartments, or in my inner apartments, or at the cattle-shed, or in my carriage, or in my gardens—wherever I may be, my informants should keep me in touch with public business . . . I must promote the welfare of the whole world, and hard work and dispatch of business are the means of doing so.

In the 7th Pillar Edict he says:

> On the roads I have had banyan trees planted, which will give shade to beasts and men, I have had mango groves

planted and I have had wells dug and rest houses built at
every eight *kos*.

As Thapar points out, 'Religious texts of the time stressed man's
responsibility to his religion and to his ancestors. To these Asoka
added yet another responsibility, perhaps the most important, that of
responsibility to one's fellow human beings . . .'[35]

His decision to spend time in meetings with 'aged folk' and
'people in the countryside' rather than in 'pleasure tours' and 'hunts'
is conveyed by Asoka's 8th Major Rock Edict, and the needs of the
'poor' and 'prisoners' are highlighted in the 5th Major Rock Edict.
'Regard for slaves and servants' is a phrase that occurs in at least three
edicts. In the 9th Major Rock Edict he places it at the head of what
he calls the 'ceremony of Dhamma,' which he says is to be preferred
to wasteful ceremonies over births, marriages, and travel. Next to
'regard for slaves and servants' comes 'respect for teachers.'

That his edicts were composed not in Sanskrit, the language of
the learned elite, but in the people's language, Prakrit, and indeed, in
one or two instances, in a region's local language, showed Asoka's
keenness to reach the common citizen.

If his interest in humble folk provides a contrast to the
Mahabharata's 'stars,' Asoka also explicitly devalues two goals nursed
earlier by him and exalted in the epic. The 10th Major Rock Edict
says that the emperor 'sets no store by fame or glory,' except in so
far as it assists him in propagating Dhamma.

Significantly and even humorously, Asoka adds here that Dhamma
is 'particularly difficult for the highly placed,' a remark that may also
be seen as questioning the importance traditionally given to birth and
position. Thapar reminds us that the titles used for the emperor in
the edicts, Beloved of the Gods and Piyadassi, the amiable-looking
one, are modest compared with descriptions of other kings reigning
near Asoka's time.

Also departing from the epic's seeming values of pride and
intolerance is this advocacy, in Asoka's 12th Major Rock Edict, of
courteous dialogue:

> One should honour another man's sect, for by so doing one
> increases the influence of one's own sect and benefits that of
> the other man . . . Whosoever honours his own sect or
> disparages that of another man, harms his own sect even
> more seriously . . . Concord is to be commended, so that
> men may hear one another's principles.

'It is hard to do good,' the emperor disarmingly admits in the 5th Major Rock Edict. Yet perhaps the most interesting text of all is contained in the 3rd Pillar Edict:

> Thus speaks the Beloved of the Gods, the king Piyadassi: One only notices one's good deeds, thinking, 'I have done good,' but on the other hand one does not notice one's wicked deeds, thinking, 'I have done evil,' or, 'this is indeed a sin.' Now, to be aware of this is something really difficult.

As will be remembered, the Mahabharata in contrast yields to the human inclination to spotlight the other man's evil and one's own virtues.

*

Most of the edicts end with an expression of the hope that the emperor's sons and grandsons will follow the Dhamma. However, there is little indication that this happened. Moreover, the empire launched by his grandfather and consolidated by Asoka ended fifty years after his death. Pusyamitra Sunga, the Brahmin commander-in-chief, killed his king Brhadratha, seventh successor to Asoka, and captured the throne, ending the Maurya dynasty.

For a time Pusyamitra defended the empire's western borders against the Bactrian Greeks but finally Punjab and Sind were lost. Around 73 BC, Devabhumi, tenth king of the Sunga dynasty, was killed at the instance of his minister, Vasudeva. Despite Asoka's gallant bid, history was repeated, the Mahabharata reenacted, and the empire broken up.

Historians have tried to explain the Maurya disintegration: Brahmins resented Asoka's policies; for all its innovations, Asoka's was a centralized state revolving round the ruler's personality and requiring a ruler of exceptional ability; no bureaucratic network was created that could have sustained the empire without a succession of outstanding rulers; the empire was unwieldy; neither in its heartland, Magadha, nor elsewhere in the empire was a national feeling present; the loyalty that existed, or was espoused by Kautilya's *Arthasastra*, was either to a king or to a social order, not to a nation or state. And so forth.

These explanations or their validity are not the focus of our study. What we can note is both the brightness and the seemingly short life of the lantern that was Asoka. We can see it now, and see some truths with its help, because, long centuries after it was apparently extinguished, the lamp was re-lit by history's servants, who were no doubt aided by Asoka's own ancient exertions over rocks and pillars.

But for a moment perhaps we should pause with a common criticism that the seed of the Mauryan demise had in fact been sown by Asoka himself, an anti-militant, anti-statist, weak Asoka who preferred sentimental peacemaking to Kautilya's hard-headed advice. Thus D.R. Bhandarkar observed:

> The effects of [Asoka's] change of policy, of the replacement of vijaya by Dharma-vijaya, were politically disastrous though spiritually glorious. Love of peace and hankering after spiritual progress were no doubt engendered, and have now been ingrained in the Indian character . . . Asoka's new angle of vision, however, sounded a death-knell to the Indian aspiration of a centralised state and world-wide empire.[36]

Offered by scholars like Bhandarkar but also by others allergic to any hint of 'softness' or 'meekness,'[37] this criticism presumes a greater devotion to peace in India over the ages than is noticeable to a student of history. Where is the evidence that Indians have generally hesitated to fight the invader? By contrast, there is plenty of evidence that they have been keener to fight one another, thereby easing the invader's passage. Asoka did not err in striving to bridge the divisions among Indians.

Answering Bhandarkar in *Asoka and his Inscriptions*, a 1946 study[38], B.N. Barua pointed out that empires or kingdoms that followed the Mauryan, including those of the Guptas and the Mughals, also died sooner than some would have wished, even though no philosophy similar to Asoka's preyed on the minds of the Guptas or, later, on Aurangzeb, the last of the famous Mughals. Kautilya's 'statecraft [had] guided . . . the large majority of the Indian states, but . . . to what end?' Rejecting the suggestion that Asoka ever disbanded his armies, Barua argued that it was 'no sound reason to make Asoka pay the penalty for the weaknesses of his successors in the line.'

As we have done, Barua also compares Asoka's Kalinga war with the Kurukshetra war in the Mahabharata, and underlines the barrenness left by the latter:

> The Kurukshetra war resulted in the destruction of all great

warriors, the destruction of the Kurus, the descendants of the Pandavas, the annihilation of the Yadavas; . . . and the general emasculation of humanity . . . The new world sought to be created through the battle of Kurukshetra was a world of desolation and despair, the inhabitants whereof began to utter in their helplessness the pitiful cry of Haa Krishna, Haa Krishna![39]

*

On a summer day in 1996, I visited the site of the Dhauli Rock Edict, at the foot of Dhauli Hill, seven kilometres east of Bhubaneswar. The river Daya flows close by. Above the rock with the edict are other rocks, out of one of which an elephant has been finely carved, dating, archaeologists tell us, from Asoka's time.

Standing on a rock above the elephant, one faces wide vistas on all sides. Apart from the Dhauli Hill, where now a Buddhist Peace Temple stands, and also a Siva temple built next to it, all one sees is flat land, flat as a sheet of glass.

This was Kalinga country and possibly a site for the ancient carnage. According to the inscriptions near the Peace Temple, which was built by the Japanese Buddhist priest, Fuji Guruji, and his followers, it was while Asoka was resting on or near Dhauli Hill after the war that breezes from the river Daya brought home to him the dimensions of the bloodshed he had been part of.

As I stood and walked on that soil—the grass was green that day, the trees were in flower and the birds were trilling—, I tried to recall that violent past and also the contrition and the conviction that followed.

A century or so after Asoka's death, the Kalinga king Kharavela, who it seems was a Jaina, had attacked and defeated Magadha. Avenging the defeat administered by Asoka would no doubt have been part of Kharavela's motivation. But I noted that Asoka's Edict had remained where it had been, in hostile territory, even though he, the invader, had died, the Maurya empire had gone, and Kalinga had revived under Kharavela.

*

Lanka and Dutugemunu. Asoka's remorse in Kalinga found an extraordinary parallel a century later in Sri Lanka. In, apparently, 161 BC, the Sri Lankan king Dutugemunu, a Buddhist thanks to Asoka's initiatives, vanquished Elara, a Tamil king from the Chola line, killed an immense number of Tamils, became the sovereign of all of Sri Lanka, and brought the whole island under his sway as a Sinhala-Buddhist nation. However, he was conscience-stricken. In a portion probably composed in the fourth century AD, the Mahavamsa states:

> Sitting there on the terrace of the royal palace, adorned, lighted with fragrant lamps and filled with many a perfume, magnificent with nymphs in the guise of dancing girls, while he rested on his soft and fair couch, covered with costly draperies, he looking back upon his glorious victory, great though it was, knew no joy, remembering that thereby was wrought the destruction of millions (of beings).[40]

Divining Dutugemunu's feeling of guilt, some monks assured him that the 'Tamils he killed were not only barbarians and heretics but their deaths were like that of cattle, dogs and mice.'[41] But the king's feelings were not eased, for he knew that Elara was a righteous king. The Mahavamsa states that Elara acted 'with even justice towards friend and foe, on occasion of disputes of law,' and that once, when a chariot he was riding had accidentally damaged a Buddhist stupa, Elara leapt out, asking that his own head should be severed as penalty. His ministers not permitting this, Elara spent a fortune repairing the stupa.

Dutugemunu not only ordered a ceremonial funeral for Elara; he seems to have erected an 'Elara image-house' on the model of a Buddhist shrine. In a stimulating reflection on Dutugemunu's conscience and the actions stemming from it, Gananath Obeyesekere suggests that Elara, older than Dutugemunu by about twenty-five years, was seen as a father-figure by Dutugemunu, who as a red-blooded youth had rebuked his father Kavantissa for the latter's seeming softness towards the Tamils.

Asked by his father to take the oath, 'Never will we fight the Tamils,' the twelve-year-old Gamani, as he was known in boyhood, had flung away the food his father was offering him, gone to his bed, and lain there curled up. When his mother asked why he was not stretching his limbs, Gamani gave what Obeyesekere calls 'his famous reply':

> Over there beyond the river (Mahavali) are the Tamils and on the other side is the ocean, how can I lie with outstretched limbs?[42]

Kavantissa died some years after this incident, but according to some accounts Dutugemunu was absent during his father's final hours and also missed the funeral.

In Obeyesekere's analysis, the 'unprecedented honour accorded [by Dutugemunu to] a fallen enemy' flowed from Dutugemunu's 'unconscious identification of the noble Elara with his own well-intentioned and loving father.'[43] Juxtaposing Dutugemunu's response to his violent victory over Elara with Asoka's reaction in Kalinga and Arjuna's quavering at Kurukshetra, Obeyesekere reminds us that in his youth Asoka too had killed his eldest brother, the rightful heir and in South Asian culture a father figure; and that in his protests about the impending war to Krishna, Arjuna recoiled above all from the thought of killing the father figure, Bhishma. In all three cases, guilt vis-à-vis a father or a father figure seemed powerfully linked to the contrition about violence.

Some Lankan histories omit Dutugemunu's guilt after his victory over Elara, even as they exclude references to Elara's virtues. The view of the monks who tried to expel Dutugemunu's sadness by stressing the supposed degraded status of the Tamils would find growing acceptance in the centuries that followed; and an ideology arguing that Buddhist principles could and perhaps should be jettisoned for defending a Buddhist state struck root. The stance resembles some positions taken in the Mahabharata by Krishna and the Pandavas.

Dutugemunu is a much-used symbol in modern Sri Lanka but what he stands for is contested. Obeyesekere refers to 'a Sinhala book written by liberal and concerned intellectuals entitled *War or Peace: Lanka's Ethnic Problem*,' the cover of which shows Dutugemunu and Elara on their royal elephants, spears in hand and locked in combat. Inside the book a poet implores 'the two kings to get off their elephants and sit together.'

However, another modern book, sponsored by staunch Sinhala nationalists, claims that Dutugemunu was not troubled by his conscience. Ignoring Elara, this book 'focuses on the plunder and destruction of places of worship by Tamils.'[44] Concluding his reflection, Obeyesekere writes:

> I have some sympathy for [Dutugemunu] but none for the monks who consoled him. To say that the killing of one's enemy is justified is a perversion of Buddhism, and those who condone such acts . . . have not understood the profound moral significance of the conscience of Dutthagamani Abhaya (the fearless Dutugemunu).

I also think the conscience of the king is not a Sri Lankan story alone. Who among us can ignore [its] wider import . . .? It does not matter whether we are talking of the Jews and Arabs, of the Basques and the Spanish, or Irish Catholics and Irish Protestants, or the Evil Empire and the Good . . .

It is not an easy task to reconcile one's conscience with the workings of the world. It is easier to emulate the immature youth Gamani, curled up in bed in the fetal position, saying, 'How can I lie with outstretched limbs with the ocean on one side and the Tamils on the other?' than the mature Dutthagamani whose conscience, disturbed by dying and killing, saw goodness on the other side of the divide.[45]

*

Arjuna and Asoka. Armies have raced along Indian soil a number of times, in a number of directions, and for a number of reasons, including plunder, conquest and occupation. Often they have raced from outside into Indian soil, generally from the northwest.

Asoka's attack from Magadha into Kalinga in the third century BC was part of a known pattern, and destined to be frequently repeated during the two millennia to follow. But Asoka's reflections after the Kalinga conquest, and Dutugemunu's after Elara's defeat, were uncommon; and perhaps they are as significant as Arjuna's reflections before the Kurukshetra war.

At Kurukshetra, his bow Gandiva slipped from Arjuna's hand as he surveyed the arrayed ranks of relatives, friends and teachers, and contemplated the suffering that lay ahead. At Kalinga, Asoka looked with guilt at the devastation he had caused, with doubt at the sword at his side, and with courage into his heart. Ensconced there were his idols of fame and glory. His worship of them had produced the scene around him on the flat fields of Dhauli—dead, groaning, or sorrowing human beings. He saw danger in the idols—and hope in the message of the Buddha.

The Guptas, the 'Golden Age' and the Gita. Disintegration and waves of invasions from the northwest marked the long period between the end of the Mauryan empire in the second century BC and the start, with Chandragupta I, of the Gupta dynasty in the fourth century AD. The disintegration encouraged the waves, which also brought new ethnic groups into the subcontinent; equally, the invasions accelerated the disintegration.

Samudragupta, son of Chandragupta I and the second Gupta monarch, was a conqueror, poet and musician. His feats were preserved in a poem written by his poet laureate Harisena and engraved on an Asokan pillar standing at Prayag (Allahabad). So a tale of conquest, composed in polished classical Sanskrit, stood next to Asoka's exhortation for peace, composed in common Prakrit.

The written Mahabharata seems to have made its entry at about this time.[46] If an engraved record of physical conquest mocked Asoka on the Buddhist emperor's own stone, the epic of war and revenge was now available on parchment to contend, in people's minds, with the doctrine of tolerance. We may be certain that the epic was sponsored by a warrior-conqueror like Samudragupta.

When the Bhagavad Gita made its first appearance does not seem to be clear. In part at least the Gita too appears to have been a response to Buddhism and Jainism, in this case a brilliant philosophical response.[47] The Gita admitted value in the renunciation exalted by Buddhism and Jainism and incorporated the ideal, without referring to the Buddha or Mahavira. It claimed, however, that what had to be renounced was not action or duty or desire, but the desire for fruits from action.

In the preceding chapter we had seen that kshama or forgiveness had a place in the Gita, an inclusion for which Buddhism and/or Jainism might have been responsible, though we cannot be certain. The Gita can thus be seen as representing, to some extent, a fusion with heterodoxy.

Going further, one scholar calls the Gita 'one of the earliest . . . attempts to accommodate, and, one might even say, to emasculate Sramanical religious culture, whose potency had been clearly demonstrated not only by its impact upon the Brahmanical tradition but also by the immense popularity achieved by Buddhism during the millennia extending from the fifth century BC to the fifth century CE.'[48]

Yet acceptance and accommodation may weaken a rival ideology without any wish to emasculate it. The Gita possessed two great advantages in its competition with Buddhism and Jainism. Unlike the latter, it offered a Supreme Being, a God, to whom weak and weary individuals could turn. Secondly, again unlike Buddhism, which in India at least tended to elevate asceticism, and Jainism, which seemed to do the same, the Gita could be interpreted as an affirmation of life.

When these advantages were combined with the doctrine—

perhaps adapted, as has been suggested, from Buddhism or Jainism—, of renouncing all concern with the fruits of action, the result was a message of considerable power, which would reverberate for centuries. The Gita's weakness, however, was that it seemed to retain caste. Where the Buddha and Mahavira emphasized an individual's role and choices, the Gita's notion of duty was frequently that of caste duty, the role of a Brahmin, a Kshatriya, a Vaishya, or a Shudra, rather than, simply, the duty of an individual.

We may guess that in a period such as that of the Guptas, when strong kings subdued and ruled over large portions of India, notions of compassion and reconciliation would have had a hard time battling the power of a revivified Mahabharata, especially if the latter could also appropriate the Gita with its notable appeal.

Lasting a little under two centuries and encompassing much of northern and central India, the Gupta empire enabled the flowering of painting, sculpture and literature, on the one hand, and medicine, mathematics and astronomy, on the other. Written texts of the Mahabharata and the Ramayana; the Puranas; and *Shakuntala*, *Meghaduta* and other creations of Kalidasa are among the classics that probably belong to these or adjacent times, often called the Golden Age of Hinduism. The temples and paintings in the caves of Ajanta and Ellora apparently came shortly after the Gupta dynasty.

A fair part of our knowledge of the Gupta period comes from the account of the Chinese traveller, Fa-hien, who was in India early in the fifth century. He noticed that intoxicants and meat were not consumed much, a sign of the continuing influence of Buddhism and Jainism, and commented positively on the free hospitals he saw. However, he also found that Pariahs and Chandalas lived outside the city walls; if entering a city, they struck a gong to warn others of approaching pollution.

It was during the reign of Samudragupta's son, Chandragupta II, that Fa-hien visited India, Kalidasa and other famed scholars flourished, and northern India was in touch with Greece, Persia and China. In the middle of the fifth century, during the rule of Skandagupta, Huns and related tribes flowed into India from the northwest, and the Gupta slide commenced. By 550 AD the Gupta empire was 'reduced to a mere name.'[49]

Harsha. Ruling from 606 to 647 AD, Harshavardhana, or Harsha, appears to have treated two cities as capitals, Kanyakubja or Kannauj on the Ganga and Thanesar in Kurukshetra country. Thanks to

Harsha Charita, a historical romance by Bana, a writer in Harsha's court, and the accounts of the remarkable Chinese traveller, Hsuan Tsang, who, desiring to know the soil that had produced the Buddha, spent sixteen years in India, visiting Kashmir, Saurashtra, Assam and the Tamil country, Harsha is better known than any of the Gupta kings. But he did not leave behind a dynasty, and an attempt by him in 620 AD to enter the South was successfully resisted by the Chalukya king, Pulakesin II.

Bana and Hsuan Tsang have much to say about Harsha, who was a scholar-king, his courtesies towards the Chinese visitor, and his reign. We learn about the 10,000 students in the university city of Nalanda, and about other towns and villages in his kingdom. In addition, Dandin's *Dasakumaracarita*, a seventh-century prose-romance, provides rich information about the ordinary person's life in Harsha's time, including descriptions of 'gambling, burglary, cunning, fraud, violence, murder, impersonation, abduction and illicit love.'[50]

Interestingly enough, Bana inveighs with passion against those who regard 'as an authority Kautilya's *Arthasastra*, merciless in its precepts, rich in cruelty' or 'to whom brothers, affectionate with natural cordial love, are fit victims to be murdered.'[51]

For our purpose, however, we should note the relative brevity of the periods of stability, enabling bursts of creativity, under the Guptas and Harsha—like the relatively brief period of the Mauryas. We may mark, too, that Hsuan Tsang's accounts suggest a less orderly land than the one earlier portrayed by Fa-hien. Hsuan Tsang himself was more than once attacked on the highways, and was fortunate to escape with his life.

Hindu-Buddhist bitterness was evident, and Harsha was blamed for encouraging Buddhists. At a religious assembly convoked by Harsha at Kannauj, the wooden structure built for housing a Buddha image was burnt down by a group of Brahmins, and a bid was made to kill Harsha.

At debates in Harsha's court a part was sometimes taken by his widowed sister, whom the king had rescued from the funeral pyre after her husband's death in battle. If this discloses an enlightenment ahead of its time, we should also note that while announcing a public debate at the Kannauj assembly Harsha had added that if anyone spoke against the Master of the Law—Hsuan Tsang—, his tongue would be torn out by the roots! Obviously, rather than a debate, what Harsha had organized was a function to honour the visiting Master.

*

Buddhism's fate in India. Not long after Harsha, Buddhism seemed either absorbed into Hinduism or exiled out of India. A factor in Buddhism's decline in India was the apparent similarity between the Mahayana or Greater Vehicle school of Buddhism, which grew between 150 BC and 100 AD, and Hinduism. Mahayana Buddhism, the form in which the Buddha's message would be accepted in Tibet, China, Japan and Korea, saw the Buddha 'as a glorified, transcendent being,'[52] enabling Hinduism, by around the sixth century, to accept and appropriate the Buddha as the ninth avatar of Vishnu, the successor to Rama and Krishna.

Orthodoxy's willingness, noted above, to adopt renunciation as a value, and espouse the ideal of a householder who in spirit was a renouncer, also served to blur the distinction between Hinduism and Buddhism. A similar effect was produced when the brilliant ninth-century theologian and strong critic of Buddhism, Sankara, a Brahmin from the Kerala country, propounded a philosophy that took over some key Buddhist concepts and also launched a Hindu brotherhood of celibate priests, paralleling the Sangha or association of Buddhist monks.

In Buddhism's recession, a role was also played by the separation between the Buddhist monks and nuns on the one hand, for whom strict rules were prescribed, and the laity on the other. While Hinduism 'wove itself into the fabric of society through the caste sytem,'[53] and Brahmin priests were required to legitimize every ritual of birth, marriage, or death, the connection of Buddhist monastic centres with ordinary Buddhists was looser and weaker.

What, however, is significant for our study is the fact that though Buddhism was being absorbed into Hinduism, there was little indication that Indian society was accepting the primacy of the values of compassion and non-retaliation.

We may note at this stage that the Mahayana or Greater Vehicle Buddhism exported from northwestern India and accepted in Tibet, China, and Japan emphasized the notion of a heavenly Buddha called Amitabha, as well as the concept of Bodhisattvas, previous incarnations of the Buddha who for the sake of ordinary human beings declined the nirvana option and chose to remain (as spirits) in the world.

Amitabha and the Bodhisattvas were usually seen as embodiments of kindness to whom human beings in need could appeal, and in Tibet the compassionate Bodhisattva, Avalokiteswara, was regarded as the figure of whom successive Dalai Lamas were reincarnations.

While Indian Buddhism tended to preoccupy itself with questions of rebirth and with freedom from cycles of birth and death, the Tibetans and East Asians who turned to Buddhism seemed to regard as its 'fundamental aim, the deliverance of people from suffering.'[54] As the Japanese Buddhist scholar, Hirakawa Akira, sees it,

> [R]ebirth is not a necessary tenet of Sakyamuni's teachings. Although he did not reject rebirth, Sakyamuni was primarily concerned with liberation from the suffering of existence.[55]

Possibly Indian Buddhism, and perhaps, as well, some other sections of Theravada Buddhism (the Buddhism 'as taught by the elder or first teachers'), allowed a lapse into intellectualism and complex speculations about rebirth, losing the focus on compassion and the life of the community, aspects that remain noticeable in some Buddhist societies outside India.

Like the Buddha, Vardhamana Mahavira had also become, by about the first century AD, an object of warm loving devotion or bhakti, and Jaina monks took the faith to western and southern India. Jainism never spread across the world the way Buddhism did, but in India it performed better than Buddhism against Islam's onslaught and Hinduism's absorptive capacity. Until about the eleventh century, several major rulers in South India had supported Jainism. In the twelfth century, King Kumarapala in Gujarat became a Jaina.

Thiruvalluvar, 'most probably a learned Jaina divine,' authored the Tamil classic *Kural* in perhaps the sixth century.[56] A riveting manual of compassionate ethics, politics and psychology, the *Kural* features to this day in South India's discourse.

But a great wave of devotional Hinduism focusing on the God Siva pushed Jainism out of most southern kingdoms, and in Gujarat too Hinduism returned with strength. Yet, thanks to 'carefully regulated observances and the pastoral care of the monks,' lay Jainas seemed more closely bound to their faith than India's lay Buddhists.[57] The fact that Jaina ranks included some prosperous and well-knit merchant communities helped survival.

Hindu-Buddhist and Hindu-Jaina struggles in South India were not necessarily peaceful. One scholar points out that

Tamil literature makes it painfully clear that the foundations of the medieval synthesis were soaked in blood from battles that established the temple-centered, devotional Brahmanic religious ceremonial practice at the centre of agrarian order.[58]

Gail Omvedt thinks that 'in Tamilnadu, where brahmanic orthodoxy managed finally to coopt or absorb a very powerful indigenous [and heterodox] tradition, it did so in a process of a historically shadowy but apparently powerful conflict with Jainism.'[59] We can hear the conflict in the background in these lines in praise of Siva by Sambandar, the famous Tamil poet of perhaps the seventh century:

> Those Buddhists and mad Jains may slander speak/ Such speech befits the wand'rers from the way/ But He who came to earth and begged for alms,/ He is the thief who stole my heart away./ The raging elephant charged down at Him;/ O marvel! He both took and wore its hide./ Madman men think Him, but He is the Lord/ Who in Great Bamapuram doth abide.[60]

It would appear that Kun Pandiyan, king of Madura, had become a Jaina. The queen, whose name was Mangaiyarkkarasi, supported by the premier, sent for Sambandar the poet, who reconverted the king; and there is a suggestion that all Jaina teachers were executed by impaling.

Destruction of images of the Buddha in Kashmir at the end of the eleventh century, during the reign of one of the territory's Hindu rulers, is also recorded in Kalhana's *Rajatarangini*, written in the middle of the twelfth century.[61]

3

The Charge of Islam: Rage, Reflection and Coexistence

SEVERAL TIMES OVER a span of eight centuries, starting with the eleventh AD, plunderers and conquerors flying the flag of Islam raced down the passes of the Hindu Kush, and down the plains and deserts of India, killing those in their way, smashing numberless idols in temples, including images of the Buddha, and seizing gold and sparkling stone. Sometimes they returned whence they came with their booty. Sometimes they remained and ruled.

But they did not seem to reflect before or after their battles. Swords or guns did not slip from their hands, or invite doubt. If they looked into their hearts, and there found awkward idols of fame, glory and wealth, and uglier idols of lust and greed, they also seemed to see, next to these, another, more comforting idol, or call, as they preferred to think of it.

This was the idol or call of duty, religious duty. Their duty was to smash the images of metal, stone or wood in the India that they were racing across, and to foster the worship of humanity's and the universe's One God. If they performed this duty well—so the call seemed to say to them—, their sin in worshipping the idols of fame, glory and wealth, or even those of greed and lust, might be cancelled.

'To every vein of falsehood, every Muslim was a knife.' This is God speaking in *Jawab-i-Shikwa* ('Reply to the Complaint'), composed by one of South Asia's most famous modern poets, Iqbal.[1] To a presumed religious duty or the call of truth, the response, whether in deed or verse, was violent.

These invaders, plunderers and conquerors had some advantages over the Indians standing in their way. In zeal and enthusiasm for their faith, weaponry, horses and horsemanship, and unity of command, they scored over the Hindus and Buddhists of India. Most significantly, perhaps, thanks to the caste system, a majority of the Indian population seemed indifferent to the fate of their ruling elites at the hands of the attacker.

We have already noted that the word mleccha, meaning barbarian, was used both for foreigners and for the Indian outcastes. 'Below the Sudras were the degraded races called the *Mlecchas*,' says *The Gazetteer of India* in its description of castes.[2] 'Even the resistance against the Greeks, the hated *Mlecchas*, was not an organized one,' writes Thapar, referring to the period of Alexander and the Greeks that succeeded him in northwestern India.[3] Centuries later, resistance against the Turks and Afghans, too, could not be organized across Indian society because many at the bottom remained separated from the rest and in squalor.

Since for centuries after Asoka, and again after the Guptas, India was divided into numerous pieces with shifting boundaries, the banner of Islam under which the forces of Ghaznavi and Ghauri and their successors rode across India was countered not with an Indian, Hindu or Buddhist banner, but with the standard of a relatively small fiefdom. Those rallying under it, while often heroic, were generally recruited from a few 'fighting' clans and castes; they did not represent the area's people as a whole.

Whether or not the heart of the Gita's message, the call to Kshatriyas to fight was generally acknowledged, but such a belief also implied that other castes did not have the duty to take up arms. Moreover, in the contest between Kshatriya duty and Islamic fervour the edge often belonged to the latter, for while the former could set Kshatriya against Kshatriya, Islamic fervour usually set Muslims against non-Muslims.

*

Divinization and Demonization: Indian princes braving an attack from the northwest were at times likened by court poets or chroniclers to Rama, the hero of the Ramayana epic, and the invader to Ravana, the demon overcome by Rama. The Ramayana legend, comprising the struggles of the noble prince Rama, his wife Sita, brothers Bharata and Lakshmana, and devoted monkey-lieutenant, Hanuman, first against a jealous stepmother and then against Ravana, the demonic king who abducts Sita, had affected India 'from at least the fourth century AD,'[4] offering ethico-social ideals of a monogamous prince, a faithful wife, and sons obedient to parents, and a political norm that a king should be succeeded by his eldest son. The principles were not always followed but found a place in the Indian psyche.

However, something new and significant happens, as Sheldon Pollock has pointed out, from about the twelfth century—'kings *become* Rama.'[5] Indian princes are divinized and the alien attacker demonized. Simultaneously, temples devoted to the Rama figure emerge in different parts of India, sponsored by princes frequently described as Rama's reincarnations or direct descendants.

Thus a stone inscription in Dabhoi in Gujrat, circa 1253 AD, ascribes divinity to Lavanaprasada, feudatory and minister to Bhima II (AD 1178-1242) of Gujrat and a victor in some battles over Muhammad Ghauri:

> How could he be a mere mortal who defeated the king of
> the mlecchas whom no other mortal could defeat?[6]

An inscription circa 1168 AD, originally found in Hansi in modern Haryana and recounting the deeds of Prithviraj II and his commander and maternal uncle, Kilhana, makes a similar point. Kilhana having defeated Ghauri in Hansi, Prithviraj II is described in the inscription as a reincarnation of Rama. According to the inscription, Prithviraj thought of 'the mighty Hammira warrior (Ghauri) as a thorn in the side of all the world.'[7]

Written between 1191 and 1193 by Jayanaka or Vinayaka Pandita, in either case a Brahmin scholar of Kashmiri origin, and celebrating the resolve of the Rajput prince, Prithviraj III, to repulse Ghauri, *Prithvirajavijaya* offers the clearest example of the divinization-demonization reaction.

In this poem Brahma complains that the mlecchas have polluted Ajayameru (Ajmer) and in particular Pushkar, the sacred lake and pilgrimage site. Where 'heavenly courtesans' were forbidden to bathe, there 'now bathe the menstruating wives of these lowest of men' and the mleccha army drink waters meant only for those who feed on nectar.[8]

Another passage in *Prithvirajavijaya* acknowledges that 'every king in the northwest is as powerful as the wind,' the reference being to India's Turkic invaders, and speaks of Mahmud of Ghazni, who had attacked and desecrated the great Somnath temple on India's western coast in 1026 AD, as one having 'true courage' and 'so surpass[ing] all others.' The author recalls that Ghazni's kingdom in the northwest was extinguished by 'the evil Ghori,' reads the name Ghauri or Ghori as Go-ri, which in Sanskrit means 'the enemy of cows,' and informs us that the mleccha Ghauri was heedless enough to send an ambassador to Prithviraj, who had vowed to exterminate all 'demon-men.' (The mlecchas thus are here rakshasas as well.)[9]

Kalhana's famous Sanskrit poem chronicling Kashmir's Buddhist and Hindu dynasties, *Rajatarangini*, written between 1148 and 1150, after Shaivite Hinduism had supplanted Buddhism in Kashmir, also refers to Mahmud of Ghazni and to his battles a century and a half earlier with Hindu princes in the northwest, some of whom, like a section of Kashmir's rulers in this period, may have been Turkic by race.[10] The resistance to Mahmud offered by prince Trilochanapala, who may have had a Brahmin ancestor, is feelingly sketched, but Kalhana does not describe it as a Hindu-Muslim clash.

Curiously enough, *Rajatarangini* makes no mention of Somnath or Mahmud's raid there, to many a key event in the history of the Hindu-Muslim encounter. Also of interest is the opinion of *Rajatarangini's* learned translator that Mahmud's 'victories on the Oxus and in India were gained with the help of Hindu battalions under Hindu officers.'[11]

Referring at times to the Mahabharata, the Ramayana, the Buddha and Asoka, and on occasion reminding the listener of the seas to India's west and the east, of the Vindhya mountains, of Assam in the northeast and the river Godavari in the south, the *Rajatarangini* offers rare historical and all-India perspectives. But the princes it depicts, and the women they are entangled with, are more often than not sunk in debauchery, treachery and murderous plots, and seem incapable of defending their territories or subjects. If even a portion of India's ruling classes in the tenth, eleventh and twelfth centuries resembled some of Kalhana's pathetic protagonists, then it is small wonder that the land was conquered.

To return, however, to *Prithvirajavijaya*, Muhammad Ghauri, and Ghauri's ambassador at Prithviraj's court, the poet calls the visitor a cow-killer and adds: 'The colour of his beard, his eyebrows, his very lashes was yellower than the grapes that grow in his native region . . . Horrible was his speech, like the cry of wild birds; . . . all his phonemes were impure, impure as his complexion . . . He had what looked like skin disease, so ghastly white he was . . .'[12]

While the ambassador was with Prithviraj, word came—the poet informs us—that 'these demons with the bodies of men' had overrun a fort in Marwad, whereupon

> there appeared on Prithviraja's face a terrible frown—the boundary line of security for the world—announcing it was

now the moment to span the bows of war.[13]

Elsewhere in the poem, Prithviraj III is described as a reincarnation of Rama. In 1191 Prithviraj defeated Ghauri in Tarain, but in the following year Ghauri returned and was able to overcome Prithviraj and his allies in another battle in Tarain.

In another composition in praise of Prithviraj and his victories, Vinayaka Pandita says:

> I have little relish for paying homage to Siva, no desire to worship Krishna; I am stiff when it comes to bowing down to Siva's consort, indifferent to the worship of Brahma . . . [I]t was through King Prithviraja that we were protected from enemy destruction, and so I worship the very grass on the streets of his capital.[14]

Thus divinized, Prithviraj became a hero of folk ballads as well. At about the same time, Jayachandra of the Gahadavala dynasty was described as 'Narayana descended to save the earth.'[15] Some decades later, Ramachandra, the Yadava king of Devagiri in Maharashtra (ascended 1271 AD), was spoken of as a modern Rama,[16] and a 1304 Jaina text referred to mlecchas as rakshasas.[17] Then in 1346 the Vijayanagar kingdom was established in the south, a Hindu kingdom that successfully resisted Muslim invaders and, significantly enough, gave an important place to Rama worship. Vijayanagar's rulers were described as reincarnations of Rama.

Also instructive is a passage from the 1153 AD drama *Lalitavigraharaja* by Somadeva. In lines clearly drawn from real life, an ambassador representing a Turkic ruler cites to Vigraharaja IV a Sanskrit verse to the effect that a king, any king, contained a part of Vishnu.[18] The ambassador is making a case for the legitimacy of mleccha rule, but we may note that for the sake of such a rule he has studied an alien language and text.

This ambassador was clearly in the tradition of the remarkable scholar Alberuni, who had joined some of the expeditions of Mahmud of Ghazni, spent ten years in India, and closely studied its intellectual, social and religious life, even while others in the expeditions abducted Indians into slavery.

The divinization of Indian kings notwithstanding, one of Alberuni's findings was that some Hindu philosophers were 'entirely free from worshipping anything but God alone.'[19] Another was that because of their ruination at Mahmud's hands, the Hindus 'cherished the most inveterate aversion towards all Muslims.' Alberuni also noted that the Hindus, while seemingly resigned to their humiliation, looked upon the invaders as outcastes and 'recoiled from the touch of the impure barbarian Muslims.'[20]

We see that the Turkic ambassador portrayed by Somadeva is very different from the author of *Prithvirajavijaya*, who also describes a Turkic visitor. The Indian author of *Prithvirajavijaya* ridicules the 'impure' speech of the Turk, but Somadeva's Turk has learnt the speech of the Indian. Like some Greek and Chinese visitors to India in earlier centuries, like Alberuni in the eleventh century, and like several Europeans in the future, the Turk in Somadeva's drama is interested in India's language, thought and beliefs. The Indian poet, the author of *Prithvirajavijaya*, on the other hand, judging the Turk and what he represents to be contemptible, disregards him.

We know that the curiosity of the visitors to India was connected with a wish to conquer or control, and we may assign a positive value to India's traditional lack of interest in conquest, but not to Indian incuriosity regarding actual or potential attackers. When it came to defending an Indian kingdom from an alien invader, contempt and demonization proved ineffectual substitutes for knowledge.

The Greeks, the Chinese, the Arabs, the Central Asians and Europeans who surveyed, scrutinized and described facets of India were seldom studied by the subjects of their curiosity who as a result also became political subjects. The human body excited the curiosity of the ancient Indians, as did the firmament, and so did the mystery of numerals—medicine, astronomy and mathematics flourished. Invaders took India's notable discoveries in these sciences to the Middle East, Central Asia and Europe.

But a different breed of human beings, people with an unfamiliar colour, appearance and language, or the life and culture of such a people, aroused no interest in a race fatally self-satisfied, not even when the alien was threatening to stay put and rule over the natives.

*

Indianization: Within two years of the defeat of Prithviraj III in Tarain, the Gahadavala ruler, Jayachandra, was killed in battle with the Turks, and the holy city of Banaras or Varanasi was raided. In the following decades, Ghauri's commanders and clansmen extended their sway towards the east and south of India, a succession of princes and idols yielded before force, and a sultanate of Muslim rulers was established in Delhi. Later (1296-1309), Alauddin Khalji or Khilji marched south and defeated many including the Yadavas of Devagiri.

Though none of them erected pillars with a message similar to Asoka's, some of the Muslims who won battles in India and chose to stay did build magnificent structures—mosques, forts, gates, towers and mausoleums—and gracious gardens. From their interaction and commerce with Hindus a new language emerged, Urdu, the vocabulary of which was largely Indian.

The truth was that with time some of the invaders and conquerors had become Indian. Seeking a less tense relationship with the subjugated Hindus of India, they were perhaps aided by the Hindu belief, cited by the Turk in Somadeva's drama, in the sacred character of a king. In the Mahabharata, Bhishma states that 'the king is appointed by (God) Vishnu himself, and he partakes of his divinity and is, therefore, to be obeyed.'[21] The belief enabled Brahmins (and other Hindus) to serve Muslim—and, later, British—rulers.

Tension was eased, too, by Islam's mystic or Sufi wing, which, presenting a face of piety rather than the sword, tried to reconcile Hindus with Muslims, and Hinduism with Islam.

The exercise was not easy. The Hindus felt that rough feet had ridden over them, their temples and their feelings. Though successful in battle, the Muslims on their part felt the sting in day-to-day life when caste Hindus avoided them: the touch of a Muslim was thought to pollute a Hindu or any vessel from which the Muslim ate or drank.

Nor was the exercise quite safe from the angle of Islamic purity, for to reach their goal the Sufis often invoked the doctrine of wahdat-ul-wujud, or unity of being. While congenial to the Hindus, who found wahdat-ul-wujud akin to their own philosophy of the oneness of all life, advaita or non-dualism, the doctrine troubled the ulama, Islam's orthodox scholars, who, arriving in India with some of the Muslim armies, were as cool to the Indian Sufis speaking of wahdat-ul-wujud as they had been to its best-known proponent in the Muslim world outside India, Ibn-al-Arabi (d. 1240).

Not all Sufis in India propounded the doctrine; many concentrated on leading austere, contemplative or helpful lives, made no distinction between Muslims and Hindus, and refrained from philosophizing. But the ulama wondered whether Islam would have a role in India if some Sufis preached that God was in everything and everyone, including, presumably, in Hinduism and Hindus, while in the eyes of other Sufis a Hindu was the same as a Muslim. In anxiety for unity with Hindus, would Islam lose its identity?

Refusing to worry along these lines, Muslim Sufis struck roots in India and, chiefly through the simplicity and devotion of their lives, won the goodwill of many Hindus. Not merely an 'Indian' Islam but varieties of Islam grew on the subcontinent, accommodating local traditions and practices.

A founder figure in Islamic mysticism in India is Shaikh Muinuddin Chishti (d. 1236), who reached India before Ghauri battled with Prithviraj in Tarain, and whose tomb in Ajmer attracts Muslim and Hindu visitors to this day.

Asked about the highest form of devotion to God, Shaikh Muinuddin is said to have answered: 'Redressing the misery of those in distress, and feeding the hungry.' A chain of eminent successors descended from Shaikh Muinuddin. His famous disciple, Shaikh Qutb-ud-din Bakhtiyar Kaki, had an equally well-known disciple, Shaikh Farid, who taught Shaikh Nizamuddin Auliya (d. 1325), after whose tomb one of New Delhi's major railway stations is named.

The Chishti chain was only one of a number of Sufi orders, or silsilas. Several Sufis adopted Hindu customs or practices such as eschewing meat. Some wrote, while others inspired, poetry that unveiled Hindus and Muslims as human beings. While many Hindus converted to Islam because of the Sufis, other Sufi achievements were greater. One lay in narrowing the Hindu-Muslim divide at the grassroots, a feat that should be seen against the history of Islam's entry into India, including the violence and the iconoclasm that marked it; another in helping Muslims to see India's soil, culture and history as their inheritance as well.

Thus Amir Khusrau (1253-1325) called India his 'motherland,' praised it as 'a paradise on earth' even though non-Muslims formed its majority, and suggested that Muslims might find much to admire if they probed the heart of the seeming idol-worshipper and of the woman willing to enter the fires consuming her deceased husband.[22]

In due course we will see the ulama's opposition to what they saw as attempts to dilute and pollute Islam.

*

Humanization: Rage and terror, two of the first reactions of Hindus to the Muslim onslaught, were gradually joined by soul-searching. Why did the Hindus lose their battles? Were the gods defaced in their temples weaker than Islam's God? Rama images had proved no more effective than other idols or other temples in sending back the invader, and divinized and often-heroic princes had fallen in battle.

Did Indians have the wrong gods? Or was theirs too a powerful God, yet one neglected or unrecognized, or shut out at times by chants and the smoke of incense? When prostrating before images in their temples, did not the Hindus in fact often appeal to God the creator, the sustainer, and the destroyer of the world and its inhabitants? Piercing the layers of ritual and ceremony, the insight of the alien Alberuni had discovered this. Could the Hindus focus on it too?

Indeed, was Rama or Krishna no more than the name of a present or past earthly prince? In a deeper sense, was not Rama or Krishna a word for something beyond the world, a sound, a sigh, for the God beyond all gods? Was it not time for Indians to reach out more wholeheartedly to this God behind all gods? Instead of divinizing their princes, and demonizing the invaders, could Indians not humanize this God? Finally, and equally importantly, had they not hurt themselves by ostracizing the lower castes and the outcastes? Surely a touch of humanity was called for in this relationship as well. And also, hard as it was, in the Hindu-Muslim relationship?

Soon the soul-searching left the rage and the terror behind, or calmed the rage and banished the fear. Reflection sparked creativity, and devotion to the rediscovered God fanned the young flame to the great and warm fires of Bhakti poetry, kindling ideals of compassion, service and equality.

While real, the reflection did not necessarily go far enough. It seemed not to touch some painful practices such as the one the law-maker Manu had prescribed, possibly in the second century AD. Eight, he laid down, was the ideal age for a girl's marriage,[23] a recommendation apparently followed for centuries.

The reflection did not take in the plight of the child-bride who frequently became a child-widow, was barred from marrying again, and suffered great torments for the rest of her life—or the ordeal of the widow pushed into the flames around her dead husband's body. Such tribulations were not uncommon for girls and women even in the 'golden' Gupta age, or in later periods.

One who had reflected more than most was the fourteenth-century mystic Ramanand, who was influenced by the teachings of the twelfth-century South Indian philosopher, Ramanuja. Arguing that man should recognize his sinfulness and surrender himself to God, Ramanuja approached God through the name Vishnu.

While residing in heavenly regions, Vishnu or God was seen as incarnating himself on earth for the sake of its residents. Rama and Krishna were two of his, God's, recent incarnations. Reciting Rama's name and adoring Krishna were the recipes for the salvation of sinners. Such in essence was the teaching of the Vishnu or Vaishnavite school.

Ramanand passed on Ramanuja's teaching in North India in Hindi—he wished to reach the common people—and collected a remarkable band of disciples, including Kabir the weaver, Raidas the cobbler, Dhanna the Jat farmer, Sena the barber and Pipa the Rajput. The disciples, who had broken the caste barrier, wrote and sang poetry that teased the mind and moved the heart.

In their songs of Bhakti or devotion, God was called Rama or Krishna in the Hindu fashion, or Rahim or Karim in Muslim style; the 'religious' divide too had been crossed. Though not portrayed with forms or attributes, the God of these poets offered mercy, succour and grace to human beings, not because humans were virtuous but because God was loving. Also this God, in some ways the God of the Gita but unencumbered with the Gita's concern over caste purity, seemed to deplore distinctions between human beings.

This was a God that Muslims too could recognize and accept. Indeed, Muslim concepts of God may have played a part in the discovery or rediscovery of the God of the Bhakti poets. On the other hand, we should also note an opinion that Abu Yazid al-Bistami, who lived in the ninth century, had access to the advaita strand in Hindu philosophy, and that by way of al-Bistami advaita could have influenced the Sufi doctrine of wahdat-ul-wujud.[24]

Be that as it may. When in 1518 Kabir, who had been raised by a Muslim weaver in Varanasi, died, the Hindus sought the body for cremation and the Muslims for burial. Disciples of the Bhakti poets wrote poetry in turn; some were Muslims. Describing the common yearnings of Hindus and Muslims, these poets were helping the difficult process of coexistence.

Not content with a Nirguna God—a God without any features or with only a name—, other Bhakti poets portrayed in vivid detail the charisma and doings of Rama or Krishna. Among many in North and East India who sang of a God with attributes, or a Saguna God, we can name Surdas (1483-1563), Mira (1498-1546), Chaitanya (1486-

1533), Sankaradev (1449-1569) and Tulsidas (1532-1623).

People in North, West and East India gave their hearts to Tulsi's monumental and magnificent rendering of the Ramayana in folk verse. Much earlier, perhaps towards the end of the twelfth century, South Indians had similarly been captured by the story of Rama written in Tamil verse by Kamban. Both Kamban and Tulsidas owed much to Valmiki's Ramayana in Sanskrit, written probably in the first or second century AD.

On the other hand, love for Krishna and Krishna's success in tormenting those seeking to love him form the themes of the verses of Surdas, Mira and Chaitanya.

To these representations of God in human form and with consorts, orthodox Muslims, with their belief in a formless God who was not born and did not beget, could not respond with warmth. For the Hindu families who heard Tulsi's story of·Rama, however, the form of God was not the question or a problem. What seeped into their hearts were a set of virtues—of fulfilling a promise, obeying a parent, loving a brother, remaining faithful to one's partner, and, if need be, sacrificing comfort in the process.

In no verse did Tulsi inflame anger or stoke revenge. There was nothing even remotely anti-Muslim in his story, which in any case depicted a previous age that contained no Muslim. Because Tulsi's story tended to foster kindness, loyalty, endurance and sacrifice, it turned out to be an ally to the poetry of Kabir and Raidas and the other poets of the Nirguna school.

The thrust of Tulsi's message comes across in an episode in his Lanka canto. The demonic king Ravana's brother Vibhishana, an ally of Rama, is troubled at the contrast between a Ravana riding a strong chariot and a Rama who is barefooted and chariotless. How can Rama vanquish so well-equipped an adversary, asks Vibhishana. Replies Rama:

> Listen friend, the chariot that leads to victory is of another kind. Valour and fortitude are its wheels; truthfulness and virtuous conduct are its banner; strength, discretion, self-restraint and benevolence are its four horses, harnessed with the cords of forgiveness, compassion and equanimity. . . Whoever has this righteous chariot, has no enemy to conquer anywhere.

Tulsi again reveals himself, and his goal of reconciliation, by excluding from his Ramayana the provocative episode in Valmiki's version where Rama kills the 'untouchable' youth Shambuk for trying to emulate the way of life of the higher castes—for 'stepping out of his place'. Where Valmiki mirrors the cruel realities of caste, even through the character of his hero Rama, in Tulsi's hands Rama becomes a compassionate man-God who cannot possibly be party to brutal inequality.

Nevertheless, a verse in Tulsi's Ramayana states that 'a Shudra, a dull-witted person, a beast, and a woman merit chastisement.' Commenting on the verse, Gandhi, who loved much of Tulsi's text and often used it in his twentieth-century discourse, was to point out that Tulsi's Rama 'not only never raised his hand against Sita, he did not even displease her at any time.'

Even if it could be shown, Gandhi added, that 'Tulsidas himself used to beat his wife, . . . the practice [did] not cease to be reprehensible.' Verses by Tulsi that were derogatory to Shudras and women had to be rejected, even as 'we should reject any erroneous statements of a geographical character' in Tulsidas's text.'[25]

Gandhi's ability to disregard offending items in the Tulsi Ramayana was clearly shared by most Hindus, who were riveted by its plot and moved by the characters of Rama, Sita, Bharata and Lakshmana.

The ethical teaching of the Krishna poetry was subtler, and harder to put into simple words, but its impact was to increase the ardour in the listener's love of God. While, like the Rama story, the Krishna poetry might have sounded un-Islamic to the Muslim ear, Islam was not an issue in it either, and the poetry did not teach intolerance. Therefore, whether taking a Saguna or Nirguna stance, Bhakti songs, like Sufi attitudes, seemed to favour mutual accommodation.

We have interpreted the flowering of Bhakti in the fifteenth and sixteenth centuries as a reaction to Islam as well as a process that in a measure Islam might have aided. But Bhakti has ancient roots in India. Most scholars link its beginnings to the devotion first to Siva and later to Vishnu in South India in the first few centuries after Christ, when Nayanars singing emotionally about Siva were paralleled by Alwars who preached loving adoration of Vishnu.

In the twelfth century, Basava, prime minister of a Karnataka kingdom, started the Virasaiva or Lingayat movement which believed in Siva as the Supreme God and opposed caste. A century after Basava, Maharashtra produced the remarkable Jnanadev (Jnaneswar or Gyanesvar), whose commentary on the Gita was written when he was in his teens. Devoutly recited to this day, the Jnaneswari should be seen against the background of preceding Turkic invasions in India's north and west—even, possibly, as a response to questions about India's faith that Alberuni might have raised during his ten-year stay.

While Jnaneswar was a Brahmin, his contemporary Namdev, who addressed his songs to a Nirguna God, belonged to the low caste of cloth-painters and was a murderer sensitized by the laments of his victims' widows. Whereas Jnaneswar and Namdev preceded Kabir and Tulsi, three other poet-saints of Maharashtra, Eknath, Tukaram, who was a farmer's son, and Ramdas, like Eknath a Brahmin, came after the two North Indians.

Not confining himself to spiritual questions, Ramdas or Ramdas Samarth (b.1608), seems to have urged the Maratha hero, Shivaji, to found a Hindu kingdom. A sanctuary for Hindu practices was needed, Ramdas said, when a Muslim sat on the Delhi throne and Muslim chieftains controlled much of South India as well. Writing for Shivaji a Ramayana version quite different from Tulsi's, Ramdas presented Aurangzeb as Ravana.

*

Guru Nanak

Ramdas was not the first mystic in India to speak openly of the political scene. Guru Nanak (1469-1539), the founder of Sikhism, had written of the early sixteenth-century bloodshed associated with Babur, founder of the Mughal dynasty, much of it taking place not far from where Nanak was:

> The Kal age is a knife, and kings are butchers;
> Justice hath taken wings and fled
> In this completely dark night of falsehood,
> The moon of truth is never seen to rise.

Addressing Babur directly, Guru Nanak wrote:

> Deliver just judgments, reverence holy men, forswear wine and gambling . . ./ Be merciful to the vanquished, and worship God in spirit and in truth.

Perspective and compassion ruling his heart, the Guru added:

The Primal Being is now called Allah
the turn of the Shaikhs hath come . . .
Babur ruled over Khorasan and
hath terrified Hindustan.
The Creator taketh no blame to Himself;
it was Death disguised as a
Mughal who made war on us.
When there was such slaughter and lamentation,
didst not Thou, O God, feel pain?
Creator, Thou belongest to us all.[26]

The Guru cries out to God, holds the age and Death responsible, and does not weigh down his soul with lasting wrath against Babur, or against Muslims. Babur to him is neither a contemptible mleccha, a strange figure with a strange speech from a place unworthy of being named, nor the great enemy, but a great sinner. Hindus and Muslims are not natural enemies either; the Primal Being is not only 'ours,' and Allah not only 'theirs.' In fact, the Creator belongs to 'us all'— there is no 'we' and no 'they.' We are reminded of Asoka in Kalinga—and of the contrast with exclamations and oaths in the Mahabharata.

Accommodation and its limits: Thanks to Nanak, Kabir and other saint-poets from different parts of India, the Muslims, whether of alien origin or converts, found a large measure of acceptance at the grassroots. The mleccha label was withdrawn; the Muslim too was accommodated in Indian society. Despite the blood he had spilled, even the foreigner/invader/conqueror could be accepted; in the Eternal Being's inscrutable plan, the conqueror's 'turn had come.' But he should repent of his cruelty and desist from coercion—the Indian should be free to worship in any way and to call God by any name.

Most Bhakti poets voiced, and thereby promoted, an acceptance of Muslims. This acceptance had other significant implications, whether or not fully realized by the poets. One was that, along with the Muslim presence, facts were being accepted, including unwelcome facts of invasion, inequality, division and defeat. Acceptance of facts could lead to reform in Hindu society, and to a better performance next time an invader appeared. And acceptance of Muslims could help bring about their integration in the Indian polity.

As pointed out before, the poets did not necessarily go far enough in reconciliation. For instance, only rarely did they call for

Hindus and Muslims, or for people of all castes, to break bread together. Here Nanak and the Sikh Gurus who followed him provided a notable exception, requiring all who were desirous of accepting the new faith to eat together, forgetting caste.

Nor did the Bhakti poets quite say that God would forgive human beings *only* after they had forgiven one another. Elsewhere in the world, as Hannah Arendt has noted, Jesus and the early Christian church had indicated that far from being exclusively divine, forgiveness had to be 'mobilized by [human beings] toward each other before they can hope to be forgiven by God also.'[27]

Shriver, for one, has stressed that 'eating together' and forgiveness went together in the accounts about Christ:

> One can only be struck by the many connections throughout these stories between the physical presence of alienated people, the offer of forgiveness around a table, and the simple act of eating together.

Social taboos are broken, superiority is humbled, and forgiveness exchanged, as Christ, tax-gatherers, sinners and divided apostles eat together. According to Arendt and Shriver, the early church successfully tested the 'conviction that mutual forgiveness would ensure the continued existence of a fractured or fracturable human community.'[28]

The Bhakti poets did not do all this or revolutionize their world. Yet, goading Hindu society to face itself and its inequalities, proclaiming an identity between the God of the newcomers and that of the natives, fostering acceptance of the newcomers and their native adherents, and refusing to fall into impotent rage or blind revenge, the Bhakti poets probably influenced the future beyond their hopes. Without them, even modest Hindu reform and Hindu-Muslim coexistence might have proved impossible.

The Indianization initiated by the Sufis and the acceptance offered by the Bhakti poets did not lead to an integration comparable, say, to that between England's native and invading races in the period following the Norman conquest of England, which occurred in 1066 AD, i.e. between Ghazni's and Ghauri's Indian raids. Like the Turks who came down the northwestern passes in force, their contemporaries crossing the English Channel in large numbers, the Normans, were adept horsemen and warriors keen on treasure and territory, and if some of the Turks built towers in India to mark their conquests, the

Normans built tall cathedrals in England.

But the religious gulf between attacker and resident was wider in India than in England, and the level of destruction higher. Another difference, however, may have been more significant. After an encounter that was humiliating for one side and glorious for the other, England's Anglo-Saxons and Normans learned first to tolerate and then to marry one another, and 'compromise, give-and-take, live-and-let-live [evolved into] a national habit.'[29] In India, on the other hand, mutual contempt separated elite newcomers from elite natives, with, as we have seen, the Turks detesting the Indians' temples, and the Indians distancing themselves from the 'impure' Turks.

In the view of one British historian, England's 'hard-won toleration . . . rested in the last resort [on a belief] in the sanctity of the individual [and on] the thesis that every man . . . was a soul of equal value in the eyes of God.'[30] Assiduously though they proclaimed such a belief, India's Sufis and Bhakti poets failed to persuade the elites in the different communities that the Other was a soul of equal value.

*

The Sikh scripture: Guru Nanak was born in a Khatri family in Talwandi in the part of the Punjab that went to Pakistan in 1947. Though the name suggests a Kshatriya connection, Khatris in the Punjab have been traditionally engaged in trade and the professions.

The Guru's disciples found that he gave little or no importance to rituals, images, pilgrimages, Sanskrit, the recitation by Brahmins of ancient texts, or caste rules. Since meditation upon the divine Name and an interior devotion to a formless God lay at the heart of Guru Nanak's teaching, as was the case with Kabir, the Guru is often seen alongside the Nirguna tradition.

His devotional poetry, written in the language of the common person, is a further reason for many to see Guru Nanak and Kabir together. While Kabir's followers also created a sect, that of the Kabir-panthis, Guru Nanak's followers would eventually form a larger, worldwide community, that of the Sikhs, or disciples, drawn from a number of castes but with a significant infusion of the Jats of central Punjab.

'There is no Hindu; there is no Mussalman.' Believed to be the Guru's first utterance after a mystical experience, these words may be variously interpreted—as a rejection of any Hindu-Muslim divide, a lament that true Hindus and true Muslims were no longer to be found, or an expression of faith in a third way. Nominating, before his death, a successor from among his disciples, Guru Nanak seemed to endorse the emergence of a new fold.

Part of the subsequent history of the north of the subcontinent would revolve around the relationship of this fold and its ten successive Gurus with the Muslims and Hindus living next to them, and their relationship with Lahore, the capital of the Punjab, and Delhi, the capital of India.

We will be looking at some of this history. Here let us note three significant and related events in the Sikh story: the compilation of the Sikh scripture, its installation in Amritsar, and its designation as the deathless Guru.

The Adi Granth, the Sikh scripture, was compiled by the fifth Guru, Arjan Dev, during the years 1603-04. It contains, among other texts, Guru Nanak's Japji, thought of as the scripture's quintessence, and a great number of devotional verses, arranged under different ragas (melodies). The verses are by Guru Nanak and other Gurus; prayer songs by Namdev, Kabir and Raidas and a composition attributed to Ramanand are included, and also hymns and couplets from two Sufis, Shaikh Farid and Bhikhan.[31]

In 1604 the holy book was installed in Amritsar at the site of the Harmandir Sahib, or the Golden Temple, the land for which was evidently given by the Mughal emperor Akbar, Babur's grandson, in 1576. Before his death in 1708, Guru Gobind Singh, the tenth Guru, declared that the line of human Gurus had ended with him but the Adi Granth would remain forever as the Guru Granth Sahib.

*

Akbar: Born in 1542 in Umarkot in Sindh while his father Humayun was in flight, Akbar, third in the Mughal dynasty, became king at fourteen and ruled India for forty-nine years until his death in 1605.

His early years were terrifying: thrice separated from Humayun, who was being pursued by his younger brothers and other seekers of the Mughal throne, the child Akbar was rescued each time. Though the rivalry ended in his father's favour—in 1555 Humayun re-entered Delhi and re-occupied the throne—, Akbar's boyhood witnessed the banishment of one uncle, Askari, the slaying of another, Hindal, and the blinding of a third, Kamran.

A lover of books and libraries, Humayun was destined to have an illiterate heir. The Mughal court's finest tutors failed to budge the child or boy Akbar from his refusal to be educated. Within a year of his return to Delhi, Humayun died, and the illiterate boy, a natural marksman and rider (of elephants, camels and horses), was crowned.

He named as prime minister, with full control over civil and military affairs, his guardian Bairam Khan, who as a Shia in a Sunni-dominated court was less likely than others to covet the shaky throne bequeathed by Babur. Among those eyeing the throne were descendants of the Afghan Sher Shah Sur, who after Babur's death had briefly ruled over Delhi and Agra, the Mughal kingdom's twin capitals.

Akbar and the royal army were chasing one of the descendants, Sikandar, in the Punjab when tidings were received that another of the Sur clan, Adil, or rather Adil's Hindu prime minister, Hemu, had effortlessly captured Agra and also taken Delhi after defeating its royalist garrison.

Originally a grain merchant, Hemu had risen to his place next to Adil Sur through administrative and military skill. After capturing Delhi, Hemu, who had several Rajput and Afghan chieftains as allies and was seen by some as 'an aspirant to independent kingship,' assumed the royal title Vikramaditya, which evoked memories of earlier Hindu power and valour.[32]

A majority of Akbar's officers favoured a retreat to Kabul but Bairam Khan proposed an immediate move to the east to attack Hemu, and Akbar backed his guardian and prime minister. On 5 November 1556, in the second battle of Panipat—in Kurukshetra country—, Akbar's forces led by Ali Quli Khan Shaibani, an Uzbek, and Bairam Khan defeated the Rajput-Afghan alliance led by Hemu and employing a huge number of elephants. The Pakistani writer S.M. Burke describes the end:

> Hemu fought valiantly on his mountainous elephant Hawai ('swift as the wind') but suddenly an arrow pierced . . . one of his eyes [and] its point emerged from the back of his head. Seeing their chief thus disabled, his men . . . fled the field. Hemu was captured and brought before his victors.

> Bairam Khan invited Akbar to earn merit by killing the infidel with his own hand. Akbar displayed an aversion to striking the already grievously wounded prisoner but . . . touched the head of the captive with his sword. Bairam

Khan then drew his sabre and severed Hemu's head with a
single stroke. A minaret of the heads of the slain was erected
to mark the victory and the title of Ghazi ('vanquisher of
infidels') was added to Akbar's name.[33]

But Akbar was too masterful to allow Bairam Khan a long spell of
power. Four years after the Panipat battle, Bairam Khan was isolated,
provoked into a fight, and ousted. He was on his way to exile in
Mecca when a band of Afghans nursing an old injury killed him in
Patan in Gujrat in January 1561.

Quli Khan, chiefly responsible for Akbar's success at Panipat,
and other influential, and therefore potentially dangerous, figures
were also eliminated.

In the autumn of 1567, Akbar attacked Mewar in Rajasthan,
ruled by the ancient Sisodia clan that had never submitted to a
Muslim ruler. Taking the town of Chittor was no problem for
Akbar, but Rana Udai Singh, whose father Rana Sanga had given
Babur his toughest fight in India, scorched the countryside and took
to the hill next to the town. The hill was surmounted by a broad,
thick and well-watered fort. It was only at the end of the following
February, after a long, bloody and costly battle and the construction
of mines and tunnels, that Akbar secured the fort.

Akbar was personally brave in this battle and nearly lost his life;
there were many Hindus in his army and many Muslims who fought
with the Sisodias; but the battle produced terrible bloodshed. After
the Mughal victory, in disregard of the principle of mercy to the
vanquished, 'a general massacre was ordered and no less than 30,000
of the enemy were mercilessly slaughtered. This number included the
peasants who had fought beside the Rajput warriors.'[34]

But Udai Singh escaped and harried the Mughals until his death
in 1572. His son Rana Pratap continued to challenge the Delhi
throne. In 1576, on the field of Haldighat, 'a grim battle in which
bravery on either side rose to the highest pitch'[35] ended in Pratap's
defeat, but he was unbowed. As Mughal pressure subsided because of
disturbances in the Empire's northwest, Rana Pratap improved his
position in Mewar, and built for himself a new capital. He died in
honour in 1597.

But Akbar's march continued in all directions. Kabul was annexed,
Kashmir taken, Bengal conquered. Revolts were suppressed wherever
they occurred. The Empire's southern boundaries were extended,
though with heavy losses. Akbar became lord of an immense territory.

Some historians think that his 'aggressions' were 'made without the slightest regard to moral considerations,' that he nursed 'earth-hunger.'[36] Perhaps, as has been said, he only did what others around him also wanted to do, except that he was much better at it. Akbar himself thought that 'a monarch should ever be intent on conquest, otherwise his neighbours rise in arms against him.'[37]

Yet the carnage linked to Akbar's conquests sullies his image and always will. After he secured the Chittor fort he fulfilled a promise he had made and went to the Chishti tomb in Ajmer to give thanks to God; it is not known whether any penitence accompanied the gratitude.

What is known is that he was content in many cases to be an overlord, not insisting on direct rule, and also that, like Asoka eighteen centuries earlier, he saw himself as being responsible for all the people and not merely a section of them. Akbar would be the protector not of India's Muslims alone but of everyone, and many Hindus acknowledged him as such. Though the Sisodias fought him without ceasing, a great number of Rajputs joined his army, and several Hindus his administration.

That a group of Rajputs had stood their ground even when a rogue elephant ridden by Akbar lunged towards them had impressed him. The group, led by Raja Bihari Mall, the ruler of Amber, had been invited to Delhi by Akbar because of Bihari Mall's role in saving a Mughal garrison attacked by followers of Sher Shah Sur.

Later, in February 1562, threatened by a Muslim chieftain in his neighbourhood, Bihari Mall sought Akbar's protection and offered to the emperor the hand of his eldest daughter. Akbar, then nineteen, accepted the offer. The Rajput wife, who remained a Hindu, gave birth to Salim, the crown prince who would eventually succeed Akbar.

Bihari Mall's son Bhagwan Das and the latter's adopted son Man Singh enlisted in the imperial forces on the day of the marriage. Fourteen years later it was Man Singh who commanded the Mughal forces that defeated Rana Pratap in Haldighat. Burke comments:

> The generous treatment accorded to the [Bihari Mall] family induced several other Rajput chiefs to seek marriage alliances with the Emperor and [later] his sons. They could see that Akbar had no desire to annex their territories or to humiliate them. All they had to do was formally to acknowledge the Mogul Emperor as their overlord.[38]

In Burke's view, the Afghans, whom the Mughals had displaced as India's rulers, were Akbar's 'most persistent adversaries,' but 'the greatest danger' to him was posed by some who in theory were his vassals—'turbulent and ambitious nobles' in Central Asia, 'including his half-brother Hakim.'

His most dependable allies, Burke claims, were the Shias, belonging to a minority sect and 'totally dependent upon him for their positions.' However, the Emperor's 'stoutest allies proved to be the Rajputs.' 'And once this warrior class had accepted the Mogul monarch as their own, the rest of the Hindu community, comprising the vast majority of his subjects, followed suit without much difficulty.'[39]

Akbar recognized what Hemu's failed yet remarkable bid and the unceasing resistance of Mewar had shown—the continuing strength of Hindus despite three centuries of pre-Mughal Muslim rule in Delhi. Akbar saw that he had to obtain Hindu acceptance. This he sought through marriage alliances, by inducting Hindus in offices of state, by refusing to interfere in Hindu beliefs and practices, by participating personally in Hindu festivals and abjuring meat for portions of the year, and by abolishing taxes that offended the Hindu sentiment.

In 1563, a year after marrying Bihari Mall's daughter, Akbar abolished the pilgrim tax, and the following year he withdrew the jizya, a discriminatory levy on Hindus. In a letter to the Shah of Iran, Akbar explained his reasoning:

> Divine mercy attaches itself to every form of creed . . . The eternal God is bounteous to all souls and conditions of men. Hence it is fitting that kings, who are the shadow of divinity, should not cast away this principle.[40]

As we shall soon see, Akbar was drawn to Sufi tolerance, but his religious views probably influenced him less than the practical consideration of gaining Hindu acceptance. His success in doing so meant that the Mughals were before long seen as an Indian dynasty, whereas the Muslims who had ruled Delhi earlier had been viewed as aliens who had captured power.

An indication of the extent of Akbar's success came over two-and-a-half centuries after his death, during the 1857 Rebellion against the British. By that time Akbar had been followed by several other Mughals of varying quality who also differed in their commitment to the cause of religious tolerance. Among them was Aurangzeb, zealous for Sunni Islam, under whose rule from 1659 to 1707 Hindus faced severe hardship. Even so, the most ardent Hindus among the 1857 rebels chose to rally under the banner of the titular Mughal emperor of Hindustan, Bahadur Shah Zafar. If the Mughals had become Hindustanis, it was thanks above all to Akbar.

*

Christians, at the time almost all European, Zoroastrians, Jains and Sikhs were also part of Akbar's expanding world. Rounding the Cape of Good Hope, Vasco da Gama, the Portuguese, had landed in Calicut in 1498, twenty-eight years before Akbar's grandfather Babur had defeated Ibrahim Lodi at Panipat. Thus Europeans preceded the Mughals on Indian soil.

European Jesuits invited to explain Christianity to Akbar have left behind detailed portrayals of the Emperor, his religious attitudes, personality and policies. Between 1580 and Akbar's death in 1605, three Jesuit missions spent long periods with the Emperor, in Fatehpur Sikri, the new capital that Akbar had built near Agra, in Lahore, in Kashmir, and elsewhere.

A member of the first mission, Father Monserrate, thought that Akbar's visage was such that 'one could easily recognize, even at first glance,' that he was the king. He was 'sturdy, hearty and robust.' His shoulders were broad and his somewhat bandy legs were 'well-suited for horsemanship.' He shaved his beard but wore a short moustache and kept the hair on his head long.[41]

Frequently the Christian Fathers felt that Akbar was close to accepting Christ; and the Pope was persuaded to write to Akbar expressing interest in his conversion. Though not literate, the Emperor had a deep spiritual curiosity; saying repeatedly that no faith seemed to satisfy him fully, he sought proof of the superiority of any one faith over others.

The Fathers' rejection of gifts of money, willingness to die for their faith, and simple lifestyle impressed Akbar, who also seemed to enjoy their company, but the hopes of each of the three missions were belied. The Fathers finally claimed that Akbar's unwillingness to reduce the number of his wives to one was the chief stumbling block, but the Emperor had political and intellectual difficulties as well. His conversion to Christianity would have invited rebellion; also, his mind was apparently unwilling to accept that Christ was God's only son, born of a virgin.

Akbar, who honoured ascetics, holy men and dervishes of all backgrounds, studied Hinduism, Jainism, Zoroastrianism and Sikhism as well but did not embrace any of them. As the Fathers on the first mission put it, Akbar 'holds firmly that there is no divinely accredited form of faith, because he finds in all something to offend his reason and intelligence.'[42] He was troubled, too, by the irreligious ill will of the religious. Father Monserrate quotes Akbar:

> [T]he followers of each religion regard the institutions of their own religion as better than those of any other. Not only so, but they strive to convert the rest to their own way of belief. If these refuse to be converted, they not only despise them, but also regard them for this very reason as their enemies. And this causes me to feel many serious doubts and scruples.[43]

We are reminded of Asoka's edicts by Akbar's concern at intolerance and by his attitude that 'there are wise men to be found and ready at hand in all religions,' that truth could not be 'confined to one religion and creed,' and that as Emperor he should aim at Suleh-kul, or Peace with All.

Yet the attitude was anathema to the ulama and its influential supporters in the court and administration. The Fathers concluded that Akbar escaped assassination by Muslim fanatics only because 'his army was a heterogeneous mixture of indigenous and foreign races and included Hindus in whom he reposed much confidence.'[44]

In 1578 Akbar claimed that while on a hunt in the Punjab he had experienced a spiritual ecstasy similar to what Sufis often spoke of. Perhaps because he was emboldened by this experience, or for other reasons, Akbar launched in 1582 the religious innovation known as Din-i-Ilahi, or the Divine Religion. Whether, as some have held, Din-i-Ilahi was indeed a new religion, clearly separate from Islam, that Akbar tried to propagate, with himself as its founder or messiah, or merely a Sufic order within the broad world of Islam, as others maintain, is a debate we need not go into.

But we can note Din-i-Ilahi as an item in the bitter and lasting dispute between the orthodox ulama on the one hand and Akbar and the Sufis on the other. One of Akbar's sharpest critics was Abdul Qadir Badauni, a writer and translator in the Emperor's service from 1574 until Akbar's death. His trenchant *Muntakhabut Tawarikh*, a history of India's Muslim kings with special attention to Akbar's reign, balances the tributes of the famed *Akbarnama*, written by the Emperor's talented friend, Abul Fazl.

Badauni claims that he wrote his book from 'sorrow' and 'heartburning' over 'the deceased Religion of Islam'; it is clear that he holds Akbar responsible for the supposed decease. However, Badauni's attacks on Akbar should perhaps be seen alongside the intemperate remarks he also made about Hindus, Shias and Sufis.

In Akbar's time, orthodox unease about his religious views was joined to resentment, which was directed at Rajput influence in the palace and the army, at Akbar's personal warmth towards his friend Birbal, the Hindu poet and court wit, and at the standing of Akbar's 'foremost expert in financial and revenue administration,'[45] Todar Mall, an orthodox Hindu. Previously assisting Sher Shah Sur, Todar Mall 'rose to be Ashraf-i-Diwan (literally, the noblest diwan) and was virtually the prime minister for some time.'[46]

Conspicuous they might have been, but the Hindus in Akbar's court and administration were always a small minority. As Burke points out, 'it is amazing how little Akbar actually needed to give away in order to win the confidence of the Hindus.'[47] Out of 415 mansabdars—the Empire's principal officers, serving at the Emperor's pleasure in any civil or military duty assigned to them—only 51 were Hindus.

Yet the trust of Hindus was gained, largely because they were not penalized by the state for remaining in their faith. They could worship freely, and their religious poets, including Surdas and Tulsidas, wrote freely during Akbar's reign. Also, the Hindus noticed in the Emperor and some of his companions an effort to understand Hindu practices. Thus, regarding 'idol-worship' by Hindus, Abul Fazl would write that the images before which Hindus bow were 'fashioned as aids to fix the mind and keep the thoughts from wandering, while the worship of God alone is required as indispensable.'[48]

After Akbar's death (he was buried as a Muslim and with Islamic rites), a Jesuit Father wrote:

> Indeed he was a great king, for he knew that the good ruler is he who can command, simultaneously, the obedience, the respect, the love, and the fear of his subjects. He was a prince beloved of all, firm with the great, kind to those of low estate, and just to all men, high and low, neighbour or stranger, Christian, Saracen (Muslim), or Gentile (Hindu); so that every man believed that the King was on his side.[49]

Men like Badauńi thought that Islam was hurt in the bargain. A similar charge made by the influential Islamic thinker, Shaikh Ahmed of Sirhind (d. 1624), has stuck over time. One result is that in a country like Pakistan, Akbar, emperor for forty-nine years in a famous Muslim dynasty, is 'not mentioned in any school textbook from class one to matriculation.'[50]

'On the other hand, Aurangzeb appears in different textbooks of social studies and Urdu language as an orthodox and pious Muslim copying the Holy Quran and sewing caps for his livelihood.' The Shaikh of Sirhind is featured for opposing Akbar's Din-i-Ilahi.

But in books for college-level courses Akbar is mentioned—adversely. I.H. Qureshi criticizes Akbar's incorporation of non-Muslims in his administration. Another writer, Shaikh Muhammad Rafiq, alleges that '[Akbar] favoured the Rajputs so much that his nobles lost confidence in him.' Shaikh A. Rashid in *A Short History of Pakistan* writes:

> In the final analysis, if the Muslims were to forget their uniqueness and come to absorb, as Akbar did, contradictory tendencies and beliefs from other religions, could the Muslim nation continue to exist as a separate entity?[51]

Against this appraisal must be placed Akbar's success in gaining Hindu acceptance of Islam's presence in India. As Burke observes, 'Akbar gained far more by conciliating the mass of the Hindus than he lost by alienating a section of Muslims.'[52]

Without Akbar, the resentment of the Hindu majority might eventually have crippled Islam's position on the subcontinent. If he had not made Islam optional or voluntary, and other faiths acceptable and legitimate, a counter-struggle might have eliminated Islam by force from India. Instead of such an outcome, Islam, whether orthodox, Sufistic or of another sort, has a voice today in India, Pakistan, Bangladesh and Sri Lanka. Part of the credit belongs to Akbar.

4

Empire and Conscience: Mughals, Sikhs and Marathas

THIS CHAPTER TRAVERSES the two centuries that followed Akbar, the seventeenth and the eighteenth. We will focus on two challenges to Mughal rule that marked the period, one mounted by the Sikhs and the other by the Marathas, and also glance at a battle for the Mughal throne that affected Hindu-Muslim relations.

The Sikh and Maratha enterprises are significant as assertions of conscience and efforts towards nation-building, though what was being built was a Maratha or a Sikh nation, rather than India. Equally, the Mughal-Sikh and Maratha-Mughal conflicts indicate that the India coming gradually under European gaze was in fact several Indias.

Akbar's son Jahangir (1569-1627) and the latter's son Shah Jahan (1592-1666) were half-hearted about the legacy of tolerance left by Akbar. Unable to resist the temptation of appeasing the ulama, they also lacked Akbar's independence and innovative capacity.

Jahangir failed in an important relationship, that with Arjan Dev, the fifth Guru of the Sikhs. We saw that Akbar had gifted the land in Amritsar where Guru Arjan had installed the Sikh scripture and built a temple. The gesture seems to have aroused hopes that the Emperor might accept Sikhism, but no conversion occurred. Equipped with hindsight, and aware that Akbar's religious curiosity took him in different directions but never very far, we are not surprised.

Succeeding to his father's throne, Jahangir took offence at the warmth the Guru showed to the Emperor's rebelling son, Khusrau; but evidently the Emperor was also put out by the growing size of Guru Arjan's following. J.P.S. Uberoi has quoted from Jahangir's memoirs:

> [Clothed] in the garments of sainthood and sanctity, [Arjan Dev] had captured many of the simple-hearted of the Hindus, and even of the ignorant and foolish followers of Islam, by

his ways and manners . . . They called him Guru, and from all sides stupid people crowded to worship and manifest complete faith in him . . . Many times it occurred to me to (a) put a stop to this vain affair or (b) to bring him into the assembly of the people of Islam . . .

At last, when Khusrau passed along this road, this insignificant fellow . . . came out and did homage to him. He behaved to Khusrau in certain special ways, and made on his forehead a finger-mark in saffron . . .

When this came to my ears and I clearly understood his folly, I ordered them to produce him and handed over his houses, dwelling-places and children to Murtaza Khan, and having confiscated his property commanded that he should be put to death.[1]

The execution and, as Sikhs believe, inhuman torture of Guru Arjan in 1606 is a crucial milestone in the story of the clash between uniformity and pluralism on the subcontinent. Acknowledging that at some point Guru Arjan 'laid aside the garments of a faqir,' 'wore a sword in his belt,' and 'turned the voluntary offerings of his Sikhs into a treasury of the community,' which enabled him to hire 'soldiers as well as officials,' Uberoi adds:

The fifth guru may not have meant to give offence to, much less wage war upon, the emperor, but he was effectively urging the claims of pluralism versus . . . one single central rule in culture as well as power, religion, civil society and political economy, as a matter of conscience.[2]

Guru Hargobind, son and successor, at the age of eleven, to Guru Arjan, signified his commitment to autonomy by carrying two swords in his belt at the investiture. According to G.C. Narang, Guru Hargobind explained the meaning of the pair of swords in these words: 'one to avenge my father, the other to destroy the miracles of Muhammad.'[3] Or, as has been said, one symbolized temporal power (miri), the other spiritual power (piri).[4]

Subsequent history has prompted some questions that are difficult to answer. Was executing the fifth Sikh Guru the only way in which Jahangir could protect his throne? In a similar situation, how would Akbar have acted? If suspecting an alliance between a rebelling son and the leader of a (partially armed) religious group, would Akbar have ordered the religious leader's death? Did the Guru's 'false' religion bother Jahangir, or was he primarily seeking to punish an abettor in Khusrau's treason?

Again, was there any alternative to Guru Hargobind's pledge, 'I will avenge my father,' a reaction supported by an enraged community?

What is plain is that after Guru Arjan Dev's execution the Sikh-Muslim relationship no longer remained a matter of inter-religious or inter-community dialogue. Drenched in hate and suspicion, the relationship turned into a political battle. The Sikhs in the Punjab perceived persecution from the centre's Mughal rulers, and attempted to carve out a safe space for themselves, if necessary by battling the Mughals. The latter, on their part, perceived a threat from Sikhs, and strove to stamp it out.

In the previous chapter we referred to the Sikh belief that immediately after experiencing a divine revelation Guru Nanak had uttered the sentence *'Na koi Hindu na Musalman'*—'There is no Hindu and no Muslim.' Assigned to 1499, or one hundred and seven years before the execution of Guru Arjan, the remark seemed to underscore Nanak's concern with a person's inner intention, rather than the outer label, and also with Hindu-Muslim amity. Discussing Nanak, Uberoi writes:

> The folk wisdom of India has surely got [his] message right, e.g. in the Urdu and Hindi saying about [Guru Nanak's] mission and reputation: *'Nanak Shah faqir:/ Hindu ka guru,/ Musalman ka pir.'* ('Nanak the master/renunciate is a teacher to Hindu and Muslim.')

As to what his followers, the Sikhs, should strive for in this world, Guru Nanak's answer, it has been said, was, 'Work, worship and sharing.' After Guru Arjan's martyrdom and from Guru Hargobind's time, however, there seemed a stress on additional objectives: 'temporal power, honour and revenge.'[5]

Yet this interest in power, honour and revenge, as well as the future story of the Sikhs, would bear a distinctive mould; it would be shaped by the fifth Guru's martyrdom. In an insightful phrase, Uberoi distinguishes 'the soldier and the hero,' who try 'to be stronger than the other,' from 'a martyr or a saint' who tries 'to be stronger than oneself.'[6]

The very similarity in certain areas between Islam and Sikhism, implying ease in moving from one to the other, spelt conflict. Unambiguous belief in the One God, disbelief in idols, the notion of equality among men, simplicity in the place of worship, repetition of God's name as a form of prayer, a fusion of the spiritual and the worldly, and reverence for the Holy Book and for the founder of the community—these features marked both faiths. Jahangir and his Mughal successors might well have feared the crossing over to Sikhism of fresh ranks of 'ignorant and foolish followers of Islam.' In contrast, common ground between Hinduism and Islam seemed much smaller, offering less room for stepping on one another's toes.

*

Dara Shukoh: Shah Jahan lives on through the Taj and the mosques and forts in Agra and Delhi, but the killing of male relatives that marked his ascension returned to haunt Shah Jahan in his last days in Agra Fort. After reigning for thirty years, he was incarcerated there by his son Aurangzeb, who then proceeded to trap, chase and destroy his brothers Dara, Shuja and Murad, and seize the throne of Hindustan.

The triumph of Aurangzeb over Dara Shukoh, Emperor Shah Jahan's eldest son and designated successor, represented also the defeat of Akbar's policy of tolerance; and the clash symbolized the conflict between an Islam that interacted freely with the culture of India and its exclusive, insulated version.

While as sympathetic towards Hinduism as his great-grandfather, Dara was also, unlike Akbar, an able scholar. His study of the Upanishads and the Gita persuaded Dara that Hinduism was a 'twin brother of Islam' and could indeed assist in providing a fuller understanding of Islam.[7]

A Persian translation of a portion of the Upanishads, entitled *Sirr-i-Akbar* ('The Great Secret'), was sponsored and possibly even translated or edited by Dara. This initiative by Dara was destined to carry Indian thought to the West: early in the 19th century, a Latin version of *Sirr-i-Akbar* introduced the Upanishads to Europe for the first time.

In *Majma al-Bahrain* ('Mingling of the Oceans'), a Persian work written by him, Dara dissents from the ulama when he 'takes it for granted that Hinduism is basically monotheistic' and claims that indirectly the Koran itself refers to the 'first heavenly book'—the Upanishads.[8]

Aware that the Empire his forebears had created could not long survive without Hindu trust, and ready for a fresh bid in Akbar's spirit for Hindu-Muslim cooperation, Dara was moreover a prince loved by the poor of Agra and Delhi, and a patron of painters and poets. We may note, too, that as a boy Dara had as his tutor the Lahore Sufi, Miyan Mir, who had evidently been present when, under the aegis of Guru Arjan Dev, the foundation stone for Amritar's Golden Temple was laid. According to some, Mir laid the stone himself.[9]

Such a Dara, however, lost out to a more focused and ruthless brother, who was aided by betrayers of Dara. On 29 August 1659, by Aurangzeb's order, the captured Dara was humiliatingly paraded on the back of an elephant in the streets of Delhi and then executed on trumped up charges. In a 1910 appraisal, Abul Kalam Azad, an outstanding reconciler himself, called Dara

> a man of excellent taste. The overwhelming proof of his taste is that in pursuing his goal he lost the distinction between the temple and the mosque.[10]

With some justification, a modern poet ascribes to Dara the following vision for the Mughal dynasty:

> Each Moghul advancing his precursor's efforts/Some physic to bring for India's deep hurts/ . . .Till our people's pain abates . . .
>
> In a purpose so pure, so selfless and true/As would of course ensure our line, but also hew/Trust out of suspicion.[11]

Aurangzeb: However, winning India's trust was not a serious goal, neither were Hindus 'our people,' for Aurangzeb, the brother with a sharp mind, an interest in books, and austere habits who prevailed over Dara and ruled India for forty-nine years (1658-1707).

Aurangzeb's victory over Dara produced seeming stability and an extension of the Empire's boundaries, but at great price. His overcentralized, overstretched, discriminatory and puritanical rule invited discontent and prepared the soil for the eventual demise of the Empire founded by his forebears.

Muslims—to be precise, Sunni Muslims—were the people he was chiefly concerned with. For acting properly with them, he sought counsel from the sharia and interpretation from the ulama. The jizya levy that Akbar had abolished was reimposed by Aurangzeb in 1679—it helped distinguish between subjects, the Muslims, from second-class subjects, the Hindus, and was moreover 'a heavy tax, . . . exacted in a humiliating manner.'[12]

Many Hindu temples were destroyed during Aurangzeb's reign, partly because of the bigotry to which his mind had yielded and also because the destruction fetched him support in influential ulama quarters. In 1668 he banned Hindu religious fairs.

The emperor won new territory in the east, and firmed up border areas in the northwest, but his offensive and defensive battles with Rajputs, Marathas, Sikhs, Jats and Bundelas, and with Muslim chieftains in the South, drained the empire; and his policies induced hate in Hindus and Sikhs.

*

The Gurus and the Mughals: The sixth Sikh Guru, Hargobind, who had raised an army and built in Amritsar a small fort, Lohgarh ('Iron Castle'), was for some time imprisoned by Jahangir. During Shah Jahan's time, Guru Hargobind's force thrice fought Mughal soldiers; but after 1634 the Guru settled into a quieter life on the slopes of the Shivalik hills in eastern Punjab, and died there ten years later.

This ten-year span saw the start, scholars tell us, of a significant relationship between Sikhism and the Hindu cult of the goddess or Devi who protected and avenged her devotee, a cult holding sway in and around the Shivalik region, as place-names such as Kalka, Chandigarh and Ambala would confirm.

Guru Hargobind was succeeded by his grandson, Har Rai, who was followed by his young son, Har Krishan. On Guru Har Krishan's death, Guru Tegh Bahadur, a son of Guru Hargobind, became the ninth Guru.

In chapter one we saw how one of Guru Tegh Bahadur's preachings recalled a rare tribute to forgiveness in the Mahabharata, and also how the Guru seemed to exceed the Mahabharata in his willingness to forgive a nephew, Dhir Mall, who had coveted the Guru's throne and was involved in an attempt on Guru Tegh Bahadur's life. While a difference between a king's throne and a Guru's may be conceded, we should mark the contrast between Jahangir's reaction to Khusrau and Guru Arjan Dev on the one hand, and Guru Tegh Bahadur's attitude to Dhir Mall on the other.

It is of some interest, and perhaps not unconnected with his valuation of forgiveness, that Guru Tegh Bahadur, whose grandfather had been tortured to death under Jahangir's orders and whose father had vowed revenge and struggle against the Mughal king, appears to have associated for a period with Aurangzeb's forces in Assam.[13]

Yet, as we saw in the introduction, this magnanimous Guru Tegh Bahadur, the ninth Guru of the Sikhs, was destined to be executed, on Aurangzeb's orders, opposite Delhi's Red Fort in 1675. If Tegh Bahadur's father, Hargobind, was eleven when his father, Guru Arjan Dev, was done to death, Tegh Bahadur's son, Gobind, was but nine when the severed head of his father was brought to him by a faithful band of humble Sikhs.

And if the 1606 martyrdom set freedom of conscience against state power, the 1675 event witnessed, as we noted previously in the introduction, the offering of life for the freedom of one's weaker fellow-humans. Coercion against Pandits in Kashmir, including forcible removal of the tilak and the janeu, was what had impelled Guru Tegh Bahadur to confront Aurangzeb.

Following his execution, many in the Punjab 'began to burn with indignation and revenge.'[14] In the spirit of his grandfather Guru Hargobind, Guru Gobind Singh made it known before long that he would shoulder the burden of redressal. He wrote:

> For this purpose was I born: to uphold righteousness, to
> protect those worthy and virtuous; to overcome and destroy
> the evildoers.

The language was that of the Gita, but the young Guru warned that anyone calling him the Supreme Being 'shall suffer in hell,' and added: 'Recognize me as God's servant only.'[15] However, he would be a militant servant.

*

Guru Gobind Singh: Maturing in the east Punjab foothills and doubtless encouraged by the Devi cult, Guru Gobind Singh prescribed training in, and the worship of, arms. In his compositions, as Harbans Singh puts it, 'God and Sword became interchangeable terms.'[16] He called God *Sarbloh* ('All-steel') in the opening line of the congregational prayer prepared by him, *Ardas:* 'Having first remembered the Sword (God), meditate on (or turn your thoughts to) Guru Nanak.'

This exaltation of arms becomes the more meaningful when it is remembered that Guru Nanak, the first Guru of the Sikhs, seems to have called on his followers to wield no weapon and to rely on the efficacy of the Divine Name.[17]

Interesting though it is, we will not here join the debate on the degree to which the transition to militancy in Sikhism may have been aided by the traditions of the Jats of the Punjab who, attracted by the social equality for which Guru Nanak and succeeding Gurus stood, had entered Sikh ranks in large numbers. That these Jat traditions included directness in speech, a similar lack of inhibition in recourse to arms, generosity with guests, and 'an insistence upon their right to take revenge' seems widely accepted, as is the view that to some extent at any rate Jat infusion brought these traits into the Sikh community.[18]

The Guru's personality and the composition of the Sikh community combined to produce a hardy fighting force that controlled Anandpur and its environs in the east Punjab foothills, even as the ranks of his followers across the Punjab grew.

Announcing, towards the end of his life, that he would be the last in the line of Gurus, and that after him the Sikh scripture, the Granth Saheb, would guide the community as the Guru Granth Saheb, Guru Gobind Singh also baptized, at Anandpur in the year 1699, those who were willing to be loyal unto death to him and to become true Sikhs—'Singhs,' or lions, as he now called them.

After initiating five Sikhs (from different castes) with baptismal water purified by a double-edge sword, Guru Gobind Singh insisted, 'with folded hands,' that the five 'administer the same baptismal rite' to him. With these gestures the tenth Guru was not only promoting social equality and binding Sikhs to one another; he was also indicating that after him authority would be transferred to a collectivity of Sikhs, the Khalsa. His designation, a few years later, of the Granth Saheb as the deathless Guru, meant that leadership would vest, as Uberoi puts it, in 'the scripture-in-the-community.'[19]

Apparently it was at the same 1699 ceremony that Guru Gobind Singh asked male Sikhs to keep on their persons the five k's—kesh (unshorn hair), kangha (comb), kirpan (sword), kara (steel bangle), and kachh (thigh-length shorts).

Against impossible odds, Guru Gobind Singh and his Sikhs fought the Mughals. His attitude was defended in a letter he is said to have written to Aurangzeb: 'When all avenues have been explored, all means tried, it is rightful to draw the sword out of the scabbard and wield it with your hand.'[20] The Guru and his men also fought Hindu rajas in the Himalayan foothills. In Uberoi's words:

> [T]he so-called feudal hill rajas, Hindus of the Himalayas, . . . with the single possible exception of Mandi, remained from the first to the last implacable enemies of Guru Gobind Singh and the Sikh cause, as implacable as the Mughal imperial authority. The Hindus always seem to have implicitly charged the guru with trying to set up a third tradition of his own, instead of restoring their true one . . .; while the Muslims chiefly accused him of sedition and trying to undermine the state or the empire . . .[21]

Possessing a radiant face and princely bearing, fearless in battle, undaunted in adversity, unexcelled as a horseman or as a shot, steel-like in grief, blessed with the gift of poetry—it is in such terms that Guru Gobind Singh is perceived by the Sikh community. While Sikh belief does not grant any separation or even distinction between one Guru and another—the ten Gurus are seen as constituting a single personality—, who would dispute that Guru Nanak and Guru Gobind Singh tower in the Sikh imagination?

It is the blows that he took that strengthen Guru Gobind Singh's hold over us. The trauma at age nine of his father's execution was to be succeeded by a series of cruel strokes.

In December 1704, five years after he had initiated the Khalsa at Anandpur in the Himalayan foothills, the Guru, now thirty-eight and seen as a foe both by the Hindu hill rajas and by Mughal officials, was, it would seem, forced out of Anandpur. Mughal forces pursued him. Striving to keep ahead of them, the Guru departed from the town of Sirsa after evidently leaving instructions that two minor sons of his, Zorawar and Fateh, and their grandmother (the Guru's mother), be taken under escort to Delhi.

Then disaster struck. Sikhs believe that the boys and their grandmother were betrayed into the hands of Wazir Khan, the governor of the important Mughal province of Sirhind (comprising much of the state of Punjab in today's India). One version states that the boys, who bore themselves defiantly, were then 'bricked up alive' in Sirhind, the city that gave the province its name. According to another version, the boys were executed.[22] The shock killed their grandmother.

Soon thereafter, in Chamkaur, the Guru's older boys, Ajit and Jujhar, 'also died fighting valiantly . . . in single combats.' One account states: 'The Guru had insisted . . . that if not the first, his sons must not be the last to die.'[23]

Two Pathans, Nabi Khan and Ghani Khan, are believed to have saved the Guru's own life in the wake of the Chamkaur battle by describing him as a fasting Muslim Pir to a Mughal patrol looking out for the Guru. Escape, however, was followed by shock; the Guru learned of the fate in Sirhind of his younger boys and mother. Thereupon, Sikhs believe,

> The Guru, composed as ever, bent upon his knees and lifting his hands to God in prayer uttered: 'These two, Thy trust, I have rendered unto Thee'; and digging up a shrub with his knife he made this prophecy: 'Just as I've torn this shrub from its roots, so shall this tyrannous empire be destroyed, root and branch.'[24]

*

One more oath of revenge on the soil of the Punjab, not all that far from Kurukshetra country, a natural and inexorable oath—how else could a father react?—, a powerful oath reverberating across the smog of time, its rising echoes drowning the relevance of any efforts to establish 'the facts' of the story, drowning the relevance of any distinction between legend and history. One more oath igniting generations of the faithful—and destined to kindle new pain and new oaths.

For a moment the scene softens a bit, for Sher Muhammad Khan, the Nawab of Malerkotla, not far from the town of Sirhind, wrote to Emperor Aurangzeb protesting against the execution of the minor boys and describing it as being contrary to the law of Islam and its Prophet.[25] The long-term consequences of this brave dissent against inhumanity have been described as follows:

> The Sikhs under Banda Singh Bahadur kept this act . . . so much in their memory that whereas they destroyed Sirhind utterly, and butchered Wazir Khan and his entire family, they spared the state of Malerkotla altogether. Even during the worst communal holocaust of many centuries that occurred in 1947, when Hindu, Sikh and Muslim populations of the divided Punjab migrated en masse . . . amidst much carnage, no Muslim of Malerkotla was touched, and they were pathetically persuaded to stay in India.[26]

We will ere long come to Banda Singh Bahadur, but, to stay with softened scenes, we can look at an attempt made almost three centuries later to reach out to hearts still hurting from what had been done to Guru Gobind Singh's boys. A man named Zakir Husain, whose Pathan forebears had migrated to India at about the time that the boys were killed, made the attempt. In May 1967 Zakir Husain became the President of India. Later in the year, in Patiala, he laid the foundation-stone for the Guru Gobind Bhavan of the Punjabi University, and addressed a largely Sikh audience.

Twenty years earlier, during the 1947 riots, Zakir Husain, though a distinguished educator known for a stand against Partition, had come close to losing his life on a train in east Punjab, but the exertions of three men, one of whom was a Sikh, saved him. Having lost four brothers in his childhood and, later, his three-year-old daughter, Zakir Husain knew what the death of young ones meant. He also knew history. Said he:

> The whole life of Guru Gobind Singh is a unique story of sacrifice, toil, educative activity, military talent, unrivalled valour, boundless graciousness, unfathomable love. There are in this story accounts of hardships suffered such as shake the heart and of success that fills it with hope . . . This story will make it clear . . . that the life of a man of God, a beautiful, pure and noble life, cannot be bought cheap.

> For what was there that this man of God did not bring as an offering before God's throne? His father; the light of his eyes, his beloved sons; recklessly brave comrades, to whom he was more gracious than to his own offspring; all were offered up to him.[27]

The eyes of Zakir Husain and of some in the audience were seen to be moist.

*

Deaths of Aurangzeb and Guru Gobind Singh: From 1679 until his death in 1707, Aurangzeb lived far to the south of Delhi, coping with rebellions. Apparently it was in Ahmadnagar in 1705 that two of Guru Gobind Singh's 'trusted Sikhs, Daya Singh and Dharam Singh,' personally delivered the Guru's letter, referred to above, to the emperor.

Entitled *Zafarnama* ('Letter of Victory'), the letter was strongly worded. It warned the Emperor that though 'thou hast killed my four sons,' Sikh fire was alive. 'Hear me, do not employ the sword to murder the innocent,' said the Guru, adding a reminder that God's 'vengeance is terrible.' Evidently the Guru also said, 'I wish I could speak to thee face to face.' According to Gopal Singh, who reproduces the averred letter, 'the emperor expressed a wish that the Guru might come and see him, but before the two could meet, news was received that the emperor was dead.'[28]

In *History of the Panjab*, a work first published in 1889, Syad Muhammad Latif claims that the *Zafarnama* was a response to a 'mandate summoning the Guru to his presence.' Acknowledging that the *Zafarnama* pointed out to Aurangzeb that 'the day of reckoning would at last come, when the oppressor would have to account before the Creator for the wrongs done by him to the helpless and the oppressed,' Latif says that after reading it the Emperor again desired the Guru's presence, whereupon 'the Guru set out to meet Aurangzeb, but, on the way, he heard of the aged monarch's death.'[29]

Having overcome but not crushed his empire's Muslim and Hindu rebels in the Deccan, Aurangzeb died there in February 1707. Shortly before his end, the seventy-eight-year-old Emperor—a pious Sunni Muslim who dutifully made copies of the Koran and sewed caps—seems to have sensed that he had invited long-term hostility for Islam and its representatives in India. In a letter to a son, he wrote:

> Son of my soul . . . Now I am going alone. I grieve for your helplessness. But what is the use? I have greatly sinned, and I know not what torment awaits me . . : Let not Muslims be slain and reproach fall on my useless head. I commit you and your sons to God's care. I am sore troubled.[30]

The apparent willingness for a dialogue on the part of Aurangzeb as well as Guru Gobind Singh places at least a faint question mark on the oft-expressed assessment of 'an undying feud of the deadliest kind' between Sikhs and Muslims in India, or the view that Sikhism, departing from its early origin, 'became an implacable adversary of Islam.'[31] That the assessment should be qualified is also suggested by the fact that several Muslims were among the Guru's followers[32], and by what Uberoi calls Guru Gobind Singh's 'loving familiarity with the tradition of Islam,' revealed, for example, in the names the Guru gives to God, which in many cases resembled names found in the Islamic tradition.[33]

Recalling also the features, noted earlier in this chapter, that seem common to Islam and Sikhism, a scholar like Uberoi speaks of the Sikhs' 'unity of goal' with the Muslims, and proceeds to express a bold thought:

> Sharing the 'unity of origin' with the Hindus, so to say, and the 'unity of goal' with the Muslims, or with some of them, Sikhism could produce for that very reason a negotiation, mediation or reconciliation in history . . .[34]

To return, however, to Guru Gobind Singh, Sikh and Muslim scholars agree that the Guru met Aurangzeb's successor, Bahadur Shah. According to Latif, 'the new emperor received the Sikh Guru with distinction, and bestowed on him presents, and appointed him to the command of five thousand men . . .'[35]

However, Gopal Singh states that the Guru, aware of Bahadur Shah's reputation for tolerance of Shias and Sufis, which contrasted with Aurangzeb's narrowness, had sent 'a detachment of two to three hundred horses' in support of Bahadur Shah's claim to the Mughal throne. After securing the throne, Bahadur Shah received the Guru in Agra 'with great courtesies, presented him with a jewelled scarf and robe of honour,' thanked him for the assistance rendered, and 'requested to spend some time with him. The Guru gladly accepted this invitation.' Gopal Singh also cites two notings in Mughal chronicles to the effect that the Guru accompanied the new emperor and the royal cavalcade on their journey to the Deccan.[36]

According to Gopal Singh, during one of their conversations the Guru asked the emperor to dismiss and prosecute Wazir Khan, the governor of Sirhind. Bahadur Shah explained that he could not act against a powerful provincial chief 'till his rule was firmly established.'

Travelling southwards more or less alongside the imperial forces, the Guru reached Nanded, in Marathi-speaking country, where took place the enlistment in his cause of the bairagi or renunciate, Madho Das. Born into a Rajput family in Poonch in Kashmir and hungry for a purpose, Madho Das had wandered to the south. His person-to-person encounter with the Guru was to have immense consequences.

At the Guru's call, he became a Sikh, renounced his renunciation, accepted a sword and five arrows, and offered to fight the tyrants of the Punjab as a 'Banda' or slave of the Guru. Madho Das thus became Banda Bairagi (Banda the ascetic), or Banda Bahadur (Banda the brave) or Banda Singh Bahadur (Banda the brave lion). The Guru

directed him 'not found a sect of his own, to look upon . . . associates
. . . as equals, and never their superior.'

> Thereupon (writes Gopal Singh) the Guru gave [Banda]
> detailed instructions to proceed to the Punjab along with
> three other Sikhs, . . . [and] to wait for reinforcements
> (which the Guru would arrange) . . . and, later, . . . to march
> on Sirhind, lay siege to the city and seize and personally
> execute Wazir Khan . . . [and thereafter] to settle accounts
> with the chiefs of the hill states . . . The Guru himself would
> join them at a later stage.[37]

Banda Bahadur left for the Punjab, but Guru Gobind Singh was
stabbed in Nanded by a Pathan suspected of links with Wazir Khan.
He died in October 1708, even though, as some Sikh writers believe,
'the emperor, who was camping near Nanded, . . . sent his personal
surgeons, one of them an Englishman, to treat the wound.'[38] Following,
thus, the pattern set by his great-grandfather, Guru Arjan Dev, and
emulated by Guru Tegh Bahadur, his father, Guru Gobind Singh
became the third Sikh Guru to be martyred, but not before laying
down firmly that after him the Granth Saheb would be the Guru of
the community.

*

Stirrings in Maharashtra: While remaining in Maharashtra, we will go
back a little in time. In 1296 and 1307 the forces of Alauddin Khalji,
the Sultan of Delhi, attacked the Hindu kingdom of Devagiri, ruled
by the Yadavas and comprising portions of modern Maharashtra; in
1313 Devagiri was annexed to Delhi.

The saint-poet Jnaneswar or Gyaneswar (1275-96), to whom we
referred in the previous chapter, was a subject of Devagiri. He died
in the year of the first Khalji attack. Though Ghazni's raids early in
the eleventh century and Ghauri's invasions at the end of the twelfth
century (a hundred years before Jnaneswar's time) had stopped far to
the north of Devagiri, we can assume that accounts of the attacks had
filtered down across time and distance to the sensitive young poet,
without losing their capacity to sting.

Though his world had been shaken, Jnaneswar's poems breathe
equanimity and faith. Of anger, or a thirst for revenge, there seems
no trace whatever. As we saw in the previous chapter, the Bhakti
poets seemed to respond to the challenge from Islamic Central Asia

not by venting fruitless steam at the invaders but by examining themselves and the society around them. Though he preceded most of the Bhakti poets by two centuries or more, this was Jnaneswar's response too.

Also born in the latter half of the thirteenth century, but in a family of the 'untouchable' Mahars and thus barred from entering temples, Chokhamela wrote poems reflecting anguish at the abhorred status of Mahars like him and seeking relief from suffering through devotion to the god Vitthala.

Asking why Hindus had become weak and how they could become strong, the Bhakti poets came up with answers like, 'Deepen your relationship with God,' or 'Treat no one as high or low.' At times they seemed to imply, even if only indirectly, that the humiliation of alien rule had been invited by the excesses of a privileged minority, the priestly class.

Occasionally a Bhakti poet would name the aliens, and do so pejoratively, to evoke not anger, however, but introspection, devotion or faith. It seemed understood that devotion would lead in the end to relief. Thus one of the verses of the poet Namdev (1270-1350) says: 'The people, having found the Yavanas unendurable, are singing the praises of God; for these are the means of redemption.'[39] (Yavana, used originally for a Greek, had come to mean any foreigner.)

A remarkable leap from annoyed recognition of the alien ruler to a dialogue with him was taken by the Brahmin Bhakti poet Eknath (1533-1599) in his 'Hindu-Turka Samvaad' (Hindu-Turk or Hindu-Muslim Conversation). In the verse, the Turk calls the Hindu a kafir or infidel. 'Your touch is polluting,' replies the Hindu. 'You Hindus are idolatrous,' the Muslim retorts. 'You are no different,' the Hindu says. 'Don't you venerate Pirs and worship at their tombs?' 'At least we don't condemn whole sections of humanity as untouchable,' the Muslim points out.

> But then emerges the conclusion that God is one, whether
> . . . called Khuda or Allah or Rama or Krishna, for He has
> created all, Muslims as well as Hindus . . .[40]

In another notable dialogue, Eknath brings a Mahar and a Brahmin together, and shows how the Mahar teaches the way of devotion to the arrogant Brahmin. Eknath had a Sufi counterpart, Shaykh Muhammad, who after studying Hindu systems produced a text called *Yogasamgraha* and wrote poetry in praise of God that is 'included among the works of the saint-poets of Maharashtra.'[41]

Perhaps the most popular Bhakti poet in Maharashtra was Tukaram of the Kunbi or peasant caste. His songs reflected 'harassment by family obligations and by the orthodox Brahmanas' and carried 'an anti-caste theme' but also affirmed 'a life in the world rather than renunciation.'[42]

The role of Maharashtra's Bhakti poets is not free of controversy. Some have argued that the attention given to the Bhakti poets devalues the contribution of the twelfth-century Mahanubhav or Manbhav sect that opposed caste more directly than Bhakti poets ever did. Others have emphasized the differences, including over caste, within the Bhakti tradition. Some of the sharpest debate is over Ramdas (1608-1681). It has been contended, for instance, that in urging 'a strong political regeneration of religion,' Ramdas departed from the preference of most Bhakti sants for an 'interiorised form of devotion.'[43]

While Bhakti may have meant different things to different people, and to different social groups, it is probably safe to accept that it weakened high-caste domination, strengthened popular faith, and brought Maharashtra's varied groups—including, in some cases, Hindus and Muslims, and upper castes and low castes—closer to one another.

*

Shivaji: The Bhakti tradition was part of the culture that nurtured Shivaji (1627-80), son of Shahji Bhonsle (1594-1664), who was a fief-holder under Muslim courts at Ahmadnagar and Bijapur and maintained his own soldiers.

For about 350 years, from the early fourteenth century to the time of Shivaji's youth, different parts of the Marathi-speaking country in the Deccan—the South—had been ruled by a variety of Muslim kings or nawabs. These Muslim rulers could be Shia or Sunni, native-born or originating in West or Central Asia or East Africa. Occasionally a ruler was a convert from Hinduism.

Conflict among them was usual, and boundaries between them changed constantly. While a Deccan nawab generally acknowledged the suzerainty of the ruler in Delhi or Agra, the degree of his obedience depended on the ruler's preoccupations and the intentions of other Deccan nawabs.

These Muslim rulers in the Deccan were not particularly loved by their subjects. While more the exception than the norm, cases of forced conversion, destruction of temples, and violation of Hindu women had occurred in the region; the jizya had at times been levied; and cows were being killed and eaten. Offended and aggrieved, the Hindu majority tended to view the rulers as well as the Muslim minority, which included a number who had converted to Islam or were born in families of converts, with dislike or contempt.

Yet Muslim rule was accepted. On its part, Muslim rule accommodated various layers of Hindu sub-rule: without the support of Hindu chiefs like Shivaji's father and Hindu officials, no administration was possible. Moreover, the Muslim rulers of Bijapur 'had taken Hindu women into their harems and patronized local languages and literatures.'[44] It is true, too, that their influence in the Deccan's Muslim courts gave men such as Shahji confidence, and stoked ambitions.

Born nine years after Aurangzeb, Shivaji, we can be sure, liked the taste of the modest power commanded by his father, and desired more of it. Ambition, in this instance, was joined by opportunity, for there was conflict between the Mughal centre and the Deccan kingdoms. First as Viceroy for the Deccan under his father Shah Jahan, and later as emperor, Aurangzeb was striving to curb the southern kingdoms. Internal squabbles had weakened one of them, Bijapur. Moreover, after decades of showing tolerance towards Hindus, the Muslim court of Bijapur had turned anti-Hindu and lost public sympathy.

But ambition, opportunity and shifts in sympathy avail nothing when ability is absent. In Shivaji's case, it was abundantly present. Astute, resourceful and ingenious, he was also willing to think and act dangerously.

By the time he was twenty, Shivaji had broken free of handed down constraints and struck out. Seizing forts, nibbling at poorly guarded territories, collecting fresh revenues, and creating diversions in favour of Deccanis attacked by Aurangzeb, he multiplied his father's fiefdom. After three centuries and a half of submission in Maharashtra, a Hindu chief was finally proclaiming a desire to control the world around him.

The controversial incident involving Afzal Khan, the general leading the army of the Deccan kingdom of Bijapur against Shivaji, occurred in Pratapgadh in 1659, when Shivaji was thirty-two. Afzal Khan was invited to Shivaji's camp, embraced by his host, and supposedly killed by steely claws that Shivaji had concealed on his hands. That Afzal Khan had intended to employ foul means against Shivaji, who was forced to eliminate Afzal Khan before being eliminated himself, is the justification that has come down.

The climax of this phase of Shivaji's career was his sack in 1664 of Surat, far into the north from his bases in the hills around Poona. The next year, however, the Rajput general Jai Singh, appointed the Deccan's Viceroy by Aurangzeb and provided with masses of Mughal troops, overpowered Shivaji and compelled him to sign the treaty of Purandhar. Surrendering twenty-three forts to the Mughals, Shivaji agreed to be a vassal of the Emperor.

A year later he presented himself at the Mughal court in Agra. However, not having been received with sufficient dignity, he complained, found himself in detention, and escaped famously in a basket of sweets.

Aurangzeb's zeal for 'pure' Islam and distaste for Hinduism was now growing but his control over the far-flung Empire was not. In 1670 Shivaji repudiated his allegiance, recovered lands he had ceded, plundered Surat a second time, raided Mughal territory, and repulsed Mughal generals sent against him.

Moving from defence to offence, and raids to occupation, Shivaji had himself crowned at Raigadh on 5 June 1674. He was called Chhatrapati or emperor; if Aurangzeb could thus style himself, why not Shivaji?

On the ground that Shivaji was merely a Maratha and not a Kshatriya by caste, Maharashtra's Brahmins had refused to conduct a sacred coronation. However, a Brahmin from Kashi performed the ceremony, after which Maharashtra's Hindu majority found themselves with a kingdom of their own, extending along the west coast from southern Gujrat to Goa and including pockets like Gingee Fort and Vellore in the Tamil country, and Bellary on the Tungabhadra.

*

In Shivaji's remarkable achievement, a role was clearly played by the hills of Maharashtra. In their homeground, Shivaji and his soldiers knew better than their adversaries how to hide while defending, and surprise while attacking.

The remoteness of Agra and Delhi was also a factor. For the Emperor, suppressing rebellions by the Rajputs, Jats, Satnamis and Bundelas, which took place closer to the Mughal capital, was one thing; sending an army to the Deccan was a longer, costlier and riskier exercise, riskier because the army might be cut off, or its commander tempted to rebel himself.

Enjoying advantages of terrain and location, Shivaji benefited, too, from a sense of unity that had grown on Maharashtrian soil thanks to the waters of Bhakti teaching. From Jnanadeva to Namdev to Eknath to Tukaram to Ramdas, the Bhakti poets had for numerous decades sung of the equality before God of all, of the unimportance of caste, and of God's love for all humans as His children.

We have seen that there were differences of emphasis among the poets. As suggested above, Ramdas, a Brahmin, 'preached a militant Hinduism, a gospel that called on its followers to cease suffering persecution abjectly and deliver blow for blow.'[45] He and Shivaji are stated to have first met two years before Shivaji was crowned. (We should, however, note a claim that 'there is no historical evidence that [Shivaji] ever met Ramdas and his own seals give no such description.'[46]) On hearing of Shivaji's triumphs, Ramdas seemed to hail, we might say, a retributive Providence:

> The sinners are all lost,/ The land of the Hindus is now strong./ The unbelievers are on the decline . . ./ The sinful Aurangzeb is destroyed,/ The mlecchas are destroyed . . .[47]

However, not God's righteous anger but his love, warmth and protection was what Tukaram (1608-1649), son of a 'middle' caste farmer, sang of:

> Doth not a mortal mother love her child the more/ When he is weak, and sad? Thou art better, wiser, stronger, Lord, than she:/ Then save Thy wandering child, and bring him home.[48]

Familiarity with Bhakti teaching gave Shivaji's soldiers and non-combatant supporters pride in their ideals and a sense of the umbrella of Providence. Contributing to a feeling of unity beyond caste and to faith, the Bhakti poets had also fostered the spread of the Marathi language. A Maharashtrian nation was emerging. All it needed was a leader and a rallying point, and the singular Shivaji appeared.

*

Guru Tegh Bahadur's martyrdom and Shivaji's coronation were separated only by a year. But a difference between Maharashtra and the Punjab is immediately obvious. Where Guru Gobind Singh was himself both the spiritual and the political/military leader of the Sikhs, Shivaji only took the political/military command. The saint-poets supplied what was needed on the spiritual side.

After Aurangzeb reimposed the jizya in 1679, Shivaji wrote to him a letter that reveals a refusal to accept an inferior status for Hindus, as well as an indication of elements in Islam that Shivaji could respect. Reminding Aurangzeb that his great-grandfather Akbar had abolished the jizya and that neither Jahangir nor Shah Jahan had brought it back, Shivaji added:

> The infamy will quickly spread from west to east and become recorded in books of history that the Emperor of Hindustan, coveting the beggar's bowls, takes jizya from Brahmins and Jain monks, paupers and the famished . . .

> Many of your forts and provinces have gone out of your possession, and the rest will soon do so, because there will be no slackness on my part in ruining and devastating them . . .

> Well, your majesty! If you believe in the true Heavenly Book and word of God (i.e. the Koran), you will find there *Rabb-ul-alamin* (God of all men) and not *Rabb-ul-Musalmin* (God of Muslims) . . . To show bigotry is like altering a word in the Holy Book.[49]

In the well-known finding of Jadu Nath Sarkar, Shivaji

> proved by his example that the Hindu race can build a nation, found a state, defeat enemies; they can conduct their own defence . . .[50]

Considering that in his age Shivaji's was a rare example of a Hindu-run state, Sarkar's interpretation is surely valid. But it needs to be fleshed out. Thus it should be remembered that, as a goal for the ardent spirits whom he was attracting, Shivaji the devout Hindu used the expression *Hindawi Swaraj*, which translates as 'native' or 'Indian' independence, not as 'Hindu' independence. A term like 'dharmic' or 'Hindu' *Swaraj* was not employed. The claim that Shivaji had founded a 'Hindu raj or rashtra'—not merely a state largely run by Hindus—was, it would seem, 'ideologically contested even in the nineteenth century.'[51] Also relevant is the fact that

Within the territories under his control Shivaji showed exemplary tolerance towards the Muslims. He not only protected places of Muslim worship but also made endowments to them and supported the holy men of Islam as well as employing Muslims in his own administration.[52]

Again, after political control was wrested by the Hindus, there was 'little evidence of [any] Hindu desire for retaliation against Muslims for their former acts,' though the Muslim was 'still looked on as a "stranger" or "foreigner." '[53]

Sambhaji, Rajaram and Tarabai: At the age of fifty-three, six years after being crowned, Shivaji died. He was succeeded by his eldest son Sambhaji (1680-89), who had 'saddened the last year of Shivaji's life by going over to the Mughals.'[54] This fact and Sambhaji's 'inconsiderate treatment of many of the officers of his father created great dissatisfaction and weakened the solidarity of the newly found kingdom.'[55]

Sambhaji blundered, too, in welcoming Aurangzeb's rebelling son Akbar, who had asked for Maratha protection. In March 1682 Aurangzeb arrived in the Deccan with a large army. His objectives were to crush Sambhaji and Akbar, who, as far as the emperor was concerned, were in mutinous alliance—in a Mughal's eye, no offence was greater—and to conquer the Muslim kingdoms of Bijapur and Golconda—'the Hinduised states of Golkanda and Bijapur,' as a Muslim writer describes them.[56] Sambhaji was captured, tortured and executed.

His defiance before meeting his end restored to Sambhaji a place in Maratha hearts; because of the torture, those hearts harboured rage as well.

The throne at Raigadh went to Rajaram (1689-1700), Sambhaji's half-brother, but by this time Aurangzeb's forces had occupied most of the Deccan. After sieges, Bijapur fell to the emperor in 1686 and Hyderabad in 1687. Though Rajaram escaped to Gingee in the far south, Raigadh fell to the Mughals, and Sambhaji's widow and young son were taken prisoner. Led first by Rajaram and later, after his death in 1700, by his widow Tarabai, bands of Marathas, receiving no pay but surviving on lands they attacked, continued the battle.

Aurangzeb's overstretched armies in different parts of the South were harassed and disabled by them. By 1706 these guerrilla attacks by the Marathas were occurring in western and central India as well. When, after a back-breaking campaign, Aurangzeb died in the Deccan in 1707, his armies and officers were hardly in full control of their extensive empire.

The Peshwas: Released in 1707 after eighteen years in the Mughal camp, Sambhaji's son Shahu claimed the Maratha throne from Tarabai's son Shivaji II. But real power in the kingdom soon shifted from Shivaji's descendants to a man in Poona, Balaji Vishwanath, an able and adroit Chitpavan Brahmin who had backed Shahu's claim. In 1713, Balaji was appointed Shahu's Peshwa, or premier. Future Peshwas would come from his family and function from Poona; at times they would be called rulers or kings.

Supposedly the Marathas' masters, the Mughals were embroiled in rivalries after the death in 1712 of Aurangzeb's son and successor Bahadur Shah. Raids by Jat and Muslim chieftains in the vicinity of Delhi harried them. From a confused and enfeebled Mughal court, Vishwanath succeeded in obtaining a firman or order of Swaraj that enabled Shahu's regime to levy taxes in return for certain services to be rendered to the Emperor.

Succeeding to the Mughal throne in 1713, Farrukhsiyar repudiated the firman but the sick Rafiuddarajat who dethroned Farrukhsiyar reinstated it in 1719, providing the Marathas with the opportunity to re-establish their state and expand it. Becoming the Peshwa in 1720, Vishwanath's son Balaji Bajirao revealed military skills as well as statecraft in keeping threatening neighbours at bay and the Mughals in good humour.

Interested in the political exercise of Maratha 'consolidation and expansion' and adding to 'their own power,'[57] the Peshwas were not fighting a Hindu-Muslim battle. They cultivated Muslim friends in and around the Mughal court and were prepared, in the Deccan, to make deals with Muslim neighbours. Muslims were employed as soldiers and guards in the Maratha state; by now there was 'a general acceptance of the Muslim as a part of a larger society' in Maharashtra; and some 'forms of Muslim political organization as modified by Mughal and Deccani Sultanate practice' as well as of 'dress [and] polite address' were adopted. The word Peshwa was itself Persian in origin.[58]

Yet the Peshwas' Hinduness (and Brahminness) must have come across, for one Hindu mahant seems to have addressed Bajirao as 'a Hindu raja, . . . [an] incarnation of the epic hero Parashurama, protector of Brahmins and cows, . . . and defender of the honour of the Hindus.'[59]

Over a century and a half later, the figure of Parashurama, the Brahmin who in ancient times had supposedly wrought a terrible revenge on Kshatriyas, was again recalled when an influential intellectual, Vishnu Shastri Chiplunkar, referred to the military prowess of the eighteenth-century Peshwas and their Brahmin clansmen:

> Those people who traditionally were priests and are now clerks threw away in that century their priestly functions and pens and became Kshatriyas. Some became kings, some became soldiers. This was an unprecedented and remarkable change in which Parashurama's [descendants] demonstrated their bravery . . .[60]

Because Brahmins, especially Chitpavan Brahmins, had risen to dominant positions in the military and the bureaucracy and in banking, Peshwa rule, or the Peshwai, as it was known, was also called 'Brahmanya raj,' and it has been suggested that whereas Shivaji had kept a balance between Brahmin administrators and Maratha soldiers, under the Peshwas the state was Brahmanized.[61]

From an independent kingdom to occupied territory to a self-governing Mughal dominion towards a loose confederacy of autonomous Maratha rulers steered by the Peshwa and eyeing the power-centre that seemed to be slipping from the Mughals' grip—such was the journey of the Maratha state after it was founded by Shivaji in the last quarter of the seventeenth century.

*

Eyeing the Mughal throne: But other journeys were also being made on the subcontinent, some by Europeans: there was a scramble for succession to the Mughals' disintegrating empire. Apart from the Marathas, the Portuguese, the French, the Dutch and the British were in the race. In an important round in this battle, Bajirao's younger brother Chimnaji Appa captured Bassein from the Portuguese for the Maratha state in 1737.

In 1739 another man raced from outside India towards Delhi, but his aim was to plunder, not to stay or rule. When Bajirao heard that Nadir Shah had exploded across North India, he left for Delhi to join the Muslim rulers of Hindustan in repelling the Persian. To his brother, he wrote: 'Appa, if foreign rule is established, it will engulf all.'[62] Along with many others in different parts of India,

Bajirao had accepted the Mughals as Indians.

When Bajirao died in 1740, his young son Balaji Bajirao was named the new Peshwa by Shahu. Before he died in 1749, Shahu, the king, evidently agreed to an extension of the hereditary principle to the premier's office.

Under Balaji the Maratha state extended its boundaries. The French, who were a presence in the South, Nizam Ali Khan of Hyderabad, and Mysore's Haidar Ali tried to stop the Marathas' advance southwards but met with only limited success. In a key battle in 1760, the Peshwa's cousin, Sadasiva Rao, defeated the Nizam in Udgir, but an even more crucial battle was taking place in the North.

Towards Panipat III: From 1748, Ahmad Shah Abdali, the Afghan, was making sporadic attacks from Afghanistan into the Punjab, where the Sikhs had been asserting themselves for some decades—we will soon return to their story. The Mughal court in Delhi was divided about Abdali. Seeing the Afghan as an alien interloper, one faction in the court, led by Ghaziuddin of Avadh, sought the Marathas' help to keep him out of the Punjab. As a result, in a remarkable display of Maratha reach, the Peshwa's brother, Raghunath Rao, occupied the Punjab.

But another party in the court, backed militarily by the Rohilla leader Najib Khan and ideologically by the influential Delhi intellectual, Shah Waliullah, welcomed Abdali. Breaking with tradition, Waliullah had translated the Quran into Persian; and he favoured 'a rational and broad-minded interpretation of the fundamentals of Islamic belief, thought and practice.' At the same time, he sought 'a sharper definition' of the boundaries separating Muslims and non-Muslims.[63] According to a widely-held but contested view, Waliullah was so concerned at Sikh activity and Maratha inroads that he invited Abdali to save India for Islam by invading it.[64]

Ahmad Shah Abdali pushed the Marathas out of the Punjab but they came back, led this time by the man who had defeated the Nizam at Udgir, Sadasiva Rao. Over the Maratha forces flew the bhagwa or saffron standard venerated by Hindus, but their artillery was commanded by a Muslim called Ibrahim Gardi who had trained under Bussy, the French General. The stage was set for the third battle of Panipat.

*

Flashback to Banda Bahadur: There was no rest for the Sikhs between 1707, when Guru Gobind Singh died, and 1761, when the third battle of Panipat was fought. Banda Bahadur did not merely carry out the Guru's command regarding Wazir Khan, the governor of Sirhind; he so exceeded his charge as to destroy all distinction between justice and revenge on the one hand, and revenge and carnage on the other. Sikh rage at what had been done to the Guru's boys and to the Guru himself, paralysis at the Mughal court and restiveness in the peasantry combined to enable Banda and the followers he had quickly gathered to wreak a terrible vengeance.

Even though Latif's *History of the Panjab* was written in the late 1880s—close to two centuries after the events in question and not during the heat of the violence—, its particulars cannot all be accepted. We must assume that these particulars bear a bias imparted by a continuing wrath, and also, perhaps, by resentment against Sikh rule over the Punjab, which lasted from 1799 to the 1840s. We know, moreover, that after the suppression of the 1857 Rebellion, a Muslim, Sikh or Hindu writer was frequently anxious to present 'evidence' to the Raj of the excesses or undependability of the 'other' community.

While we should allow, therefore, for exaggeration and distortion, a Muslim perception of the events of the ten years that followed Guru Gobind Singh's martyrdom should be looked at. Writes Latif:

> A sanguinary battle was fought in the neighbourhood of Sirhind, in which the imperial army was totally defeated, and Wazir Khan himself killed by an arrow which pierced his breast. Banda now entered Sirhind, and punished the city in a vindictive and barbarous manner. He commanded it to be fired, and all the inhabitants to be put to death . . . [His] followers . . . slaughtered the inhabitants indiscriminately without regard to age or sex. They butchered . . . [or] burnt alive every Mahomedan in the place.

> Elated with his success at Sirhind [in 1709-10], Banda crossed the Sutlej, carrying fire and sword wherever he went. Towns were devastated and the inhabitants plundered, and driven into the wilderness, or put to the sword . . . At Samana ten thousand men and women were mercilessly put to the sword . . .

> [In a fierce battle outside Lahore,] thousands fell on both

sides, but at last the Mahomedans gave way before superior
numbers, and at sunset they retreated towards the city . . .

From within two or three days' march to Delhi to the
environs of Lahore, the whole country [of the Panjab] was
ravaged.[65]

According to Latif, violating Guru Gobind's Singh's injunctions,
Banda had taken the title of Guru, and, while eluding the Mughal
forces sent after him, appeared sometimes 'in the richest and most
showy garments' of 'a prince' and at other times in 'the guise of a
jogi or sannyasi.'

Another interpretation, however, offered in 1980, sees Banda as
a recluse who was won over to a life of action by Guru Gobind
Singh, and likens the conversion to that obtained in Arjuna by
Krishna at Kurukshetra.[66]

Banda's forays bore the marks of a peasant revolt as well. 'At one
stage during this revolt Mughal authority was almost completely
obliterated in the Panjab and it was not until the capture of Banda
in 1715 that the revolt was finally crushed.'[67]

Escaping several times, concealing himself in forests or hills,
launching surprise attacks to hurt or humble the Mughals and
mobilizing the peasantry, Banda was finally captured and brought to
Delhi with a number of his followers. In describing the cruelty and
horror of their execution in 1716, Latif's version is similar to the
eyewitness account of a British mission that was visiting Delhi.
Members of this mission saw a procession of 'some 800 live Sikh
prisoners' along with about '2,000 fresh bleeding heads of the rebels
borne aloft on poles.' Evidently 'the Sikhs vied with one another in
precedence of death.'[68]

It was the Mahabharata all over again.

*

After Banda's execution, the regrouped Mughals 'sought to strengthen
their ascendancy over the scattered Sikhs.' Sikh tradition sees this
period as one in which the Mughals, seeking counter-revenge,
attempted to 'exterminate the Panth.'[69] The attempt was frustrated in
1739 by the invasion of Nadir Shah. The Sikhs took full advantage
of the Nadir Shah-Mughal clash. On Nadir Shah's return journey,
they plundered the Persian's baggage of loot. In the Punjab's villages,
the cry of 'Raj Karega Khalsa'—'The Khalsa Shall Rule!'—began to be
heard.

Abdali and Panipat III: Abdali's attacks on North India soon followed. By 1753 Mughal power in the Punjab seemed a thing of the past. Thereafter, Abdali's targets were the Sikhs and the Marathas. In his 1756 assault, Abdali desecrated the Golden Temple at Amritsar and sparked off a general Sikh uprising. Two years later, the Marathas succeeded in occupying Sirhind and Lahore.

In 1762, shortly after the third battle of Panipat, Abdali's forces 'killed more than 5,000 Singhs in a single day in a running battle in the present district of Ludhiana.' Sikhs have been marking the day of wadda ghallughara or 'the great carnage' ever since. However, thanks to roving bands of Sikhs that 'moved with speed and struck with effect,' Abdali 'found the Punjab too hot for himself.'[70] Indeed, there were phases in the 1750s and 1760s when it seemed that Sikh bands had 'brought the entire land from the Sutlej to the Indus under their control.'[71]

Even so, when the third battle of Panipat took place, the Sikhs had kept aloof—partly, perhaps, because a section of the Mughals were fighting on the Maratha side, or also 'to watch the Afghans and Marathas destroy each other's hopes of dominance.'[72] At Panipat, 'attacks and counter-attacks, rallies and sorties went on for a couple of months.'

Maratha spirits were high; only recently they had 'watered their horses in the Indus, . . . knocked at the gates of Calcutta,' and humbled Hyderabad.[73] However, the final battle, fought on 14 January 1761, resulted in the defeat of the Marathas.[74]

Apart from fighting too far from their Poona base, the Marathas had been weakened by differences between the clan of the Brahmin Peshwa and the more numerous clans linked to the descendants of Shivaji. A high point of mistrust had evidently been reached in 1749 when, following the death of Shivaji's grandson Shahu, the Peshwa, Balaji Bajirao, staged a coup and seized power.

Unexpected inheritors: Hopes of Hindu rule over India seemed to evaporate at Panipat, but the Afghan victor was not interested in trying to replace the dying power of the Mughals. Those who would succeed in doing so were not in Panipat or Delhi in 1761—at that juncture they more likely to be found in eastern and southern India. But they were not Asians. They had come to India on behalf of a trading company to which, in the last year of the sixteenth century, a White queen in a far country had given a charter.

The first Europeans to establish bases in India were the

Portuguese—Vasco da Gama had entered India thirty years before Babur. But despite a promising start and a long-lasting outpost in Goa, the Portuguese involvement with India as a whole petered out.

In the battle of Plassey of 1757, soldiers of England's East India Company had defeated the nawab who was ruling the Mughal Empire's virtually self-governing province of Bengal. Two years later, in 1759, the English routed the Dutch near Hooghly. On 16 January 1761—two days after the third battle of Panipat—the English overcame their French rivals in another crucial battle, this one in the south of India. Three years later the British won a fresh battle against Mughal-backed chiefs in Buxar in Bihar. A year later, in 1765, the Mughal court conceded to the East India Company the right to collect and spend the revenues in the provinces of Bengal, Bihar and Orissa.

Thus it was between 1757 and 1765, as the Mughals eliminated one another in Delhi, the Afghans pushed the Marathas southward, Sikh bands hung on to numerous pieces of the Punjab, the French lost out in the south, and Mughal forces (and the Dutch) were defeated in the east, that the English inherited the power escaping from the Mughal throne, and waited for the throne too to descend to them.

*

A might-have-been: In 1876, over a hundred years after the third battle of Panipat, the Bengali writer, Bhudeb Mukhopadhyay (1827-94), imagined a history that might have averted European rule.

In Bhudeb's 'utopian history,' as Partha Chatterjee terms it, a messenger from the Maratha commander comes to Ahmad Shah Abdali in the fields of Panipat even as he is engaged in battle with the Maratha forces. The messenger says that though Muslims have always mistreated Hinduism, the Hindus were prepared to forgive. Ahmad Shah can go back and take with him all Muslims who wish to leave, provided they do not return before five years are over. Abdali agrees, says he would never attack again, and the Marathas say that all Muslim nawabs, subahdars, zamindars and jagirdars can return unmolested to their estates and residences.

After this a grand council of all the kings of India takes place, which recognizes Hindus as natural sons of the soil and India's Muslims as adopted sons. Adds Bhudeb:-

> Can there be no bonds of fraternity between two children
> of the same mother, one a natural child and the other

adopted? There certainly can; the laws of every religion admit this. There has now been born a bond of brotherhood between Hindus and Muslims living in India.

As the vision proceeds, Badshah Shah Alam hands over the throne and crown to a descendant of Shivaji.

In Bhudeb's vision—or revision of history—, there is an initiative of forgiveness, an offer that seems generous and yet practical, and responses, whether or not realistic, that seem wise or gracious.

The two armies poised to fight in Kurukshetra territory remind us of the Mahabharata. A reconciliation is offered that in the epic seemed ruled out or a foregone failure. Yet it is similar to the brief reconciliation scene, viewed in the first chapter, that Vyasa creates—and swiftly banishes. As in the epic, so in the India of the eighteenth century, forgiveness seems a fancy. The facts are of revenge, and also, this time, of European rule.[75]

5

Enter Britain:
Humiliation, Dazzlement and Trust

ASSUMING THAT IT started with the Battle of Plassey (23 June 1757) in which Robert Clive, then thirty-two and representing the English East India Company, had defeated the twenty-nine-year-old Nawab of Bengal, Sirajuddaula, British rule in India lasted for 190 years.

To this jolting, bemusing and also, for some time, dazzling experience, which probably changed India as nothing before had done, we will devote three chapters. Here, in the first of these, after a few general observations, we will consider the responses to British rule of some influential nineteenth-century Indians. In the chapter that follows, we will look at a single but, for the purposes of our study, instructive episode: the British success in enlisting Sikh support within a few years of defeating the Sikhs in the bitterest battles in Britain's conquest of India. Finally, in chapter seven, we will look at the most traumatic challenge to the British—and to Indians—during their rule of nearly two centuries, the 1857 Rebellion.

*

No Indian invited the British to rule India or a part thereof, and, to be fair, few British claimed that they were in India in response to requests. Thus Penderel Moon's comprehensive survey of the Raj refers time and again, in text and chapter headings, to British 'conquests,' acknowledges that Britain took India by force, and is entitled, *The British Conquest and Dominion of India.*[1]

In the previous chapter we noted some of the key dates connected with the conquest. To those may be added the final defeat and death in 1799 of Britain's principal foe in the South, Tipu Sultan; the 1799 takeover of Lahore and much of the Punjab by the Jat Sikh chieftain Ranjit Singh, who two years later assumed the royal title of Maharaja; the defeat in 1803 of the Maratha power in central and northern India, which also brought Delhi under British control; and, in 1817, the snuffing out by the British in Poona of the last flicker of Peshwa defiance.

In 1803 Shah Abdul Aziz, eldest son of the Islamic ideologue, Waliullah, had declared that the areas under non-Muslim rule had become dar ul-harb, or the house or land of war. That was the year the British entered Delhi and established their authority there, without removing the Mughal ruler. The reaction of Aziz was provoked by the arrival of the British, the rise of the Sikhs, and the liberties that in 1803 the Marathas were still taking. It reflected the demise of Mughal power.

Non-Muslim areas continued to grow, mostly controlled by the British. Using the lure of trade to gain a foothold, the foothold to station their troops, and the troops to extend their dominion, the British also played skilfully on the resentments and suspicions between neighbouring Indian rulers. After 1817, the Punjab ruled by Ranjit Singh was the only part of the subcontinent outside British subjection. By 1849, the Punjab too had been annexed, and Sindh as well.

Until 1858, India was ruled by a trading company supervised by the British Parliament. From its Indian earnings the East India Company engaged tens of thousands of Britons to serve in India as clerks and soldiers, civil servants, police and army officers, judges and governors of Indian provinces. Steering the governors from his headquarters in Calcutta was the Company's Governor-General of India. After 1858 the Crown replaced the Company as the master of the Britons administering India.

Defeat and subjugation stung Indians' pride. British strength—a combination of pluck, arms and organization—awed them. Yet a greater, if also more confusing, impact was made by what came in the wake of the British: Western civilization, a combination of technology, culture and thought.

The steamship, the railway train and the telegraph, the printing press and the camera, cement and macadam—such elements of Western civilization were obviously overwhelming and also appealing or challenging, but so were Shakespeare and the Bible, and so were the images of Europe's powerful nation states.

We saw that it was not any nation state of India but portions of India that, piece by piece, the British had taken. The Mughals no doubt had ruled what was sometimes called Hindostan, but in the last chapter we obtained a flavour of the intensely regional nature of political and military activity in eighteenth-century India.

Britain's eventual ability to rule all of India, and a related ability to see India as a single unit, encouraged thoughts of an Indian nation that probably were outside the ken of most residents of eighteenth-century India. Also, nineteenth-century Europe's fascination with nation states produced a desire for an Indian nation that could take its position alongside the nations of Europe.

We saw at the end of the last chapter that by 1876—well after the British advent, that is—Bhudev Mukhopadhyay could visualize a Hindu-Muslim rapprochement as well as a single king in whom chiefs from all of India reposed faith. There seems to be no evidence of such dreams in the previous century.

Even in 1876 Bhudev was something of an exception. In fact, even as national feeling grew during British rule, that rule also sharpened Indians' awareness of, and at times their conflicts with, fellow Indians. Whether intended or foreseen by the British or not, this sharpening was a consequence of censuses conducted by the British Raj, requiring Indians to name their caste and religion.

The curiosity and zeal of European Orientalists, who delved, language by language, into India's culture, and the availability of histories of Europe's different peoples, whetted in Indians an appetite for sectional histories—Hindu history, Muslim history, Bengali history, Maratha history, Sikh history, and so forth.

Until the end of the nineteenth century and well into the twentieth, most Indians had difficulty deciding whether they belonged, first and foremost, to India or to a region, religion or caste. In responding to British rule, too, an individual in India could think either as an Indian or as a Sikh, a Muslim, a Bengali, a Brahmin, a Shudra, or whatever.

Before looking at some of these responses, we should note another significant result of British rule: the gradual emergence of a rule of law, replacing the whimsical rule of a local strongman. British rule was foreign rule, and there was evidence of deceit in launching it, but with time it also seemed to become fair rule, or rule in conformity with laws or principles—at least when a British administrator or judge was deciding between Indians, rather than between a White person and an Indian.

Some of the early Britons ruling India were no more than adventurers or fortune-seekers. Quite a few were corrupt though not, in the first phase, racially offensive. After British women started coming as wives or in hopes of finding husbands, British officials in India became more exclusive. However, thanks to better supervision and training, they also tended to become more committed to their duties and to the rule of law.

*

THE INDIAN RESPONSE

In at least some circles in Bengal, where British rule came earlier than in most other parts of India, that rule was, to begin with, compared favourably with Muslim rule. This was so despite the deceit and treachery that had marked Clive's success at Plassey, following which Nawab Sirajuddaula had been put to death. The 'Black Hole' episode of the previous year, in which scores of Englishmen taken prisoner by Sirajuddaula in Calcutta were alleged to have died of suffocation, had not helped the reputation of the dead nawab.

In *The Nation and its Fragments*, Partha Chatterjee quotes from Mrityunjay Vidyalankar's *Rajabali* (1808), described by Chatterjee as 'the first history of India in the Bengali language that we have in print.' While looking at Vidyalankar's comments, we should remember that he was employed by the British to teach Sanskrit at Fort William College.

Pointing out that while rajas and the praja, rulers and subjects, exist in Vidyalankar's history, a 'nation' does not, Chatterjee notes that Vidyalankar, an admirer of Akbar and a sharp critic of Aurangzeb, while using for Muslims the pejorative expression Yavanas, suggested that Yavana rule was ordained by divine will.

'The Supreme Lord's Will': According to Chatterjee, Vidyalankar calls Sirajuddaula 'cruel and lecherous,' describes his betrayal and end as 'just retribution,' and closes by saying that 'the Supreme Lord willed that the rule of the Company Bahadur be established.' To Vidyalankar the English were 'holding aloft the flag of dharma.'[2]

In a Bengali version, published in 1857-58, of J.C. Marshman's *History of Bengal*, the translator Ramgati Nyayaratna, apparently inserting some lines of his own that referred to Maratha raids on Bengal in the 1740s and 1750s, wrote:

> At that time the influence of the Marathas was so strong that everyone thought they would become the rulers of the country. But how ineffable is the greatness of the divine will! Those who had come to this country only as ordinary traders, those who were often on the verge of leaving the country for ever, those who had never even dreamed of

becoming rulers of this country—they, the English, ousted Siraj-ud-daulah . . . and have now become the virtual sovereign of all of India.[3]

'Treachery': So the British are seen as having simultaneously rid Bengal of a despotic nawab and prevented its capture by the Marathas. By 1869, however, and following the impact of the 1857 Rebellion and its suppression, the mood changed. A question and answer book published that year, written by Ramsaday Bhattacharya and also quoted by Chatterjee, contains the following sentences:

Q: How did Clive win?

A: If the treacherous Mir Jafar had not tricked the Nawab, Clive could not have won so easily.

Divide and fall: In 1870, the Bengali writer Krishnachandra Ray said that Clive could do what he wanted because the Emperor in Delhi was weak. In Ray's view, Clive had inaugurated the rule of force. Sirajuddaula is exonerated of complicity in the Black Hole deaths. Adds Ray:

If this country had been under the dominion of one powerful ruler, or if the different rulers had been united and friendly towards one another, then the English would never have become so powerful here and this country would have remained under the Musalman kings. Perhaps no one in this country would have ever heard of the English.

'Infinite benefits': However, Ray felt that 'whatever be the means by which the English have come to acquire this sprawling kingdom, it must be admitted that infinite benefits have been effected by them to this country.'[4]

*

Rammohan Roy: Some Indians responded to more than the politics of the British arrival. Rammohan Roy (1772-1833) not only seemed to become a bridge between India and the West; he showed how Indians could employ the foreign presence to understand themselves better.

Arguing that for long ages valuable Indian wisdom had been 'concealed within the dark curtain of the Sungscrit (Sanskrit) language,'[5] Roy wanted the meaning of the most important Sanskrit texts to be made available to the Hindu masses in India's popular languages, and to Europeans in English. If this happened, Indians and Europeans, Roy felt, would both come to know, for one thing, that rank superstition and idolatry did not constitute the heart of Hinduism.

Roy was conscious of the efforts of British and other European Orientalists to standardize popular Indian languages and adapt them for printing. Able himself to write in Persian, Bengali and English, and familiar with Sanskrit and Arabic, Rammohan Roy seemed to realize, too, that for some Indians English translations of old Indian texts might be as useful as they would be to Europeans. As Wilhelm Halbfass puts it,

> for Rammohan, English, the 'foreign' language, is not just a means of communicating with a foreign culture, it also serves as a medium in which he articulates his self-understanding and reinterprets his own tradition. What is more, he uses English and Bengali not simply as vehicles for translation, but also as devices for . . . opening up [the classical Indian tradition] and reclaiming it for the present.[6]

Rediscovering the home: Making a similar point, though with reference to a much later work—*Ramakrishna Kathamrita*, containing sayings of Ramakrishna Paramahansa and first published in the early years of the twentieth century—Partha Chatterjee says:

> But for both narrator and reader of the *Kathamrita*, the terrain of European thought is familiar ground—familiar, yet foreign—from which they set out to discover (or, perhaps, rediscover) the terrain of the indigenous and the popular, a home from which they have been wrenched.[7]

Or, to put it more simply, a Western ship seemed useful for a voyage to the Indian home.

A short work in Persian, *Tuhfatul Muwahhidin*, was Roy's first publication (1804). Later he wrote mostly in English and Bengali. A real estate agent, lender, broker and successful businessman, Roy founded his movement for reform, the Brahmo Samaj, in 1828.

While Roy's well-known attacks on idolatry and sati, the practice of cremating a widow along with her dead husband, made him an obvious target of Indian conservative forces, his unwillingness to embrace Christianity disappointed Christian missionaries in India and the West who had invested high hopes in him.

India and the world: Pointing out that Roy, 'in a complete

reversal of the [traditional] Indocentric attitude,' reminded his fellow
Bengalis that India in his time was 'less than "one-twentieth of the
world," and that outside Hindustan, the people of more than half the
world worship one pure supreme God,'[8] Halbfass adds:

> Rammohan's most important and, in a sense, revolutionary
> step . . . was that he tried to guide India and Hinduism into
> the open arena of the 'great wide world,' that he exposed his
> own tradition to comparisons and contrasts with other
> religions and cultural traditions, and that he called for an
> openness towards and a willingness to learn from Western
> science and the Christian ethic.[9]

*

Kalamka, taken in both its visual sense as stigma and its
verbal sense as slander, was the mark an alien will had left
on the purloined indigenous past.[10]

In this sentence Ranajit Guha conveys a sense of the injury to Indian
sentiments caused by the assumption of Indian inferiority, and in
particular by the Indian history provided by the British. It is a sense
to which, in different ways, Dayananda Saraswati (1824-83),
Bankimchandra Chatterjee (1838-94), Vivekananda (1863-1902), and
Rabindranath Tagore (1861-1940), among others, gave expression.

Dayananda, the Gujarati Swami who founded the Arya Samaj,
contended that the Vedas of the Aryas predate all historical
developments: they were originally communicated by God to the
Aryas. However, Indians had failed to preserve a proper understanding
of what was revealed to their forebears, which was a pure monotheism
and a call for mastering the secular world. In Dayananda's view, the
polytheism of the Puranas and the escapism of advaita had obscured
the pristine message.

Aryan pre-eminence: Sharply critical of Christianity and Islam,
and also of the Westernization he saw in Roy's Brahmo Samaj,
Dayananda suggested that the Europeans owed their technological
and scientific superiority not to Christianity, as some missionaries
and Orientalists tended to claim, but to the teaching that Indians had
given to Europeans in the past. Though arguing that as descendants
of the first receivers of God's truth, Indian 'Aryas' had a special place
in the world, Dayananda conceded that in modern times they should
learn from European virtues and achievements.

*

A desire to wipe out the *kalamka* or *kalank* against India and Bengal lay at the root of Bankim's oft-quoted call for a history that was truly Indian or Bengali. Evidently his severest criticism was reserved for 'Indological scholarship, especially studies of Hinduism.' He thought that while India's ancient glory was intolerable to European Indologists,[11] to redeem 'the glory of our forebears' was 'a filial duty' for Indians.[12]

Vivekananda spoke of the 'endless stream of futile abuse' of India and her culture and her past by foreigners and educated Indians alike.[13] While reviewing Akshaykumar Maitreya's 1898 book, *Sirajuddowla*, Rabindranath Tagore said:

> The English are hardly aware that the innumerable abuses addressed to the Oriental character and Oriental principles of government briefly or elaborately, vaguely or explicitly, relevantly or irrelevantly, in books written in the English language, generate a grievance, born of a sense of humiliation, in the minds of educated Indian readers.[14]

'Incapable Indians': There is abundant evidence that British superiority and Indian inferiority were basic premises with the Raj's custodians. In 1857 a British official, Robert Dunlop, wrote of 'the weak and childish but cruel and treacherous native character,' and added:

> It is a patent fact that the proud contempt which the Anglo-Saxon bears to the Asiatic has proved, to a great extent, the salvation of our Indian Empire. Nearly all men come to the country fully prepared to accord equal rights and privileges to its dusky inhabitants; but experience leads to a common conviction of their debasement.[15]

Of Dalhousie, who came to India as Governor-General in 1848 at the age of thirty-five and added substantially to the Empire's Indian territories, an author who is on the whole his admirer, Penderel Moon, writes:

> Imperious, masterful and autocratic, he was unnecessarily emphatic in the assertion of his authority . . . To him it was obvious that English government, laws, customs and manners were far superior to Indian . . . Indians were, in his opinion, 'wholly incapable of being admitted into a share of the

government' of their own country; and while he recognised that this might not hold good for ever, his thinking was governed by the assumption of their inferiority . . .[16]

*

Fear: The emotion of fear stayed close to that of humiliation. Partha Chatterjee describes a scene from a sketch staged in Calcutta in 1886 and written by Girishchandra Ghosh (1844-1912), 'the most eminent playwright and producer on the nineteenth-century Calcutta stage and a close disciple of Ramakrishna.' One of Ghosh's characters, Dokari, 'roaming the streets [of Calcutta], suddenly comes upon three Englishmen and, instinctively, turns around and runs.' As Chatterjee says, 'A mortal fear of the Englishman and of the world over which he dominated was a constituent element in the consciousness of the Calcutta middle-class.'[17]

Dismay over being ruled from a far and wholly strange country was a third reaction. Unlike Muslim rule, which saw aliens entering and controlling India, British rule gave a whole race of remote foreigners control over the country. India was now subject not just to a family or dynasty but to a race or nation. Bankim, who took care not to advocate confrontation with Britain, would note nonetheless that at times 'India's welfare was sacrificed for the welfare of Britain.' Bankim thought, too, that Indians were prevented from learning how to rule themselves. However, this handicap was balanced, Bankim felt, by the benefits of modern education, transport and communication.[18]

'*Actually superior?*' Studying nineteenth-century Bengal's response to Europe, Tapan Raychaudhuri noticed 'a fundamental anxiety' at the centre of all assessments of the West: were the Europeans, and especially the English, actually a superior race? According to Raychaudhuri, Bankim's answer to this query was unequivocal: 'In culture, education, power, wealth, and happiness—in fact in all respects, the English are superior to the Bengalis.' In Bankim's opinion, this recognition of superiority bred among Bengalis an attitude which he described in these words:

> We are particularly curious to learn what we should dislike in Europe . . . [We are told that] Bengalis . . . are not praiseworthy in any way . . . We do not know for certain if this is true. But we hear this said every day and are beginning to believe in its truth. This belief does us no good

... We hence long to hear if we are superior in any way to
the most civilized nations. But nowhere do we hear such
things. What we hear are only the words of people brought
up in the narrow traditions of our society and given to false
vanity. We cannot believe those words; they do not fulfil
our desire.[19]

Bankim here asks for genuine evidence of superiority, not the vain
boasting of revivalists who claimed that all European knowledge had
lain concealed in ancient Indian texts. Bankim's own answer was that
the Hindu past contained both bahubal ('arm-strength'), to which he
gave high value, and spiritual greatness; and he argued that a properly
understood Krishna, freed from gopis, was superior to Christ. While
the latter was incomplete, in Krishna 'every positive quality vouchsafed
to man [reached] its apogee,' that of 'a householder, politician,
lawgiver, saint, and preacher.'[20]

Quite unlike the playful Krishna that other Hindus visualized,
and differing, as Bankim underlined, from Christ and also from the
Buddha, Bankim's Krishna was interestingly enough reminiscent—
Tanika Sarkar points out—of 'another leader of a world religion
who, too, was a householder and who yet transcended his mundane
ties—Muhammad.' Bankim did not acknowledge the parallel.[21]

According to Raychaudhuri, Bankim thought that the scope and
size of the Mahabharata and the Ramayana also constituted an item
of Indian superiority, though in his own case Bankim was perhaps
touched even more by Shakespeare.

So Hindus did have a rich past, but Bankim felt that the way to
recover it was to learn all that could be learnt from the British. In
Bankim's view, while 'the central maxim of the Western civilization
[was] that "knowledge is power," ... the central maxim of the Hindu
civilization [was] that "knowledge is salvation." ' As he saw it, the
Hindus' indifference to power explained their decline. Faith in
renunciation was at the root of Indian inactivity and the major cause
of political dependence.[22]

Caution: Yet Bankim was wary of attempts to evict the British.
Guha cites Bankim's answer to a question he had asked of himself—
'Are independence and dependence then equivalent to you?'—: 'We
are a dependent nation and shall remain in a state of dependence for
a long time yet. It is not for us to debate such issues.'[23]

The younger Bankim had argued that if India under the British
was experiencing the rule of one race, earlier she had seen the rule of

one caste. He refused to concede that oppression by one's countrymen was 'sweeter' than oppression by foreigners. An older Bankim prescribed loyalty to the British but not necessarily amity. Raychaudhuri points out that Bankim was 'an admirer of Rani Lakshmibai and a man moved to tears by the memory of Plassey.' Indeed, he thought 'racial animosity' to be necessary. Competition was easier with enemies than with friends; friendship would come after the achievement of equality.[24]

Yet this inconsistent, complex, brilliant and unpredictable Bankim seemed to agree with British caricatures of the Bengali 'Babu':

> The ocean of animal nature was churned and thence emerged the Babu, like the moon, to light up the entire landscape of India.[25]

In a 'hymn to the English,' Bankim's Babu says:

> Whatever I do, it is for your pleasure; I donate [money] so that you will find me generous; I do good to others so that you will call me a philanthropist; I cultivate learning, so that you will call me learned. Therefore O Englishman, please look upon me with favour.[26]

Chatterjee warns us, however, that Bankim was always leaving it to readers to decide whether his irony was aimed at the Babu—or at the Babu's European critics.[27]

*

Recovering confidence: In an opposite response, Ramakrishna Paramahansa (1836-1886) declared that India had only to return to her ancient ideals of renunciation and self-control to demonstrate her superiority to the West. In an early biography of Sri Ramakrishna, Swami Saradananda, who significantly claimed that he was writing it in the context of 'the occupation of India by the West,' explained this diagnosis:

> Coming more and more under the spell of the West, India rejected the ideal of renunciation and self-control and began to run after worldly pleasures. This attitude brought with it the decay of the ancient system of education and training, and there arose atheism, love of imitation and lack of self-confidence. Thus the nation lost its backbone.[28]

Saradananda suggested that Ramakrishna's emergence issued from 'the compassion of the Lord,' which was aroused, he thought, by the sight of an 'India shorn of its glory and reduced to an object of contempt to foreigners.'[29] According to Partha Chatterjee, the middle-class culture of Bengal 'had, by the turn of the century, come to accept' that in spiritual matters India was superior to the West. British superiority in arms might have been confirmed by the outcome of the 1857 Rising, but Ramakrishna (and others) had helped tilt the spiritual scales in favour of India.

'Karmayoga is very hard indeed,' Ramakrishna once said, adding, 'In the Kaliyuga the best way is bhaktiyoga, the path of devotion—singing the praises of the Lord, and prayer.'[30] Chatterjee suggests that the withdrawal recommended here, the apparent warning against engaging in futile conflict, represented a strategy of survival in an age of colonial domination.

Where Bankim stressed bahubal, Ramakrishna presented the alternative of the male possessing the feminine qualities of compassion and caring. Apparently acknowledging that 'it was only owing to the Divine Mother's will that Western ideas and ideals had entered India,' Ramakrishna also seemed to imply that, as Saradananda put it, 'the Divine Mother had plans to counteract this trend as well.'[31]

*

In Ramakrishna's foremost disciple, Swami Vivekananda, we can see strands of his master's thinking and also of Bankim's. Holding that 'despite all the material achievements of Europe, India was superior to the West in her spirituality,' Vivekananda thought that 'India's special role [was] as preceptor to all mankind despite her weak, dependent, fallen state.'[32]

Referring to Vivekananda's 'unparalleled hatred of the British until he got to know them' on his overseas journeys, Raychaudhuri adds:

> Vivekananda, growing up in the period of increasingly militant nationalism, had an almost xenophobic resentment against western civilization, the British in particular. His long sojourn in the west and enthusiastic reception in America and Europe, especially by the elite, altered his attitude to one of profound admiration. It coexisted with great pride in the Indian past.[33]

Under British rule, India had seen famine, starvation and subjugation, and the British had often been callous, yet, according to Raychaudhuri, Vivekananda seemed to think that 'God had shown Indians no mercy, for they had been unbelievably cruel to their own people.'[34]

Though 'the mystic Vivekananda could be made to lose his . . . calmness of spirit by references to British rule in India,' he apparently 'despaired of physical victory' over the West's representatives in India. To him they were 'the mighty children of Virochana.' 'In direct confrontation with these masters of the material world, sons of the super-demon Virochana, Indra's challenger, [Vivekananda] saw no chance of success . . . He evidently believed in the illusion of permanence created by the Raj. His aim therefore was the religious-cultural conquest of the West.'[35]

Thus, agreeing with his master that in important areas India was, or could become, the West's superior and teacher, Vivekananda also seemed to go along with Bankim's reading that Indians had oppressed fellow Indians in the past, and with Bankim's counsel of patience with the West's rule.

*

Tenderness vs Masculinity: One who was sceptical of muscle-power in the East or the West was Keshab Chandra Sen (1838-84), a leading figure in the Brahmo movement and sympathetic to much that was linked to the West, including Christianity. In 1866, he had said in Calcutta:

> Owing to the reckless conduct of a number of pseudo-Christians (among the Europeans living in India), Christianity has failed to produce any wholesome moral influence on my countrymen. Yes, their muscular Christianity has led many a Native to identify the religion of Jesus with the power and privilege of inflicting blows and kicks with impunity.[36]

After a trip to England in 1870, Sen became more ascetic, more 'Indian', and seemed to prefer to speak in Bengali rather than in the English of which he had become a master. Partha Chatterjee informs us that in 1875 or 1876, two weeks after Ramakrishna visited Keshab Chandra Sen, an article appeared in Sen's *Indian Mirror*, an English-language daily, entitled 'A Hindu Saint.'

> We met one not long ago, and were charmed by the depth, penetration and simplicity of his spirit. The never-ceasing

metaphors and analogies in which he indulged are, most of them, as apt as they are beautiful. The characteristics of the mind are the very opposite of those of Pandit Dayanand Saraswati, the former being gentle, tender and contemplative as the latter is sturdy, masculine and polemical. Hinduism must have in it a deep source of beauty, truth and goodness to inspire such men as these.[37]

Chatterjee concludes that the piece was authored by Sen. Apparently this and subsequent articles in Sen's Bengali journal *Sulabh Samachar* noticeably enhanced Ramakrishna's appeal among the Bengali middle class.

*

'*Wait for the leader*': According to Bhudev (or Bhudeb) Mukhopadhyay, described by Partha Chatterjee as 'unquestionably the most brilliant rationalist essayist of the time,'[38] and whose 'dream history' about the third Panipat battle was seen by us in the previous chapter, the British 'did much good but they lacked sympathy or warmth for the Indian people. They loved the British race, were patriotic, and not individually selfish, but had no sympathy for the Indians. They could not win the affection of the Indian people.'[39]

However, Bhudev, while upset at Europe's 'missionaries [speaking] ill of [India's] religion and social practices,' advised Indians to wait for the emergence of 'the leader.' According to Raychaudhuri, Bhudev predicted in the year 1893 that

this leader . . . would be truly Indian in his character and outlook, conversant with what was best in Europe but untarnished by the individualistic greed of the west and the slavish imitativeness of the western educated.[40]

Bhudev thought, too, that though 'incapable of sympathy [for Indians], the Englishman [was] of heroic stature' and would honour 'those who are strong.'[41]

In his *An Indian Historiography*, Ranajit Guha tells us of the 1898 book, *Sirajuddowla*, written by Akshaykumar Maitreya. Tagore termed the book a 'blow for self-respect,' though Guha comments that 'the self-respect at issue here was the self-respect of a subject people reconciled to its subjection . . . [It] was prestige coveted by the servant in the form of recognition from the master.'[42]

'*Ambrosia from poison*': Although 'demonstrating . . . that the destruction of Sirajuddowla and his kingdom was brought about by chicanery, deceit and venality on the part of Clive and company,' Maitreya's book apparently concluded thus: 'In view of the happiness and peace which characterize the new conditions of life in contemporary India, it must be admitted that . . . poison has produced ambrosia and a new India has been brought to life—an auspicious outcome which could have hardly been possible without the help of the English merchants.'[43]

*

Sayyid Ahmad Khan: The youth of Sayyid Ahmad Khan (1817-1898) was spent in Delhi at the heart of a dead Mughal empire kept nominally alive under British surveillance. When Sayyid Ahmad produced a new version of *Ain-i-Akbari*, Abul Fazl's record of the reign of Akbar, Sayyid Ahmad's contemporary, the poet Ghalib, commented:

> You waste your time.
> Put aside the *Ain*, and parley with me;
> Open thine eyes, and examine the Englishmen,
> Their style, their manner, their trade and their art.[44]

The British presence soon attracted Sayyid Ahmad. During the 1857 events he risked much in taking the British side, just as others had risked much by joining the rebels. However, shaken by the suffering of relatives and other Muslims in the course of the Rebellion's suppression, Sayyid Ahmad seemed to feel that a British-ruled India was 'no place for a self-respecting Muslim.'[45]

But the reaction was overcome, and Sayyid Ahmad Khan would play a crucial part in bringing the Raj and the Muslim qaum closer to each other. Visiting England and Europe in 1869-70, he sent lines to the *Aligarh Institute Gazette* that might not have gone down well with the journal's readers:

> Without flattering the English, I can truly say that the natives of India, high and low, merchants and petty shopkeepers, educated and illiterate, when contrasted with the English in education, manners and uprightness, are as like them as a dirty animal is to an able and handsome man.[46]

Self-rule opposed: Perhaps the seemingly insulting words revealed his impatience with a people not living up to his hopes. Perhaps he wanted to shame them out of old habits. In any case, recovering his poise, Sayyid Ahmad contributed greatly, through writings and institutions, to Indian and Muslim self-respect. Fearful, however, of rule by the lower classes and of Hindu rule, he opposed notions of self-government and adult franchise:

> Now suppose that all the English were to leave India. Then who would be rulers of India? Is it possible that two qaums—the Muslim and Hindu—could sit on the same throne? Most certainly no . . . One of them will conquer the other and thrust it down.[47]

*

In a book of questions and answers in Bengali, *Bharatbarser Itihaser Prasnottar* (Barisal, 1870), also representing a response to the perspectives provided by British rule, the Muslim writer, Saiyad Abdur Rahim, reflected critically on the Muslim role in Indian history. Parts of his text are available to us because of Partha Chatterjee's research and translation. Wrote Abdur Rahim:

> Between Muhammad Ghaznavi and Muhammad Ghori, the latter caused greater harm to the Hindus, because whereas Muhammad Ghaznavi only looted and plundered, Muhammad Ghori robbed the Hindus of the precious treasure of independence . . .

> The benevolent Akbar had scrapped the jizya tax; the wicked Aranjib (Aurangzeb) reinstated it . . . The reason for the collapse of the Mughal empire was the bigotry and oppression of Aranjib . . .

Honest reflection. Yet perhaps it is in the following excerpt that we see the best specimen of Abdur Rahim's frank analysis:

> *Teacher:* What lesson have you drawn from your reading of the history of Musalman rule?

> *Student:* This is what I have learnt for certain . . . To rule a kingdom is to destroy one's life both in this world and in the next. To rule, one must give up for all time the God given gifts of forgiveness and mercy. How lamentable it is that one must, for the sake of a kingdom, redden the earth

with the blood of one's own brother in whose company one
has spent so many years of one's childhood . . . For your
(the kingdom's) sake, to kill one's parents or one's brothers
and sisters . . . seems a matter of little concern. Oh kingdom,
how bewitching are your powers of seduction![48]

*

Jotiba Phule: Finally, we should look at reactions of a wholly
different sort. Jotiba Phule (1826-90), who came from Maharashtra's
Mali or gardener caste, which stood close to the Maratha-Kunbi
peasant castes, was sceptical of attempts to glorify everything
indigenous. Writing, instead, of 'the history of Brahmin domination
in India,' Phule said:

> The cruelties which the European settlers practised on the
> American Indians on their first settlement in the new world
> had certainly their parallel in India in the advent of the
> Aryans and their subjugation of the aborigines . . .

In Phule's reading of history, the Aryans were indeed, as European
Orientalists argued, 'descended from conquering Indo-Europeans,
but, far from being superior, they were cruel and violent invaders
who had overturned an originally prosperous and egalitarian society.'[49]

Phule, who wrote 'almost entirely in Marathi,'[50] opened schools
for girls and untouchable boys, and in 1875 founded the Satyashodhak
Samaj ('Truth-Search Society'), which 'organized non-Brahmins to
propound rationality.' He seems to have hoped for 'a new, theistic
and egalitarian religion.'[51]

As he saw it, 'in order . . . to keep a better hold on the people,'
the Brahmins had devised a 'weird system of mythology,' the
institution of caste, and a 'code of inhuman laws.' We get an idea of
the strength of Phule's feelings from the dedication prefacing his
work, *Gulamgiri.* He offers the book to 'the good people of the
United States' for their abolition of black slavery, an event that he
hopes would inspire Indians to shake off 'Brahmin thraldom.'[52]

Perhaps the first among nineteenth-century writers to eulogize
Shivaji as a hero, Phule 'presented Shivaji as the leader of Maharashtra's
lower castes whose achievements were attributable to the strength of
his Shudra and ati-Shudra armies rather than to the intellectual skills
of his Brahmana ministers.' According to the historian Uma
Chakravarti, Phule also sought to refute 'the attempts to project

Ramdas (the Brahmin poet treated by some as Shivaji's adviser) as the actual hero of Shivaji's exploits.'[53]

Not trusting, either, the 'reformist' Brahmins of his time, Phule seemed to regard the activities of the Brahmo Samaj and also of the Indian National Congress, started in 1885, as 'elite efforts, designed to deceive the masses and establish upper-caste hegemony.'[54]

'*Evil necessity*': According to M.S. Gore, the social scientist, Mahatma Phule, as he came to be called, thought that 'the social and cultural goals of equality were more likely to be achieved under British rule.' Phule, says Gore, was 'afraid that political freedom might mean a return to Peshwa rule.' To Phule, 'British rule was an evil necessity if the shudras were to make any progress.'[55] In Chakravarti's view, 'Phule believed that the presence of the British made it possible to overturn the lower-caste exclusion from learning.'[56]

*

Ramabai: We looked not just at Phule's response to the British, but also at his response, in the light of the British presence, to Indian conditions and history.

The same can be done with Pandita Ramabai (1858-1922), born into a Chitpavan Brahmin family in Maharashtra, who became known at a young age for eloquence in expressing her views, including in Sanskrit, and later for sheltering widows, first in Bombay and then in Poona. She had shown courage in marrying a non-Brahmin from Bengal and again, after her husband's death within two years of marriage, in speaking from public platforms in Poona despite traditional and scriptural injunctions against a widow doing so.

However, Ramabai's worst offence in the eyes of many contemporaries was her conversion in 1883 to Christianity, during a stay in England. Ramabai linked the conversion to a meeting in Calcutta in the late 1870s, before her marriage, when Keshab Chandra Sen apparently advised Ramabai to read the Vedas even though the Hindu canon seemed to be against women doing so.

> New thoughts (*Ramabai would later write*) were awakening in my heart. I questioned myself, why should I not study the Vedas and Vedanta? Soon I persuaded myself into the belief that it was not wrong for a woman to read the Vedas. So I began to first read the Upanishads, then the Vedanta and the Veda.[57]

Troubled, however, by scriptural passages that seemed to slight all women as well as men from the lower castes, Ramabai began a search for satisfaction—'I wanted something more than the Shastras could give me'[58]—that in her case ended in conversion to Christianity.

'You are after all a woman': Those, including high-caste reformers, who had previously extolled her now accused Ramabai of 'fickleness,' a trait they characterized as being 'peculiarly female,' as Uma Chakravarti points out in her *Rewriting History: The Life and Times of Pandita Ramabai.*[59] The journal *Indu Prakash* wrote:

> We were all taken with awe and wonderstruck by her charms of appearance and the fluent tongue wielding the language; her modest and intelligent speeches, all so sweet and juicy, now gone and wasted. Oh Pandita Bai. You are after all a woman.[60]

Thus she was adjudged guilty of three crimes—of being a woman, of having become a widow, and of becoming a Christian. The first two were accidents but the last was her choice and therefore even more objectionable. As Uma Chakravarti puts it, after her conversion Ramabai 'represented not the glory of the ancient Maitreyi,' who had shunned wealth for learning and mastered Sanskrit at a time when women received little education, 'but a discordant voice who spoke for the subjugated woman of nineteenth century India.'[61]

Widely denounced for her conversion, the independent-minded Ramabai was also soon engaged in battles with English clerics and colonial administrators. Among her few defenders was Phule, who argued that Ramabai's break with Brahmanic Hinduism followed a discovery that the Shastras were biased against low castes and women.

Uma Chakravarti's study of Ramabai, which is also a study of widowhood in India, cites an essay written in 1907 by Sushila Devi, evidently a North Indian, that describes the life of a girl married at the age of nine to a forty-year-old man. The child-bride is first 'ripened'—fed with 'cream and curds'—but when the beautiful and youthful girl is widowed all the people around her mount a ceaseless surveillance designed to save her from any joyous company, sight or moment. All she can look forward to is a life of drudgery, near-starvation and abuses.

Distrust and trust: Chakravarti stresses the fact that shortly after her marriage and before her widowhood, the girl was broken into the 'distrust system' in which a man is always represented by the older womenfolk as a wolf in sheep's clothing and always to be shunned. The woman is made out to be still worse in this system. She is a 'burning fire' so dangerous that to glance at one, even during the day, causes destruction to man.[62]

The man, the woman, the untouchable, the stranger—hazards were posed by all. She or he would scorch, pollute, destroy. Safety lay in suspicion, surveillance, distance, walls and Lakshman Rekhas. The logic of the 'distrust system' was widely soaked up. But it was not a nineteenth-century idea. We saw that its seeds—and bitter fruits—were there in the Mahabharata. And intervening centuries had shown that these 'safety devices' of distrust had never failed to cause suffering, or evoke an equal or greater counter-distrust.

In such a climate, sanctified by tradition, of distrust, the British were successful in winning the trust of insecure groups of Indians, who credited the British with the power as well as the willingness to curb any oppression from other Indian groups.

To return, however, to Ramabai, the popular if contestable notions that Hinduism and nationalism were synonymous, and that Christianity and colonialism were also one and the same, marginalized her voice for a long time. Yet that voice, and Phule's, articulated the tensions, hierarchies and struggles existing within a colonized India and within Hindu society. Ramabai and Phule tried to declare that oppression was not confined to the Muslim-Hindu and the colonizer-colonized relationships—that privileged Hindus also were capable of oppressing weaker Hindus.

*

New windows and old wounds: We have noticed that reaction to British rule often seemed joined to feelings about Muslim rule. The encounter with the West had reopened older wounds, even as it opened new windows.

The stigma against which Bankim rebelled was, in his view, 'a mark given both by British and Muslim historians, and it was the latter's judgments that were used by the British, which made the Muslim historians the bigger culprits.'[63] According to Ranajit Guha, Bankim characterized the Muslim historians as 'liars' and 'Hindu-haters.' To him India's nationhood seemed to have a 'purely Hindu identity.'[64]

Rammohan Roy, on the other hand, had seemed better disposed towards Islamic culture; and in circles around Ramakrishna there appeared to be a positive place for Islam. Thus Saradananda's venerational biography of Ramakrishna, *Lilaprasanga*, while stating that all prophets or divine incarnations, with the exception of Rama and Buddha, were born in poverty, included Muhammad among the prophets born poor.[65]

Raychaudhuri quotes Vivekananda's opinion: 'The Muslim occupation of India liberated the poor and the downtrodden,' for a fifth of the population accepted Islam. 'It is madness to imagine that this was achieved only by fire and sword.'[66] In Raychaudhuri's appraisal, 'Bhudev [Mukhopadhyay] and Vivekananda had deep regard for Islam and the Indo-Islamic past. The Indian nation of their dreams included the Muslims very emphatically. Muslims to Bhudev were "foster-brothers" and Bankim alone rejected the Indo-Islamic heritage.'[67] Bhudev is quoted by Raychaudhuri as pointing out that despite differences in language or custom, 'the Indians had deep affection for their Muslim rulers.'[68] However, adds Raychaudhuri,

> [t]he nationalist literature . . . long excluded the Indo-Islamic past from its perception of national heritage. The identification of Turko-Afghan and Mughal dynasties as alien rulers and their regime as 'Muslim rule', projected in British historical writings on India, was accepted by the Bengali Hindu writers with rare exceptions. The Rajput and Maratha resistance to the Delhi-based empires was incorporated into a new mythology of Hindu patriotism. The often positive assessment of the British rule was sustained by favourable comparisons with the alleged 'Muslim tyranny.'[69]

When questioned about the hardships of Indian women, Hindu intellectuals in the second half of the nineteenth century usually ascribed responsibility for the hardships to Muslim rule. Partha Chatterjee quotes from a lecture given in Calcutta in 1876 by Bholanath Chakravarti:

> The misfortunes and decline of this country began on the day the Yavana flag entered the territory of Bengal . . . Ravaged by endless waves of oppression, the people of Bengal became disabled and timid. Their religion took distorted forms. The education of women was completely stopped. In order to protect women from the attacks of Yavanas, they were locked up inside their homes.[70]

Women internalized the explanation. Widows interviewed early in the twentieth century in western India seemed inclined to attribute practices like the early marriage of girls, tonsuring of widows, sati, purdah and the denial of education to the 'fear of Mussalmans abducting women,' especially 'good-looking widows.'[71] The explanation could not be entirely convincing. Marriage at the age of eight was after all Manu's ancient prescription; Hindu tradition had always frowned on widow remarriage; and sati featured in the Mahabharata and had been recorded during Harsha's seventh-century reign[72], well before Islam's advent.

The truth was that the West's advent had caused serious unease in Hindus over some aspects of their tradition and revived Hindu memories of Muslim excesses. Not everyone could resist the urge to blame Muslims for more than their excesses, including for some embarrassing Hindu weaknesses.

*

It is worth pausing with the realization that many of those we have looked at qualified their desire for confrontation with the uncongenial rule of the British with the caveat, 'But not yet!' Behind Bankim's caution a feeling seemed to exist that Muslims might benefit from any Hindu-British clash. Vivekananda appeared to suggest that until times were more favourable Indians should concentrate on what they seemed good at—and what their past had evidently prepared them for—, viz., spirituality. And Bhudev counselled waiting for the right leader.

Jotiba Phule feared that early self-government for India would transfer power to high-caste Hindus, who, having accepted Western education, were well-positioned to take over from the British and block the low-caste majority's progress. Reckoning that in any democratic system of self-government Hindus would rule over Muslims, and the ill-mannered over the aristocratic, Sayyid Ahmad Khan advised a continuance of British rule, distasteful as it was.

Thus, though repeatedly humiliated, enraged or outraged by British rule, some of the proudest and most sensitive Indians of the nineteenth century still saw that rule as being, on balance, a force for unity and progress.

6

To Crush and Conciliate:
The Raj and the Sikhs

AN ACCOUNT OF the Punjab of the 1840s and 1850s is included in this study for three reasons. It enables us to pick up the thread of the Sikh story. It enlightens us about how the British won, and Indians lost, some crucial and fierce battles. Finally, it shows how a ruling power enlisted the support of a recently-defeated and bitter foe.

Before becoming the Sikh king, Ranjit Singh Sukarchakia was one of numerous Sikh chiefs each of whom headed a misl, or band of committed fighters, and sought domination over bits of a Punjab no longer under Mughal control. In the 1770s there evidently were more than sixty Sikh 'territories' between the Jamuna and the Indus. But by 1799 Ranjit Singh's misl had managed to subdue or subjugate most rival misls and to capture Lahore from three Sikh chieftains separately governing partitioned portions of the city.

Two years later Ranjit Singh declared himself a Maharaja. In 1805 he captured Amritsar. But in 1809 the British pushed him into signing the Treaty of Amritsar. While this treaty recognized Ranjit Singh as the sole sovereign ruler of the Punjab, in return he had to agree that the Sutlej rather than the Jamuna would be his southeastern boundary, and that the Sikh principalities to the south and east of the Sutlej (such as Patiala, Faridkot and Nabha), earlier conceding his suzerainty, would submit to the British.

Discussing the negotiations regarding these cis-Sutlej principalities between Ranjit Singh, then twenty-seven, and the Governor-General's twenty-three-year-old representative, Metcalfe, Penderel Moon says that Ranjit Singh's

> contention that he, rather than the British, was their suzerain could not be rebutted by Metcalfe except by recourse to untruth.[1]

In Moon's view, Ranjit Singh yielded to the British because of his 'considerable dread of their military power.' Adds Moon:

> The British for their part, having extended their sovereignty
> from the Jumna to the Sutlej with the minimum of trouble
> and expense, were relieved of further anxiety about their
> north-west frontier by the existence of a strong and friendly
> Sikh power in the Punjab.[2]

Non-interference from the British enabled Ranjit Singh to bring
within his sway the Hindu rajas in the hills between the Beas and
Sutlej rivers, as well as Muslim chieftains towards, and later beyond,
the Indus. He took over Multan in 1818, Kashmir a year later, Dera
Ghazi Khan in 1831, and Peshawar in 1834. Many of these exercises
involved clashing with the Afghans. In the words of J.S. Grewal:

> Before his death in 1839, Ranjit Singh's authority over all
> the conquered and subordinated territories between the river
> Satlej and the mountain ranges of Ladakh, Karakoram,
> Hindukush and Sulaiman were recognized by the rulers of
> Kabul as well as by the British rulers of India.[3]

Only around 10 per cent of the population of the areas controlled by
Ranjit Singh were Sikhs, half of whom were concentrated in a core
region comprising the upper Bari, upper Rachna, and Jullundur
doabs. The Bari, Rachna and Jullundur doabs refer, respectively, to
the land between the rivers Beas and Ravi, between the Ravi and the
Chenab, and between the Sutlej and the Beas. The space between the
Indus, to which the other five are tributaries, and the Jhelum, is the
Sindh Sagar doab, and that between the Jhelum and the Chenab, the
Chaj doab. Throughout history, these five spaces, and their varying
access to water, have had major economic, political and military
implications.

In parts of the core region mentioned, which included the cities
of Lahore, Amritsar and Jullundur, Sikhs were about a third of the
population; their percentage in the remaining portions of Ranjit
Singh's Punjab was much below 10. Despite this disadvantage in
numbers and ratios, Ranjit Singh (and, for about three decades before
him, the numerous Sikh misls) had established control.

Why Ranjit Singh succeeded: Without going into details, we can
look at some of the reasons for Ranjit Singh's success in creating a
large state and sustaining it until his death. The dominance of Ranjit
Singh's own Sikh Jats in the Manjha—the Sikh heart of the core

region—was one. Fierce as horsemen and in face-to-face combat, they were also hardy farmers. Their loyalty and skills were valuable assets for Ranjit Singh.

His skill in subjugating other chiefs (mostly fellow Sikhs but also Hindu Rajput and Muslim chiefs) and, thereafter, in enlisting their support as vassals or officers of his state was another. Grewal thinks that Ranjit Singh was able to 'reconcile all important sections of his subjects to his rule.'[4]

The size of his ever-growing army, which finally numbered around 50,000 (of whom a great many but by no means all were Sikh) and employed nearly 300 pieces of artillery, was a third factor.

Aware that 'friendly' Britain would one day want the Punjab as well—'The British had long cast covetous eyes on it,' according to Moon[5]—, Ranjit Singh took into his service 'a stream of European officers, French, Italian, Greek, Spanish, English and Eurasian.'[6] Their large salaries were a burden for Ranjit Singh and an irritant for the soldiers, but the European officers made a difference to the army's efficiency.

Before he became king and abolished the misls, Ranjit Singh and the misls had been helped by the social equality and the doctrine of the Guru-Panth urged by Sikhism. In practice equality was limited, but the notion that members of the Sikh community together constituted the Guru strengthened morale. By 'ensur[ing] the right of every Singh to fight, to conquer and to rule',[7] the Guru-Panth doctrine injected a sense of responsibility in every leader and soldier, even if it also, perhaps, worked against clarity of command.

But Ranjit Singh was pragmatic after establishing his kingdom: every Sikh was not going to rule in the new state. Those claiming a special right to interpret the Sikh tradition would not rule either. Only Ranjit Singh would. A believing Sikh had established Khalsa Raj, but he would run the state on modern and secular lines, rejecting the option of a theocratic state.

Though Sikhs, and among them the Jats, were dominant in his army, it also contained many Hindus, Muslims and lower caste Sikhs. Several leading positions in the kingdom were occupied by Hindus, including some from outside the Punjab, and Muslims. These included relatives of the Jammu Raja Jit Singh—Kishora Singh and his sons, Gulab Singh, Dhian Singh and Suchet Singh. The four had joined Ranjit Singh's service as common troopers before he ousted their relative, Jit Singh.

According to Grewal, 'the Hindus, Muslims and the Sikhs of the core region constituted the large majority of the ruling class.'[8] Persian was the court language, and also the language in which Muslim writers composed their encomiums to Ranjit Singh. Under him Mughal patterns of administration and revenue collection were continued, as was the practice of rewarding a supporter or conciliating a former foe with a jagirdari—a land area with the right to its revenue. In return the jagirdar would acknowledge the king and supply soldiers to him.

Indian historians have generally credited Ranjit Singh with success in winning the loyalty of the Punjab's Muslim majority, but this judgment has to be set against the negative image that modern Pakistanis seem to have of Ranjit Singh. In Lahore, notices in mosques and monuments tell the visitor that the places were used as stables during Sikh rule.[9] Yet Ranjit Singh could not have ruled over the Punjab for as long as he did without at least a measure of support from Muslim chieftains, jagirdars and subjects.

But this ruler with a glass eye, clear head and strong drive did not prepare a successor. As Khushwant Singh has put it, 'when he died on the evening of 27 June 1839, there was no one fit to step into his shoes and guide the destinies of the state.'[10] Also, his army had drained the treasury, and the soldiers were fearful and restive. Worst of all, the Lahore durbar was shot through with intrigue and factionalism.

Even so, Bankim would claim later in the nineteenth century that after the Vedic and the immediate post-Vedic period, there were only two instances of 'nation-formation' taking place in India. The Marathas and the Sikhs, he said, had achieved this 'nation-formation,' 'each for a short while, under their respective leaders, Sivaji and Ranjit Singh.'[11]

*

Powerlust and revenge: Within ten years of Ranjit Singh's death, however, the British succeeded in subjugating and annexing the Punjab. During this period the Sikh kingdom had provided facilities and soldiers for British campaigns in Afghanistan, but this fact did not constrain the British, whose ascendancy was aided by a sequence of power-clashes and revenge-killings in the Lahore Durbar.

The new king, Kharak Singh—his father's eldest and only legitimate son—was a feeble-minded opium eater whom several, including Kharak Singh's son Nau Nihal, wished to supplant. After

Kharak Singh's wazir, Dhian Singh (one of the three Dogra brothers elevated by Ranjit Singh), apparently acting with the connivance of Nau Nihal, killed Chet Singh, a favourite of the king, Nau Nihal Singh in effect replaced his father.

But on 5 November 1840, the day on which his father died, Nau Nihal was himself killed when the arch of the palace gateway collapsed on his head while he was returning from the funeral. Suspicion was directed at Dhian Singh—the Sikh aristocracy had never approved of the influence enjoyed by the Dogras—but it is improbable that Dhian Singh caused the murder. He himself was almost killed in the collapse, which also took the life of Dhian Singh's nephew.

In the struggle for succession, Dhian Singh supported Sher Singh, the eldest of Ranjit Singh's sons from concubines. Though many leading Sikhs pressed for the installation of Kharak Singh's widow, Chand Kaur, Sher Singh won the backing of most of the army by promising large increases in salaries, and was crowned, with Dhian Singh as wazir.

In June 1841 Chand Kaur was killed by her female attendants, but others too were obviously involved. Revenge came two years later. On 15 September 1843, Maharaja Sher Singh and his young son Partap Singh were assassinated just after the king had reviewed some troops freshly raised by Ajit Singh Sandhanwalia, who was related to Ranjit Singh and had championed Chand Kaur's cause. After the march past was over,

> Ajit Singh came up to the platform on which Sher Singh was sitting and on pretence of presenting him with a new double barrelled gun suddenly pointed the weapon at him and shot him dead. He then cut off his head and stuck it at the end of his spear. Meanwhile his uncle, Lehna Singh, killed the young lad, Partap Singh, and likewise mounted his head on his spear. The two of them then rode back to the city with their trophies.[12]

Dhian Singh, though not 'altogether displeased'[13] at the regicide, was inveigled into the fort and shot in the back. Every one in his small bodyguard was also killed.

The deeds were immediately avenged. 'In the cantonments, the army panches (representatives) met and resolved to punish the malefactors. They chose as their leader Hira Singh, the son of Dhian

Singh, who had appealed to them to help him avenge the death of his father.'[14] In another revenge demand that recalls the Mahabharata,

> Dhian Singh's widows refused to allow the cremation of their husband's corpse until the heads of the Sandhanwalias were placed at its feet.[15]

Next day the fort was stormed and Ajit Singh and Lehna Singh along with several hundred of their troops were slain. The severed heads of the Sandhanwalias were then duly laid at the feet of the dismembered body of Dhian Singh, and the widows, their condition met, readied themselves for sati. The chief widow said to Hira Singh: 'When I meet your father, I will tell him that you acted as a brave and dutiful son.' Then flames consumed the dead and the living. We should mark that the incident occurred ten years *after* the death of sati's foe, Rammohan Roy.

The Kshatriya son had done his duty, and the widows, young and old, had done theirs, even as, earlier, the Sandhanwalias had been faithful to Chand Kaur and to their memory of Ranjit Singh. For yet another time, duty had erased mercy, and young hopes and old bones were alike crushed.

A six-year-old boy, Dalip Singh, Ranjit Singh's son by 'a favourite concubine, the comely Rani Jindan,'[16] was named king, with Hira Singh as wazir. About Hira Singh it has been said that Ranjit Singh had preferred the Dogra youth over all his numerous sons. He had been raised as Ranjit Singh's 'own child' and 'invested with the Persian title, Farzand-i-Khas (Special and well-beloved son).'[17]

Among Hira Singh's enemies now was his uncle Suchet Singh, who hoped to replace him as wazir. But 'the nephew had no hesitation in eliminating the uncle,'[18] who died fighting against overwhelming numbers in March 1844. Hira's luck was not destined to last, however. His mentor, Pandit Jalla, made scandalous remarks about the moral character of Rani Jindan, whereupon the Rani and her brother, Jawahar Singh, appealed to the army panches and roused their wrath against 'the insolent Brahmin'[19] and his perceived protector, Hira Singh.

Hira and Jalla both fled from Lahore with a large Dogra escort towards Jammu, where Hira's uncle Gulab Singh could provide sanctuary, but pursuing Sikh soldiers caught up with the escapees. Along with a thousand Dogra soldiers, Hira and Jalla were killed on 21 December 1844. Their heads were impaled on spears and paraded through Lahore streets.

In Lahore the vacuum was now filled by Rani Jindan, her brother Jawahar Singh, who became wazir, Lal Singh, apparently the Rani's paramour, and by the army panches.

Within nine months, however, Jawahar Singh too had to die. He was suspected of a role in the murder of another of Ranjit Singh's sons, Prince Pashaura Singh, who had wanted to overthrow Dalip Singh and Rani Jindan. The army panches summoned Jawahar Singh, who took his nephew Dalip along with him on his elephant, hoping to gain from the soldiers' sentiment for the boy-maharaja.

> But the army were not to be deflected from their vengeance. [Jawahar Singh] was separated from the Maharaja and put to death. The next day four wives mounted his funeral pyre and died cursing the 'Khalsa' and prophesying that it would be overthrown and that the wives of the men of the army would be widows.[20]

*

Treachery: Like Gandhari's curse on Krishna and his kinsmen, this one worked too. In two wars fought between the Sikh kingdom and the British, one in 1845-46 and the other in 1848-49, tens of thousands of Punjabi soldiers, of whom most were Sikh but quite a few were Muslims, perished, but not before they had given the British, in Penderel Moon's words, 'a severe fright' and killed thousands of the enemy's white and brown soldiers.

In the first war, treachery at high levels aided the curse's power, as did the urge to get even. Lal Singh, the wazir, and Tej Singh, the commander-in-chief of the army, which numbered 1,20,000 in 1844 compared with 85,000 at the end of Ranjit Singh's reign[21], were in touch with the British, as was Gulab Singh, the surviving Dogra chieftain. Rani Jindan's liaison with Lal Singh and a letter the latter wrote to the British requesting them 'to consider him and the Bibi Saheba as their friends' placed a question mark against her role as well. According to Khushwant Singh,

> There is nothing concrete to implicate Rani Jindan . . . Nevertheless the feeling among many people was that the Durbar and Jindan were primarily responsible for egging the soldiers into hostility and then letting them down—the object being to teach them a lesson for having executed her brother, Jawahar Singh.[22]

Afraid that the army's demands would eat into their jagirs, many in the Sikh aristocracy hoped for a war in which the British defeated and dispersed the army and made the Punjab safe for the aristocrats. On their part, the British were only awaiting a suitable pretext for eliminating the Sikh kingdom, and had collected soldiers and boats on the frontier. Thus the first war started by tacit mutual consent.

On 11 December 1845, Tej Singh crossed the Sutlej and moved towards Ferozepur, which contained an isolated British force of no more than 7,000. But, as Moon's record of the event puts it, 'he refrained from attacking and secretly informed the British of his goodwill.'[23] By this time, however, the Governor-General, Lord Hardinge, had declared war, taken over by proclamation the Lahore Durbar's few possessions south of the Sutlej, and personally enlisted to serve as second in command under the British commander-in-chief, Gough.

More patriotic than their leaders, the soldiers in the Sikh army wanted actual fighting. The first battle took place at Mudki, twenty miles from Ferozepur, where the Sikhs were repulsed with heavy casualties. But there were 900 killed and wounded on the British side, and the British suddenly realized the fighting qualities of the Sikhs.

And when Gough ordered an immediate attack on Ferozeshah, where the main Sikh force was entrenched, the Sikh reply was so fierce that the British expected to lose. Hardinge even sent instructions for his private papers to be destroyed in the event of defeat. However, after courageous fighting from both sides, the British won, chiefly thanks to abrupt withdrawals by 'the irresolute or traitorous Tej Singh,' as Moon describes him.

Indian sepoys, 'the Hindustanis,' constituted more than half of Gough's force of 17,000, but, aware that for several decades the Sikhs had never lost in clashes in the Punjab, they were less willing than the White boys to move up to the Sikh soldier. The result was that

> The Sikhs were deeply impressed by the toughness of the British soldiers and never forgot it. The Hindustani sepoys they despised.[24]

Gough recognized that there were two other reasons for the sepoys' seeming reluctance to fight. Firstly, a disastrous British campaign in Afghanistan in which they had recently taken part had demoralized them; secondly, like many others in India, they did not wish to see the only remaining independent native government overthrown.

However, after the British victory and Sikh defeat in Ferozeshah, the morale of the sepoys rose, and they gave a much better account of themselves in subsequent battles.

It was in Sabraon on 10 February 1846 that the bloodiest battle of the first war was fought. With the river Sutlej behind them, the Sikh forces had dug themselves in. However, Henry Lawrence, newly appointed as the British Political Agent in Ludhiana in cis-Sutlej or 'British' Punjab, had 'been able through intermediaries to get from the treacherous Lal Singh sufficient information to prepare a rough sketch of [the Sikh entrenchments in Sabraon].'[25] After a savage battle, to quote from Moon's account,

> the Sikhs were forced back inch by inch towards the river. The traitor, Tej Singh, fled across the pontoon bridge almost at the first assault, but most of the Sikh generals and army fought on bravely.[26]

The collapse of a section of the pontoon bridge on which numerous retreating yet battling Sikhs were crowded added greatly to the loss of life. Many of the Sikh wounded were 'mercilessly slaughtered,' says Moon, 'because at Ferozeshah and in the earlier stages of [the Sabraon] battle, they had barbarously mutilated any wounded soldier who fell into their hands.'[27] The scene was later described by Hardinge's son, who had taken part in the battle:

> The river seemed alive with a struggling mass of men. The [British] artillery, now brought down to the water's edge, completed the slaughter. Few escaped; none, it may be said, surrendered. The Sikhs met their fate with the resignation which distinguishes their race.[28]

If the Sikhs had their traitors, they also had a hero. Old Sham Singh Atariwala, 'a white-bearded veteran of Ranjit Singh's armies,' clad in white and riding a white mare, was killed with fifty others in a desperate last stand. Disgusted with the Lahore Durbar but unable to accept foreign domination, he had vowed that he would not leave the battlefield alive.

Nearly 10,000 of the Sikh force in Sabraon were killed or drowned, all the guns they had moved across the Sutlej were captured, and about 2,400 died on the British side. But the British victory was complete. Two days later the British crossed the Sutlej, occupied Kasur, about thirty miles from Lahore, and considered the terms they should impose for peace.

Gulab Singh: For one astute man, the moment offered an opportunity that he was willing to seize. In the war Gulab Singh had remained neutral but in touch with both sides. The Durbar authorized him to negotiate on their behalf with Hardinge in Kasur.

Hardinge did not want to annex the Punjab—the British were in no condition yet to fight the numerous battles that occupation would invite. But he was resolved to weaken and control the Punjab. The Darbar was called upon to cede the rich territory between the Beas and the Sutlej, the Jullundur doab; to forego all claims to any cis-Sutlej pockets; to reduce its army to 20,000 infantry and 10,000 cavalry; to host in Lahore a British Resident and a contingent of British troops; and to pay an indemnity equivalent to a million and a half sterling. If the conditions were met, Dalip Singh could stay on the throne, with his mother as the regent and Lal Singh as the wazir.

The Durbar was willing to accept all the terms but unable to act on the last, for its treasury was empty. Gulab Singh, whose cofffers were not empty, had a solution. If, in lieu of the indemnity, the Lahore Durbar ceded to the British the vast hill territories between the Beas and the Indus, he would buy the lands from the British. The deal made, Raja Gulab Singh of Jammu was transformed into the Maharaja of Jammu and Kashmir. Had he taken all the area on offer, he would have become the Maharaja of Jammu, Kashmir and Hazara, but he did not wish to be saddled with Hazara.

It is worth noting that before and during this war, the British were secretly approached, and publicly reproached, by every faction—by Rani Jindan, the Sandhanwalias, Gulab Singh, and others. With some, e.g. Gulab Singh, the British made a deal. With others such as Tej Singh and Lal Singh an understanding was reached. The advances of others were rejected. But the fact that all sides sought British support, even while railing publicly at the firanghis, signified that the British were expected to control the future.

*

Henry Lawrence, the first Resident in Lahore, and his brothers, George, who was the eldest and posted at this time in Peshawar, and John, the youngest, who was given charge of the Jullundur doab and adjoining hill areas, have earned fame as the Lawrence brothers standing at the head of the so-called Punjab school. The school refers to a band of British officers perceived as having laid—with firmness, dedication and sympathy for the Punjab peasantry—the foundation for the Punjab province that would remain stable for two years short of a century, from 1849 to 1947, the pride of the Raj that supplied the rest of India with grain and the Empire with soldiers.

The Second Anglo-Sikh War: But before we examine the record of this school, we should look at the origins of the second Anglo-Sikh war, which led to the 1849 annexation. First Lal Singh was ousted as wazir because it was apparently proved that he had instigated an eventually unsuccessful bid by the Durbar's governor of Kashmir, Imamuddin, to deny the territory to Gulab Singh.

Next, a new treaty forced by the British on the Durbar—to have effect until 1854, when Dalip Singh would attain the age of sixteen— laid down that the British Resident would direct and control all the Durbar's departments. A liberal allowance was announced for Rani Jindan, but she was elbowed out as regent and excluded from a new Council of Regency imposed on the kingdom, over which the British Resident would preside.

In a letter to his Resident, Hardinge made it clear to Henry Lawrence that 'the native prince is in fetters and under our protection, and must do our bidding.'[29]

Jindan did not like her wings being clipped, but being at the mercy of the army that had killed her brother was something she liked even less. To Henry Lawrence she expressed gratitude for what had been done for her. 'Sullen acquiescence in the British protection, which they hated even while they craved for it,'[30] was the attitude of many Punjabi leaders.

Hardinge left and was succeeded as Governor-General by a young, driven and shrewd politician, Lord Dalhousie. Earlier in this chapter we had occasion to note the views of the Empire's new, thirty-five-year-old proconsul in Calcutta. Convinced of Indian inferiority, Dalhousie held the view 'that the more of the map of India that could be coloured red, the better it would be for everyone.'[31]

But he did not expect early showdowns. Shortly after arriving in India he wrote: 'Everything is quiet, and the only discontent I have heard of in the Punjab is that of the little Maharaja, who complains that [the tutors arranged by the British] give him too many lessons.'[32]

Yet trouble soon arose in Multan. To begin with, the dispute was between the Lahore Durbar and its governor in Multan, Diwan Mulraj, a Hindu. The Durbar wanted Mulraj to put up a substantial nazrana or 'offering' for being confirmed as governor in succession to his capable father, Diwan Sawan Mal, who as Diwan had enhanced the province's cultivation and revenue and also his own wealth. The Durbar and Mulraj failing to agree on the amount of the offering, Lahore appointed a new governor, Kahan Singh.

Two young British officers, Vans Agnew and Lieutenant Anderson, and 500 Durbar troops accompanied Kahan Singh to Multan, where local soldiers loyal to Mulraj, outnumbering the Durbar troops, refused to acknowledge Kahan Singh and killed Agnew and Anderson, cutting them to pieces. There was no evidence that Mulraj had incited his soldiers—'he seems to have been virtually a prisoner of his own soldiers,' who apparently thought they were losing their jobs along with Mulraj.[33]

All the same, the Durbar/Multan dispute had swiftly turned into one between Punjabis and firanghis, and the Durbar troops, who felt little warmth for the British, were induced to stand under the Mulraj banner, ready to face the foreigner.

Though it was summer, the British could have sent a force to deal with Multan, but it seems that Dalhousie was 'very willing to allow the Sikhs ample time and opportunity to rise in general revolt, as this would give him a good excuse for conquering and annexing the Punjab.'[34]

However, some of Lawrence's British officers in the Punjab were unwilling to delay a reply to the murder of Agnew and Anderson. One of them, Herbert Edwardes, at the time posted across the Indus, had received a letter written by Agnew shortly before his death in which help was sought. Edwardes mobilized Pathans and Baluchis and the Nawab of Bahawalpur against Multan and the Sikhs. Facing Edwardes and his allies, Mulraj and his force of Sikh, Muslim and Hindu soldiers were obliged to take refuge within Multan's city walls.

Tensions were raised by two other events. Suspecting Rani Jindan of an attempt to tamper with the loyalty of Hindustani sepoys stationed in Lahore, Currie, the acting Resident (Henry Lawrence was on leave in England), banished the Rani to Benares. Currie had to admit to Dalhousie, however, that 'the Khalsa soldiery on hearing of the removal of the Maharani were much disturbed.'[35]

The second disturbing event was in the region beyond the Jhelum in the northwest. There the Durbar's governor, Chattar Singh Atariwala, found himself in bitter conflict with officers of the Punjab school, especially Captain James Abbot and Captain John Nicholson, whose sole aim now was to prevent or quell any rebellion against the British.

Distrusting the governor, Abbot raised levies of Pathan tribesmen
by playing on their memories of Sikh violence. Later he would admit
that he

> called upon [the tribesmen] in memory of their murdered
> parents, friends and relatives to rise and aid me in destroying
> the Sikh forces.[36]

The Atariwalas enjoyed prestige as clan chiefs and fighters; more
important, Chattar Singh's daughter had been betrothed to the
young maharaja. A revolt led by the Atariwalas could be a serious
affair.

However, the British seemed confident of the loyalty of Chattar
Singh's son, Sher Singh Atariwala, who was asked by Currie to lead
a Durbar force for capturing Mulraj. They were in for a shock. On
14 September 1848, 'Sher Singh and his whole force of 7,000 men
went over to Mulraj.'[37]

Sher Singh switched partly because his father had written 'telling
him of the way he had been slighted by upstart foreigners and
exhort[ing] him to join his countrymen in fighting them to a
finish.'[38] He was probably also influenced by the popularity of Bhai
Maharaj Singh, a religious leader from the Manjha, the Sikh heartland,
who moved from village to village predicting the return of Khalsa Raj
and the end of British influence, and recruited several hundred men
for fighting the British.

In a proclamation asking all Punjabis to rise against the foreigners,
Sher Singh Atariwala, prospective brother-in-law of the Maharaja,
spoke of the

> oppression, tyranny and violence [with which] the firangis
> have treated the widow of the great Maharaja Ranjit Singh
> and [the] cruelty they have shown towards the people of the
> country.[39]

On pain of expulsion from the fold, Sikhs were exhorted 'to rise up
and kill the firangis, cut off the postal systems and proceed to Multan
without delay.'[40]

But Mulraj would not trust Sher Singh, a leading light of the
Durbar that had tried to squeeze him, and the British did not miss
any chance to deepen the suspicion.[41] The result was that 'the gates
of Multan fort remained firmly shut against Atariwala. Sher Singh
lost patience with Mulraj and on 9 October struck camp to go north
to join his father.'[42]

In his meticulous study of mid-nineteenth-century Punjab, Andrew Major examines why in the late 1840s some Sikh chiefs fought the British while others did not. Some of Major's findings are worth pausing with:

> A number of chieftains opted for either resistance or collaboration as much out of a desire to humiliate and destroy personal enemies as out of a desire to either expel or retain the influence of the firangis . . . For instance, the descendants of Sardar Sham Singh Atariwala (the hero of Sabraon) actively participated in the war against Chatar Singh Atariwala and his sons . . . in order to avenge an old family dispute.

> Most significantly, the leaders of the rebellion eventually identified their rivals at the darbar—rather than the British— as their real enemies . . .[43]

*

Dalhousie had now got his opportunity. In private he expressed delight that matters had been 'brought . . . to the crisis I have for months been looking for,' but he managed to inject righteous passion into his riposte to Sher Singh:

> Unwarned by precedents, uninfluenced by example, the Sikh nation has called for war, and on my word they shall have it and with a vengeance.[44]

So it was with yet another *oath* of revenge that the second Anglo-Sikh war was proclaimed. Dalhousie had shown that the British were as faithful to the spirit of the Mahabharata as the sons of the soil.

On 14 January 1849, the first engagement of the new war, fought in ravines and scrub-jungle near the village of Chillianwala on the banks of the Jhelum, went wholly in favour of Sher Singh's forces. After losing nearly 3,000 officers and men and achieving nothing, the British withdrew. In all their time in India, they had not seen a worse defeat. However, a week later Mulraj surrendered before a British attack, and on 21 February the final clash took place not far from the town of Gujrat.

For this encounter Chattar Singh's forces had joined those of his son, and Chattar Singh had even secured support and soldiers from the Afghans in Kabul. But the British came with their strongest artillery. The Sikh positions were subjected to a fierce cannonade. In Moon's version,

> After a short, fierce fight, [the Sikhs] gave way, their retreat was turned into a rout and they fled in disorder, leaving in the hands of the British their camp equipment, ammunition and nearly all their guns.[45]

A British writer noted, however, that in Gujrat as in Chillianwala,

> [the] Seikhs caught hold of the bayonets of their assailants with their left hands and closing with their adversary dealt furious sword blows with their right . . . This circumstance alone will suffice to demonstrate the rare species of courage possessed by these men.[46]

The Sikh army laid down its arms on 13 March 1849. For many a Sikh soldier and officer, the moment of parting from their horses and weapons, which was also the moment of the end of the Sikh kingdom, was hard. On 29 March, at a ceremony in the Hall of Audience in Lahore Fort, ten-year-old Dalip Singh 'stepped forward and affixed his signature and seal to the document that deprived him and his heirs and successors of "all right, title and claim to the sovereignty of the Punjab, or to any sovereign power whatever." '[47]

Belonging, before the phases of misl rule and the Sikh kingdom, to one empire, the Punjab was now part of another. Henry Elliot, Foreign Secretary to the Government of India and sent to Lahore to negotiate the terms of annexation with the Durbar, would later recall:

> As I left the Palace, I had the proud satisfaction of seeing the British colours hoisted on the citadel under a Royal salute from our own artillery—at once proclaiming the ascendancy of British rule and sounding the knell of the Khalsa Raj.[48]

*

From revenge to support: There is much in common, we shall see in the next chapter, between the events in the Punjab of the 1840s described above and the Great Revolt of 1857, which swept across much of northern and central India but in which the Punjab did not join. Historians seem agreed that if in 1857 the Punjab had joined the rebels of what is now U.P., Bihar, Delhi and Central India, British rule might not have survived.

Instead of linking forces with the rebels, the Sikhs of the Punjab as a whole—those in the erstwhile kingdom as well as the cis-Sutlej and Jullundur doab Sikhs—lent crucial support to the British in 1857. In only eight years, the Sikhs had turned around from revenge to accommodation in their attitude to the British. How did the switch occur?

For one thing, the British seemed earnest about governance. A Board of Administration comprising Henry Lawrence, John Lawrence and Charles Mansel was set up in 1851, and forty-nine carefully selected civil and military officers of the East India Company were asked to serve under the Board in every corner of the province.

These officers were instructed to rule directly over the countryside, with as little reliance as possible on chiefs and local potentates. They were authorized to act on the spot as they saw fit, and allowed 'an extremely flexible interpretation of basic administrative concepts.'[49] These concepts were indeed spelt out in printed codes and circulars, yet the autonomy given to the Punjab's local officers constituted the core of what would be called the 'Non-Regulation System' of the Empire's new Indian province.

Seven Commissioners, each heading a large division of the province, reported to the Board. They had judicial, police and revenue responsibilities, but it was the Deputy Commissioner (DC), the chief officer of each district within a division—'a little king in his own domain, subject to loosely defined limitations'[50]—, who was the Raj's face to the people of the Punjab. In idealized perceptions, the DC 'spent most of his day on horseback, touring his district, . . . listening to the grievances of "his people," and always on the lookout for any sign of political unrest.'[51]

The DC had two aides, an Assistant Commissioner (AC) and an Extra Assistant Commissioner (EAC). All officers were British but Indians were allowed entry into the EAC ranks. Major's study revealed that 'in 1852 nineteen out of thirty and in 1855 twenty-four out of forty-two EACs were Indians.'[52] Of the 1855 Indian EACs, eleven were Muslims, eleven Hindus and two Sikhs.

Each district was divided into four or five tahsils, and an Indian tahsildar, the link between the Raj and the village, was in charge of each tahsil. Much depended on the relationship between the DC, to whom the tahsildar was immediately responsible, and the tahsildar, but the DC was also expected to get to know 'his people.'

Along with the autonomous district officer, the post office, the telegraph office, the improved road, and—above all—the canal also appeared on the Punjab scene. In 1853 an anonymous article in the *Calcutta Review* claimed that reforms that had required twenty-five years elsewhere in India had been implemented in the Punjab in four. The article went on to say:

> We know not where else to look, in order to find a parallel
> to this metamorphose, from riot to tranquillity, to peace
> from misrule, that has taken place in India, before our very
> eyes, over the plains of the Punjab.[53]

Secondly, the British succeeded in large measure in disarming the Sikhs, in accordance with Dalhousie's instruction to disarm 'this turbulent population while they are still disheartened and in fear of punishment.'[54] While ten regiments of the Durbar's army and three batteries of artillery were taken into the Raj's service, scores of thousands of others were disarmed, paid up, and disbanded. The infirm and long-serving were granted pensions.

To prevent the possibility of guerrilla warfare, the general population too was required to surrender its arms (within a year of annexation nearly 1,20,000 weapons, mostly swords and matchlocks, were gathered) and 172 of the 248 mud forts in the Lahore division were demolished. Dacoity was sternly punished: in the first year after annexation, 37 sentences of capital punishment, almost all for dacoity, were awarded in Amritsar district. In Ranjit Singh's time mutilations rather than death sentences were ordered; the British ended punishment by mutilation.

Bhai Maharaj Singh, who did not cease talking of ejecting the British, was captured and sent to a jail in Singapore, where he died in 1856. Diwan Mulraj was tried, declared guilty of murder, and given life imprisonment. Chieftains like Chattar Singh Atariwala, whose lives had been spared following their surrender, were sent out to Indian jails far from the Punjab. When released after a few years, they were broken men with few supporters.

Thirdly, the British consciously introduced some levelling tendencies in Punjab society. Chiefs who had fought the British found their jagirs gone or truncated, and their palaces confiscated or destroyed. The privileges of chiefs who had not battled against the British were not greatly curtailed, but in almost every case they were changed from hereditary to lifetime privileges.

This question of how to deal with traditional chiefs and aristocrats bitterly divided Henry Lawrence, who was sympathetic towards them, from his brother John. Henry, in fact, had opposed annexation. Denying the boy maharaja his kingdom because of acts of other people over whom he, as a minor, had no control did not seem just to Henry. He felt, too, that the chivalrous treatment of British prisoners and especially their wives by Sikh chiefs who had seized them during the war had to be factored into the chiefs' punishment. The proposal infuriated Dalhousie.[55]

In disputes between the Lawrence brothers, Dalhousie almost always backed John as against Henry. This meant that the Punjab would move from chiefs' rule to rule by the bureaucrats of the Punjab. However, Henry Lawrence succeeded in obtaining Dalhousie's sanction to his plan of rewarding loyal cis-Sutlej chiefs; the more important ones among them were exempted from the jurisdiction of the Raj's new civil and criminal courts.

Some Muslim chieftains were better treated. Though the forces that had fought the British in the Punjab had included Muslims, the British knew that they could tap the unease about Sikh rule that the Punjab's Muslim majority had always harboured. As Major puts it,

> In the western Muslim-majority districts especially, the collaboration of individual tribal patriarchs was sought quite deliberately. In Shahpur district, for example, the Tiwana Maliks were rewarded for their past services and bound to the new regime by the creation of new jagirs in their ancestral tracts.

Fourthly, the British seemed to take the peasant and his needs seriously. Work was started on 'the first great modern canal in the Punjab,' the Upper Bari Doab Canal, which would take water from the Ravi to the districts of Gurdaspur, Amritsar and Lahore. Apart from large schemes of this sort, Henry Lawrence claimed that 'light assessments, simple laws, and general non-interference in village concerns'[56] were his objectives, and also the objectives of his brother John, despite their differences on other questions.

In their third report, the Board of Administration made this assertion:

> The policy of the Sikh Government was to tax heavily the agriculturalists, and to make large assignments of Revenue to the nobility as payment for service and support. But the policy of the British Government is to tax lightly the

agriculturalists, to pay its servants from its own Treasury, to excuse the native nobility from service, and to gradually reduce their assignments of Revenue.[57]

In Grewal's view, 'periodic settlements [of revenue] and records of [land] rights' were the 'major planks' of the British agrarian system.[58] Another finding, by Andrew Major, is that the adjudications of British officials on revenue assessments and land titles led to a greater 'levelling of rural society than the Sikhs had been able to achieve.'[59]

To a fair extent, the British succeeded in giving the impression to the peasants that rule by the Punjab school also meant simple laws, the rule of law, and a measure of justice. Seeking, in addition, a humane image, the Board adopted three calls that John Lawrence had propagated in the Jullundur doab between the two wars:

> *Bewa mat jalao.* (Do not burn widows.)
> *Beti mat maro.* (Do not kill daughters.)
> *Korhi mat dabao.* (Do not bury lepers alive.)[60]

*

The Board had been abolished, Henry Lawrence had moved to Lucknow, and brother John was in unquestioned command as Chief Commissioner when, on 12 May 1857, a telegram agitatedly tapped out in Delhi by William Brendish, a British army signaller of mixed race, informed Lahore that sepoys who had arrived from Meerut were burning down bungalows in Delhi. Then the line went dead.

For some time previous to this, the Punjab's British had been hearing of unrest over greased cartridges among Indian sepoys in the Bengal Army—the army deployed across North India, including the Punjab. The receipt of the telegram and its abrupt termination indicated the tasks falling on the British in the Punjab:

To assemble men and supplies and send them to Delhi; to preclude a rebellion by the 37,000 or so potentially mutinous Hindustani sepoys based in the Punjab; to guard from the Afghans a long and turbulent frontier in the Northwest; and to keep the Punjab's civilian population under control.

To order the sepoys to disarm was to risk an instant mutiny, yet a few Punjab-based sepoy units were disarmed in this way. This proved possible because in May 1857 about half of all the British in the Bengal Army were stationed in the Punjab. Backed by the British soldiers' superior weapons, the call to disarm was obeyed by the sepoy.

For sepoys in the Punjab running to join their colleagues in Delhi, and there were many who tried to do this, the Sikhs' dislike for the Purabiahs, as the sepoys were disparagingly called, stemming from the wars the Sikhs had fought against the British, was effectively if brutally used. Sikhs in the Manjha were offered a reward of fifty rupees for every escaping sepoy caught dead or alive. As Montgomery, who had replaced Mansel as the third member of the Board of Administration, would later say:

> The smothered martial spirit of the people was kindled into a flame; escape for a deserter was hopeless, for every village became to him as a nest of hornets.[61]

Even more effective was the strategy of offering opportunities in the British army to Sikh chiefs and their clansmen, even to chiefs who had fought against the British. As soon as he heard of the massacres in Meerut and Delhi, John Lawrence personally wrote to the leading chieftains who had been deprived of their jagirs on account of their disloyalty in 1848-49, inviting them to Lahore with a specified number of retainers. 'As the chieftains came in, Lawrence organised them and sent them off to join the British camp on the Ridge above Delhi.'[62]

Apart from these Punjab Irregulars, as the levies provided by the chiefs came to be called, Lawrence and his fellow-officers also raised eighteen new infantry regiments—about 34,000 men—in the Punjab in 1857. Many of the new recruits were from the Manjha.

> The fiercer spirits were everywhere enrolled, and the very class most likely to create disturbance at home was drained off to serve abroad.[63]

We will find later that Sikh regiments played a crucial part alongside British troops in the eventual suppression of the 1857 rising, but in 1857 this alignment was not the only possible one. The inhabitants of the Punjab, so used to disturbances, changes of regimes and convulsions, were waiting to see which way the wind blew. In such a situation, as Thornton, Commissioner of the Jhelum division, understood,

> a prudent man would be observant and profess loyalty until he saw his way clearly.[64]

In the end the Punjabis placed their bets on the British because, in the summer of 1857, Lawrence and his colleagues displayed a mix of toughness, promptness, conciliation, inventiveness and boldness. An example of the last-named quality was John Lawrence's preparedness to leave Peshawar unguarded if its defenders too were needed in Delhi.

A role in the Sikhs' decision was also played by the manner in which the Punjab had been ruled in the eight years after 1849. The levels of peace, order and law that the British had brought to the Punjab between 1849 and 1857 contrasted sharply with the well-remembered anarchy that followed Ranjit Singh's death. And if the two Anglo-Sikh wars had yielded their considerable quota of bitterness, they had also produced mutual respect, for each thought the other brave.

The Anglo-Sikh alliance of 1857 owed something also to the fact that the Sikhs felt little love or loyalty for Delhi's Mughal 'ruler,' who had been proclaimed King of Hindustan by the rebels. The executions of their Gurus under Mughal rule had not been forgotten by the Sikhs.

The Punjab's Muslims had less reason to reject the claims of the Mughal throne; but they too had memories of a century and a half of Mughal ineffectiveness in the Punjab after the death of Aurangzeb. To exchange the steady British rule that they were experiencing for an uncertain Mughal revival dependent on rebelling sepoys did not seem to them an attractive bargain. The result was that many Punjabi Muslims too enlisted under the British.

Also favouring the British was the fact that the spring of 1857 had seen a bumper harvest in the Punjab, an abundant harvest, moreover, that did not cause prices to fall, for markets were not overstocked—the spring and autumn harvests of 1856 had not been bountiful. In the summer of 1857, the Punjab peasantry was not restive.

Finally, the Sikhs had only recently done their fighting with the British. Their '1857' had taken place in 1848-49, life had been a little more secure for them since then, and they had little interest in a renewal of war.

7

The 1857 Trauma and its Meaning

STUDYING IN DETAIL the 1857 Rebellion, the theme of numerous books and dissertations, is not our purpose. But we will seek to understand its causes, look at some of its ups and downs, and attempt also to understand its meaning in South Asia's history.

When the Rebellion began, a mixed British/Indian army was being maintained by each of the three 'presidencies' of the East India Company: Bengal, Bombay and Madras. (By now barred by the British Government from trading, the Company served as the Government's agent in India.) In addition to the Company's three armies, some units of the British Army—the Queen's Regiments as they were called—were also stationed in India.

In 1856, seven years after the Punjab's annexation, there were six Indian soldiers to one British in the Company's armies, a change from an earlier three-to-one ratio. Indians in the armies were mostly sepoys (infantrymen) or sowars (cavalrymen), and the seniormost Indian officer was junior to the juniormost British officer.

Deployed in northern, northwestern, central and eastern India—from Peshawar and Karachi to Calcutta and further east—, the Bengal Army found most of its Indian recruits in Avadh or, in British spellings, Oudh or Oude.

Avadh had achieved de facto independence from the Mughal empire in 1722 when its governor, Saadat Khan, a Shia Muslim of Iranian origin, chose to disregard Delhi's crumbling Mughal throne. Following the British victory in the 1764 Battle of Buxar (in Bihar), Avadh consented to British protection. In 1801 half of its territory was taken over by the British and half retained by the ruler of Avadh, who remained submissive to the British. The districts left in Avadh included Lucknow, Sitapur, Hardoi, Kheri, Unnao, Rae Bareli, Sultanpur, Barabanki, Pratapgarh, Faizabad, Gonda and Bahraich.

With Lucknow as its capital, Avadh became a convenient buffer state for the British, hosting a Resident and a body of British troops, contributing an income, and providing soldiers to the Bengal Army.

Of every four in the Bengal Army's Indians, three, roughly speaking, were Hindus and one a Muslim. Among the Hindus most were Rajputs or vegetarian Brahmins. Their pay of seven rupees a month, though less than a third of what a White soldier earned, was decent enough; and in Avadh's villages their prestige was considerable.

The sepoys and sowars wore an uncomfortable uniform, including a thick red coat and a heavy headgear, which they shed whenever they could. They were put off also by the Englishman's interest in beef and brandy. On his part the White soldier or officer too thought some Indian practices peculiar. Yet bonds had evidently been formed. In *The Great Mutiny*, Christopher Hibbert quotes from a pre-1857 observation by a British officer:

> You might see the sepoy, watchful and tender as a woman, beside the sick-bed of the English officer, or playing with the pale-faced children [in] his captain's bungalow. There was not an Englishwoman in the country who did not feel measureless security in the thought that a guard of sepoys watched her house or who would not have travelled, under such an escort, across the whole length and breadth of the land.[1]

*

Causes: Here are some well-understood causes of the explosion that nonetheless occurred in 1857:

—the suspicion of Hindu sepoys that the greased wrapping which had to be bitten into for pulling out cartridges for the new Enfield rifle contained extracts of beef, and of Muslim sepoys that it contained pork; and the consequent fear in Hindu and Muslim alike of being polluted out of their community

—the fear that, official statements to the contrary notwithstanding, individual British officers were scheming to convert the sepoys to Christianity

—the suspicion, given the taboo against 'crossing the seas,' that service for the Empire outside India, for which sepoys were required to be willing, would also destroy one's caste

—the annexations that made the Punjab and Sind internal to

British India and therefore deprived the sepoys of the 'external service' allowance for serving in the Punjab and Sind

—Dalhousie's annexation of Avadh in 1856 and the deposition and exile of its ruler, Wajid Ali, causing restiveness in the principality and unsettling its talukdars (corresponding to the Punjab's jagirdars, Avadh's talukdars were chieftains with rights to the revenue of the tract conceded to them and the duty to provide fees and soldiers to Lucknow), general public and sepoys

Then there was Dalhousie's Doctrine of Lapse, by which an adopted heir was barred from inheriting a throne without the Governor-General's consent. When, in 1848, the dying and heirless Raja of Satara, the last lineal representative of Shivaji, adopted a son, Dalhousie withheld consent to the adoption, so that Satara became British when the Raja died. Jhansi suffered the same fate in 1853, and Nagpur in 1854.

The death in 1851 of Baji Rao, the last Peshwa, who as we saw belonged to a dynasty of Peshwas, invited a similar response from Dalhousie. After his defeat at British hands in 1818, Baji Rao had been living in forced exile in Bithur, near Kanpur (Cawnpore), and receiving from the Company a handsome pension of Rs 8 lakhs a year. However, Dalhousie rejected the claim of Baji Rao's adopted son, Nana Sahib, to his father's pension, titles and honours.

Thus the India of the 1850s contained several influential individuals reacting against dispossession and rejection, and other chiefs and princes who feared a similar fate. When in 1856 their ranks were joined by Wajid Ali of Avadh, sadness in his kingdom was widespread, even though 'the Nawabs who succeeded Saadat Ali Khan, one after the other, [had] increasingly abandoned the attempt to govern and returned into the zanana, where they amused themselves with wine, women and poetry.'[2] Dirges were sung, and the departing king was 'followed all the way to Kanpur.'[3]

Wajid Ali and his predecessors had not administered Avadh well, and corruption was rife, yet Avadh had not seen the anarchy that had marked the Punjab after Ranjit Singh's death. Moreover, the annexation violated an 1837 treaty between the Avadh ruler and the Company that included a promise not to take over Avadh.

British officials arriving in Lucknow in 1856 were therefore not greeted with the relief felt by at least part of the population in

Lahore when Henry Lawrence arrived there as Resident in 1845-46.

Oddly enough, it was Henry Lawrence who in March 1857 took charge in Lucknow as the Chief Commissioner of Oudh. Conscious as Lawrence was of the risks in alienating traditional chiefs, in Avadh he had to preside over the land and revenue policy favoured by his brother John and prescribed by Dalhousie. This policy, tried out with apparent success in the neighbouring North-Western Province (the north-western part of modern U.P., with Agra as its capital) aimed at curtailing the influence of talukdars and jagirdars, and settling revenue and land questions directly with the village community or the village proprietor.

In accordance with the new policy, the annexation of Avadh was followed by a stringent inquiry into the titles of the province's talukdars, as a result of which a number of them lost large portions of their tracts. Some of them Muslims and many of them Rajputs, the talukdars of Avadh had 'enjoyed an independent right to a share of the produce and controlled law and order through their own militia.'[4]

In his valuable study of the Avadh of 1857-58, Rudrangshu Mukherjee, while cautioning against romanticizing the talukdar-peasant link, refers nonetheless to 'the well-knit relationship between lord and peasant and the care and protection the former provided' in return for the peasant's labour, loyalty and willingness to take up arms on the talukdar's behalf.[5] Of course, fear and force also entered the relationship.

Following annexation and the new settlements, talukdars like Beni Madho and Hanwant Singh, destined to play significant roles in the Rebellion, lost about half their villages. Even so their peasants did not become pro-British. Bewilderment rather than gratitude was their reaction to the dispossession of their masters and the deposition of their king.

The perturbation did not leave untouched the sepoys, who at bottom were only Avadh peasants in a queer uniform. Moreover, the sepoys were members of caste fraternities where important matters were decided upon in common, communication was swift, and dissent punished with ostracism or worse. At least one farseeing Englishman, W.H. Sleeman, had indeed 'warned Dalhousie that annexation would lead to mutiny in the Bengal Army, for Oudh was "the great nursery of the sepoys." '[6]

*

The sepoys' dilemma: On Sunday 29 March 1857, in Barrackpore near Calcutta, Mangal Pandey, an Avadh sepoy in the 34th Native Infantry, who later admitted under examination that he had been taking opium and bhang, threatened British officers with a loaded gun and exhorted his fellow sepoys to join him. 'It is for our religion,' Pandey shouted. 'From biting these cartridges we shall become infidels.'

Ordered to shoot at Pandey, other sepoys refused. A White officer was told that 'the sepoy was a Brahmin and no one would hurt him.'[7] In his excitement Pandey shot himself but survived. Eventually he was overpowered, tried and executed.

The incident sparked off widespread disaffection. Officers in far-apart cantonments noticed that sepoys would murmur or hiss when told of Mangal Pandey's execution. That they could be executed for refusing to risk pollution seemed both alarming and outrageous, and they suddenly wondered whether the British were not coercing them out of their caste or religion.

In previous chapters we paused at times to mark the success of the British in eliciting trust from different sections in India. In 1857, arriving on top of an annexation that had come across, even to the sepoy, as a breach of trust, the cartridge question jolted, in the core of the sepoy's being, his faith in the British; it injected panic and deep anxiety into that core.

Towards his British officer the sepoy harboured some positive feelings. If the sepoy performed chores for the officer, and when necessary for the officer's wife and children, the officer was at times personally thoughtful towards the sepoy. The words 'nigger' or 'suar' ('swine') and similar racial slurs were on occasion hurled at sepoys,[8] yet this did not always prevent the sepoy from feeling grateful for what an officer might do for him, or from recognizing that he and his family were eating the Company's salt.

Yet in the summer of 1857 it seemed to the sepoys that in order to remain true to their salt, they had to become false to their blood. Salt versus race, loyalty versus religion, a personal bond versus a terrible fear—such were the hopeless terms in which the sepoys saw their dilemmas.

In the Mahabharata, Karna chooses Kaurava salt over his Pandava blood, and salt binds Bhishma and Drona even when inclination draws them towards the Pandavas. But Karna had powerful grudges against the Pandavas, and in remaining loyal to the Kauravas Bhishma and Drona did not have to betray their clan or religion.

The sepoys' dilemma seemed fiercer. It did not take long for alarm to turn into arson. Pandey's death was followed by a spate of fires that destroyed stores, offices and bungalows in several Bengal Army stations across northern India. However, while troubled and perplexed, most British officers were inclined to dismiss any possibility of *their* sepoys mutinying.

*

'*To Delhi !*': On 24 April sowars of the 3rd Light Cavalry in Meerut, of whom a majority were Muslims, made plain their unwillingness to handle the new cartridges. Truthful explanations that the cartridges were now free of beef or pork were disbelieved. On 9 May, before an assembly of all the soldiers in Meerut, including European troops with their guns and rifles loaded, eighty-five disobedient Indian soldiers of the 3rd Light Cavalry were 'stripped of their uniforms; their boots were removed and their ankles shackled.'

The next day a number of British officers and soldiers and the wives and children of many of them were killed in Meerut by mutinying sepoys and sowars, who had been joined by some town ruffians, and the eighty-five soldiers serving punishment in jail were freed.

A British lieutenant heard galloping hoofs and a voice shouting, 'Quick, brothers, quick! Delhi, Delhi!' Men of the 3rd Light Cavalry were on their way to Delhi, where they hoped to secure the blessing of Bahadur Shah Zafar, the Mughal Emperor under British protection. They hoped, too, to secure the support of the three native Bengal Army regiments located in Delhi, which, as the sowars seemed to know, contained no British troops that day.

Meerut had not quite been taken over by the rebels, but, reeling from the day's assaults, its British force was unable or unwilling to pursue the Delhi-bound horsemen.

Bahadur Shah, poet and lover of animals and birds, was eighty-two. Consuming no beef, he took part in Hindu festivals and appointed Hindus to offices in his household. Along with a vast body of near and distant relations, he lived in Delhi's Red Fort. If his personal quarters were comfortable, most of the relatives resided in varying degrees of squalor.

He had no power, but his British masters, who were providing him with a pension, treated Bahadur Shah with great courtesy and kept up the fiction that he was a sovereign.

On the morning of 11 May the king was disturbed by the 3rd Cavalry sowars. 'Help, O King!' they cried up to his windows. 'We pray for assistance in our fight for the faith.' Not knowing the rebels' strength, Bahadur Shah played for time; he also managed to send word to the British at Agra that rebels from Meerut were pressurizing him.

More sowars arrived from Meerut, and soon all of Delhi seemed to be in revolt. Europeans, Anglo-Indians and Indian Christians were slaughtered. Yielding to the rebels' urgings, Bahadur Shah declared his independence from the British and allowed himself to be proclaimed King of Hindustan. A large number of British women and children were also killed in Delhi, including several within the Red Fort's walls, but a few European fugitives, sometimes ingeniously aided by a dhobi, bhishti or sweeper, trudged furtively to safety in Meerut or Karnal.

The firanghis were destroyed or thrown out of Delhi but were able, as we saw earlier, to send a telegram to the Punjab. They also managed to fire the magazine on the Ridge to the north of the city walls. An immense store of ammunition was stored in the magazine; the explosion shook all of Delhi and its neighbourhood.

*

Making a choice: Mutinies in Aligarh, Etawah, Mainpuri, Etah and Lucknow, in that order, followed the Delhi massacre. As Mukherjee puts it, 'It was as if the mutinies were travelling down the Ganges valley from Meerut and Delhi.'[9] In June more units revolted in the area north of the Jamuna between Delhi in the west and Ghazipur in the east—this was the rebellion's core territory, and May and June 1857 the core period.

The infection did not stay confined to the sepoys. Towards the end of May, an Indian agent informed the British that newly-recruited policemen serving near Lucknow had said to him that they would not fight the rebelling sepoys. They had added:

> Kala kala admee sab eyk hyn. Deen kee bat hyn. Hum log kahi ko bey dhurm ho? ('All black men are one. It is a question of our faith. Why should we lose our religion?')[10]

So at least in some places the mutiny was turning into a racial clash between black and white. The remark also hints at remembered humiliation.

Mukherjee suggests that 'the sadistic cruelty' by Indians in 1857 could have been a 'replicat[ion of] the mercilessness and violence they (the sepoys) had seen in the sahib.' 'Sepoys,' he says, 'had had to tolerate abuse and kickings, disgrace in front of comrades, and floggings; they had seen their comrades blown from guns.'[11] That the British indulged in such cruel practices is clear from the records; whether these practices were the norm before the 1857 slayings of Britons in Meerut, Delhi, and, later, in Faizabad, Sitapur, Sultanpur, Kanpur and elsewhere is less clear.

Yet it seems pointless to ask whose cruelty came first in 1857, and whose qualified as replication or retribution. Mercifully there is evidence that here and there in 1857 impulses of pity and ingenuity preserved lives that seemed doomed.

Hanwant Singh, the Kalakankar talukdar, sheltered an officer called Captain Barrow, but soon felt he had to join the rebels. Recorded by Barrow, his words to the latter on the eve of his rebellion tell us much about 1857 and its causes. In their righteous resentment, the words also recall the eve-of-the-war scene in the epic where Karna turns down Krishna's plea that he should desert the Kauravas. Said Hanwant Singh to Barrow:

> Sahib, your countrymen came into this country and drove out our King (the Avadh ruler). You sent your officers round the districts to examine the titles to the estates. At one blow you took from me lands which from time immemorial had been in my family. I submitted.

> Suddenly misfortune fell upon you. The people of the land rose against you. (As Mukherjee points out, this is a reference to Avadh's sepoys.) You came to me whom you had despoiled. I have saved you. But now—now I march at the head of my retainers to Lakhnao to try and drive you from the country. (By country he appears to mean Avadh.)[12]

*

From 1856 the Governor-General in Calcutta had been Lord Canning, who had succeeded Dalhousie, the 'man of firm, decided views and of masterful disposition.'[13] Canning had been a member of different governments in London, and his father had died as Prime Minister. Enraged by the news of the Meerut and Delhi massacres, the British in Calcutta attacked Canning for his supposed leniency towards the rebels. In a letter to Queen Victoria, Canning described their mood:

> There is a rabid and indiscriminate vindictiveness abroad,
> . . . which it is impossible to contemplate without a feeling
> of shame for one's own countrymen . . . Not one man in ten
> seems to think that the hanging and shooting of forty
> thousand or fifty thousand men can be otherwise than
> practicable and right.[14]

To the Governor of Ceylon, Sir Henry George Ward, Canning
wrote of 'the rabid unreasoning spirit of blood and vengeance . . .
activating the European community.'[15] Another of Canning's letters
indicates his keenness to remain level-headed:

> As long as I have breath in my body, I will pursue no other
> policy than that which I have been following, not only for
> the reason of expediency but because it is just. I will not
> govern in anger. Justice, and that as stern and inflexible as
> law and might can make it, I will deal out. But I will never
> allow an angry or indiscriminate act or word to proceed
> from the Government of India as long as I am responsible
> for it.[16]

Brave and wise words, in line with words in similar vein from Vidura
or Yudhishthira, and perhaps not much more effective in taming a
storm of blood and vengeance. Yet Canning's stand and policies, and
the backing he received from Victoria, probably helped in guarding
some areas from the storm's destructiveness. The British in Calcutta
tauntingly called him 'Clemency' Canning and petitioned the Queen
for his recall, but Victoria, who rejected the petition, seemed willing
to learn from the trauma. In a letter to Lady Canning, the Queen
said:

> I think that the greatest care ought to be taken not to
> interfere with their (the sepoys') religion.[17]

*

'Cawnpore' and Lucknow: Cruelty and vengeance reached terrifying
heights in Kanpur in June and July. Though lacking the history
possessed by cities like Delhi, Agra, Benares and Lucknow, Kanpur
had for decades served as an army station for the British and by 1857
grown into an important commercial town of about 60,000 people.

Part of the North-Western Province, it lay on the Ganga's western bank. Across the river was Avadh.

There were four Indian regiments in Kanpur, giving Indian soldiers a ten-to-one edge in numbers. Moreover, many of the Europeans were invalids. However, led by a sixty-seven-year-old Major-General, Sir Hugh Massy Wheeler, British officers seemed to believe in the loyalty of Kanpur's Indian regiments; and they derived additional comfort from the special relationship they seemed to enjoy with Dhondu Pant, better known as the Nana Sahib, the adopted son of the last Peshwa.

We noted earlier that for thirty-three years, Baji Rao, the last Peshwa, had lived in Bithur, twenty or so miles away from Kanpur, on a princely pension from the Company, and that Nana Sahib had resented the pension's discontinuance on his adoptive father's death. The thirty-five-year-old Nana Sahib inherited his father's palace, retainers, horses, elephants and other assets, but the British refused to concede to him either the title of Maharaja of Bithur or the right to a salute as the Peshwa's heir.

To obtain these honours the Nana Sahib had spared no effort. He had even sent to London an emissary called Azimullah. But the British had not budged, and the Peshwa, as Nana Sahib felt himself to be, nursed a deep grievance.

If despite this some of the British felt strengthened by Nana Sahib's proximity, it was in part because he had been friendly and hospitable to a series of British officers calling at Bithur, who were impressed with the Nana Sahib's skill at billiards and called him the Maharaja even if Calcutta and London did not, and also because General Wheeler's wife was an Indian of the same caste as the Nana.

In May, Nana Sahib 'arrived at Cawnpore with three hundred men, cavalry and infantry, and protestations of support for the English cause.'[18] Visiting Lucknow a few days earlier, he had aroused the suspicions of Avadh's Financial Commissioner, Martin Gubbins, and of Chief Commissioner Henry Lawrence, but Wheeler apparently saw 'no reason to distrust the man . . . who was always perfectly agreeable with him.'[19]

Nana Sahib was asked by Wheeler to take charge of the Government Treasury in Kanpur's suburb of Nawabganj. All the British in Kanpur, civilian and military, men, women and children, had by this time been assembled in the army barracks to the east of the city, about a mile from the river bank. Comprising two main buildings, one with a thatched and the other with a pukka roof, and some outhouses, the barracks area was surrounded by a trench and a four-foot-high mud wall. Its inmates called it the Entrenchment.

On 5 and 6 June Kanpur's Indian regiments mutinied. The 2nd Cavalry made for the Treasury, where Nana Sahib's men helped them to take over. A rebel deputation called on Nana Sahib and asked him to lead them. Though he evidently wrote later that he had 'joined the rebels from helplessness,' the appeal to lead caught his imagination.

Apparently, when the leader of the rebel deputation told Nana Sahib, 'Maharaja, a kingdom awaits you if you join our enterprise, but death if you side with our enemies,' Nana Sahib's reply was:

> What have I to do with the British? . . . I only pretended to help them. At heart I am their mortal enemy . . . I am altogether yours.[20]

Led by Nana Sahib, the four regiments were on the road to Delhi, intending to fight the British under the Mughal banner, when the Nana was apparently advised, chiefly it seems by his confidant Azimullah, that leading the rebels in and around Kanpur would suit his prestige more than serving a decrepit Muslim king as a subordinate.[21] The rebels returned to Kanpur, and General Wheeler was informed on the morning of 6 June that his Entrenchment would soon be attacked.

A rebel administration took over Kanpur and its environs; a rebel subedar, Tika Singh, was appointed General and Commander-in-Chief; the Entrenchment, cut off from Lucknow and everywhere else, was shelled and besieged, and casualties daily occurred in it.

Being chronic diarists, and being resourceful, moreover, in protecting diaries from disasters, the British managed to bequeath to the future portrayals of the heat, starvation, injuries and deaths in the battered Entrenchment. We can look at some fragments:

> All through the first day's bombardment the shrieks of the women and children were 'terrific,' but after that ordeal of initiation, 'they never uttered a sound except when groaning from the horrible mutilations they had to endure' . . .

> The General's son, Lieutenant Godfrey Wheeler, his 'favourite darling son,' as his father called him, was sitting on a sofa, recovering from a wound while one of his two sisters fanned

his face, when a round-shot came hurtling over the mud wall and knocked his head clean off.[22]

The Entrenchment survived longer than anyone expected. Into a well just outside the trenches the British tipped 250 of their bodies before the siege was over. But on 25 June a Eurasian woman arriving in a palanquin brought an offer signed by Azimullah that General Wheeler and the other exhausted survivors accepted:

> All those who are in no way connected with the acts of Lord Dalhousie, and are willing to lay down their arms, shall receive a safe passage to Allahabad.[23]

The acceptance of the terms of surrender and safe passage, the trudge to the river of several thin, half-naked, one-armed, one-legged men and women and their more fortunate companions, all weary and yet none entirely without hope, a procession in which, in Trevelyan's words—

> Step was not kept . . . Little was there of martial array, or soldier-like gait or attitude. Lace might not be seen, nor embroidery, nor facings, nor uniforms . . . The show was not such as would dazzle a vulgar eye: but in the soul of those with whom glory is not skin-deep, the retinue of an imperial coronation would fail to inspire the reverence excited by that ragged and spiritless cavalcade—,[24]

The entry of some of them into boats at Satichaura Ghat, the sudden shooting, the swinging sabres and clubs, the falling bodies, the Ganga's reddening waters, the burning boats, the escape of a few British, the arrest of the remainder—these scenes of 27 June 1857 have been described in more than one book.

So have the scenes that occurred in the second week of July in the Bibighar, fifty yards from the hotel that Nana Sahib was now occupying—the announcement that the survivors of Satichaura Ghat and other European hostages would be slaughtered; the threat of the women of Nana Sahib's household to leap out of upper windows if more killings occurred; the slayings that nevertheless took place, including of women and children; the dragging of the dead by the hair; the filling of the Bibighar well with the dead, and in some cases still living, bodies; and more.

Between these dates, Nana Sahib had been crowned Peshwa, rewards to the troops had been announced, Kanpur had been illuminated, and a proclamation informed the populace that 'by the kindness of God' all the Christians in Delhi and 'at other places' had been 'destroyed and sent to hell by the pious and sagacious troops, firm in their religion.'[25]

Meanwhile, however, two hard-nosed British officers, General Henry Havelock, sixty-two and no more than five feet tall, and Colonel James Neill, who thought himself a worthier commander than 'Mr Pomposity,' as Neill's staff referred to Havelock, were advancing with their separate columns from Calcutta towards Kanpur—and Lucknow. There too the British were under siege, although the Residency into which the British in Lucknow had withdrawn provided a somewhat better defence than Kanpur's Entrenchment.

Havelock's and Neill's summer marches through Bihar, Benares and Allahabad and intervening country; the fierce battles and the cruel punishments meted out sweepingly to rebels and their supposed supporters during these marches, especially by Neill's soldiers, well before they learned of the Kanpur massacres; the reinforcement and eventual relief of the British in Lucknow, where Henry Lawrence, however, had been killed by a shell; and the unspeakable cruelties that followed Neill's discovery of the Satichaura and Bibighar outrages are also well known.

We should however mention Neill's remark that he could not control his feelings in Kanpur after seeing ladies' and children's slippers, petticoats, straw hats and prayer-books covered with blood, and his resolve 'to punish with the most savage ferocity'[26] the people he presumed were responsible for the outrages. Neill ordered that

> every stain of . . . innocent blood shall be cleared up and wiped out, previous to their execution, by such miscreants as may be hereafter apprehended, who took an active part in the mutiny . . . The task will be made as revolting . . . as possible, and the Provost-Marshall will use the lash in forcing anyone objecting to complete his task. After properly cleaning up his portion the culprit is to be immediately hanged [at] gallows . . . erected close at hand.[27]

In obedience to this order, the victim, before being hanged, was required to kneel down and lick clean a square foot of the Bibighar floor covered with dried blood, 'which would previously be moistened with water by natives of the lowest caste.' Kept in force for three months, the order resulted in the humiliation and hanging in the Bibighar of dozens and perhaps hundreds of Indians, including a large number 'who had no direct connection with the murders.'[28] As Hibbert notes,

> Private Metcalfe of the 32nd said that the Highlanders knelt down on being taken into the building and 'took a Highland oath that for every one of our poor creatures who were thus slain, 100 of the enemy should bite the dust, and I need not add that they kept their vow.'[29]

Once more, then, despite 'Clemency' Canning, sacred oaths of revenge, invited by ghastly sights and ghastlier rumours. Clergymen supported calls for vengeance. The rebels had 'imbrued their hands in the innocent blood of women and children,' the Rev John Rotton wrote, '. . . and that very blood was appealing to heaven for vengeance.'[30] When a volunteer was sought for executioning a mutineer thought to be involved in the Kanpur massacres, 'every man in the company stepped forward to offer his services.'[31]

*

In Lucknow, the sepoys mutinied on 30 May, and the Residency into which all the Europeans of the city and 700 Indian soldiers had crammed themselves was under constant bombardment. On 2 July a shell exploded in Henry Lawrence's room, and he knew the end had come. Several times before his death, which occurred two days later, he asked that his tomb should state, 'Here lies Henry Lawrence who tried to do his duty. May the Lord have mercy on his soul.'[32]

Those enforcing the Lucknow siege included the mutinying sepoys and a league of Avadh's talukdars, each of whom brought a personal army to the city. In rebel ranks a special position was held by Begum Hazrat Mahal, one of the wives of the exiled and now imprisoned Avadh ruler, whose ten-year-old son Birjis Qadr was crowned king to provide a symbol for the rebellion. Proclamations issued in Qadr's name asked for Hindu-Muslim unity and for the killing of Europeans and Christians. A Maulvi from Faizabad called Ahmadullah imparted fiery zeal to the effort in Lucknow.

Interestingly enough, Mughal suzerainty was admitted during Qadr's coronation—the rebels wanted to confront the British Empire with the prestige of another, older empire. This had been true in

Kanpur as well. Though Nana Sahib had changed his mind about proceeding to Delhi, he took care to refer to Bahadur Shah as the King of Hindustan.

Lucknow's population and the Avadh countryside seemed to sympathize with the rebels and expected them to succeed in ousting the British; a year later a British official would estimate that 'probably three-fourths of the adult male population of Oudh had been in rebellion.'[33]

Even so, the British at the Residency twice managed to slip out an agent, a sepoy pensioner called Angad Tewari, to find out whether help was on its way. From his first mission Tewari had returned with the message that Havelock had Lucknow in mind but was not likely to arrive in less than twenty-five days. Tewari was sent out again 'with a letter which he concealed in a quill in his rectum.'

> Just before midnight on 22 September, . . . Angad came rushing through the lines, fired on by rebel sentries. He had exciting news to impart: Havelock had crossed the Ganges and would be at Lucknow within a few days.[34]

On 25 September, British and Sikh troops arrived in Lucknow. They were led by Havelock, Neill and General Sir James Outram, appointed Chief Commissioner of Oudh in succession to Lawrence; Outram elected to serve under Havelock, in rank his junior. The troops fought their way inch by inch along Lucknow's streets and lanes to the Residency. On the way they faced 'sheets of fire shooting out from the houses,' 'storms of grape,' and 'showers of musket balls.'

Neill was killed, shot by a rebel who 'fired a rifle held at arm's length,' as were about five hundred others on the British side and hundreds of rebels, but Havelock led the survivors to the Residency, where he was welcomed as a saviour. Vandalism and looting by the British and Sikh soldiers followed this success.

On 17 November Sir Colin Campbell, newly-appointed Commander-in-Chief of the British forces in India, also reached Lucknow with the Highlanders and other regiments from Calcutta. Every major palace, graceful building and fortification in the city was fought for. In face-to-face, room-by-room and merciless battles, with revenge as the British watchword and the rebels believing that to kill was the only way to survive, thousands on both sides were done to death, often brutally.

The slaughter inside Lucknow's Sikandar Bagh was 'appalling.'

Lieutenant Cubitt of the 5th Fusiliers wrote:

> There were hundreds of sepoys dead and dying . . . While
> there I saw 64 collected, drawn up and bayonetted with yells
> of 'Cawnpore'. God forgive us . . .[35]

Also referring to Sikandar Bagh, Lieutenant Fairweather would write
to his family:

> You may think me a savage, but I gloated over the sights of
> this charnel house. Who did not who saw the slaughter at
> Cawnpore?

Fairweather provided evidence that in Sikandar Bagh the British did
not refrain from killing women:

> Among the corpses were those of several women . . . I saw
> the body of a woman . . . and by her a dead baby also shot
> with two bullet wounds in it. The poor mother had tied the
> wounds round with a rag. McQueen (of the 27th Native
> Infantry) told me that he had seen a Highlander bayonet
> another woman . . .[36]

Despite the reinforcements, Campbell concluded that the British
position in Lucknow was highly vulnerable, and evacuating most of
the British unavoidable. The Residency was abandoned, but 4,000
British soldiers under Outram fortified themselves in Lucknow's
Alambagh estate.

Escorted by heavy guns and a large body of troops, a sprawling
procession of camels, horse-carts and ox-carts carrying British women
and children with their Indian servants and their belongings moved
out of Lucknow for Kanpur on 27 November. Havelock, however,
had died in Lucknow on 24 November following an attack of
dysentery.

Such was the strength of the rebels in Avadh and Lucknow that
it was not until March 1858 that a fresh force under Campbell
relieved Alambagh and recaptured Lucknow. The destruction, plunder
and drunken revelries into which the British and supporting troops
threw themselves in Lucknow troubled some of the British. Lieutenant
Ashton Cromwell Warner wrote to his family:

> Lucknow used to be the finest city in India and beat Delhi
> into fits. Some of the buildings are the finest I saw anywhere

in the world . . . But it is a most miserable looking city
now.[37]

The *Times* estimated that plunder worth a million and a quarter
sterling was collected by the British troops in Lucknow.[38] Little of it
was shared; the 'average' soldier or officer got next to nothing; but
certain estates in England, Scotland or Ireland found new owners.
Some accounts of Lucknow's orgiastic plunder could bring to mind
the excesses in Dwarka at the end of the Mahabharata.

One of those killed during the oft-risky exercises of plunder was
a man whose earlier role in Delhi we shall soon look at. Apparently
smelling booty, Captain William Hodson 'had dashed into a room
[in Lucknow's Begum Kothi], sabre in hand, and had staggered back,
shot through the liver.'[39]

*

A flaw: Before viewing the Delhi events and completing our
abbreviated account of the Rebellion, let us pause to recognize a flaw
which affects our grasp of it. Many of the diaries and letters that
numerous Britons wrote at the time are available to us. From these
documents the British victim or victor of 1857 comes across to us in
all his or her humanity. We get to know his or her name, family,
hopes, terrors, sorrows, doom or relief. In a word, we know 1857's
British cast in flesh and blood.

Not so with the Indian victims of 1857, who in numbers were
many times the victims on the British side. Few of the Indians appear
in diaries, letters or epitaphs. Though each possessed a face, a name,
hopes, memories, a personality, and loved ones, these are now
beyond recall. All we seem to have are rough numbers of the Indians
hanged, shot, bayoneted and blown off gun-mouths. Those on the
rebel side, or their relatives, did not favour posterity with diaries or
letters. Apart from a difference in education and an old Indian
disdain for recording what one sees or feels, surviving rebels were
probably wary of being caught with incriminating material.

Much of what we do know about the Indian victims comes from
references in British diaries or letters. Thus we learn that 'the sepoys
were of more imposing physique than the European soldiers.' Since
there was never a shortage of recruits, 'commanding officers were
able to choose only the strongest, tallest and most presentable-
looking men.'[40]

Almost every British account acknowledges the rebels' forbearance in the face of death. Thus a lieutenant wrote of 'a decrepit old man' who was 'severely wounded in the thigh' by a British sentry in Lucknow and captured:

> He was brought out and soon surrounded by a noisy, gaping crowd of soldiers, who clamoured loudly for his immediate execution . . . The only person of the group who appeared unmoved and indifferent to what was going on was . . . the old man himself whose stoicism one could not but admire . . .
>
> He must have read his fate a hundred times over in the angry gestures and looks of his captors but never once did he open his lips to supplicate for mercy or betray either agitation or emotion . . . He was given over to two men who received orders to 'destroy him.'[41]

Also in Lucknow's Sikandar Bagh, a Highlander called 'Quaker' Wallace shot someone firing from a tree. The body that fell was clothed in a tight-fitting red jacket and rose-coloured silk trousers. 'The breast of the jacket bursting open with the fall showed that the wearer was a woman.' She was armed with a pair of heavy pistols. Apparently Wallace burst into tears when he realized that he had killed a woman.[42]

The British observed that those hanged in Kanpur also took their end with dignity, and sometimes with defiance. A trooper called Potiphar wrote of a sepoy of the 10th Native Infantry who was condemned to hang:

> The man of the 10th before being hung spoke to the crowd, which was immense of both natives and Europeans. He made use of the words that he was satisfied to die and we need not think we were going to beat the Sepoys because they would yet beat us. [He was] then swung into eternity.[43]

One F.A.V. Thurburn, witnessing the hanging of a native officer from his regiment who had been adjudged guilty of mutiny, recorded that the Indian officer called out to him, saying, 'When you write to the adjutant remember me very kindly to him.' After uttering these words, the Indian, 'springing from the platform, . . . launched himself into eternity with the greatest nonchalance and coolness.'[44]

Also noted down by the British were some incidents when friendly sepoys 'protected their officers from harm, knocking down the muskets of others who would have shot them, or fetching carriages in which they could escape.' One officer, whose wife was also rescued by friendly sepoys, wrote:

> Three sepoys caught hold of me, and said they would try and save me. They threw off my hat, tore off my trousers, . . . and covered me with my horsecloth . . . Putting me between two, the third walked in front . . . We got through all the sentries and crossed the river.[45]

Havelock, whose long marches and relentless battles for relieving the Europeans in Kanpur and Lucknow had made him a hero in England, Europe and North America, was one of those who prescribed execution by the method of blowing from guns. Stating this in his *The Raj, the Indian Mutiny and the Kingdom of Oudh*, John Pemble adds:

> Two sepoys captured in Oudh were destroyed in this way. 'They were both extremely fine men,' wrote Major North, 'in the flower of their age, tall, athletic, graceful, with finely moulded limbs—almost resembling antique statues in bronze.'[46]

Also humanizing Indian victims and their loved ones is a reference by Frederick Roberts, who afterwards became Field Marshal Earl Roberts and commanded British forces in the Boer War in South Africa. In a letter to his sister from India in 1857, Lieutenant Roberts wrote:

> I came on three women watching the dead bodies of their husbands, none of them Sepoys I believe. It was such a sad sight, however, that I felt quite unhappy . . .[47]

Unlike the ordinary rebel, 1857's principal Indian characters have been written about in independent India, though not perhaps always with the detail and frankness that lends credibility to a portrayal:

> Kunwar Singh, the brave old leader of the rebels in what today would be called western Bihar and eastern U.P.;
>
> his relative Beni Madho Singh, the talukdar who became a folk hero in Avadh;

Begum Hazrat Mahal, who rallied Avadh;

Maulvi Ahmadullah, who roused anti-European and anti-Christian feelings but seemed to want nothing for himself;

Firoze Shah, the Mughal prince who, being out of Delhi at the time, had avoided Hodson's vengeance, and who later boldly spread disaffection among the residents of Avadh and the North-Western Province;

Nana Sahib, the Peshwa heir, who prevented neither the Satichaura massacre of those whose escape he had guaranteed nor the Bibighar massacre of his hostages;

Khan Bahadur Khan, the Rohilla chief; and, perhaps above all,

the heroic Rani Lakshmibai of Jhansi, who continued to give battle until the moment when she was killed in the summer of 1858, and

Ramchandra Panduranga, better known as Tatya Tope, the best of the rebel generals, always harrying and often surprising the British, whose unrelenting rebellion was cut short by a betrayal and consequent execution in the summer of 1859.

Narrating the major doings of these persons is outside this study's scope, but we will briefly touch on some of those named after taking another look at Delhi, which we left in May 1857, in the hands of the rebels and their king, Bahadur Shah Zafar.

*

Delhi retaken: Eliminated from Delhi in May, the British held on to their position on the Ridge to the city's north, and awaited reinforcements from the Punjab, where, as we saw, John Lawrence was collecting Sikh and Muslim recruits to add to all the European soldiers he could assemble.

If the British could breach or scale Delhi's walls, recapture the city, and dethrone Bahadur Shah, rebel prestige would evaporate, but despite Lawrence's keenness and, from Calcutta, Canning's urgings for speedy action, it took time for sufficient soldiers and a siege-train to arrive from the Punjab. Meanwhile the British on the Ridge, suffering losses from shelling and firing from the city walls and from illness, thought at times of forgetting Delhi and pursuing other objectives.

General Barnard, in command at the Ridge, died early in July. A fortnight later his successor, General Reed, handed over the command to Brigadier Wilson. British morale was not fully restored until the arrival from the Punjab, in the middle of August, of Brigadier John Nicholson and a large body of troops.

In the Punjab, Nicholson, a man with a massive chest, powerful limbs and a haughty air, had largely done civilian duty, mostly among warlike frontier tribes. Apparently the tribesmen had been impressed by 'the strength, talent and resolution' that his 'frame and manner' seemed to convey. The thirty-four-year-old Nicholson exercised a similar awe on the British on the Ridge.

Many of them probably shared Nicholson's view that those who had killed European women and children in Delhi should be 'flayed alive, impaled or burnt.' 'The idea of simply hanging' them was 'maddening' to Nicholson.[48] Another young officer with a reputation for toughness and retribution, Lt. William Hodson, had arrived from the Punjab two months earlier and taken over intelligence.

Spies had brought word to the Ridge that life in the city was disorganized, with soldiers demanding pay increases from the king and extorting merchandise from shopkeepers. Intense rivalry among the king's offspring, especially for control over the army, was also reported. Some order over the soldiers was apparently restored by Muhammad Bakht Khan of Bareilly, who had won Bahadur Shah's confidence.

While Bakht Khan prepared for a confrontation with the British, the king's physician, Ahsanullah Khan, was advising negotiations, a course probably favoured by Bahadur Shah. Feelers, however, were rejected by the British; and on 12 September Delhi was abuzz with talk that the king himself would lead a huge assault on the Ridge, and that by force of numbers the British would be defeated.[49]

Instead, it was the British who attacked. Constructing heavy batteries close to the city walls, they launched a cannonade that felled portions of the walls, and on 14 September four separate columns launched forth to enter Delhi, two to storm over shattered walls in the Kashmiri and Water Bastions, the third to blow Kashmiri Gate in, and the fourth to attack the suburbs outside the Kabul and Lahori Gates. Reserve forces would follow Nicholson who was to command all the columns once the assault was under way.

Disorganized though they were, the rebels worked and fought furiously, filling the breaches with stone and sand, occupying every height, crevice and vantage, and raining shells, bullets and masonry on the British and Sikh forces that tried to blast or climb their way in. Among the large number of officers and men fatally wounded on the British side was John Nicholson, shot in the back at Lahori Gate when, having turned around to face his men, he was urging them to press on.

Some of them needed urging, and Wilson in fact considered a recall. When Nicholson, who was 'slowly dying in his tent,' heard of Wilson's cogitations, he evidently 'cried out in fury, "Thank God, I have strength yet to shoot that man, if necessary." '[50] But Wilson did not order a recall, the assault continued, and though British losses were immense—over 3,800 British and supporting Indians died in the battle for Delhi between May and September, and over 21 per cent of the troops involved were killed between 8 and 20 September—, Delhi fell. Backed by greater firepower, and 'sapping forward from house to house,'[51] a force of 5,000 had captured a walled city defended by 40,000 men.

Many rebels and residents managed to get out of Delhi, and Bahadur Shah took refuge with his family in Humayun's Tomb, six miles south of the city. Learning from his spies of the royal family's move, Hodson, with Wilson's consent, went after them with a cavalry detachment and negotiated the king's surrender. Bahadur Shah was promised his life and taken into custody.

The next day Hodson obtained the surrender of two of the king's sons and a grandson without assuring them their lives. On the way to the city, Hodson shot the three dead with his own hands. To his family, Hodson wrote:

> Today, more fortunate still, I have seized and destroyed the King's two sons and a grandson (the famous, or rather infamous, Abu Bukt), the villains who ordered the massacre of our women and children, and stood by and witnessed the foul barbarity; their bodies are now lying on the spot where those of the unfortunate ladies were exposed. I am very tired, but very much satisfied with my day's work.[52]

'I have done it!' Bhima roars on killing Duhshasana. 'The oath I swore against this great sinner has been redeemed.' 'We have done our duty!' an exhausted Ashwatthama says to Kripacharya and

Kritavarma after their night's work of slaughtering the children of Draupadi and Dhrishtadyumna in their sleep. 'Let us go and give the glad news to Duryodhana before he expires. Let him die pleased.'

With similar eagerness, Hodson conveyed his glad news to his family. Not surprisingly, Hodson was silent about the basis, judicial or any other, for his conclusion that the princes had ordered and witnessed the massacres.

We may also note that one of Hodson's associates, MacDowell, recorded that the Sikhs accompanying Hodson 'shouted with delight' at the killing of the Mughal princes.[53] They did so because, among other things, they remembered the beheading in Delhi, almost two centuries earlier, of Guru Tegh Bahadur. Like the three princes' bodies, the Guru's body had also lain exposed for a time on Chandni Chowk.

A few days later, an additional twenty-one Mughal princes were hanged. Delhi was thoroughly plundered, and many of its inhabitants massacred. In Penderel Moon's words:

> The celebrated sacking of Delhi by the Persian, Nadir Shah, 118 years earlier, was rivalled now by British, Sikhs, Pathans, and Gurkhas. Every house and shop was ransacked, the soldiers ferreting out all articles of value and smashing whatever they could not carry away.[54]

The poet Ghalib, who had criticized the Rebellion, cried, 'The dust of Delhi thirsts for Muslim blood.'[55] With every suggestion of approval, a British official wrote at the time:

> All the city people found within the walls when our troops entered were bayoneted on the spot; and the number was considerable, as you may suppose when I tell you that in some houses forty or fifty persons were hiding. These were not mutineers but residents of the city, who trusted to our well-known mild rule for pardon. I am glad to say they were disappointed.[56]

An order to spare women and children was, as Moon put it, 'not always observed.' Moon quotes an assistant commissioner of Gurgaon called Clifford, whose sister had been killed in Delhi in May, as claiming to a friend that 'he had put to death all he had come across, not excepting women and children.'[57]

After being confined for eighteen months in a small Red Fort room, where he was stared at as a curiosity by European visitors, old Bahadur Shah Zafar, Babur's last reigning descendant, was tried by a military court for abetting the mutineers and allowing himself to be proclaimed India's king and sovereign, found guilty on 29 March 1859, and transported for life to Rangoon, where he died in 1862.

*

Before drawing some broad lessons from the Rebellion, let us look briefly at some others who played prominent roles in it. Described by Hibbert as a 'Rajput noble' who was 'generous and well-liked,' and by Moon as 'one of the best guerilla leaders produced by the Mutiny,' Kunwar Singh, the old talukdar of Jagdishpur, eluded British troops time and again, and led several damaging attacks on British positions in western Bihar and eastern U.P. These continued until the end of 1858, beyond Kunwar Singh's death.

Kunwar Singh's granddaughter was married to the son of an important Avadh talukdar, Rana Beni Madho Singh, who became the focus of rebellion in southern Avadh. A large number of peasants rallied under the banner of Beni Madho Singh, who, as Mukherjee puts it, became 'a folk hero . . . exalted in rustic songs.'[58]

Khan Bahadur Khan pestered the British in the Rohilkhand area around Bareilly for months until his defeat in May 1858 by Campbell's force. Maulvi Ahmadullah, who had escaped from Lucknow when the British re-took it, was even more irksome, raiding one British station after another in different parts of Avadh and also in Rohilkhand. For a while styling himself King of Hindustan and Khalifatullah, or Deputy of God, the Maulvi was killed early in June 1858 in Avadh by soldiers of the pro-British Raja of Pawayan, whose fort he had attacked.

For a period Firoze Shah, the Mughal prince, bolstered the efforts of the Maulvi and of Hazrat Mahal, who too had eluded the British, before being forced into exile in Mecca, where he died in poverty in 1877.

The pacification of Avadh was to prove a lengthy process. The rebels' frequent success in denying capture exasperated the British, who as a result were harder-hearted with those who were seized. Hibbert quotes the comment of one officer, Garnet Wolseley:

> Altogether I am thoroughly tired of this life. As long as any honour or glory was attached to it, of course I liked it, but now that the row or whatever it should be called has

degenerated down into pursuing small bodies of rebels without cannon and annihilating not fighting them, I take no interest whatever in the work . . .[59]

By the end of 1858, however, diligent operations led by Generals Colin Campbell and Hope Grant combined with promises to rebel leaders that surrender would not automatically lead to loss of their lands ended the resistance. Rebels refusing to surrender were driven into Nepal, where they were not welcomed by the ruler, Jung Bahadur. However, Hazrat Mahal and her son Birjis Qadr, who crossed into Nepal at the end of 1858, were allowed to stay.

Many rebels perished in the mountains of Nepal. In all probability, one of them was Dhondu Pant or Nana Sahib, though no evidence of his death appeared. After Kanpur was recaptured by the British, Nana Sahib had retreated to jungle hideouts, leaving his seal with Tatya Tope. During his flight, Nana Sahib, always thinking of himself as the rightful successor of the Peshwas who, but for the British, might have taken over India, sent fruitless pleas for support to rulers in different parts of India and even to Emperor Napoleon III of France.

Speculating on Nana Sahib's fate in his book *Cawnpore*, published in 1865, George O.Trevelyan wrote:

> Dhoondoo Panth . . . escaped across the Nepaulese marshes to a life of suspense, and toil, and privation amidst the Himalayan solitudes. The end of that man we know not, and may never know. Perchance, as they hover over some wild ravine or wind-swept peak, the eagles wonder at the great ruby which sparkles amidst the rags of a vagrant who perished amidst the snows of a past December. Perchance another generation will hear . . . that the world-noted malefactor is at last to expiate misdeeds already classical.[60]

Trevelyan's faint hope of Nana Sahib's capture was, as we have seen, denied, but the feeling vibrating from his sentences gives an idea of the impact of the Satichaura and Bibighar events on British minds at the time. Later British writers stated that Nana Sahib's direct responsibility for those events was never established, and suggested that the severity of preceding British punishments could have contributed to the Kanpur massacres.[61]

The reference by Trevelyan to Nana Sahib's 'great ruby which sparkles' offers an uncanny parallel to the 'shining jewel' which was part of Ashwatthama's forehead, and which Draupadi wanted prised out and fetched. Despite Trevelyan's wish, Dhondu Pant's ruby remained out of British reach, whereas Arjuna, Bhima and Krishna delivered Ashwatthama's jewel into Draupadi's hands.

Yet there are similarities. Both were sons of Brahmin warriors. If Ashwatthama killed Draupadi's young sons with his own hands, Nana Sahib failed to prevent the killing of British children who were in his custody. Both Ashwatthama and Dhondu Pant had taken revenge, and both invited retribution—in the Nana's case, on others as well as on himself. In the end, both wandered in the Himalayan solitudes.

*

Married when fourteen to the much older Gangadhar Rao, the Raja of Jhansi, Lakshmibai lost a baby before being widowed in 1853. Though a son had been adopted, the British did not recognize him as Gangadhar Rao's heir or Lakshmibai as regent. Jhansi was annexed and Lakshmibai given a pension. While resentful at the rejection of her pleas for recognition, the Rani seemed friendly to British officials, who noticed her popularity as well as 'the force and charm of her personality.'[62]

Early in June 1857, the sepoys at Jhansi mutinied, killing their British officers, opened the gaol gates, and made for the city fort where forty-odd Europeans and Eurasians, including women and children, had taken refuge. The British, who evidently thought that the Rani would come to their relief, were, however, all killed on 8 June, after the rebels had succeeded in entering the fort.

In a message to Major Erskine, Commissioner of the Sagar division, the Rani regretted the massacre and the 'faithlessness, cruelty and violence' of the rebels but pleaded helplessness before them. They had threatened to blow up her palace if she defied them, she said.[63]

Erskine agreed that until British replacements reached Jhansi, the Rani should 'manage the District for the British Government.' But when in March 1858 a large army led by Major-General Sir Hugh Rose and intent on revenge arrived in Jhansi, the Rani 'determined to fight' the British.[64]

In the fierce battle that followed, she was aided by the arrival of a force of 20,000 rebels led by Tatya Tope, but Rose's men succeeded both in forcing their way into the Jhansi fort and in repulsing Tatya

Tope's army. Destruction followed; every rebel who looked older than sixteen was killed if caught; rebels unable to escape threw their women and children into wells and then jumped in themselves; a room near the stables into which forty sowars had crowded themselves was set on fire, and in a re-enactment of a Mahabharata scene all the sowars were killed while rushing out in their burning clothes.

The European women and children had been avenged, and Jhansi was in ruins, every square ablaze 'with burning bodies and the city [looking] like one vast burning ground,'[65] but Lakshmibai had escaped and joined Tatya Tope's forces.

At Kalpi, where a strong fort was protected by deep ravines, the rebels were reinforced by the Nawab of Banda and his men and by Rao Sahib, a nephew of Nana Sahib. But the British were again successful, and the Rani of Jhansi, Rao Sahib and Tatya Tope were pushed to Gopalpur near Gwalior.

Jiyajirao Scindia, the ruler of Gwalior, had chosen to back the British, who he thought would defeat the rebels. It looked as if the Rebellion was over, but Tatya Tope had other ideas. Arguing that Gwalior's soldiers would join the rebels irrespective of the maharaja's preference, the irrepressible Tatya Tope decided on an attack on Gwalior.

The audacious plan worked. With their 11,000 men and twelve guns, the rebels, led by Tope, Rao Sahib and the Rani of Jhansi, forced the maharaja and his personal bodyguard to flee to Agra and won over the Gwalior soldiers to their side.

Daring as it was, the victory was short-lived. Rose and his men attacked the rebels' expanded forces, and on 17 June 1858, Rani Lakshmibai was killed after being shot in the back and then run through with a sword. When mortally attacked she was dressed as a man, using her sword with both hands, and holding her horse's reins between her teeth.

Canning would record that though her face was marked by smallpox, the Rani's eyes and figure were beautiful, and that 'when taken to die under the mango clump,' she distributed the pearl necklace she was wearing among her soldiers.[66]

Tatya Tope and Rao Sahib had, however, once more escaped, and for months British columns sent in pursuit failed to catch either of them. Tatya Tope's 'small but disciplined army' was helped by its excellent horses and by villagers who refused to betray them despite promises of large rewards.

In April 1859, Man Singh, the Raja of Narwar, who had a dispute with the ruler of Gwalior and thus seemed to be on the anti-British side, tricked and betrayed Tatya Tope. In a message to Tatya Tope, the raja said he needed advice on whether or not to join forces with Firoze Shah, who was continuing to elude the British; would Tatya Tope grant an interview? Tatya Tope agreed to meet Man Singh. 'As [Tope] lay down to sleep after a long talk with Man Singh,' the raja's soldiers 'closed in silently and pounced upon [Tope] and his two attendants.'

After Tatya Tope had been pinned down, Man Singh himself joined in shackling him. A quick trial took place, and Major Reade, who had induced Man Singh to betray Tatya Tope, read out the sentence of death by hanging. Hibbert quotes a British eyewitness of Tatya Tope's execution:

> He mounted the rickety ladder with as much firmness as handcuffs would allow him; was then pinioned and his legs tied, he remarking that there was no necessity for these operations; and he then deliberately put his head into the noose . . . [Later,] a great scramble was made by officers and others to get a lock of [Tope's] hair.[67]

Remorselessly though they had pursued the Rani and Tatya Tope, the British could not avoid respecting them. As Pemble puts it in his study,

> Rebel leaders who had fought with bravery and honour were not denied the final accolade of the admiration of their enemies.[68]

Rao Sahib kept himself safe from the British until 1862 when, like Tatya Tope, he too was betrayed and hanged.

*

Lessons and consequences: Now that we have surveyed the Revolt, we can attempt some generalizations about the Rebellion's lessons and legacy. It is clear, for one important thing, that the rebels saw their defiance as a war for religion. Whether issued in the name of Bahadur Shah Zafar, Firoze Shah, Birjis Qadr, Nana Sahib, or the sepoys, the Rebellion's proclamations invariably called for the protection of Hinduism and Islam, which were perceived as threatened, and warned Indians, as one of Feroze Shah's proclamations put it, that the British intention was 'to eradicate Hindooism and Mahomedanism and to make all people embrace Christianity.'[69] Once reprisals commenced, the sepoys' war also became one of survival.

Restoration was a key impulse for the rebels' major supporters. Thus Hazrat Mahal and her son wanted Avadh restored to them, Rani Lakshmibai wanted Jhansi back, Nana Sahib desired the Peshwa's title and pension, and the talukdars of Avadh wanted their lands returned. Though rebel leaders frequently spoke of eliminating the British and at times of restoring the kingdom of Hindustan, neither the independence of India nor the freedom of individual Indians, in the sense in which later Indian leaders were to speak of these concepts, appeared to feature in their minds.

As against the rebels attached to the status quo, the British seemed to be 1857's radical party. Confined to north and central India and receiving wide popular backing in Avadh, the Revolt aimed at destroying the British, but not at providing either an alternative set of rulers or an alternative way of ruling.

The reasons for the Revolt's failure are well known. By quickening communication, deployment and reinforcement, the telegraph wire saved the British. The new Enfield rifle, whose cartridges triggered the Rebellion, and heavier guns gave the British the edge in combat.

The rebels were hurt by their limited awareness of British strength and numbers. A few of them believed in the daydream that the British Isles' manpower had been used up. Noticing the Highlanders coming to fight in their kilts, some of the rebels seem to have 'cried with joy that the men of England had been exhausted, and that the Company had been reduced to call out the women.'[70]

If underestimating the foe proved costly, more crucial was the fact that not many in the India of 1857 shared a concept of Indian nationality. Surendra Nath Sen emphasizes in his study that while the people of India might have felt in 1857 that 'they had something in common as against Englishmen,' Bengalis, Marathas, Punjabis, 'Hindustanis' and South Indians thought of one another not as kinsfolk but as strangers.[71]

A history of the Revolt written in Bengali by Rajanikanta Gupta, *Sipahi Juddher Itihas*, published in 1880, and excerpted by Ranajit Guha in his *An Indian Historiography of India*, includes the following observations:

In the event, the rebellion was limited to sepoys alone . . . Indians as a whole were not seized by the madness of

insurgency. Educated Indians, in particular, had nothing to
do with it . . . [The Bengalis] were never lacking in loyalty
. . . The Bengalis never allowed anything to blemish their
loyalty to the Raj.[72]

Writing not long after the suppression of the Revolt, Gupta is
anxious to establish Bengali loyalty. The mutiny of infantry regiments
in Chittagong and Dacca in November 1857 and of cavalry regiments
in Madariganj and Jalpaiguri in the following month is not allowed
to affect his argument. Yet in essence his conclusion seems valid, and
not just for Bengal.

Though only fragments have been cited in the foregoing pages,
evidence that the British sedulously practised divide-and-rule is
plentiful. We saw how the Sikh-Purbiah discord was worked on, but
the British missed few opportunities of reminding Indians of their
histories of conflict with other Indians.

During the Rebellion and for some years thereafter, a majority
of the British tended to assign 'most of the blame' to Muslims.[73]
Before the Rebellion, too, it had been lamented that 'the Crescent of
the Eastern Imposter still flies over the Hindostan.'[74] In the eyes of
quite a few British, the role played in 1857 by the Meerut sowars, the
Red Fort killings, and the prestige given to the Revolt by figures like
Bahadur Shah Zafar, Hazrat Mahal, Firoze Shah and Maulvi
Ahmadullah suggested Muslim dominance in the Revolt.

However, this view, from which some British dissented even
during the Rebellion, was gradually modified, and Hindus were held
to be as responsible as Muslims for it. The opinion of fellow-Britons
that the Rebellion had been instigated by 'ambitious [Muslim] zealots
[who] had never forgiven us for ousting them from their ancient pre-
eminence' was challenged by Trevelyan, who pointed out that the
mutineers in Kanpur had 'unanimously saluted the Nana as their
Rajah, and proceeded forthwith to choose [Hindu] leaders [to]
command them in the field.'[75]

Those ascribing the Revolt to Muslims were soon equalled in
influence if not in numbers by Englishmen who saw its roots in the
brains of wily Brahmins, underscored the preponderance of high-
caste Hindus in the Bengal Army, and warned that few Indians were
more dangerous than the Hindus pretending to be jogis or fakirs—
'the bloated, filthy, sensual wandering friars of the East; wild-looking
fellows, in orange or salmon-coloured linen, if by good luck they
deigned to wear any clothes at all.'[76]

The anti-Hindu findings of some Britons, and the anti-Muslim conclusions of others, would for decades provide ammunition for the disputes between Hindus and Muslims that broke out in the aftermath of the Rebellion. The joint Hindu-Muslim front witnessed in 1857-58 disintegrated following defeat. Now Hindus and Muslims separately sought a positive relationship with the British, highlighting *their* acts of loyalty in 1857-58 and, often, the rebellious deeds of the 'other' community.

We saw that the Revolt's incidents often recalled episodes from the Mahabharata. Terrifying bloodletting and revenge, deceit, treachery, and the dutiful role of greybeards and whitebeards were common to the Revolt and to the epic's battles. Particularly striking perhaps is the dilemma, reflected in both, over loyalty.

Some sepoys admitted after capture that a feeling of guilt had sapped their valour in battle. A British officer was told by them:

> Sahib, it has been all the work of fate. After what we had done, we never could fight. No matter whether your troops were black or white, native or European, we could not stand against them; our salt choked us.[77]

Also significant is a proclamation of Firoze Shah in which he stated that 'the killing of women and children had worked against the insurgents.' Quoting Firoze Shah, Mukherjee holds that 'in pragmatic terms the sepoys' sense of guilt undermined their morale.'[78]

We have seen a sense of guilt about *their* excesses coming across from some British comments during the Revolt. Reflecting on what he had witnessed in India in 1857-58 and on other battles he had covered, William Howard Russell of the *Times* came up with the following judgment:

> Conduct warfare on the most chivalrous principles, there must be a touch of murder about it, and the assassin will lurk under fine phrases. The most civilized troops will commit excesses and cruelties, which must go unpunished . . .[79]

If, as Russell observed, bloodlust was aroused during the Rebellion, and vengeance played its grisly part, we saw that a key role was also played by fear and panic. After rising in revolt, the rebels thought that they had to kill to survive; and fear clearly intensified the severity with which rebels were eliminated in the Punjab, as well as the cruelty displayed by the marching columns of Havelock and Neill.

The reluctance with which many of the Revolt's leading figures plunged into it is also of interest. As was the case with Mulraj in the Punjab in 1848-49, Bahadur Shah Zafar, Nana Sahib, Rani Lakshmibai and Kunwar Singh seemed to have been pushed into revolt by soldiers. The tail wagged the dog; the sepoys were the prime movers. The generalship of Tatya Tope, the courage of the Rani of Jhansi, and the defiance of Firoze Shah appeared in the later stages of the Revolt, too late one might say—after Delhi, Lucknow and Kanpur had been recaptured by the British.

Let us also mark that hurt pride and a breakdown of trust lay behind several switches in loyalty in mid-nineteenth century India. Mulraj and Chattar Singh Atariwala in the late 1840s and Hazrat Mahal, Nana Sahib and the Rani of Jhansi in 1857-58 all felt dishonoured and let down by the British. The consequences of their sense of betrayal gave the British much to think about, yet we should not forget the confidence in the British that preceded the feeling of betrayal. As we have noticed, trusting the British had become customary in nineteenth century India.

*

For averting future rebellions, some British voices urged a tougher military control over India, and others asked for the Christianization of Indians and the abolition of caste. Instead, a quite different approach was adopted, one for which 'Clemency' Canning and several other British officials in India had argued.

While conceding that Europeans should no longer be heavily outnumbered in the Indian Army, Canning and his supporters held that the Rebellion had sent a deeper lesson, which was that it was neither feasible nor wise to attempt to coerce Indians to alter their religious beliefs or customs sanctioned by religion or caste. In Hibbert's words, it was realized that 'the friendship of the Indian people was to be desired, not their enforced submission.'[80]

Arguing that the British could earn this friendship, Canning and his friends pointed out that thousands of Indian soldiers and camp-followers had fought alongside the British, much of India had remained calm, and in 1857 itself the universities of Bombay, Calcutta and Madras had been founded.

Read out on 1 November 1858 at every British station in India, a proclamation by Queen Victoria, approved by the British Parliament, seemed to suggest that London had backed the views of men like Canning. It was declared that the East India Company was abolished and that India was now ruled directly by the British Government. Also, the Government would honour all treaties the Company might have made with Indian princes, and refrain from annexing any more territory.

Victoria also assured religious freedom—'all shall alike enjoy the equal and impartial protection of the law.' Old customs would be respected—'In framing and administering the law, due regard [would] be paid to the ancient rights, usages, and customs of India.' Indians 'of whatever race or creed [would] be freely and impartially admitted to office in our services.' Finally, rebels who had not joined in murdering Europeans would be pardoned.[81]

Pemble, for one, suggests in his study of Avadh that in line with the last item penitent rebel talukdars were 'generally treated with leniency.' Divested of their lands but given small pensions, they were sent out of Avadh. Pemble's figures show that in Avadh 364 people in all were tried for rebellion. 'Of these 23 were executed, 115 transported, 13 imprisoned for less than three years, 27 flogged, 47 fined and 139 acquitted.' Fifty or so talukdars and small co-sharers lost their lands.[82]

When compared with the mass executions that followed the recapture of Delhi, Lucknow, Kanpur, Jhansi and other places, these figures indicate, as Pemble puts it, 'a mild reprisal.' Adds Pemble:

> The hysterical screams for vengeance had subsided with the fear that had inspired them, and as the British reasserted their strength and repaired their damaged pride their attitude grew more constructive and magnanimous. The old rancour and hatred disappeared.[83]

'War is at an end,' Canning, who after the proclamation became Viceroy as well as Governor-General, claimed in July 1859, adding: 'Rebellion has been put down . . . Order is re-established; and peaceful pursuits have everywhere been resumed.' Two years later Canning said that Avadh, which had been the heart of the Rebellion, was now 'so thriving [and] so tranquil that an English child might travel from one end of it to the other in safety.'[84]

Whether made a century and a half ago by a British Viceroy or in the 1970s by a British scholar, such unqualified assertions of transformation are bound to be disputed, yet the success of the British in regaining prestige and control was underscored on 1 January 1877 when, at a grand Delhi Durbar, Victoria was proclaimed Empress of India.

Indian princes responded warmly to the idea of a paramount ruler over them. In any case, following the Rebellion, they and India's landed aristocracy were treated with greater consideration by the British. The policies of Henry Lawrence, who had died, seemed to triumph over those of his younger brother, even though, two years after the retirement of Canning in 1862, John was appointed Viceroy. India's attachment to old values and ways was acknowledged.

Twenty years after the Delhi Durbar—that is, forty years after the outbreak of the Rebellion—, when Victoria celebrated her golden jubilee, the *Hindu* of Madras would say (22.6.1897):

> Everywhere Her Majesty's name is blessed and cheered to the echo by millions upon millions of voices of Hindus. In every Hindu temple and home, prayers . . . are being raised to the feet of the Almighty to bless our gracious and noble Queen-Empress.

Muslims expressed similar sentiments. True, the Indian National Congress, aiming to represent all sections of India and pleading for a role for Indians in the governance of India, had been formed in 1885. Still, every Congress session commenced with a reiteration of loyalty to the throne. Moreover, led by Sir Sayyid Ahmad Khan, the founder of what was to become the Aligarh Muslim University, a large section of Muslims seemed wary of the Congress. Fearing Hindu dominance in elected bodies, they seemed to prefer direct rule by British officials.

During the Rebellion, Sayyid Ahmad Khan, forty at the time, was in Bijnor in Rohilkhand, which had passed from Avadh rule to the British in 1801. Pluckily confronting the Muslim nawab who had taken over Bijnor on 20 May 1857, Sayyid Ahmad obtained a safe exit for the European men, women and children trapped in the area, including the collector of Bijnor, a man called Shakespeare.

Mahmud Khan, the nawab, asked Sayyid Ahmad to join the rebels, but Sayyid Ahmad is supposed to have replied: 'By God, Nawab Sahib, I say that British sovereignty cannot be eliminated from India.' After being proved right, Sayyid Ahmad, shattered by British reprisals, declined an offer from Shakespeare of rights over a rebel talukdar's lands, yet he had said in 1859 that it was his

> heartfelt desire and prayer to God that our Government and
> the people of India be so connected together as to be of one
> accord.[85]

In Etawah, not far from Bijnor, the British magistrate, a man called
Allan Octavian Hume, showed courage first in capturing rebels and
then in ensuring that 'they received as impartial a trial as the
circumstances allowed.' Also, he saw to it that 'methods which
caused the least suffering' were used for the seven who were to be
hanged.[86]

Hume's was the crucial role in the emergence thirty-seven years
later of the Indian National Congress. Aware that Indians involved
in political debate were more likely to keep thoughts of rebellion at
bay, Hume also sought, in his words, 'the fusion into one national
whole of all the different elements that constitute the population of
India.'[87] We can thus see that the Rebellion gave birth to two
significant political tendencies, one represented by Hume and the
Congress, and the other by Sir Sayyid Ahmad Khan.

But we should not forget another consequence. After 1857,
divide-and-rule became the cornerstone of British policy in India.

*

The American Civil War, in which even more blood was shed, and
the Indian Rebellion took place on opposite sides of the globe at
virtually the same time—the year 1856 heard the rhetoric that
triggered the Civil War, and General Robert E. Lee signed his
surrender in 1865. Yet few seem to have viewed the two coeval
contests together.

The differences are obvious. The Civil War was a clash between
Americans; the Rebellion set Indians against the British, Asians
against Europeans. The Civil War lasted longer, covered a larger land
mass, stirred a higher percentage of the population, took more lives.

As it progressed, slavery emerged as the central question of the
Civil War. Was an issue of comparable significance at stake in India
in 1857-58? We have seen that the rebels were not really fighting
either for the independence of India or for the freedom of individual
Indians.

Christians fought Christians in the American conflict. In the
Rebellion, although a number of Hindus and Muslims stood alongside

the British, Hindus and Muslims were repeatedly exhorted by the rebels to defend their faiths, while many among the British, officers and soldiers, thought that Britain had been charged by Providence to bring Christianity to a heathen land. They would fight to preserve the ability to do so.

It is this question related to religion that gives to the Rebellion a deeper meaning. That slavery was the issue was not obvious to many Americans when the Civil War started. The integrity of the Union and the rights of States seemed to be the questions in the foreground. Similarly, it took time for the British to realize that what was at stake in India was the right of Indians to their religious beliefs.

As we have seen, after the Rebellion the British rulers of India were persuaded to admit this right and to assure it through Victoria's proclamation. Many British, no doubt including several involved in governing India, continued to think that India needed Christianity, but pressure for this was given up. Their religious belief was a question to be left to Indians.

In time, this policy was backed by some missionaries as well, who argued that the moment coercion accompanied it, Christianity ceased to be Christianity. The separation of religion from the state, and of compulsion from Christianity, was thus the fruit of the Rebellion's bitter, crimson-coloured buds.

'Both read the same Bible and pray to the same God, and each invokes His aid against the other.' Lincoln's words about the irony of the Civil War cannot apply to the Rebellion. Perhaps, too, reconciliation in America after the Civil War was aided by the fact that the two sides subscribed to the same religion, and one, moreover, that exalted forgiveness.

It was harder, perhaps, for India's Hindus and Muslims and Christians from Britain to find reconciliation, but the explicit divorce of coercion from religion reduced the difficulties a little.

Improving the Indians' position in the European-Indian equation, this acknowledgment of their right of belief was, at the same time, a step in the direction of equality. The assurance in the 1858 Proclamation that positions in the Raj would be open to Indians can be seen in this light. Along with freedom of religion, an admission of eventual equality also, thus, came out of 1857.

So far we have looked at what the British learnt from the Rebellion, but Indians too had much to think about in the years that followed. Instead of uprooting the British, a fierce rising had brought misery to immense numbers of Indians. Were there other ways of restoring Indian rule? Linked to this was the difficult question of just what the Indian attitude to British rule should be.

Also, when and how would Indians think of themselves as one? They had not done so in 1857; even in North India, Avadh apart, the 'common Indian' had been reluctant to join the rebellion. Finally, if the question of greased cartridges, which impinged on religion-related taboos, could cause such an upheaval—in the end hurting Indians even more than it hurt the British—, did Indians also need to re-examine their attitude to religion, as the British were obliged to?

The questions were not immediately faced, and there were not many Indians, even during the decades that followed, who were willing to confront the entire range of them.

8

Freedom and *Reconciliation?*
Gandhi's Large Bid

NO SCHOLAR OF Gandhi seems to have noted the impact of the 1857 Rebellion on him, even though Gandhi himself indicated that the Rebellion was often on his mind. In his autobiography, first published in the mid-1920s, Gandhi relates how as a student in London he was rebuked on his poor knowledge of Indian history by Frederick Pincutt, 'a Conservative who nonetheless was helpful to Indian students,' and asked by him to read 'all the volumes of Kaye and Malleson' on the Mutiny. Adds Gandhi:

> I could not read Kaye and Malleson's volumes in England, but I did so in South Africa as I had made a point of reading them at the first opportunity.[1]

Gandhi probably read the six volumes in Pretoria during his first year in South Africa (1893-94), a phase of intensive reading that ended when in 1894 he founded the Natal Indian Congress. In one of the first issues (9.7.1903) of *Indian Opinion*, the journal Gandhi started in South Africa, Gandhi referred to the 1857-58 events and came out squarely on the rulers' side:

> [1857-58] was a year of great anxiety and trouble. At one time the cloud looked so black that even the final result had been a matter of uncertainty. An appeal was made to the worst superstitions of the people of India, religion was greatly brought into play, and all that could be possibly done by the evil-minded was done to unsettle the people's minds.

> At that time of stress and trouble the great mass of the Indian people remained absolutely firm and unshaken in their loyalty . . .

> [John Lawrence] turned to the very best account the loyalty of the martial races of the Punjab who had, only a few years

before, offered stubborn resistance to the British army at the
historic field of Chillianwala. (*Collected Works*, 3:357-58)

The article containing these lines was primarily political, not historical:
the thirty-four-year-old Gandhi was asking the Empire to protect
Indian rights in South Africa, and reminding London of Victoria's
1858 Proclamation which had assured equality to Indians. However,
his later deeds and words show that Gandhi's disapproval of the
Rebellion was more than an expediency. Two years after the article
cited above, he returned to the 1857 events and this time paid a
tribute to Henry Lawrence.

'The English people have progressed because men like him are
born amongst them,' Gandhi said. Referring to Henry Lawrence's
bravery, piety and sense of duty during the forty-eight hours when
he awaited death in Lucknow, Gandhi also acknowledged the fortitude
of the British and the Indians who jointly withstood the siege there.
(Gujarati *Indian Opinion*, 14.10.1905; 5:102-03)

In this 1905 article Gandhi noted that Henry Lawrence had
condemned 'the atrocities' the British perpetrated following the
Rebellion.

In a talk to the Emerson Club in London in 1909, while visiting
England on behalf of the Indians of South Africa, a Gandhi who by
now had discovered satyagraha, or nonviolent struggle, said that war

demoralizes those who are trained for it. It brutalizes men of
naturally gentle character. It outrages every beautiful canon
of morality. Its path of glory is foul with the passions of
lust, and red with the blood of murder. This is not the
pathway to our goal. (On 8.10.09, published in *Indian
Opinion*, 12.2.10)

The short, sharp, epigrammatic sentences no doubt owed much to
Gandhi's experiences while heading an ambulance corps in the turn-
of-the-century Anglo-Boer War in South Africa and a similar corps
in the 1905-06 Zulu War. But we can also perhaps link them to
Gandhi's study of the volumes by Kaye and Malleson detailing the
1857-58 bloodletting in India.

A year earlier, in 1908, after a bomb aimed by Indian
revolutionaries in Bihar at a British official ended the lives of two
Englishwomen, Gandhi had commented:

The bomb now thrown at Englishmen, will be aimed at Indians after the English are there no longer.[2]

Eight days before Gandhi's arrival in England for his 1909 visit, Madanlal Dhingra, an Indian student, had killed Sir Curzon Wyllie, ADC to the Secretary of State of India, at a reception in London to which the National Indian Association had invited Wyllie. Cowasji Lalkaka, a Parsi doctor who had tried to save Wyllie, was also killed.

Dhingra's deed had been inspired and perhaps aided by two men who were influential among Indian students in London at the time, Shyamji Krishnavarma, an ex-dewan of Udaipur, and Vinayak Damodar Savarkar, who wanted young Indians to be trained in bomb-making in Europe and who would soon write of the 1857 Rebellion as *India's First War of Independence*. The statement that Dhingra read at his trial was drafted by Savarkar. Varma and Savarkar eluded the British police but Dhingra was given a death sentence. Gandhi condemned Dhingra's deed in the clearest language:

> It is being said in defence of Sir Curzon Wyllie's assassination that it is the British who are responsible for India's ruin, and that, just as the British would kill every German if Germany invaded Britain, so too it is the right of any Indian to kill any Englishman ... The analogy of Germans and Englishmen is fallacious. If the Germans were to invade Britain, the British would kill only the invaders. They would not kill every German whom they met. Moreover, they would not kill an unsuspecting German, or Germans who are guests ... (*Indian Opinion*, 14.8.09; 9:302)

In 1919-20, after the Jallianwala and Khilafat events, Gandhi formally broke with the Empire, and the nonviolent Non-cooperation Movement of 1920-22 was launched. It challenged and shook British rule as nothing before had done, and Hindus and Muslims fought nonviolently from a common front. But Gandhi called off the struggle after an incident in Chauri Chaura in eastern U.P. in which a mob shouting slogans in support of the Gandhi-led movement had killed twenty-three of the Raj's Indian policemen.

Shock and demoralization followed the stoppage. In Chauri Chaura, after a trial of over a hundred accused, nineteen were hanged.[3] Arrested in Ahmedabad, Gandhi was charged with sedition. One of his articles cited to substantiate the charge had referred to the 1857 Rebellion and the excesses in its wake.

It is high time (*Gandhi had written*) that the British people
were made to realize that the fight that was commenced in
1920 is a fight to the finish, whether it lasts one month or
one year or many months or many years and whether the
representatives of Britain re-enact all the indescribable orgies
of the Mutiny days with redoubled force or whether they do
not. ('Shaking the Manes,' *Young India*, 23.2.22; 22:458)

Composed at the peak of the struggle against the Empire, the article
was a direct response to two utterances, a speech in Parliament by
Lord Birkenhead that warned India of Britain's 'hard fibre,' and an
assertion by the Secretary of State, Edwin Montagu, that

If the existence of our empire were challenged, . . . then
India would not challenge with success the most determined
people of the world.

Gandhi's reply referred also to empires 'intoxicated with the red
wine of power,' a remark that recalled the drunkenness marking the
1857 reprisals in Delhi and Lucknow by the victorious British. To
stand up to an intoxicated empire but to do so unitedly, fearlessly
and nonviolently, without any reenactment of 1857—this was what
Gandhi was asking India to do.

There was an echo of the 1857 Rebellion in Churchill's famous
comment on Gandhi in 1931. When, after Gandhi's successful Salt
March, he held talks with Irwin, the Viceroy, Churchill expressed
outrage that Gandhi, 'this former Middle Temple lawyer, now a fakir
of a type well known in the East,' had been invited to stride up the
steps of the Viceroy's palace to parley on equal terms with the
representative of the king-emperor. And this too shortly after Gandhi's
campaign had, in Churchill's words, 'inflicted such humiliation and
defiance as has not been known since the British first trod the soil of
India.'[4]

Churchill's reference to 'a fakir of a type well known in the East'
was suggestive of a British appraisal, noted in the last chapter, that
the 1857 Rebellion emerged from the brains of wily Hindus, and that
few Indians were more dangerous than jogis or fakirs.

Thanks to a seditious fakir's Salt March, Churchill was insinuating,
1857 had been repeated in 1930. He was unwilling to acknowledge
the wholly nonviolent character of the 1930 defiance. But the British
public, which had noticed the absence of violence, gave Gandhi an
extraordinary welcome in 1931 that contrasted sharply with the anti-

Indian rage witnessed in Britain in 1857.

In the last phase of his life, when Gandhi saw hate and violence swirl around him, he again recalled the horrors of 1857. On 24 July 1947 he said in Delhi:

> . . . we are nurturing attitudes that will result in [Hindu-Muslim] war and if this drift is not stopped we shall find ourselves in a conflict much more sanguinary than the Mutiny of 1857 . . . God forbid that! (88: 416)

*

Gandhi's guidelines: Not only was the Rebellion imprinted on Gandhi's mind; his life showed that unlike most of his compatriots, he faced the hard questions left by the Rebellion and its aftermath. The conclusions he came up with were as follows:

One, Indians had to be reconciled with one another if they were to free themselves. Not only across religion—Hindus, Muslims and the smaller minorities, Sikhs, Christians, Jains, Parsis and Jews—but also across caste and class. Untouchability was a great offence and blot, but caste Hindus had to be carried along in journeys of political and social reform. Given India's attachment to religion, the only realistic goal was to bring Hindus, Muslims, Sikhs and Christians together on common platforms; de-Hinduizing the Hindus or de-Islamizing the Muslims was not a practical proposition.

Two, independence had to free and empower the weak Indian, not transfer strength to those rich in arms, land and gold. As Gandhi put it in *Hind Swaraj*, India could not mean 'its few princes. To me it means its teeming millions.' In fifteen words written in 1909, each of a single syllable, Gandhi put his finger on a key weakness of the Indian elite:

> Those in whose name we speak we do not know, nor do they know us. (*Hind Swaraj*, Ch. 13)

In 1942, on the eve of Quit India, he claimed that the Indian revolution would be different from the French and the Russian. 'Though theirs was a fight for the people, it was not a fight for real democracy . . . My democracy means every man is his own master.' (76: 377-81)

Shortly before independence, in June 1947, he commended Jawaharlal Nehru, Vallabhbhai Patel, Rajendra Prasad and Rajagopalachari, Congress's leading figures in the interim government, to the people. But he added that if despite cooperation from the public and traders, India 'cannot have enough food and clothing,' then 'you can remove [the leaders] from office.' (88: 56)

That is, unless it empowered the citizen, independence was not worth much.

The third guideline was that the British had to be fought nonviolently. 1857 had shown that violent uprisings would be swiftly and ruthlessly suppressed. But there was another reason for nonviolence: violence would become a habit. 'The bomb now thrown at Englishmen will be aimed at Indians after the English are there no longer.'

Gandhi's nonviolence or ahimsa ('non-injury') was lifted from long-standing Hindu, Jain and Buddhist traditions but infused with new meaning. It implied active love (for the neighbour, the stranger, the weak) and also struggle.

How nonviolence became a central theme in Gandhi's life is not a question on which we will linger here. It has been gone into by several, including, in *The Good Boatman*, by this author. Suffice it here to say that for Gandhi nonviolence was both a principle and a strategy, and also that he reacted against the assault on life that violence represented and against its presumptuousness.

As Gandhi saw it, a killer assumed the status of God, ascribing to his stand a perfection no human could claim, and to his victim an irredeemability that no human could pronounce. Since all humans were fallible, no human being had the right to kill another.

We mentioned earlier that Gandhi's attitude was probably influenced by his familiarity in South Africa with the wounds of war. This inference is strengthened by Gandhi's remark about Tolstoy, whose long *Letter to a Hindoo*, urging Indians to resist England nonviolently, was translated by Gandhi into Gujarati in 1909. In a preface, Gandhi described the Russian as 'one of the clearest thinkers in the western world, one of its greatest writers, *one who, as a soldier, has known what violence is and can do.*' (10: 4-5)

Gandhi's control over the freedom movement and his insistence on nonviolent means probably laid the basis for the ascendancy of civil over military power for at least fifty-one years in free India. If guns had wrung independence from the British, those with guns might have ruled the new India.

Not that the independence that came in 1947 was solely attributable to the nonviolent campaigns he led and in which great numbers took part. Indians believing in violence also contributed to

the final outcome, as did British fatigue at the end of the Second
World War.

Gandhi's fourth guideline was that, for all the humiliation of
alien rule, the British could not be blindly opposed. Many sections
in India trusted the British; in some ways they were a cementing
factor. Also, the British held powerful cards, and evoking their
enmity could invite disruption.

In March 1918, three years after his return from South Africa,
Gandhi disclosed his innermost thoughts to a key recruit and aide,
Mahadev Desai:

> I have to cruelly suppress my urges. Ever since I read the
> history of the East India Company, my mind refuses to be
> loyal to the British empire and I have to make a strenuous
> effort to stem its tide of rebellion. The first thought that
> rises up in the mind is that the British should be driven out
> of India bag and baggage; but a feeling deep down in me
> persists that India's good lies in [the] British connection, and
> so I force myself to love them.[5]

The 'history of the East India Company' is a reference to the first
volume of Romesh Dutt's *Economic History of India*, published in
1901, but more relevant is Gandhi's sense, in 1918, that snapping 'the
British connection' could be risky.

Hence his insistence that opposition to British rule should not
mean violence, hate or dislike against British individuals or officials.
Or, as he put it in simpler terms, 'Hate the sin, not the sinner.'

Debatable maxim: On occasion, and especially in *Hind Swaraj*,
Gandhi also offered another maxim. To Indian militants eager 'to
expel the English by force of arms' Gandhi said: 'Your hatred against
them ought to be transferred to their [modern] civilization.'(Ch. 14)
Don't dislike the British, reject their civilization.

Gandhi's thesis was that nonviolence suited the genius of India,
whereas violence was inseparable from modern or Western civilization.
With support and encouragement from Leo Tolstoy, the Russian
thinker, Gandhi spelt out the thesis in *Hind Swaraj*.

His misgivings about modern civilization antedated *Hind Swaraj*
by many years. When he was twenty-five he wrote pejoratively in
the *Natal Mercury* of 'the dazzling and bright surface of modern
civilization. (3.12.94; 1: 139-40) The following year, in 1895, he spoke
of the 'utter madness of materialism [and of] . . . a civilization

[whose] greatest achievements are the invention of the most terrible weapons of destruction.' (*Natal Advertiser*, 1.2.95)

Yet Gandhi was also aware of the political potential of his thesis. It strengthened Gandhi in his confrontations with the Empire, enabling Indians fighting under Gandhi to feel that they held the moral high ground, above the violent British.

In his lifetime, the formulation also strengthened Gandhi in his clash with the Indian school of violence, a contest in which he was seen as the authentic Indian and his opponents, the pro-violence Indians, as the West's imitators.

Accepted in Gandhi's time and for some years later by numerous Indians, the thesis tended, however, to feed an old vein in India of self-righteous superiority, the notion that India was older, wiser and more spiritual than the materialistic West.

We know from Gandhi's life and doings that this was not his belief. In 1918 he reminded his British friend Charlie Andrews that 'incarnations' in Indian legends were 'bloodthirsty, revengeful and merciless to the enemy,' (14:474-75) and in 1946, in remarks in Noakhali, he again recalled the violence in India's past. (*Harijan*, 8.10.46; 86:134.)

We know too that though in *Hind Swaraj* he attacked railways, law courts and hospitals, he did not hesitate to use the railways to spread his anti-Raj views, a British-run hospital to have his appendix removed (in 1924) and his legal skill to protect the interests of the Indian National Congress in negotiations with the Raj.

In June 1920 Gandhi translated for *Navajivan*, his Gujarati journal, an item from the *Bombay Chronicle* claiming that 'the Hindus invented the decimal system, Geometry and Algebra were first developed in India, and so too Trigonometry,' that 'the first five hospitals to be built were in India,' that 'the physicians of ancient Europe used Indian drugs,' that 'the Ramayana and the Mahabharata remain unrivalled,' and so forth, and added this comment:

> I do not know how far these statements are true but this I know, that if the late Justice Ranade were alive today and heard such talk of India's past glory, he would certainly have asked, 'So what?' (20.6.20)

Yet *Hind Swaraj* had perhaps encouraged such non-productive talk of India's past glory.

*

Deduced by us from his life, the four planks of Gandhi's platform did not present themselves to him suddenly or as a revelation. Our linking them to the events and lessons of 1857 may be reasonable, but Gandhi did not emerge one day from a study of the Rebellion saying, 'Eureka.' His experiences, study and reflections—from 1892, if not earlier, until 1909—led Gandhi to the guidelines.

In what follows, we will focus on two of his guidelines: do not oppose the British blindly, and reconcile Indians with one another. We will try to see how Gandhi arrived at, pleaded for and adhered to his guidelines, and how India responded.

DEALING WITH THE BRITISH

Born in the port town of Porbandar in western India in 1869, ten years after the Rebellion ended, Mohandas Karamchand Gandhi seemed to have thought as a boy that with greater physical strength, attainable through meat-eating among other things, Indians could drive out the British. But studying in England became a passion with the lad; overcoming strong family and caste objections, he sailed for London in 1888. In a diary he kept in London, Mohandas wrote:

> I had a secret design in my mind of coming here to satisfy my curiosity of knowing what London was. (1:3)

He has a strong urge to know the foe. Also linked to the visit, however, was a hunger for 'reform.' Thanks to what *The Kathiawar Times* published in an 1888 issue, a translation of Mohandas's Gujarati remarks, we know what he said at the age of eighteen years and seven months at a formal send-off organized by his friends at Alfred High School in Rajkot:

> I hope that some of you will follow in my footsteps, and after your return from England you will work wholeheartedly for big reforms in India. (1:1)

England's rule was a humiliation; from England big reforms could be learnt. In Gandhi and others in India, this ambivalence never disappeared. As we have seen, Gandhi eventually resolved the paradox by deciding that he would oppose British rule but not hate the British; he would battle the British, nonviolently, and also seek reconciliation with them.

'Dear London': There is no evidence, in the autobiography, in his London diary or in later recollections of his student years that the

student Mohandas was slighted in England because of his race. During his three years of study he tried and gave up 'aping the English gentleman'—playing the violin, wearing the clothes in vogue, learning ballroom dancing—and became, thanks to some British friends, a vegetarian by choice, closely followed Irish politics, and despite some teetering on the brink kept to the vows against 'meat, drink and women' that his mother had insisted upon. We know of his reaction on leaving England:

> I could not make myself believe that I was going to India until I stepped into the steamship *Oceana* of the P. & O. Company. So much attached was I to London and its environments; for who would not be? . . . [It] was not without regret that I left dear London. (1:50-51)

On the voyage home he wrote, for the first and last time in his life, a couple of amusing articles that were published in *The Vegetarian* of London, and he seemed to toy with the idea of a literary career. But he had forebodings. In the autobiography he describes the state of his mind as the ship carrying him neared India in the late summer of 1891.

> The sea was rough . . . all the way from Aden. Almost every passenger was sick; I alone was in perfect form, staying on deck to see the stormy surge, and enjoying the splash of the waves. The outer storm was to me a symbol of the inner . . .

His anxiety was justified. Arriving in Bombay, he learnt that his mother had died. Some months later he received another shock, one that 'changed the course of [his] life.'

*

Humiliation: Charles Ollivant, the Raj's powerful political agent in Kathiawad, was a man Mohandas had met in England and found friendly enough. When Mohandas's brother Laxmidas heard of this contact, he was excited, for Ollivant was at this time examining an allegation that had blocked Laxmidas's advancement in Porbandar's princely court. (Karamchand, the father of Laxmidas and Mohandas, had been prime minister to the rulers of Rajkot and Porbandar, and Laxmidas felt entitled to a promotion.)

Mohandas was pressed by his brother to intercede with Ollivant. At first Mohandas declined, arguing that it would be unbecoming to take advantage of an acquaintance obtained in England. Laxmidas, who had helped finance Mohandas's studies in England, answered:

> You do not know Kathiawad, and you have yet to know the world. Only influence counts here. It is not proper for you, a brother, to shirk your duty, when you can clearly put in a good word about me to an officer you know.

Giving in, Mohandas asked for and secured an appointment. In the autobiography, Gandhi has recorded what followed:

> I reminded him of the old acquaintance . . . The Political Agent owned the acquaintance, but the reminder seemed to stiffen him. 'Surely you have not come here to abuse that acquaintance, have you?' appeared to be . . . written on his brow. Nevertheless, I opened my case. The sahib was impatient. 'Your brother is an intriguer. I want to hear nothing more from you. I have no time. If your brother has anything to say, let him apply through the proper channel.'
>
> The answer was enough, was perhaps deserved. But selfishness is blind. I went on with my story. The sahib got up and said, 'You must go now.' 'But please hear me out,' said I. That made him more angry. He called his peon to show me the door. I was still hesitating when the peon came in, placed his hands on my shoulders and put me out of the room.
>
> The sahib went away as also the peon, and I departed, fretting and fuming. I at once wrote out and sent over a note to this effect: 'You have insulted me. You have assaulted me through your peon. If you make no amends, I shall have to proceed against you.'
>
> Quick came the answer through his sowar: 'You were rude to me. I asked you to go and you would not. I had no option but to order my peon to show you the door. Even after he had asked you to leave the office, you did not do so. He therefore had to use just enough force to send you out. You are at liberty to proceed as you wish.'
>
> With this answer in my pocket, I came home crestfallen, and told my brother all that had happened. He was grieved but was at a loss as to how to console me. He spoke to his vakil friends, for I did not know how to proceed against the sahib.

Sir Pherozeshah Mehta happened to be in Rajkot at this time, having come down from Bombay for some case. But how could a junior barrister like me dare to see him? So I sent him the papers of my case, through the vakil who had engaged him, and begged his advice.

'Tell Gandhi,' he said, 'such things are the common experience of many vakils and barristers. He is still fresh from England, and hot-blooded. He does not know British officers . . . Let him tear up the note and pocket the insult. He will gain nothing by proceeding against the sahib, and will very likely ruin himself.'

The advice was bitter as poison to me, but I had to swallow it. I pocketed the insult, but also profited from it . . . *This shock changed the course of my life.* (Emphasis added.)

The clarity with which, in the autobiography, Gandhi remembers the details of a thirty-three-year-old incident confirms its importance in his life. We may mark, incidentally, that Ollivant's answer was sent through the sowar or horseman, a graphic symbol of power and, in 1857, of rebellion.

After the Ollivant episode, a literary career appeared to Gandhi an indulgence he could not afford. British officials in India were not like the people he had befriended in 'dear London.' Haughtiness ruled India, and Gandhi would have to fight it. In 1924, Gandhi recalled what it was that scotched his youthful interest in writing:

At the earliest period of my life it became one of storm and stress. It commenced with a fight with the then political agent of Kathiawar. I had therefore not much time for literary pursuits. (*Young India*, 4.9.24)

Also, after the clash with Ollivant, Gandhi could no longer contemplate practising law in Kathiawad. Ollivant was, among other things, the judge at the region's chief court, and Gandhi had no desire to milord the sahib there. When, therefore, Abdulla & Co., a Pretoria-based firm with Porbandar connections, asked if Gandhi would help with a case in South Africa, he at once agreed to go. As he puts it in the autobiography, 'I wanted somehow to leave India.'

Reflection: In the last chapter we looked at the rebuffs that the Nana Sahib, who had socialized with British men and women, received at British hands, the revenge he sought to exact, and the flames of violence in which his life disappeared.

The anger of the twenty-two-year-old Gandhi, 'fuming' at being rejected and ejected by Ollivant, was not less than that of the Nana Sahib. Like the latter, Gandhi was a proud man conscious of his pedigree and of the prime ministers from whom he had descended. In 1907 he told Joseph Doke, the Presbyterian minister who befriended Gandhi in Johannesburg: 'One of my earliest memories is connected with the learning and repetition, as a child, of the family pedigree, with all its ramifications and offshoots.' (Doke:19)

He wanted to punish Ollivant, but when Mehta advised against a legal proceeding, Gandhi 'pocketed the insult.' Also, he drew lessons from the episode. One he mentions in the autobiography:

> 'Never again shall I place myself in such a false position,
> never again shall I try to exploit friendship in this way,' said
> I to myself, and since then I have never been guilty of a
> breach of that determination.

Thus Gandhi was willing to reflect on a bitter encounter, to examine where he too might have been at fault. We may note here the contrast that this provides to the Mahabharata, where, as we saw, the heroes reflected but rarely.

It is apparent, also, that Gandhi did not let his anger at Ollivant affect his faith at the time in the Empire. He said to Doke in 1907 that 'while, now and then, some British official [in India] had shown himself brusque or overbearing (doubtless a reference to Ollivant), nothing, so far, had happened to chill his loyalty (to the Empire).'[6]

How Gandhi coped with his anger at Ollivant is not recorded, but we can look at some of Gandhi's references to anger in other contexts:

> Anger wells up in my breast when I see or hear about
> misdeeds . . . All I can humbly claim is that I keep these
> passions and moods under fair subjection. (*Young India*,
> 14.7.27)

> I am also a human being and feel enraged but I swallow my
> anger. (In 1947; 89:174, *Collected Works* reference and
> explanation given earlier)

'Do you get angry?' he was once asked by G.D. Birla, the industrialist who was his friend and helper. Gandhi's reply was, 'Yes, I do. But

I try to become a witness to my own anger.'[7]

Sometimes he sought to banish his resentments by thinking of others whose hurts were greater or more unjust than his. Thus he writes in the autobiography that when in South Africa a barber refused to cut his hair (because Gandhi was not white), or he received other knocks to self-respect, he overcame the hurts by remembering how untouchables were treated in India. '[The] conviction that it was the punishment for our own sins saved me from becoming angry.'

In his biography of Gandhi, written in 1907-08 after conversations with his subject, Joseph Doke says:

> The twelve months spent in Pretoria were a distinct gain.
> He learned self-restraint . . . [and] to bear the insults which
> attached to his race and colour until . . . he almost gloried
> in them, and, gradually, pride of birth and education gave
> way before the humility of sacrifice. (45)

Pride in his background was giving way—the contrast with the Mahabharata is again of interest—, and the young man was dissolving his hurts in the common humiliation of the Indians in South Africa. Soon he would organize them for struggle and discover satyagraha. Led by him, thousands of men and women would defy unfair laws nonviolently, if necessary braving beatings and prison.

But fighting and forgiving could go together. When a White policeman in Pretoria 'pushed and kicked' Gandhi without the slightest warning, a man called Coates who noticed the incident reprimanded the policeman, who apologized. 'I had already forgiven him,' Gandhi would claim in the autobiography.

*

Gandhi and Churchill: In the India-Empire clash, Gandhi's opposite number was Winston Churchill. The only time the two met was in 1906, when Churchill was Britain's under-secretary for the colonies. Gandhi called on him in London and informed him of the problems faced by Indians in South Africa.

A few years earlier, Churchill too had gone to South Africa, to cover the Anglo-Boer War as a correspondent. He was aware of an incident in Durban in 1897 when Gandhi had come close to being lynched by a White mob. In his book *My African Journey*, published in 1908, Churchill touches on the conflict between Whites and Indians in South and East Africa. To Churchill the interests of the two races were, in his phrase, 'irreconcilable.' Writing that the

Whites in Africa felt threatened by competition from Indian immigrants, Churchill added that the White man believed that 'he could strike down [the Indian immigrant] with his hands.'

We can fairly speak of a fifty-year clash, from 1897 to 1948, between Churchill's concept of the power of a physical blow and Gandhi's location of power in the consciences of thousands of Indians. Churchill's famous lament of 1931, after the successes of the Salt March, that 'the half-naked fakir' was being allowed to 'stride up the steps of the viceregal palace' has already been noted by us, as also his complaint of the same year that appeasement had been extended to those inflicting unprecedented humiliation and defiance on the British in India.

Here we have the admission of Churchill, who in ten years would confront Hitler in the Second World War, that Indians who could be struck down by bare White hands had by their nonviolent action inflicted a blow on the Empire greater than anything occurring earlier, including, presumably, the 1857 Rebellion.

When Gandhi visited London shortly after signing his pact with Irwin, a still-indignant Churchill refused to meet him. But in 1935 Churchill indicated to G.D. Birla that he felt uneasy about his refusal to meet Gandhi in 1931. 'It was then rather awkward,' Churchill said, adding, 'Mr Gandhi has gone very high in my esteem since he stood up for the untouchables.' This was a reference to Gandhi's nationwide campaigns against untouchability in 1932-34.

Receiving Birla's account of his talk with Churchill, Gandhi authorized Birla to write to Churchill that he retained 'a good recollection of Mr Churchill when he was in the colonial office,' a reference to their 1906 meeting in London. In 1937 Birla again called on Churchill, who asked the Indian to 'give your leader my greetings.'[8] But any Gandhi-Churchill understanding that might have emerged was torpedoed by Hitler's war.

Churchill, now Prime Minister, claimed in September 1941 that the Atlantic Charter, spelling out the right to national independence, would not apply to India. And in November 1942, after Gandhi's Quit India call in the summer of that year, Churchill declared that he had 'not become the King's First Minister in order to preside over the liquidation of the British Empire.'

Earlier in 1942, when Churchill's cabinet colleague Stafford Cripps visited India with proposals for the future, Gandhi had given Birla his assessment that Churchill had made up his mind not to 'abandon [India] voluntarily.'[9]

General Jan Smuts of South Africa was dining with Churchill on 7 August 1942 when the All India Congress Committee began its Quit India deliberations in Bombay. Lord Moran, Churchill's physician, entered the conversation into his diary:

> Smuts spoke of Gandhi: 'He is a man of God. You and I are mundane people. Gandhi has appealed to religious motives. You never have. That is where you have failed.' PM (with a great grin): 'I have made more bishops than anyone since St. Augustine.' But Smuts did not smile. His face was very grave.[10]

Two days later, after Gandhi had been arrested, Winston Churchill 'pouted' to Moran: 'We have clapped Gandhi into gaol.' Gandhi's release in May 1944 followed consultations between Wavell, the Viceroy in New Delhi, and London. Gandhi had been seriously ill with malaria and dysentery, and the Raj did not want to take chances. Eight weeks after the release, Churchill, according to the Viceroy's diary, sent Wavell 'a peevish telegram to ask why Gandhi hadn't died yet.'[11]

In the spring of 1945, Churchill spoke to Wavell of dividing India into 'Pakistan, Hindustan and Princestan.' That summer British voters sent Churchill into opposition. When he called again on Churchill, Wavell was exhorted to 'keep a bit of India' even if independence was unavoidable.[12] Gandhi, on his part, sought to prevent a partition.

Muhammad Ali Jinnah, president of the Muslim League, established a line to Churchill, who exerted his influence in partition's favour. Hate and violence disfiguring the subcontinent in August and September of 1947, Churchill rubbed in the shame that Gandhi was experiencing. He said:

> The fearful massacres which are occurring in India are no surprise to me. We are, of course, only at the beginning of these horrors and butcheries, perpetrated upon one another with the ferocity of cannibals, by the races gifted with the capacities for the highest culture and who had for generations dwelt side by side in general peace under the broad, tolerant, and impartial rule of the British Crown and Parliament. I cannot but doubt that the future will witness a vast abridgment of the population [on the subcontinent] . . . (89:253)

Taking criticism: Gandhi's reaction to these formidable phrases from Churchill reveals his character, and also how he coped with an adversary. Despite the history of Churchill's attitude towards him, Gandhi called Churchill 'a great man,' acknowledged that there was 'no doubt' that Churchill had 'saved the British Empire' in the Second World War, and admitted that 'a few lakhs in India had taken to the path of barbarism,' Gandhi however asked Indians to 'prove Mr Churchill's prediction wrong.' Also, he took Churchill to task for describing the killings in India with, as Gandhi put it, 'such relish and gross exaggeration.' (89:253-55)

Thus in Gandhi's rhetoric there was no tit for tat in 1947, just as there had been none in 1931. Churchill's words were taken seriously but also subjected to scrutiny.

When, in 1931, Churchill had spoken of Gandhi as a 'half-naked fakir,' Gandhi commented that he was indeed trying to identify with India's naked millions. The remark suggested a sense of humour and also of political ju-jitsu, an ability to derive advantage from the opponent's move.

Because of his large ears, the poetess Sarojini Naidu called him Mickey Mouse, a label Gandhi was happy to accept; and he similarly took in good part comments from close associates like Vallabhbhai Patel and Chakravarti Rajagopalachari that he was 'cruel' or a 'tyrant faddist.'[13]

Patel, Rajagopalachari and Sarojini Naidu were colleagues, not adversaries, yet Gandhi's ability to laugh, his eyes twinkling, at a joke or half-jokes at his expense, and his attitude to harsh remarks from a foe like Churchill provide a contrast once more to the characters of the Mahabharata, who seemed to think that not to avenge an insult was to lose one's status as a man and as a warrior.

Mahadev Desai's record of Gandhi's term in Yeravda jail in 1932-33, when he and Vallabhbhai Patel were Gandhi's prison-mates, offers instances of Patel's merciless leg-pulling. It also discloses a keenness in both Gandhi and Patel to read the British mind from officials visiting the prison. Weighing a remark by Poona's (British) Police Commissioner, Gandhi wondered whether it was innocuous, a feeler, or, as he put it to Patel and Desai, 'an echo of the table-talk of the ruling class.'[14]

In an earlier chapter we saw how in her long history India had sometimes dismissed alien conquerors as an uncivilized mass not worthy of curiosity, study or differentiation. However, Gandhi took them seriously and as individuals. When, also at Yeravda, Patel said, referring to Ramsay MacDonald, the Prime Minister at the time, 'They are all birds of the same feather,' Gandhi's comment was, 'Still I think he has his own convictions.'[15]

*

Jallianwala: Nothing tested Gandhi's commitment to a principled fight against the British more than the 1919 massacre at Jallianwala Bagh in Amritsar.

Let us recall the background. Early in 1919, an anti-sedition committee chaired by an English judge, Sir Sidney Rowlatt, recommended a series of tough provisions including, for suspected seditionists, arrests without trial or trials without appeal, and a two-year sentence for an offence like carrying a seditious leaflet in one's pocket.

When, despite Indian protests, the Viceroy went ahead with the proposals, Gandhi called for satyagraha, a nonviolent defiance. In March and April 1919, for the first time ever, an all-India stir took place; and prominent Indians signed a pledge to disobey the Rowlatt measure and also to 'refrain from violence to life, person and property.'

On 8 April the Raj prevented Gandhi from entering Delhi and the Punjab and forcibly sent him back to Bombay. In Amritsar, where the situation was tense, two important leaders of the Punjab, Dr Saifuddin Kitchlew, a Muslim, and Dr Satyapal, a Hindu, were arrested under the orders of the Lieutenant-Governor, Michael O'Dwyer.

The arrests sparked off violent disturbances in Amritsar and Gujrat. In attacks by demonstrators and firing by the police and the military, Indians and Englishmen lost lives. On 14 April, unaware as yet of what had happened in Amritsar the previous afternoon, Gandhi spoke as follows to about two thousand men gathered outside his Ashram:

> Brothers, I am ashamed of the events of the last few days. Those responsible have disgraced me. In the name of satyagraha, we burnt down buildings, forcibly captured weapons, extorted money, stopped trains, cut off telegraph wires, killed innocent people, and plundered shops and homes . . .
>
> We should repent and do penance. I would also advise you,

if it is possible for you, to fast for 24 hours in slight
expiation of these sins . . . My responsibility is a million
times greater than yours . . . I will therefore fast for 72
hours.

*If a redress of grievances is only possible by means of illwill for,
and slaughter of, Englishmen, I for one would do without
Swaraj and without redress.*[16] (Emphasis added.)

Four days later he announced a suspension of the defiance.

In Amritsar a demonstration against the arrests of Satyapal and
Kitchlew was fired at. In revenge the infuriated crowd killed five or
six Englishmen in their offices and assaulted a British schoolmistress,
Miss Sherwood. Next day Amritsar was taken over by a Simla-born
British general, Reginald Dyer, who prohibited meetings. However,
his ban was apparently proclaimed only in English, and on the
afternoon of 13 April over 10,000 people, Sikhs, Hindus and Muslims,
assembled in Jallianwala Bagh, a public ground enclosed by five-foot-
high walls.

We need not repeat here the oft-told story of the massacre and
repression that followed, the worst in the annals of British rule in
India, producing a seemingly unbridgeable chasm between India and
its British rulers.

Gandhi declared that Indians would build a memorial at
Jallianwala, not to express 'illwill or hostility to anyone' but as 'a
symbol of the people's grief' and a reminder of 'the sacrifices,
through death, of the innocent.' (16:468). Donations seemed slow in
coming until Gandhi said he would, if necessary, sell his Ashram in
Ahmedabad to finance the memorial.

At the end of 1919, the Indian National Congress held its annual
session in Amritsar, on a site adjacent to Jallianwala Bagh. The able
Brahmin lawyer from Allahabad, Motilal Nehru, presided, and those
present included the respected Lokmanya Tilak, the colourful Ali
brothers, who were recently released from British prisons, Annie
Besant, the Irishwoman who had made India her home and Indian
home rule her mission, Calcutta's Bipin Chandra Pal and Chitta
Ranjan Das, Pandit Madan Mohan Malaviya from Benares, and
Bombay's gifted barrister, Muhammad Ali Jinnah.

Also at Amritsar was Gandhi, whose call for a struggle over the
Rowlatt question had earned him nationwide fame. But he was not
yet the pre-eminent figure he later became, and he was ill.

With the memory of Jallianwala so fresh and, in Amritsar, so intimate, anti-British feelings ran high at the session. K.M. Munshi, another Bombay lawyer who was present, would later recall the mood and a remarkable intervention:

> A resolution was moved in the Subjects Committee condemning both the massacre of Jallianwala Bagh and the mad frenzy of the crowds. The hearts of most of us revolted at the latter part of the resolution . . . This must have been Mrs Besant's work, most thought; she was after all British.

> One Punjab leader gave expression to this feeling rather crudely: no one born of an Indian mother, said he, could have drafted this resolution. Lokmanya too was indignant and so were Pal and C.R. Das; and the latter part of the resolution was lost by an overwhelming majority.

> Next day the President wanted the committee to reconsider the resolution, as Gandhiji, he said, was very keen on it. There were vehement protests. Ultimately Gandhi was helped to the table to move that the resolution be reconsidered. He spoke sitting. Out of respect the house sat quiet but with ill-concealed impatience.

> Referring to the remark that no son born of an Indian mother could have drafted the resolution, Gandhiji stated that he had considered deeply and long whether as an Indian he could have drafted the resolution, for indeed he had drafted it. But after long searching of heart he had come to the conclusion that only a person born of an Indian mother could have drafted it.

> And then he spoke as if his whole life depended upon the question . . . When he stopped, we were at his feet . . . The resolution was reconsidered and accepted in its original form.[17]

Indians felt proud to have a leader who laid down demanding standards, even though they also frequently rebelled against his norms. Read with his Ahmedabad remark that he for one would do without Swaraj if killing vulnerable British individuals was the only way to get it, his insistence at Amritsar that despite the Jallianwala massacre such violence against the innocent or the weak had to be condemned gave a devastating nobility to the struggle that Gandhi was leading. In the end, the British had no answer to it.

With this stamp of honour that Gandhi managed to imprint on it, India's freedom movement of 1919-47 found a distinctive place in modern history. Its participants seemed to be fighting not for revenge but for a nation's birthright; willing to take injury, they were resolved never to inflict injury; and they were willing to obey their leader if, noticing or fearing violence, he called a halt.

At times grumblings accompanied their obedience—this was particularly so in 1922, when, following the Chauri Chaura killings, Gandhi suspended the Non-cooperation Movement at its peak. Demoralization led to fears of collapse, but before too long, in 1930, came the spectacular Salt March and its all-India follow-up.

*

Loving, or trying to love, the enemy: Some of Gandhi's British adversaries remained skeptical of his goodwill. General Archibald Wavell, the penultimate Viceroy and the one who, as Britain's Commander-in-Chief in India, had to face Gandhi's Quit India challenge in 1942, wrote in 1946 that he felt 'malevolence' in Gandhi. According to Wavell, Gandhi was 'the most formidable' of the opponents 'who have detached portions of the British Empire in recent years'; the Viceroy also thought that Gandhi's goal was 'a Hindu Raj.'[18]

Other Viceroys or Secretaries of State did not notice illwill in Gandhi. Irwin, who first arrested Gandhi after the Salt March and later signed a pact with him, said that he could always trust Gandhi's word. According to Louis Fischer, the American journalist who met Gandhi a number of times in the 1940s, Gandhi 'had no animus.' Added Fischer: 'He was incapable of hatred . . . He wanted to liberate India in order to liberate England from India.'[19] Remarks in a similar vein were made by some other Whites who encountered Gandhi.

As we saw in the comment that Gandhi made to Desai in 1918, the reality was perhaps more complex. The excesses and humiliation of British rule were not easy to live with; no wonder Gandhi had to force himself to love the British. The surprise was that he so often succeeded.

Perhaps his closest British friend was Charlie Andrews. On 7 August 1942, when Gandhi presented his Quit India plan to the All India Congress Committee, he reiterated his opposition to any ill will against the British and recalled Andrews, who had died in 1941:

We must remove any hatred for the British from our hearts. At least in my heart there is no such hatred . . . At a time when I am about to launch the biggest fight in my life, there can be no hatred for the British in my heart . . . You should not resort to violence and put nonviolence to shame . . . If you don't understand this it will be better if you reject this resolution.

Then there is the sacred memory of Charlie Andrews which wells up within me at this moment. The spirit of Andrews hovers about me . . . I enjoyed closer relations with him than with most Indians. I enjoyed his confidence. There were no secrets between us. We exchanged our hearts every day . . . He is unfortunately gone. He was a fine Englishman. I know that the spirit of Andrews is listening to me. (76:377-81)

Five years later, something of Gandhi's attitude to the West as a whole was revealed in his talk to leaders of the emerging Asia in April 1947, four months before India's independence. Jawaharlal Nehru had invited them to New Delhi. Gandhi told them that India's wisdom could be found in an untouchable's 'humble cottage in a humble village,' not in 'Delhi, Bombay, Madras, Calcutta, Lahore.' Killings in the Punjab and Bihar were in the news, and Gandhi admitted that 'the carnage that is going on before our very eyes is a shameful thing.'

But, recalling that men from the East had taken wisdom to the West, he urged his listeners to reject the temptation of vengeance against their departing European rulers:

The first of these wise men was Zoroaster. He belonged to the East. He was followed by the Buddha who belonged to the East—India. Who followed the Buddha? Jesus, who came from the East. Before Jesus was Moses who belonged to Palestine though he was born in Egypt. After Jesus came Mohammed . . . I do not know of a single person in the world to match these men of Asia.

If you want to give a message to the West, it must be the message of love and the message of truth. I want you to go away with the thought that Asia has to conquer the West through love and truth . . .

In this age of democracy, in this age of awakening of the poorest of the poor, . . . you will complete the conquest of the West not through vengeance because you have been exploited, but with real understanding. (87:190-93)

On 15 August 1947, when independence was finally won, Gandhi, opening his eyes in free India in a Muslim's house in one of Calcutta's poorest quarters, wrote a letter to an English friend, Agatha Harrison:

You know, my way of celebrating great events, such as today's, is to thank God . . . and therefore to pray. This prayer must be accompanied by a fast, and then, as a mark of identification with the poor . . . there must be [extra] spinning . . . My love to all your friends. (89:43-44)

So on independence day the Empire's chief adversary penned his love to British friends.

Princess Elizabeth of England, whose grandfather, George V, Gandhi had met in 1931, was married three months after Indian independence to Philip, nephew of Mountbatten, the last Viceroy in India. At the request of India's leaders, Mountbatten had stayed on as Governor-General. In consultation with the Mountbattens, Gandhi decided he would send, as a wedding gift to Elizabeth and Philip, a small tablecloth woven from thread his hands had drawn on a charkha. He requested Mountbatten to carry the present:

Dear Lord Mountbatten: This little thing is made out of doubled yarn of my own spinning. The knitting was done by a Punjabi girl who was trained by Abha's husband, my grandson. Lady Mountbatten knows Abha. Please give the bride and the bridegroom this with my blessings, with the wish that they would have a long and happy life of service to men. Yours sincerely, M.K. Gandhi (9.11.47; 89:507)

RECONCILING INDIANS WITH ONE ANOTHER

From Mohandas's London diary we know that Muslims were among fellow-students who saw him off at Rajkot and at railway stations between Rajkot and Bombay; and we know too that in London he joined the Anjuman-e-Islamia, an association of Muslim students.When a young Hindu anxious to preserve his vegetarianism joins the Anjuman-e-Islamia in London, we infer an attempt for reconciliation.

We know from our survey of India's past that a reconciler had his job cut out, but, as Sumit Sarkar points out, Gandhi was fortunate to find in South Africa, where he lived from 1893 to 1914, an India in miniature that he could learn from, work with, and work on. Writes Sarkar:

> The peculiar conditions of South Africa allowed the amalgamation into a successful movement of . . . Hindus, Muslims, Parsis and Christians, Gujaratis and South Indians, upper-class merchants and lawyers as well as Newcastle mineworkers who Gandhi led in a memorable strike and cross-country march in October 1913 . . .

> [This] experience made Gandhi into potentially much more of an all-India figure from the beginning of his work in India than . . . other politician[s], all of whom (like Tilak, Lajpat Rai or Pal, for example) had essentially regional bases. Gandhi's life-long recognition of the necessity and possibility of Hindu-Muslim unity certainly goes back to his South African movements . . .[20]

Important sections in the India to which Gandhi returned in 1915 were wary of independence. The rajas, hundreds of whom ruled over pockets in different parts of India, thought independence could lead to revenge by the praja; Muslims feared that force of numbers would produce Hindu rule; landlords were apprehensive of the anger of tenants and the landless; and the untouchables feared caste Hindu domination.

These sections felt no particular love for the British, but, afraid of the consequences of independence, they were inclined to support British rule as against any pro-independence parties. If they combined their resources and numbers, such groups were capable of blocking a freedom movement.

Gandhi was able to prevent such a combination. For the sake of independence but also for its own sake, Gandhi strove for reconciliation among India's divided groups, using the Indian National Congress as his principal instrument. Addressing the All India Congress Committee (AICC) two months before his death, Gandhi recalled his attempt:

I am an Indian to the last. Ever since I returned from South Africa, I have tried to serve the Congress in every way . . . I have tried to understand Indians from different walks of life, have lived with them, eaten with them, and loved them . . . (90:38)

THE HINDU-MUSLIM QUESTION

Gandhi to Mahadev Desai, 1918: Though we do say that Hindus and Muslims are brothers, I cannot conceive of their being brothers today . . . Something within tells me that Hindus and Muslims are going to unite as brothers one day, that there is no other course open to them, and they have but to be brothers. If we go on remembering old scores, we would feel that unity is impossible, but at any cost we ought to forget the past.[21]

Gandhi in 1939 to Muslims who had stood by him and the Congress in the NWFP: If you could dissect my heart, you would find that the prayer and spiritual striving for the attainment of Hindu-Muslim unity goes on there unceasingly all the twenty-four hours without even a moment's interruption, whether I am awake or asleep.

Note the fourfold underscoring in the second quote. His striving, he claims, goes on all the twenty-four hours; it is unceasing; it is never interrupted; it is a night and day thing. Added Gandhi:

Let no one imagine that because the Hindus constitute the majority community, they can win swaraj for India . . . without the backing of the other communities . . . I resign myself utterly to His grace. Who knows, in spite of my incessant heartprayer, I may not be found worthy for this great work . . . Pray for me that my dream may be fulfilled in my lifetime . . . (70:22-24)

In his bid to reach a goal he knew to be difficult, Gandhi employed a variety of means. At the political level, he sought an understanding and alliance with Muslim groups for gaining Swaraj and obtained Congress's commitment to equal rights for Muslims under Swaraj. Socially, he popularized a reconciling Hinduism, a version similar to that of the Bhakti poets, and insisted that Muslims were in no way less Indian than Hindus, while also asking Muslims to respect the Hindu conscience. At the grass-roots level, he strove to heal the wounds of communal violence.

Gandhi's temporary success and eventual failure to build a solid Hindu-Muslim front for independence; the campaigns against British rule that he nonetheless launched, including the Salt March in 1930 and Quit India in 1942; the consequent unease in many Muslims; the unsuccessful yet revealing Gandhi-Jinnah talks of 1944; and Gandhi's 1947 proposal, for saving India's unity, of a Congress-backed Jinnah-led government, a proposal undermined by Mountbatten and rejected by Nehru and Patel—these items are relevant to our discussion. But having been dealt with in *The Good Boatman*, they are excluded here.

*

Pain and healing: Though neither Gandhi nor anyone else succeeded in averting bloodshed and Partition, his stand and initiatives in 1946-48 contained the cruelty that was abroad, preserved India as a home for all its residents, whether Hindu, Muslim, Sikh, Christian or whatever, protected their equality under law, and healed wounds.

The last eighteen months of his life, from August 1946, when the Great Calcutta Killing occurred, to 30 January 1948, when he was assassinated in Delhi, were divided between Noakhali in East Bengal, where Hindus were victims, Bihar, where Muslims had suffered, Calcutta, where both communities were hit, and Delhi, where Muslims were at the receiving end.

We will see from the following narrative that to victims Gandhi strove to bring courage and succour; to attackers, shame and repentance; to the strong, restraint; to the weak, strength; to majorities, respect for a minority's rights; to all, non-retaliation; to the subcontinent, a summons to sanity and decency. At no stage did Gandhi prescribe an absolute or doctrinaire nonviolence. Self-defence was justified by him, but he warned against revenge and against a love of violence.

Noakhali: Asking the area's Hindus to stay and fight, Gandhi said that it would have been manlier for the Hindus in Bihar who had attacked innocent Muslims in their province to take on Noakhali's Muslim assailants. On 7 November 1946, speaking to a Muslim-majority audience of 15,000, he frontally criticized forcible conversions, forcible feeding of beef, forced marriages, abductions and the destruction of idols.

Asked in the village of Paniala whether he did not think that Muslim neighbours had saved Hindu lives and property in Noakhali, Gandhi answered on 22 January 1947 that what was wanted was 'repentance that there were enough Muslims found in Noakhali who lost their heads' and committed terrible crimes. 'If more mischief was not done, God alone was to be thanked, not man.' However, he would freely concede that, 'be it said to their honour, there were Muslims who afforded protection to Hindus.' (86:382-83)

When Hindus in Noakhali asked how they could forgive or forget, Gandhi replied, 'Remember Bihar.' A number of Noakhali's Hindus returned to the homes they had abandoned. Overcoming fear of Muslim neighbours, many found courage to sing Hindu prayers at Gandhi's prayer sessions. Hindu women wore vermillion and bangles again.

Joining Gandhi while he walked in the village of Bhatialpur, 'a number of Muslim youths expressed gratification at his work in Noakhali' and assured him, according to the *Amrita Bazar Patrika* of 19 January that 'they would stand guarantee' against a repetition of what had happened. (86:354-55)

'Forgive me': But if Gandhi's voice was reaching out to others, an inner voice seemed always to admonish him on his own life. His grand-niece, Manu Gandhi, who was with Gandhi for much of his Noakhali and Bihar endeavours, recorded an apology he made to her in the pre-dawn hours of 10 January 1947. Having earlier accused Manu of something (what it was is not mentioned), Gandhi told her early on 10 January:

> I tell you I was absolutely wrong in accusing you. I am so much older than you. I am your grandfather. What pardon can I seek from you? Still there is nothing wrong in my asking for it.

Gandhi added that while it was a wonder that God had kept him going thus far, his end could come any moment. He wanted to make his confession before it came.[22]

Contrition, confession and apology—notes avoided, we saw, by the Mahabharata characters—seemed to punctuate Gandhi's life. His secretary and companion Mahadev Desai recorded a 1932 conversation in Pune's Yeravda prison that also involved Vallabhbhai Patel, a fellow-prisoner, and Gandhi's wife Kasturba:

10.4.32: It was now a couple of minutes to three (when

Gandhi was to commence a 24-hour period of silence). Therefore Vallabhbhai said: 'You have now a few minutes of speech. So tell us if you have any instructions to give.' I remarked: 'You are talking as if Bapu has now to make his last will and testament.' Bapu: 'All right, I will tell you. Please pardon me if I have offended you in any way.'

Saying this he began to laugh. His laugh was occasioned by a sweet remembrance of his. He said, 'Ba (Kasturba) said to me, "Please pardon me if I have offended you in any way".' Vallabhbhai asked, 'When was that?' Bapu: 'When I was arrested, of course. She said this with tears in her eyes. She was afraid we might never meet again on this side of the grave and was anxious not to die unforgiven.'[23]

*

Bihar: The loss of life and property in Bihar much exceeded the Noakhali levels but the province's ministers and Congress leaders did not seem greatly perturbed. In fact there were indications that some Congressmen had connived at the violence.

The explanation that Bihar's Hindu leaders offered to Gandhi was the mirror image of what he had heard from Noakhali's Muslims. Goondas, not Hindus, had misbehaved; Muslims had supplied provocation; many Hindus had gone to the aid of Muslims; 'innocent' Hindus were being harassed by the police; and so on. Gandhi's response was as forthright as it had been in Noakhali. At a meeting on 19 March with Congress workers, he said:

> Is it or isn't it a fact that quite a large number of Congressmen took part in the disturbances? How many of the 132 members of your committee were involved? . . . I have also worked in the Congress . . . I know the Congress inside out.

> I wish to ask you, how could you live to see an old woman of 110 years being butchered before your eyes?

One of the leaders admitted that 'we have become vicious, the whole atmosphere has been vitiated' and that some Congressmen were 'carried away by the tide.' (87:118-21) Earlier, Gandhi had told Bihar's Congress leaders and Ministers that from what he had heard 'the Bihar massacre was like the Jallianwala Bagh massacre.'

Warmth was interwoven with directness in his Bihar discourse.

Quoting 'the English saying "The greater the sin, the greater the saint" ' to a prayer meeting audience of over one hundred thousand on 5 March, Gandhi asked for 'honest reparations greater in magnitude than their crimes.' If these were forthcoming, Bihar would 'hold her head high' again. Abducted women, stolen goods and illegal weapons should be surrendered—to the police if possible or, if necessary, to him, Rajendra Prasad (the Bihari who had joined Gandhi in 1917 and would become India's President in 1950), or Syed Mahmud (the Congress Muslim who had pressed Gandhi to come to Bihar). (87:43-46)

As in Noakhali, he went to Bihar's affected villages. As in Noakhali, he taught through prayer meetings. In Bihar these were at times attended by tens or even hundreds of thousands. On 11 March he explained the dynamics and folly of retaliation:

> If I am starving and you feed me, the contentment in my eyes will brighten your face too. But suppose I am starving and demand food from you by abusing you. You will drive me away, saying, 'Go and starve yourself to death.' My abuses will not get me food. They will, however, make me feel that I am a brave man. Again, if you ask your gatekeeper to beat me up for my abuses, that will sow the seeds of hatred against you in my heart . . . The next day I shall gather a few friends and retaliate. If you manage to kill me, it will create among my relations and friends a feeling of revenge against you . . . The world has reached the stage of atomic warfare in returning violence for violence. (87:70)

Biharis were proud of their role for Quit India in 1942. Acknowledging it, Gandhi contended that its violent component had aided the communal violence of 1946-47. 'Once the evil spirit of violence is unleashed, by its inherent nature it cannot be checked or even kept within any prescribed limits. All violence inevitably tends to run to excess.' (87:424) To those who argued that their own hands were clean, Gandhi said: 'Everyone of us is equally guilty of what anyone of us has done.' (87:55)

Hindu men gave money and Hindu women their jewels for Gandhi's fund for Muslims. In the village of Siparah, Gandhi was given a purse, a letter of apology, and an assurance that returning Muslims would be protected. Many Hindus wrote to him confessing their guilt. Fifty persons wanted in connection with the riots surrendered themselves in Masaurhi the day after Gandhi's arrival there.

*

Calcutta: At the end of August 1947, after greeting independence day in Calcutta, Gandhi was all set to return to Noakhali when a violent demonstration at Hydari Manzil, the Muslim home where he was staying, changed his plans. A lathi and brick aimed at Gandhi, who had come out to meet the Hindu demonstrators, missed him, but there were killings elsewhere in Calcutta later that night and the next day. Fifty lost their lives and nearly five hundred were injured. Visiting the affected areas, Gandhi saw, as he told the Press, 'two dead bodies of very poor Muslims,' victims of a grenade attack on a truck in which they were fleeing.

Gandhi announced a fast by him, to 'end only if and when sanity returns to Calcutta.' If Calcutta responded to his fast, he said, he would go to the Punjab, where terrible events had occurred. Meanwhile, the fast might speak to the Punjab also, to both parts of it.

'Can you fast against the goondas?' Rajagopalachari, the governor of West Bengal, asked. Gandhi's reply was that his fast could 'touch the hearts of those behind the goondas,' without whose 'sympathy and passive support the goondas would have no legs to stand upon.'

The fast began on the evening of 1 September and at once triggered action. Hindus and Muslims marched for peace. About five hundred members of the North Calcutta police force, including Britons and Anglo-Indians, went themselves on a twenty-four-hour sympathy fast while remaining on duty. The Shanti Sena, or Peace Brigade, was born, comprising young men willing, at jeopardy to their lives, to intervene in a clash.

'University students would come up to us,' a professor later recalled, 'and ask to be excused from attending their classes [as] they felt disturbed [because] if anybody had to suffer for the continued killing and betrayal in the city, it was not Gandhiji.' Added Amiya Chakravarty:

> Some even gathered weapons from streets and homes at great personal risk and returned them to Gandhiji. Men would come back from their offices in the evening and find food prepared by their family ready for them; but soon it

would be revealed that the women of the home had not
eaten during the whole day . . . They could not understand
how they could go on when Gandhiji was dying for their
own crimes.[24]

Rammanohar Lohia, the socialist leader, brought to Gandhi a body
of Hindu youths who admitted complicity in violence and surrendered
a small arsenal of arms. A gang of goondas followed and asked for
'whatever penalty you may impose.' Only 'you should now end
your fast.' Gandhi asked them to go 'immediately among the Muslims
and assure them full protection.' (89:151) He wanted to put the
changed sinners to immediate use.

At 6 p.m. on 4 September, Suhrawardy, the ex-Premier of Bengal
under whose rule Calcutta had experienced the Great Killing a year
earlier, escorted a deputation of Hindu Mahasabha, Muslim League
and Sikh leaders to Gandhi's bedside. When they pleaded that he end
the fast, Gandhi asked them if they would risk their lives to prevent
a recurrence of communal killings. The deputation withdrew to
another room, conferred, and returned with a pledge. After reminding
them that 'above all, there is God, our witness,' Gandhi broke his
fast, which had lasted 73 hours.[25]

'Gandhiji has achieved many things,' Rajagopalachari said on
5 September, 'but in my considered opinion there has been nothing,
not even independence, which is so truly wonderful as his victory
over evil in Calcutta.' (*Statesman*, 6.9.47)

Communal violence would not return to Calcutta for years.
Thanking the people of Calcutta and acknowledging the martyrdom
of two young men, Sachin Mitra, who was killed on 1 September
while defending Muslims, and Smritish Banerjee, who lost his life on
3 September while protecting a peace procession, Gandhi boarded,
on 7 September, three weeks after Independence, a train for Delhi, en
route, as he informed Jawaharlal in a wire, to the Punjab.

*

Delhi: But Delhi detained Gandhi.

The city was under curfew. Thousands had been killed.
There was looting and firing. All bazars were closed. People's
rations were exhausted . . . Localities like Karol Bagh,
Sabzimandi and Paharganj were being emptied of Muslims.
(Brij Krishna 3:278)

Gandhi decided that he could not go to the Punjab until Delhi 'regained its former self.' (89:166-67) Within twenty-four hours of his arrival in the capital, Gandhi had visited the camp near Humayun's Tomb where Muslim Meos from Alwar and Bharatpur had taken refuge, the Jamia Millia, where many of Delhi's Muslims were huddled, and camps filled with Hindu and Sikh refugees from West Punjab at Diwan Hall, Wavell Canteen and Kingsway.

Angry faces and shouts of 'Go Back!' greeted Gandhi in almost all the camps, Muslim and non-Muslim, but the anger of the latter seemed greater. He was told that he was for the Muslims, that his heart was of stone. He had not suffered the way they had, his near and dear ones had not been killed, he did not have to beg for his food.

Gandhi said to his companion and aide Brij Krishna that he was happy the refugees could lighten their sorrows by abusing him. Through their outspokenness, the critics' 'anger is spent and their hearts are cleansed,' and they would 'work wonders' if his response managed to convince them. (89:367) To the refugees, Hindu, Sikh or Muslim, Gandhi offered the strong truth that God who gave life also took it; all were to die one day, and the only remedy was to live right while one lived.

When, in September, it rained, and later as winter approached, he would shiver thinking of the uprooted and unprotected ones in Delhi's camps. People sought out and killed in a hospital, a man stabbed in a train and thrown into a river, another killed while he was opening the little shop where he repaired spectacles, trainloads of refugees stopped and butchered, all because they belonged to the Other religion and none because of any offence committed, all before approving or silent onlookers—such were the incidents related to Gandhi, often by those directly bereaved.

'There is a constant stream of visitors,' he wrote to a friend in November. 'How can I refuse to listen to their sorrows? Very often my own grief becomes overwhelming.' (89:510) Shame joined pain. 'I do not wish to be a witness to these things. I do not wish to see such a downfall.' (89:271) And guilt too, for he identified with the attacker as well as the victim. 'When someone commits a crime anywhere, I feel I am the culprit.' (90:133)

Confronting the fearful reality around him, collecting blankets for the refugees, digging out his deepest thought for each caller or audience, he also turned more than ever to God. Recalling the Mahabharata, he likened his state to Draupadi's when the Kauravas had tried to disrobe her in a public chamber, and remembered that Draupadi's prayer had been answered:

> I saw your letter only now (Gandhi wrote to a friend in November 1947), after listening to the sweet and sad bhajan containing Draupadi's prayer . . . Draupadi had mighty Bhima and Arjuna and the truthful Yudhishthira as husbands; she was the daughter-in-law of men like Dronacharya, Bhishma and Vidura, and yet amidst an assembly of people it appeared she was in a terrible plight. At that hour she did not lose faith and prayed to God from her heart. And God did protect her honour.
>
> Today I also am seated in a palatial house surrounded by loving friends. Still, I am in a sad plight. Yet there is God's help, as I find each day. (89:464-65)

Fear, he often insisted, was the real foe. 'I have just a handful of bones in my body,' he said on 24 September, 'but my heart belongs to me. So do your hearts belong to you.' (89:231)

Ready for anything, he expected to be killed, and hoped to harbour goodwill for his likely assassin. In October he said to a group of Muslims, including several old friends, who called on him on the day of Bakr-Id:

> It is my constant prayer to God that He may give me the strength to intercede even for my assassin. And it should be your prayer too that your faithful servant may be given that strength to forgive. (89:411)

Few things affected him more than the abduction of women in both parts of the Punjab, and uncertainty about their acceptance after recovery:

> The number could be in hundreds or even thousands . . . [I]t is still doubtful whether they will be accepted by their families. This is very bad . . . If my daughter has been violated by a rascal and made pregnant, must I cast her and her child away? . . . These girls are innocent. (90:301-02)

*

Tackling the RSS: The morning after Gandhi's arrival in Delhi a Sikh taxi-driver had told Brij Krishna:

> If Gandhiji had waited some more days before coming to
> Delhi, all the Muslims here would have been eliminated.
> (Brij Krishna 3:282)

Gandhi confronted the RSS chief, M.S. Golwalkar, with the reports
he had received of the body's hand in the Delhi violence. Golwalkar,
who called at Birla House on the morning of 12 September, assured
Gandhi that 'this was untrue.' When Golwalkar affirmed that the
RSS did not stand for the killing of Muslims, Gandhi asked him to
issue a statement to that effect. Golwalkar said Gandhi could quote
him. This Gandhi did in his prayer speech that evening, but he told
Golwalkar that the statement ought to come from him.[26]

Four days later he met, at his own initiative, a number of RSS
activists. He told them that Hinduism would be destroyed if Muslims
in India were treated as slaves; and Islam would be finished if Hindus
in Pakistan were enslaved.

Asked by one of the activists whether Hinduism did not permit
the killing of an evildoer, Gandhi answered: 'How could a sinner
claim the right to judge or execute another sinner?' Only a properly
constituted government could exercise the right of punishing an
evildoer. (89:177 and 193-95); and Brij Krishna (3:294-97)

He repeated that last thought on his birthday: 'I would appeal to
the people not to take the law into their hands but leave it to the
government to decide.' (89:275) This rather than nonviolence was his
emphasis in the final six months, though he continued to recall
nonviolence as the ideal. Excerpts from his prayer speech of 12
September give a fuller picture of what he was trying to say and how
he said it:

> The very first thing I want to tell you is that I have received
> disturbing news from the Frontier Province . . . I am amazed
> that the Hindus and Sikhs there cannot live [there] in peace
> . . . What I think to myself I may as well convey to you,
> that is, we should not get angry. We can, of course, feel the
> pain. We ought to feel sympathy . . .
>
> It is natural to feel, 'Why not kill the Muslims because our
> brothers have been killed.' But I for one cannot kill even the
> actual murderers of my brothers. Should I then prepare
> myself to kill other innocent people?

I am also a human being and feel enraged but I swallow my anger. That gives me strength . . . How should I take revenge so that they feel repentant for their crimes?

The people of Pakistan resorted to ways of barbarism, and so did the Hindus and the Sikhs . . . He who does good to one who has been good to him is a mere Bania and a pseudo-Bania at that . . . A true human being is one who does a good turn for evil. I learnt this in my childhood. I still believe in the rightness of this. I would like you to return evil with good. (89:173-77)

The news of many Hindu and Sikh women in West Punjab who chose death over dishonour stirred him:

They have gone with courage . . . Not that their lives were not dear to them, but they felt it was better to die with courage rather than be forcibly converted to Islam by the Muslims and allow them to assault their bodies. And so those women died. They were not just a handful, but quite a few. (89:202)

Yet revenge against India's Muslims was folly. If all of them were driven out, which was not possible, the Hindus would fight one another. 'This is inevitable. Once one has a taste of killing, one can't resist the temptation.' (89:386)

In November and December he made an unsuccessful bid to persuade Muslims in Panipat, sixty miles north of Delhi, and close to Kurukshetra, not to migrate to Pakistan. Though at first willing to stay on, they changed their minds when Hindu and Sikh refugees who had come from West Punjab to Panipat demonstrated against their presence. Gandhi went twice to Panipat and met with the Muslims and with the non-Muslim refugees. To the Muslims he said on 2 December:

Gandhi can only tell you that you should stay, for India is your home. And if your brethren should kill you, you should bravely meet death . . . Still, if you are resolved to go, . . . there is nothing further I can say to you . . . Having heard you and seen you, my heart weeps. Do as God guides you.

Returning to Delhi, Gandhi described an encounter in Panipat with a boy who had escaped from West Punjab:

> Today a small boy confronted me. He was wearing a
> sweater. He took it off and stood glaring at me as if he
> would eat me up . . . 'You say that you have come to
> protect us,' he said, 'but my father has been killed. Get me
> my father back.' . . . I can imagine that if I had been of his
> age and in his position, perhaps I would have done the same.
> (90:153-61)

Thanks to Gandhi's exertions, a bid to send the Muslim Meos of
Bharatpur and Alwar to Pakistan was abandoned. 'How shameful it
is for us,' Gandhi had exclaimed at an AICC meeting in November,
'that we should force them to trudge three hundred miles on foot!'
(90:42) To Gandhi, India belonged to its Muslims too.

Coming across a couplet by a Muslim in an Urdu magazine
asking for 'a new Ghaznavi to avenge the renovation of the Somnath
temple,' Gandhi spelt out his position on the past's wrongs:

> It is painful to think that such a thing can issue from the pen
> of a Muslim . . . [But] I cannot return evil for evil . . .
> [Hindus] must not remember the wrong that Ghaznavi did.
> Muslims must realize and admit the wrongs perpetrated
> under the Islamic rule. (25.12.47)

*

The meaning of honour: He wanted to go to Pakistan. On 23
September he had said: 'I want to go to the Punjab. I want to go to
Lahore . . . I want to go to Rawalpindi . . . Let me tell you that once
peace descends on Delhi, I shall not stay here even a day longer.'
(89:225)

'When I go to Pakistan, I will not spare them. I shall die for the
Hindus and the Sikhs there. I shall be really glad to die there. I shall
be glad to die here too. If I cannot do what I want to do here, I have
got to die.'

Recounting the 'evil deeds of Pakistan . . . won't help the Hindu
or the Sikh sufferers,' he said on 24 November. 'Pakistan has to bear
the burden of its sins, which I know are terrible enough.' (90:99) But
the future of Pakistan and the honour of Islam were relevant
questions.

Pakistan or Islam cannot mean that non-Muslims cannot live

there. The Muslim empire [had] spread far and wide; but nowhere was it laid down that non-Muslims cannot live there. (89:206)

On 30 December he asked whether Pakistan had 'become Islamistan where no non-Muslim may live or where he can only live as a slave.' (90:327)

Finding that 'now there are even some Congressmen who think that Muslims should not live [in India],' Gandhi insisted on a clear statement of Congress's position. Addressing the AICC in November, he explained what he understood by India's honour and Hinduism:

> There are many places today where a Muslim cannot live in security. There are miscreants who will kill him or throw him out of a running train for no reason other than that he is a Muslim . . . I am ashamed of what is happening today; such things should never happen in India . . .

> We would be betraying the Hindu religion if we did evil because others had done it . . . [V]iolent rowdyism will not save either Hinduism or Sikhism . . . Hinduism cannot be saved by orgies of murder. (90:37-43)

Following his intervention, Congress committed itself to 'develop this great country as a democratic secular state where all citizens enjoy full rights, . . . irrespective of the religion to which they belong.' Coercing minorities to leave India or Pakistan was also condemned, and a call issued for efforts to enable refugees 'ultimately to return to their homes and to their original occupations under conditions of safety and security.'

*

'*My heart will dance*': On the morning of 13 January he began a fast that would continue until he was satisfied that there was 'a reunion of hearts of all communities.' He claimed that God sent the fast, that 'the peremptory call of conscience and duty' required it, that it came 'out of felt agony.' Added Gandhi:

> The loss of her soul by India will mean the loss of the hope of the aching, storm-tossed and hungry world.

> Death for me would be a glorious deliverance rather than that I should be a helpless witness of the destruction of

India, Hinduism, Sikhism and Islam . . .

I would beg of all friends not to rush to Birla House (where Gandhi was staying) nor try to dissuade me or be anxious about me. I am in God's hands. Rather, they should turn the searchlight inwards. (90:409-10)

Both India and Pakistan seemed affected by the fast. Ghazanfar Ali Khan, a member of the Pakistan cabinet, said in Lahore that 'the fast should open people's eyes not only in India but also in Pakistan to the shame that they had brought upon themselves.'

After a meeting with two of Gandhi's friends, Jehangir Patel and Dinshaw Mehta, who, with Gandhi's consent, had gone to Karachi to explore the possibility of Gandhi visiting Pakistan, Jinnah sent a message urging Gandhi to 'live and work for the cause of Hindu-Muslim unity in the two Dominions.' Sent via Sri Prakasa, the Indian High Commissioner in Karachi, Jinnah's message, an indirect appeal against the fast, was also conveyed to Gandhi by Zahid Hussain, Pakistan's High Commissioner in New Delhi.[27]

Enquiries from Pakistan heartened him, but a gruesome attack in West Punjab on 13 January on a train filled with Hindu and Sikh refugees threatened to undo the effects of the fast. 'If this kind of thing continues in Pakistan,' said Gandhi on the 14th, 'how long will the people of India tolerate it? Even if a hundred men like me fasted, they would not be able to stop the tragedy that may follow.'

Decades earlier, said Gandhi, he had read outside the Red Fort the verse, 'If there is paradise on earth, it is here.' He did not find the Fort to be paradise. 'But,' Gandhi added, 'I should love to see that verse with justice inscribed on the gates of Pakistan at all the entrances.' Again he painted a picture of an ideal India and Pakistan and said:

I hope everyone who listens to me or reads these lines will forgive me if stretched on my bed and basking in the sun, inhaling lifegiving sunshine, I allow myself to indulge in this ecstasy . . .

When I was young [and] never even read the newspapers, could read English with difficulty and my Gujarati was not satisfactory, I had the dream that if the Hindus, Sikhs, Parsis, Christians and Muslims could live in amity not only in Rajkot but in the whole of India, they would all have a very happy life.

If that dream could be realized even now when I am an old man on the verge of death, my heart would dance. Children would then frolic in joy. (90:425)

Meeting one of Gandhi's conditions for breaking his fast, the Indian cabinet agreed to release Rs 55 crore owed to Pakistan under an agreement, signed in November 1947, for sharing the assets and liabilities of undivided India. Earlier, citing the conflict in Kashmir, the Indian government had announced that it would withhold the payment. Gandhi had asked for commitments from Delhi's citizens as well:

Muslims should be allowed to hold their annual fair at the mausoleum of Khwaja Qutb-ud-din. Mosques converted into temples and gurdwaras should be returned. Muslims should be ensured safety in their homes and on trains. The economic boycott imposed against Muslims in some Delhi localities should be lifted. (90:440)

Leaders of Delhi's Hindu, Sikh and Muslim communities, including representatives of the Hindu Mahasabha and the RSS, accepted the terms, and over two hundred thousand citizens signed a pledge and a plea for the fast to end.

According to Brij Krishna, Gandhi's lined and shrunken face was radiant as he broke his fast on 18 January. Prayers—Hindu, Muslim, Sikh, Christian and Buddhist—were recited in Gandhi's room in Birla House, and silence reigned while Gandhi extended his bony hand at 12.25 p.m. to hold the glass of orange juice handed to him by Maulana Azad and drank from it. Then, amid noises of joy and congratulation, all present, at Gandhi's instance, partook of fruit.[28]

His duty by Delhi done, Pakistan seemed Gandhi's next arena of action. Hoping that the Pakistan government would 'tell me that I can go and carry on my work there,' he said: 'Even if any one of the provincial governments of Pakistan invites me, I shall go.' (90:494)

To Ismat Iftikharuddin in Lahore, 22.1.48: I assure you I am eager to go to Lahore as soon as my convalescence is finished and the way is open for me to go to Lahore. (90:475)

*

Clashing visions: Seven men in a conspiracy to kill Gandhi joined his prayer meeting on 20 January. As planned, one man, Madanlal Pahwa, set off a bomb behind Gandhi, which was to be the cue for another conspirator, Digambar Badge, to throw a grenade at Gandhi's face, but Badge lost his nerve. The courage of a woman named Sulochana Devi led to Pahwa's apprehension but the other six slipped away. Gandhi was unhurt.

The attack on his life was also an attack on Gandhi's vision for India and version of Hinduism, and a test of his commitment to goodwill towards assailants. At the end of his prayer meeting the next day, Gandhi responded:

> Let me first deal with the bomb incident of yesterday. People have been sending me wires congratulating me and praising me. In fact I deserve no congratulations. I displayed no bravery. I thought it was part of army practice somewhere. I only came to know later that it was a bomb and it might have killed me if God had not willed it that I should live . . .
>
> You should not have any kind of hate against the person who was responsible for this. He had taken it for granted that I was an enemy of Hinduism. Is it not said in Chapter 4 of the Gita that whenever the wicked become too powerful and harm dharma, God sends someone to destroy them?
>
> The man who exploded the bomb obviously thinks that he has been sent by God to destroy me. I have not seen him. But I am told that is what he said when questioned by the police.
>
> But . . . if we do not like a man, does it mean that he is wicked? . . . If then someone kills me, taking me for a wicked man, will he not have to answer before God? . . . When he says he was doing the bidding of God, he is only making God an accomplice in a wicked deed . . . Those who are behind him or whose tool he is should know that this sort of thing will not save Hinduism.
>
> If Hinduism has to be saved it will be saved through such work as I am doing. I have been imbibing Hindu dharma right from my childhood. My nurse . . . taught me to invoke Rama whenever I had any fears . . .

Having passed all the tests, I am as staunch a Hindu today as intuitively I was at the age of five or six . . . Do you want to annihilate Hindu dharma by killing a devout Hindu like me?

Some Sikhs came to me and asked me if I suspected that a Sikh was implicated. I know he was not a Sikh. But what even if he was? What does it matter if he was a Hindu or a Muslim? May God bless him with good sense. I have told the Inspector-General of Police not to harass the man. They should try to win him over. (90:472-73)

Jehangir Patel and Dinshaw Mehta had meanwhile returned from Karachi. The two Parsis were accompanied by a third, the khadi-wearing Karachi-based helper of refugees, Jamshed Mehta, of whom Jinnah had once said, 'I know he is a Gandhian at heart but I cannot do without him.'[29]

As long as he did not ask for reunion, Pakistan would welcome him, Gandhi was told; but he would have to accept protection by Pakistan's police. Gandhi resisted the second condition but yielded when pressed by Mehta. By 27 January the three Parsis were back in Karachi and talking with Pakistan's leaders. The second week of February was proposed for Gandhi's arrival in Pakistan.

On 29 January about forty Hindus from Bannu in the Frontier province saw Gandhi. Injured in body and spirit, they took out some of their resentment on Gandhi, who referred to the meeting in his prayer speech in the evening:

One of them said I had done enough harm already and that I should stop and disappear from the scene . . . I asked him where he wanted me to go. He said that I might go to the Himalayas . . . I can only do as God bids . . . God is the help of the afflicted, but an afflicted person is not God . . .

Why do you presume that because I am a friend of the Muslims I am an enemy of Hindus and Sikhs? I cannot run away because anyone wants me to run away . . . God will do what He wills. He may take me away . . . My Himalayas are here. (90:524-25)

But to his companions Gandhi said:

You can take that as notice served on me . . . We should

accept curses from a sorrow-laden heart like that as the voice
of God. (Brij Krishna 3:571)

The following evening, while walking to prayer, his hands joined
together to greet fellow-worshippers, Gandhi was shot thrice at
point-blank range by Nathuram Godse, one of the men who had
planned to kill Gandhi on 20 January.

The words, 'Ram, Ram,' escaped from Gandhi as he fell. Within
minutes he was dead. We will never know for certain whether he
forgave Nathuram before life left him, but Gandhi's mind was on
prayer when he was shot, and his joined hands suggested goodwill as
well as greeting. We have seen, too, that he had prayed to die
forgiving and forgiven.

CASTE, HIERARCHY AND UNTOUCHABILITY

Alien rule and Hindu-Muslim discord were not Gandhi's only foes.
Hindu society's hierarchy, culminating in untouchability and dividing
Hindus from one another, was another. Though sometimes criticized
as being keener on Swaraj than on social justice, Gandhi contested
the charge. Thus he wrote to his friend Charlie Andrews in 1921:

You are doing an injustice to me in even allowing yourself
to think that for a single moment I may be subordinating
the question [of untouchability] to any others . . . It is a
bigger problem than that of gaining Indian independence but
I can tackle it better if I gain the latter on the way. It is not
impossible that India may free herself from English
domination before India has become free of the curse of
untouchability . . . (29.1.21; 19:288-90)

In 1932, when Gandhi and Ambedkar, the leader of the untouchables,
signed their Poona Pact in a British prison, Ambedkar confessed to
Gandhi that he was 'surprised, immensely surprised' that there was
'so much in common' between the two, and added, 'If you devote
yourself entirely to the welfare of the Depressed Classes, you would
become our hero.'[30]

Andrews, who wrote in October 1932 that love for the
untouchables 'may be said to be the deepest thing in all his (Gandhi's)
life,' invited Gandhi, in 1933, to do just what Ambedkar had asked.
Suggesting that Gandhi had 'been trying to serve two masters,'

Andrews urged him to concentrate on untouchability removal 'for the whole remainder of your life, without turning to the right or to the left.'[31]

Gandhi did not heed the advice of Andrews. For all his feeling for the untouchables, he could not drop his concern for freedom and Hindu-Muslim unity. But he attacked untouchability in language seldom emanating from a caste Hindu. Thus in 1916, a year after his return to India, he said in Madras:

> Every affliction that we labour under in this sacred land is a fit and proper punishment for this great and indelible crime that we are committing. (16.2.16; 13:232-33)

In 1921, at the peak of the agitation against the Punjab wrongs, Gandhi spoke as follows at a Suppressed Classes Conference in Ahmedabad:

> What crimes for which we condemn the government as Satanic have not we been guilty of towards our untouchable brethren? . . . We make them crawl on their bellies; we have made them rub their noses on the ground; with eyes red with rage, we push them out of railway compartments— what more than this has British rule done? What charge that we bring against Dyer and O'Dwyer may not others, and even our own people, lay at our door? (13.4.21; 19:572)

In an article in *Navajivan*, Gandhi used even stronger words. Cruelties to the untouchables did not merely equal the Punjab atrocities; they constituted 'an outrage grosser than that in the Punjab against which we have been protesting.'

> We . . . segregate them, . . . drive them to live on the outskirts of the village, [are] not concerned whether they live or die, . . . give them food left over by others. (19:331)

The suggestion that Indians in South Africa were paying for Indian untouchability was repeated by him throughout his life:

> Has not a just Nemesis overtaken us for the crime of untouchability? Have we not reaped as we have sown? (*Young India*, 19.1.21)

Our sins have a strange way of coming home to roost. We turned a portion of ourselves into pariahs and today the whites of South Africa are doing the same to our compatriots there. (Speech to AICC, Bombay, 7.7.46; 84:422-23)

At times he spoke of wider consequences:

In the history of the world religions, there is perhaps nothing like our treatment of the suppressed classes . . . God does not punish directly. His ways are inscrutable. *Who knows that all our woes are not due to that one black sin?* (Emphasis added.)

He was fiercely attacked in 1920 when the university he had started, Gujrat Vidyapith, decided not to accept students from schools that excluded untouchables. Gujarati journals and whispering campaigns alleged that Gandhi had imposed the decision under the influence of Christians, and the leaders of orthodoxy declared that they would oppose his movement against the Raj if the decision was not annulled. Gandhi answered his critics in *Navajivan:*

The advice I receive from one and all is that if I do not exclude Antyajas (the untouchables) from the national schools, the movement for swaraj will end in smoke. If I have even a little of the true Vaishnava in me, God will also vouchsafe me the strength to reject the swaraj which may be won by abandoning the Antyajas. (5.12.20; 19:73)

Gandhi's wife Kasturba, his brother Laxmidas, and some of his closest Ashram associates objected to Gandhi's notions of social equality and on occasion spoke of parting company. In 1915, when Gandhi's Ahmedabad Ashram admitted a family of Dheds, who were seen as untouchables, Kasturba and some others rebelled. Describing the incident, Gandhi wrote to V.S. Srinivasa Sastri:

There was quite a flutter in the Ashram. There is a flutter even in Ahmedabad. I have told Mrs Gandhi she could leave me and we should part good friends . . . I might have at no distant time to carry out the idea of shifting to some Dhed quarter and sharing their life with the Dheds . . . [The incident] is of importance to me because it enables me to demonstrate the efficiency of passive resistance in social questions, and when I take the final step, it will embrace swaraj, etc. (23.9.15; 13:127-28)

In the event Kasturba and the other rebels revised their attitude, and Gandhi and the Ashram did not have to move.

*

If Gandhi hoped to shame the caste Hindus, he also strove to counsel the untouchables. In 1921 he told them:

> I [do not] expect you to cease to have misgivings about the Hindus. How can they deserve to be not mistrusted having wronged you so much? . . .

> You must not ask the Hindus to emancipate you as a matter of favour. Hindus must do so, if they want, in their own interests. You should make them feel ashamed by your own purity and cleanliness . . .

> You should now cease to accept leavings from plates, however clean they may be represented to be. Receive grain only— good, sound grain, not rotten grain—and that too only if it is courteously offered . . .

> The Hindus are not sinful by nature—they are sunk in ignorance . . . May God give you strength to work out your salvation. (13.4.21; 19:569-75)

If here Gandhi seems to discourage confrontation, we should remember his remark to Sastri about the possibility of 'passive resistance (satyagraha) in social questions.' In 1924 he backed a satyagraha, which won partial success, against a long-standing denial to untouchables of the use of public roads adjacent to a temple and Brahmin residences in the town of Vaikom in the princely state of Travancore.

The Vaikom effort may have had a part in encouraging the Mahad satyagraha of 1927, which was guided by Bhimrao Ambedkar, a brilliant scholar and lawyer born in a family of untouchable Mahars of Maharashtra and educated in England and America. Untouchables gathering in Mahad for a conference surged forward and drank water from the Chawdar tank, from which untouchables were barred despite a resolution of the Mahad municipality for its opening to all.

Later in the year, between 10,000 and 15,000 untouchables gathered again in Mahad. A copy of the Manusmriti was burned on this occasion. According to Gail Omvedt, scholar of the Dalit movement, Ambedkar 'had a soft spot' for Gandhi at this juncture, though he was disappointed that Gandhi was 'not giving as much weight to untouchability removal as to Hindu-Muslim unity.' The tent for the December rally 'featured Gandhi's photo.' Two years earlier, Ambedkar had evidently said to an untouchable gathering at Belgaum: 'Where no one else comes close, the sympathy shown by Mahatma Gandhi is by no means a small thing.'[32]

*

Gandhi and Ambedkar: Some of his closest political colleagues viewed Gandhi's involvement with untouchability as a risky distraction. Jawaharlal Nehru seemed to feel this way in the early 1930s, and Vallabhbhai Patel's advice in March 1933, recorded by Mahadev Desai, was that Gandhi should not allow himself to be crushed between 'the upper and nether stones of the orthodox Hindus and the followers of Ambedkar.' He should stay clear and 'let the two parties quarrel among themselves.'[33]

Disagreeing, Gandhi thought that he could not 'let the millions of [untouchables] feel that they have been left to their fate.'[34]

Apart from deploring Gandhi's unwillingness to concentrate solely on attacking social inequality among Hindus, Ambedkar had other criticisms. In his view, Gandhi attacked untouchability but neither the caste system nor Hinduism and was therefore not radical enough. Politically, by attracting untouchables to Congress, he was diluting untouchable solidarity. Asking caste Hindus to admit untouchables to temples, Gandhi was being paternalistic.

Ambedkar's biggest fear, however, was that Swaraj would lead to caste Hindu domination and worsen the position of the untouchables. It was an old anxiety. In 1917, before Ambedkar became the leader of Maharashtra's untouchables, a deputation of the untouchables of western India had told Edwin Montagu, Secretary of State for India, who was visiting Bombay:

> We shall fight to the last drop of our blood against any attempt to transfer the seat of authority in this country from British hands to the so-called high-caste Hindus.[35]

The untouchables' fear was understood and in fact shared by Gandhi. In August 1931, he had said:

> If we came into power with the stain of untouchability unaffected, I am positive that the 'untouchables' would be

far worse under that 'Swaraj' than they are now, for the simple reason that our weaknesses and our failings would then be buttressed by the accession of power. (2.8.31, in Ahmedabad)[36]

A conference in London in 1931 saw a sharp clash between Gandhi and Ambedkar. His Majesty's Government (HMG) had invited representatives of a number of Indian interests to confer with one another and their British rulers. Gandhi represented Congress, Ambedkar the Depressed Classes League. Ambedkar asked for, and Gandhi opposed, a separate electorate and reserved seats for the untouchables in any new constitution for India.

Separate electorates for Muslims and Sikhs were included in the 1916 Lucknow Pact between Congress and the Muslim League which Tilak and Jinnah had helped forge and Gandhi had backed. But Gandhi refused to accept a division of the Hindu electorate. It would destroy the slender bridge he had helped construct between caste Hindus and untouchables, impede the reform that had commenced amongst caste Hindus, and expose untouchables to heightened hostility. At the conference he said:

> It (the separate electorate for scheduled castes) means the perpetual bar sinister. I would not sell the vital interests of the untouchables even for the sake of winning the freedom of India. I claim myself in my own person to represent the vast mass of the untouchables . . .

> Today there is a body of Hindu reformers who are pledged to remove the blot of untouchability. Sikhs may remain as such in perpetuity, so may Mohammedans, so may Europeans. Will untouchables remain untouchables in perpetuity?

Referring to 'the two divisions' in every village that separate electorates would entrench, Gandhi suggested that those demanding a separate electorate 'do not know their India, do not know how Indian society is today constructed.' He ended with a declaration:

> I want to say with all the emphasis that I can command that if I was the only person to resist this thing, I would resist it with my life. (48:297-98)

During a discussion at Friends House, the Quaker centre, he was more candid:

The untouchables are in the hands of superior classes. They can suppress them completely and wreak vengeance upon the untouchables who are at their mercy. I may be opening out my shame to you. But . . . how can I invite utter destruction for them? I would not be guilty of that crime. (48:258)

In London Gandhi tried to win Ambedkar, sending his son Devadas to him to arrange a meeting. A message he addressed to Sir Mirza Ismail, also a participant in the conference, shows Gandhi's anxiety:

It will be a great triumph of yours if you can convert Dr A. Having suffered like him in [South Africa], Dr A. always commands my sympathy in all he says. He needs the gentlest treatment. (22.10.31; 48:208)

In a speech to the Indian Majlis in London, Gandhi spelt out the sympathy:

I have the highest regard for Dr Ambedkar. He has every right to be bitter. That he does not break our heads is an act of self-restraint on his part . . . The same thing happened to me in my early days in South Africa where I was hounded out by the Europeans wherever I went. It is quite natural for him to vent his wrath. (48:224)

Did Gandhi see that it was also natural for Ambedkar to seek British support, even as Gandhi had sought it for Indians in South Africa? Sixteen years later, in February 1947, even someone like Jagjivan Ram, the untouchables' leader serving as a Congress minister in India's interim government, would ask the departing British Viceroy, Wavell, not to throw his people 'to the mercy of the majority communities,' adding that they 'would miss British protection and British justice' and would have preferred that the British 'should remain for another ten years or so.'[37]

Passion, confidence and irreverence marked Ambedkar's performance in London. He rejected Gandhi's right in respect of the untouchables. Other delegates said that Gandhi could not speak for Muslims, Christians, Anglo-Indians and India-based Europeans.

On 13 November 1931, the Minorities Pact was announced. Signed, among others, by Ambedkar and the Aga Khan, the Pact demanded separate electorates for Muslims, untouchables, Christians, Anglo-Indians and Europeans. Within hours Gandhi made the

declaration, quoted earlier, that he would 'resist' a separate electorate
for the untouchables 'with my life.' HMG reserved judgment on this
but made it clear that Gandhi's demand for independence would not
be conceded.

A fast, a pact and a change: Returning to India, Gandhi announced
the resumption of disobedience and was imprisoned. Tens of thousands
followed him into the Raj's jails or received blows from its police.
Following his truth, Ambedkar continued to press for a separate
electorate. Six months after the London conference, he was in that
metropolis again, urging HMG not to yield to Gandhi.

Writing from prison in March 1932, Gandhi had reminded the
British Premier, Ramsay MacDonald, of his oath. In August HMG
announced that the untouchables would have a separate electorate. In
September Gandhi said, from prison, that he would fast unto death.
HMG made it plain that it could revise its award only if caste Hindus
and the untouchable leadership agreed on an alternative.

Gandhi insisted that his fast was above all directed at caste
Hindus. He wished, he claimed, to 'sting the Hindu conscience.' If
the Hindu mass mind showed remorse, the untouchables' leaders
might relent. But if the Hindus were not prepared to banish
untouchability, they should sacrifice him 'without the slightest
hesitation.' Added Gandhi:

> My life I count of no consequence. One hundred lives . . .
> would, in my opinion, be poor penance done by Hindus for
> the atrocious wrongs they have heaped upon helpless men
> and women of their own faith.[38]

Many sent telegrams pleading with Gandhi not to fast. Replying to
C. Rajagopalachari, Gandhi said: 'I expect you to rejoice that a
comrade has a God-given opportunity for a final act of satyagraha in
the cause of the downtrodden.'

He warned caste Hindus that this was but the beginning.
Henceforth 'an increasing army of reformers' would resist 'social,
civic or political persecution of the Depressed classes.' The issue was
of 'transcendental value, far surpassing Swaraj.'

To the untouchables, Gandhi clarified that he would accept
reserved seats, though he doubted their usefulness. He hoped they
would forgo the separate electorate.

The fast began inside Yeravda prison on 20 September.
Responding, caste Hindu leaders resolved in Bombay that 'one of the

earliest Acts of the Swaraj Parliament' would be to guarantee to untouchables equal access to 'public wells, public schools, public roads and all other public institutions.' (53:130)

To save Gandhi's life one caste Hindu leader after another asked for a change in customs. Across India temples were opened overnight to untouchables. Brahmins and untouchables dined together. Padmaja Naidu wrote of 'a catharsis' cleansing Hinduism of 'the accumulated corruption' of centuries, and Tagore spoke of a 'wonder' happening 'before our very eyes.'

The Raj permitted negotiations around Gandhi's bed under a mango tree in the jail compound. Ambedkar came. His first words were, 'Mahatmaji, you have been very unfair to us.' 'It is always my lot to appear to be unfair,' replied Gandhi. Gandhi's secretary, Pyarelal, saw that 'the redoubtable Doctor, strongly supported by his colleagues, fought every inch of the ground.'

Gandhi's acceptance of reserved seats had given the negotiations a good start. Agreement was reached on the seventh day. Untouchable leaders and caste Hindu leaders signed an accord to which Gandhi had agreed; HMG sent word that it would be honoured; and Gandhi broke his fast, sipping orange juice handed to him by Kasturba.

From behind bars a prisoner had jolted a nation's customs and imposed his will on an empire. The Yeravda or Poona Pact, as it came to be known, gave the scheduled castes double the seats that HMG had offered and merged caste Hindus and untouchables in a single stream.

After the fast was broken, Gandhi suggested that 'a meeting of hearts' had taken place, conveyed his 'Hindu gratitude' to Dr Ambedkar, Rao Bahadur Srinivasan and Rao Bahadur M.C. Rajah, the untouchable leaders, and said, referring to them:

> They could have taken up an uncompromising and defiant attitude by way of punishment to the so-called caste Hindus . . . If they had done so I at least could not have resented their attitude and my death would have been but a trifling price exacted for the tortures that the outcasts of Hinduism have been going through for unknown generations. But they have chosen a nobler path and . . . have followed the precept of forgiveness.[39]

Thus Gandhi felt that forgiveness rather than revenge had emerged from the untouchables' leaders. On his part, Ambedkar gave 'a large part of the credit . . . to Mahatma Gandhi himself.'

But the Yeravda spirit was not destined to last. The years from 1933 to 1947 saw another round of conflict between Gandhi and Ambedkar. Despite Ambedkar's exhortation, Gandhi could not devote himself 'entirely' to the cause of the untouchables. He could not forget Swaraj or Hindu-Muslim unity. Ambedkar, on the other hand, was clear that 'social democracy was more vital than independence from foreign rule.'[40]

*

Gandhi's strategy over caste: Radical Dalits have blamed Gandhi for alleged softness towards caste Hindus, and for statements that could be construed as defending the caste system even while attacking untouchability. Asked by Gandhi in 1933 to send a message for the opening number of *Harijan*, Gandhi's journal for tackling untouchability, Ambedkar replied that he did not think that Hindus would 'treat any message from me with respect.' But he sent a 'statement':

> The outcaste is a bye-product of the caste system. There will be outcastes as long as there are castes. Nothing can emancipate the outcaste except the destruction of the caste system.

Gandhi published the statement with a comment:

> Untouchability is the product, not of the caste system, but of the distinction of high and low . . . The attack on untouchability is thus an attack on this 'high-and-low'ness. The moment untouchability goes, the caste system itself will be purified . . .' (*Harijan*, 11.2.33; 53:259-61)

By 1935, however, Gandhi started criticizing the caste system itself. In fact, even his earlier 'defence' of the system was of an ideal that Gandhi admitted did not exist in practice. As for verses from scripture quoted by defenders of orthodoxy, Gandhi was clear from 1917 that these 'cannot be above reason or morality':

> It is no good quoting verses from Manusmriti and other scriptures in defence of this orthodoxy. A number of verses in these scriptures are apocryphal, a number of them are quite meaningless. (1917; 14:345 and 73-77)

Light was thrown on Gandhi's strategy regarding caste and untouchability by Nehru. He told Tibor Mende in January 1956:

> I spoke to Gandhi repeatedly: why don't you hit out at the caste system directly? He said that he did not believe in the caste system except in some idealized form of occupations and all that; but that the present system was thoroughly bad and must go. I am undermining it completely, he said, by my tackling untouchability . . . If untouchability goes, he said, the caste system goes. So I am concentrating on that . . .

Asked by Mende if Gandhi could be called 'a genius in finding the common denominator,' Nehru replied: 'There was more than that. The genius [lay] in finding . . . the weakest point of the enemy, the breaking of his front.' Gandhi thus seems to have been candid with Nehru about his dislike of the caste system and strategy for finishing it. He would have united pro-orthodox ranks in opposition if he had commenced with an attack on caste. He chose to zero in on an evil none could defend.

Nehru told Mende that while 'all the old reformers . . . just functioned in the air, . . . this man powerfully moved the masses and created huge social changes.' By making 'untouchability the one thing on which he concentrated,' he 'affected ultimately the whole caste system.'[41]

Going by the verbal and physical attacks it launched against Gandhi, orthodoxy certainly felt threatened by him. When, after his release in 1934, Gandhi campaigned across India against untouchability, champions of orthodoxy waved black flags and shouted slogans against him. In Pune, a car thought to be carrying him was bombed; Gandhi was not in it but seven others were injured. His meetings were broken up, his character was reviled in pamphlets, in Benares his portrait was burnt. In Karachi a Hindu with an axe was apprehended before he could use it against Gandhi.

Those with close ties to him took offence. His sister Raliat voiced displeasure. An old family friend, Ranchhoddas Patwari, whose loan had helped with Gandhi's voyage to London in 1888, demanded precise replies to eighty-eight questions, predicted that Gandhi's stand against untouchability would destroy his position in the country and wreck Congress, suggested that Gandhi had 'completely forsaken dharma,' and finally spoke of a break between them.

Yet Gandhi uncannily foresaw that the purists were isolating themselves, and that the bulk of the Hindu community would follow him. To Jawaharlal he wrote:

> The fight against [orthodoxy] is becoming more and more interesting if also increasingly difficult . . . The abuses they are hurling at me are wonderfully refreshing. I am all that is bad and corrupt on earth. But the storm will subside. For I apply the sovereign remedy of ahimsa—non-retaliation. The more I ignore the abuses, the fiercer they are becoming. But it is the death dance of the moth round a lamp. (53:309-10)

*

Harijan to Dalit: From 1931, 'Harijan' ('Person or persons of God') had been Gandhi's term for 'untouchable' in *Navajivan,* his Gujarati journal which the Raj banned in 1932. In 1933 he started the English-language weekly *Harijan,* which was soon followed by the Hindi *Harijan Sevak* and the Gujarati *Harijanbandhu.* The opening issue of *Harijan* had a piece entitled, 'Why "Harijan" ':

> It is not a name of my coining. Some years ago, several 'untouchable' correspondents complained that I used the word 'asprishya' in the pages of *Navajivan.* 'Asprishya' means literally untouchable. I then invited them to suggest a better name and one of the 'untouchable' correspondents suggested the adoption of the name 'Harijan,' on the strength of its having been used by the first-known poet-saint of Gujrat (Narsinh Mehta) . . . I thought it was a good word.

> 'Harijan' means 'a man of God.' All the religions of the world described God pre-eminently as the Friend of the friendless, the Help of the helpless and the Protector of the weak . . . In India who can be more friendless, helpless or weaker than [those] classified as untouchables? If, therefore, any body of people can be fitly described as men of God, they are surely these helpless, friendless and despised people.

> Not that the change of name brings about any change of status, but one may at least be spared the use of a term which is itself one of reproach. When caste Hindus have of their own inner conviction . . . got rid of the present-day

untouchability, we shall all be called Harijans, for caste Hindus then will have found favour with God. (11.2.33; 53:266-67)

For about fifty years, until the late seventies, 'Harijan' was perhaps the most widely employed and accepted term for the 'untouchables,' though official documents tended to use the phrase 'Scheduled Castes.' In the eighties and the nineties 'Dalit' ('oppressed') increasingly replaced 'Harijan,' and seemed to be the expression preferred by the community's representatives. Reflecting the community's radicalization, the change has sometimes been accompanied by an attack on Gandhi's motives for employing the term 'Harijan' but only rarely by an awareness of how he came to use it in the first place.

*

Ambedkar's warning: Five years after the Poona Pact, in the 1937 elections to provincial assemblies, no party could equal Congress's performance in the seats reserved under the Poona Pact for the untouchables. Ambedkar's followers won 11 out of 15 seats in Bombay but Congress was comfortably ahead everywhere else. Of the 20 reserved seats in the U.P., Congress won 16. In Bihar it got 11 out of 15, and in Madras 26 out of 30.

Ambedkar linked Congress's success to the caste Hindu vote but the truth was that Gandhi and the freedom movement had found a response among the scheduled castes as well. This became even more obvious nine years later, when Congress swept the Scheduled Caste seats in the 1945-46 polls. By this time Quit India had taken place, and Ambedkar's image had been damaged by his being a member of the Executive Council that sought to suppress Quit India.

From time to time, Ambedkar warned that he and his followers would exchange the Hindu faith for another. When Ambedkar spoke along these lines in 1933, Gandhi commented:

If this doctrine of utmost superiority and utmost inferiority, descending from father to son for eternity, is an integral part of Hinduism, . . . then I no more want to belong to it than does Dr Ambedkar. But . . . there is no superiority or inferiority in the Hinduism of my conception. (on 14.2.33; 53:306)

On another occasion Gandhi said that religion was 'not like a house or a cloak, which can be changed at will.' It was 'a more integral part of one's self than one's body.' As for conversions, Gandhi urged Ambedkar to consider the reaction of caste Hindus, amidst whom, 'for good or ill,' the untouchables found themselves.[42]

Gandhi's ultimate appeal, however, was not to loyalty or prudence but to the mind and the soul:

> I invite Dr Ambedkar to shed his bitterness and anger and try to learn the beauties of the faith of his forefathers. Let him not curse Hinduism without making an unbiased study of it, and if it fails to sustain him in the hour of need, by all means let him forsake it. (14.2.33; 53:307)

Ambedkar's reply was that the Hinduism which the Dalits found around them was alienating. He had hoped, he said, that Gandhi would 'attain dictatorship in social affairs,' but Gandhi had refused to strive for it. 'India wants,' added Ambedkar, 'a dictator like Kemal Pasha or Mussolini in social and religious matters.'[43] When, eight years after Gandhi's death, Ambedkar took hundreds of thousands of his people from Hinduism to Buddhism, he spoke of a word he had evidently given to Gandhi. This was that when the time came, he would 'choose only the least harmful way for the country.' By adopting Buddhism he had ensured, Ambedkar said, that the conversion would not dislocate India.[44]

*

Enlisting Ambedkar: Between 1937 and 1946 Gandhi was severely attacked by Ambedkar. Gandhi and the Congress were deceiving and suppressing the untouchables; Gandhi was not frontal and thoroughgoing enough in his criticisms of caste; and so on. 'Caste Has to Go' was Gandhi's title to an article he wrote in *Harijan* in November 1935. The article discussed the best way 'to destroy caste' and stated: 'The sooner the better.' (*Harijan*, 16.11.35; 62:121-22) But Ambedkar was not satisfied.

As independence drew near, Gandhi advised Nehru and Patel to include Ambedkar in the new nation's first cabinet. When there was hesitation, Gandhi evidently reminded Jawaharlal that power was coming 'to India, not to Congress.'[45] According to G. Ramachandran, 'both Nehru and the Sardar were not in favour, saying that this man had been attacking and maligning the Congress.' In Ramachandran's view, Gandhi saw Ambedkar's inclusion as an 'atonement' that India had to make to her untouchables.[46]

Ambedkar's skills had also influenced Gandhi. One of Ambedkar's biographers, C.B. Khairmode, has referred to a conversation in Bombay in December 1946 between Ambedkar and Muriel Lester, one of Gandhi's English friends. Lester had been present at a Gandhi-Ambedkar meeting in London in 1931. She evidently informed Ambedkar that 'Gandhi was keen that the Congress should include Ambedkar in the Central cabinet and use his learning and leadership . . .' According to Khairmode, after Lester had given Gandhi an account of her talk with Ambedkar, Gandhi asked Patel and Nehru to invite Ambedkar into the cabinet.[47]

There was magnanimity in Ambedkar's willingness to join the caste Hindu-dominated Congress cabinet. As Law Minister, chairman of the Drafting Committee, and pilot of the Constitution Bill, his role in the construction of the Indian Constitution was greater than anyone else's.

Yet it is legitimate also to see the rights the Constitution guarantees to the weak and the underprivileged as proof of Hindu India's assent. Gandhi had pledged these rights in London in 1931, at the Karachi Congress earlier that year, and on numerous other occasions. Led by his colleagues and followers, the Constituent Assembly enshrined the rights at the heart of the Constitution, thereby implying caste Hindu acceptance of untouchable rights. Daily life would be different from law, yet law at least was amenable to Gandhi's strategy.

*

Inhumanity under Swaraj: In the last two years of his life, Gandhi lived as much as he could in untouchable settlements: in New Delhi amidst sweepers in the Balmiki colony, in Noakhali in the homes of weavers, cobblers and fisherfolk. His grasp of reality in grass-roots India was revealed in a letter he wrote in August 1946 to Vallabhbhai Patel, who was about to take over as Home Minister in India's eve-of-independence interim government:

> Who are the people who beat up Harijans, murder them, prevent them from using wells, drive them out of schools and refuse them entry into their homes? They are Congressmen. Aren't they? It is very necessary to have a clear picture of this. (1.8.46; 85:102)

Underscoring his acceptance of intermarriage, he said in Patna in April 1947 that he had 'long ago made it a rule not to be present at or give his blessings for any wedding unless one of the parties was a Harijan.' (24.4.47; 87:350) When, two months after Gandhi's death, Ambedkar married a Brahmin doctor, Patel wrote to him: 'I am sure if Bapu were alive he would have given you his blessings.' Replied Ambedkar: 'I agree that Bapu, if he had been alive, would have blessed it.'[48]

In June 1947, Gandhi was asked, 'Who will be the President of the Indian Republic? Should we not have Jawaharlal Nehru?' Replied Gandhi:

> If I have my way, the first President of the Indian Republic will be a chaste and brave Bhangi girl. If an English girl of seventeen could become the British Queen and later even Empress of India, there is no reason why a Bhangi girl of robust love of her people and unimpeachable integrity of character should not become the first President . . .
>
> She should be chaste as Sita and her eyes should radiate light. Sita had such radiance that Ravana could not touch her . . . If such a girl of my dreams becomes President, I shall be her servant . . . I shall make Jawaharlal, Sardar Patel and Rajen Babu her Ministers and therefore her servants. (27.6.47; 89:223-25)

In September 1947, when Gandhi returned to Delhi from Calcutta, refugees from Pakistan were occupying the space in the sweepers' colony that he had become used to. Patel and others decided that he would have to live at Birla House. Gandhi thanked the Birlas, admitted that they had met his expenses at the Balmiki colony, but added that he was 'greatly pained' at the change of lodging. (10.9.47; 89:167)

Two months later, he exposed the denial of untouchable rights in free India:-

> It is a matter of shame for us that . . . in Rohtak district . . . there are Jats and perhaps Ahirs too [who] felt that the Harijans were their slaves . . . They may be given water and food but they can get nothing by right . . . We feel that we can even intimidate a judge if we are brought before him . . . The result is that the Harijans are ruined. (23.11.47; 90:92)

In December 1947 he backed a fast by Sane Guruji that enabled Dalits to enter Maharashtra's famed Pandharpur temple. When some priests started a counter-fast to revive the bar, Gandhi criticized them and expressed his view that 'as long as the Harijans were barred from the temple, it had not been really consecrated.' (30.12.47; 90:327)

Three days before his death he wrote an article for *Harijanbandhu* deploring the bar against Harijans in some Jain and Swaminarayan temples in Gujrat. His last public utterance in relation to the untouchables was about a Harijan basti in Ajmer. Rajkumari Amrit Kaur, the Health Minister, had seen it and described its pitiable condition to him. Gandhi referred to it in his post-prayer speech on 27 January:

> We have secured our independence but it is of no value if we cannot stop such a thing. And it can be done in a day. Can we not provide a piece of dry land for the Harijans? If they must remove garbage, . . . must they be also made to live in it? . . . We have become heartless. (27.1.48; 90:508)

On the day of his death, when a delegation of East Punjab's Jat leaders came to see him, he asked them about the province's Harijans. He had lived to see his old prediction coming true, that Dalit suffering would continue after Swaraj.

*

During his life Gandhi often spoke of cheerfully putting up with any abuse that Dalits might throw at a caste Hindu like him. Caste Hindu conduct over the centuries had invited it, he said. In the decades since Gandhi's death several Dalit spokespersons have indeed castigated him, alleging that Gandhi used Dalits instead of empowering them.

At the end of 1997, however, the writer Kancha Ilaiah, who refers to his birth in the 'shepherd caste' and calls himself one of the 'Dalitbahujans'—'people and castes who form the exploited and suppressed majority'[49]—wrote:

> Did the Congress nationalists, barring Gandhi himself, even oppose untouchability? Was not Gandhi alone in addressing untouchability within the Congress? . . .

Ilaiah's comment, part of a review of Arun Shourie's critique of

Ambedkar, *Worshipping False Gods*, concludes with this remark:

> Perhaps it is pertinent to remind Shourie that Gandhi was
> killed not by a Dalit or a Muslim—the wretches and
> worshippers of false Gods—but by a high-born Hindu.
> (*Biblio*, New Delhi, November 1997)

*

Gandhi's bid was huge. One wonders whether anyone before him in
India's long history had aimed for so much, or asked so much—in
terms of changes in entrenched attitudes, customs and conduct—of
the Indian people. And though his success was neither complete nor
necessarily lasting, the values that Gandhi strove for seem to have
entered India's soil and air, which however are hospitable to contrary
values too.

Disappointed with post-independence South Asia, some have
looked for flaws in the chief of the independence movement. Gandhi
has been criticized as being not macho enough, or not Hindu
enough, or too much of a Hindu, or not radical enough, or not
modern enough, charges levelled by, respectively, militant nationalists,
staunch Hindus confusing Hinduness with dislike of non-Hindus,
Muslims unable to come to terms with Hindu numbers, votaries of
equality angered by continuing caste and class injustices, and admirers
of the economic progress of Western and westernizing countries.

In some ways these criticisms are more revealing of the critics,
of their sectional or partial concerns, than of Gandhi, who was
candid about his commitment to Indians (and, after August 1947, of
Pakistanis) of all kinds, including the poor and the needy, and,
despite his passionate Indianness, to a world beyond nationalism. No
South Asian future could be constructed, Gandhi insisted, without its
Dalits, or its Muslims, or its caste Hindus, or its women.

More significant, perhaps, is the question that the African-
American educator Stuart Nelson asked Gandhi in Calcutta two or
three days after independence: why was it that 'Indians, who had
more or less successfully gained independence through peaceful
means, were now unable to check the tide of civil war'? (89:62)

'This is indeed a searching question that I must answer,' Gandhi
said. Then he offered this explanation:

Indians harboured illwill and anger against their erstwhile

rulers, while they pretended to resist them nonviolently . . .
The attitude of violence which we had secretly harboured,
in spite of the restraint imposed by the Indian National
Congress, now recoiled upon us and made us fly at each
other's throats when the question of the distribution of
power came up. (89:62)

There is no evidence that the same people took part in nonviolent
campaigns for freedom and the communal violence of 1946-47.
Strictly speaking, therefore, Gandhi's diagnosis was not accurate.
What is true is that the urge in him—natural, pressing, irresistible—
for India's independence caused Gandhi from time to time to lose
sight of India's potential for violence—of which, as we have seen, he
was well aware—, or on occasion to disregard or risk that potential.
This is what he was acknowledging to Nelson.

Though India's (and South Asia's) capacity for violence had
troubled Gandhi deeply, its eradication was not the chief goal of
Gandhi's life. India's independence was, closely followed, or equalled,
by Hindu-Muslim unity and the end of caste inequalities.

We need not speculate on India's possible fate if, disregarding
India's subjugation, Gandhi had concentrated solely on curing Indian
violence. He could not ignore that humiliation; for the world as a
whole, it is perhaps well that he could not.

Yet South Asia, though wanting freedom, needed reconciliation.
It did not come free with freedom; as Gandhi told Nelson, the new
nation(s) had to build it:

India was now free . . . Now that the burden of subjection
had been lifted, all the forces of good had to be marshalled
in one great effort to build a country which forsook the
accustomed method of violence in order to settle human
conflict whether it was between two States or between two
sections of the same people. (89:63)

9

Why Partition Occurred, and the Wounds of 1947

THERE IS NO need to quote here from the ample evidence showing that Britain found Indian divisions congenial and useful. (Among the several works that offer the evidence, Bipan Chandra's *Communalism in India* may be mentioned.) But it does not follow that the divisions were a colonial creation, or that the British did not try, when their rule was not in danger, to unify India. A month before independence, Gandhi candidly acknowledged Britain's role in Indian unity:

> The British carried on their rule in India for 150 years . . . and also tried to develop it as a nation and to some extent succeeded also. Before them the Moghuls had made a similar effort but they were less successful. *Having first unified the country*, it is not a very becoming thing for them to divide it. (Emphasis added; 88:281)

After over fifty years of independence, it is surely time to admit openly that for all the divide-and-rule gleefully practised by the British, the India they left behind was a good deal more united than the India they had found in the eighteenth century. While this truth of history is privately conceded by many Indians, there is less readiness to acknowledge another awkward graph from history, which suggests that every step forward in the struggle for independence also turned out to be a step in the direction of partition.

Not that those who sought independence also sought division. Far from it. Most of them went ahead firmly convinced that Indian divisions were a British import, and that Indian unity would flow from independence and from struggles for it. But our overview of the India of the eighteenth, nineteenth and twentieth centuries has indicated that there was always some Indian section or another that feared the end of British rule, and placed greater trust in the British than in a dominant Indian group.

If the British were to go, more than one Indian section desired a separate state or status for itself and was reluctant to be part of a united or centralized India, A subcontinent of mistrust had invited alien rule. A continuance of mistrust divided the independent subcontinent, politically into India and Pakistan, and emotionally into several religious, sectarian, caste, ethnic or linguistic groupings in both countries.

There were three ways in which the 1947 Partition might have been avoided. One, by Gandhi and Congress winning the trust and allaying the fears, justified or unjustified, of the Muslim League. But we have seen that Gandhi's attempts were unsuccessful, and also that his closest colleagues blocked his last-minute proposal of a Jinnah ministry for saving Indian unity. Two, by a British willingness to hand over power to India's largest party, Congress, regardless of the League's views, but this was lacking not only in Churchill but also in post-war Britain's Labour government. Three, by Congress coercing Muslim-majority areas to remain with India, but for this Congress had neither the desire nor the capacity.

Non-coercion or self-determination was an article of faith with Gandhi. He also felt, to quote from his comment on the League's opening call for Partition, that 'compelling the obedience of eight crores of Muslims to the will of the rest of India' was not possible. (*Harijan*, 6.4.40) Following Gandhi's lead, Congress explicitly committed itself to self-determination in 1942. Bodies such as the Hindu Mahasabha made no such commitment, though the Mahasabha president, Savarkar, had argued in 1937, three years before the League's Pakistan resolution, that Hindus and Muslims were two nations.[1] However, the Mahasabha lacked the strength to enforce its vision of a single, Hindu-controlled India.

Congress's 1942 declaration in favour of self-determination made it plain that that right belonged to non-Muslims as well. East Punjab and West Bengal and the Punjab's Sikhs could not be forced to join a Muslim homeland. The principle of non-coercion and British unwillingness to transfer power to Congress produced the 1947 Partition of India, the Punjab and Bengal.

The preceding paragraphs seem to answer the historical 'why' of Partition; the 'how' of it, the story—touched upon in the last chapter—of the interaction in 1919-1947 between nationalism, colonialism and separatism, or between Congress, the Raj and the Muslim League, has been spelt out in several different versions,[2] and need not be repeated here.

Gandhi and Partition: Pointing out that the Gandhi claiming to be non-coercive had not refrained from using 'coercive' fasts to obtain a change in the Hindu position, some of Gandhi's Hindu critics demanded to know why he had not fasted to prevent Pakistan, especially since he had said in 1940, 'Vivisect me before you vivisect India.' (*Harijan*, 22.9.40) He who had always stood for the unity of India and for the sanctity of one's word, why was he not fasting unto death for One India?

When Partition stared him in the face, Gandhi was agonized enough to think of a fast. On 5 June 1947, he said, 'I feel as if I [have been] thrown into a fire-pit and my heart is burning.' Yet he felt that to die by self-immolation 'in order to prove that I alone was right' would be 'mad.' (88:84) Though he did not say so, we can assume that he did not expect that Jinnah and the League would be moved by a fast against the creation of Pakistan, or by his death from such a fast, whereas such a death was bound to spark off large-scale Hindu-Muslim killings.

'The Muslims have given me up,' he admitted on 4 June. By this time it was also clear that the Sikhs and Hindus of the Punjab and the Hindus of Bengal, and Congress as a whole, preferred the Partition solution. On 5 June, Gandhi said:

> Lately I have been receiving a number of letters attacking me. A friend points out how ineffective were my words when I said that vivisection of the country would be the vivisection of my own body . . . But when the popular opinion is contrary to mine, should I force my own view on the people? . . . I can say with confidence that if all the non-Muslims were with me, I would not let India be divided. But I must admit that today the general opinion is not with me, and I must step aside and stay back. (9.6.47; 88:117-18)

We may conclude that Gandhi was willing to be regarded by some as a betrayer but not willing to expand and intensify civil war. Perhaps we should also recall that Gandhi's fasts seemed aimed at awakening the consciences of people sympathetic to what he stood for, not at forcing large sections of India to change their opinions.

*

Religion and Partition: That a journey towards independence that did not also set Muslim anxieties at rest was bound to lead to Partition is not as yet a respected or popular explanation. Other theories seem more in fashion. One is that Partition and the carnage that accompanied it derived from 'religion' and in particular from Gandhi's 'introduction of religion into politics.'

In August 1998, the theory was arrestingly restated by the celebrated writer, Arundhati Roy, who said that Gandhi sought to harness 'tremendous bursts of political energy'

> when he rubbed the magic lamp and invited Ram and Rahim to partake of human politics and India's war of independence against the British. It was a sophisticated, magnificent, imaginative struggle, but its objective was simple and lucid, the target highly visible, easy to identify and succulent with political sin . . .
>
> [Now] the genie is out of its lamp, and won't go back in . . . Yes, it won us freedom. But it also won us the carnage of Partition. And now, in the hands of lesser statesmen, it has won us the Hindu Nuclear Bomb.[3]

While Roy states that Gandhi invited Ram and Rahim, others have been less inclusive in their criticism, some blaming Gandhi chiefly for bringing in Ram, and others for the hospitality offered to Rahim. Thus Ainslee Embree has argued that Gandhi's 'use of a religious vocabulary—inevitably Hindu in origin' damaged the prospects of Indian unity. We saw at the start of the previous chapter that Gandhi was well aware of the hazards of religious politics, and noted his 1903 comment on the 1857 Rebellion, in which he had referred pejoratively to the 'appeal . . . made to the worst superstitions of the people of India' and to the fact that 'religion was greatly brought into play.'

But was it possible to imagine an India, even a political India, that evicted religion? Even if Gandhi did not invite Ram, others would. If not Ram, they would invite someone else. Indeed, India's political air was thick with religion when Gandhi returned to India in 1915. Tilak had invoked Ganpati in the late 1890s, and Aurobindo Ghose had solicited Durga just thereafter.

Religious metaphors flew like missiles in the skies of Bengal when, in 1905, the presidency was partitioned into Muslim-majority and Hindu-majority parts, and again in 1911, when Bengal was reunified. Appealing to the Raj in the name of religion, the Muslim League had secured separate electorates for Muslims in 1909.

Aware that it was impossible to toss religion out of the maidan,

Gandhi sought to give a new spin to it, or rather to rectify its spin. In his view, Hinduism and Islam both taught fraternity, not hate. If Indians reflected a little, they would see, as Kabir had seen five centuries earlier, that Ram and Rahim were one. By inviting the two together, Gandhi hoped to deflect and overcome Hindu-Muslim suspicion.

Certainly Gandhi spoke as a Hindu. Significantly, however, and with fair success, he spoke as a reconciling Hindu. Unlike, for example, Tilak and Aurobindo, Gandhi took great care to assure Muslims that they had nothing to fear from his Hinduness. Bringing Hindus and Muslims closer was one reason why he wanted to reach the Hindu heart, which his Hinduness enabled him to do. Indeed Gandhi seems to have tried to link religion to its forgotten goal of spreading goodwill, despite the history of its use to spread hate.

That Gandhi's Hinduness helped him in 1920-22 to forge a Hindu-Muslim partnership was freely acknowledged by the Muslim leaders of the time. But Hindu-Muslim trust was a casualty of the eventual failure of the 1920-22 struggle, and thereafter Muslim League leaders found it advantageous to paint Gandhi as, above everything, a Hindu.

Gandhi took every chance to explain his Hinduness to Muslims, but he could not give it up. He knew that India's masses, Hindu or Muslim, could be stirred, whether for good or ill, only by individuals or movements connected to their faiths and loyal to their cultural and religious inheritance. This inheritance needed touchstones of ethics and common sense, and Gandhi used these touchstones to remodel Hinduism, yet the inheritance could not be thrown overboard.

That Gandhi had employed his Hinduness for the goal of pluralism was amply confirmed when independent India's Constituent Assembly, dominated by his lieutenants and followers, forbade discrimination on the basis of religion and stipulated a secular state.

An opposite criticism, welcoming Ram (or its version of Ram) but suspicious of Rahim, holds that, far from being too much of a Hindu, Gandhi appeased Muslim extremists. The fact that Jinnah left Congress at the end of December 1920 is cited to suggest that Gandhi encouraged communal Muslims against secular ones such as Jinnah, thereby estranging him, and the start of Pakistan is seen in Gandhi's endorsement of Khilafat.

There is no evidence, however, to suggest that Hindu-Muslim relations would have turned for the better if Gandhi, Congress and other Hindus had refrained from supporting Khilafat. No matter how strange or purposeless it seems in hindsight, the Muslim passion over Turkey and Khilafat was a powerful reality owing nothing to Gandhi. It was a factor in Jinnah's 1913 decision to join the Muslim League, and in Tilak's 1916 decision to sponsor a Congress-League pact that conceded separate electorates to Muslims.

Moreover, Jinnah's 1920 difference with Gandhi was not over Khilafat. In September 1920 Jinnah spoke of 'the spoliation of the Ottoman empire and the Khilafat, a matter of life and death.'[4] What he was opposed to was the changing of Congress's goal from 'Swaraj within the Empire' to just 'Swaraj' and to Gandhi's willingness to experiment with mass defiance of laws.

Endorsing Jinnah's objection to large-scale civil disobedience, some critics see a connection between the disobedience that Gandhi inaugurated in 1919-22 and the violence and Partition of 1947. However, just as there is no evidence that Congress or Hindu aloofness from Khilafat would have improved Hindu-Muslim relations, there is none either that the pre-Gandhian technique of lawful protest would have kept Hindu-Muslim relations on an even keel.

Marked by us in an earlier chapter, Sayyid Ahmad Khan's sharp opposition to the activities of the 'constitutional' Congress, which he feared would invite Hindu rule, and the Hindu-Muslim bitterness over partitioning Bengal antedated Gandhian satyagraha by years.

The lesson, rather, is that a joint struggle against the British was an inadequate cement for the Hindu-Muslim relationship. In the absence of trust, a struggle for freedom would have aroused suspicions irrespective of whether the struggle was lawful or defiant of laws, peaceful or violent, focused on Khilafat, Jallianwala, land revenue, democratic rights, the salt tax or something else.

Not Ram and Rahim but a failure of trust, and the resultant fear and hate, produced Partition and its carnage. Five decades later, mutual fears constructed the nuclear bombs of India and Pakistan. If India's 1998 bomb can be linked to Gandhi's hospitality to Ram and Rahim in 1920, presumably Russia's bomb of the 1950s should be connected to the turn-of-the-century religious pacifist Tolstoy, rather than to Stalin and his successors, France's nuclear arsenal to Joan of Arc, who claimed to hear divine voices, and America's to Lincoln, who brought God repeatedly into his civil war discourse.

*

Nationalism's side effects: The apparent verdict of history that India's advance towards independence was at the same time a move towards partition does not show that the cry for independence was 'wrong.' The spirit of an age does not ask to be judged—we might as well judge winds and waves, or the urge for air, water and food; that spirit only asks to be understood, and the understanding has to extend to its effects.

The urge of an age does not ask to be judged, but eras end, and new urges are called for. Yet such was the power of the Quit India cry, by which I mean not merely the 1942 movement but the sentiment against alien rule, that it had some unintended and hurtful side effects. We have seen that Partition was one. Also, the nationalist cry submerged other sounds sent forth by Indian hearts, such as the cry of the untouchables and women for justice. Again, the power of Quit India lingered long after the age that required it had ended—long after the British had quit and India was free.

As far back as in 1921, Rabindranath Tagore, troubled by the Non-cooperation Movement, had warned Gandhi of nationalism's negative consequences. Admitting that he was 'ply[ing his] boat where the current is against me,' Tagore said he desired 'a true meeting of the East and the West.' He disapproved, he added, of 'the intense consciousness of the separateness of one's own people from others.' Claiming that nationalism was a Western rather than an Indian idea, Tagore went on:

> We, the famished, ragged ragamuffins of the East, are to win freedom for all Humanity. (*Modern Review*, May 1921)

Replying to Tagore, Gandhi said that a negative was often necessary— 'weeding was as important as sowing'—and added:

> Nor need the Poet fear that non-cooperation is meant to create a Chinese wall between India and the West. On the contrary, non-cooperation is intended to pave the way to real, honourable and voluntary cooperation. (*Young India*, 1.6.21)

Regardless of what Gandhi intended, nationalism did at times build a wall between India and the West. Moreover, if, in Tagore's phrase, Indians could become 'intensely conscious' of their 'separateness' from the British, a Muslim, Dalit, Assamese, Tamil or another group in India could also be roused to a fierce awareness of its separateness from others in India.

After 1947, a new spirit was needed for new times, a spirit willing to look at hurts inflicted, now and in the past, by Indians on fellow Indians, or, as Tagore might have said, by humans on fellow-humans, rather than the hurts Indians received from their European masters, a spirit exploring reconciliation among Indians with different and often conflicting interests, perceptions and versions of history. Yet lingering nationalism resented any sustained focus on Indian weaknesses, wanting always to link those to the evil of colonialism.

It was not in India alone that the spirit of nationalism ruled an age. Asians and Africans disliked being ruled by races from remote lands even as Europeans in the eighteenth, nineteenth and twentieth centuries disliked being ruled by near neighbours. And in every country the self-respect that was a component of the spirit has survived the departure of the European ruler. Though civil wars, massacres and cruel dictatorships have scarred many an independent country in the second half of the twentieth century, no nation so far has asked the United Nations or an outside power to manage its affairs.

This unwillingness we can honour, but we cannot celebrate the failure in reconciliation, which, among other things, is also a failure to acknowledge that the portion of Asia or Africa that a European colonizing power conquered was not necessarily at peace with itself at the time, and has not always been at peace following the foreigner's exit.

*

Carnage and its impact: It was in fear and trembling that the Hindus and Sikhs of West Punjab and the Muslims of East Punjab opened their eyes on the morning of 15 August 1947. Before the day ended, some of them were dead. Before the year ended, between four hundred thousand and half a million had perished in the Punjab.[5] This is the estimate of Gopal Das Khosla, whose *Stern Reckoning* remains one of the most objective accounts of the 1947 killings.

Whether the parity was divine or devilish, the loss of life was about the same in East and West Punjab: non-Muslim deaths equalled Muslim deaths.[6] By the middle of 1948, about five-and-a-half million Sikhs and Hindus had moved from West Pakistan to India, and roughly the same number of Muslims from India to West Pakistan. In the process, West Punjab and the NWFP lost virtually all its Sikhs and Hindus, and East Punjab nearly all its Muslims.

The Great Migration, a two-way trudge for humans and bullock-carts in lines that were often more than a mile long, was panic-triggered, sudden and completely unplanned. In both parts of the Punjab, the route to safety was controlled by a hostile majority, and the only neutral military force available, the Punjab Boundary Force set up by the departing British, was hopelessly overstretched.

At one stroke of the midnight hour, every Hindu or Sikh official in West Punjab, and every Muslim official in East Punjab, ceased being a helper and became utterly helpless, wondering how to move with his family to the other side. Most Muslim officials in West Punjab, and most non-Muslim officials in East Punjab, became fiercely partisan. As for the general public, thousands were slaughtered when their trains or convoys moving towards 'safety' across the border were attacked.

For hundreds of thousands in end-of-the-century India and Pakistan, including many in government, defence, the media and academia, the events of 1947 are part of family history, so agonizing a part that even after fifty years many prefer not to speak of it. Though most have tried to suppress or expel memories of the trauma, that trauma perhaps remains a lasting influence.

Sought to be pushed down or pushed out of the mind, the trauma inevitably loses all details. Only a central fact survives: '*they*' committed the unspeakable horrors. Not a set of individuals, from whom other individuals of their group might be different, but '*that lot*'—'*those*' Hindus (or Sikhs or Muslims). Such summing-ups and attitudes, often passed down from one generation to the next, are part of the legacy of the unhealed traumas of 1947.

At first fiction or poetry alone could form an outlet for the nightmares witnessed and suppressed. In the nineties, however, some survivors have been willing to speak of what they saw and went through, and their recollections have been published. Much earlier, Khosla had tried in his *Stern Reckoning* to give an even-handed overview of the sequence, nature and scale of the killings.[7]

We will not attempt an overview or summary here. In its outlines if not in detail, the harrowing story of the revenge, plunder, cruelty, ingenuity, bravery and endurance that marked the Punjab in 1947 is widely known.

Children were pitilessly killed by both sides and women were raped, kidnapped and forcibly converted. In some cases, military sepoys escorting an escaping column of the threatened and the weak did nothing as young women were selected, grabbed and carried off by armed men of the Other, dominant side.[8] This was a replication of the Mahabharata scene after Krishna's death, viewed by us in the opening chapter, when Arjuna, the 'invincible' Gandiva at his side, was unable to prevent the abduction of women from the column he was escorting.

> Do not cut my throat. Do not cut my throat. You have already killed my parents. Take me with you!

On the afternoon of 26 August, the child thus pleading was killed in a hospital in Sheikhupura in West Punjab. The man who recorded the entreaty, Sheikhupura's civil surgeon, was hiding twenty yards away.[9] On the other side, the Sikh leader, Master Tara Singh, acknowledged that Muslim women and children had been killed in East Punjab.

Lives saved: After recounting other inhumanities, the Sheikhupura civil surgeon, a Hindu, added:

> In the end I feel honour-bound to record that the lives of my children and of about six hundred educated Hindus and Sikhs, male and female, of the Civil Lines were saved by the efforts of some God-fearing Muslims who gave them shelter in their homes, even at the risk of their lives.[10]

Reproducing the civil surgeon's report but not providing his name, Khosla—by profession a judge—adds that the accounts included in his study were chosen 'on grounds of sincerity and for their lack of exaggeration.'[11]

Lives were saved on the other side as well. In 1947, Dr Khushdeva Singh was the medical superintendent of the Hardinge Sanatorium in Dharampore on the Kalka-Simla road in East Punjab, and tuberculosis adviser to the princely state of Patiala. Dharampore and three hill cantonments in its vicinity, Kasauli, Dagshai and Subathu, all had sizable Muslim populations, including TB patients, ex-patients seeking the hill air, shopkeepers, grocers, hospital and military contractors, fruitsellers, tongawallas, and porters.

Early in September 1947, Sikh and Hindu refugees arrived in Dharampore, looking for space and jobs and narrating their gruesome experiences in West Punjab. Some of them told Khushdeva Singh, who was also Dharampore's honorary magistrate and Small Town Committee president, that if he did not move the town's Muslims out, the refugees 'would finish them all in a day.'

Khushdeva Singh answered that he would resist such an attempt. Meanwhile he 'would have nothing to do with them.' Later, however, when it became certain that Dharampore's Muslims would be attacked, Khushdeva Singh arranged two trucks for their departure to Subathu, to join a Muslim camp that seemed to enjoy 'some sort of protection from the military regiment stationed there.'

The trucks and their drivers arrived, and the Muslims were about to leave on 8 September when Khushdeva Singh learnt that the four-mile road to Subathu had been blocked with tree trunks and tar drums, the drivers had been bribed, and miscreants were moving about near the blockades.

> My entire plan was upset. I went home in great distress. I wept and prayed to God to show me the way so that I could save the lives and honour of these people. For a while it all looked dark, and then a thought flashed which gave me a ray of hope. Why not send them to Dagshai which was [also] four miles from Dharampore [but] in a different direction? There was no Muslim camp there. Nobody was thus likely to forestall the move.

Moreover, Dagshai was 'a cantonment where their protection was more or less guaranteed.' Securing two new drivers, and sending the original drivers 'to my hospital on some pretext,' Khushdeva Singh packed the Muslims into the trucks and sent them on their way to Dagshai, while the would-be attackers waited at their blockades on the Subathu road.

> Everyone, including the Muslims on the trucks, was surprised . . . All the Muslim residents of Dharampore were transported to Dagshai without the loss of a single life . . .

Thereafter, Khushdeva Singh, obtaining support from others in the Simla hills and adroitly sidestepping the angry elements, succeeded in evacuating all the Muslims in Dagshai, Kasauli and Subathu, even while doing what he could for the Sikh and Hindu refugees from West Punjab. 'I love Muslims as my own kith and kin,' Khushdeva Singh said.

Later, he would receive 317 letters from or on behalf of Muslims whose lives he had saved. Visiting Oslo for a tuberculosis course in 1949, he stopped in Karachi on his way and again while returning. In Karachi six Muslim constables, including some who had known Khushdeva Singh in the Simla hills, offered him betels, accompanied him right up to the plane, stood in a line, and saluted him as he entered the aircraft. After fastening his seat belt, a moved Khushdeva Singh said to himself:

> Love is stronger than hatred, love is far stronger than hatred, love is far stronger than hatred at any time and anywhere. It was a thousand times better to love and die, than to live and hate.[12]

*

Memory, pain, remorse: If sixty or more as the twentieth century ends, a Sikh, Muslim or Hindu Punjabi is likely to possess some memories of the pain, suspense and migration of 1947. If willing to speak about these memories, he or she is also likely to mention (so I have found in numerous interviews) an intervention that relieved, even if only fleetingly, the torment of 1947. Often the relieving ray of humanity was silently, ingeniously and bravely brought by a neighbour or stranger from the fold of the 'enemy.' If lives were not always saved, at least a glimpse of a compassionate attempt softened the agonizing scene.

Hindus and Sikhs who in 1947 moved east, and Muslims who moved west, testify to such interventions. They also mention, again almost invariably, their awareness, and in many cases their direct observation, of cruelty from their own fold against helpless 'enemies.' Thus several Hindus and Sikhs who managed to survive the train journey from Pakistan to India—as indicated earlier, refugees on trains in either direction were often blocked and slaughtered—have, in interviews with me, spoken of the killing of Muslims and pools of Muslim blood they witnessed after their train crossed the border and entered East Punjab.

Muslims interviewed in Lahore likewise admitted the slayings and plunder against Hindus and Sikhs they saw in Pakistan. Five non-Muslims I interviewed—a Hindu owning a small printing press in Delhi, a Sikh farmer in Rajasthan, a Hindu who retired in Delhi as a railway official, a Hindu Punjabi settled in Maryland, USA, and a Punjabi woman writer now living in Salem, Oregon—spoke of close relatives killed by Muslims and also of their decision to fight feelings of revenge.

How those more directly involved in the violence of 1947 may be feeling fifty years later was indicated in a report by the writer Suketu Mehta, who talked in June 1997 with old Sikhs living in Attari, twenty miles from Lahore on the Indian side of the border between the two Punjabs. Mehta was told that Attari's Sikhs were enraged in 1947 by accounts of trains coming from Pakistan with bodies of Hindus and Sikhs and by the murder by Muslims of a local Sikh, an old man, who was walking to buy milk. To quote from Mehta's account:

> Gurdev Singh (not his real name) was a student then, a 'leader type,' as he refers to himself. Ten Sikh men, four from Gurdev Singh's family, gathered to seek vengeance. Before they went on their expedition, they went to the gurudwara, and took an oath not to kill or molest women and children.
>
> They went to the Muslim part of the village. One member of their band grabbed a Muslim woman, but he was reminded of his oath by the others . . .
>
> Gurdev Singh did not tell me what happened next. 'My mind went mad for one day,' is all he would say . . .
>
> Finally, Balbir Singh (I have changed his name too) . . . another of that band of ten men—he has done well with his wheat and rice farms, has a daughter in the US and a son in Toronto—told me what happened the day their minds went mad.
>
> 'There was much junoon (madness). It lasted fifteen to twenty days . . . Then when the old man was killed, nobody could hold back.'
>
> They got guns, swords, spears, scythes. Then they went to the Muslim village. 'It lasted just a few hours.'
>
> The Sikhs rounded up the Muslim men, and gathered the women and children to one side. 'We killed one third of the people in that village. About 50-60 were killed in those few hours. The women and children were put to one side but they were watching; they were screaming.'
>
> Balbir Singh was weeping profusely by now, his handkerchief going now to one eye, now the other. It was obvious he was saying some things for the first time.
>
> 'I don't get angry on anybody else but myself. I didn't sleep

all that night. I didn't stop thinking about it for a single minute. That's the worst memory for me.'

Mehta writes that Gurdev Singh was saddened in 1947 to watch Muslim families he knew cross over to Pakistan. 'Pieces of my heart are going across,' he felt. Adds Mehta:

> Balbir Singh's way of atonement has been through a constant searching out of the Other, a series of highly emotional meetings with his former enemies. He has crossed the border three times since then, a feat whose magnitude can be appreciated by any Indian trying to get a visa at the Pakistani embassy in Delhi . . .

> I looked for Muslims in Attari and found none. They had all fled . . . Gurdev Singh pointed out to me the houses they had inhabited, their quarter. Then he led me to the place he used, until quite recently, to come every day to pray at. It is a grave—the tomb of the fakir Gulab Shah. Gulab Shah was a Muslim.

> Every Thursday (this is June 1997) people come from all the surrounding countryside to ask for favours at the oblong tiled tomb of the saint inside a light green building within a grove of fruit trees . . . They are all Sikh and Hindu.

> All over the Punjabi countryside are the tombs of Muslim holy men, venerated by Sikhs and Hindus. Attari has a full-time keeper of the Muslim tombs, Arjun Singh, who claims to be 111-years-old.

In Mehta's view, the minds of men like Gurdev and Balbir Singh and others with memories of violence and uprooting, whether as victims or attackers, 'are the battleground between the need to forget and the need to remember.'[13]

*

Panipat, 1998: Identified with Kurukshetra and remembered for its sixteenth and eighteenth-century battles, Panipat also contains the tomb of the thirteenth-century Sufi saint, Qalandar Sahib, who attracted students from Iran, Hejaz, Turkey and Central Asia. In the last chapter we noted Gandhi's unsuccessful attempt in November 1947 to persuade Panipat's Muslims to remain in India. Exactly fifty years later, some of them, now Karachi-based, gave a warm welcome to a visiting lawyer from Panipat, Ram Mohan. At Ram Mohan's suggestion, a Pakistani group with previous Panipat links travelled to the town in March 1998.

> They stepped hesitantly (*writes Syeda Saiyidain Hameed*) on the soil of their janmabhoomi. In the fifty years gone by, they had sunk their roots in their new karmabhoomi . . . There were some grey-haired men, some stately grandmothers, some young girls aged seventeen and eighteen, some strapping youths, some middle-aged professionals. Twenty-three in all—hailing from Karachi, Lahore and Islamabad.
>
> The visitors spent their own money for travel, the hosts found them places in guest houses, hotels and private homes. People of the city put on feast after feast. Whether it was breakfast or lunch, there were more than three invitations for each, including the last day when they were to have 'high tea' at seven places! . . .
>
> A nineteen-year-old walks to the podium. She has long flowing hair and her complexion glows. Among the audience are the small businessmen, the retired engineers, the newspaper proprietors, the school teachers, the city elders— men and women who have tried to identify and recognise their neighbours and friends.
>
> The girl says that she will recite a poem that the famous poet of Panipat, Shugan Chand 'Roshan', wrote and sent to her grandfather as an expression of the pain of parting when he and his family said their last farewells to Panipat.

The 1947 poem urged the breeze to inform 'those who in unhappiness had left us' that their departure had changed Panipat. Its flowers had lost their fragrance, its thorns no longer pricked, its berries bloomed no more. 'My grandfather had cried when he received Shugan Chand's poem,' said the Pakistani girl. She was embraced by an elderly woman, who told her:

> I am Shugan Chand Roshan's daughter. I remember that after your grandfather left, Babuji never smiled again.

Older visitors touched on bits of Panipat's history that the 1998 audience had never heard of, and 'the listeners were breathless as one visitor rattled off the names of fifty-one villages surrounding Panipat.' Connections were made with the past; much of it, of course, had been lost for ever. Yet, adds Syeda Hameed,

> the present was here and now, the girl with the long straight flowing hair, her tall handsome brother who was looking splendid in a dhoti he had worn for the first time, the women fingering fabrics in the Khadi Gramodyog Bhandar, little girls, big girls, riding the crest of time.[14]

10

Two Cheerful Decades: India 1947-67

AT THE END of 1946, Jawaharlal Nehru offered three predictions to a French journalist and asked the journalist to 'remember' them: 'One, India will never be a Dominion, two, there will never be a Pakistan, three, when the British go there will be no more communal trouble.'[1] A year later, proved wrong on all three scores, Nehru was big enough to recall his hollow prophecies to the same journalist.

In Jawaharlal Nehru, Prime Minister from 1947 to 1964, free India possessed a leader with unusual gifts. The masses loved him for his sacrifice and courage. Students and intellectuals appreciated his ability to place Indian events in a global as well as a historical context, outline a vision for the future, and come up with inspired utterances. His industry and energy shamed most of his political colleagues. His experience included terms as chairman of the Allahabad municipality and as Congress president. Crucially, Indians of all kinds and ages seemed fond of him and willing to overlook his mistakes.

Though the lines are familiar to many Indians, what he said in the first minutes of independence is worth looking at, for it reveals an ability to match a historic moment as well as the largeness of Nehru's mind, apart from being an example of his writing and speaking style:-

> Long years ago we made a tryst with destiny, and now the time comes when we shall redeem our pledge, not wholly or in full measure, but very substantially. At the stroke of the midnight hour, when the world sleeps, India will awake to life and freedom. A moment comes, which comes but rarely in history, when we step out from the old to the new, when an age ends and when the soul of a nation long suppressed finds utterance. It is fitting that at this solemn moment we take the pledge of dedication to the service of India and her people and to the still larger cause of humanity.

At times Nehru's interest in history and human greatness sent his thoughts all the way back to the Buddha and Asoka. 'As India's first Prime Minister looking for a model of inspiration,' writes Bhikhu Parekh, Nehru 'seems to have chosen Asoka whom he had earlier described as a wise ruler, a lawgiver to his people, and a man of peace with a message for the world.'[2]

Jawaharlal would strive for a reconciler's role as Prime Minister. The seeming extremist of the 1920s and the 1930s who had demanded immediate and complete independence, scoffing at dominion status, and declared himself a socialist and a foe of maharajas, landlords, capitalists and the Raj's Indian Civil Service (ICS), now appeared willing to put up with such enemies.

Under him independent India remained in the Commonwealth, headed by the British monarch. On its part, the Commonwealth altered its rules to retain India, opening membership for the first time to a republic, which is what India became in 1950. Earlier, for the first two-and-a-half years of independence—from 15 August 1947 to 26 January 1950—India had functioned as a free dominion.

From August 1947 to June 1948, Louis Mountbatten, cousin to the British king, continued as free India's Governor-General. For several months British officers headed free India's army, navy and air force, and while almost all White members of the ICS chose to retire on the considerate terms on offer, the new Indian government did not disturb the pre-eminence of the ICS in the Indian bureaucracy.

The continuities were unavoidable in an India having to cope with the transfer of power and the Partition upheaval. In gaining the loyalty of the ICS and of senior police and military officers—of men the Raj had employed to suppress Congress's campaigns and to gaol persons like himself—, Nehru received crucial help from Vallabhbhai Patel, the Deputy Prime Minister, who held the portfolios of Home and States. Civil servants fell under Home; moreover, Patel had leverage over Congressmen and could prevent them from hitting back at civil and police officers. When some Congress members of the Constituent Assembly attacked the ICS and objected to articles in the draft constitution that protected the state's servants, Patel retorted:

> If during the last two or three years most of the members of the Services had not behaved patriotically and with loyalty, the Union would have collapsed. If you have done with [the ICS] and decided not to have this service, I will take the service with me and go. They will earn their living. They are capable people.

Today my secretary can write a note opposed to my views
. . . I have told [my secretaries]: 'If you do not give me your
honest opinion, then please you had better go.' (10.10.49)[3]

After this the party fell in line. Even more important was Patel's role
in obtaining the accession to India of the hundreds of small and large
princely states whose future was left unclear by the agreement that
brought independence. It seemed as if the ruler of each state was free
to join India or Pakistan or claim independence; free India could have
been destabilized at birth if princely pockets across India had exercised
the last option.

That danger was averted by Patel, who employed his conservative
image to woo the rulers. But he also warned that failure to settle with
him and Nehru would oblige the maharajas and the nawabs to
negotiate later with a more radical leadership in New Delhi, and he
skilfully used Mountbatten to draw the rulers towards a merger with
India. After acceding to India, the rulers were also persuaded to
merge their territories with other acceding states next to them or
with an adjoining non-princely province. Within thirteen months of
independence, India was unified. It was a signal feat.

Sharp differences and clashes, including a bitter one over the
presidentship of Congress in 1950, marked the relationship between
the Premier and the Deputy Premier. Earlier, Nehru's appointment,
following an intervention by Gandhi, as Congress president in 1946,
which positioned him for India's Premiership, had hurt Patel, who
was fourteen years older than Nehru and appeared to be the party's
choice for presidentship. Swallowing the disappointment, Patel gave
invaluable backing to Nehru. Writing to Nehru in August 1947,
Patel had said:

My services will be at your disposal, I hope, for the rest of
my life and you will have unquestioned loyalty . . . from me
. . . Our combination is unbreakable and therein lies our
strength.[4]

Unquestioned, yes, but not unquestioning loyalty. Patel did not
suppress his disagreements. In Patel, who controlled the party and
the services, and Nehru, who enjoyed the confidence of the masses
and the intelligentsia, India possessed an ideal pair at the helm until
Patel's death at the end of 1950.

Complementing each other in abilities, influence and perspectives
and frank to each other about their views, Nehru and Patel ran a

successful duumvirate for more than three years. Each was useful to the other, and aware of the other's usefulness to him and to the country. We can say that together the two provided a notable example in accommodation despite conflicts, and despite ardent 'Nehruites' and 'Patelites' in Congress and the media who at times pushed for a break.

*

Kashmir: With three princely states, however, there were problems. The largest, Hyderabad, and the small state of Junagadh in Kathiawad (Saurashtra) had Muslim rulers but an overwhelmingly Hindu population. In Jammu and Kashmir, a Hindu raja ruled over a sizable and strategically located Muslim-majority state. The Nawab of Junagadh acceded to Pakistan but revolt by a populace emboldened by Indian security forces stationed at Junagadh's borders undid the accession in November 1947.

Pushed by the Razakars, an extremist group committed to Muslim dominance, the Nizam of Hyderabad strove for independence, but Indian troops ended that dream in September 1948.

Kashmir's ruler, Hari Singh, also toyed with independence but the fear that as a Hindu he might join India prompted Pakistan to sponsor an armed raid into Kashmir in October 1947. When the raiders approached Srinagar, the capital, the maharaja signed an instrument of accession to India, and Indian troops flew into Srinagar and pushed the raiders back. Fighting continued for over a year. When, with the help of the United Nations, a ceasefire was finally agreed to on 1 January 1949, Pakistan was left in control of slightly more than a third of the territory of Jammu and Kashmir, and India with the rest.

With respect to all three states, Hyderabad, Junagadh and Kashmir, India's stand was that popular will rather than the ruler's wish should finally prevail, and referendums held in Junagadh and Hyderabad endorsed merger with India.

Kashmir's popular leader, Sheikh Abdullah, had long been a friend of Nehru, who was a scion of Kashmiri Pandits, and of Gandhi. Abdullah had also led a campaign for democracy in Kashmir, which resulted in his being arrested by the maharaja. Released by Hari Singh in September 1947, Abdullah led a grass-roots resistance to the attack from Pakistan and became the Premier of Kashmir. If conducted in the late forties or early fifties, a plebiscite in an

Abdullah-led Kashmir would probably have gone in India's favour, but the opportunity was missed.

By the mid-fifties, India-Pakistan relations and the Kashmir question were fully entangled with the Cold War between the West and the Soviet Union, to which India and Pakistan made divergent responses. While India sought to stay clear of the Cold War, Pakistan signed a defence treaty with the USA in 1954 and soon thereafter joined the West's defence pacts in the Middle East and South-East Asia. Nehru seemed to think that India was entitled, in this altered context, to review its plebiscite commitment.

In March 1948, Jinnah, who headed the state, the Constituent Assembly and the ruling party in Pakistan, had acknowledged to a Swiss journalist that it was 'of vital importance to Pakistan and India as independent sovereign states to collaborate in a friendly way jointly to defend their frontier.'[5] Even so, India and Pakistan made no serious attempt to develop a joint view of world affairs. Given the wounds of Partition, this failure was understandable. Yet it would damage the future.

Matters worsened in Kashmir because the Nehru-Abdullah relationship broke down. In 1953 a mistrusted Abdullah was removed from office and put behind bars. Eleven years later, however, the relationship was revived, and Nehru sent Abdullah to Pakistan to explore an Indo-Pak rapprochement and a solution to the Kashmir question.

It seemed as if Abdullah had made some progress in talks with General Ayub Khan, Pakistan's military ruler, but Nehru's sudden death in May 1964 destroyed hopes of a Kashmir accord. By 1964, India had expended lives and resources on a large scale in Kashmir and saw it as an inseparable and integral part. Only someone with Nehru's prestige and popularity could have persuaded Indians to modify their relationship with Kashmir.

*

Nehru and Indian democracy: Ten years before independence, in October 1937, an article about Nehru, then the Congress president, had appeared in Calcutta's *Modern Review*. Signed by 'Chanakya,' the article stated that Nehru had

> all the makings of a dictator in him—vast popularity, a
> strong will directed to a well-defined purpose, energy, pride,
> organizational capacity, ability, hardness, and with all his

love of the crowd an intolerance of others and a certain contempt for the weak and the inefficient . . . [Also, an] overmastering desire to get things done and sweep away what he dislikes and build anew . . . [In that process] he may keep the husk [but he sees to it] that it bends to his will . . .

He calls himself a democrat and a socialist, and, no doubt, he does so in all earnestness, but every psychologist knows that the mind is ultimately a slave to the heart and that logic can always be made to fit in with the desires and irrepressible urges of man. A little twist and Jawaharlal might turn a dictator sweeping away the paraphernalia of slow-moving democracy.[6]

Yet throughout seventeen years of unchallenged power and popularity, from 1947 to 1964, Nehru kept that 'little twist' at bay and remained a democrat. Perhaps one reason for his success was his alertness to the danger—the 'Chanakya' authoring the article was Nehru himself.

Democracy was what Congress had sworn itself to during the freedom movement, and the Constitution of independent India drafted between 1947 and 1949 and promulgated in January 1950 sought to entrench democracy in black and white. Nehru's distinctive contribution was to provide India with a flesh-and-blood demonstration of democracy.

Free India's first cabinet of fourteen, formed by Nehru and Patel in consultation with Gandhi, was a model of pluralism. It included seven from outside Congress—Ambedkar, Syama Prasad Mookerjee from the Hindu Mahasabha, Baldev Singh from the Akali Dal, John Matthai from the private sector, C.H. Bhabha to represent Parsis, the former Raj loyalist Shanmukham Chetty, and Rajkumari Amrit Kaur, a Christian who had worked closely with Gandhi. Two Muslims, both from Congress, Maulana Azad and Rafi Ahmed Kidwai, and two from the Scheduled Castes, Ambedkar and Jagjivan Ram, were included.

Taking Parliament and parliamentary norms seriously, Nehru ensured that opposition MPs, of whom there were not many to begin with, were given their say. The judiciary's independence was scrupulously observed. The Press and its freedoms, too, were respected, even though on occasion Nehru expressed resentment at the ownership of newspapers by Big Business, and even though a 1951 constitutional amendment empowered the government to deal with incitement of violence by the Press.

Nehru was wise, in addition, in not interfering with the governance of provinces, renamed 'states.' India's regional and linguistic variety, the realities of India's distances, and the advantages of accessible government were well recognized by the Constitution, which gave ample powers to the states. However, the prestige that grew around Nehru was such that he could have overridden the states, their legislatures, and their chief ministers. That he refrained from doing so was part of Nehru's contribution to Indian democracy.

A difficult test was the demand for a redrawing of state boundaries so as to correspond to linguistic boundaries. The demand was spearheaded by speakers of Telugu, who formed part of the multilingual Madras presidency in the South, but wanted a state called Andhra, comprising the Telugu-speaking areas of Madras and of the former princely states of Hyderabad and Mysore.

Though Congress had declared itself in favour of linguistic states as far back as in 1917, Nehru and his cabinet colleagues in independent India were at first perturbed by the demand for Andhra and its nationwide implications. The migrations sparked by Partition had coloured their reaction. But linguistic states had unmistakable popular backing, and when a grass-roots Congress leader, Potti Sriramulu, died fasting for the creation of Andhra, Nehru and his colleagues yielded. Andhra was separated from Madras in 1953 and joined in 1956 by the Telugu-speaking parts of Hyderabad and Mysore.

New boundaries created separate states for the speakers of Marathi, Gujarati, Kannada, Malayalam and Tamil. The speakers of Bengali, Oriya, Assamese and Kashmiri lived already in states of their own, while those who spoke Hindi or its various regional forms were distributed among U.P., Bihar, Madhya Pradesh, Rajasthan and Delhi.

Punjab: The speakers of one important language, Punjabi, felt left out of this rearrangement, for East Punjab, where they lived, could not claim Punjabi as its sole state language: a large number of Hindi-speakers lived in East Punjab's eastern and southern districts, later separated as Himachal Pradesh and Haryana. The long-sustained demand for a Punjabi suba (state) divested of its Hindi-speaking portions was clearly also a demand for a Sikh-majority state.

Once more Partition's unpleasant memories contributed to the resistance to a Punjabi suba, but in the end it did not prove possible either to postpone indefinitely the application to East Punjab of the linguistic principle, or to deny the Sikhs a state where they could feel a majority's strength. As the Sikhs saw it, the subcontinent's Muslims had obtained Pakistan, and the Hindus had India; were the Sikhs not entitled even to a province of their own within India? The Punjabi suba came into being in 1966.

Tamil separatism: Though to begin with some 'nationalists' in the South had opposed the separation of Andhra, fearing that it would divide Indians from one another, the emergence of Tamil Nadu as a linguistic state for the Tamils played a part in weakening the separatist tendency that had existed in the Tamil South from the 1930s.

Supporters of this tendency saw the Tamil South as the subcontinent's Dravidian home, Indian history as a struggle between Aryans and Dravidians, and South Indian Brahmins as Aryan agents in Dravidian territory. Their leader was E.V.R. Ramaswami Naicker (1879-1973), known as Periyar or senior leader, who also strove for self-respect and unity among the non-Brahmins of the Tamil country, and inspired political parties championing Dravidian interests and on occasion an independent Dravida state.

Thanks to early opportunities in English-language education, Brahmins, a small minority among Tamilians, had secured an edge in the civil service, professions and politics, but democracy and free voting soon produced non-Brahmin dominance in the Tamil Nadu legislature and government, which was accompanied by the progress of non-Brahmins in other areas as well. The demand for a separate Dravida state lost force as a result, and when in 1962 all of India was agitated because of Chinese troops sweeping into Assam, the main Dravida party, the Dravida Munnetra Kazhagam (DMK), led by C.N. Annadurai (1909-1969), took the chance to abandon formally its secessionist platform.

*

In the early period of independence, India's Muslims were understandably apprehensive. Many of them had lent their sympathy to the call for a Muslim homeland, but they soon found that Pakistan was far away and of no help to them, and also that they were being blamed by a section of Hindus for Pakistan's creation. Nehru's clarity that India belonged to all its residents and his frequent reminders, to Muslims and Hindus and to officers of the state, that India's Constitution and laws bestowed equality irrespective of religion seemed to restore a sense of security to India's Muslims.

Hindu criticism: A vocal Hindu element, destined to grow in strength after Nehru's death, charged that Nehru and the government he led were appeasing or pampering the Muslims, an accusation that figures of Muslim percentages in government jobs or legislatures would not corroborate. Thus there were 37 Muslims in the 425-member U.P. Assembly in 1957, a less than 9 per cent representation in a state where 15 per cent were Muslims. In 1952, the 530-member Lok Sabha contained 22 Muslims, a representation of under 4 per cent against a population percentage of 10. Likewise, Muslims in the Indian Administrative Service (IAS), the successor to the ICS, were 3.27 per cent in 1980, and in all government services the Muslim percentage was 6.01, against a population percentage of about 11.[7]

However, many Hindus disbelieved or disregarded such figures. Nehru's efforts to 'win' popular approval for his policies and approach were perhaps least successful with a core of Hindu hardliners and their supporters, who remained convinced that Nehru and Congress were appeasing Muslims.

A Left-leaning rhetoric and some socialistic measures, including centralized planning, a steeply progressive income-tax and the reservation of some industries for the state sector, brought Nehru the goodwill of much of India's Left, though extremist groups in Andhra, West Bengal and Bihar pursued a militant and at times violent agenda against landlords and the government. In time, the criticism that Nehru harboured a naive and misplaced faith in the public sector, while failing to see the potential of the private sector to create growth and provide jobs, would eclipse attacks on his policies from the Left.

Ambedkar's alienation: An important failure in Nehru's bid for an all-India consensus occurred in 1951, when Ambedkar, the brilliant lawyer and leader of the Scheduled Castes Federation, who was Nehru's colleague in the Indian cabinet from 1947 and the key figure in the construction of the Indian Constitution, resigned from the ministry.

Ambedkar's induction into free India's first cabinet and role over the Constitution seemed for a while to symbolize a new relationship between the Indian high castes and the untouchables. In the thirties and forties, Ambedkar had denounced Hindu society, attacked Gandhi and Congress as instruments for hoodwinking and softening the untouchables, and declared that social change was more important for India than political independence, but, as we saw earlier, in 1947

Gandhi, Nehru and Patel sought a partnership with Ambedkar, who was invited to join the cabinet.

Ambedkar agreed. The high castes being prepared to have an 'untouchable' as India's lawmaker, and the leader of the untouchables being willing to work for India as a whole, suggested a step forward in justice and reconciliation in Indian society. But the break came over legislation to reform some family and social customs of the Hindus, Ambedkar feeling that Nehru was weak before conservatives in Congress who wanted to stall the legislation. The legislation would eventually go through in 1955-56, but in 1951 Ambedkar resigned.

The issue of Hindu reform apart, Ambedkar also felt that he was being taken for granted. By the end of 1950, when Patel died, Nehru was both enormously popular and almost wholly unchallenged. In September 1951 he accepted the presidentship of Congress, even though a year earlier he had said that he was

> quite convinced that it would be improper for me to accept this great honour and responsibility [of the party presidentship] so long as I remain Prime Minister. (*Hindustan Times*, 8.8.50)

Nehru's popularity, and that of Congress, extended to the Dalits, and in the early fifties it seemed that Congress did not particularly need 'outside' help from leaders like Ambedkar. In October 1956, Ambedkar converted to Buddhism along with hundreds of thousands of followers and declared that the conversion signified their rejection of Hindu society. Two months later he died. Three decades after his death he would become an icon for India's Dalits, and political parties of varied hues, eyeing Dalit votes, would vie with one another for installing Ambedkar's portraits and statues. But when Ambedkar resigned in 1951, neither Nehru nor most observers of the Indian scene sensed what was at stake.

The middle castes: Another trend unnoticed when it began in the early fifties involved the so-called backward castes. These groups occupying the middle ground between the Hindu high castes and the 'untouchables' made up about half the Indian population, but they enjoyed neither the social status of the high castes nor the quotas in education, government employment and legislatures that the 'untouchables' and tribals had secured. Land reforms, however, had bolstered the peasant groups in this cluster of middle castes, and whetted their desire for political strength.

One of the first to start mobilizing them in north India was the socialist, Rammanohar Lohia (1910-67), from the late forties a sharp critic and foe of Nehru.

*

Comparing India's post-independence condition with Pakistan's, Mushirul Hasan wrote in 1998:

> In 1947 India went on to consolidate itself as a democracy; . . . a constitution came into force on January 26, 1950. On the other hand, it took nine years for the Pakistan Constituent Assembly to agree to a constitution . . . Still, no national elections were held under the 1956 constitution. Two years later, Pakistan fell prey to military rule.

> So, what explains the differences in the experiences of India and Pakistan? . . . The man who probably made the greatest difference of all was Mohandas Karamchand Gandhi. Although assassinated by a Hindu fanatic just when the country had tasted the fruits of freedom, his legacy lived on in the hearts and the minds of the people . . . Similarly, Nehru, the natural successor of the Mahatma, . . . more than anybody else among his contemporaries, was able to keep the fissiparous tendencies in check . . .

> It was easy to project Islam as a cementing bond at the height of the Pakistan movement, but the real task at hand was to mediate between conflicting interests and contending identities that surfaced soon after the birth of Pakistan . . .[8]

Congress under Nehru: Hasan's suggestion that mediation between conflicting interests and contending identities was attempted in India seems valid, as does his assessment of the roles of Gandhi and Nehru, but success in mediation or reconciliation in India was incomplete even in the fifties and sixties. And perhaps Nehru's most important failure was in relation to Congress.

Founded in 1885 and named the Indian National Congress in hopes of representing all who lived in India, Congress underwent, in Gandhi's hands, a crucial transformation in the 1920s and the 1930s. Firstly, it became broader-based and more democratic, with elected units in provinces, districts, towns and villages. Secondly, it became more efficient, with provincial and all-India committees and a round-the-year national executive, the Working Committee. Thirdly, Congress members seemed to strive, with varying degrees of commitment, to remain in touch with the Indian people.

Writing in 1972, and emphasizing the first development, the scholar J.C. Heesterman argued that Gandhi reshaped Congress to give expression and scope to India's social pluralism. Under him Congress embodied the diversity and conflicts of India. To Heesterman this was probably 'Gandhi's greatest achievement.'[9]

But in addition to embodying India's variety and conflicts, Congress in Gandhi's time possessed a sizable team of leaders. Even with Gandhi present, and despite the unique respect given to him, the Working Committee was never a one-person show. A realist Vallabhbhai Patel frequently stood up to an impulsive Jawaharlal Nehru, in 1938-39 a Rajagopalachari favouring another round of negotiations with the British contested a Subhas Bose who wanted to issue an ultimatum to the Raj, a conservative Rajendra Prasad opposed, in 1936, the socialism advocated by a Jawaharlal Nehru, or a socialist Rammanohar Lohia argued in 1947 with a Nehru-Patel duo reconciled to Partition. Moreover, there were several occasions in the twenties, thirties and forties when the Working Committee rejected Gandhi's recommendations.

Not that differences between leaders in Congress were always amicably resolved. In 1939 Subhas Bose felt compelled to resign from the Presidentship he had won earlier in the year. Still, debate and dissent were common in meetings of local Congress committees and in the Working Committee.

After Gandhi's death, dissent tended to diminish, and independent-minded Congressmen began to feel uncomfortable. Jayaprakash Narayan, Rammanohar Lohia, Narendra Deva and other socialists were the first to leave the organization. Vallabhbhai Patel was perhaps more responsible than Nehru for their departure, which took place in 1948, but even Nehru did not press the socialists to remain in Congress. J.B. Kripalani, who had joined Gandhi in 1915 and was Congress President in 1947, left Congress shortly afterwards to lead a party of his own.

In 1949, referring to himself, Vallabhbhai Patel, Maulana Abul Kalam Azad, Rajendra Prasad and Rajagopalachari, all of whom had joined Gandhi and Congress three decades earlier, Nehru had written: 'The public generally have looked up to us five as the old guard of the Congress.'[10] But the five did not or could not work as a team of equals.

Patel's death in December 1950 removed the only serious counterweight in Congress to Nehru. Rajendra Prasad's elevation in January 1950 as India's President had cut him off from Congress affairs. At the end of 1951, Rajagopalachari, then a cabinet colleague in New Delhi, felt that Nehru did not need him (which is what Ambedkar had also felt) and left for his home in Madras. In 1954, Rajagopalachari withdrew from Congress; five years later, he formed the Swatantra party. By this time Maulana Azad, who was Congress president first in 1923 and then from 1940 to 1946, and thereafter a minister in the Union government, had died.

Congress's five-man guard had been reduced to one individual, but a crucial, and possibly unwise, change had occurred some years earlier, well before Azad's death or Rajagopalachari's secession, when, in 1951, Nehru accepted the Congress chair in addition to that of the Premier. A vacancy had arisen because the incumbent, Purshottamdas Tandon, a conservative stressing Hindu culture who was elected President in 1950 with the support of the now-deceased Patel, had resigned following differences with Nehru.

The experience with Tandon seemed to persuade Nehru that government and party ought to speak with one voice—that any pronounced divergence would stymie progress. Accordingly, Nehru headed both the government and the party from 1951 to 1954, when his nominee, the unassertive U.N. Dhebar of Gujrat, was made the party president, a position occupied by Dhebar until early 1959, when he was replaced by Nehru's daughter and only child, the young Indira Gandhi.

Concentration of authority in an individual was the tendency in almost all decolonized nations, in Africa and nearer home in Pakistan, where, as we noted, Jinnah (who died in September 1948) had kept most powers with himself. An abridgment of democratic rights and procedures accompanied the trend. Despite Nehru's commanding presence, India was different, and stood out. Writes Judith Brown:

> From 1947 to 1967 Congress was [India's] major and totally dominant party. But its dominance was unlike the one-party rule which so often followed independence in other newly independent states and in effect silenced legitimate opposition. . . . [Other] parties functioned freely . . . Furthermore Congress by its very nature helped to encourage and organize

the exchange of opinion and the airing of interests which are central to democratic politics.

It was often called an 'umbrella party' or a whole party system within itself, for it contained and allowed free expression of a wide range of political opinions and interests. In its many internal ideological and factional conflicts a bargaining and reconciliation process was at work which produced an all-India consensus based on the articulation of diversity and conflict, not its suppression. Its inclusive quality owed much to its pre-independence role as a welder of a national movement out of disparate groups, and also to the presence at its helm of Jawaharlal Nehru.[11]

In view of what we have noted, Professor Brown's assessment has to be qualified. Nehru was unable to retain dissent and debate in the Congress High Command, and he acquiesced in the growing identification of Congress with himself. The failures blemish, even if they do not erase, the image of Nehru as almost the only head of government in the group of nations decolonized after the Second World War able to keep democracy going.

*

A new role for Congress? In the twenties, thirties and early forties, the goal of freedom and a focus on the common Indian had bonded Congress workers with the people of India. Was it possible to sustain this relationship after independence, when power, jobs and influence beckoned Congress members?

Immediately before his death, a Gandhi troubled by reports of 'the moral degradation' of Congress legislators who were accused of 'making money by the use of influence' and of interfering with officials and judges[12] had thought of a radical step. He wondered whether, its role discharged with the winning of independence, Congress as a political body should not dissolve itself and 'flower into' an association for gaining 'social, moral and economic independence.'[13]

In this daring vision, Gandhi saw a new Congress tackling illiteracy, ill-health, unemployment, untouchability and communal intolerance in every village in the land. In the political field, the vacuum left by Congress's exit would be filled by old and new parties from the Left to the Right, as well as by those members of Congress who were unable to survive without politics.

However, Nehru, Patel and their colleagues gave little consideration to what may be regarded as Gandhi's deathbed proposal. No doubt they were fully stretched. In addition to the rush of challenges that came in the wake of Partition, they now had to face the implications of Gandhi's assassination.

But the old man who was no more had passed on a key insight. If Indian conditions were to be improved—in education, health, employment, social equality, Hindu-Muslim relations or wherever— the Indian people had to be involved, for the task was well beyond the capacity of government departments. And if the Indian people were to be involved, Congress workers, with their reach and a stock of popular sympathy that was not yet exhausted, had a crucial role. Could they deepen their bonds with the people, and use those bonds for promoting 'social, moral, and economic independence'?

Necessary as this transformation of Congress might have been, it was a daunting undertaking, and Nehru did not attempt it. At times, however—oftener, perhaps, in the early years of independence—, he expressed sadness at the fall he saw from ideals, as in this letter to a ministerial colleague, Mohanlal Saxena, in September 1949:

> As I see things happening in India, in the Constituent Assembly, in Congress, among young men and women, which take us away step by step from those ideals, unhappiness seizes me. Gandhiji's face comes up before me, gentle but reproaching. His words ring in my ears. Sometimes I read his writings and how he asked us to stick to this or that to the death, whatever others said or did. And yet those very things we were asked to stick to slip away from our grasp. Is that to be the end of our lives' labour, . . . the curious finale to our careers?[14]

It was only in 1963 that a Nehru who seemed in declining health attempted something with Congress that faintly—very faintly—recalled Gandhi's 1948 advice. The move was connected to K. Kamaraj (1903-1975), the chief minister of Tamil Nadu. Concerned by the growth of anti-Congress sentiment in his state, Kamaraj offered to resign and take up party work. Accepting the offer, Nehru invited other chief ministers as well as his cabinet colleagues in New Delhi to emulate the exercise and tender resignations under what was called 'the Kamaraj Plan.'

These resignations were duly if not wholeheartedly offered, and Nehru accepted six of them, those from four central ministers (Morarji Desai, Lal Bahadur Shastri, Jagjivan Ram and S.K. Patil) and two chief ministers (Partap Singh Kairon of East Punjab and Biju Patnaik of Orissa). Nehru hoped that the exercise would be seen as an example in self-denial by Congress leaders, but cynics suggested that space was being created for Nehru's daughter Indira, and that politicians capable of blocking her were being stripped of power.

To summarize the argument of this section, we may say that against Nehru's considerable achievements for democracy and consensus in India should be set his failure with Congress. Independent India required a reorientation of Congress, which, apart from the machinery of the government, was the only link that Nehru and his colleagues had with the Indian people, but Nehru shrank from the challenge.

The state and its officers: Nehru did not also try to reconstruct the governmental machinery inherited from the Raj. Representing a colonial power whose primary concern was its authority, the government functionary under the Raj, whether a policeman, a tax collector or any other enforcer of rules and regulations, was inclined to see the citizen as a supplicant of whom he, the official, was the master. Independence led to a large increase in the government's role in development, and therefore in the numbers of officials with whom the citizen had to interact, but the official-citizen relationship remained what it was during the Raj.

How to rectify this relationship, or instill a sense in officials that they existed to serve and assist the citizen, rather than the other way round, were difficult questions that Nehru was not able to address. The problem became more acute after Nehru committed Congress and the government, in the middle and late fifties, to socialistic goals. These called for a plethora of new rules and regulations that gave additional powers to bureaucrats, further weakened the citizen in his equation with officials, and led to what Rajagopalachari, in 1959, called a licence-permit-quota raj.

Deficiencies in the agencies of the government and the inability to reform Congress added up to a failure in reconciling India's rulers with the people, a failure that in time would be reflected in widespread disappointment with the progress of independent India. Sometimes the disappointment was expressed in violence.

*

The succession question: In an assessment offered when Nehru was alive, a warm but not uncritical admirer, Rafiq Zakaria, wrote:

> The tragedy of his leadership is that, unlike Gandhiji, he has not produced the leaders—young, active and dynamic—who can carry on his mantle.[15]

At the end of 1928, when Jawaharlal was barely thirty-nine, Gandhi first expressed a sense that Nehru would be his successor, and in subsequent years he repeated the statement in different forms.[16] But he also took care to groom—and in the process commend, recommend, defend or chastise—several others, including Patel, Subhas Bose, Rajagopalachari, Rajendra Prasad and Azad, and the Congress socialists Jayaprakash Narayan, Lohia and Narendra Deva.

At the end of 1947, when J.B. Kripalani relinquished the Congress presidentship that he had assumed on Nehru taking ministerial office, Gandhi had proposed Jayaprakash, then forty-five, or Narendra Deva, fifty-eight at the time, as a successor, but the idea was dropped after Patel expressed opposition and Nehru seemed unenthusiastic.

However, even in 1946, a year before independence, Nehru had thought that Jayaprakash, or JP as he was called, who was thirteen years younger than him, might be a possible future Prime Minister.[17] Later, in February 1948, Nehru referred to JP in a national broadcast and added:

> I am sure that a time will come when he will play a very important part in shaping India's destiny.[18]

For some more years Nehru continued to think in this vein, and early in 1953 he made some efforts—we do not know how strenuously—to obtain the association of the younger man and his socialist colleagues. However, talks to explore a partnership led nowhere.

A commitment on constitutional amendments, land reforms and nationalization of key industries desired by the socialists was not something that Nehru could give on his own. Moreover, any move by Jayaprakash towards Nehru was prevented by the stand of Rammanohar Lohia, who insisted that a Congress-Socialist partnership would have to start at the grass roots, not at the top. In his biography of JP, Ajit Bhattacharjea has written of

> Lohia's suspicions that JP was willing to give up the path of struggle in return for a senior ministerial position and the

unwritten assurance that he would succeed Nehru as Prime Minister.[19]

The suspicions were proved false—JP did not join any Nehru cabinet. Yet it is by no means established that India's cause would have been hurt by a Nehru-JP alliance in the early or mid-1950s, possibly followed by JP obtaining the Prime Ministership after Nehru. Almost as charismatic as Nehru, with a record of bravery and suffering in the freedom struggle that could compare with Jawaharlal's, JP was committed to human rights in India and the world and alert to the state's potential for oppression.

In a 1948 letter to the U.P. chief minister, Govind Ballabh Pant, Nehru had written of JP as 'one of the straightest and finest men I have known.'[20] A man for all Indians in the tradition of Nehru and Gandhi, a seeker of India-Pakistan friendship, an opponent of communalism, casteism and majoritarianism, and sympathetic towards the marginalized, Jayaprakash might have made a reconciling prime minister of India, and one perhaps capable of summoning from the Indian people the better part of their nature.

One of JP's socialist colleagues, N.G. Goray, noted in 1954 that he had 'heard eminent judges of the Supreme Court, high dignitaries in the Army and civil administration and discerning men in other walks of life . . . say that Jayaprakash Narayan was the only person whom they could think of as a worthy successor to Nehru.'[21]

To some, JP indeed appeared 'cross-grained' and 'woolly-minded',[22] but the utterances that invited such criticism emanated from one who was sensitive to human hardship, understanding of human failings, and uninterested in power for himself. If needed, tough and unsentimental politicians could have been found without much difficulty to take their positions alongside JP.

In the event, after Nehru's death in 1964, India's Prime Ministership went for eighteen months to Lal Bahadur Shastri, who was followed by Indira Gandhi. Nehru's daughter would spend sixteen years in all as Prime Minister, almost the same length of time as her father.

*

Indira Gandhi: As the only child of her parents, and losing her mother in 1936, when she was nineteen, Indira was extremely close to her father, though there were long periods when his imprisonment separated them. In 1942, after stints of learning in Santiniketan and

Switzerland, she married Feroze Gandhi, a U.P.-based Parsi. When on independence Jawaharlal became Prime Minister and moved into the mansion built for the Commander-in-Chief of Britain's forces in India, Indira joined him there and served as her father's hostess and aide.

Seated quietly near Nehru when Indian politicians and foreign dignitaries called on him, presiding at the dining table when he entertained, and usually accompanying her father on his travels within and outside the country, including on election campaigns across India in 1952 and 1957, Indira received a priceless education in politics.

In 1953, when her father was Congress President as well as Prime Minister, Indira was given the responsibility of organizing the women's wing of the Congress; there is no evidence that this happened at Nehru's initiative. In 1956, when Dhebar was the party chief, she was made president of the Allahabad Congress Committee, and in 1957 a member of Congress's Central Election Committee, a powerful body in an election year.

At the end of 1958 some Congress leaders proposed the forty-one-year-old Indira as the next all-India President, and Nehru did not demur. Others were taken aback but said nothing. In Congress's 1958 climate, querying a proposal for elevating Nehru's daughter was unthinkable. Indira's appointment was duly announced.

Was Nehru consciously preparing a succession by Indira to the Premiership? Raising the question, one of his biographers, M.J. Akbar, who does not hide his fervour for Jawaharlal, says:

> He never promoted her in politics himself, but he never restrained anyone else from promoting her . . . Jawaharlal may have been careful about not being seen to take any initiative personally, but he quite evidently used trusted lieutenants from Allahabad like Lal Bahadur Shastri to nudge his daughter's political career along.[23]

In an oft-quoted study, *After Nehru, Who?*, published a year before Nehru's death, the American writer, Welles Hangen, referred to Indira as one of eight possible successors. The others mentioned by him included Jayaprakash Narayan, Morarji Desai (1896-1995), who would become Prime Minister in 1977, and the man who did follow Nehru in the Prime Ministerial chair, Lal Bahadur Shastri (1904-66). For his study Hangen had interviewed Indira in 1962. Asked who was likely to succeed her father, she apparently replied, without any hesitation, 'Mr Shastri.'[24] By 1962 her political instincts had been well honed.

Indira Gandhi's Premiership (1966-77 and 1980-84), on which we will spend more time in the chapter that follows, won her great support as well as great opposition, but here a limited question may be raised: was Nehru wise in assenting to his daughter's rapid promotion in Indian politics?

The claims of Indira—and of India: The point may be relevant for our study of reconciliation, or a consensus, in India. When Nehru, a man for all Indians, allowed himself to be seen as a man advancing his daughter, did he perhaps damage his bond with the rest of India?

This question of political judgment has deeper overtones and reminds us of a possible link between reconciliation and renunciation. Nehru, who sometimes spoke of himself as an agnostic, was nonetheless stirred by a spirit that came down from the past of India. In the famous 'last will and testament' composed before his death, Nehru would write:

> And though I have discarded much of past tradition and custom, and am anxious that India should rid herself of all shackles that bind and constrain her and divide her people, . . . yet I do not wish to cut myself off from that past completely . . . I am conscious that I too, like all of us, am a link in that unbroken chain which goes back to the dawn of history in the immemorial past of India; that chain I would not break, for I treasure it and seek inspiration from it.

Perhaps nothing from India's past moved Nehru so much as the life and thought of the Buddha, to whom he would often return in his writings and speeches, prompting some to suggest that informally Jawaharlal was a Buddhist. Writing about the Buddha to his fourteen-year-old daughter in 1931, Nehru had explained that

> he condemned the sacrifice of all manner of things to gods, and said we must sacrifice, instead, our anger and hatred and envy and wrong thinking.[25]

As Nehru doubtless knew, partiality, too, was something that the Buddha wanted sacrificed, as one of four impulses behind wrong deeds, the other three being enmity, stupidity and fear.[26] Though too large-hearted a man to desire a dynasty, Nehru may have convinced himself that his daughter was more likely than others in Congress to continue the policies that he saw as fundamental.[27] Whether he was sound in this judgment, and whether in his attitude to Indira's promotion he advanced the democratic spirit, were, however, questions that would only be answered after his death.

*

China's attack: Led by Nehru, Congress had easily won the elections of 1952, 1957 and 1962. But after the 1962 elections he fell ill and had to stay in bed for most of April. By now many in India were troubled by Chinese nibbling in the Himalayas, which had occurred through the fifties and become pronounced in 1961, and by Chinese policies in Tibet, which had forced the Dalai Lama to escape with many of his followers to India in 1959.

Earlier, in 1958, the Chinese had announced the completion of a 750-mile road in western China of which a 112-mile segment lay in Aksai Chin, territory that India saw as part of Jammu and Kashmir and therefore of India. But it was only from Beijing's announcement that India learned of the road and of the annexation it seemed to represent—the Chinese had managed to work for months on Indian land without India coming to know!

Critics targeted Nehru's defence minister, V.K. Krishna Menon (1896-1974), who appeared to minimize the significance of Aksai Chin and, generally, the threat from China. Menon's favours to one officer, Brigadier B.M. Kaul, and his overall performance as defence minister had alienated many senior army officers, but Nehru protected Menon even as small-scale incursions continued in the Himalayas.

On 20 October 1962 the Chinese Army made a swift and massive move into India's northeast across the McMahon Line (the international boundary agreed in the 1914 Simla Convention). The outnumbered Indian soldiers on the heights of the eastern Himalayas were not only poorly armed; they were also poorly clothed and poorly shod. After inflicting a humiliating defeat and descending with ease into the foothills of northern Assam, the Chinese declared a ceasefire in December and returned to their October positions.

By this time Menon had been sacked as defence minister, but Nehru's own prestige too had taken a beating. His China policy had been shown up as disastrous, and political opponents were attacking him as both naive and feeble. Moreover, swallowing humble pie,

Nehru, who had always denounced arms agreements between an Asian country and the West, had been forced to ask the Americans and the British for help in defence against China. Indeed, there were indications that China's withdrawal might have been influenced by a warning from the United States.[28]

Nehru saw China's attack as a betrayal, for right from 1949, when the Chinese Communists won the civil war and captured power, he had personally campaigned for Beijing's right to China's seat in the United Nations, and to a place of prestige on any global platform. More than that, he had believed that as neighbours and as Asians with no history of territorial conquest but similar memories of injury at European hands, India and China could work together for world peace.

Earlier in this chapter we noted Nehru's desire to serve as 'a man of peace with a mission for the world.' The desire led him to advocate peace and coexistence between nations with different systems and ideologies, and to prescribe, to the nations of Africa and Asia, a refusal to align with either the West or the Soviet Union in the Cold War that had followed the Second World War.

A tilt? To Nehru, peaceful coexistence and non-alignment were extensions on the world stage of the nonviolence that persons like him had employed in India's struggle for independence. But just as the Raj on occasion charged that Congress's nonviolent campaigns led to violence, critics of Nehru's non-alignment saw in it a tilt at times in favour of the Soviet Union.

The accusation was not wholly baseless. A fascination with socialism and Marxism when he was young plus the natural reaction of any nationalist with memories of the West's affronts to the East, and, perhaps most importantly, a down-to-earth awareness that the Soviet Union and China were geographically close to India, while the West was far, combined to make Nehru hesitant to embrace the West even when it seemed to be in the right, or offend the Communist powers even when they seemed to be in the wrong.

Thus, there was some truth in western criticism in 1956 that while Nehru's India had condemned the Anglo-French attack that summer on Egypt, it merely deplored the Soviet Union's invasion of Hungary that took place a little later in the same year. Yet the fact remained that Nehru had spoken out, even if in restrained terms, in favour of Hungary's independence. The international reconciliation being advocated by Nehru was by no means synonymous with appeasement of the Soviet Union; mixed into it were pleas for justice.

Costlier than the perception of a tilt was the inability of India
and Pakistan to adopt a common approach to the rest of the world.
At no time was this inability more glaringly exposed than in 1959
when General Ayub Khan (1907-74), Pakistan's military ruler,
proposed a joint defence pact between India and Pakistan.[29]

'Joint defence against whom?' Nehru responded,[30] in the year
when the Dalai Lama was forced into exile in India, and three short
years before Chinese troops raced down the Himalayas in 1962.
When, following this intrusion, the USA and Britain provided India
with some aid, Pakistan, guided by Ayub Khan and his foreign
minister, Zulfiqar Ali Bhutto (1927-79), edged closer towards China,
without disrupting its ties with the West.

Death of Nehru: The Chinese attack had destroyed some of
Nehru's fondest dreams, upset his world, hurt his image and also
affected his health, yet he sought valiantly to meet the new realities.
On 6 January 1964, however, he suffered a stroke—but seemed to
recover, and to reflect.

His reflections involved Kashmir, his friend Sheikh Abdullah
who was in detention since 1953, and Indo-Pak relations. To Lal
Bahadur Shastri, who was recalled from his exile under the Kamaraj
Plan and made minister without portfolio, Nehru seems to have said:

> I have wronged Abdullah. We must release him.[31]

Abdullah was freed, invited to Delhi, where Indira received him at
the airport, and taken to Nehru. In his autobiography, Abdullah
claims that Nehru 'expressed his deep sorrow' at what had happened.[32]
The two agreed that Abdullah would go to Pakistan with Nehru's
endorsement and explore the possibility of a solution for Kashmir.
At a press conference on 22 May, Nehru said:

> Sheikh Abdullah is going to Pakistan the day after tomorrow,
> I think, and he will have some exploratory talks there. It is
> best that these talks take place without any inhibition . . .
> He looks upon the Kashmir issue not as one by itself but as
> one between India and Pakistan. He thinks it is important
> that India and Pakistan should come nearer to each
> other . . .[33]

At this conference, a journalist asked Nehru, 'Why don't you solve
the succession problem in a democratic manner in your lifetime?'
Nehru replied: 'My lifetime is not ending so very soon.'[34]

Abdullah went to Pakistan, talked with Ayub, and informed Nehru over the phone that Ayub was willing to come to New Delhi for discussions with Nehru. But the fates, tempted by Nehru, were unkind: on 27 May, Jawaharlal, for three decades and a half the object of the Indian people's affection, suddenly died. With him died the hope of an Indo-Pak rapprochement and a solution for Kashmir, for, as we noted before, only someone like Nehru could have reconciled India to even a partial change over Kashmir.

We have touched on Nehru's failures with Congress and with the machinery of the Indian state, yet for seventeen years he symbolized a unity beyond class, caste, religion and language that contributed to the holding together of India, and he showed that a country freed of colonial rule can pursue progress without abandoning democracy. Another person in his place might not have achieved the same results.

*

Lal Bahadur Shastri: Speculation over Nehru's successor had started after the January stroke. The field seemed confined to three: the minister without portfolio, Lal Bahadur Shastri, who was sixty, the sixty-eight-year-old Morarji Desai, who like Shastri had left the central cabinet the previous year under the Kamaraj Plan, and Indira, forty-seven and a widow, her husband Feroze having died in 1960. Desai seemed certain that his seniority, experience and ability entitled him to the prize, but apart from indications that Shastri had been Nehru's choice, Desai was handicapped by an image of self-righteousness and stubbornness that had alienated several powerful Congress leaders.

In the end Shastri was chosen; after ascertaining, in one-on-one conversations, the opinion of every Congress MP, Kamaraj, the Congress president, declared that the party preferred Shastri. Meanwhile, however, Shastri had offered to support Indira, who at the time held no party or ministerial position, 'if she wished to succeed her father.'[35]

Behind the offer was Shastri's belief that 'Nehru's innermost wish was that Indira Gandhi should become Prime Minister,' though not necessarily an 'immediate successor,'[36] as well as a recognition of Indira's standing in Congress and the country as Jawaharlal's sole offspring who with her father's blessing had recently headed Congress. While declining the first position, she joined Shastri's cabinet as minister for information and broadcasting.

Small in size and humble in demeanour, Lal Bahadur Shastri possessed a quiet self-confidence, shrewdness, judgment and courtesy that made him an excellent Prime Minister. His first broadcast as Prime Minister struck a statesmanlike note:

> For too long India and Pakistan have been at odds with each other . . . We must reverse the tide.[37]

The sentiment was shared by JP, whom Nehru had included in his initiative related to Abdullah, and for whom Shastri had a deep respect—for one thing, Shastri seemed to think that the chair he was occupying could and perhaps should have gone to JP.[38] In any case, Shastri supported a visit that JP made to Pakistan in September 1964. JP's belief that his talks with Ayub had gone well seemed corroborated when the Pakistanis gave a warm welcome to Shastri as he stopped in Karachi in October on his return from a journey to Egypt.

The 1965 war: But the mood was not destined to last. Sharp criticisms of the Indian government made by Abdullah while travelling in Europe and North Africa in early 1965 did not help. On his return to India, Abdullah was again detained, and Indo-Pak relations also plummeted. Over 2,000 ceasefire violations occurred in Jammu and Kashmir in the first half of 1965, and Indo-Pak skirmishing took place in the desolate salt marshes of Kutch, between Pakistan's Sindh province and India's Gujrat. Helped by the UN, the two sides accepted a ceasefire at the end of June.

For three weeks in August-September 1965, however, India and Pakistan fought a regular war that included a bid by Pakistan to seize Kashmir by force. Brought to an end because of shortage of ammunition on both sides, the hard-fought war salvaged, for India's soldiers, some of the pride that had been lost in 1962. Also, it revealed a tough Shastri who ordered an extension of the war across the Punjab border, as well as a canny leader who, not wishing to provoke enmity against India among the people of East Bengal, resisted urgings for an Indian attack on East Pakistan.

The understanding that seemed to have grown between China and Pakistan troubled the Soviet Union, which proposed an Indo-Pak summit in Tashkent in the Soviet republic of Uzbekistan. Shastri and Ayub agreed to the idea. Assisted by Prime Minister Alexei Kosygin of the Soviet Union, the Indian and Pakistani delegations argued for a week before Shastri and Ayub signed the Tashkent declaration on 10 January 1966.

Shastri's place in India's story: Though Kashmir was not resolved at Tashkent, an agreement was reached on the vexed question of returning the bits of territory that India and Pakistan had gained from each other during the three-week conflict, and also on rejecting force as a means of solving disputes. L.P. Singh, a senior civil servant who worked closely with Shastri, has recalled a conversation on 10 January 1966:

> Shastri said that . . . if relations betwen India and Pakistan remained strained, holding the potential of another armed conflict, India would take the path of military glory, and our unique heritage, the ideals of nonviolence, truth and human brotherhood bequeathed to us by Gandhiji, would be lost. Peace and good relations with Pakistan, he said, were essential if India was to preserve her soul.[39]

After the two signed the agreement, Shastri accepted Ayub's invitation to break journey in Pakistan on his way back. Some hours later, however, a sudden and massive heart attack killed the sixty-one-year-old Lal Bahadur Shastri. Less than nineteen months earlier, Nehru had died when an understanding with Pakistan appeared close. Shastri's death in an almost identical setting made more than one person wonder 'whether a mysterious fatality overhangs Indo-Pak relations.'[40]

The man who died in Tashkent in January 1966, Lal Bahadur Shastri, though India's Prime Minister for less than two years, has a place in the story of reconciliation in South Asia that will not easily be erased. Firmly and capably concentrating on war while it lasted, Shastri left it behind the moment it ended, and sought for the future a glory greater than may be won by lethal arms.

*

Two questions left by 1967: Political leverage in India when Shastri died was largely in the hands of Kamaraj, the Congress president, and the chief ministers, whose word counted with party MPs. Looking for a new Prime Minister, their eyes settled on Indira, who, lacking a faction of her own and being not merely a woman but a widow, seemed influenceable. Morever, fresh elections were only a year away, and as Nehru's daughter and a woman she would be a promising mascot.

The idea was opposed, however, by Morarji Desai, who had

been thought of as a future Premier when Nehru was alive, and whom Shastri had had to prevail over. This time Desai demanded open voting: 186 Congress MPs voted for him, 355 for Indira. If Nehru had indeed desired Indira to succeed him, but after an interregnum, the wish had been fulfilled with remarkable precision.

Early in 1967, elections were held to the Lok Sabha and to several state assemblies. A devaluation of the rupee and a reassessment of Indira's supposed pliability had been the two principal features of her year as Prime Minister. Much to the dismay of Congress's chieftains, Indira had displayed a mind of her own.

But she failed to perform the electoral magic expected of her. Two decades after independence, the apparent identification of Congress with India was broken. Congress won 279 seats in a house of 515, obtaining a majority of only 20, compared with a majority of over 200 in 1962. Opposition alliances, in many cases representing newly-assertive caste or religious groups, gained power in six states—West Bengal, Bihar, Orissa, Tamil Nadu, Kerala and the Punjab. In April, Charan Singh (1902-87), championing U.P.'s peasant and 'backward' castes, left Congress, thereby toppling the state's Congress ministry, and became an opposition chief minister of India's largest state.

Twenty years after freedom, the results confronted Indian democracy with two critical questions of political accommodation. One was whether Congress, so accustomed to unquestioned power, could live with strong opposition. The other was whether the myriad parties opposed to Congress could live with one another. The two questions—sharing political space with dissenters, and sharing political power with allies—would nag India for the rest of the twentieth century.

11

The Unreasonable Other: South Asia After Independence

IN THE FIRST half of 1999, six of Asia's most influential women were nursing a common fire of memory. The father or husband of each had been violently killed—in one case, father *and* husband had been killed.

The father of Chandrika Kumaratunga, the Sri Lankan Premier since 1994, was stabbed to death in 1959 by a Buddhist monk; her husband was gunned down by militants in 1988. The father, S.W.R.D. Bandaranaike, was the Sri Lankan Prime Minister when killed; the husband, Vijaya Kumaranatunga (or Kumaratunga), was a film-star-turned-politician wishing to heal Sri Lanka's ethnic wounds.

The father of Sheikh Hasina, the Bangladeshi Premier in 1999, was killed with his wife and all but two of his children in the early hours of 15 August 1975. Sheikh Mujibur Rahman was Bangladesh's President at the time. Three-and-a-half years earlier Mujib had cheated the gallows; returning to Dhaka from a Pakistani death row, he was mobbed as his people's deliverer.

The father of Benazir Bhutto, in 1999 Pakistan's leader of the opposition and twice her country's prime minister, had been hanged, judicially murdered as her daughter and many others saw it, in 1979. Zulfiqar Ali Bhutto was Pakistan's Prime Minister from 1971 to 1977.

The husband of Khaleda Zia, Bangladesh's Premier from 1991 to 1996 and in 1999 the leader of the opposition, was shot dead in May 1981. Ziaur Rahman had ruled Bangladesh as a general or a president from 1975 to 1981.

The husband of Sonia Gandhi, in 1999 the president of the Indian National Congress, was gunned down in the summer of 1991. Rajiv Gandhi had served as India's Prime Minister from 1984 to 1989 and was expected to regain the Premiership in the 1991 elections.

Though Burma is outside the scope of our study, let us nevertheless note that the father of Aung San Suu Kyi, Burma's popularly-elected but militarily-curbed leader, was shot dead along with several cabinet colleagues in July 1947. General Aung San was Burma's Premier at the time and had been the leader of his country's freedom struggle.

In 1999, several of the six were yet to be satisfied that the killers of husband or father had all been tracked down, or had received their deserts. But if some of the women were still thirsting for justice, they could take heart from knowing that in South Asia murderers did not for long profit from the politics of murder. Here justice was undoubtedly weak and retribution slow, yet sympathy was strong, and capable sooner or later of bringing a murdered leader's spouse or offspring to high office.

This snapshot of Asia's violently bereaved women of influence confirms that if independence gave relief, it also meant upheaval. In this chapter we will look at post-independence Sri Lanka, Pakistan and Bangladesh, and at post-1967 India.

SRI LANKA

Sources differ on details when it comes to dividing Sri Lanka's population by religion or language. Giving rounded off and therefore only approximate figures, one source suggests that 70 per cent of the island's roughly 20 million people (1998) are Buddhists, 15 per cent Hindus, 7.5 per cent Muslims, 7.5 per cent Christians. As for language, the same source believes that 74 per cent (Buddhists plus many Christians) speak Sinhala, and 25 per cent (Hindus, many Christians, and a majority of Muslims) Tamil.[1]

Sinhala speakers, first appearing in history 2,000 or more years ago and traditionally separated into low-country Sinhalese (60 per cent) and Kandyan (40 per cent), are found in the island's south, west, centre and east. A majority of the Tamils live in the north and the east, their home for centuries (or, as some assert, for 2,000 or more years); of these two groups the eastern Tamils are said to have known a greater interaction with the Sinhalese.

Tamils living in the tea-growing central highlands descend from more recent (nineteenth-century) immigrants from South India, belong to 'lower' castes, and are sometimes referred to as estate Tamils. Following an Indo-Lanka agreement, a number of estate Tamils were disfranchised and repatriated to India in the 1960s and 1970s, reducing the island's Tamil percentage from, roughly, 33 to about 25. In modern times, popular Sinhalese belief has imagined

> a Sinhala-Buddhist reality equat[ing] ethnic community
> (Sinhalese Buddhists), religion (Theravada Buddhism),
> language (Sinhala), race (Aryan Sinhalese), and nation (Sri
> Lanka). In this reality, the island nation of Sri Lanka is the
> land of the Sinhalese, a Buddhist nation of Sinhala-speaking
> people of the Aryan race.[2]

According to Jayadeva Uyangoda,

> The Sinhalese nationalist ideology is a peculiar combination
> of a nativized Theravada Buddhism, the self-understanding
> of a 'superior' (Aryan) and 'chosen' race, and a near-
> apocalyptic fear of being overrun by Dravidian Tamils.[3]

A precise history comes with the popular belief: the legendary King
Vijaya came to Sri Lanka in the sixth century BC, arriving on the day
of the Buddha's death to fulfil Gautama's supposed deathbed wish
that the island and its inhabitants nurture his true doctrine. Vijaya is
seen as a North Indian Aryan from the Buddha's Sakya clan.

But Vijaya could not have been a Buddhist, for it was only three
centuries after him that Mahinda, son of Asoka, took Buddhism to
Sri Lanka. According to the scholar Douglas Allen,

> Vijaya, who was not a Buddhist, did not establish some
> pure, homogeneous, North Indian Sinhalese group. Properly
> speaking, Sinhala and Tamil are linguistic (i.e., not racial)
> terms, the former related to its Indo-European Sanskritic
> roots and the latter to the Dravidian family of languages. As
> a social classification, Sinhala originally referred only to the
> king and his immediate kin group. Its identification with a
> large ethnic group of Sinhalese was a much later development.

> The continual references to Sinhalese and Tamil 'races' have
> no historical basis. From the beginning, Sinhala speakers and
> Sinhalese kings mixed with others and the term 'race' was
> not even part of Sinhala and Tamil vocabularies. The
> Sinhalese-Buddhist-Aryan racial identification was a
> nineteenth- and twentieth-century innovation.[4]

Another study also holds that to begin with there was 'little
differentiation between the two religions as Hindu gods were

recognized and worshipped in Buddhist temples.' One surmise is that the difference may have first arisen 'in about the seventh century in South India when a new militant form of Hinduism appeared, and showed hostility to Jainism and Buddhism. Then only was it possible to connect Sinhala identity with Buddhism, and present the Tamils as enemies of Buddhism.'[5]

Historians agree that from the seventh century if not earlier there was a Tamil presence and note an independent Tamil kingdom in the island's north from 1215 to 1621, representing the 'golden age' of Sri Lankan Tamil culture. Thus a sense has existed of a Tamil territory in Sri Lanka. But history also mentions Tamil kings who protected and patronized Buddhism, while a Sinhalese ruler, Rajasinghe I (1581-93), embraced Shaivism and gave land to Hindu Brahmins.[6]

Allen is not alone in contending that Sinhala, or the lion people, was initially a political term referring to the ruling family. Later it became a phrase implying a separate racial, cultural and linguistic group[7] and denying a history of ethnic mixture. According to an eminent Sinhalese scholar,

> Though the initial Sinhala migrants were probably Indo-European language speakers who arrived over 2,500 years ago, practically all later arrivals were South Indians (mostly Tamil speakers) who were assimilated into the Sinhalese Buddhist community. The South Indian influence is omnipresent among Buddhists. On a level of popular religiosity, Buddhists propitiate Hindu gods like Vishnu, and Skanda, the son of Siva. However the Buddhists view these gods as totally subservient to the Buddha, while the Tamils view the Buddha as an avatar of Vishnu . . . The call for a separate state of Tamil-speaking peoples is thus a contemporary historical phenomenon.[8]

Some Tamils see history quite differently. On 31 March 1984, _India Today_ summarized their (possibly modern) version:

> Six hundred years before Christ, when Sri Lanka was an obscure island, sparsely inhabited by a sedate, peaceful population of Tamils, an event of great significance took place. Prince Vijaya from Bihar invaded the island with his conquering armada . . . Says Tamil lawyer and rebel ideologue S.P. Ruthramoorthy: 'Vijaya's first act was a genocide of the Tamils. He slaughtered thousands. Then he founded the

Sinhala race and kingdom. So deep and old is our distrust of the Sinhala people.'[9]

Partisans in the modern conflict do not like to admit either that 'Buddhism was a virile religion in South India from first century AD to seventh century AD,' or that 'Tamil Buddhist monks contributed . . . to the enrichment of both Tamil literature and Pali literature'— or that Buddhist pilgrims outnumber Hindus at Kataragama, in Sri Lanka's northeast, where the Hindu god Skanda or Muruga is enshrined.[10]

*

A recent divide? The modern Sinhalese-Buddhist-Aryan identification owes much to Anagarika Dharmapala (1864-1933), who led a powerful movement against the island's British rulers and Christian missions, and launched a new form of political Buddhism. In a response to the British advent that paralleled Indian reactions seen in chapter five, Dharmapala also advocated a new code of Buddhist ethics with room in it for Victorian Protestant values. As Gananath Obeyesekere puts it, Dharmapala

> instituted an ethic of this-worldly asceticism, reaffirmed the Buddhist identity, treating Christians and non-Sinhalas as alien outsiders . . . Dharmapala also used the term Aryan not in its traditional meaning of 'noble,' but in its racist sense. It is Dharmapala who identified non-Sinhala civilian populations for attack: the Muslims, Borah merchants, and especially the Tamils, whom he referred to as *hadi demalu*, filthy Tamils . . .

Dharmapala claimed that the first arrivals on the island with Vijaya

> were Sinhalese in heart and mind before they left their motherland. They brought with them, within them, rather, the ripened fruit of centuries of civilization, literature and art, poetry and music; and Aryan culture was bodily transported to create and enrich the virgin civilization of Sri Lanka.[11]

Obeyesekere sees Dharmapala as having 'paved the way for the emergence of a specific modern Sinhala-Buddhist national consciousness.' Before long a universal message directed towards the individual and not restricted to any specific group or race was turned into a racial or 'national' rallying cry,

> laying bare for many (Obeyesekere continues, referring to
> present times), especially for those who live in modern
> overcrowded cities, the dark underside of Buddhism without
> the mitigating humanism of the Buddhist conscience. Not
> only slum dwellers but middle-class people and monks are
> equally vulnerable. Many condone violence against Tamils,
> and some would openly say that the solution to the ethnic
> problem is to kill Tamils.[12]

Arumuga Navalar (1822-79) was the Tamil counterpart of Anagarika
Dharmapala. He 'campaigned against missionary proselytisation and
westernised life-styles and manners' and founded schools for providing
Hindu, and in particular Shaivite, education. Unlike Dharmapala,
however, Navalar wanted Hindu children to be educated in English.[13]
Embracing English education ahead of the Sinhalese, the Tamils had
better access to government jobs and the professions, which would
be resented by the Sinhala majority. Scholars have nonetheless found
that, as Douglas Allen puts it, the

> identification of Tamil Hindus as the threatening 'other' is
> actually quite recent . . . Originally, modern Sinhala-Buddhist
> revivalists identified the English-speaking, more privileged,
> Christian minority as the main threat.[14]

Kumari Jayewardene points out that for some time the Christian and
Burgher (Eurasian) female provided the stock image of the 'other,'
figuring in diatribes and in satirical fiction. The Burgher woman
became the standard stereotype of the immoral temptress who not
only appeared in public with men, but danced and drank with
them.[15] Until the third or fourth decades of the twentieth century,
Sinhalese and Tamils seemed united in an anti-Christian and,
sometimes, anti-Muslim front, as Muslim influence in trade was
resented.

In 1936 Hitler was praised by some Sinhalese nationalists as a
champion of Aryans and of racial purity.[16] In December 1948, A.E.
Goonesinha, a prominent labour leader, declared in parliament:

> If for the protection of the interests of the nationals of this
> country, the interests of hundreds of thousands of workers
> of this country, I have to be racial then I am indeed racial
> and I shall continue to be racial.[17]

But in 1948 Goonesinha was targeting Malayali workers, not Tamils. Until the mid-1950s, in fact, there was relatively little by way of organized anti-Tamil campaigning. The targets were Bohra and Sindhi traders, Coast Moors, Malayalis and Christians.[18] In fact, a Tamil, Arasaratnam, had written in 1944:

> Far from presenting themselves as a communal colossus,. . .
> the Sinhalese appeared to be an unorganized disadvantaged
> people.[19]

Increasingly, however, the Tamils, including those of South India, became the 'other.'

As against the notion of a Sinhala-Buddhist Sri Lanka, the island's Tamils have thought of Lanka as a plural society with separate but equal communities living in a peaceful equilibrium, and not as a special haven for Sinhalese Buddhist culture.

According to some, Tamil identity in Lanka in recent times has consisted of language, a sense of territory, and a third component, the Shaivite or Shaiva Siddhanta strand of Hinduism, even though some might dispute this feature, citing the leadership exercised over the Tamils for many years by a Christian, S.J.V. Chelvanayagam.[20]

*

'Sinhala only': It was probably the language campaign for 'Sinhala only' in the mid-1950s that started the island's modern conflict. In the view of Jehan Perera,

> The most grievous blow to an united Sri Lanka that explicitly
> mobilized communal solidarity and support was that struck
> by the cry for 'Sinhala only.'[21]

Quoting Erik Erikson's comment that identity is 'located in the core of the individual and yet also in the core of his communal culture,' Perera adds, 'Communal identity eases the problem of anonymity and weakness.'[22] Active participants in the 'Sinhala-only' campaign included non-English-knowing Sinhala language schoolteachers, Sinhala students, ayurvedic physicians in villages and small towns, and Buddhist monks.

What seemed justice to the Sinhalese—a redressal of the privileges enjoyed by English-speakers under colonialism—, came across to the Tamils as degradation to second-class status. Earlier, in 1944, J.R. Jayewardene, a future President, had supported both Sinhala and

Tamil as official languages, while in 1949 Prime Minister D.S. Senanayake of the United National Party (UNP) had asserted:

> Nor again should it be forgotten that our essential task is to create a nation, and that our people speak not one language but two or perhaps three.[23]

When the 'Sinhala only' Bill was introduced in 1956 by S.W.R.D. Bandaranaike, the newly-elected Prime Minister and leader of the Sri Lanka Freedom Party (SLFP), some leftists opposed it and warned of dire consequences. Thus Leslie Goonewardena said:

> If those people (the Tamils) feel that a grave and irreparable injustice is done to them, there is a possibility of their deciding even to break away from the rest of the country. (8 June 1956)

Colvin R. de Silva argued that parity of language was the road to freedom and unity and added:

> Two torn little bleeding states may yet arise out of one little state . . . (14 June 1956)[24]

But the Bill was passed. In the words of Kumari Jayewardene:

> The Sinhala leaders were able to delude the Sinhala public that a progressive step had been achieved. Instead, what happened was a quick descent into ethnic violence.[25]

Shaken by the violence, Premier Bandaranaike, an Oxford-educated Anglican Christian converted to Buddhism, entered into an accord with S.J.V. Chelvanayagam, the leader of the (Tamil) Federal Party, the so-called 'B-C Pact,' which provided for parity to Sinhala and Tamil and greater authority to provincial councils in the north and the east. But the United National Party, ousted from office in 1956, could not resist the temptation to blast the accord as a sell-out.

The UNP campaign was led by J.R. Jayewardene, earlier a supporter of parity, and blessed by prominent monks. After months of violence, the B-C Pact was repudiated in 1958, and in September of the following year, Bandaranaike was assassinated by a monk.

Killings unlimited: Many more political killings, and a great many violent deaths, would mark Sri Lanka in the rest of the century. By the end of 1999, perhaps 38,000 would be killed in various ramifications of the Tamil-Sinhala conflict—and perhaps even more in intra-Sinhalese clashes between new leftists and state forces.[26] We may note a 1996 comment by the scholar Valentine Daniel that violence in Sri Lanka

> is no longer inter-ethnic, but intra-ethnic, with more Tamils killing Tamils and Sinhalas killing Sinhalas; with the Sri Lankan state killing the most, Tamils and Sinhalas.[27]

Also worth absorbing is another stark perspective, offered in 1998 by an Indian scholar of Lankan affairs:

> Throughout the colonial period, there was no ethnic conflict, with the sole exception of the 1915 Sinhalese-Muslim clashes, in which, strange as it may seem today, the Tamil leadership took the side of the Sinhalese.[28]

*

Let us look at some milestones and features of the modern Sinhala-Tamil tragedy:

1. After 1960, the Left, finding that it could have a share in power by allying with one of the two major Sinhalese parties, UNP or the SLFP, lost the confidence of the Tamils won earlier by its stand on language parity.

2. The repatriation to India of a number of estate Tamils in the 1960s and 1970s affected Tamil confidence.

3. Affirmative action begun in the early 1970s reduced Tamil presence in colleges. In 1969, 78.8 per cent of those admitted to engineering as well as medical faculties were Tamils; in 1974, after affirmative action, the Tamil percentages fell to 16.3 in engineering and 25.9 per cent in medicine.[29] By 1978-9, unemployment in the educated was significantly higher among Tamils: 41 per cent as against 29 per cent among the Sinhalese.[30]

4. In the late 1970s and early 1980s, the Jatiya Sevaka Sangamaya (JSS), or National Workers Organization, a large trade union led by Cyril Mathew, Minister of Industries, fuelled anti-Tamil sentiment and used muscle power to bring officials and politicians into line. Mathew's line was that the minority Tamils controlled everything in Sri Lanka; whereas they had India to go to, the Sinhalese, the country's original and indigenous people, only had the island of Sri Lanka. The JSS supplied a political and nationalist ideology to marginal people in cities who until then had only a precarious sense of identity.

5. The 1972 constitution made Sinhala the official language and declared that 'the Republic of Sri Lanka shall give Buddhism the foremost place.' While other religions were assured their rights, Buddhism was given a unique status.

6. Several Tamil groups rejected the nonviolence that had characterized the fight led by Chelvanayagam, who wanted the Tamils to adhere to Gandhian norms. In 1976 a young man, Velupillai Prabakaran, founded the Tamil New Tigers, later renamed the Liberation Tigers of Tamil Eelam (LTTE). That same year the former Federal Party was transformed into the Tamil United Liberation Front (TULF), with the declared goal of a separate Tamil state rather than protection for Tamils in a federal Sri Lanka.

7. A policy of settling Sinhalese in traditional Tamil and Muslim areas sharpened the estrangement.

8. In 1978 the LTTE was proscribed, and in the following year a Prevention of Terrorism Act gave wide-ranging powers to security forces.

9. In the summer of 1981, Jaffna Library, containing 'priceless manuscripts pertaining to the identity of Tamils of Jaffna,' was burnt with the apparent connivance of security forces angered by the murder by the LTTE of a Tamil member of the UNP and two policemen.[31]

*

The JVP's class war: A parallel struggle pitted radical Sinhalese rural youth and their (Sinhala) bourgeois and intellectual sympathizers against the Lankan state. The radicals fought under the banner of the Janatha Vimukthi Peramuna (JVP), or the People's Liberation Front, which was founded in 1965 in the context of a growth in the number of youth without jobs or land, with Rohan Wijeweera, who had studied at Patrice Lumumba University in Moscow, as its leader.

In the JVP's campaign, a Marxian thrust was joined to attacks on alleged Indian expansionism. To begin with, the JVP specially targeted the estate Tamils as an alien group depriving Sinhalese youth of jobs in the central highlands. In 1970-71, the JVP threatened to overthrow the government of Sirimavo Bandaranaike, which was supported by traditional leftists, but the insurrection was crushed.

The summer of 1983 saw a serious escalation of the Tamil-Sinhalese conflict. A sequence of violent incidents involving the LTTE culminated in an ambush in Jaffna on 23 July when thirteen Sri Lankan soldiers were gunned down. The arrival of their bodies touched off a week-long pogrom of Tamils in Colombo and anti-Tamil violence in other Sinhalese strongholds.

There was evidence of methodical planning and of army and police inactivity as about 2,000 Tamils were killed, and about a hundred thousand Tamils were driven into temporary camps. Unfortunately, neither sympathy for the victims nor condemnation of the attackers was voiced by President Jayewardene. In the north, many Sinhalese were ruthlessly killed, while about 24,000 fled to the south.

The Tamil Nadu factor: The condition of Sri Lanka's Tamils became a major political issue in the Indian state of Tamil Nadu, which received a number of Tamil refugees from Sri Lanka, after having coped earlier with the return of the island's estate Tamils. Mindful of Tamil Nadu politics, the Indian Prime Minister, Indira Gandhi, was also looking for ways to apply pressure on President Jayewardene, whose approaches to the West, China, Pakistan and Israel had troubled her.

Gains on both the Tamil Nadu and Jayewardene fronts were perceived in a policy initiated by Indira Gandhi of supporting and training some of Sri Lanka's militant Tamil groups, including the LTTE. After Indira Gandhi's assassination in 1984, the policy was modified by her son and successor, Rajiv Gandhi, who continued support for the LTTE but also sought a settlement of Sri Lanka's ethnic conflict.

Indian negotiators found that both the Sri Lankan government and the LTTE were hard to budge. At the end of 1986, Tamil Nadu-based LTTE cadres were disarmed and asked to leave India. Many of them returned to Jaffna, where it was announced that the LTTE was taking over the administration. To this threat of de facto independence, Colombo replied with a tight economic blockade. Starvation in Jaffna seemed imminent, and there was pressure in Tamil Nadu for action to avert it.

Rajiv-Jayewardene Pact: In response, the Indian government sent five transport planes with foodgrains, backed by two fighter aircraft, to Jaffna, an action that became a factor in the willingness of President Jayewardene, hitherto a critic of Indian interference in Lankan affairs, to seek Indian help. At the end of July, Jayewardene signed a pact with Prime Minister Rajiv Gandhi in which India recognized Sri Lanka's unity while Colombo admitted that Lanka contained a Tamil homeland comprising the north and perhaps the east as well.

It was agreed that power in Sri Lanka would be devolved, and that a referendum in the Eastern province would decide the question of that province's links with the Northern province. A significant provision called on India to send a Peace-Keeping Force (IPKF) to the island to disarm the Tamil militants in the north and the east.

*

JVP's second bid: Some ministers of the Lankan government, led by Premier Ranasinghe Premadasa, showed their displeasure by staying away from the signing of the pact, and the SLFP alleged that Jayewardene had capitulated to India, but the fiercest opposition from the Sinhalese side came from a resurrected JVP. The 'illegal, treacherous, murderous, fascist, Jayewardene-Thondaman' government was bitterly denounced (a member of the government, Thondaman represented estate Tamils), and Sinhalese youth were exhorted to launch a 'Patriotic War' against the Colombo government.[32] A bloody conflict ensued, with terrible reprisals and counter-reprisals. Poor unemployed Sinhalese youths once more constituted the JVP's chief support base.

According to one scholar, the JVP-government clashes 'resulted in the deaths of from 20,000 to 60,000 people between 1987 and 1990.'[33] Bruce Kapferer adds:

> The attack by the JVP on the families of state forces quite consciously brought forth the revenge structure of the 'victim.' . . . A hero of the JVP destruction was Deputy Inspector General of Police Udugampola. Members of his close family were destroyed by a mine set by the JVP. He was depicted in the press at the time as a demonic figure of vengeance executing a righteous revenge.[34]

In its propaganda, the JVP invoked Vijayabahu, a medieval Sinhala king whose deeds of conquest and Lankan unification are recounted in the Culavamsa, an extension of the Mahavamsa. As Kapferer points out,

> Vijayabahu [was selected as] the nom de guerre of the leader of the JVP military wing . . . Vijayabahu, more than Dutugemunu (*discussed in chapter two*), is through-and-through a warrior, a man capable of uncompromising violence. He is ruthless against Tamils and also against his own people who refuse his power . . . [In him] there is none of

Dutugemunu's Buddhist quietitude or ultimate commitment to Buddhist values as conditioning the state.[35]

Some scholars see the JVP rebellion as having posed 'the deadliest threat, so far, to Sri Lanka's democratic system,'[36] presumably even more serious than that posed by Tamil secessionism. In November 1989 Rohan Wijeweera was killed by the police, and by 1991 the JVP was crushed for the second time, yet great if suppressed angers and oaths have probably been bequeathed to Sri Lanka by the JVP-state conflict of the late 1980s.

Meanwhile, the IPKF, instructed to disarm but not quite finish the LTTE, was engaged in conflicts that produced heavy casualties for the IPKF as well as the LTTE. The latter, however, managed to wipe out rival groups of Tamil militants. In October 1987 the IPKF captured Jaffna after stiff fighting with the LTTE, which retreated into jungle sanctuaries in the north and the east, from where it continued for two years to harass the IPKF. It was only in March 1990, following Indian elections in which Rajiv Gandhi's Congress party was defeated, that the IPKF was recalled by a new Indian government led by V.P. Singh.

By this time Premadasa, an opponent of the 1987 accord and of the IPKF's presence in Sri Lanka, had become the Lankan President. As the nominee of Jayewardene's UNP, he had narrowly defeated Mrs Bandaranaike of the SLFP in elections held in 1988.

Chain of assassinations: Thus the Tamil question was not solved either by the 1987 accord, or by the IPKF's entry into Lanka, or by the change in governments in India and Sri Lanka. Violent clashes between state forces and the LTTE continued, and the LTTE continued to target perceived informers, betrayers, and enemies.

In June 1991, Rajiv Gandhi, who seemed likely to return to power in India, was assassinated at an election meeting in Tamil Nadu by suspected LTTE cadres. Three months earlier, a bomb blast believed to have been engineered by the LTTE ended the life of the Lankan defence minister, Ranjan Wijeratne. In 1993 President Premadasa and a prominent UNP Minister, Lalith Athulathmudali, were assassinated, again, apparently, by the LTTE. In the following year, another senior UNP leader, Gamini Dissanayake, was killed, also, it would seem, by the LTTE. In the words of a Pakistani scholar:

The most terrifying of all Tiger (LTTE) operations have

been the suicide bombers: cadres who tie explosives to their
bodies and blow themselves up and their victims. Tamils
who oppose the Tigers are intimidated and terrorized . . .
Thus the Tigers have gained notoriety as a vengeful and
cruel terrorist organisation.[37]

Significantly enough, it emerged that 'the heroic tales from the
Mahabharata [were] employed [by the LTTE] to instil a love for
martyrdom.'[38] Also worth noting is the support the LTTE was able
to extract from many in the substantial Lankan Tamil diaspora in
North America, Western Europe, South-East Asia and Australia,
which was enlarged in the seventies and eighties by the island's civil
war.

*

After being elected President in 1994, Chandrika Bandaranaike,
daughter of two former heads of government, tried what had rarely
been attempted in Sri Lanka. She asked the Sinhalese majority to
understand why the island's Tamils had long felt alienated. As for the
LTTE, she declared that her government was willing to enter into
negotiations but would have to suppress violence. The subsequent
period has been marked by fierce if sporadic clashes between the
government and the LTTE, with heavy casualties and claims by both
sides of losses and gains, interspersed with reports of likely talks
failing to materialize.

Generalizations: We may end this brief survey of independent Sri
Lanka with some generalizations. As Kingsley de Silva points out,
'one of the crucial weaknesses of the Sri Lankan party system—and
this is as true of the UNP as it is of its opponents—has been the
reluctance if not refusal of the leadership to accept dissent as a
necessary factor in the life of a political party . . . The UNP and
SLFP have a common flaw. There is no inner-party democracy in
either of them . . .'[39]

In the Lankan polity as a whole, this reluctance to accept dissent,
or difference, meant that neither the Tamils nor the unemployed
Sinhalese youth received the place or the attention to which they
were entitled. Explosions followed. There was a shortage of political
leaders sympathetic to both sides of the divide, whether ethnic or
economic.

Secondly, tending to be philosophical on the one hand and racial
or 'nationalist' on the other, Sri Lankan Buddhism seems to have

devoted insufficient attention to the Buddha's calls for compassion and nonviolence.

Thirdly, the apparently unending chain of violence in Sri Lanka and the LTTE's merciless elimination of dissent seem to prove the truth of Gandhi's warning that it is the character of violence to beget more and more of itself, and less and less of freedom.

When considered along with the appraisal, viewed earlier, that 'throughout the colonial period, there was [on the whole] no ethnic conflict' on the island, the continuing violence in independent Sri Lanka obliges us to identify the features in alien rule that were conducive to inter-ethnic peace.

One, possibly, was the fact that in firepower the alien authority had a decisive edge over any local group or combination of groups. More importantly, however, having no natural cause to prefer one local group to another—even if between white and brown they were inclined to favour the former—, the alien rulers could obtain the trust of all local groups. As outsiders, they were also better able to view Sri Lanka as a whole, even if an insider was more closely acquainted with his or her part of the island.

While alienness denied British rulers the chance to win affection or allegiance in Sri Lanka, it also brought a detachment and a perspective that elicited the trust of different, and potentially mutually hostile, groups of Lankans. Tragically, leaders of independent Sri Lanka on either side of the ethnic divide were reluctant to strive for that detachment, impartiality or breadth of view, and hesitated to be firm towards 'their' side.

PAKISTAN

One way of starting to comprehend Pakistan, as Shahid Javed Burki points out, is to see it as a migration site and recognize the impact of the migrations.[40] First there was the 1947 migration, when perhaps about six million Hindus and Sikhs left for India, and about an equal number of Muslims moved to Pakistan. Many of the newcomers, or Muhajirs (migrants) as they were called, more educated, urbanized and entrepreneurial than the residents, found influential roles in the new nation.

Their preferred destination, Karachi, the great port city on the Arabian sea and Pakistan's commercial as well as political capital, was transformed by the influx. Elsewhere in Sindh, Hyderabad and

Sukkur also became Muhajir-majority cities.

Then, in the 1950s, perhaps two or three million Punjabis and Pathans migrated from their provinces in Pakistan into Karachi, once more altering the city's ethnicity. Scope was created for ethnic tensions in the future; in 1995, nearly 2,500 would be killed in Karachi's ethnic clashes.

After the Soviet invasion of Afghanistan in 1979, 3.5 million Afghan refugees migrated into Pakistan, altering the ethnic balance in Balochistan and the NWFP. This migration, and Pakistan's involvement in the war to oust the Soviets from Afghanistan, flooded Pakistan with guns and drugs.

In 1970s and 1980s, a large number of Pakistan's poor migrated for jobs in the Gulf and other parts of the Middle East, earning foreign exchange for Pakistan and also creating new socio-economic groups which would vie with landed interests.

Shahid Javed Burki gives the following figures for Pakistan in 1997. Population: 138-140 million, which is more than four times the number (32 million) living in the same space in 1947. At 3 per cent, Pakistan's annual rate of population growth is one of the largest in the world. In 2050 AD, Pakistan may hold 400-500 million people. Rapid urbanization has also been taking place; in 1997 more than 50 million (35 per cent) lived in towns.

Until hit by sanctions that followed the subcontinent's nuclear tests in May 1998, Pakistan enjoyed an annual growth rate of 4.5 per cent, but, lacking a robust savings rate, it has relied on remittances from Pakistanis earning in other lands, and on foreign aid. Fully half of those in schoolgoing age do not go beyond the fourth grade—45 per cent of the boys and 55 per cent of the girls.

Forty per cent do not have access to safe water, and only 30 per cent have access to sanitation. In 1995, the infant mortality rate was 95 for 1,000 live births, a very high figure.

Wheat and rice production was greatly increased by the green revolution of 1967-75, and in the 1980s another green revolution boosted cotton production. The two phases created a new socio-economic class of successful farmers.[41]

*

Three conflicts: But we should outline the country's trajectory since independence. Muhammad Ali Jinnah (1876-1948), Pakistan's remarkable founder, was the new country's head of state, president of the Constituent Assembly (or CA, which served also as Pakistan's legislature), and president of the Muslim League (ML). This concentration of power in one person was however to prove a mistake, for Jinnah died within thirteen months of Pakistan's emergence, well before a constitution for the new country could be drawn up, or a proper succession arranged.

On Jinnah's death Liaqat Ali, who was functioning as Premier, became head of the Muslim League as well, but the Governor-General's position went to East Pakistan's Khwaja Nazimuddin, and the CA presidentship to Maulvi Tamizuddin Ahmed, also from the eastern wing. Liaqat thus lacked the authority that Jinnah had possessed; it has been suggested that 'the transfer of effective power to Liaqat Ali during Jinnah's lifetime might have advanced the process of Pakistan's political development.'[42]

In October 1951 Liaqat was assassinated in Rawalpindi. The man who killed him was murdered on the spot, and the story of the assassination was never put together. One suggestion was that some landed interests of West Punjab, supported by sections of the Army, wished to end Muhajir or 'external' influence, which Liaqat was seen to represent.

Pakistan's course was determined by three interacting conflicts. One had a regional/linguistic dimension and involved West Pakistani, East Pakistani and Muhajir interests. Though born in Karachi, Jinnah was in some ways a Muhajir himself, having mostly lived in Bombay and Delhi. Fuelled by the insecurities of Muslims living amidst Hindu majorities, the drive for Pakistan had been led by men like Jinnah and Liaqat and by others in the Muslim League who now were Muhajirs in Pakistan.

Yet it was impossible for West Pakistan's Punjabis, Pathans, Sindhis, and Balochis—or for East Pakistan's Bengalis—to endlessly accept Muhajir leadership. Still, thanks to Muhajir influence in the Muslim League and the advantages that Muhajirs seemed to possess in business, the bureaucracy and the professions, Muhajir dominance lasted for several years.

Though East Pakistan's population exceeded that of the western wing, its representatives in the Pakistani establishment lost their clout because their East Bengali base was slipping from under their feet. After opposition parties routed the Muslim League in East Pakistan in 1954, the contest for central power was restricted to West Pakistanis and Muhajirs.

But East Bengal had been estranged by this time, indeed before Jinnah's death.

> In failing health, Jinnah had made the strenuous journey to East Bengal, not to celebrate the country's independence, but to chastise Bengalis for their rejection of Urdu as the national language. The polarization of East and West Pakistan began after that event.[43]

Bengali had its place in the province, said Jinnah, but only Urdu, 'embodying the best . . . in Islamic culture,' could be the common language between the two wings. 'We are Muslims, we are Pakistanis,' Jinnah stressed.[44] But 'Bengali Muslims and Hindus believed they, not Islam, were in danger, and their energies were directed towards the protection of their exclusive heritage.'[45] In 1954 both Urdu and Bengali were recognized as national languages by the CA, but the damage had been done.

A second conflict was over the role of Islam in the new state. Though he had used the 'Islam in danger' cry to attain Pakistan, Jinnah was also strongly secular in some ways, and in an oft-quoted speech to Pakistan's Constituent Assembly on 11 August 1947 he had said:

> You may belong to any religion or caste or creed—that has nothing to do with the business of the state . . . We are starting with this fundamental premise that we are all citizens and equal citizens of one state . . . Now, I think we should keep that in front of us as our ideal and you will find that in the course of time Hindus would cease to be Hindus and Muslims would cease to be Muslims, not in the religious sense, because that is the personal faith of each individual, but in the political sense as citizens of the state.[46]

While such an attitude seemed inconsistent with the two-nation theory that Jinnah had espoused in his bid for Pakistan, of greater practical consequence was its conflict with the demand of many of Pakistan's ulama for an Islamic state. Ironically enough, while the Muhajirs only recently in the vanguard in the fight for a Muslim homeland seemed to prefer a secular state—which was also the Bengali choice—, the Punjabis and Pathans, late joiners in the battle for Pakistan but with a tradition of close links with local religious leaders (Pirs), seemed keener on a clear Islamic orientation.

The hands of West Pakistanis desiring an Islamic constitution were strengthened after the 1951 census revealed that non-Muslims left in West Pakistan were far fewer than was thought. Hardly any Hindus or Sikhs remained in Punjab and the NWFP. Sindh did have a few lakh Hindus, but Muslims made up 95 per cent of West Pakistan.

If conflicts involving regions and religion (and the constitution) influenced Pakistan's history, so did disputes over democracy. In particular, West Pakistan's landed interests enjoyed blood and kinship ties in the army and were skeptical of the virtues of elected legislatures.

After Liaqat's assassination in 1951, high offices in Pakistan witnessed rapid changes, and the indigenous/Muhajir competition intensified while the stock of politicians fell. In 1956 a constitution was brought into force that acknowledged Allah's sovereignty over man, declared that laws would have to conform to the Qur'an and the Sunnah, and laid down that the country's President had to be a Muslim.

Iskander Mirza, a retired general raised in Bombay, was the first President under the 1956 constitution and Chaudhri Muhammad Ali, a seasoned civil servant, the Prime Minister. Though a Muhajir, Muhammad Ali was from Jullundur and so a Punjabi; his Premiership was a half-way house in the transition from Muhajir to indigenous rule.

Also in 1956, prominent politicians native to West Pakistan but kept out of power by the Muslim League came together to form the Republican Party; some of them, such as Dr Khan Sahib, former chief minister of the NWFP, had been unenthusiastic if not critical about Pakistan. In 1958 a top West Punjabi politician and landlord, Malik Feroz Khan Noon, became Prime Minister, ending Muhajir rule.

But Noon was not destined to stay in office for more than a few months, for on 7 October 1958, encouraged by President Iskander Mirza, General Ayub Khan, the Army Chief, staged a coup d'état. Under Ayub's military rule, Punjabi and Pathan dominance would eclipse the Muhajirs, and East Bengal's alienation would deepen.

*

The Ayub years: The cabinet, the national assembly and political parties were dissolved by Ayub, who, three weeks after the coup, removed Mirza as well. Ayub went on to make some shrewd and even sensible moves.

One was to provide land to the large number of refugees from East Punjab, who were scattered all over West Punjab and Sindh. Many of these East Punjabis were already enlisted in the Pakistan army, which worked energetically to rehabilitate other refugees from East Punjab, mostly ex-farmers who in comparison with the Muhajirs from urban areas in the U.P., Delhi, Bombay, and central India had received little attention thus far. The resettlement of farmers from East Punjab appeared to bring vigour to West Pakistan's agriculture.

Another of Ayub's moves was to set up a system of representative local government, or Basic Democracies, that small landlords and middle peasants in Punjab and the NWFP found attractive, and to which bureaucrats, hitherto restricted to law and order duties, were also assigned. Having created a sizable constituency for himself, Ayub made a third move: he launched a political party of his own, the Pakistan or Convention Muslim League, and in some measure restored political activity.

Also, Ayub decided that Pakistan's capital would move from Karachi to a spot near Rawalpindi in the region across the Punjab-NWFP border that had supplied the Raj's forces with recruits and was providing the Pakistan army with numerous soldiers. So the capital went 'from the city of Jinnah's birth to a city that was only forty miles from Rehana, the birthplace of Ayub Khan.'[47]

The last of Ayub's major moves, the constitution of 1962, was neither popular nor successful. This envisaged a strong President, elected by Basic Democracies and not by the people, and a weak National Assembly; the office of Prime Minister was done away with. Though in 1964 Ayub was elected President, rather narrowly defeating the candidate of the combined opposition, Jinnah's sister Fatima, the new constitution had put too great a distance between the government and the people, whose disenchantment was only a matter of time.

The downswing in Ayub's fortunes can also be connected to the 1965 clash with India, which we looked at in the last chapter, and towards which he had apparently been prodded by some close associates including Zulfiqar Ali Bhutto, a young Western-educated Sindhi landlord brought into government by Ayub.[48] After the Tashkent agreement of January 1966, however, Bhutto resigned, hinting that too much had been given away to India.

A heart attack in early 1968 sent Ayub out of action for several months, yet instead of handing over to Abdul Jabbar Khan, the East Pakistani speaker of the National Assembly, who under Ayub's own constitution was entitled to act for a sick President, Ayub allowed a group of civil servants to hold the reins. A chance to earn East Bengal's goodwill was missed.

By this time Pakistan's rate of growth had come down, as had the prestige of the army, which ten years earlier had been welcomed as an honest and efficient substitute for squabbling politicians; Muhajirs, the middle classes, industrial workers and intellectuals seemed in alliance against Ayub; and Bhutto was drawing attention to the quick enrichment of a few families.

*

Alienation of East Bengal: More ominous, however, was the scene in East Bengal, which had nursed resentments almost from the start. Identifying Islam with Arabic and Persian, West Pakistanis had attacked the Bangla language as being not Islamic and also as strange and unpronounceable. Ayub himself was said to have 'remarked several times' on the 'evil influence' of Hindu culture in East Bengal and banned the playing by Radio Pakistan of Tagore's songs, loved by East Bengalis, because he was a Hindu.[49] When Bengalis clung to their language, which was 'their primary inheritance, their only real property,' they were 'accused of irrational behaviour.'[50]

Accompanying this disdain over language was a sense of superiority, based on a lighter skin-colour and a larger physique, that many West Pakistanis, including politicians, civil servants, and army officers, seemed to entertain.

On the economic front, while East Bengal's jute fetched the bulk of Pakistan's export earnings, government revenues were largely spent in the west wing, and on a military that was predominantly Punjabi or Pathan. Politically, the eastern province contained 55 per cent of Pakistan's population, yet 'parity' between the two wings had been imposed at the centre by merging—in 1955—all the provinces, territories, and princely states of the western wing into the so-called 'One Unit' of West Pakistan. A deeper malaise affected both wings:

> The [Muslim] League assumed it had the right to govern indefinitely and treated other parties with contempt . . . Thereafter, each party gaining control of the government, whether at the centre or in the provinces, assumed it had the right to strangle the others. In this way, confrontation and political warfare replaced flexibility and compromise. The opposition parties were judged life-threatening, not only to the party in power, but to the nation as well . . . The party

in power began to think of itself as the *only* responsible and
patriotic organization in the country. Opposition politicians
were the enemy, and internal warfare, not free debate,
consumed the energies of all involved.[51]

Seeing East Bengal through West Pakistani or 'Urdu' eyes, the
politicians of the western wing blundered again and again, and forced
three Bengali politicians with conflicting agendas and personalities to
come together: Fazlul Huq, the mover of the 1940 Pakistan resolution,
Maulana Bhashani, who had organized Bengal's poor and landless
Muslims, and Suhrawardy, the last chief minister of a united Bengal.

In 1950, Fazlul Huq quit the Muslim League; in 1952 students
agitating for the Bangla language were killed by security forces; and
in elections in 1954 for an East Bengal government, a United Front
of opposition parties defeated, and seemed to finish for all time, the
Muslim League.

The Hindus of East Bengal, roughly 20 per cent in 1950, were a
factor. Founded in 1949, the Awami League admitted non-Muslims
from 1956-57, and campaigned for joint (i.e. Muslim-Hindu) electorates
in both wings of Pakistan. A practical consideration necessitated such
a stand: with separate electorates, East Bengal's political parties were
condemned to minority status in Pakistan's National Assembly.

West Pakistanis reacted to this plea for joint electorates by
accusing the Awami League of 'plotting the destruction of Pakistan.'[52]
Maulana Abul Ala Maudoodi, founder of the Jamaat-i-Islami, asked:-

Why did the Muslims create a separate state of their own if
it was to be no different from any other?[53]

Men like Maudoodi were blind to what was happening in East
Bengal. In the winter of 1955-56, Maulana Bhashani attacked both the
provincial and the national government at a massive rally in Dhaka
and warned of 'secession.' In September 1956, the Awami League
won control of the East Bengal government, with Ataur Rahman
Khan as the chief minister and Sheikh Mujibur Rahman (b. 1920) as
its real leader. Ten days later, the shifting sands of Pakistan's national
politics in the mid-fifties made Suhrawardy, who was linked to the
Awami League, Prime Minister.

Shouts of 'Muslim-Hindu Bhai Bhai' and 'Joint Electorates
Zindabad' filled the halls of the East Pakistan legislature in
October 1956.[54]

However, with Mujib in East Bengal demanding autonomy and charging that 'the history of East Pakistan is the history of exploitation,'[55] Suhrawardy had a difficult time at the centre. West Pakistani politicians accused him of sheltering secessionists. Yet when he dissociated himself from some of East Bengal's demands, Bengali allies like Ataur Rahman 'upbraided Suhrawardy.'[56]

In October 1956, after Bengal politicians asked for the dissolution of the west wing's 'One Unit,' which they saw as a device for neutralizing East Bengal's numerical superiority, Dr Khan Sahib, the chief minister of West Pakistan, Iskander Mirza, the Governor-General, and Ayub Khan, the Commander-in-Chief, forced Suhrawardy out of Pakistan's Premiership. They could not see that Suhrawardy was trying to keep Pakistan together and might have carried Mujib with him.

Suhrawardy was followed as Prime Minister first by Ismail Chundrigar, a Muhajir, and then by Malik Feroz Khan Noon. In May 1958, Dr Khan Sahib of the NWFP, the One-Unit chief minister and a power behind Noon, was assassinated. Ayub's takeover came in October.

The coup was presented as an answer to political instability at the centre and also to disorder in East Bengal. In an incident in September that would prove handy to the army, Shahid Ali, deputy speaker of the East Pakistan assembly, had died after being hit in the face by a spinning tile of wood ripped off from one of the assembly chairs and flung like a discus by a member.

*

Emergence of Bangladesh: If the army had been supplied with excuses for taking over, the takeover hardened the Awami League. During the long period of Ayub's rule, while West Pakistani politicians hoped for his departure, Mujib and the Awami League moved towards the goal of complete autonomy if not secession.

In 1966, when West Pakistani politicians sought Mujib's support for joint opposition to Ayub, Mujib asked them if they would agree to turn Pakistan into a federation where the federal government dealt only with defence and external affairs, and East Bengal had its own currency, the sole power to tax, the right to trade directly with other countries, and a separate militia.

These demands, incorporated into Six Points by the Awami League, were rejected by the startled West Pakistani politicians, who

in any case were too absorbed in their local affairs to gauge the depth
of Bengali feeling. Denounced also by Ayub, the Six Points were
however increasingly embraced by East Bengal's people. Warning of
'civil war,' Ayub had Mujib arrested and then, in December 1967,
charged, in the so-called Agartala conspiracy case, with conspiring
with the Indian government for the dismemberment of Pakistan.

'Although the allegations were dramatic, the evidence was flimsy
at best.'[57] The trial of 1968 and the effort to discredit him only made
the incarcerated Mujib more popular. Meanwhile, in West Pakistan,
Bhutto had launched his Pakistan People's Party (PPP), adopted a
populist, anti-rich platform, and stepped up criticism of an ailing
Ayub. Disturbances, often violent, were rocking both wings.

In March 1969, Ayub finally decided to quit, transferring power
to the army chief, General Yahya Khan. Thereby, Ayub believed,
though cornered and defeated, he had preserved the unity of Pakistan
that was being recklessly questioned by the now-released Mujib, the
Awami League, and so many in East Bengal.

Unlike Ayub, who had given bureaucrats important roles, Yahya
seemed to rely exclusively on the military, but he was aware that
after ten years of army rule the people in both wings were impatient
for popular government. He therefore announced that elections at
central and provincial levels would be allowed, but also that he
would dissolve the National Assembly if a new constitution, which
could permit autonomy but would have to be acceptable to him, was
not produced in four months. Pakistan had to know who was boss.

In his bid to placate popular opinion, Yahya made two additional
decisions. One was to scrap 'One Unit'—which had made little
administrative sense and barred many doors to politicians—, and
provide Punjab, the NWFP, Sindh and Balochistan with their separate
governments.

Yahya's other decision was to concede due weightage at last to
East Bengal's numbers: out of 313 in the new National Assembly,
169 would be from the eastern wing. It appears that Yahya was
relying on the competitive nature of Bengali politicians:

> Yahya seemed to appreciate the genuine nature of the
> Bengali autonomy movement but he was not convinced
> Mujib was its sole leader. His plan called for prompting
> other Bengali leaders to challenge Mujib.[58]

A huge cyclone, more furious than anything seen in East Bengal for decades and apparently taking a million lives, forced a postponement of elections. The Yahya administration's response to the disaster was seen as grudging and scanty and as proof of the case for autonomy.

Held in December 1970 and January 1971, the elections destroyed Yahya's hopes while fulfilling those of Bhutto and exceeding Mujib's fondest dreams. In the National Assembly, the Awami League won 167 out of East Bengal's 169 seats, while of West Pakistan's 144 seats, Bhutto's PPP got 83, all in Sindh and Punjab. In the 300-strong East Bengal assembly, the Awami League won 288 seats.

This was not a scenario that Yahya or Bhutto had thought of, but the independence of Bangladesh was not necessarily written into it. Mujib seems to have indicated on 7 March 1971 that the Awami League would stop short of full secession if Yahya and Bhutto accepted its majority in the National Assembly and right to the Premiership,[59] but West Pakistan's military ruler and political victor, while disagreeing on several issues, were firmly united in their resolve to prevent an Awami League government for Pakistan.

To these two, the voter was not king. Apparently agreed, moreover, that firepower rather than acceptance or accommodation should protect Pakistan's unity, Yahya and Bhutto agreed on a crackdown. Tanks rolled, guns boomed, and Mujib and hundreds were arrested.

The crackdown targeted Awami League leaders, Hindus, students, trade union activists and East Bengali soldiers of the Pakistan army. The scholar Ziring claims that he was told by General M.A. Osmani, who became commander-in-chief of the Bengali Mukti Bahini or Liberation Force and was known earlier as 'East Bengal's most formidable mind in the Pakistani army,' that

> save for this brutal and unprovoked attack by West Pakistani troops, the Bengal forces would have remained neutral.[60]

While Mujib and many others were arrested, several Awami League leaders eluded the Pakistan army and organized a liberation movement from East Bengal hideouts or from exile in Calcutta, and Bengali civil servants, judges, and police followed Awami League instructions rather than the commands of the Pakistan army.

On 25 March, Yahya and Bhutto flew together from Dhaka to Karachi while the Pakistan army strove to crush what now was an inexorable—and insurmountable—resolve for independence. Emerging from the plane in Karachi, Bhutto said, 'Pakistan has been saved.'[61]

He could not have meant the Pakistan still on the map in March 1971, the Pakistan that came into being in 1947. Perhaps he meant that West Pakistan had been saved from Mujib's Premiership, or perhaps his instincts told him that the Premiership of what would remain of Pakistan had been saved for Zulfiqar Ali Bhutto.

In 1965 he was accused of a role in goading Ayub into the clash with India that, in retrospect, started Ayub's political decline. Six years later, he would be blamed for encouraging the Yahya crackdown that, as hindsight knows, tore Pakistan into two.

Though he had draped the PPP in socialist cloth, Bhutto, scion of an old line of landlords, had, in Ziring's words, an 'elitist, authoritarian personality' and a poor opinion of Mujib, 'who he believed was uneducated.' In addition, 'like other West Pakistanis, Bhutto, too, questioned the character of the Bengalis and harboured suspicions about their enduring loyalty.' Mujib, on his part, 'saw in the Sindhi landlord the epitome of the arrogance he associated with Pakistani leaders.'[62]

*

Bhutto spares Mujib's life: Though several million Bengalis fled to India, repression was met with struggle by a large number, including many who returned from India with arms and training. By the autumn of 1971, 'tens of thousands of Bengalis had joined the guerrilla army'—the Mukti Bahini.[63] Early in December the Indian army intervened, and received full Bengali support. On 16 December the Pakistan army surrendered, and about 94,000 of its soldiers were taken prisoner by India.

The previous day, Bhutto, who had joined the Yahya administration as Deputy Prime Minister, had vowed an unending war with India after failing to persuade the United Nations Security Council to condemn India's action:

> We shall tell our children and they will tell their children. We will fight for a thousand years . . . I am leaving your Security Council. I find it disgraceful to my person and my country to remain here a moment longer.[64]

The emotional speech stirred Pakistanis and lifted Bhutto to supreme status in his country. On 20 December he replaced the defeated Yahya Khan as Pakistan's President.

During the months of repression and struggle in East Bengal, perhaps a million or more Bengalis were killed, many with great savagery, and almost ten million, of whom a large proportion were Hindus, sought safety in India.[65] When, after the creation of Bangladesh, the refugees were free to return to their homes, a high percentage of Hindus chose to remain in India, permanently reducing the Hindu presence in Bangladesh.

'The Bengalis also drew innocent blood.' Thousands of non-Bengalis domiciled in East Bengal were killed, often by horrible methods. 'Although some non-Bengalis [had] actively aided the Pakistani army, and others assisted the troops in the slaughter of Bengalis,'[66] in most cases the reason for killing the non-Bengalis, or Biharis as they were referred to, was that ethnically they were the Other.

One of Bhutto's earliest acts as President was to invite Sheikh Mujib, who was in army custody, for secret talks in Islamabad. Bhutto could have ordered Mujib's execution but did not. On 8 January 1972, Mujib was released unconditionally and allowed to return to what now was the new nation of Bangladesh. That Bhutto spared Mujib is remembered by history, but neither Mujib nor Bhutto was fated to die naturally.

*

The Bhutto years: 'In politics, democracy; in the economy, socialism; in religion, Islam.' With these slogans, the charismatic Zulfiqar Ali Bhutto had launched the PPP in 1967. However, his first task as President was to obtain the release of the 94,000 Pakistani soldiers in Indian custody.

He accomplished it by signing in July 1972 a pact with Mrs Indira Gandhi, the Indian Prime Minister, that demarcated a Line of Control in the territory of Kashmir (which some saw as 'a quasi-permanent frontier'[67]) and stipulated that any questions that remained or occurred between the two countries (including, Pakistan would later insist, Kashmir) would be resolved without the use of force and through bilateral negotiations.

The condition of bilateralism, and the fact that the pact was signed in Shimla in the Indian Himalayas, signified the change in Indo-Pakistan relations occurring since 1966, when Ayub and Shastri had reached their agreement in Tashkent in the presence of the Soviet Premier, Alexei Kosygin. Bhutto's response to the change was to pursue diligently a strategic goal that he had espoused from the time when he was Ayub's foreign minister: deepening Pakistan's relations with China.

The secession of Bangladesh had brought to the forefront a question that East Bengal's unrest had pushed off-stage: Punjab's dominance in what used to be the west wing and now was Pakistan. Helped by his Sindhi origin, Bhutto obtained a consensus among political parties, including those that were influential in the less populous provinces, for a new constitution that, among other things, seemed to give status to each province and strength to the centre.

This 1973 constitution sought to balance a national assembly with seats according to population, which would give Punjab's numbers their weight, with a national senate with equal provincial representation. In addition, Bhutto offered his solemn word that the non-PPP governments that were in office in Peshawar in the NWFP and Quetta, the Balochistan capital, would not be disturbed.

However, in February 1974 Bhutto removed the Quetta government, charging that it was inciting Balochis against the central government. In sympathy, and doubtless believing its days to be numbered, the NWFP ministry also resigned.

The consensus for the 1973 constitution had also provided for a role for Islam in politics and for a parliamentary form of government, though a no-confidence vote against the prime minister was virtually ruled out for ten years. Bhutto became Prime Minister, with Fazal Elahi Chaudhry, a Punjabi politician, filling the President's post.

Over Islam, the new constitution went beyond the 1956 and 1962 constitutions and laid down that 'Islam shall be the State religion of Pakistan' and that only a Muslim could be President or Prime Minister. It also said that the state 'shall endeavour to preserve and strengthen fraternal relations among the Muslim countries based on Islamic unity.'

When Bangladesh became independent, Bhutto had commented that Pakistan's 'geographic focus' and 'geo-political perspective' had 'significantly altered.'[68] This apparent hint that Pakistan's destiny lay more with West Asia than with South Asia found an echo in the provision about Muslim countries in the 1973 constitution.

Bhutto's willingness to play 'Islamic politics' was also revealed when with his support the National Assembly declared in 1974 that Ahmadis (or Ahmadiyas or Qadianis), members of a sect founded in 1889 by Mirza Ghulam Ahmad and denounced as heretical by orthodox ulama, were non-Muslims. A Sindhi looking for enduring support in Punjab and the NWFP, Bhutto had pulled out the Islamic card.

The caution of Pakistan's founder, Jinnah, about 'Islamicizing' politics in Pakistan may have stemmed from an awareness that it was perhaps impossible to Islamicize laws without doing so in accordance with the specific doctrines of one of Islam's several schools. To Islamicize was to sectarianize, and thus divide, Pakistan.

As one born into a family that was neither Sunni nor mainstream Shia but belonged in fact to one of the Gujarati-speaking factions of the Khoja or Ismaili community of Shias led by the Aga Khan, and as an acute lawyer, Jinnah was more sensitive than most to the scope that 'Islamicization' would offer to discord. However, Jinnah himself, or at least his cause of Pakistan, had profited from Islam's political possibilities, and it is these, rather than the potential in Islamicization for discord, that registered with Jinnah's successors in Pakistan, including Bhutto.

Endowed with a handsome appearance and high social status, schooled in Berkeley and Oxford, immaculate in attire and gifted in speech, suave where needed and rousing before a crowd, his rhetoric often socialistic or populist, Bhutto could sometimes bring Nehru to mind, and at other times Sukarno, Peron or Castro.

In January 1972, within two weeks of becoming President, Bhutto nationalized thirty-one enterprises, including industries and banks. Labour reforms, encompassing the small sector as well as big enterprises, were brought into force in February, and in March life insurance companies were taken over by the state. He hoped to reduce inequalities but ended up hurting investment and giving the bureaucracy a tight grip over business.

Bhutto arrested and hanged: Bhutto's tragic end was preceded by elections in 1977 to the national and provincial assemblies. The opposition—'a loose confederation of the old ruling establishment, Islamic fundamentalists, and ethnic minorities'[69]—seemed disorganized, and Bhutto expected an unchallenged passage. However, a nine-party Pakistan National Alliance (PNA) that included the fundamentalist Jamaat-i-Islami and the Left-leaning National Democratic Party quickly came into being, drew large crowds, and looked likely to enter the assemblies in strength.

But when results were declared in March, the PNA had won only 32 out of the 192 National Assembly (NA) seats it contested, including just 8 from Punjab, which had 116 NA seats. 'The opposition cried foul and took to the streets.'[70] In an operation called

'Fairplay,' the army arrested Bhutto as well as PNA leaders and took over the country. A man of unassuming appearance called General Ziaul Haq headed the army, having been appointed chief the previous year by Bhutto.

To begin with, General Zia gave Bhutto 'protective custody' in the former Premier's own home, claiming that he had to be shielded from popular wrath. Set free for a while for elections that Zia promised would be held in October 1977, Bhutto was rearrested on a charge of murder. It was alleged that Bhutto had been the chief culprit in a 1974 conspiracy to kill Ahmad Raza Kasuri, a former Bhutto protege who had turned into a foe. In addition, the military government published White Papers spelling out the Bhutto administration's supposed misdeeds.

But it was also alleged that Pakistan's judges were no longer independent, and the elections promised were not held. In March 1978 a court in Lahore pronounced Bhutto guilty and sentenced him to death. A year later, by a four-three verdict, Pakistan's Supreme Court confirmed the sentence. While the four judges upholding the guilty verdict and the death sentence were from Punjab, two of the three who favoured acquittal were Sindhis. The third was a Parsi.

On 4 April 1979, eight years after he had spared the life of his Bengali prisoner, Sheikh Mujibur Rahman, Zulfiqar Ali Bhutto of Sindh was hanged in Rawalpindi jail, for Zia, the Punjabi whose prisoner he was, preferred to let Bhutto hang.

*

The Zia reign: Given the army's firepower and the fact that the 1977 election results had been angrily challenged, Zia's takeover was not a difficult exercise, but his reign would not have lasted for eleven years without Zia's native shrewdness, which he masked under a deferential air.

The foundation of his survival policy was a refusal to hand over command of the army to any other individual. Zia the Martial Law Administrator or President would also always remain the Army Chief. Secondly, he kept the air force and the navy out of the power structure. Zia would control the army, which would control Pakistan, while other forces were kept at a distance.

Islamicization, far more extensive than anything Bhutto might have thought of, was another central feature of the Zia years. Claiming that Islam was to Pakistan what Judaism was to Israel, Zia declared, 'Take Islam out of Pakistan and make it a secular state, it would collapse.'[71] In February 1979, new 'Islamic' courts were empowered to punish crimes with lashes, amputation, stoning or public hanging, and to pronounce on the Islamicness of existing laws.

Six months later came an ordinance containing an implicit warning that political parties could be debarred from any future elections if their manifestos excluded Islamic provisions. Then in March 1981 Zia promulgated a Provisional Constitutional Order in the name of Islamicizing the political structure.

This Order brought into being, firstly, a Majlis-e-Shura, a Federal Council nominated by Zia for debating policies and laws, presumably from the Islamic standpoint. Secondly, it retroactively invalidated all court judgments against the Zia government. Thirdly, it protected military courts and cases from the jurisdiction of any civil court. Finally, it required all judges to take a new oath of office, with a more detailed Islamic content. Judges unwilling to recite the new oath were dismissed, including the Chief Justice of the Supreme Court.

A reaction was inevitable. It was led by the Movement for the Restoration of Democracy (MRD), joined by eleven parties, including the PPP. On 12 August 1983, Zia countered by declaring that he too wished to restore democracy and elections, but he would not commit himself to details.

The Zia 'bombshell' was aimed at pre-empting a campaign that he knew the MRD was about to launch. Begun on 14 August (Pakistan's independence day) in 1983, the MRD campaign was particularly strong in Sindh, where the Bhutto memory refused to die. By the end of the year, Zia admitted that about 5,000 MRD supporters had been arrested and more than 60 killed in Sindh. Larger figures were claimed by the MRD.

But Zia alleged that the movement was a Sindhi bid against Pakistan's central government, not a fight for democracy. Because Sindh was the centre of MRD activity, many were inclined to believe the charge, especially in Punjab, and Zia also employed to his advantage a statement by Indira Gandhi, the Indian Premier, that the struggle for democracy in Pakistan had her support. In another 1984 gambit, aimed at cementing bonds with fundamentalists, the Zia regime forbade Ahmadis from using Islamic symbols.

Refusing to contemplate a 'democratic' set-up not regulated by him, Zia obtained, at the end of 1984, a 'mandate' to continue as President for five more years. This he did through the device of a referendum in which the public was asked whether or not, for the sake of 'Islamicizing Pakistan,' Zia should stay on as President. Announcing that 98 per cent had voted for his continuance, Zia also claimed that 62 per cent of those eligible had taken part in the referendum. His opponents asserted that the turnout was about 10 per cent.

Finally, in February 1985, non-party elections to the national and provincial assemblies were held. This time the report of an over 50 per cent turnout seemed genuine. But voting results suggested that Islamicization was no longer popular: only eight out of the sixty candidates openly sponsored by the Jamaat-i-Islami won.

On 23 March, Zia announced that Muhammad Khan Junejo, one of those elected, a Sindhi and a close associate of Sindh's most powerful religious leader, the Pir of Pagaro, would be Pakistan's new, democratically chosen, Premier, but by this time two other major decisions had also been taken. The 1973 constitution was amended to make the President all-powerful and the Premiership dependent on the President's pleasure; and Zia declared that he would remain Chief of the Army Staff.

In choosing Junejo, Zia aimed at neutralizing the influence in Sindh attaching to the memory, as well as the living relatives, of Bhutto. This time, however, the astuteness backfired. Revealing a mind of his own, the mild-looking Junejo revived the Pakistan Muslim League in January 1986, and took several League members into his cabinet.

To begin with, Zia appeared to welcome Junejo's initiatives as evidence of the democracy he had promised to restore, but he knew he had to act when Junejo, who also held the defence portfolio, evidently 'held up the promotion of a couple of generals considered to be close Zia associates' and even suggested that the President should let someone else serve as the Army Chief.[72]

Earlier, the two had disagreed over Afghanistan, where different factions, including some heavily backed by Pakistan, were battling the Soviet presence. While Zia felt that only a military victory would empower the groups that Pakistan favoured, Junejo seemed to prefer a negotiated settlement. To that end Junejo had convened an all-party conference in March 1988, attended, among others, by Bhutto's daughter, Benazir.

Zia's plans to remove Junejo were finalized in May 1988, while the Premier was visiting China and Japan. On his return to Islamabad on 29 May, while Junejo was addressing a press conference at the airport, Zia informed another group of journalists that Junejo and his ministerial colleagues were being dismissed, and existing assemblies dissolved.

Zia claimed, too—with what sincerity we do not know—, that fresh elections would be held 'within ninety days.' But on 17 August 1988, a C-130 aircraft carrying Zia, several army generals including General Akhtar Abdur Rahman, the ex-chief of the Inter-Services Intelligence (ISI) who had played a major role in Afghanistan, and Arnold Raphel, the American ambassador, exploded in mid-air near Bahawalpur, in southern Punjab, killing all aboard.

Investigators, including some belonging to America's FBI, concluded that a bomb had been placed in the plane when it was parked at the airport outside Bahawalpur, but 'none of the investigating teams was prepared to speculate about the identity of the assassins.'[73]

* .

The Zia years—an analysis: Zia's eleven-year reign and its longevity have been copiously analysed. It has been argued, for one thing, that Zia's power was based, the army apart, on the 'bazaar bourgeoisie'— a 'middle class of retail and wholesale merchants, import and export traders, contractors, renters, real estate agents, traders in contraband groups, and smugglers.' According to Hassan Gardezi, members of this 'class,' having 'a common need to acquire social acceptability and a clean front,' are a natural constituency for the politics of Islamicization.[74]

This constituency welcomed Islamicization's alliance with nativization during the Zia years. Mustapha Kamal Pasha suggests that non-westernized or vernacular sections of Pakistan used Islamicization to attain dominance over the westernized elements. In Pasha's view, Zia was the first representative of the vernacular class to lead Pakistan. Adding that 'the confluence of patriotism and Islamization offers nearly limitless possibilities for illiberal politics,' Pasha describes the 'antinomies of Zia's eleven-year rule':

> Zia's tenure was littered with glaring contradictions: glitter and ostentation mixed with entreaties to frugality and a spartan life-style; an unending chorus of religiosity through the media amidst massive corruption and graft; drug trade (often with state connivance or malevolent neglect); and wholesale human rights violations . . . in the name of Islamic justice . . .

[D]uring the Zia years, the main emphasis was on outward conduct: prayer (and the building of mosques); fasting and the enforcement of moral purity during the month of Ramadhan; public flogging for 'crimes'; rectification campaigns; and [for women,] chaddar (veil) and chardivari (four walls), or the repression of women's rights to curb any possible expression of female sexuality.[75]

Also striking is that Zia's Islamicization had no room for any analysis of Bangladesh's secession. Pasha points out that

the dominant classes shunned a deeper introspection into the real reasons for the creation of Bangladesh in favour of rewriting national history from the vantage point of 'new' Pakistan's rediscovered primal religious, cultural and geographical proclivity to West Asia and the Middle East. In essence, the role of Bengali Muslims became relegated to an historical footnote once the holy alliance with the Gulf states—especially Saudi Arabia and the UAE—had been fully consummated.[76]

However, 'these (Islamicizing) intellectuals have managed to inject a religious vocabulary into the most diverse forms of social communication, ranging from politics to science to public morals...'

Particularly significant, in the light of our study, is the teaching of history, though it should be remembered, as Khursheed Kamal Aziz underscores in his 1993 critique of Pakistani textbooks, that the abolition of history as a subject in schools occurred during Ayub's time. 'Social studies' for classes 1-8 and 'Pakistan Studies' for classes 9-12 filled history's place.[77]

According to Aziz, in each Pakistani province a Textbook Board prescribes textbooks for each class. Some of these carry 'a warning issued by the Chairman of the Board that the students must not buy or use any "additional" textbooks.' These books 'are the only source of information for millions of students whose education stops at or before the 12th class.' (pp. 1-2) Aziz quotes from a West Punjab textbook for class 2:

q: How did Jinnah come to think of creating Pakistan?
a: Pandit Nehru said that after independence there will be a government of the Hindus in India. The Quaid-i-Azam said that Muslims also lived here [and] Muslims should have a separate government. (from p.4 of textbook; p.9, Aziz)

Some other textbook sentences quoted by Aziz are:

> In the 1971 India-Pakistan war the Indian forces were defeated
> everywhere . . . In the 1965 India-Pakistan war India sued for
> peace after having been defeated soundly by Pakistan. In
> 1947 the Hindus and Sikhs massacred many Muslims. (118-
> 19)

That 1947 also saw identical massacres of Hindus and Sikhs in West
Pakistan is not indicated. Adds Aziz:

> The Red Shirts movement of the NWFP and the Unionist
> party of the Punjab are not mentioned in chapters on these
> provinces. The 1971 break-up of Pakistan is dismissed in a
> few lines or one paragraph, and is always made out to be the
> result of an Indian invasion . . . The Bengalis' role in the
> political, educational and cultural history of Muslim India is
> ignored . . . The Indian National Congress [is called] a
> Hindu political party, [and it is written that] in 1937 the
> Indian National Congress won the provincial elections by
> chance. (120-21)

In Aziz's strong words, 'history has been manipulated, polluted, ill-
used and trampled under foot' in the textbooks. (121) Thus the 1857
clash is presented as 'a war of independence waged by the Muslims
against the hated British' (126), but Aziz asks how the war of
independence and its strong critic, Sayyid Ahmad Khan, can both be
simultaneously praised.

More serious is Aziz's finding in respect of Pakistan's 1971
break-up. The textbooks for 'classes five up to B.A. offer a standard,
repetitive, false, spurious and monotonous' explanation:-

> [I]t was imprudent and mischievous of the people of East
> Pakistan to oppose Urdu as the national language; the
> Hindu population of East Pakistan was disloyal; India
> engineered riots through her agents; India invaded East
> Pakistan from all four sides, and the Pakistan army had to
> surrender. (154)

To follow the government in office, support military rule, glorify
wars, hate India, and welcome the imposition of a new culture on
Pakistan are among the books' direct or indirect exhortations to
young Pakistanis. (188-203) According to Aziz, the books contain

nothing about the theory and philosophy of history, or about economic, social, intellectual and literary history, or even modern Islamic thought.(228-29) We may note here that comparable scrutinies of history textbooks in other South Asian lands, including India, do not seem to exist.

Before moving to the post-Zia scene, we should mark that the three intertwined conflicts we had identified as influencing Pakistan's course since its creation—one over region/language, another over the military's role, and the third over the place of Islam—retained their significance during the Ayub, Bhutto and Zia years. When a need for coping with another region/language became pressing—when, e.g., Ayub and Yahya faced unrest in Bengal, or Bhutto needed support in Punjab, or Zia encountered disaffection in Sindh—, the temptation was to turn to firepower or Islam or both. Accommodation or power-sharing—doubtless risky, for an inch offered could whet appetites for a foot—was seldom seriously explored. A 1998 study, published in Pakistan, notes:

> As an independent nation, Pakistan largely ignored the social diversity of its people and the economic disparities of its regions. It constructed a 'national ideology' based on a mechanical notion of unity and simplistic ideas of cultural homogeneity. This neglect of social diversity and disregard of ethnic and regional interests has exacted a heavy cost from Pakistan.[78]

*

Benazir/Sharif/Benazir/Sharif: As long as they were assisting the West vis-à-vis the Soviet Union, Pakistan's military rulers were fine in American eyes. Zia's stock rose in the USA when, following the Soviet Union's invasion of Afghanistan at the end of 1979, Pakistan opened its doors to around three-and-a-half million Afghan refugees, and Zia suggested that Afghan Mujahideen groups fighting for their country's independence could be trained in, and aided from, Pakistani soil.

Some of the dollars sent for the struggle in Afghanistan were lost in transit in Pakistan. Two other side effects of the Afghan struggle were less fortunate for Pakistanis. One was the siphoning off of a large number of guns meant for Afghanistan and their use for crime, political violence and sectarian strife in Pakistan. The other was an escalation in drug-trafficking.

The Soviet Union being not far from its own demise when Zia died, the USA was willing to press for a movement towards democracy in Pakistan. In elections held in November 1988, Bhutto's daughter Benazir led the PPP to power at the centre and became Prime Minister. In August 1990, however, Benazir was dismissed by President Ghulam Ishaq Khan, who alleged massive corruption and a failure to control violence in Sindh.

New elections saw Benazir's defeat and the coming to power of a Punjabi industrialist, Nawaz Sharif of the Muslim League. Though the 1988 and 1990 results were disputed by some participants, in 1990

> Pakistan did achieve a more or less regularised transfer of political power from one civilian government to another, arguably the first since independence.[79]

In 1993 President Ghulam Ishaq Khan dismissed Sharif, accusing him of corruption, and elections held later in 1993, after a few months of technocratic rule, brought Benazir Bhutto back to office. Three years later, another President, Farooq Leghari, removed Benazir from office, citing large-scale violence in Karachi, incompetence and corruption. After another spell of rule by technocrats, elections held in February 1997 returned Nawaz Sharif to power, who used his majority to annul the President's power to dismiss the Premier.

Since Zia's death, the Pakistan army has remained in the wings, no doubt with eyes wide open but remembering the unpopularity of Zia's military rule. Democratic rule has thus proceeded without interruption for over ten years, but 1999 saw suggestions that alternatives were again being weighed. Under Sharif's instructions, the army enforced order and held trials in Sindh, and controlled the national board for water and power, prompting speculation about a larger role.

The surmise received a boost in the summer of 1999, when it was suggested, in the context of Indo-Pak battles around the Line of Control in Kashmir, that the army rather than Nawaz Sharif was directing policy.

*

Ethnic conflicts have continued to hound Pakistan in the nineties. The army has fought Sindhis offended by grants of land to Punjabi farmers and by Muhajir dominance in the cities of Sindh. Armed Muhajirs in Karachi, Hyderabad and other Sindhi towns have clashed with soldiers trying to subdue them, or with Sindhis resentful of their numbers, or with Pathans or Punjabis contending for influence in Karachi. Balochi tribesmen have fought army units.

A critical issue is the ethnic composition of Pakistan's armed forces. Ishtiaq Ahmed, a Pakistani scholar trying to gather information on regional percentages (the military withholds such information), was told by some Sindhis that 85 per cent in the army were of Punjabi origin. Others, however, told Ahmed that the Pakhtun (Pathan) ratio exceeded 30 per cent. Ahmed cites Khalid bin Sayeed's estimate that in the 1960s, 65 per cent were Punjabi and 35 per cent Pakhtun but in the late 1970s the Pakhtun representation in the armed forces was a good deal less, between 15 and 20 per cent.

An unnamed source quoted by Ahmed claimed that in 1990 54,857 recruits were taken from Sindh in the army's non-commissioned posts. Of these 70 per cent were Urdu-speaking (Muhajirs) and 30 per cent Sindhis.[80] In the view of another writer, Feroz Ahmed,

> Given the ethnic specificity of the armed forces and the spending of the largest portion of the budget on defense, a more equitable distribution of resources among ethnic communities is unthinkable without drastically altering the ethnic composition of the military and/or reducing the military budget . . . The civil bureaucracy has been [relatively speaking] more amenable to ethnic diversification.[81]

Sectarian clashes matching ethnic ones, Sunnis have fought Shias or fellow-Sunnis in various parts of Punjab and in Karachi. Observers have felt that foreign support was available to numerous sectarian groups—Iranian assistance for Shia bodies and Saudi aid for Sunni groups. Methods of killing were modern, but rival militant groups were not necessarily representative of citizens. The killings occurred not in riots involving large numbers or neighbours but usually through drive-by shooting.[82]

According to Mumtaz Ahmad, long periods of suppression of political activity, identity politics and institutional collapse are among the causes of violence, including Shia-Sunni and intra-Sunni violence (involving Deobandis, Barelvis, and Ahl-e-Hadith). At times, rulers have found Shia-Sunni conflicts useful for claiming the role of umpire or peace-enforcer. Bazaar merchants finance the violent activity, which is executed by madrassa students or unemployed youth.[83]

Noting that dissatisfaction was widespread, some observers feared in 1998-99 that it could flare up along the regional fault-line and take a Punjab-versus-the-rest shape.[84]

The Islamic card remains attractive to Pakistani politicans but perhaps its hazards are now plainer to see. The severe codes imposed in 1997-98 on the people of Afghanistan by its Taliban rulers have not gone down well in Pakistan, where women, intellectual and social elites and professionals, including in the army, appear to prize personal freedom and opportunities.

The Taliban is more a military organization than a political movement, and covert Pakistani support for the Taliban has been broad in its scope. In the 1980s and 1990s, links were forged between the Taliban on the one hand and the Inter-Sevices Intelligence (ISI), the transport 'mafia,' and some Islamic parties in Pakistan on the other. In the summer of 1999, questions were also raised about tendencies towards Talibanization in the army.

According to Ahmed Rashid, the extent of the Taliban's influence in Pakistani society can have major repercussions on Islamabad's future. The idea of an Islamic revolution in Pakistan could appeal to Pakistani madrassa students who have fought alongside the Taliban in Afghanistan.[85]

If this could be sobering, so is the likelihood that any Islamic rule would be the rule of a particular sect or school of Islam, a prospect bound to escalate and intensify the sectarian violence that has already taken a large number of Pakistani lives.

Shias may form only 8 to 20 per cent of the Pakistani population—no official figures seem to exist, and non-official figures vary a great deal—but are prominent in the professions, education, the bureaucracy and the army. And the majority Sunnis are distributed among several sects. In such a situation, Islamicization might prove to be more divisive, and perhaps violently so, than unifying.

*

Revenge: The revenge threads in Pakistan's story are obvious. Nawaz Sharif and Benazir Bhutto seem to feature in criminal and inimical shapes in each other's minds. As Prime Minister, each has sought to send the other behind bars, and the regional backgrounds of the two lend an ominous Punjabi-versus-Sindhi character to their conflict.

Benazir offers a prime example of the closeness between power and pain, fame and reproach. Twice a young Premier of a large nation, she lost her father through hanging and two brothers through killing, yet when her brother Murtaza was killed in Karachi in September 1996, Murtaza's wife Ghinwa accused Benazir's husband Asif Zardari of a hand in the murder.

Killings in the Shia-Sunni sectarian strife have followed a retaliatory pattern, and revenge as well as a struggle for power also seemed underlined in the bloody in-house clashes within the Muhajir Qaumi Movement (MQM), which has espoused the rights of Muhajirs.

From time to time Pakistani officials have alleged an Indian hand, in particular that of the Research and Analysis Wing (RAW), in sectarian or ethnic clashes, while the Indian government has frequently accused Pakistan and its ISI of instigating violence in India's Punjab, the Northeast, and elsewhere in the country, and of training, arming and recruiting militants for Kashmir's secession from India.

At this book's start we looked at the introduction of evocative symbols of the eight centuries old Prithviraj-Ghauri battles into the Indo-Pak missile competition of the 1990s. It is obvious that inserting history's scores and their correction as a legitimate item into the agendas of modern Pakistan and India would escalate the hazards from the nuclear capability banged out by both countries in May 1998.

BANGLADESH

In simplified terms, the story of Bangladesh is one of adoration for the Bangla language, respect for oneself, and enmity for the unjust ruler of the day. Earlier in this chapter we saw how an unthinking pressure for Urdu from Pakistan's ruling circles and disregard for Bangla had triggered separatism, and how an unwillingness to concede equal rights to residents of East Bengal had led to the emergence of Bangladesh.

Pakistanis accused East Bengalis of putting Islam in danger by privileging a 'Hinduized' language, Bangla, but we have noted the Bengalis' belief that rather than Islam they were at risk in a country that pushed down their language. Their language was a heritage beyond price; it distinguished them from other peoples; they would protect it at any cost.

That the language linked them to West Bengal, an Indian and Hindu-majority entity, could not be helped and was not necessarily a disadvantage. They saw no conflict between their language and

Islam, which in fact seemed to toughen their defence of Bangla, and were disinclined to forgive the West Pakistanis who had offended them. Mujib's electoral sweep of January 1970 was fair and square, and accomplished under rules set by Yahya's army regime.

Within ten months of Mujib's return in January 1972, a committee headed by law minister Kamal Hosain had drafted a constitution for Bangladesh—in Bangla. In letting language and self-respect shape its identity, Bangladesh has resembled Sri Lanka, but in letting enmities mould its politics, Bangladesh bears a likeness to Pakistan. Hailed on his return as a deliverer, Mujib soon attracted hostility, for even as Pakistani rulers had sought to suppress East Bengal's voice, he tried to suppress criticism from fellow Bengalis.

Mujib, 1972-75: The Bengalis have been spoken of as 'tenacious and willing to endure hardship, cherishing life yet extolling its torments, emotional, sentimental, expressive, passionate and romantic, but also not afraid of reality.' Ziring portrays Mujib as having several of these traits, a person with 'street-fighting abilities, a willingness to accept punishment, and a defiance of authority' but lacking in administrative skill and consensus-building arts. In Ziring's view, Mujib was also suspicious of those around him and could not work with colleagues who saw things differently.

Not only was Mujib charged with having become 'most dependent on New Delhi'; it was even suggested that he was toying with an association with Bhutto and his 'new' Pakistan. Ziring contrasts Mujib's alleged attempts to build ties with non-Bangladeshis like Indira Gandhi and Bhutto with a lack of similar exertions with fellow-Bengalis.

His absence in a Pakistani prison during the struggle for Bangla independence and unfamiliarity with the changed scene handicapped Mujib. An early blunder of his was to select 'as his press secretary a journalist who worked for the Pakistani propaganda machine during the war.' An uproar forced Mujib to cancel the appointment, but the man was named an ambassador.[86]

Acknowledging a failing, Mujib seems to have said once that if he obtained strength from 'his capacity to love human beings,' he was also 'weak because this love was excessive.'[87] Or perhaps he was poor in assessing people.

Within a year of returning as a hero, Mujib was blamed for the new country's problems—incompetent administration, siphoning off of foreign aid, corruption, and intimidation by armed groups that claimed descent from the liberation struggle. Prominent among these groups was the Rakhi (or Rakshi) Bahini set up by Mujib, which functioned as an armed wing of the Awami League and under his ultimate supervision.

These weaponized Bahinis frightened and at times extorted the citizenry, and it 'became difficult to distinguish between marauders and the terrorist wings of political parties,' to quote from a joint study by Muntassir Mamoon, a Bangladeshi professor, and Jayanta Kumar Ray of Calcutta University. Properties abandoned by rich West Pakistanis were violently contested for and 'a culture of plunder began to vitiate the civil society of Bangladesh.'[88]

Even more importantly, the Rakhi Bahini alienated the army, which felt threatened by it. Moreover, army officers prevented by their posting in West Pakistan from joining the liberation struggle resented the promotions that had turned pre-1972 subordinates who had fought the Pakistanis into superiors.

Mujib was accused of surrounding himself with sycophants, of allowing relatives to enrich themselves, of not consulting others and of scapegoating colleagues when threatened by public discontent.[89] The expulsion from his cabinet of Tajuddin Ahmad, a former Prime Minister who was regarded as incorruptible if also pro-Indian and pro-Soviet, gave offence to many.

Greedier Awami League politicians flourished and the party as a whole was increasingly seen as aiming for 'autocratic dominance.' At one stage M.A.G. Osmani, who had led the Mukti Bahini, seems to have told Mujib: 'I have watched Ayub Khan and Yahya Khan and don't want you changed into Mujibur Rahman Khan.'[90] But this remark was an exception. Most of Mujib's Awami League colleagues refrained from questioning him.

In one view, neither Mujib alone nor the Awami League as a party but the country's middle class as a whole, civil and military, was accountable for the let-down felt by Bangladeshis:

> Their dominance or influence is determined by their ability to manage for themselves, . . . first and foremost to see to their personal and familial needs. Government positions, military station, commercial endeavour [had] one common objective, the protection of self and the accretion of personal wealth.[91]

The Mujib government's socialist rhetoric and treaties with India and the Soviet Union inviting criticism, Mujib responded by attending in

1974 a summit of Islamic countries held in Lahore and visiting Washington. The charge of Mujib's dependence on India was sometimes accompanied by wild allegations against India. Mamoon and Ray write:

> The weekly *Hak Katha* of Maulana Bhasani specialised in preaching that during the period of Awami League rule India looted from Bangladesh a larger amount of resources than the British did in course of two hundred years . . . No opposition party had the honesty to praise India for accelerating the liberation of Bangladesh, and for repairing, at the request of the Awami League government, hundreds of bridges and culverts with extraordinary rapidity . . . Nor did any opposition party register appreciation for withdrawal of Indian troops from Bangladesh in less than three months . . .[92]

Mujib was hit, too, by the 1973 oil shock that multiplied Bangladesh's import bill. The following year saw a drought and a flood. In the view of Mamoon and Ray, 'the despotic tendencies' displayed by Mujib, culminating in his assumption of extraordinary powers in 1974, were 'a not unnatural although far from desirable' response to these shocks as well as to 'the corruption and incompetence' of Awami Leaguers, and 'the vicious propaganda' against him.[93]

After proclaiming a state of emergency at the end of 1974, Mujib abrogated fundamental rights, dissolved parliament, banned all but four newspapers, and finally launched a new political vehicle, Baksal, which was to supersede the Awami League and become the sole party in a single-party state. The sequence of steps invited bitter hostility, and many of Mujib's detractors saw in their once-respected leader the biggest threat to Bangladesh's future.

On 15 August 1975, a group of officers and soldiers of the army invaded Mujib's house in Dhanmandi, Dhaka, and shot him to death. Also gunned down with him were Mujib's wife Faizilatunnessa, his sons Kamal, Jamal and Russell (who was nine), Sultana, the wife of Kamal, Parveen, Jamal's wife, and Mujib's youngest brother Naser. Elsewhere in Dhaka the same day, Mujib's brother-in-law Abdur Rab was killed along with several of Rab's relatives, guests and servants; and the same end was meted out to Mujib's nephew Fazlul Huq Moni and Moni's pregnant wife.

Because they were out of the country, two daughters of Mujib,

Hasina and Rehana, survived this onslaught against Mujib's progeny and relations.

Behind the killing: Even after twenty-four years, the assassination of Mujib, his family and relatives, though the subject of several books, is yet to be fully solved. Three majors were openly involved. It has been suggested that one of their grouses was Mujib's alleged failure to settle an altercation that the wife of Major S.H. Dalim had had with an Awami League leader. Another explanation focuses on the dismissal by Mujib of Dalim and another officer, Major S.H.M.B. Noor, following charges that after having caught some Awami League leaders in smuggling, Dalim and Noor had humiliated the leaders. Referring to the three majors, Ziring writes:

> Their act, as barbaric as the record shows, was not a lone effort, nor was it done to seize power for the triumvirate (of the three majors). The decision to destroy Mujib was also a decision to introduce the military as the true governors, indeed the only possible governors of Bangladesh . . . The Majors sought refuge not control, and . . . they seized the first opportunity to slip back into the shadows from where they had emerged.[94]

Also minimizing the role of personal revenge, Mamoon and Ray argue that the operation in which Mujib and his family members were killed 'required elaborate and lengthy planning' and a wider conspiracy. In any case, high circles in Bangladesh and outside welcomed Mujib's elimination. Forty-two days after the murders, the new President, Khandaker Mushtaque Ahmed, officially indemnified the killers, who were allowed to leave the country. China and Saudi Arabia now recognized Bangladesh, and 'relations with Pakistan and the United States registered improvements.'[95]

Whoever they all were, the conspirators aimed at Mujib's seed and also at his legacy. On 3 November 1975, four Awami League leaders were killed in the jail in Dhaka where they were being kept: former Vice-President Syed Nazrul Islam, former Premiers Tajuddin Ahmad and Mansur Ali, and former minister A.H.Q. Qamruzzaman.

*

Ziaur Rahman, 1975-81: Rivalries infecting the army as well, on 3 November a contingent of infantry loyal to Brigadier Musharraf arrested General Ziaur Rahman, the Chief of Staff, whose voice over the radio had announced Bangladesh's independence in December 1971. Army officers forced President Mushtaque to resign, and Chief Justice Abu Sayem became President, but rank and file soldiers overthrew and killed Musharraf, who was accused, without evidence, of being India's nominee. Abu Taher, a colonel seen as an egalitarian and termed a 'people's officer,' seemed likely to take over as Chief of Staff, but a group of jawans freed Ziaur Rahman, and Taher joined in inviting Zia to lead.

Zia's leadership was quickly and widely accepted in the army. A meticulous and intense officer, he had spent his boyhood and much of his army life in West Pakistan, specializing in intelligence and also commanding a battalion in the 1965 Indo-Pak war. Posted in the East during the 1971 repression, he chose Bangla independence over loyalty to the Pakistan army, and like several other East Bengali officers broke free at an opportune moment.

Restored as Chief of Staff, Zia moved fast. His rival, Abu Taher, was arrested and hanged for revolutionary activities in the summer of 1976, and Zia was alleged to have ordered the killing of a large number of soldiers loyal to Taher.[96]

On 21 April 1977, Zia took over as President. Some have alleged a Zia hand in the Mujib assassination. Ziring, who cites several of Zia's accomplishments and is sharply critical of Mujib's failings, writes:

> Zia sanctioned the action that destroyed Mujib. He was also its immediate beneficiary . . . The belief that Mujib had to be forcefully removed made Zia a party to the act of conspiracy.

Ziring adds:

> Mascarenhas and Lifschultz are more direct in assigning blame for Mujib's death to Zia.[97]

Mamoon and Ray write:

> There is no proof about Ziaur Rahman being directly responsible for Mujib's murder. It was, nevertheless, true that he had information about the conspiracy against Mujib.[98]

In 1979 the Zia-controlled parliament declared that all the acts of Bangladesh's rulers since 15 August 1979 were valid, confirming the immunity that Mushtaque had conferred, under duress or otherwise, on Mujib's killers. Since Zia did not want them in the country, some ended up in the Bangladesh foreign service, while two ring leaders, Colonels Farooq Rahman and Rasheed, found employment under President Gaddafi of Libya.

Less committed than Mujib to a secular polity, Zia moved towards an Islamic orientation. The 1972 constitution had explicitly mentioned secularism as an ideal. General Zia had it deleted in 1977. 'Trust and faith in the Almighty Allah' was inserted in its place, and Islam declared the state religion.

In the 1972 constitution, citizens of Bangladesh were called 'Bengalis' but in 1977 they were redefined as 'Bangladeshis.' Zia wanted no one in Bangladesh, India or anywhere else to confuse his country and its people with the Bengalis of India's West Bengal. Not that Mujib had desired such a confusion, or thought of a closer political relationship with West Bengal. The linguistic nationalism that swept away West Pakistan's rule was a controlled tide, not intended to destroy the walls separating Muslim-majority East Pakistan from Hindu-majority India. Bangladesh's linguistic identity had a religious bottom line.

Zia, who foiled several mutinies and escaped several bids against his life, shored up the Islamic bottom line, for domestic political reasons and also to strengthen relations with the oil-rich lands of the Gulf. In another departure from Mujib's stance, Zia clarified that his government would pursue 'economic and social justice' rather than 'socialism.' A 'referendum' that was scarcely credible ratified Zia's presidentship at the end of May 1977 but he functioned also as Chief Martial Law Administrator and Chief of the Army Staff.

In the summer of 1978, craving the legitimacy so often desired by military rulers, Zia got himself elected to the presidentship that he was occupying, comfortably defeating his main opponent, General Osmani. Later that year he floated the Bangladesh National Party (BNP), which won the parliamentary elections held in February 1979, securing 41 per cent of the vote and 207 seats, while the Awami League obtained 24.6 per cent of the vote and 39 seats.

Zia had astutely sensed that Bangladesh, where existing parties were perceived as pro-Left, pro-Islam or pro-India (fairly or not, Mujib's Baksal and Awami League were given the last label), offered space for a party of Bangladeshi nationalism.[99] Martial law was lifted in April 1979, but Zia continued as defence minister, while General H.M. Ershad served as Chief of the Army Staff from the end of 1978. However, in 1981, a little more than four years after he had become President, Zia too, like Mujib before him and others in Bangladesh's ruling establishment including Tajuddin Ahmed, Nazrul Islam, Musharraf and Abu Taher, came to a violent end. In the early hours of 30 May 1981, Ziaur Rahman was shot and killed in Chittagong's Circuit House by soldiers under the command of Major General Mansoor, the GOC in the region, who nursed grievances against Zia. The soldiers had attacked the Circuit House, and the President was in his pyjamas.

Mansoor was an intimate of Abu Taher, the two having escaped from Pakistan together when the civil war erupted. Each had fought as a sector commander in the liberation battle, as had Zia. Apart from his grievances and a wish to avenge Taher's death, Mansoor may have also wanted to replace Zia as the country's ruler; after Zia's murder he seems to have announced a takeover from Chittagong radio.

Units in Chittagong went along with Mansoor, but not in the rest of the country; never-to-be-substantiated rumours of an Indian hand in the Zia murder circulated, and General Ershad, the Army Chief, ordered Mansoor's capture. Sympathy for Zia in the countryside surrounding Chittagong prevented Mansoor from escaping across the border to Burma.

Troops loyal to Zia found Mansoor 'in the coolie quarters of a tea garden'[100] and shot him dead. Zia's body, hidden by his killers, was retrieved, and he was given a state funeral in Dhaka. More than a million attended it. Zia was credited with bringing stability to Bangladesh, and taking steps for the welfare of peasants and towards Gram Sarkar or village government.

Also, he improved or strengthened Bangladesh's relations with the USA, China, South-East Asia, and the Islamic world, and enabled many Bangladeshis to find jobs in the Gulf. The cooperation he observed among the nations of South-East Asia encouraged Zia to espouse a South Asian Association for Regional Cooperation (SAARC), a regional grouping with which Zia's name will remain linked.

Though untouched by any charge of personal corruption, Zia could not check the growth of 'an affluent elite whose extravagant life styles built on aid and borrowed money surpassed those of their Pakistani forebears,' to quote Rehman Sobhan, one of Bangladesh's leading economists and administrators.[101]

However, regard for Zia survived such failures and also the ruthlessness with which he eliminated perceived enemies; referring to an aborted coup in October 1977, the writer Anthony Mascarenhas claimed that 'no general in the history of the subcontinent massacred his own troops the way that General Zia did.'[102] Zia also introduced a measure of democracy and was seen as having 'almost brought order and discipline to the armed forces.'[103] Yet some saw him as a culprit, too.

*

Ershad, 1982-90: Zia had made his fatal trip to Chittagong against the advice of some officers who had scented danger, but the fact that Ershad, who would succeed Zia in less than a year, did not stop Zia from going prompted speculation about how much Ershad knew of the plot. As was true of Zia in relation to Mujib, General Ershad, who would rule Bangladesh for eight years, was aware that he was the beneficiary of an assassination and suspected by some of involvement in it.

The deaths of Zia and Mansoor brought to an end the freedom fighters' phase in the Bangladesh army. In 1981 not more than two of the fifty or so higher echelon officers were identified with the liberation struggle. The rest, Ershad included, were repatriates from Pakistan or new officers.

In November 1981, standing with Ershad's blessings on a BNP ticket, Abdus Sattar, the acting President, won an election for the presidentship with 66 per cent of the vote. His majority was widely viewed as inflated but given the sympathy for the BNP generated by Zia's death it is unlikely that his leading opponent, Kamal Hosain of the Awami League, could have won.

On 24 March 1982, however, Sattar was removed by the man in control, Ershad. Promising a lean and clean government, Ershad announced the closure of several departments and directorates and spoke of a 'parliament of soldiers,'[104] presumably more efficient than an assembly of politicians.

Ershad made much, too, of his version of grass-roots government and declared that the sub-district or upazila would be his administration's cornerstone. However, a vehement protest by students in 1983 marred the picture he hoped to present, and the emergence at about the same time of two women provided a challenge that eventually overcame Ershad, though he kept it at bay for several years.

The women were Hasina Wajed, one of Mujib's two surviving

daughters, under whom the Awami League seemed to be reviving, and Khaleda Zia, the widow of Zia, who claimed the BNP as her legacy. While Hasina had at least observed 'the game of politics' from her vantage point in Mujib's home, Khaleda had been 'really a soldier's wife with no exposure to politics or governance of any sort.'[105] The lack in experience was more than made up, however, by a fire in each heart, lit by a certainty that a great murder, of a father in one case and a husband in the other, was yet to be fully uncovered, and fanned by the indignant belief that parties to the murder had been rewarded.

In combination, the two fires might have burnt Ershad's rule to ashes in a short time, but a union was exceedingly difficult, for apart from human rivalry, Khaleda's late husband Zia was the man on whom Hasina's ire in relation to her father's assassination and the killing of most of her family had perhaps focused the most. Yet if Hasina could never think of Khaleda solely as a victim, Khaleda would often accuse Hasina of not being firm enough against Ershad.

But there was scope for joint protests, which often took the form of nationwide hartals. In December 1983, Ershad responded to one wave of demonstrations by styling himself President, while also continuing as the Chief Martial Law Administrator. Seeking legitimacy like Zia, Ershad first formed the Janadal party as a political vehicle and then, in 1986, the Jatiyo party. In 1984 he held and won local elections where opposition parties were hardly free to campaign.

To say that in the middle eighties Bangladesh witnessed a triangular Ershad-Hasina-Khaleda contest is to simplify greatly, for there were times in this period when, in addition to Ershad's groups, the country had a fifteen-party alliance led by the Awami League, a seven-party alliance led by the BNP, a twelve-party alliance led by Khandaker Mushtaque, and an eleven-party alliance led by Ataur Rahman Khan, who had served in the fifties as East Bengal's chief minister.

A sequence of demands and protests from Khaleda and Hasina and the other politicians, of concessions made and withdrawn by Ershad, and of floods and cyclones that never leave Bangladesh alone, saw the eighties through. The period also saw an escalation in the siphoning-off of foreign aid. One estimate suggested that if in some other lands 8 per cent was the typical 'handling' loss, in Bangladesh about 30 per cent of the aid vanished along the way.[106]

In 1986 Ershad achieved a success of sorts when the Awami League and the BNP attacked each other over a proposal by him for parliamentary elections. After agreeing to make a joint response, Hasina announced at the last minute that the Awami League would participate, while the BNP declared a boycott, and each accused the other of betrayal.

Ershad's Jatiyo party was declared to have won 153 seats to 76 for the Awami League. Though massive rigging was observed, Hasina chose at first to participate in the Sangsad or parliament, but was frustrated by Ershad's refusal to reopen issues relating to Mujib and his killers.

Hasina and Khaleda boycotted the presidential election that Ershad held in October 1986, which re-elected Ershad with, supposedly, more than four-fifths of the vote. Interestingly enough, a contestant in this election was Colonel Farooq Rahman, who had found sanctuary under Gaddafi after his role in the Mujib assassination. Rahman was credited with 4.5 per cent of the vote.

With Ershad's re-election, martial law was declared ended. Retiring from the army, Ershad ruled in civilian dress, but democratic rights were nullified by a series of amendments to the constitution approved by the Sangsad in 1986-87 and by a local government law passed in the summer of 1987 that authorized army officers to sit on sixty-four district development committees throughout the country.

Khaleda and Hasina, the latter now boycotting parliament, declared that Ershad was aiming at a 'permanent garrison state' and jointly called for a siege of Dhaka, while Hasina even urged security forces to ignore Ershad's orders. Hartals, strikes and street demonstrations were however repressed by the army and the police, though martial law was not reimposed, and there was violence in Dhaka, Chittagong and Mymensingh.

'Determined not to be run out of office by unconsolable women,'[107] Ershad placed Hasina and Khaleda under house arrest for some weeks, proclaimed a nationwide emergency, and dissolved the Sangsad, but an indication of the national mood was the resignation of Bangladesh's leading poet, Shamsur Rahman, from the editorship of the government-controlled daily, *Dainik Bangla*.

On 24 January 1988, security forces opened fire on a meeting in Chittagong that Hasina had addressed, killing eleven on the spot and injuring fifty-six, of whom several died later. There was a mammoth mourning procession, and the deaths seemed a reminder of the clashes that preceded Bangladesh's liberation, but Ershad obtained a new lease of life when Hasina and Khaleda failed to sustain their unity.

While 'Ershad must go' was Khaleda's single-point programme, Hasina demanded a restoration of a parliamentary democracy as spelt out in Mujib's 1972 constitution, which did not enthuse Khaleda, who seemed comfortable with the presidential system worked by her late husband Zia. 'Elections' that Ershad again conducted in 1988, first for parliament and then for the presidency, were boycotted by the entire opposition, but unprecedented floods in 1988 and 1989 swallowed the energy of a civil society disheartened by the Khaleda-Hasina rivalry. Meanwhile, amending the constitution, Ershad had Islam declared as the state religion.

In 1989 Bangladesh received $2.3 billion in foreign aid, bringing total aid since independence to $30 billion, but while the common citizen's life seemed untouched by it, several personal coffers had swollen, and the rule of law seemed a far cry. As Rehman Sobhan puts it:

> Ershad was seen by the people to stand at the apex of all the corruption . . . The system was tailored for individuals [and] did not permit for any precedents which could guide the process of governance . . . He or his wife could call banks in the middle of the night to have the overdraft of a particular businessman renewed . . .
>
> A law could be amended for twenty-four hours to enable a particular business house to bring in a consignment and then reversed to shut down further imports so that the businessman could make a windfall killing . . .
>
> The system of governance in Bangladesh had degenerated into a form of functional anarchy, where efficiency and resource mobilization were substituted by a dependence on the largesse and direction of the donors.[108]

*

Ershad's fall: By 1990, however, the world suddenly became less congenial for leaders lacking in legitimacy. The Soviet Union was breaking up, the USA appeared to be giving a push for democracy in the third world, and Bangladesh's donors were not only demanding to know where their aid was going; they asked for political reform in Bangladesh. Moreover, in neighbouring India, Rajiv Gandhi, the third-generation Premier from the Nehru-Gandhi dynasty, had lost a general election in November 1989, while in Pakistan General Ziaul

Haq had died in a crash, and Benazir Bhutto, the daughter of the man hanged under Zia, had been elected to power.

In such a climate some Bangladeshi civil servants and one or two of Ershad's ministers began to mutter dissent or even resigned, student resistance intensified, and young supporters of the Awami League, the BNP, and the Left parties, forming themselves into the All Party Students Unity (APSU), declared that the 'residences of Khaleda and Hasina would be subjected to a siege if even at that juncture they failed to unite for toppling Ershad.'[109] Cooperation between Hasina and Khaleda finally came in November 1990.

'Faced with a call for a non-stop hartal to be enforced till the government resigned,' Ershad proposed a return to martial law; but the army commanders asked him 'to settle this matter politically with the opposition.'[110] By now the only settlement the opposition and the people were prepared for was Ershad's ouster. In the words of Mamoon and Ray:

> The period from 27 November to 4 December 1990 was full of glory for the civil society. On 27 November, journalists stopped the publication of newspapers . . ˙. On 29 November, teachers of Dhaka University resigned . . . Men got killed and injured in clashes with security forces and ruling party thugs. But processions on streets became larger and larger . . . Government employees marched out of the Secretariat on 3 December. At last, on 4 December, Ershad tendered his resignation.[111]

But we should also look at Ziring's reflection on the end of the Ershad phase:

> Several hundreds had died in this last campaign to oust the President, but it was doubtful that they would be the last victims of Bangladesh's ongoing effort to find and set an acceptable political course.[112]

*

Khaleda Zia, 1991-96: Serving as acting President, Chief Justice Shahabuddin enlisted fifteen professionals—two active and seven retired civil servants, a retired judge, a lawyer, a doctor, an economist, and two professors—in a caretaker government. Conducting a free and fair election was its principal task. The fifteen were supported by a three-judge election commission. Between them, the government and the commission organized a fully credible election.

> I have covered eleven general elections in my reporting
> career of nearly five decades (*wrote Nikhil Chakravartty*), and
> not one of them came up to the level of being as free and fair
> as that I saw with my own eyes on February 27 in Bangladesh.
> It was indeed a massive upsurge, overwhelmingly free of fear
> and violence, tension and clashes.[113]

Though polling a smaller vote share, 30.87 per cent against 33.87 per cent obtained by the Awami League and its allies, Khaleda's BNP secured 140 seats to 100 for the front led by the Awami League. Ershad was in custody and under trial, but his Jatiyo party got 11.9 per cent of the vote and 35 seats (including five won by Ershad in his home district of Rangpur), while the Islamic party, the Jamaat, won 18 seats and an 11.9 per cent vote share.

Falling, Ershad had removed the only reason for cooperation between Khaleda and Hasina, and Khaleda's government was under Hasina's fire from the word go. Rejecting, not surprisingly, an Awami League demand for revising the warrant of precedence that gave superiority to the army chief and the cabinet secretary over MPs, Khaleda was also unwilling to revoke the immunity to Mujib's killers.

When, early in 1994, Khaleda refused to give a commitment that the next election would be conducted by an independent caretaker government, the opposition parties boycotted the Sangsad and launched a movement against the Khaleda government. Towards the end of the year, members from the Awami League, the Jatiyo party, and the Jamaat resigned from the Sangsad.

Popular protest exacted a price. In the first nine months of 1995, Bangladesh saw 144 hartals, each lasting for anything from six to ninety-six hours, at an estimated daily cost to the nation of 250 crore takas.[114] Ports and airports, trains, buses, boats, government offices, hospitals, colleges, all were disrupted.

American and British diplomats joined for a year in exertions in Dhaka for a Khaleda-Hasina rapprochement, but to no avail. After the Sangsad had functioned for twenty-three months as a one-party legislature, a general election was again due but Hasina and others in the opposition refused to participate, for Khaleda rather than an independent body was going to conduct it.

Estimates of participation in the February 1996 poll, where

virtually every seat was 'won' by the BNP, ranged from 5 to a maximum of 25 per cent. Acknowledging the unreality of her position, Khaleda resigned and handed charge to neutral civilians.

Hasina Wajed, 1996-: The June 1996 elections gave the Awami League 176 seats, BNP 113, Jatiyo Dal 33, the Jamaat 3. Now it was Hasina's turn to rule and Khaleda's turn to cry foul. The Hasina government acted promptly to revoke the indemnity law, arrest those of the Mujib murder suspects that were in Bangladesh, including Farooq Rahman, and try all suspects, including, in absentia, some believed to be in Libya, Germany, Canada and the USA. While four of the accused, including Khandaker Moshtaque, were deceased, one, an army major, was extradited from Bangkok.

Also, the Hasina government announced investigations into the 1975 killings in jail of four prominent Awami League leaders, the execution of Colonel Taher in 1975, and the 1981 deaths of General Ziaur Rahman and General Mansoor.

In November 1998, after a 148-day trial, fourteen of the accused in the Mujib family killings were sentenced to death by Sessions Judge Kazi Golam Rasul. There was provision for appeal, but, interviewed after the judgment, Hasina said that she felt that a 'curse' of inaction and immunity had been 'finally removed.' Adding that she had 'prayed to the Almighty for 23 years for justice,' Hasina broke down.[115]

Out of custody since January 1997, Ershad, whose Jatiyo party has been supporting the Awami League government in the Sangsad, commented that 'the nation has to accept' the judgment.[116] His involvement in the Mujib assassination also being alleged, Ershad denied it, claiming that he was in New Delhi when the killing occurred. On her part, Khaleda, who called for a hartal against the Awami League government in March 1997, continues to believe in Ershad's involvement in her husband's murder, while Hasina remembers that it was Khaleda's husband who gained power following the Mujib murder.

In a heartening development in December 1996, India's foreign minister I.K. Gujral and his Bangladeshi counterpart signed in Dhaka a treaty on sharing the waters of the Ganga, putting an end to a long-festering dispute between neighbours. A sell-out was alleged on both sides of the border, but the treaty, to which patient non-governmental efforts in both countries had contributed, seems to have held.

Big floods and calls, now made by Khaleda, for hartals and fresh polls have continued to mark Bangladesh. Under the heading, 'O these women,' Kuldip Nayar would write in December 1998:

> The hatred of one against the other has not lessened over the years . . . Khaleda has publicly asked why Islamabad, 'which killed three million Bangladeshis during the liberation struggle, spared Sheikh Mujibur Rahman.' For Sheikh Hasina, this is the unkindest cut. She weepingly told the National Assembly after the assassins of the Sheikh were brought to book, 'Why did they kill all members of my family, including my ten-year-old brother?'
>
> Her sufferings—she has been in the wilderness for 21 years—have made her bitter and even intolerant. Nearly 8,000 cases have been registered against the BNP leaders and its activists. One of her cabinet ministers defended her by arguing that she had undergone so much 'torture' at the hands of successive governments, including the BNP, that 'she is paying them back in their own coin.'
>
> [The feud has produced] cracks within the bureaucracy, the police and the armed forces . . . The fear is that [Khaleda] and the opposition parties may push the country into a long spell of hartals . . . (*Indian Express*, New Delhi, 8.12.98)

INDIA: 1967-1999

It remains to pick up the Indian story, which we left in early 1967 at the end of the last chapter, and bring it to the present day.

Indira Gandhi, 1966-77: The 1967 election results demanded a capacity in political parties to share power with allies. For the first time since independence, Congress had lost its monopoly. In the Lok Sabha it won only 54 per cent of the seats, and its performance in the states was much worse.

In eight state assemblies, Congress found itself in a minority, and in two other states on the borderline. Yet only two states gave a majority to an opposition party or a pre-existing opposition front: Tamil Nadu, where the Dravida Munnetra Kazhagam (DMK) humbled Congress, with a student leader defeating Kamaraj, the Congress president who had only recently, in 1964 and 1966, masterminded the selection of India's Premier; and Kerala, where a Communist-led front was the clear victor.

In four states, West Bengal, Bihar, the Punjab and Orissa, opposition parties with divergent aims formed coalitions, while Congress headed governments of motley groups in Haryana, Uttar Pradesh, Madhya Pradesh and Rajasthan.

Forming and sustaining a coalition was a new exercise. However, the politicians, whether in or out of Congress, failed to summon the tolerance and compromise called for. Defections from an opposition coalition to a Congress-led one, or vice versa, forced President's rule and fresh elections in several states.

Congress was found wanting, too, when its capacity to stomach dissent was tested. Elected President in 1967, Zakir Husain had died in office in 1969, and a successor was needed. The uneasy relationship between Indira Gandhi, who had been re-elected as Prime Minister in 1967, and her senior Congress colleagues made the choice difficult.

At first described, wishfully, as a 'dumb doll' or a 'babe in the woods,' Indira by this time had shown a will of her own, and party chieftains feeling cheated by her independence but also disquieted by her evident mistrust of colleagues desired a President who if needed would stand up to her. Their choice, confirmed by the Congress Parliamentary Board (CPB), was a former party head, Sanjiva Reddy of Andhra Pradesh.

Indira, who had voted in the CPB against this choice, signed a nomination paper in Reddy's favour—a Congress Premier was expected to propose the Congress candidate's name. Nonetheless, taking the CPB decision as a snub and a challenge, she proceeded to work for the election of V.V. Giri, the Vice-President, who had thrown his hat in the ring as an independent candidate. Also a son of Andhra, Giri had been a prominent Congressman before becoming Vice-President.

The choice between Reddy, Giri, and a third candidate, C.D. Deshmukh from Maharashtra, a former finance minister sponsored by 'right-wing' parties, was left by the Constitution to members of the two houses of Parliament (MPs), and members of all the state assemblies (MLAs), though an MLA's vote had less value than an MP's.

Indira's backing for Giri, and a call made on her behalf for a 'conscience' rather than a party vote, split Congress into two. Depicting her opponents in Congress as pro-rich, and stripping her Deputy Premier Morarji Desai, a Reddy supporter, of the finance portfolio, Indira also ordered at this juncture the nationalization of fourteen leading banks.

She had presented herself as the friend of the poor, and several

Left and regional parties offered their support to her and to Giri. The variety of parties and alliances filling Parliament and the state assemblies made the election for the Presidency wholly unpredictable, but in the end Giri edged out Reddy, with Deshmukh in third place.

A strengthened Indira emerged from the tempest—she had turned a fence into a springboard. However, the 1969 split was Congress's most serious rupture since its founding in 1885. Though painted in ideological colours, the split had been caused by a clash over power and its sharing. Viewing a Reddy presidency as a limitation upon her personal power, Indira had hit back with populism, not minding either the break-up of Congress or the injury to the tradition of accommodation left behind by her father.

The Emergency, 1975-77: While it is reasonable to regard 1969 as a watershed, it was six years later, in 1975, that the unappeased hurts, fears and hungers of 1969 wrought their worst damage. Earlier, in 1971, employing the slogan 'Garibi Hatao' ('Banish Poverty') and putting her populist appeal to work, Indira had secured a large majority in a snap election that caught the opposition parties napping.

But disillusionment surfaced before long, and Gujrat and Bihar in particular saw vehement student-led protests against the governments of the Indira Congress or the Congress (I), as her party was called. In both states, corruption and official callousness supplied the issues for protest, and Jayaprakash Narayan, or JP, now seventy-two, came out of self-imposed retirement to provide a charismatic rallying point.

On 12 June 1975, in this climate of growing criticism, the Allahabad High Court found Indira guilty of two election-code violations in her 1971 election to the Lok Sabha. Though the violations seemed minor, the verdict meant a loss of her seat in Parliament and a consequent loss of her Premiership.

A second blow came even as Indira petitioned the Supreme Court's 'vacation' judge, Krishna Iyer—the court as a whole was in summer recess—, for an immediate and complete stay of the Allahabad judgment. Results from new elections in Gujrat showed that the JP-blessed Janata (People's) Front of parties opposed to the Indira Congress, including Morarji Desai's Old or Organization Congress, Congress (O), and the pro-Hindu Jan Sangh, had humbled the Indira Congress.

Amidst calls from all sides for Indira's resignation, Justice Krishna Iyer ruled on 24 June that while Indira could remain as Prime Minister until the Supreme Court considered her appeal against the

Allahabad verdict, she could neither vote nor speak in Parliament.

The Premier's chair was still hers, and a legal avenue for recovering what she had lost lay in front of her, but, as in 1969, she had been snubbed and challenged. As in 1969, Indira hit out and hit back, except that this time she targeted the institutions of democracy rather than her Congress colleagues.

On the night of 25 June, 676 opposition politicians including JP and Morarji Desai were arrested under the Maintenance of Internal Security Act (MISA) and electricity to Delhi's newspapers was cut off. In the pre-dawn hours President Fakhruddin Ali Ahmed meekly signed a piece of paper; in the morning a state of emergency was proclaimed; and Indira addressed the nation:

> There is nothing to panic about. I am sure you are conscious of the deep and widespread conspiracy which has been brewing ever since I began certain progressive measures of benefit to the common man and woman of India . . . We learn of new programmes challenging law and order throughout the country . . .[117]

A tight Press censorship was imposed, a total of 1,10,806 persons were arrested under emergency regulations and detained without trial, several organizations were banned, including the RSS, the Jamaat-i-Islami, and Naxalite groups, and fundamental rights were abrogated.

While citizens were denied court protection, Indira had the electoral law amended for her benefit by a tame Parliament (thirty or so MPs were in jail). The offences of which the Allahabad High Court had found her guilty were retroactively erased from the law, rendering it unnecessary for Indira to seek the Supreme Court's help.

Indira's most influential adviser at this juncture was her second son, Sanjay, 28, who had insisted on the emergency solution. Sanjay's advent, while holding no public office, as India's second most powerful person in 1975-77 symbolized the departure from democracy. chief ministers, cabinet ministers and senior civil servants took orders from this young man.

At Indira's behest, and perhaps on Sanjay's instigation, Parliament's life had been extended, but in January 1977 Indira unexpectedly announced elections. Intelligence agencies assured her of success, yet Sanjay had been opposed to the move. Indira's rejection of his advice was proof of a chink in her dictatorial armour: she desired validation in India and abroad.

Jails opened, politicians were let out, censorship was lifted and elections were held. For candidates opposed to Congress, these were the cheapest elections in Indian history, with the public providing whatever seemed needed—fuel, a roadside stage, a sound system, cloth for banners or volunteers to serve at booths.

Sanjay's misgivings were well-founded. Bolstered by an ailing yet determined JP who had nearly died while in detention and by a dramatic last-minute defection from Congress of Jagjivan Ram, the Scheduled Caste leader from Bihar who had served in almost every Indian cabinet since independence, the opposition coalescing against Congress won massively. Congress's defeat included the loss by Indira and Sanjay of the seats they personally contested.

In the summer of 1980 Sanjay died when a single-engine plane he was flying crashed. By this time, however, Indira was Prime Minister again, thanks to the incapacity of those defeating her to stay together.

*

Morarji Desai, 1977-79, and Charan Singh, 1979: Five groups had come together for the alliance that won over 300 seats in 1977: the Congress (O) led by Morarji Desai; the pro-Hindu Jan Sangh; the Lok Dal, supported by many of North India's peasant castes and led by the Jat leader, Charan Singh; the Socialists; and Jagjivan Ram's breakaway group, the Congress for Democracy (CFD). Shortly after the elections, the five groups 'merged' into a single Janata Party, but their separate identities remained.

Desai, Ram and Singh were in the running for the Premiership. Since voting could have split the fledgling party, JP and an older veteran of the freedom struggle, Acharya Kripalani, were asked to choose the leader. The two selected Desai, a prime ministerial candidate, as we have seen, from the time of Nehru's death in 1964.

Less impulsive and more flexible than Desai, the long-surviving Ram might have provided a stabler Janata government, but, exemplifying a tension between Dalits and the peasant castes that would influence Indian politics for years, Charan Singh had declared that he would not serve under Ram. His having been a member of Indira's 'emergency' cabinet had also gone against Ram.

Goodwill for Janata was enormous, and its prospects seemed bright. After new assembly elections held within a few months of the parliamentary poll, Janata captured several states from Congress. Eyebrows were raised, however, at what led to the assembly elections—

the removal under Article 356 of Congress-ruled state governments, on the argument that the parliamentary poll had proved their unpopularity.

Sanjiva Reddy, whose nomination for the Presidency in 1969 had invited an onslaught from Indira, now became India's President. A constitutional amendment made a declaration of emergency harder. And a year after its 1977 defeat, Congress, which had 154 MPs in the Lok Sabha, split, with the Congress (S), a group led by Swaran Singh and Y.B. Chavan, separating from Indira and regretting the emergency.

The Indira Congress seemed in hopeless decline but it was Janata that succumbed to a death wish. Its leaders squabbled shamelessly. Sanjay spotted Charan Singh's restiveness under Desai and signalled that Congress might support a government led by Charan Singh if with his followers he broke away from Janata.

Wanting an issue on which to part company with Desai, Charan Singh and his supporters found one in Janata's ex-Jan Sangh component. Former Jan Sangh MPs were asked by Charan Singh's supporters to prove that they were not enjoying 'dual membership' of the Janata Party and the RSS.

That these MPs with a Jan Sangh background should quit Parliament if they did not resign from the RSS was a demand that could not be satisfied. When the demand was turned down by the Jan Sangh, a 'secular' faction, styling itself Janata (S) and including many from the former Lok Dal and Socialist components, walked out of the ruling party, which was reduced to a minority.

In July 1979, Desai resigned and Charan Singh became Prime Minister, heading a government of the Janata (S) in alliance with the Congress (S)—and supported by MPs of the Indira Congress!

By now, though not perhaps soon enough, Desai had handed over the Janata Party leadership to Ram, who asserted, before Charan Singh's installation, that he commanded greater backing in the Lok Sabha than Charan Singh. But President Sanjiva Reddy, like Charan Singh a leader from a peasant caste, rejected Ram's claim and swore Charan Singh in as Prime Minister. Perhaps Reddy recalled that in 1969 Ram had been Indira's ally and Reddy's foe.

Charan Singh, however, was not destined to last as Premier. Having served the purpose of sinking the Desai government, he was no longer of value to the Indira Congress, which withdrew its support. Sick of Janata's quarrels, India's voters brought Indira back to power when fresh elections were held during the last days of 1979.

Indira Gandhi, 1980-84, and the Punjab: Emulating Janata's example, Indira had Janata-led state governments dismissed in 1980, contending that the Lok Sabha poll had shattered their legitimacy. Later governments have also improperly used Article 356 to remove inconvenient state governments, though not quite as sweepingly as in 1977 and 1980, but a crucial Supreme Court ruling in 1994 allows dismissed state governments to seek judicial redress.

Following this ruling, the removal of a state government by the Union cabinet may be blocked by the President (who however cannot withhold assent to a second request from the cabinet), the Supreme Court, or either house of Parliament.

Sanjay's sudden death in June 1980 might have broken another mother, but Indira endured it, with support from her older son, Rajiv, an airline pilot hitherto aloof from politics.

Nowhere in India was Indira's 1975-77 emergency more strongly opposed than in the Punjab, where the Akali Dal, the principal political party of the Sikhs, spearheaded the opposition. The emergency, however, was not the Akalis' only complaint.

Though, after a hard struggle, the Akalis had secured in 1966 a Sikh-majority state, to their frustration it was Congress that had frequently ruled the Punjab, by uniting the support of Mazhabi (untouchable) and some other non-Jat Sikh groups to that of a majority of the Punjab's Hindus, who were 40 per cent or more of the population. While the Akalis sought the backing of every Sikh caste and sect, Jat Sikhs formed the Akali backbone; and often there was scope for an Akali alliance with non-Congress Hindu parties such as the Jan Sangh.

Religious extremism among the Punjab's Sikhs was fuelled by the Akali-Congress rivalry and also by the fear that with modernization Sikhs might lose their identity, that, e.g., young Sikhs might abandon the tradition of not cutting their hair. It is in this perspective that we should see the Akalis' demands in the 1970s and 1980s, which included a declaration of Amritsar as a holy city and the recitation of Sikh devotional songs on All India Radio, as well as additional autonomy for the Punjab, assurances on water, and the merger of Chandigarh city with the Punjab.

But the Akali Sikhs were not the only ones tempted by the religious route to political success. Thus his knowledge of Sikh lore and links with religious Sikhs proved useful to Congress's Giani Zail Singh, the Punjab's chief minister from 1972 to 1977, a Sikh from the Ramgarhia caste.

It has been widely suggested, too, that following Congress's loss to the Akali-Jan Sangh alliance in the 1977 Punjab assembly elections, Sanjay Gandhi and Zail Singh encouraged a young extremist with a religious appeal, Sant Jarnail Singh Bhindranwale, to bite into the Sikh 'religious' vote. In 1982, two years after Congress was back in office in the Punjab, a *Times of India* article referred to Bhindranwale's growing influence, anti-New Delhi rhetoric and support of violence, and added:

> The irony, of course, is that the Sant was originally a product nurtured and marketed by the Centre to cut into the Akali Dal's spheres of influence. (22.9.82)

Belonging to a family of poor Jats, Bhindranwale denounced rich landlords, Hinduized (or modernized) Sikhs, drinking, and immorality, and attracted unemployed youth as well as several former Naxalites who had survived clashes with the police in the 1960s and 1970s. A 1978 incident when his supporters clashed with members of the breakaway Nirankari sect—to Bhindranwale and many Akalis a heretical group—made Bhindranwale something of a folk hero.

While eating into Akali support, Bhindranwale had also fed Sikh resentments and Hindu alarm, emerged as the guide and rallying point of Sikh militancy, and contributed to terrorizing violence. Incidents where Hindu passengers were separated from Sikhs in public buses and shot triggered calls for firm measures from the state, which in turn seemed to widen the Sikh-Hindu divide.

Extra bitterness was produced when Sikhs entering New Delhi for the 1982 Asian Olympics were subjected, irrespective of rank or position, to rigorous and at times rude checking.

In October 1983, following a chain of killings, Indira had the Punjab's Congress ministry dismissed, and the state was brought under President's rule. Central emissaries opened negotiations with Akalis, but if some Akali leaders felt that New Delhi was offering little that was new, others, aware of militancy's long arm, refrained from entering into an agreement with the centre.

Bhindranwale, meanwhile, had entrenched himself in Amritsar's Golden Temple, along with several hundred armed followers and allies, converting that venerated bastion of Sikhism into an armoury and a sanctuary from where he directed attacks of terror. Meanwhile, clandestine bodies in India and some Sikh groups abroad raised the cry of Khalistan, an independent Sikh state.

Unable to get at Bhindranwale, the central government moved in

March 1984 against the Akali president, Harchand Singh Longowal, charging him with sedition. Though in competition with Bhindranwale the Akalis had escalated their demands on New Delhi, they still were the Punjab's moderates. The central action pushed them closer, in sympathy at least, to the extremists.

The clear risks of attacking Bhindranwale in his hideout inside Sikhism's holiest shrine had thus far overruled the clamour for action, but pressures mounted with the killing in the Punjab of over two hundred in the first five months of 1984. On the night of 5-6 June 1984, in Operation Bluestar, the Indian army moved in.

Any expectations of a quick surrender by Bhindranwale's forces were at once belied. In numbers and arms, the extremists surprised the Indian army, and the pitched battle lasted until the morning of the 7th. According to official figures, at least 576 were killed, including 83 soldiers, but several hundred more may in fact have perished.

Bhindranwale's body was found in a basement of the Akal Takht, along with that of Major-General Shahbeg Singh, who had been charged with corruption and dismissed from the Indian army just before his retirement. A rebellion against the Indian state had been crushed, but, as so often before in the Punjab's history, revenge was pledged by many in the community.[118]

The government's explanation that by his activities there it was Bhindranwale who had desecrated the shrine got lost amidst images of the Indian state invading the Golden Temple with its armour, officers and soldiers. Four of the six generals in charge of Operation Bluestar were Sikhs, and Indian TV showed soldiers taking off their shoes as they advanced into the Temple, but Sikh rage could not be mollified. From some army centres in different parts of the country, deserting Sikh soldiers (raw recruits in many cases) headed for the Golden Temple. Several hundred were detained, and 55 were apparently killed in shoot-outs with loyal army units.[119]

On 31 October 1984, about five months after Operation Bluestar, Prime Minister Indira Gandhi was gunned down at her residence by some Sikhs in her personal bodyguard. As counter-revenge, three days of arson, loot and murder followed, the worst carnage in Delhi after 1857. Up to three thousand innocent Sikhs were killed. Even in 1947, so many had not been done to death in the capital in the space of three days.

Sikh homes, shops and taxis were destroyed, men had their beards and hair pulled and cut, and some Sikhs were hacked or burnt to death before their families. Only rarely did the police intervene, and there was delay in summoning the army, which eventually quelled the rioting. The involvement of some Congress politicians was immediately alleged, but despite promises by a sequence of governments, very few have served sentences for a role in the 1984 Delhi riots.

The Punjab after Indira: Zail Singh, who had followed Reddy as President, swore Rajiv Gandhi in as Prime Minister even before the cabinet or the Congress Parliamentary Party named him as the leader. Rajiv's demeanour during his mother's last rites evoking sympathy and admiration in millions of TV viewers, Congress, led by him, overwhelmingly won the Lok Sabha elections held at the end of 1984.

Although the Congress campaign, and some of Rajiv's own rhetoric, had played on Hindu anger at Sikh extremism, and the RSS appeared to lend its backing to Congress, after the elections Rajiv strove for an accord with the Akalis. The effort seemed to bear fruit, for in August 1985 he and the Akali president, Sant Harchand Singh Longowal, who was released from detention, signed a pact.

Among other things, the accord laid down that Chandigarh, the joint capital of the Punjab and Haryana, would go to the Punjab in exchange for Hindi-speaking bits of the Punjab, the state's water demands would be referred to a tribunal, Sikhs would not be discriminated against in the military, and the Punjabi language would be promoted.

Longowal declared that 'the long period of confrontation is over,'[120] and elections for a new Punjab state assembly were announced for late September. In the middle of the campaign, however, Longowal, dubbed a traitor, was killed by Sikh extremists. Steered by moderates standing by the accord, the Akalis were nonetheless voted to power.

But the accord was not implemented. Haryana made tough demands on Rajiv, the Akalis under their chief minister, Surjit Singh Barnala, were a divided lot, and the extremists were back in business. In May 1987, accusing it of inability to control terrorism, the centre removed the Barnala government.

From 1987 to February 1992, a succession of Governors, serving under a succession of Prime Ministers—Rajiv Gandhi, V.P. Singh, Chandra Shekhar and P.V. Narasimha Rao—, administered President's rule in the Punjab. In 1992, elections to the Punjab assembly were held after a seven-year gap, but the Akalis boycotted them. Polling was less than 25 per cent, and a Congress ministry under Beant Singh, a Jat Sikh, took office.

Tough if selective action against the militants under the Beant Singh government produced some results, and the Akalis entertained second thoughts about staying out of the political process. Extremism was not extinguished, however, and in the summer of 1995, Beant Singh was assassinated, his widow replacing him as chief minister.

In a subsequent round of assembly elections in February 1997, an Akali-BJP alliance scored a comfortable victory over Congress, and the Akali leader, Parkash Singh Badal, became chief minister. While extremism seemed contained, factional rivalry within the Akali camp has persisted. So has bitterness among Sikhs towards Congress.

Rajiv Gandhi, 1984-89, and the Northeast: During Rajiv's Premiership a law to check defections was enacted, and a commitment made for self-governing villages and towns. Also, Rajiv sought to replicate his accord with Longowal in areas of ethnic tension in another corner of India, the Northeast.

Some of these areas, notably Nagaland and Mizoram, with populations that saw themselves as ethnically, historically and culturally different from Indians, had for years experienced insurgency. The Naga struggle, initiated in the late 1940s by Zapu Phizo, was the oldest, and an agreement signed during Indira Gandhi's Premiership had failed to end it. Still, many Nagas were participating as politicians, government employees or citizens in the Indian state of Nagaland, which was formed in 1963 by detaching Naga areas from the territory administered as Assam.

Begun in the middle sixties, the Mizo insurgency acquired a sharp edge in the late 1970s and early 1980s and received some backing from outside. But in 1986 Laldenga, the leader of the rebelling Mizo National Front, signed an agreement with Rajiv's government whereby the insurgents ceased their battle in exchange for amnesty, protection of Mizo traditions, and a separate statehood, as Mizoram, for the Mizo portion of Assam.

Two years later, in 1988, Rajiv signed an agreement with leaders of a tribal insurgency in Tripura. A state where tribals, once in a majority, are now heavily outnumbered by Bengali-speakers from the plains, including many Hindus migrating from East Bengal, Tripura is the Northeast's metaphor for anxiety. The fear is of the whole region being swamped by Bangladeshis escaping their country's overcrowdedness and poverty. It can only be allayed through a regional understanding that involves Bangladesh.

Despite periodic irritants, the Mizoram and Tripura agreements seem to have held, but not so an accord with representatives of Assam that Rajiv Gandhi announced on 15 August 1985.

The state of Manipur witnesses a hill versus plains tussle that pits Nagas and Kukis against the valley's Meiteis, who constitute Manipur's majority, a Naga versus Kuki fight over access to border trade with Burma, and an effort to unite Meiteis, Nagas, Kukis and others in a so-called Mongoloid front against India. Rejecting the Meitei conversion to Vaishnavaism in the eighteenth century is part of the pan-Mongoloid agenda. Caught in the crossfire between insurgents and the Indian state, Manipuris have also been hit hard by AIDS.

Formed in 1979, the United Liberation Front of Assam (ULFA) remains an active and often violent force. Yet who ULFA sees as the ethnic Other or foe has not always been clear. The targets of alleged ULFA attacks, and of ULFA rhetoric, have included businessmen of non-Assamese as well as Assamese origin, Muslim and Hindu immigrants from Bangladesh, Nepalis (who are almost all Hindus), Assam-based tribals, and, sometimes, all 'outsiders,' including Bengalis, Marwaris and other non-Assamese Indians.

Feeding on Assam's steady truncation over the years and on allegations that Assam's electoral rolls contain a huge number of foreigners (mostly Bangladeshis), militant Assamese rhetoric nonetheless asserts at times a non-Indian identity, an alienation unaffected by the fact that most ULFA leaders are Hindus. Links have been alleged between ULFA, some Naga extremist groups, and ethnic insurgents seeking secession from Burma. Moreover, China, Pakistan and Bangladesh have been accused at different times of involvement in the Northeast's insurgencies.

Assam's complaints against New Delhi, which include a charge of poor recompense for its oil and tea, are paralleled by grievances against Assam by several tribal groups that continue to inhabit truncated Assam. The demand of the Bodos, a substantial group in the plains of Assam, for a state of their own has led to numerous incidents of violence involving security forces, Bodos, Assamese and other ethnic communities.

Perhaps the bloodiest fight over land between neighbouring ethnic groups, or between old and new settlers, occurred in Nellie in Assam's Nagaon district in 1983, when over a thousand immigrant Muslims, including women and children, were killed in attacks by Lalung tribals.[121] Bodos have clashed over land with Assamese villagers and with Santhals, Kukis with Tangkhul Nagas, and so forth. Pushed out of Bangladesh, the mainly-Buddhist Chakmas have faced attacks in their Arunachal Pradesh refuge from tribals jealous of their ancestral land.

The Northeast's conflicts also owe something to distance from, ignorance in and neglect by New Delhi, and to misgovernance, including large-scale corruption, by the region's state governments. But the conflicts are perhaps best understood as a failure in accommodation. The party ruling at New Delhi has tended to undermine regional parties and their governments in the Northeast, and dominant regional groups in the Northeast have been similarly inclined to squash weaker ethnicities. Spread over four decades or more, the conflicts have left a legacy of pain, revenge and despair.

A legacy of a different sort was bequeathed by the process that led to the birth in 1968 of the hill state of Meghalaya, with Shillong as its capital, made up of parts of Assam where the Garo, Khasi and Jaintia tribespeople lived. Meghalaya's emergence amidst unusual goodwill was preceded by a purely nonviolent struggle and constructive talks. The leaders seeking a hill state strove to maintain sound relations with the political leaders of Assam even as they asked for separation, and an apology for bitterness made by the Khasi leader, Stanley Nichols-Roy, to the chief minister of Assam, B.P. Chaliha, eased negotiations at an important stage.[122]

In later years, ethnicity has often tended to upstage accommodation in Meghalaya, but something of the spirit of the late 1960s seems to survive.

Sri Lanka and the Indian Peace-Keeping Force (IPKF), 1987-90: Rajiv's attempts at conflict-resolution were least successful, perhaps, in Sri Lanka, where, after secret talks had produced a Rajiv-Jayewardene agreement on Tamil autonomy in a united Sri Lanka, an Indian Peace-Keeping Force (IPKF) was sent in 1987. As earlier seen, however, many in the island, including Prime Minister Premadasa and other rivals of the Lankan President, Jayewardene, opposed the IPKF's arrival.

This Sinhalese opposition was, among other things, linked to the sanctuary and training that Tamil militants belonging to the island's Liberation Tigers of Tamil Eelam (LTTE), as well as cadres of rival guerrilla groups, had received in Indian camps earlier in the eighties, during the rule of Rajiv's mother. On its part the LTTE too resented the IPKF's presence.

A Colombo-Prabakaran agreement with both parties inviting India to enforce it would have made much more sense. But Prabakaran was not a party to the Rajiv-Jayewardene accord, there was no Colombo-Prabakaran understanding, and the IPKF did not always seem to know whether its mission was to subdue the LTTE, or to pressurize Colombo and the LTTE together.

In the event, the IPKF, at one stage comprising more than 50,000 soldiers, stayed for over two years, suffered large casualties at LTTE hands, and managed to offend Sinhalese as well as Tamils. When in March 1990—after Rajiv Gandhi had lost power in India—, the officers and soldiers of the IPKF finally vacated an island more embittered than the one they had entered, they could only wonder what they had accomplished.

*

V.P. Singh, 1989-90, and Ayodhya: After serving a five-year term as Prime Minister, Rajiv Gandhi lost the elections held in November 1989. The combination that played a large part in Congress's defeat greatly resembled the Janata Party of 1977-79. It included peasant caste parties, Socialists, other Janata remnants, and breakaway Congress groups, all eventually 'merging' into what became known as the Janata Dal (JD), which allied with some influential regional parties in a National Front (NF).

JD's and NF's chief aim, defeating Congress, was shared by the party championing Hindu interests, the Bharatiya Janata Party (BJP), formed around Janata's Jan Sangh constituent, and also by parties of the Left. In 1989, the NF, the BJP and the Left, while differing sharply on some issues, made sure that anti-Congress votes were not divided. When results were out, Congress was restricted to 197 seats, well short of a majority. The NF, of which the JD was the largest constituent, won 145, the BJP 85, and the Left 45.

With outside support from the BJP and the Left, the National Front formed the government. It was headed by Vishwanath Pratap Singh, a Rajput by caste, who had served as a Congress chief minister in U.P. and as a Congress minister at the centre. The leading light of the JD, V.P. Singh had aroused widespread hope by resigning from Rajiv Gandhi's cabinet on a question of corruption.

Two JD rivals denied him peace, however. One of them, Devi Lal, an old enemy of Congress, formerly a colleague of Charan Singh in the Lok Dal and a father-figure to many Jats in Haryana, deemed V.P. Singh too recent an entrant into the ranks of Congress's foes and resented his leadership. However, Devi Lal agreed to join the

Singh government as Deputy Prime Minister.

The other, Chandra Shekhar, was like V.P. Singh a Rajput from Uttar Pradesh and a former Congressman. However, unlike Singh, Chandra Shekhar had for long opposed Indira Gandhi, leaving Congress to become a JP ally and later heading the Janata Party. Publicly rejecting V.P. Singh's leadership, Chandra Shekhar stayed out of his cabinet.

In the summer of 1990, eight months after Singh had become Premier, the BJP, whose support was crucial to the government, issued its own warning. Even as Chandra Shekhar and Devi Lal compared notes on how to oust Singh, and Devi Lal, to buttress his position, announced a huge peasant rally in Delhi, Singh was told that the continuance of BJP support would hang on Singh's non-interference with the BJP's drive for replacing Ayodhya's Babri Mosque with a Rama Mandir or temple.

The campaign was literally a drive. Lal Krishna Advani, the BJP president, was heading towards Ayodhya, the city of Rama's birth, in a Toyota truck that had been converted to resemble an epic-era chariot and designated the Rama Rath. With unconcealed symbolism, Advani had started from Somnath, the temple in Gujrat vandalized and desecrated by Muslims early in the 11th century, but he was not seeking the shortest route to Ayodhya. The BJP aim being to stir emotions in as wide an area as possible, the chariot traversed western, central and eastern India en route to Ayodhya where, in the BJP's unproven and perhaps unprovable belief, the Mughal emperor Babur had in the year 1528 razed a Rama temple and built a mosque.

History had to be redressed, said the BJP and its politico-cultural allies: the mosque had to go, and the infant Rama's site returned to him. The message intertwined Muslim wrong with Hindu piety, the memory of spoliation at Muslim hands with the warmth for the Rama-child felt in the Hindu heart. The mix was powerful.

Yet was it safe or sound to compel a correction of the past? Muslims disputed the story of Babur, the temple and the mosque. So did quite a few Hindus, while others held that the past had to be left behind, not argued over.

In any case, the JD's leaders and cadres, all descended from Indian politics' secular or pluralist schools, had assured Muslims that the mosque would be protected—the assurance was spelt out in the JD manifesto for the 1989 elections. The non-interference demanded by the BJP was beyond Singh's capacity to provide.

Mandal: Searching for a riposte that might simultaneously foil the BJP, Chandra Shekhar and Devi Lal, V.P. Singh came up with his Mandal missile. Out of the blue he declared, in August 1990, that his government would implement the ten-year-old recommendation of a commission headed by B.P. Mandal for reservation of government jobs for the 'other backward castes' (OBCs).

Dalits—Harijans or SCs—had reservation, and so did the adivasis or tribals, the STs. He, V.P. Singh, would now extend the benefit to the OBCs, which for the large part meant the peasant castes that were being championed by Devi Lal and by the politicians that Devi Lal was trying to enlist. Moreover, the religiously-minded OBCs seemed also to be the constituency to which the BJP was directing its temple appeal.

Nobody knew for sure how many OBCs India had. Certainly Mr Mandal did not offer a figure in his report. All he had said was that a large percentage of Indians were neither high caste Hindus, nor Muslims, nor SCs, nor STs. And most in this remainder, suggested Mandal, were socially or economically backward. The Constitution having provided for preferential action for 'certain backward classes,' the OBCs, Mandal said, were entitled to job quotas, even as SCs and STs were.

Ten years later, but with a timing that torpedoed the Devi Lal rally, V.P. Singh delivered the gift to the OBCs. It was a masterstroke, voices said in the Press and in Parliament. But even as he was hailed as the benefactor of the lowly, V.P. Singh, the Rajput, was attacked as a traitorous enemy of the high castes. The latter too, it was pointed out, had their poor. To light up their hurt, some students immolated themselves.

Only a few hundred persons a year were expected to benefit from Mandal's new quotas in the central government's jobs, but the political appeal of the Mandal move was too strong for any political party to persist in opposing it. The courts on their part upheld the legality of OBC quotas.

Exploding simultaneously in the 1990 summer, Mandir and Mandal sharpened India's religious and caste divisions. They did not exactly polarize society, for there were those who supported both Mandal and Mandir, while some were uneasy with both. But India's polity and society were embittered by the parallel campaigns; illwill between communities, castes and political parties increased.

It was claimed that Mandal had brought 'social justice' to the centre of the Indian agenda, and, elsewhere, that Mandir did the same for 'Hindu sentiments.' But neither 'explosion' had room for a discussion with those it affected. The abruptness with which Mandal was pulled out of the hat ruled out any consultation with the 'high-castes' who were to be hurt by it, while the stubbornness with which Mandir was pursued ruled out a genuine Hindu-Muslim dialogue.

And if V.P. Singh failed to explain either the suddenness of his concern with social justice, or Mandal's appearance bang on the eve of a challenger's rally, Advani and his BJP colleagues also had no answer when asked why Ayodhya had not been raised earlier by them, including in 1977-79, when they were part of the Janata government. Mandir and Mandal were thus similar in divisive consequences, exclusionary manner, and questionable motives.

To return, however, to the fate of the V.P. Singh government: the Mandal move failed to divert either the Shekhar-Lal duo or the BJP from their purposes. When Advani's Ayodhya-bound Rath Yatra reached Bihar, Laloo Yadav, the state's Janata Dal chief minister, acting in consultation with V.P. Singh, had Advani arrested. As the drive had done, the arrest triggered violent incidents in different parts of the country. It also extinguished the BJP's support to the Singh government, which fell in November 1990.

But before moving to Singh's successors we should look at Kashmir, which was in considerable ferment during, and shortly before, his Premiership.

Kashmir: Despite calls for rebellion from Pakistan, and despite their frustration with state governments that usually were fraudulently elected to power as well as corrupt, Kashmiris had on the whole remained quiet until the late eighties. In March 1987, however, state-level elections in which the National Conference, led by Farooq Abdullah, son of the late Sheikh Abdullah, had joined hands with Congress, caused restiveness.

The NC-Congress tally of sixty-six seats out of seventy-six was attacked as having been secured by rigging, but more serious was a feeling that Farooq, the chief minister, had surrendered his autonomy to Congress and New Delhi. Capitalizing on this sentiment in the summer of 1988, groups of militants, especially the Jammu and Kashmir Liberation Front (JKLF), which had been engaged in sporadic action from the 1970s, launched bomb attacks on government establishments and called for strikes and demonstrations.

The response was large. More blasts followed, anti-Indian slogans appeared everywhere, and homes and shops of Hindus were attacked. When elections to the Lok Sabha were held in November 1989, the militants' call for a boycott was overwhelmingly obeyed in the

Kashmir valley, with only some 5 per cent voting.

Replacing Rajiv Gandhi as Prime Minister, V.P. Singh gave the crucial Home portfolio to Mufti Muhammad Saeed of the Janata Dal, a former leader of Congress in Kashmir. Within days of Saeed's appointment, however, his daughter, Rubiyya, was kidnapped by JKLF militants.

Five JKLF activists in custody were released and Rubiyya was set free, but bomb blasts alternated with cries for independence. New Delhi's response was to dismiss the Farooq government and impose central rule. Jag Mohan, a former bureaucrat who had previously served as Governor in Kashmir, was sent there again.

Whether, as some hold, Jag Mohan's stern measures helped save Kashmir for India, or, as others believe, he deepened popular alienation, he was recalled after six months, following the death from paramilitary firing of fifty-seven participants in a mourning procession occasioned by the killing by unidentified gunmen of an eminent religious leader, Mirwaiz Farooq.

Meanwhile, in 1989 and 1990, the Pandits of Kashmir valley, Hindu Brahmins who shared a common language and culture with the more numerous Kashmiri Muslims, had in large numbers migrated to Jammu, Delhi and elsewhere. Home—for centuries the land of their forefathers—was no longer safe for them. Kashmiri Muslims, on their part, accused Indian security forces of persistent human rights violations.

Returning as Kashmir's chief minister in 1996, Farooq Abdullah contrived to remain on the right side of successive Prime Ministers. In 1993 Prime Minister Narasimha Rao had said he was willing to discuss the Kashmir question with his Pakistani counterpart, a declaration repeated in 1998 and 1999 by Prime Minister Atal Behari Vajpayee, but no settlement seems in sight.

In May 1999, an Associated Press story, written by Amir Zia and datelined Muzaffarabad in Pakistan-held Kashmir, referred to the training imparted by fundamentalist groups to militants 'at dozens of camps on Pakistani territory [in] the mountains that divide disputed Kashmir between India and Pakistan' and mentioned '2,200 religious schools across Pakistan where students learn Islam and prepare for jihad' over Kashmir. (*Times of India*, 31.5.99)

Also in May 1999, the Indian army and air force mounted a large-scale attack to dislodge hundreds of militants intruding into high-altitude territory around Kargil on the Indian side of the Line of Control in Kashmir's Kargil sector. To sever a crucial road link between Srinagar and Leh seemed to be one of the intruders' aims. New Delhi alleged that the Pakistani army was guiding the intruders, who were said to include Pakistani regulars as well as Pakistani, Afghan and Kashmiri Mujahideen.

Chandra Shekhar, 1990-91: We have strayed far from the Premiership of V.P. Singh, which was ending when we proceeded to look at Kashmir. When the Singh government fell in November 1990, Chandra Shekhar was heading a 58-strong group in the Lok Sabha, consisting largely of Janata Dal MPs he had drawn away, including Devi Lal. Offered Congress support, Chandra Shekhar served as Prime Minister from November 1990 until March 1991, when, sensing a shift in the Congress mood, he resigned.

Rajiv Gandhi's assassination, May 1991: The Janata Dal having shown an apparent inability to govern, the contest in the elections forced in the summer of 1991 was largely between Congress and the BJP. In the end Congress won a 37.6 per cent vote share (down from 39.5 per cent in 1989) and 227 seats, while the BJP secured a 21 per cent vote share (up from 11.4 per cent in 1989) and 119 seats. Congress's tally would probably have been smaller by twenty seats or so but for Rajiv's assassination at an election meeting in Sriperumbudur in Tamil Nadu on 21 May, just after the first round of elections, which secured sympathy votes for Congress in later rounds.

Evidence seemed conclusive that an LTTE suicide squad had killed Rajiv. His mother had been gunned down to avenge the Indian troops' assault on the Golden Temple, and he, it appeared, to avenge the IPKF's assaults on LTTE strongholds in northern Lanka. Evidently the LTTE had decided not to let Rajiv return as India's Premier.

Narasimha Rao, 1991-96: The man who became Premier instead of Rajiv, seventy-year-old P.V. Narasimha Rao, had to be recalled from semi-retirement. In earlier years he had served as chief minister of Andhra and India's foreign minister. Now, in 1991, he gained from having few enemies in Congress. Along with his finance minister, Manmohan Singh, Rao won notice for placing India on the path of economic liberalization and globalization, but he shied away from confronting the BJP's thrust against the Babri mosque in Ayodhya in Uttar Pradesh.

In the 1991 polls, this thrust had secured for the BJP the support of numerous Hindus formerly voting for Congress, most noticeably in U.P., where the BJP had captured the state government. Following the elections, the BJP, backed by several political and cultural associates, intensified the drive for a temple to replace the mosque. Other political parties and Muslim bodies moved the courts for injunctions against such a bid, and pressed Rao for assurances that he would prevent it.

In turn, Rao and the courts asked for assurances from the U.P. chief minister, Kalyan Singh, who promised that the structure would be protected. Confidence in that word was shaken, however, when Kalyan Singh declared that tens of thousands of Hindu extremists would be allowed to assemble in a rally in Ayodhya in the first week of December 1992.

The Babri mosque: Though pressed either to dismiss the Kalyan Singh government or to order a central takeover of areas adjoining Ayodhya, Rao chose to sit out the threat. On 6 December, as the entire BJP leadership looked on from ringside seats, and hundreds of policemen standing on duty did likewise, while many in India and the world watched on television, thousands of activists, armed with pickaxes and rods and working to design, demolished the 424-year-old mosque.

One of their cheerleaders was an ochre-robed young woman, Sadhvi Rithambhara, who kept shouting:

> *Ek dhakka aur do, Babri Masjid tor do.* ('Heave once more, the mosque must go.')

After the mosque's three domes came crashing down, many of these avengers of ancient wrongs slaked the rest of their thirst by burning the stalls and homes of Muslim vendors in Ayodhya and killing several Muslims. The BJP's allies took out victory celebrations in many parts of India, their delight unaffected by the dismissal, after the demolition, of the U.P. government and the dissolution of the state assembly.

Hindu-Muslim violence followed in many places but instances of protection under risk were not lacking. A woman of humble means who had concealed Muslim neighbours in her home in Kanpur even as she watched other Muslims being cut down told a TV interviewer some days later that Hindu militants had asked her to shout, 'Jai Shri Ram!' ('Victory to Rama').

> I couldn't (*she added*). Not after what I had seen. The words refused to come out of my throat.[123]

After scores of Muslims protesting in Bombay's streets were shot above the waist by the police and killed, the revenge for that and for the Ayodhya demolition came on the afternoon of Friday, 12 March 1993. Explosions occurred in thirteen different places in Bombay, killing over two hundred persons and seriously damaging a number of buildings including four well-known landmarks, the Bombay Stock Exchange, Air India, Century Bazaar and the Plaza cinema. The blasts were executed by Muslim extremists in the city, with the aid of expatriate associates in the Gulf.

The Hindu-Muslim polarization seeming to occur at least in parts of India was accompanied by disillusionment with Congress, and countered by the use of the caste card by some parties. If the BJP sought to mobilize all Hindus against the Other, who was understood to be, if not always spelt out as, the Muslim, social democratic parties in U.P. and Bihar and elsewhere—peasant-caste or OBC parties in some cases and Dalit-based parties in others, sometimes supported by Communist parties—tried to rally Hindu low-castes, the Hindu poor and all Muslims against an Other of a different sort, the high-caste Hindu.

The strategy succeeded in elections to the U.P. assembly held in 1993, when an alliance of Mulayam Singh Yadav's peasant-caste Samajwadi Party (SP) and the the Dalit-based Bahujan Samaj Party (BSP) led by Kanshi Ram and Mayawati handily defeated the BJP. Abandoned by most sections in U.P., Congress wound up a distant third.

But the SP-BSP alliance proved hard to sustain, with personality clashes between leaders matching the grass-roots friction between peasant castes and landless Dalits, frequently the former's servants. Skilfully exploiting the divide, the BJP succeeded in winning the BSP to a deal whereby the two parties would support each other and by turns provide a chief minister. With this move, the BJP broke the 'alliance of the deprived' that had been put together.

Deve Gowda, 1996-97: With Congress continuing to lose support, and the other non-BJP groups—regional, caste-based and Left parties—showing no signs of uniting in a common front, the BJP was confident of winning the 1996 elections. However, while the tally of BJP and committed allies exceeded 190 seats, an increase from 1991 of more than 70 seats, it did not come close to the crucial figure of 272 needed for a majority, and the BJP was unable to secure partners.

Congress, reduced to 136 seats, declared its backing for a government of a United Front (UF) of 177 MPs and thirteen parties that had hurriedly been assembled, but these parties had to agree on a leader. Their choice finally fell on the Karnataka chief minister at the time, H.D. Deve Gowda of the Janata Dal, who became Prime Minister and pledged to protect the Indian farmer.

Keeping the BJP out of office, the shared objective that had brought Congress and the UF together, was however a weak glue. To Sitaram Kesri, who had succeeded Rao as the Congress chief, Deve Gowda seemed not merely ungrateful but hostile towards the party that was keeping his Premiership alive.

I.K. Gujral, 1997-98: In April 1997, the UF grudgingly yielded to Kesri's pressure, and Inder Kumar Gujral, a former Congressman from the Punjab who had served in several governments and was Gowda's foreign minister, replaced Gowda as Premier. Declaring better relations with neighbours, including Pakistan, as his chief goal, Gujral tried to implement a policy of unilateral gestures towards South Asia's smaller countries, the so-called Gujral doctrine.

Gujral lost his position for reasons that had nothing to do with him. Following the report of a commission inquiring into Rajiv Gandhi's assassination, some Congress leaders demanded dismissal of the DMK government in Tamil Nadu, led by M. Karunanidhi. Though the report did not charge Karunanidhi with complicity or neglect, he had been chief minister in 1991 when Rajiv was killed.

The DMK being a key constituent of the United Front, and also because no case had been made against Karunanidhi, Gujral and his United Front colleagues did not act against him. Congress thereupon withdrew its support and the Gujral ministry fell.

A.B. Vajpayee, 1998—: Though in new elections Congress increased its Lok Sabha strength to 166 seats, the party that had really gained was the BJP, which had named seventy-four-year-old Atal Behari Vajpayee, a spellbinding orator and a poet with roots in U.P. and Madhya Pradesh and a moderate image, as its Prime Ministerial candidate. Through pre-poll and post-poll alliances struck with numerous regional parties (Vajpayee's image helped), the BJP was able to secure a tiny majority in the Lok Sabha.

As quid pro quo, the regional parties were allowed sway in the states and, if they wished, places in Vajpayee's central government. In addition, three contentious items on the BJP platform, relating to the Ayodhya temple, Kashmir's special status and a uniform civil code, were kept out of the new government's National Agenda, as it was called.

Not quite satisfied, however, and giving full-throated expression to their demands and grievances, the BJP's allies cornered media attention until the second week of May 1998, when underground nuclear explosions were conducted in Pokhran in the Rajasthan desert by the Vajpayee government. Euphoria erupted, and Mr Ashok Singhal of the Vishwa Hindu Parishad proposed a nationwide distribution of ash from the explosions' site, as also the erection there of a shrine dedicated to Shakti, or Power.

The glory drums soon became quieter, however, for sanctions against India were announced by much of the world community, and, before the month of May was over, Pakistan responded with its own nuclear blasts in Balochistan's Chagai Hills.

While Congress sought recovery under the leadership of Sonia Gandhi, Rajiv's Italian-born widow, a rift or rifts seemed to surface within the Sangh parivaar, the family that included the BJP, the RSS, the VHP, and other bodies. For how long, some voices in the parivaar asked, was the BJP going to allow its Hindu hands to be tied down by allies? More significantly, it was asked whether Vajpayee himself was nationalist enough in economics, and Hindu enough in politics.

Part of the answer seemed to come when, in response to attacks on Christians in Gujrat and Orissa, Vajpayee announced that he would fast as atonement on 30 January 1999, the anniversary of Gandhi's assassination. The following month saw a bigger gesture for reconciliation, this time between India and Pakistan.

What did Vajpayee do? Well, he took a bus to Lahore, that's all, inaugurating a service between Delhi and Lahore. He did an ordinary thing, and that was its significance. The bus ride showed that it was normal for Indians and Pakistanis to meet and befriend one another. What was abnormal was aloofness and rejection.

Politicians had flown across the Indo-Pak border a number of times in the past without arousing a hundredth of the hope the bus visit sparked. The latter was a people-to-people, street-level move, one that could become part of South Asia's daily life. Any ordinary person could take a bus and visit neighbours.

Moreover, the ground covered by the bus was also the soil where the 1947 Punjab killings had taken place. Reminding Indians and Pakistanis that historical enemies were actually neighbours, the bus journey, and the welcome it received from Pakistanis, suggested the possible triumph of geography over memory.

'This is a defining moment in South Asian history,' Vajpayee said on arrival in Lahore. At a banquet that night in Lahore Fort, he added:

> My regret is that we have spent so much time in mutual bitterness. It is unworthy of two nations the size of India and Pakistan to have wasted so much time in mutual ill will . . .
>
> There is nothing which cannot be solved through goodwill and direct dialogue. That is the only path. I am convinced that there is nothing in our bilateral relations that can ever be resolved through violence.
>
> As we approach a new millennium, the future beckons us. It calls upon, indeed demands upon us, to think of the welfare of our children and their children and of the generations that are yet to come. (*Hindu*, 21.2.99)

At another enthusiastic Lahore reception the following day, Vajpayee spoke of having been cautioned by some Indian advisers against visiting Minar-i-Pakistan, the site in Lahore where, in March 1940, Pakistan was first formally demanded, for it could signify 'a stamp of approval' for Pakistan's separation. Added Vajpayee:

> But I insisted on going . . . I said it loud and clear to them that Pakistan did not require my stamp for its entity. Pakistan has its own stamp . . .
>
> We have had enough of enmity, let us live in amity . . . Friendship knows no end, while enmity brings one to a stage where one is bound to get fed up. (*India Abroad*, 26.2.99)

On 17 April, however, Vajpayee was defeated in Parliament by a single vote, the floor test having been precipitated by the defection from his side of the former Tamil Nadu chief minister, Jayalalitha, and the MPs she controlled. Putting together an alternative government proving impossible, yet another reference to India's voters was ordered.

When in May the incursion by Pakistan-backed forces into Kargil in Indian-administered Kashmir occurred, and Vajpayee—asked by President Narayanan to continue as Prime Minister pending new elections—was roundly attacked for 'being taken in' by the Pakistanis, he refused to concede that the February bus ride had been an error. In June in fact he associated himself with another bus service, this one linking Calcutta to Dhaka. India's borders—Vajpayee seemed to suggest—would be defended, and intruders evicted, but a bid for friendship across borders was not a sin in February 1999 and could not be tabooed in the future.

However, Kashmir, tragic yet sparkling, remained a diamond-hard nut to crack, while patriotism flooded India, with the life-tossing jawan easily displacing cricket and film stars in Indian hearts.

Culture, and in particular the cinema, had in some ways anticipated and prepared the national mood. Throughout the nineties, as Nikhat Kazmi pointed out, (*Times of India*, 24.6.99) Indian films popularized the image of a 'smiling, satisfied and well-kept India' from which misery, ugliness and unfairness were largely left out.

It was an India where youth found pleasure, age received respect and obedience, and the modern world was comfortably but discriminatingly received, while the soldier-hero successfully negotiated his dangerous trail to triumph. The 'enemy exist[ed], but only beyond the frontiers of the family and the nation.' End-millennium evil sprang only 'from two sources, unbridled westernization and belligerent Pakistan.'

Despite such conditioning, Vajpayee's Lahore initiative obtained popular support. Then Kargil happened.

COMMON FEATURES

Reluctant accommodation: Our study of independent India, Pakistan, Bangladesh and Sri Lanka has revealed some common features. After, or along with, independence, India was shorn of the Pakistan areas, Sri Lanka 'lost' many or most of its Tamils, and Pakistan had to give up Bangladesh. In all four countries, central governments could have done better, following independence, in accommodating identities seeking autonomy or status.

This has been true of India in relation to the questions of Kashmir, Punjab and several parts of the Northeast, and of segments such as Dalits and the 'backward' castes. It has been true of Pakistan vis-à-vis the Sindhis of Sindh, the Mohajirs of Karachi, the Pukhtoons of the NWFP, the Balochis of Balochistan and assertive sectarian groups, Sunni and Shia, across the country. It applies to Bangladesh, a nation from end-1971, in respect of its Hindus and the (often-Buddhist) tribals of its hill tracts. And it applies to Sri Lanka and its (not necessarily homogeneous) Tamils, as also its Sinhalese poor.

In all four countries, the central government's failures over reconciliation have often been accompanied, we have found, by an inability in the 'mainstream,' 'heartland' or majority population to recognize the hopes and hurts of a restive segment. As a result, even modest steps taken by a central government towards accommodating an unhappy segment or region have risked a majoritarian backlash.

Also, the central government's failures in accommodation have often been matched—in each of the four countries—by violence, sometimes terrorist violence, from discontented groups. Clashes between militants and state forces seeking to suppress them have taken a heavy toll and produced several pockets in South Asia where life is insecure and human rights are minimal.

Identity politics: In a broader sense, we have noticed that articulating the unreasonableness of the Other is a widespread South Asian activity. Be the Other a separatist group or the state, a caste or a religious fold, a neighbouring country or an opposing party, a political rival or a coalition partner, it is to be distrusted and vilified. It can, however, be readmitted to the pale for confronting Another Other.

In a large and varied country like India, but also elsewhere in South Asia, political mobilization around a religious, linguistic or ethnic group, or around a class or caste—in short, identity politics— has generally seemed more promising than a political effort focusing on the needs or grievances of citizens as a whole.

In the family: We have found the dominance in politics of one or two families to be another common feature in South Asia. For thirty-eight out of free India's first fifty years, the prime minister's chair was occupied by Jawaharlal Nehru, his daughter Indira Gandhi, and her son Rajiv Gandhi.

In Pakistan, Zulfiqar Ali Bhutto headed the government from December 1971 to July 1977, and his daughter Benazir Bhutto from 1988 to 1990, and again from 1993 to 1996.

In Sri Lanka, the Sri Lanka Freedom Party (SLFP) was headed by S.W.R.D. Bandaranaike from 1951 until his assassination in 1959, when his widow Sirimavo Bandaranaike became the leader of the party, a post she continues to hold. Her husband headed the Sri Lankan government from 1956 to 1959, she from 1960 to 1977, and her daughter Chandrika Kumaratunga has been President since 1994. If D.S. Senanayake of the United National Party (UNP) was Prime Minister from 1947 to 1952, his son Dudley Senanayake, also UNP, had three spells as Premier in the 1950s and 1960s.

In Bangladesh, Sheikh Mujibur Rahman was President from 1972 until his assassination in 1975; his daughter Sheikh Hasina has been Prime Minister from 1996. General Ziaur Rahman ran Bangladesh from 1975 to 1981, when he too was killed, and his widow Begum Khaleda Zia was Prime Minister from 1991 to 1996.

While giving an impression (especially, perhaps, to outsiders) of stability, the close association with power of one or two families has polarized politics in South Asian countries, attracting hostility as well as loyalty. If the Nehru-Gandhis of India, the Bhuttos of Pakistan, Sri Lanka's Bandaranaikes, and Bangladesh's father-daughter and husband-widow duos have contributed to images of continuity, they have also aroused fierce opposition. The impact of family politics on stability has thus been mixed.

Personality politics: Whether or not part of a ruling family or dynasty, personalities have loomed larger than policies or ideologies in South Asian politics. These political personalities have generally been loved or hated as individuals and not for their policies, which have often oscillated between left and right, or between liberal and undemocratic.

The salience of personalities, not restricted to Congress or India, actually makes South Asian coalitions less durable. A plethora of personalities has meant a plethora of ego clashes, capable, we have seen, of destroying power-sharing alliances.

Negative politics: We should mark, as well, the strength in South Asia of negative politics. History here has seemed a procession of one 'useless' government after another, with the incumbent's removal being deemed far more important than any look into the capabilities of the challenger(s).

Calls in India, from the mid-1960s, for an anti-Congress front, or, from 1996, for an anti-BJP front, for an anti-Indira alliance in the first half of the 1970s, or for fronts at provincial level, e.g., against Partap Singh Kairon (East Punjab, 1960s), Jayalalitha (Tamil Nadu, early 1990s), and Laloo Prasad Yadav (Bihar, 1990s) have had their counterparts in Pakistan, Bangladesh and Sri Lanka.

More often than not, elections in all four countries have sent governments out, not brought them in; incumbency has served as the kiss of death. There have been rule-proving exceptions, of course, as in India in 1984, when, riding the sympathy wave set off by Indira's assassination, Congress succeeded itself in power. A similar exception seemed likely in 1999.

The failure of incumbents to be re-elected could at first sight suggest that South Asia's political system throws up 'useless' politicians, or that its voters are either horrible at choosing, or expect more from politicians than is reasonable. More helpful than such sweeping judgments would be the recognition that South Asian politics has a tendency to get trapped in one 'crisis' after another.

Feeling threatened by rivals or foes even when elected amidst much enthusiasm, and preoccupied perennially with personal survival, South Asia's elected leaders seem unable to think of the wider public or take a longer view. Tiring of them, voters turn to another set of politicians.

Democracy and letting go: Judged by standard criteria—elections that are competitive, free and held on schedule, acceptance of electoral verdicts by winners and losers and by the armed forces, non-coercion of political opponents, and a free Press and judiciary—, India has shown more democracy than the other three, with Sri Lanka in second place. India's record was smudged, however, during the 1975-77 emergency declared by Mrs Indira Gandhi, when fundamental rights were suspended, opposition leaders detained, Press censorship was imposed, and the life of Parliament extended.

While Pakistan and Bangladesh have witnessed long spells of military rule, Sri Lanka, though engaged in a seemingly endless war betwen security forces and Tamil militants, has shown an attachment to democracy that was broken only twice. The first instance occurred in 1972, when the government of Mrs Bandaranaike postponed by two years elections that were due in 1975; and the second in December 1982, when President J.R. Jayewardene of the United National Party (UNP), who had handsomely won an election two months previously, used the constitutionally doubtful device of a referendum to extend the life of Parliament.

Though Pakistan and Bangladesh have enjoyed elected governments since the late eighties, their armies have negated electoral verdicts in the past, or removed governments serving their term, or directly exercised political power; and in Bangladesh, opposition parties, alleging rigging (often with good grounds), have employed street agitations and strikes to nullify electoral results.

India and Sri Lanka have seen governments come and go by popular choice, but defeated political parties in these countries have often resented electoral results without quite trying to defy them, and have attempted at times to topple a government by encouraging defections from it. A resistance to letting go of power may thus be noticed in all four countries, even if differences in degree have been large.

Closed curtains: Each South Asian land we looked at seemed absorbed with itself. Suspicion and hostility were often directed at the neighbour; on occasion soldiers were eyeball-to-eyeball in war; but curiosity about life and politics across the border, or an awareness of similarities, was confined to a few.

*

We are at the end of a journey begun with the Mahabharata and brought to its close—not unfittingly, it may be allowed—in Lahore, halting-place for many a past caravan, and the capital, successively in Mughal, Sikh, British and Pakistani hands, of South Asia's suffering and striving crossroads, the Punjab . . .

This was how, in April 1999, I had thought of ending this chapter. Then Kargil happened, and what riveted attention in June 1999 was not a handclasp in Lahore but a war in Kashmir.

And what a war. Young lives rushed far and high to face death in oxygen-poor battlefields, panting soldiers clawing up vertical rocks, aware that each instant in that desolate heaven could be their last instant on earth, bodies, some of them alleged to be mutilated, returning, loved ones fighting down their sorrow, a young widow, asked about her infant son, saying resignedly before a TV camera, 'I will ask him to avenge his father's death'—it was enough to break the most stoic of us.

Equally shattering was the desecration of those secluded mountains. On 20 June, the *Hindustan Times* reported excitedly:

There is absolutely no breathing time for guns. The battle . . . threatens to reach its crescendo with guns blowing fire and smoke endlessly in the mountains reverberating with blood and thunder. (20.6.99)

Even as a millennium was ending, the far mountains were trampled upon and jolted by artillery bombardment and air strikes. A sombre, untrodden place which the gods seemed to save for themselves, the Devabhumi of the Hindu imagination, was encroached upon by modern man with all his firepower and decibel-power.

For this wanton disregard of the proprieties of time and place, the intruders who had sneaked in from Pakistan and, on being discovered, invited the Indian charge, certainly bore immediate responsibility. Yet in any long view, the tragedy of Kargil, Siachen and the whole of Jammu and Kashmir was perhaps a joint Indo-Pak accomplishment.

The war died down in the middle of July. Following a meeting between President Clinton of the United States and Nawaz Sharif, the intruders withdrew even as they were being pushed back by the Indian army and air force.

Both in India and Pakistan, grief at loss of life sometimes 'turned into hot anger,' as the *Indian Express* observed while describing the scenes in NOIDA near Delhi around the body of one of the hundreds dying in battle, Lt. Vijayant Thapar. The bullet that killed the young officer was 'ricocheting inside thousands of heads,' the paper reported. (4.7.99)

A poll conducted in early July (before the Clinton-Sharif meeting) and reported in *India Today* of 12 July showed 66 per cent of the polled wanting a full-scale war with Pakistan, while a story from Pakistan in the same issue of *India Today* spoke of a clamour for a struggle against India at funeral occasions.

On both sides, those favouring war in July probably included many who had applauded the Lahore talks of February and who in a calmer future might again support reconciliation. Yet Kargil had depleted a recently-filled tank of trust and created a sense of betrayal.

In Pakistan's post-withdrawal rhetoric, extremist anger against Sharif merged with wild threats to 'smash India to smithereens.' (*Hindustan Times*, 14.7.99, quoting speakers at an Islamabad rally of the militant outfit, Lashkar-e-Toiba.) In India, the RSS journal, *Organiser*, referring to Pakistan before the latter's decision to withdraw, ran the headline 'Time to Crush the Cobra.' (11.7.99)

But the scene was not wholly bleak. Some Pakistanis openly characterized the intrusion as a folly:

> Whoever planned the Kargil phase of the Kashmir liberation struggle must be credited with a low intelligence and complete lack of foresight.—Anees Jillani, *The News*, Rawalpindi, 13.7.99. (Cited in *Times of India*, 14.7.99)

> Kargil should serve as a good learning experience, . . . should induce sobriety, balance and humility . . . These high altitude skirmishes, which could engulf the region in a horrific war, must stop.—Dr Maqsudul Hasan Nuri, *The News*, 13.7.99.

On the Indian side, when foreign minister Jaswant Singh was asked if in hindsight he regretted 'the Lahore bus diplomacy,' his reply was,

> Of course not . . . The ultimate goal has to be to live together in peace and amity. (To Kalyani Shankar, *Hindustan Times*, 4.7.99)

Indian soldiers helped bury unclaimed bodies of enemy soldiers with due propriety and openly acknowledged the bravery of individuals among the enemy. Some Indians even questioned the enemy tag. One of them was the 'mother of a slain Indian soldier,' whose reported remarks were quoted by Kalpana Sharma in the *Hindu* (4.7.99):

> The mind does not find consolation in the thought that my son gave his life for a good cause. Such consolation would have been possible if this war had been with an enemy country. Aren't people who should be loving each other now killing each other? May the mother who has lost her son ask just one thing: at least now, can't we love each other?

*

We will end this chapter with Kargil-related statements in India and Pakistan that provide an almost literal corroboration of our arguments. On 20 June 1999, following a report that the bodies of six Indian soldiers returned by the Pakistanis bore evidence of atrocities, *Panchajanya*, the RSS's Hindi journal, wrote:

> This has been going on for centuries now. Bharat's borders have always been assaulted by Islamic invaders . . . These invaders have always been ruthless and devious. They have always attacked us stealthily in the dark of the night . . . They never change their ways except when the hands of brave soldiers go for their jugular.

> This inhuman lot can never forget 1971! Like bleating goats, 94,000 jihadis had then stood, their heads bowed in abject surrender before our brave soldiers. Had it been some Islamic country in our place, it would have beheaded the entire lot and despatched 94,000 skulls to Islamabad. But true to our own civilized values and culture, we even fed milk to these 94,000 snakes. Fed on our generosity, they all returned well fattened to their homeland . . .

Six of our soldiers on patrol [were] tortured in such inhuman ways that even hearing or reading about it is intolerable. The blood of every Indian is on the boil today. From Ladakh to Kanyakumari, the entire nation is raising only one demand—Revenge! Revenge!

The time has come again for India's Bhima to tear open the breasts of these infidels and purify the soiled tresses of Draupadi with blood. Pakistan will not listen just like that. We have a centuries' old debt to settle with this mindset . . .

Arise, Atal Behari! Who knows if fate has destined you to be the author of the final chapter of this long story. For what have we manufactured bombs? For what have we exercised the nuclear option? . . .

Enough is enough. To tolerate any more would be sheer cowardice. To teach them a lesson now is the only dharma now.[124]

A piece by Narsinh Pandit in the same issue of *Panchajanya* singled out an incident from Shivaji's life:

The best way to finish off the crooked jehadis is the way Shivaji dealt with Afzal Khan

The journal's English-language counterpart, *Organiser*, carried (20.6.99) a comment by Rajendra Singh, the RSS chief, that recalled the 1675 beheading of Guru Tegh Bahadur and the inhuman killing of the Guru's associates. Singh claimed that the Pakistani 'mindset' and their 'civilization' were 'barbaric' and 'bestial' from the roots.

Dismissing the world of 1999, the comments take us to ancient and heroic times—mythical as well as historical—where 'our' ancestors were either noble martyrs or fierce, wily avengers, and 'their' ancestors were uncivilized oppressors. In the perspective of these statements, 'they,' Pakistanis and Muslims, seem flawed, all of them and for all time. Sane individuals among them, or sane phases in their history, are not recognized.

Across the border, the *Jang* group of newspapers published the following opinion sent by a Scotland-based Pakistani called Nasim Malik:

If Pakistan had not left the job undone in 1965, we would not be seeing this day. Hindu fanatics have never accepted

Pakistan and there is no way they will ever live like a peaceful neighbour. Pakistan should therefore strike India with full force and capacity and destroy their imported nuclear structure and teach them a lesson which they cannot forget for centuries.[125]

From Canada, a man of Pakistani origin named Asif Patel wrote lines partly addressed to Indians:

India is not interested in implementing the UN resolution [on Kashmir] that it signed, and had first called for. India is not interested in an honourable peace. Muslims are commanded by Allah to do jihad if an honourable treaty cannot be achieved . . . We are not afraid to die; in fact we desire to be killed in jihad. What about you?[126]

These Pakistani statements imply that Hindus are death-fearing heathens doomed to defeat at jihadist hands.

Of course, what has been cited does not necessarily reflect mainstream Indian or Pakistani opinion. Still, rejection and contempt or demonization appear to be strong notes on both sides, and many see revenge as the only possible response. A merely appropriate armed reply does not satisfy. A lesson must be taught, but no lesson need be learned. 'Enough is enough,' and what is a weapon for if it cannot finish a long chapter or impart an unforgettable lesson?

This, of course, was the mentality in the Mahabharata. There too, as on the subcontinent of 1999, the ultimate weapon was available to both sides. In the Mahabharata, for all its destructiveness, that weapon lay unused or nullified, a precedent from the epic that one prays would be observed in our time.

12

The New Century: Strategies for Reconciliation

WHAT DID OUR journey say on the questions with which we set forth? What do our findings indicate for South Asia in the twenty-first century? In this concluding chapter, these are our enquiries. To aid our consideration, we will also look briefly at some experiences and insights gained elsewhere in the world.

On the key question, we found that despite a long line of valiant proponents the heterodoxy of reconciliation did not become a dominant Indian or South Asian trait. The surmise at the start of this study that Ashwatthama's demise seemed far off was confirmed; along with other impulses towards violence, revenge was found alive and well in South Asia.

Over and over again, our survey revealed the destructive role played in South Asian history by a habit of distrust and an unwillingness to come together. In modern legislatures as on ancient battlefields, the day's common enemy appeared to provide only a transient glue. Often we saw the Other being rejected, stereotyped, or even demonized. In some instances the Other was an alien or a descendant of aliens who on his part had scorned the native; more often, the Other was a compatriot of another caste, religion or political party.

Such findings go against the widespread and dogged belief about India's age-old, surpassing tolerance, but one cannot fight with the results of research. I am stopped in my tracks, however, by the awareness, daily reinforced by the evidence of my eyes and ears, of the accommodation practised by the humble Indian, by his or her readiness to make space, in bus, train or home, for one more, whether relative or stranger, then for another, and for another still, and to share food, no matter how meagre its stock . . .

Does not this reality undermine our study's findings? I think not. What it does is to oblige us to ask fresh questions, one about the roots of the accommodation practised by so many uncomfortably-off

Indians, and another about the causes of the dichotomy, present perhaps in age after age, between one set of Indians and another. What, to continue with new questions, caused or causes this dichotomy? Does this dichotomy also reflect a tussle taking place inside each of us?

Such inquiries lie beyond present scope, but we may assume that Indians and South Asians who adapt, endure and share have drawn encouragement from the line of reconcilers we have looked at; joining that line, they in turn encourage others. Thanks to them, what in this study has been called the dissenting tradition of reconciliation continues to live; making such a culture dominant in South Asia is the major challenge before us.

To return to our study, we saw that often what came in unity's way was a failure to recognize the individual in those seen as the Other(s). The Others were pictured not as separate men and women but as a category—as an undifferentiated mass of the flawed, the low-born, or the heathen, a mass cursed with wrong ancestors, or, sometimes, as a mass of ogres—, as members of That caste, fold, race or country, or, in recent times, as Those bureaucrats or politicians, rather than as persons.

This blindness, the inability to see individuals as individuals, each with a unique mix of gifts and defects, emerged from our survey as one of South Asia's defining—and disabling—features. Not seeing, it may be realized, is the acme of rejection.

The streaks from the past we paused with in our survey—revenge, suspicion, bloodletting, demonization and rejection—are generally played down in studies of Indian and South Asian history. No doubt I will be accused of exaggerating their importance. In defence I can only plead an urge to face facts and an effort, I do not know how successful, to face them fairly.

It is easier to chronicle than to explain the weakness, in India's story, of the thread of reconciliation. Yet one may, 'in fear and trembling,' raise a question prompted by reverence for the teachers of reconciliation and for their goal. Did the weakness stem in some ways from the teachers themselves, from the Buddha down? Was he too other-worldly perhaps? Did Indians need a God that the Buddha was reluctant to speak of? Was his questioning of caste not frontal enough?

Down the centuries, the Gita—probably an intervention subsequent to the Buddha—enabled innumerable Indians to soldier on in life, not minding success or failure and placing their future in a Deity's care. However, stressing often though not always a caste category rather than the individual, and expressing a horror of caste 'pollution,' the Gita may have lacked the capacity to bind Indians to one another in mutual love and service.

As for two great rulers we looked at, we have to ask why Asoka and, much later, Akbar could not find successors or create institutions for carrying forward their vision. Again, what limited the remarkable results of the Bhakti poets and the Sufis? Though legitimate, such questions perhaps place too heavy a load on the teachers and too easily acquit the taught.

As the Mughal empire waned, notable and in some ways unprecedented bonds were forged, we saw, between leaders, soldiers and the people in the Maratha country under Shivaji, and during various phases of Sikh history in the Punjab. Yet Sikh or Maratha unity did not always last and did not extend into Indian unity. Both the Sikhs and the Marathas fought oppression with vigour and at times with success, but a bid for an India where factions or sections did not oppress one another was not on their agenda.

Later on, the British gave India political unity and, to a fair extent, the rule of law. But they had little stake or interest in Indian reconciliation, and in the end they bore significant though not sole responsibility for the 1947 Partition that undid their achievement of uniting India under a single, and in relative terms benign, rule.

The partnership among almost all Indians that Gandhi seemed to achieve proved temporary. Whether over nonviolence in the freedom movement, or Hindu-Muslim reconciliation, or justice-plus-harmony among castes, or active sympathy for the deprived, Gandhi's line was accepted by Indians more as strategy and less in the heart. His followers and supporters liked Gandhi's indictment of British rule and enjoyed their role in challenging and outwitting the British, but were less willing to listen to his uncomfortable truths about Indian society.

On his part, as Tilak once said, Gandhi, who tapped more heroism than was thought to exist, may have demanded too much of the average person. Did Gandhi sometimes, in his own life and in his discourse with the Indian people, seek more from human effort than was reasonable—and not enough, perhaps, from God's grace?

Hardships in post-colonial South Asia dampened enthusiasm when in 1997 the milestone of fifty years of independence was reached. Reflecting the change in mood, a present-day character wondered at the start of a movie on the life of a freedom movement star, Vallabhbhai Patel, whether life was not better before independence.

Gandhi and his colleagues had never promised that life would be rosier after freedom. 'As every country is fit to eat, to drink and to breathe, even so is every nation fit to manage its own affairs, no matter how badly,' Gandhi said in England in 1931.[1] Freedom was not necessarily beneficial. It was merely natural.

We saw aspects of post-independence discontent in the oppression alleged, and separatism nursed, by groups or regions in India, Pakistan, Bangladesh and Sri Lanka. Noting that though anti-colonial struggles sought liberation, they produced domination, Michel Foucault spoke of 'the hegemonic consequences of the liberating project,'[2] consequences perhaps experienced in every liberated colony. Justice and reconciliation among the people or peoples of a liberated land were not independence's inevitable fruits.

However, despite numerous causes for chagrin, no colony freed after the Second World War has sought a return to alien rule—human beings put up with much for independence, for self-respect. The question to ask is not whether subjugation was more comfortable than self-rule, but how different groups in a free and heterogenous nation can accommodate one another, and how rulers can satisfy a diverse citizenry.

Or, as Edward Said puts it in his 1999 obituary on Eqbal Ahmad, the Pakistani analyst and activist with Bihari origins, those drawn to 'two great themes, liberation and injustice,' have to figure out 'how to achieve the first without reproducing more of the second.'[3]

Battling the British to send them away, Congress, we saw, also needed to befriend the British to avert Partition, an exercise in wizardry that proved impossible in the end, though from time to time Gandhi attempted it. The dilemma is of relevance to our days, for in South Asia foes fighting one another seem finally to need one another.

Contests such as India vs. Pakistan, Dalits vs. peasant castes, low castes vs. high castes, Sinhala vs. Tamil, or Shia vs. Sunni, or Khaleda vs. Hasina, to give only a few South Asian examples, are real enough and often bitter, but the combatants are neighbours who have to live next to one another. Fighting a foe in order to work later with it, and working with a foe you earlier fought against—these are the tricks, or skills, that South Asia needs to learn.

The British period offered another lesson. We saw that in the final analysis Britain's conquest of India as well as India's Partition occurred because from 1757 right up to 1947 some Indians trusted the British more than they trusted other Indians. At the turn of the millennium, Indian elites and political parties face the challenge of winning the confidence of the Indian people in all their variety. There may only be two means of doing so, paths however that rulers in modern South Asia have on the whole shunned: trusting the people, thereby *evoking* a response of trust, and becoming trustworthy, thereby *earning* trust.

*

Nonviolence or reconciliation? The two are distinct though related concepts. Some may agree with the retired Indian general who argues that 'whatever the present ground reality, the . . . resonance of the Indian civilization for the majority of the people of India as also for those who come to it for spiritual sustenance is one of nonviolence, in the mould of the Buddha, Ashoka and Gandhi.'[4]

However, what our study points to is the need for strategies for reconciliation, not to the sanctity of nonviolence. Moreover, adversaries in nonviolent struggles may require reconciliation as much as foes in violent battles, for great hates can accompany seemingly nonviolent proceedings.

Our study has nonetheless revealed that violent struggles, e.g. the one launched in Sri Lanka by the LTTE, can take a heavier toll of the side launching them than of the enemy, and take over two decades to get almost nowhere. Making the same point, K. Balagopal, a prominent civil liberties activist in Andhra, writes: 'Systematic and calculated violence begins with the enemy but soon turns to the agents of the enemy within and among one's friends.'[5]

Moreover, starting as a means, violence quickly becomes an end in itself. A 1998 book by Daya Somasundaram, a Tamil psychiatrist from Jaffna, depicts teenage Tamil boys initiated into militancy who 'became obsessed by the need to see blood and began to derive pleasure from brutally killing people.'[6]

Looking at violent movements in different parts of the world, David Apter notes that violence 'seek[s] the moral moment in the cannon's mouth' and 'ritualizes death as sacrifice.'[7] The Other dies in punishment, the punisher as a martyr.

In a comment similar to Apter's, Wyschogrod has observed that 'it is the death event and the death world which dominates the twentieth century.'[8] This privileging of death bears little real resemblance to the ancient intuition of Socrates that 'the style of one's dying will reflect the character of one's life.' Where Socrates saw death as a window on life, a modern fascination treats life solely as a door to martyrdom.

We found in our survey that it is possible for a modern killer to link his deed to 'divine' punishments in a glorious past. 'By imitating the exemplary acts of the mythic deities and heroes man detaches himself from profane time and magically re-enters the Great Time, the Sacred Time.'[9]

What happens on the ground, however, is less than magical. Violent extremists 'bomb factories and shout about unemployment; they shoot a teacher in classroom, kill school bus drivers, kill people on campuses and then lecture us about education. They kill, maim and injure and they carry out attacks in hospital precincts and then they tell us about protecting the Health service.'[10] Though these words are about Northern Ireland, uttered by one of its leading politicians, John Hume, they are not without relevance to South Asia.

No doubt martyrs stir us if they are genuine, if before inviting death for their cause they loved life and neighbours. Thus we respond to Yeats's recall of a slice of Irish history:

> But where can we draw water/ Said Pearse to Connolly/
> When all the wells are parched away?/ O plain as plain can
> be/ There's nothing but our own red blood/ Can make a
> right Rose Tree.[11]

Yet watering may also be possible with tears of joy at lives spared.

*

'*The killer instinct*': To some, what India has lacked and missed is not reconciliation but the killer instinct. 'If we had had the killer instinct,' so the argument goes, 'Indians would have driven invaders back and won all their cricket matches. Thanks to your reconcilers, Indians became guilty about the killer instinct and lost out to every ruthless invader or aggressive team.'

How Indians could have kept the British out and yet mastered cricket presents difficulty, but the problem with the diagnosis is deeper—it is simply not true. The princes and politicians we looked at in successive ages did not repent of their killer instinct or desire their adversaries' triumph.

What they did, however, was to use their energies and weapons—their killer instinct—on brothers and allies. At times they joined hands with an alien invader to eliminate an Indian rival. Reconciliation with brothers and neighbours would have turned swords in the direction of the invader. Cooperation of this sort, or teamwork, may prove more useful than the killer instinct—even in cricket.

*

Examples from elsewhere: No country or part of the world has an impeccable record in reconciliation, and what works in one place may not necessarily work elsewhere with a different set of histories and complexities, but some accomplishments or efforts may be worth noting.

France and Germany: In 1870-71, the French suffered a humiliating defeat at German hands and adopted the slogan, 'Never speak of revenge, always think of it.' Revenge was obtained in 1918, after Germany lost the First World War, and tough terms were imposed on Germany. The European neighbours fought again during the Second World War, which like the First took an enormous toll of French, German and other lives. Coming together, however, by the mid-1950s, France and Germany have become the core of a substantially integrated Europe, their reconciliation lasting to the end of the century.

Common post-War fears of a Communist Soviet Union and the economic advantages of cooperation were powerful yet insufficient factors behind the remarkable reconciliation. Officials and citizens strove to restore Franco-German relationships at several levels, the past was faced, apologies were made and accepted, forgiveness was experienced, and French and German scholars wrote a joint history of the conflicts that had divided the neighbours.

Leading roles were played by persons like Irene Laure. A socialist who had fought in the resistance against the Nazis and whose son was tortured by the Gestapo, Irene Laure, in her words, had 'so hated Germany that [she] wanted to see Germany erased from the map of Europe.'[12] However, yielding her bitterness against the Germans for, as she put it, 'the love of tomorrow'—for the sake of French and German children—, she made Franco-German reconciliation her life's mission. In a series of visits to Germany, she reached out to people whose destruction she had longed for.

The USA: Created out of a large number of races and nations, the USA roots its nationality not in an ancient bloodline but in a modern experiment. Immigrants arrived in the USA with their eyes on the future, leaving, in a literal sense, their histories behind them. In their new country—in the New World—they found space and scope they had never dreamed of, as well as freedom from a pinching past. The result was an unprecedented explosion of energy and creativity.

But great wounds and hurts marked the American story—native Americans and African-Americans are yet to feel fully engaged in the American Experiment. Recognizing these realities, some Americans have initiated 'honest conversations' on 'race, responsibility, and reconciliation' in their cities.

A focus in these dialogues is on acknowledging the past's hurtful events. Thus an attempt was made in June 1993 to involve as much as possible of the city of Richmond in facing what had gone before. The Confederate capital in the American Civil War, Richmond had earlier functioned, from 1680 to 1780, as the USA's main port of entry for slaves, who were shipped up the river James from the Atlantic Ocean.

Modern Richmond contains sites, not always familiar to its residents, where the slaves landed, or were auctioned, or imprisoned, or committed suicide, or killed their babies rather than let them become slaves. It also contains memorials for Confederate heroes as well as the church where, before the Civil War and before the American Revolution, Patrick Henry had declared, referring to England's rule over America:

> Is peace so dear, and life so sweet, as to be purchased at the
> price of chains and slavery? . . . As for me, give me liberty
> or give me death.

What is not known even to most people in Richmond is that this historic St. John's Church was built on a native American burial ground, so that the site today conveys one thing to white Americans and another to native Americans.

In June 1993, a Unity Walk took hundreds of Americans of different races and some from outside America, including the author of these pages, to many of these sites. At each spot a griot, or traditional African-American story-teller dressed in period costume, described its significance. Then he said:

> We must mark this site, for those who fail to remember
> history are doomed to repeat it.

'Marking' the site meant acknowledging what had happened there. Depending on the walker's race, some were ashamed and others saddened. All were moved. After the site was thus 'marked,' the griot gave everyone a chance to enter a healing process by saying:

> We mark this spot as a sign of our commitment to heal the heart of America.

Never before had American whites, blacks and native Indians together acknowledged the pain that these sites reflected. Red flowers collected from each walker were then poured into the James River at Manchester Docks, a tribute to the many slaves who, preferring death to slavery like Patrick Henry, had jumped to their death before their ships could land.

At a meeting at the end of the walk, an African-American leader recited James Weldon Johnson's poem on the Black struggle in America:

> Stony the road we trod;
> Bitter the chastening rod,
> Felt in the day
> When hope unborn had died.
> Yet, with a steady beat,
> Have not our weary feet
> Come to the places for which
> Our fathers sighed?[13]

Dalai Lama and Nelson Mandela: Better known than these American 'conversations' are the bids for reconciliation made by the Dalai Lama and Nelson Mandela. While demanding Tibetan autonomy and self-respect, the Dalai Lama insists that the Chinese are his brothers and sisters, keeps his fight nonviolent, and asks for talks with the Chinese. Also, in a concession to hard facts, he accepts that Tibet would remain linked to China.

He and his Tibetan followers are yet to secure their political goals, but that is also true for most violent separatist movements. Meanwhile, thanks to the Dalai Lama's approach, the world remains aware of, and sympathetic towards, the Tibetan cause, which is not the case with every movement for self-rule.

After twenty-seven years in prison, Nelson Mandela emerged with an astonishing freedom from rancour, and with his eyes on the future. When he visited India within months of his release,

R. Venkataraman, the Indian President, told Mandela that he was praying for his health. 'Please also pray,' said Mandela, referring to South Africa's white President at the time 'for de Klerk. He is vital to our future.' Four years later, when he became South Africa's first democratically elected President, Mandela invited his White jailor to the inauguration.

South Africa's transformation, catapulting jailed seditionists into office and sidelining White masters, was preceded by patient dialogue at several levels, involving Mandela and de Klerk, Mandela's African National Congress (ANC) and de Klerk's National Party, the ANC and the party championing Zulu interests, Chief Buthelezi's Inkatha Freedom Party (IFP), business organizations, professional bodies, trade unions and others.

The Truth and Reconciliation Commission (TRC) that was later instituted, chaired by the Nobel laureate, Archbishop Desmond Tutu, enabled many South Africans to face and admit cruelties they had perpetrated, while other South Africans could see the acknowledgment as a step of justice.

Even if not everyone was fully satisfied with its proceedings or findings, the TRC provided some moving demonstrations of apology and forgiveness. That truth and reconciliation had to go together, that one without the other would spread bitterness or be an empty gesture, was in itself a key message that Mandela, Tutu and their associates managed to convey to South Africa and the world. In Tutu's words:

> If we look only to retributive justice, then we could just as well close up shop. Forgiveness . . . is practical politics. Without forgiveness, there is no future.[14]

*

Our study and these examples underline the importance of *dialogue*, which is needed in South Asia across numerous divides. These divides have been referred to in the text and need not be named again, but let us remind ourselves of a major and oft-overlooked South Asian divide, that between those who order tasks, and others who perform them. The highest ambition of many of our doers—craftspersons, creators and restorers—is to become order-ers and command-ers, yet South Asia's future perhaps requires that commanders also become doers, and vice versa.

Crucial to dialogue is *listening*, with the heart as well as the ear, to what is said and also to what is unsaid. Is listening natural to the South Asian? A Japanese friend once said to me:

> For fifteen years I have been attending international conferences and seminars. Africans, Europeans, Asians, Americans, all take part. Do you know the biggest difficulties that the person in the chair faces? One is to persuade the shy Japanese delegate to say something. Another is to persuade the Indian delegate to end his speech.

Next, in the light of what we have seen, let us mark *acknowledgment or acceptance*. It is only rarely that we can choose our neighbours, or those with whom we would work, study, do business or do politics. This applies to individuals, groups and nations. Most of the time there is no alternative to accepting those next to us or opposite us. This does not mean we agree with them or accept all their views. We accept their presence.

Similarly, we may have to accept the past, including its pain, wounds and consequences. To fight one who invades my home or country, or oppresses me or my people, is an age-old, natural, human and universal instinct. Ancient Indian as well as non-Indian texts, e.g. the Old Testament books, tell of clashes between peoples, of prayers for 'national' victories and defeats, of yearnings for aid against the enemy. It is a sentiment that has not died with passing centuries. Invaders and oppressors have to be resisted.

But when invaders settle down amongst us and breed new generations—e.g. the Aryans, assuming they came from outside India, or the Turks, Afghans, Arabs and Persians who entered India a long time ago, or the Tamils entering Sri Lanka—, their progeny have to be accepted as part of us, of our nation; the progeny are not the invading or oppressing race. Again, if locals adopt some customs, practices or religious beliefs of the invader or immigrant, they and their descendants do not thereby become foreign. Not, at any rate, after centuries have elapsed since the invasion. If it were otherwise, every country in the world would be doomed to eternal conflict, for every people are a product of the past's invasions, migrations, oppressions and wars.

Acknowledgment also needs to extend to events in the past. It is unnatural not to fight an invader, but it is only silly, not patriotic or loyal, to deny an old event—a result, defeat or misdeed. Mahmud of Ghazni, Tamerlane and Aurangzeb were destructive, even if there was more to them. Untouchability and sati were cruel customs. Babur won in Panipat in 1526, Clive in Plassey in 1757, India's freedom was won in 1947, Pakistan was won the same year, and Bangladesh in 1971-72. Indira Gandhi lost in 1977 but won in 1980. The BJP-led alliance won in 1998. Regrettable or pleasurable, these facts are undeniable.

And also unalterable. Even God cannot change the past. As Amos Oz, the Israeli writer, cautions us, attempts to 'burn' the past can only set fire to the present. Nor are we barred from profiting from what a previous conqueror (or electoral victor) may have brought—new ideas and institutions, new policies or technologies, new links with other parts of the world, or new blood. He or she may have brought harmful things too, of course, which can be heartily rejected.

Reconverting into a temple a mosque that centuries ago may have replaced a temple does not change the past, though it can unsettle the present. It is a type of controversy that Israel also faces. Thus in 1998 the *Jerusalem Post* published the following letter from David Wilder, a spokesman for the Jewish community in the Israeli town of Hebron, in response to an article by David Kuttab, a Palestinian politician:

> Kuttab refers to the 'Ibrahimi mosque.' This building is known to the Jews as the Machpela cave, the second holiest site to the Jewish people throughout the world. This site has served as a mosque only since 1267. The building was originally constructed as a site for Jewish worship, built by Herod, king of Judea, 2000 years ago.

Quoting the letter in an article in the *New Yorker* (25.5.98), David Remnick adds: 'The key phrase here, of course, is '*only* since 1267.'

While a restoration or restitution offered of one's own free will may help towards healing history's wounds, it is obvious that forcibly obtained 'rectifications' of history, such as the Babri Masjid demolition of 1992, can only create new wounds.

*

In addition to acceptance and dialogue, reconcilers can use the maxim, '*What we are for, not who we are against.*' Our study showed that in ancient power struggles as well as in modern electoral politics, South Asians seemed impelled more by feelings against someone than by conviction for something. A related test is, 'Am I, are we, fighting today's war, or yesterday's?'

Also, reconcilers have to suspect any We-and-They discourse. In the *New Yorker* piece referred to above, David Remnick quotes an unnamed friend of Binyamin Netanyahu, then the Israeli Premier, on the Premier's father, Benzion Netanyahu:

> The father always talked about They. *They* don't understand a thing. *They* are naive. *They* are fools. Always, *they*, them.

'They' and 'them' here mean the liberal and leftist Israelis that Benzion Netanyahu would not abide, not Arabs. I quote the sentence here because it is language that falls easily from South Asian mouths—about, e.g., the BJP, or Congress, or Sharif's supporters, or the PPP, or a neighbouring country, or whoever the 'enemy' is. Fortunately, South Asia also has some counterparts of another Israeli quoted by Remnick, the liberal film-maker, Ronit Weiss-Berkowitz:

> We Israelis think (Weiss-Berkowitz said) we have a monopoly on blood, tears, and pain, but, of course, this is not true. We know our side in this story. I wanted to present the other side—loudly.

While victimization can lead to 'the incapacity of an ethno-national group, as a direct result of its own historical traumas, to empathize with the suffering of another group,'[15] reconcilers manage to *go beyond Us-and-Them*.

Recognizing that 'inhumanity is part of being human,'[16] reconcilers strive to identify even with an inhuman Other. 'The real issue,' Christopher Hollis asked in relation to Europe, 'is whether the Jew and the Nazi were two of God's children sharing a common humanity or whether they are different sorts of being, irrevocably at war with one another.'[17]

Answering similar posers about South Asia's Hindus and Muslims, or Brahmins and Untouchables, Guru Nanak, Kabir and Gandhi said that all were God's children, sharing a common humanity.

How alike We are to Them came across in a BBC programme on India, Pakistan and Kashmir shown on the night of 10 January 1999, with footage from Lahore, Amritsar and both sides of the Line of Control in Kashmir. Mirror images of hate, bravado and versions of history were presented, and an identical rhetoric about holding heads high and about the prestige that comes from strength was heard from both sides.

'We should have done more harm than we did (in 1947),' an auto-rickshaw driver said in Lahore. Recalling that his mother and seven siblings were killed in anti-Muslim riots in Jullundur in 1947, he added, 'Our children will die in this continuing battle, there will have to be war.'

With hand, chin, gun and goosestep, the Pakistani border guards made exaggerated, even ludicrous, gestures of bravado and machismo. 'Our men are lions compared with the Indians,' a Pakistani onlooker commented.

Across the fence, 'Worship the bullets' and 'No victory greater than death' were lines in a marching song that an RSS unit offered from Amritsar. The unit's men, some of them overweight and all in an incongruous uniform of black caps, white shirts and khaki shorts, exercised ostentatiously with lathis.

Captain Bali of the Rashtriya Rifles in Kupwara in Indian Kashmir articulated the doctrine of strength. 'The villagers will be loyal to the stronger side—to us, not the militants,' he said. The gun rather than good governance was to win loyalty.

What scenes will a BBC team visiting India, Pakistan and Kashmir shoot in 2009, 2059, 2999 . . .?

*

Time and grace: It takes time to recover from trauma and find healing, and it seems necessary for survivors to dismiss the authors of their suffering from their minds. The evil-doers merit no place, not even as targets for revenge. As Esther Muzawayo, a survivor of the 1994 Rwanda massacres and counselor with the Association of Widows of the April Genocide (AVEGA) in Kigali, Rwanda's capital, said in 1998:

> There are people who are strong enough to keep others going and who are bringing back [to us] a bit of faith, a bit of this faith in humanity—and it is not an easy thing . . . We feel such strength when we come together to say 'No, please let us be alive, alive—we can't allow those who could not get our bodies to get our inside—those who have not been able to take our bodies, they can't take our humanities.'[18]

These honest, courageous and moving words hint at a wonderful alchemy taking place, pointing to the role in healing of grace, or a gift from God. Perhaps the words also suggest that grace might descend where there are 'people who keep others going.'

*

Apology: Can an apology provide some healing? With respect to two relatively recent events, one, the Indian Government's assault on the Golden Temple in 1984, and the 1919 Jallianwala killings under British rule, gestures in the direction of an apology were made.

Speaking in Chandigarh in February 1998, and clearly addressing the Sikh community though not naming it, Sonia Gandhi, who had just been elevated to the presidency of Congress, said that she 'understood the pain and anguish of Operation Bluestar,' and added:

> As a widow and a mother, I can feel exactly how it hurts
> . . . this should not have happened.[19]

Another Congress leader and India's finance minister from 1991 to 1996, Manmohan Singh, said:

> If any section can be soothed by someone expressing regret
> on behalf of the Indian nation, it should be done.[20]

Though not a member of the government in January 1998 or in June 1984, Sonia Gandhi was to some extent qualified to speak of the 1984 event. She was the leader of Congress, the political party that in 1984 had ruled India, her mother-in-law, Premier Indira Gandhi, had authorized the 1984 assault, and her husband, Rajiv Gandhi, had advocated it.

If Sonia Gandhi's words did not have the effect that some had hoped for, it was partly because she was making an election speech, seldom taken entirely at face value. Secondly, the words of regret she used were not seen as unqualified by those who were at the receiving end of the 1984 assault. On the other hand, some who thought the assault inescapable in the circumstances of the time seemed to feel that Sonia Gandhi had gone too far.

Finally, and perhaps most importantly, an apology needs to emerge voluntarily from the heart if it is to have a chance of healing another's hurt heart. An apology 'on demand' is less likely to work.

We do not know whether Sonia Gandhi received a demand for an apology for June 1984, or advice that an expression of regret would be electorally helpful, but an apology for Jallianwala was publicly demanded when, earlier, word spread that Queen Elizabeth, arriving in India in October 1997 as a guest of the Government, would visit Amritsar.

The 'demand' came from several, though some confined themselves to making a suggestion. When surviving victims of the 1919 shooting and some descendants of victims were interviewed over television at the Jallianwala site, one young citizen of Amritsar said he would demonstrate what Queen Elizabeth could do. Then he folded his hands, looked into the camera, and said, 'India, I am sorry.' 'That's all we want from her,' the young man said.

In the event, although Queen Elizabeth went to Jallianwala Bagh, and stood in respectful silence in memory of the killed, and also, quite obviously, in regret for what had happened, she did not make an explicit apology; perhaps she felt her act implied it.

Matters were not improved when the British High Commissioner in India dismissed the suggestion of an apology as 'preposterous' and the Queen's husband, Prince Philip, was quoted as having questioned the figure of the killed that he saw displayed at Jallianwala Bagh.[21]

In a debate in India before the Queen's arrival, two arguments against an apology were advanced. One was that guests are not asked to apologize. The other, made by Sikhs in the Punjab, was that it was odd to ask the Queen to apologize for 1919 if the Indian Government was unwilling to apologize to the Sikhs for 1984.

The arguments were not without weight. Still, Queen Elizabeth could perhaps have helped close a painful chapter in the history of the Punjab, and of Indo-British relations, by admitting and apologizing for the wrongs from the British side in 1919. She might have stirred millions had she done so—and pricked consciences about other apologies.

We have seen that Sonia Gandhi seemed partially qualified to speak about 1984, though she had held no responsible position at the time, and that Elizabeth seemed fully qualified to speak about 1919, even though she was not even born then. Their links to the events in question were clear to all.

This may be of some relevance to the problem of healing hurts left by a past event. If some are alive who still feel the hurt, others may be alive who are linked to those who caused the hurt. Such individuals may be in a position to attempt a healing. Commenting on a recent attempt of this nature, a Delhi University professor, Uma Chakravarti, has written:

> The most courageous and moving example in recent years of living with history and *living in it*, in my view, was the apology made by the Women's Action Forum (of Pakistan) to the women of Bangladesh for the events of the 1972 war.[22]

＊

Who will be the reconcilers? What field of South Asian life is likely to rear them? Though a few political initiatives offering flickers of hope were noted by us, South Asia's politics was generally found to be negative and sterile.

Also appearing barren and negative, religion in South Asia has been willing to ally with divisive politics. We saw the employment of religion to target minorities in India, Pakistan, Bangladesh and Sri Lanka. Instances need not be repeated from all four countries, but a telling sample, which other South Asian lands can readily match or outmatch, is this announcement in April 1998 by Baikunth Lal Sharma 'Prem', national secretary of the Vishwa Hindu Parishad:

> The VHP plans to build a Rs 100 crore monument in New Delhi, located on a five-acre plot near the Qutub Minar, depicting the 'massacre of Hindus by Muslim and British invaders.' 'It will feature the atrocities committed on Hindus by invaders ranging from Mir Mohammed Bin Qasim to Lord Mountbatten,' said B.L. Sharma 'Prem'. 'The monument will ultimately tell the story of the Hindus during the past 2,000 years with authentic records of its religion and its sacrifices.'[23]

True, South Asia's religious preachers often avoid politics. Nor do they always slight other religions or their adherents. Yet their positive utterances touch but rarely on paths to reconciliation, and their concern with an individual's salvation can at times be all-absorbing. Thus a 1998 restatement of the essence of the last discourse given by the eleventh-century Vaishnava teacher from South India, Ramanunja, goes as follows:

> What is to be done to attain the Grace of the Lord? Should one do a Yajna (sacrificial rite) on a big scale? Should one ostentatiously worship in the 108 Divine Kshetras (sites)? Should one make costly offerings? Should one build temples to house the idols? Ramanuja clarified that what is needed is simple, sincere, devoted service to the Lord . . .[24]

None of the different options for attaining grace, including the last, involves neighbours or other human beings, though we are informed that when 'the Lord appeared before [Ramanuja] and assured him salvation, Ramanuja got an assurance from the Lord that all his followers and disciples should also be given salvation.' Concern for the salvation of others—for what happens to them after death—comes across here. Where the living are concerned, however, religion in India has often ignored how, for the sake of one another and for the common good, humans might cooperate.

Contrition and compassion were not unknown to the ancient Hindus, one of whom composed a morning prayer, recited to this day, that includes these lines:

> Forgive, O Merciful and Loving God of gods, all my sins, of hand or foot, body or speech, eye or ear, of commission or omission . . . I ask neither for a kingdom nor for heaven nor for salvation, but only for an end to the pain of the suffering ones.[25]

However, since those saying this prayer usually chant it in Sanskrit, its meaning probably escapes most reciters and listeners. On the other hand, the Bhakti bhajans use intelligible language to refer, as they often do, to the Other's pain.

Folk religion in South Asia, and the compassionate religion occasionally portrayed in popular movies—contemporary versions of the Bhakti bhajans—, seem more human and reconciling than 'high' or 'official' varieties. Reconciliation may thus chiefly come from the common people of South Asia, from, as we saw earlier, those who sweat, make room and give unstintingly from a scanty shelf—from those who know pain and hardship and so wish to save others from it. It probably follows that women will outnumber men among South Asia's reconcilers.

During the Mumbai riots in early 1993, a man in his fifties called Hamzabhai, who earned a living by selling nylon rope on a pushcart, lost a twenty-five-year-old son, who had been stabbed. Before dying, the son told Hamzabhai who the assailants were.

'Tell us the names,' relatives demanded, wanting revenge. Hamzabhai refused. Some months later, at a meeting in Shillong that I also attended, Hamzabhai explained: 'I did not want another father to go through what I had gone through.' He could just as easily have told himself, 'I'll make another father go through what I have gone through,' but Hamzabhai was receptive to grace.

Leaders of feuding ethnic groups heard Hamzabhai in Shillong and took his tale, which seemed a lantern of hope, to dark, stormy corners in the Northeast. Is a man like Hamzabhai an oddity? I see him as a fresh link in an old chain of sanity and reconciliation.

Though one part of him urged revenge, Hamzabhai listened to and heeded the voice of grace. It is those who listen—to others in dialogue and also to inner inspirations of grace—who may bring healing.

*

A word, finally, on Delhi, for we started this study by noting Delhi's djinns, its great load of unrepented cruelty and unshared sorrow. In many instances, while the city's killers gloried in their deeds, the killed were left unacknowledged and unmourned. The spirits of Delhi's women—mothers, wives, sisters and daughters—have cried out for healing, and continue to do so.

Can Delhi's accumulated offences be washed away? Can some atonement or penance—or some God-sent blessing or grace—expiate the guilt of centuries, and generate a breeze of forgiveness that blows away the smells of torture and revenge?

Notoriously, Delhi also suffers from physical maladies—the pollution attacking the eyes and lungs, the hazardous water, the clogged streets. 'Do you know what Delhi really lacks?' a young woman, an artist, said to me in February 1997. 'A river. The Jamna has moved, and is in any case too far for most Delhiites.'

Others articulate Delhi's desperate need for greening. A frontpage piece entitled 'How Green was my Delhi' in the *Times of India* of 21 June 1999 says:

> The Moghuls were lovers of gardens, and Delhi as their capital city was lush with greenery, nourished by the waters of the Yamuna. The British maintained the tradition and the trees they planted . . . are a fine legacy of the Raj. However, the explosive growth of its population, and the unplanned geographical spread of the city in the last three decades, is turning Delhi into a concrete jungle and the Yamuna into a sluggish sewer. The Delhi administration's plan to plant lakhs of trees is therefore welcome . . .

Every tree planted, or cubic foot of water conserved, is a celebration of life, a proclamation of the worth of the future, and a garden or a river may calm sad or angry hearts. Every caring act—of fellowship, considerateness, nursing, apology, forgiveness, greening or flowering— perhaps heals something of Delhi's torment, maybe calms one of its djinns, and a healing process in Delhi might speak to all of South Asia.

*

Begun with a look at the sanguinary pasts of Delhi and Kurukshetra, this study ended with the bloodshed in Kargil. My hope that Vajpayee's bus ride to Lahore would survive for a while as a punctuation mark in South Asia's story seemed blasted, and why not? Why should a century, or a millennium, finish with hope, or a book with a positive ending?

Yet I cannot close on such a note. In the midst of death, life persists; in the midst of darkness, light persists. Right now, at the peak of summer, I am aware of a rain-bearing, life-giving storm outside the room where I write this, and also of a flow of heavy traffic, a flow of life, that is, or of threatened life, one should perhaps say. Newspapers this coming weekend will bulge with matrimonial ads, as they did last weekend; and this evening, as I take my constitutional, I will again hear happy laughter from children, see eagerness in teenage eyes, and watch the straight-backed istri couple working away at their makeshift ironing platform, as they have done, late hour after long hour, for years.

May the Good Spirit that quickens the rain and kindles the laughter, the eagerness and the dedication use willing women and men to reconcile South Asia's ingenious, impossible and lovable inhabitants!

Notes

Introduction

1. Quoted in Gopal Das Khosla, *Stern Reckoning*, Oxford, New Delhi, 1989, p.100.
2. *The Gazetteer of India*, Publications Division, New Delhi, 2:23 and 35.
3. Michael Edwardes, *A History of India*, The New English Library, London, 1967, p.105.
4. See *The Gazetteer of India*, Publications Division, New Delhi, 1990, 2:333.
5. Harbans Singh, *Guru Tegh Bahadur*, Manohar, New Delhi, 1994, p.84.
6. W.H. McLeod, *The Evolution of the Sikh Community*, Oxford, New Delhi, 1996, pp.102-03.
7. Harbans Singh, *Guru Tegh Bahadur*, p.86.
8. Ibid., pp.86-87.
9. Edwardes, *A History of India*, p.167.
10. Ibid., p.228.
11. Ibid., p.228.
12. Narayani Gupta, *Delhi Between Two Empires: 1803-1931*, Oxford, New Delhi, 1981, p.30.
13. Quoted in Gupta, *Delhi Between Two Empires*, Oxford, New Delhi, 1981, pp.30-31.
14. Gyanendra Pandey, 'Partition and Independence in Delhi: 1947-48', *Economic and Political Weekly*, 6.9.97, p.2264.
15. Ibid., p.2265.
16. Translation of Yunus Jaffrey, in Gupta, *Delhi Between Two Empires*, p.xix.
17. Quoted by Gyanendra Pandey in 'Partition and Independence in Delhi: 1947-48', *Economic and Political Weekly*, 6.9.97, p.2267.
18. Harbans Singh, *Guru Tegh Bahadur*, Manohar, Delhi, 1994, p.84.
19. *Collected Works of Mahatma Gandhi*, 90:419 and 89:465.
20. *Collected Works*, 89:181.
21. *Collected Works*, 90:419.
22. Hugh Trevaskis, *The Land of the Five Rivers: An Economic History of the Punjab*, Oxford University Press, 1928, pp.xv-xvi.
23. S. Radhakrishnan, *Indian Philosophy*, Oxford, New Delhi, 1994, 1:546.
24. Ibid.

25. In Balkrishna Muztar, *Kurukshetra: Political and Cultural History*, B.R. Publishing, Delhi, 1978, pp.20-21; also in article by H.A. Phadke, 'Kurukshetra: Archaelogy and Early History,' in *Kurukshetra Through the Ages*, Bharatiya Itihaas Sankalan Samiti, Haryana, 1988.
26. See Muztar, *Kurukshetra*, p.12.
27. Edwardes, *A History of India*, p.93.
28. S.M. Burke, *The Greatest Mogul*, Munshiram Manoharlal, New Delhi, 1989, .p.40.
29. Muztar, *Kurukshetra*, p.27.
30. S.C. Sharma, 'Ghazni's Best-kept Secret' *Indian Express*, Mumbai, 25.4.98.
31. Sauptika Parva, verses 10-11, Annie Besant, *Mahabharata*, Adyar, p.234.

1. The Mahabharata Legacy, and the Gita's Intent

1. V.S. Sukthankar, *The Meaning of the Mahabharata*, Asiatic Society, Bombay, 1957, p.98.
2. G.C. Jhala's Introduction in V.S. Sukthankar, *The Meaning of the Mahabharata*.
3. Sukthankar, *The Meaning of the Mahabharata*, p.119.
4. Ibid., p.89.
5. Preface to her translation, *The Bhagavad Gita*, The Theosophical Society, Madras, 1977, p.viii.
6. Bal Gangadhar Tilak, *Srimad Bhagavadgita-Rahasya*, English translation by B.S. Sukthankar, 2nd edition, Poona, 1965, p.664 and p.723.
7. Quoted in J.I. Bakker, *Gandhi and the Gita*, Canadian Scholars' Press, Toronto, 1993, p.30.
8. Vinoba Bhave, *Moved by Love*, Sat Sahitya Sahayogi Sangh, Hyderabad, 1994, p.287.
9. Rajagopalachari, *Mahabharata*, Bhavan, Bombay, 1968, p.206.
10. Sukthankar, *The Meaning of the Mahabharata*, p.88 and p.97.
11. Ibid., p.95.
12. Annie Besant, *Mahabharata: The Story of the Great War*, Theosophical Publishing House, Madras, 1992, p.22.
13. P. Lal, *The Mahabharata*, p.294.
14. Rajagopalachari, *Mahabharata*, p.310.
15. Lal, *The Mahabharata*, pp.353-54.
16. See Lal, *The Mahabharata*, pp.38-39
17. Volume Two, Publications Division, New Delhi, 1990, p.XLII.
18. Donald W. Shriver, Jr., *An Ethic for Enemies: Forgiveness in Politics*, Oxford, New York, 1995, p.18.
19. Kamala Subramaniam, *Mahabharata*, Bhavan, Bombay, 1988, p.41.
20. Poem by Waman Nimbalkar, translated by Graham Smith, reproduced

in Gail Omvedt, *Dalit Visions*, Orient Longman, New Delhi, 1995, p.78.

21. Hingonekar's poem of 1989 translated by Gail Omvedt and Bharat Patankar and reproduced in Gail Omvedt, *Dalit Visions*, Orient Longman, New Delhi, 1995, pp 98-99.
22. Subramaniam, *Mahabharata*, p.16.
23. Ibid., p.393, and Rajagopalachari, *Mahabharata*, p.193.
24. Lal, *The Mahabharata*, pp.199-200.
25. Ibid., p.200.
26. Rajagopalachari, *Mahabharata*, pp.189-90.
27. Lal, *The Mahabharata*, pp.142-43.
28. From Kamala Subramaniam, *Mahabharata*, Bhavan, Bombay, 1988, p.169.
29. Lal, *The Mahabharata*, p.27.
30. Ibid., p.280.
31. Ibid., p.134.
32. Ibid., pp.144-45.
33. Sukthankar, *The Meaning of the Mahabharata*, p.74.
34. Lal, *The Mahabharata*, p.290.
35. Ibid., p.291.
36. Ibid., p.291.
37. Ibid., p.315.
38. Ibid., pp.320-1.
39. See Greg Bailey, *Humanistic Elements in the Mahabharata*, South Asia, vol. XVI; no. 1 (1993) pp.1-23.
40. From Rajagopalachari, *Mahabharata*, p.278.
41. Lal, *The Mahabharata*, p.332.
42. E.R. Sreekrishna Sarma in Bimal Krishna Matilal (ed.), *Moral Dilemmas in the Mahabharata*, Indian Institute of Advanced Study in association with Motilal Banarsidass, Delhi, 1989, p.147.
43. Lal, *The Mahabharata*, pp.343-44.
44. From Chapter One of the Gita, Annie Besant's translation.
45. Annie Besant's translation, Adyar, Madras, 1977.
46. Lal, *The Mahabharata*. p.33.
47. Vinoba Bhave, *Moved by Love*, p.184.
48. Quoted in J.I. Bakker, *Gandhi and the Gita*, p.29.
49. See Peter Della Santina, 'Conceptions of Dharma in the Sramanical and Brahmanical Traditions: Buddhism and the Mahabharata,' in Bimal Krishna Matilal (ed.), *Moral Dilemmas in the Mahabharata*, pp.106-14.
50. Except that in Chapter Eleven, where Krishna reveals his omnipotent form, two verses, 33 and 34, do ask Arjuna to fight and be the 'outward cause' of the destruction of his foes, whom Krishna has already overcome, and 'enjoy the wealth-filled realm.' In the writer's view, these exceptions do not weaken the argument.

51. Rajagopalachari in his Preface to the second edition of his *Mahabharata*, Bhavan, Bombay, 1952.
52. Sukthankar, *The Meaning of the Mahabharata*, pp.111-20.
53. *Shrimadbhagavadgita*, 38th edition, Gita Press, Gorakhpur, p.576. Tr. by author.
54. Lal, *The Mahabharata*, pp.6-7 and 50-51.
55. Sukthankar, *The Meaning of the Mahabharata*, p.34.
56. T.K. Mahadevan, citing Gandhi's Jail Diary, in G. Ramachandran and T.K. Mahadevan (ed.), *Quest for Gandhi*, Gandhi Peace Foundation, New Delhi, 1970, p.256.
57. Bakker, *Gandhi and the Gita*, p.29.
58. Preface to his *Mahabharata*, Bhavan, Bombay, 1968, p.iv.
59. Preface to her *Mahabharata*, Bhavan, Bombay, 1988, p.viii.
60. S.P. Dubey in B.K. Matilal (ed.), *Moral Dilemmas in the Mahabharata*, p.36.
61. Quoted by Sheldon Pollock in 'Ramayana and Political Imagination in India,' *The Journal of Asian Studies*, # 52, May 1993.
62. Lal, *The Mahabharata*, p.50.
63. From Subramaniam, *Mahabharata*, pp.601-6.
64. Edith Hamilton, *Mythology: Timeless Tales of Gods and Heroes*, New American Library, New York, 1969, pp.189-92.
65. Ibid.
66. Ibid., p.21.
67. Herodotus I:60 quoted in ibid., p.13.
68. Quoted by Lal, *The Mahabharata*, p.3.
69. Lal, *The Mahabharata*, p.3, and p.369.
70. Rajagopalachari's Preface, 1952, to the second edition of his *Mahabharata*.
71. Harbans Singh, *Guru Tegh Bahadur*, p.41.
72. Lal, *The Mahabharata*, p.206.
73. Quoted from C. Ball, *History of the Indian Mutiny* (London, u.d.) in R. Mukherjee, *Awadh in Revolt: 1857-58*, Oxford, New Delhi, 1984, p.172.
74. Lal, *The Mahabharata*, p.94.
75. Ibid., p.280.
76. Rev. Jon Rotton quoted in Hibbert, *The Great Mutiny*, Penguin, New Delhi, 1980, p.214.
77. Hibbert, *The Great Mutiny*, pp.209-10.
78. Rajagopalachari, *Mahabharata*, p.322.
79. Quoted in Theon Wilkinson, *Two Monsoons*, Duckworth, London, 1976, p.28.
80. Wilkinson, *Two Monsoons*, pp.31.
81. Ibid., pp.44-45.
82. Quoted in Sukthankar, *The Meaning of the Mahabharata*, p.124.
83. Lal, *The Mahabharata*, p.3.
84. Ibid., p.7.
85. Ibid., p.369.

2. A Dissenting Tradition, or the Second Thread

1. From *Dhammapada*, 3-5, 201, quoted in Ainslie Embree (ed.), *Sources of Indian Tradition*, Columbia, New York, 1988, 1:120.
2. From *Digha Nikaya*, ibid., p.115.
3. Quoted from *Majjhima Nikaya*, 1:129, by Peter Harvey, *An Introduction to Buddhism: Teachings, History and Practices*, Cambridge, 1995, p.210
4. Sukthankar, *The Meaning of the Mahabharata*, p.101.
5. From *Digha Nikaya*, ibid., p.112.
6. See Uma Chakravarti, *The Social Dimensions of Early Buddhism*, Oxford, Delhi, 1987, pp.45-46.
7. A.L. Basham in Ainslie Embree (ed.), *Sources of Indian Tradition*, vol. 1, p.129.
8. In *An Introduction to Buddhism: Teachings, History and Practices*, Peter Harvey supplies a country-wise break-up and estimates that in 1985 Asia had 495 million Buddhists.
9. See Peter Harvey, *An Introduction to Buddhism*, p.14.
10. See ibid., p.13.
11. A.L. Basham in Embree (ed.), *Sources of Indian Tradition*, Columbia, 1988, 1:57.
12. The author is grateful for information provided by Dr L.M. Singhvi, Mr L.C. Jain, Mr Gopilal Amar, and Mrs Raj K. Mahadevan.
13. Eisenstadt (ed.), *Orthodoxy, Heterodoxy, and Dissent in India*, Mouton, New York, 1984, p.1.
14. I am grateful to Rakesh Chaubey, my research assistant, for this theoretical point and for providing the reference.
15. In 'Revolution and Counter-Revolution in Ancient India,' *Dr Babasaheb Ambedkar: Writings and Speeches*, Government of Maharashtra, Bombay, 1987, 3:275.
16. See Peter Harvey, *An Introduction to Buddhism*, p.9.
17. *The Gazetteer of India*, New Delhi, 1990, 2:179.
18. See *The Gazetteer of India*, New Delhi, 1990, p.179.
19. Radhakrishnan, *Indian Philosophy*, 1:481 fn.
20. Ibid., p.482
21. These are also assumptions that historical research could test.
22. See, for example, the chapter by Peter Della Santina, 'Conceptions of Dharma in the Sramanical and Brahmanical traditions: Buddhism and the Mahabharata,' in Matilal (ed.), *Moral Dilemmas in the Mahabharata*, Simla, 1989.
23. Ibid., p.97.
24. Donald W. Shriver, Jr., *An Ethic for Enemies: Forgiveness in Politics*, Oxford, New York, 1995, pp.7-9.
25. Ibid., pp.30-31.

26. Kamenetz in Simon Wiesenthal, *The Sunflower: On the Possibilities and Limits of Forgiveness*, Schocken, New York, 1997, p.181.
27. Cynthia Ozick's comment in Simon Wiesenthal, *The Sunflower*, pp.216-17.
28. Ibid., p.247.
29. Quoted in Shriver, ibid., p.34.
30. Translation by R.S. Pandit, Sahitya Akademi, New Delhi, 1968, p.20.
31. From the text as given in Romila Thapar, *Asoka and the Decline of the Mauryas*, Oxford, New Delhi, 1990, pp.255-56.
32. Thapar, *Asoka*, p.29 and p.36.
33. Ibid., pp.257-59.
34. Ibid., pp.133-36.
35. Ibid., p.216.
36. Quoted in B.N. Barua, *Asoka and his Inscriptions*, New Age, Calcutta, 1946, p.347.
37. Nirad Chaudhuri is one of them.
38. B.N. Barua, *Asoka and his Inscriptions*.
39. Ibid., p.294.
40. *Mahavamsa*, 1912 edition, XXV, pp.101-03, quoted by Gananath Obeyesekere in Douglas Allen (ed.), *Religion and Political Conflict in South Asia*, Greenwood, Westport, Connecticut, 1992, p.136.
41. Quoted by Obeyesekere, ibid., p 136.
42. Quoted in ibid., p.137
43. Ibid., p.140.
44. Ibid., p.153.
45. Ibid., p.158.
46. See *The Gazetteer of India: History and Culture*, p.179.
47. See editor's introduction and article by P.D. Santina in B.K. Matilal (ed.), *Moral Dilemmas in the Mahabharata*, Delhi, 1989, p.ix and p.100.
48. Santina in Matilal (ed.), *Moral Dilemmas in the Mahabharata*, Delhi, 1989, p.100.
49. Sukla Das, *Socio-Economic Life of Northern India: c. A.D. 550 to 650*, Abhinav, New Delhi, 1980, p.2.
50. Quotation from S.N. Das Gupta and S.K. De, *History of Sanskrit Literature*, in Sukla Das, *Socio-Economic Life of Northern India: c. A.D. 550 to A.D. 650*, Abhinav, New Delhi, 1980, p.6.
51. Bana's remarks in *Kadambari* quoted in Rajendra Prasad, *Politico-Geographical Analysis of the Arthasastra*, Inter-India Publications, New Delhi, 1989, pp.43-44.
52. Harvey, *An Introduction to Buddhism*, p.90.
53. Ibid., p.140.
54. Hirakawa Akira, *A History of Indian Buddhism: From Sakyamuni to Early Mahayana*, University of Hawaii, 1990, p.5.

55. Ibid., p.6.
56. Nilakanta Sastri, *A History of South India*, Oxford, Delhi, 1997, p.366-67.
57. Basham in *Sources of Indian Tradition*, 1:51.
58. David Ludden in *Peasant History in South India*, p.204, quoted by Gail Omvedt, 'Hinduism, Social Inequality and the State,' in Douglas Allen (ed.), *Religion and Political Conflict in South Asia*, p.24.
59. Ibid.
60. Poem by Sambandar in *Hymns of the Tamil Saivite Saints*, The Heritage of India Series, Association Press, Calcutta, 1921, pp.27-29.
61. Kalhana's *Rajatarangini*, translated by R.S. Pandit, Sahitya Akademi, New Delhi, 1968, p.352.

3. The Charge of Islam: Rage, Reflection and Coexistence

1. Quoted in Khushwant Singh (tr.), *Iqbal's Jawab-i-Shikwa*.
2. *The Gazetteer of India*, 2:153.
3. Thapar, *Asoka*, p.211.
4. Sheldon Pollock, 'Ramayana and Political Imagination in India,' *The Journal of Asian Studies* # 52, May 1993 (pp.261-97), p.263.
5. Ibid., p.263.
6. Ibid., p.272.
7. Ibid., p.273.
8. Ibid., p.275.
9. Ibid., p.276.
10. See R.S. Pandit's translation into English, *Rajatarangini*, Sahitya Akademi, New Delhi, 1968, p.750.
11. Ibid., p.751.
12. Pollock, pp.276-77.
13. Quoted in ibid., p.277.
14. Ibid., p.274 fn.
15. Ibid., p.272 fn.
16. Ibid., p.267.
17. Ibid., p.274.
18. Ibid., p.276 fn.
19. Quoted by R.S. Pandit in his translation of *Rajatarangini*, p.751 fn.
20. Quoted in Hafeez Malik, *Moslem Nationalism in India and Pakistan*, Public Affairs Press, Washington DC, 1963, p.12.
21. T.S. Rukmani citing the epic's Shantiparva in Matilal (ed.), *Moral Dilemmas in the Mahabharata* p.29.
22. Zoe Ansari (ed.), *Life, Times and Works of Amir Khusrau Dehlavi*, Seventh Centenary National Amir Khusrau Society, n.d., p.295.

23. See Uma Chakravarti, *Rewriting History: The Life and Times of Pandita Ramabai*, Kali for Women, New Delhi, 1998, pp.18-19.
24. See Wilhelm Halbfass, *India and Europe*, SUNY, Albany, 1988, p.32.
25. Quoted from M.K. Gandhi, *The Bhagavad Gita*, Orient, Delhi, 1996, pp.11-12.
26. Quoted in J.P.S. Uberoi, *Religion, Civil Society and the State: A Study of Sikhism*, Oxford, New Delhi, 1996, pp.89-90.
27. Arendt quoted by Shriver, *An Ethic for Enemies*, p.35.
28. Ibid., p.35.
29. Arthur Bryant, *The Story of England: Makers of the Realm*, Collins, London, 1953.
30. Ibid., p.22.
31. W.H. McLeod, *The Evolution of the Sikh Community*, Oxford, New Delhi, 1996, Ch. 4.
32. S.M. Burke, *Akbar: The Greatest Mogul*, Munshiram Manoharlal, Delhi, 1989, p.39.
33. Ibid., p.40.
34. Ibid., p.57.
35. *The Gazetteer of India*, p.317.
36. Vincent Smith and Wolseley Haig quoted in Burke, *Akbar*, p.217.
37. Ibid., p.217.
38. Burke, *Akbar*, p.48.
39. Ibid., p.48.
40. Ibid., p.127.
41. Ibid., p.32.
42. Quoted in ibid., p.92.
43. Ibid., p.91.
44. Ibid., p.92-93
45. Ibid., p.65.
46. Ibid., p.127-28.
47. Ibid., p.223.
48. Ibid., p.102.
49. Father Pierre du Jarric quoted in Burke, *Akbar*, p.231.
50. Paper by Mubarak Ali at a seminar on Akbar and his Age organized by the Indian Council of Historical Research, Sahitya Akademi, New Delhi, October 15-17, 1992.
51. Ibid.
52. Burke, *Akbar*, p.223.

4. Empire and Conscience: Mughals, Sikhs and Marathas

1. J.P.S. Uberoi, *Religion, Civil Society and the State*, pp.90-91. A statement like this from Jahangir has however not prevented some Muslim writers

from rejecting the story of the Guru's execution. Thus Muhammad Akbar, in *The Punjab under the Mughals* (Idarah-i-Adabiyat-i-Dilli, 1974) writes (p.192) that Guru Arjan went to the river Ravi, 'took his bath, sat down on the bank, read his *Japji* and after giving instructions to his followers expired.'

2. Ibid., p.93.
3. Narang in his *Transformation of Sikhism*, New Book Society of India, New Delhi, 1960, quoted in Madan, *Modern Myths, Locked Minds*, Oxford, New Delhi, 1997, p.52.
4. Madan, ibid, p.52.
5. From Madan, *Modern Myths, Locked Minds*, p.53.
6. Uberoi, *Religion, Civil Society and the State*, p.97.
7. See Madan, *Modern Myths, Locked Minds*, pp.126-27.
8. See Wilhelm Halbfass, *India and Europe: An Essay in Understanding*, pp.33-34.
9. Uberoi, *Religion, Civil Society and the State*, p.92.
10. Quoted in Gopal Gandhi, *Dara Shukoh: A Play*, Banyan, New Delhi, 1993, p.202.
11. Ibid., pp.178-79.
12. Madan, *Modern Myths, Locked Minds*, p.127.
13. See *The Gazetteer of India*, Publications Division, New Delhi, 1990 edition, 2:345.
14. Quotation from Indubhushan Banerjee's *Evolution of the Khalsa* in Harbans Singh, *Guru Tegh Bahadur*, Manohar, New Delhi, 1994, p.87.
15. Quotations from Harbans Singh, *Guru Gobind Singh* (1966: Chandigarh) in Madan, *Modern Myths, Locked Minds*, p.55.
16. Harbans Singh in *Guru Tegh Bahadur*, p.89.
17. See Madan, *Modern Myths, Locked Minds*, p.56.
18. W.H. McLeod, *The Evolution of the Sikh Community*, p.11.
19. Uberoi, *Religion, Civil Society and the State*, p.73.
20. Quoted in Madan, *Modern Myths, Locked Minds*, p.56.
21. Ibid., p.87
22. Gopal Singh, *Guru Gobind Singh*, National Book Trust, New Delhi, Reprinted 1992, p.38.
23. Ibid., p.39.
24. Ibid., p.40
25. See Uberoi, *Religion, Civil Society and the State*, p.98, and Gopal Singh, *Guru Gobind Singh*, pp.38-39 fn.
26. Gopal Singh, *Guru Gobind Singh*, pp.38-39 fn.
27. M. Mujeeb, *Dr Zakir Husain*, National Book Trust, New Delhi, 1972, p.240
28. Gopal Singh, *Guru Gobind Singh*, pp.41-42.

29. Syad Muhammad Latif, *History of the Panjab*, 1889, reprinted in 1989 by Kalyani, New Delhi/Ludhiana, pp.267-68.

30. Quoted in Hafeez Malik, *Moslem Nationalism in India and Pakistan*, Public Affairs Press, Washington DC, 1963, p.86. Some Sikh writers claim that Guru Gobind Singh's *Zafarnama* helped produce Aurangzeb's contrition. See Gopal Singh, *Guru Gobind Singh*, p.42 fn.

31. Assessment and view of I.H. Qureshi cited by Uberoi in *Religion, Civil Society and the State*, p.87 and p.77.

32. See Uberoi, *Religion, Civil Society and the State*, p.98

33. Ibid., pp.76-77.

34. Ibid., p.99.

35. Latif, *History of the Panjab*, p.268.

36. Gopal Singh, *Guru Gobind Singh*, pp.47-48.

37. Ibid., pp.50-51.

38. Gopal Singh, *Guru Gobind Singh*, p.52 fn.   Latif gives a different account of the Guru's death in *History of the Panjab*, pp.268-69.

39. Quoted by Balkrishna Govind Gokhale, 'Hindu Responses to the Muslim Presence in Maharashtra,' in Yohann Friedmann (ed.), *Islam in Asia*, The Magnus Press, The Hebrew University, Jerusalem, 1984, 1:155.

40. Ibid., p.156.

41. Ibid., p.156.

42. See Uma Chakravarti, *Rewriting History*, p.11.

43. Ibid., p.12.

44. Gokhale, *Hindu Responses to the Muslim Presence in Maharashtra*, p.149.

45. Ibid., p.156.

47. Ibid., p.157.

46. Gail Omvedt, 'Hinduism, Social Inequality and the State,' in Douglas Allen (ed.), *Religion and Political Conflict in South Asia*, p.24.

48. Translated by John Hoyland. In *Village Songs of Western India*, Prinit Press, Dublin, 1992, p.53.

49. Passages from quotations of letter in Hafeez Malik, *Moslem Nationalism in India and Pakistan*, p.295, and in Gokhale, *Hindu Responses*, p.158.

50. Quoted in Gokhale, *Hindu Responses*, p.169.

51. Gail Omvedt, citing Rosalind O'Hanlon, *Caste, Conflict and Ideology: Mahatma Jotiba Phule and Low-Caste Social Protest in Nineteenth Century Western India* (Cambridge University Press, 1988), in *Dalit Vision*, Orient Longman, New Delhi, 1995, p.9.

52. Gokhale, *Hindu Responses*, p.159.

53. Ibid., pp.161-62.

54. *The Gazetteer of India*, Publications Division, 2:340.

55. Ibid., p.340.

56. Muhammad Akbar, *The Punjab Under the Mughals*, Idarah-i-Adabiyat-i-Dilli, 1974, p.207.
57. Gokhale, *Hindu Responses*, p.160.
58. Ibid., p.162.
59. Ibid., p.161.
60. Quoted in Uma Chakravarti, *Rewriting History*, p.4.
61. See ibid., p.5 and p.7.
62. *The Gazetter of India*, p.343.
63. Madan, *Modern Myths, Locked Minds*, p.129.
64. See ibid., p.129.
65. Latif, *History of the Panjab*, pp.274-75.
66. See Swami Rama, *Celestial Song/Gobind Geet*, Himalayan International Institute, Honesdale, Pennsylvania, 1980. Like the Bhagavad Gita, *Gobind Geet* is presented in eighteen chapters.
67. McLeod, *The Evolution of the Sikh Community*, pp.16-17.
68. Quoted in Uberoi, *Religion, Civil Society and the State*, p.97.
69. McLeod, *Evolution of the Sikh Community*, p.17.
70. J.S. Grewal, *The New Cambridge History of India: The Sikhs of the Punjab*, Orient Longman, New Delhi, 1990, p.89 and p.91.
71. Ibid., p.91.
72. McLeod, *Evolution of the Sikh Community*, p.17.
73. H.G. Rawlinson, *A Concise History of the Indian People*, Oxford, Madras, 1958, pp.226-27.
74. *The Gazetteer of India*, p.343.
75. Bhudeb Mukhopadhyay, 1876, quoted in Partha Chatterjee, *The Nation and its Fragments*, pp.110-11.

5. Enter Britain: Humiliation, Dazzlement and Trust

1. Sir Penderel Moon, *The British Conquest and Dominion of India*, Duckworth, London, 1989.
2. Chatterjee, *The Nation and its Fragments*, Oxford, New Delhi, 1997, pp. 77-85.
3. From ibid., p.88-89.
4. Quoted in ibid., p.91.
5. Quoted in Wilhelm Halbfass, *India and Europe: An Essay in Understanding*, p.204.
6. Ibid., p.203.
7. Partha Chatterjee, *The Nation and its Fragments*, Oxford, New Delhi, p.54.
8. From translation of Roy by D.H. Killingley quoted in Halbfass, *India and Europe*, p.206.

9. Halbfass, *India and Europe*, p.215.
10. Ranajit Guha, *An Indian Historiography of India: A Nineteenth-Century Agenda and its Implications*, pp.58-59.
11. Tapan Raychaudhuri, *Three Views of Europe from Nineteenth Century Bengal*, p.19
12. See Guha, *An Indian Historiography*, p.58.
13. Quoted in ibid., p.38.
14. Quoted in Ibid., p.53.
15. Quoted in Christopher Hibbert, *The Great Mutiny: India 1857*, Penguin, London, 1980, p.124.
16. Moon, *The British Conquest*, pp.609-10.
17. Chatterjee, *The Nation and its Fragments*, pp.56-57.
18. Quoted in Raychaudhuri, *Three Views of Europe*, p.21.
19. Bankim quoted in Raychaudhuri, *Three Views*, pp.14-15.
20. Bankim paraphrased in Raychaudhuri, *Three Views*, p.18.
21. Tanika Sarkar, 'Imagining Hindurashtra,' in David Ludden (ed.), *Contesting the Nation: Religion, Community, and the Politics of Democracy in India*, University of Pennsylvania Press, Philadelphia, 1996.
22. Bankim paraphrased in Raychaudhuri, *Three Views*, p.15.
23. Ranajit Guha, *An Indian Historiography*, pp.65-66.
24. Bankim quoted or paraphrased in Raychaudhuri, *Three Views*, p.13 and p.22.
25. Quoted in Raychaudhuri, *Three Views*, p.19.
26. Quoted in Raychaudhuri, *Three Views*, p.21.
27. Chatterjee, *The Nation and its Fragments*, p.70.
28. Quoted in Partha Chatterjee, *The Nation and its Fragments*, p.48.
29. Quoted in ibid., p.51.
30. From *Kathamrita*, quoted in Chatterjee, *The Nation and its Fragments*, p.58.
31. See Partha Chatterjee, *The Nation and its Fragments*, p.50.
32. Vivekananda quoted or paraphrased in Raychaudhuri, *Three Views*, pp.37-38.
33. Ibid., p.14.
34. Ibid., p.40.
35. Raychaudhuri, *Three Views*, p.13 and p.40.
36. Quoted in Partha Chatterjee, *The Nation and its Fragments*, p.39.
37. Quoted in ibid., p.45.
38. Chatterjee, *The Nation and its Fragments*, p.55.
39. Bhudev's views described in Tapan Raychaudhuri, *Three Views*, pp.34-35.
40. Ibid., p.36.
41. Ibid., p.35.
42. Ranajit Guha, *An Indian Historiography*, pp.53-54.

43. Ibid., p.54.
44. Quoted in Hafeez Malik, *Sir Sayyid Ahmad Khan*, Columbia, New York, 1980, p.58.
45. S.M. Ikram, *Modern Muslim India*, Institute of Islamic Culture, Lahore, p.28.
46. Quoted in G.F.I. Graham, *The Life and Work of Sir Syed Ahmed Khan*, London, 1885, Reprint, pp.125-26.
47. Quoted in Richard Symonds, *The Making of Pakistan*, Faber and Faber, London, 1950, p.35
48. From Chatterjee, *The Nation and its Fragments*, pp.106-07.
49. Quoted in Uma Chakravarti, *Rewriting History*, p.19.
50. Ibid., p.23.
51. Ibid., p.19.
52. Ibid., p.112, fn 87.
53. Ibid., pp.70-71.
54. Phule quoted in Gail Omvedt, *Dalit Vision*, Orient Longman, New Delhi, 1995, pp.17-18.
55. M.S. Gore, *Non-Brahmin Movement in Maharashtra*, Segment, New Delhi, 1989.
56. Chakravarti, *Rewriting History*, p.71.
57. Quoted in Uma Chakravarti, *Rewriting History*, p.308.
58. Ibid., p.309.
59. Ibid., p.319.
60. Ibid., p.319.
61. Ibid., p.320.
62. Chakravarti, *Rewriting History*, p.248.
63. Bankim paraphrased in Guha, *An Indian Historiography* p.59.
64. Ibid. See also p.62.
65. See Partha Chatterjee, *The Nation and its Fragments*, p.47.
66. Raychaudhuri, *Three Views*, p.39.
67. Ibid., pp.11-12.
68. Ibid., p.34.
69. Ibid., p.7.
70. Chatterjee, *The Nation and its Fragments*, p.93.
71. See Uma Chakravarti, *Rewriting History*, p.274.
72. See *The Gazetteer of India*, New Delhi, 1990, 2:148.

6. *To Crush and Conciliate: The Raj and the Sikhs*

1. Moon, *The British Conquest and Dominion of India*, Duckworth, London, 1989, p.364
2. Ibid., p.365.
3. J.S. Grewal, *The Sikhs of the Punjab*, p.103.

4. Ibid., p.113.
5. Moon, *The British Conquest*, p.590.
6. Khushwant Singh, *How the Sikhs Lost their Kingdom*, UBS Publishers, New Delhi, 1996, p.12.
7. Grewal, *The Sikhs of the Punjab*, p.93.
8. Ibid., p.114.
9. Author's observation in Lahore, February 1994.
10. Khushwant Singh, *How the Sikhs Lost their Kingdom*, p.14.
11. Quoted in Tapan Raychaudhuri, *Three Views*, p.64.
12. From Moon, *The British Conquest*, p.593.
13. Ibid., p.593.
14. Khushwant Singh, *How the Sikhs lost their Kingdom*, p.66.
15. Ibid.
16. Moon, *The British Conquest*, p.593.
17. Khushwant Singh, *How the Sikhs*, p.69.
18. Grewal, *The Sikhs of the Punjab*, p.122.
19. Moon, *The British Conquest*, p.594.
20. Ibid., p.595.
21. Grewal, *The Sikhs of the Punjab*, p.123.
22. Khushwant Singh, *How the Sikhs Lost their Kingdom*, p.109.
23. Moon, *The British Conquest*, p.596.
24. Ibid., p.599.
25. Ibid., p.600.
26. Ibid., p.600.
27. Ibid., p.600.
28. Quoted in ibid., p.600.
29. Grewal, *The Sikhs of the Punjab*, p.124.
30. Moon, *The British Conquest*, p.606.
31. Ibid., p.609.
32. Ibid., p.610.
33. Andrew Major, *Return to Empire: Punjab Under the Sikhs and British in the Mid-Nineteenth Century*, Sterling, New Delhi, 1996, p.105.
34. Moon, *The British Conquest*, p.612.
35. Quoted in Moon, *The British Conquest*, p.614.
36. Quoted in Khushwant Singh, *How the Sikhs Lost their Kingdom*, p.159.
37. Ibid., p.614.
38. Khushwant Singh, *How the Sikhs Lost their Kingdom*, p.161.
39. Ibid., p.162.
40. From Andrew Major, *Return to Empire: Punjab under the Sikhs and British in the Mid-Nineteenth Century*, Sterling, New Delhi, 1996, p.110.
41. See Khushwant Singh, *How the Sikhs Lost their Kingdom*, pp.162-63.
42. Ibid., p.163.
43. Major, *Return to Empire*, p.112-13.

44. See Khushwant Singh, *How the Sikhs*, p.165, and Moon, *The British Conquest*, p.615.
45. Moon, *The British Conquest*, p.617.
46. Thackwell's words quoted in Khushwant Singh, *How the Sikhs Lost their Kingdom*, p.177.
47. Major, *Return to Empire*, p.116.
48. Quoted in ibid., p.116.
49. Major, *Return to Empire*, p.127.
50. Quoted in ibid., p.130.
51. See Major, *Return to Empire*, p.130.
52. Ibid., p.130.
53. Quoted in ibid., p.126.
54. Quoted in ibid., p.139.
55. See Moon, *The British Conquest*, p.619.
56. Quoted in Moon, *The British Conquest*, p.620.
57. Quoted in Major, *Return to Empire*, p.155.
58. Grewal, *The Sikhs of the Punjab*, p.128.
59. Major, *Return to Empire*, p.161.
60. From Moon, *The British Conquest*, p.624.
61. Quoted in Major, *Return to Empire*, p.183.
62. Major, *Return to Empire*, p.188.
63. Quoted in ibid., p.188.
64. Quoted in ibid., p.186.

7. The 1857 Trauma and its Meaning

1. Hibbert, *The Great Mutiny: India 1857*, Penguin, London, 1980, p.49.
2. Quotation from T.R. Metcalf in Rudrangshsu Mukherjee, *Awadh in Revolt: 1857-58*, Oxford, New Delhi, 1984, p.33.
3. Ibid., p.35.
4. Ibid., p.18.
5. Ibid., pp.23-24.
6. Sleeman quoted in Hibbert, *The Great Mutiny*, p.218.
7. Hibbert, *The Great Mutiny*, p.69.
8. See Hibbert, *The Great Mutiny*, pp.36-39; S.N. Sen, *Eighteen-Fiftyseven*, New Delhi, 1958; Wayne Broehl, *Crisis of the Raj*, 1986, p.43.
9. Mukherjee, *Awadh in Revolt*, p.65.
10. Statement by Ranjit Singh Bissein in secret British files quoted in Mukherjee, *Awadh in Revolt*, p.67.
11. Ibid., p.72.
12. Quoted in Mukherjee, *Awadh in Revolt*, p.81.
13. Hibbert, *The Great Mutiny*, p.24.

14. Quoted in ibid., p.165.
15. Ibid.
16. Letter to Lord Granville quoted in Hibbert, *The Great Mutiny*, pp.166-67.
17. Quoted in Hibbert, *The Great Mutiny*, p.167.
18. Hibbert, *The Great Mutiny*, p.172.
19. Ibid., p.175.
20. Quoted in ibid., p.176.
21. Hibbert, *The Great Mutiny*, p.177.
22. Quoted in ibid., p.180.
23. Hibbert, *The Great Mutiny*, p.189.
24. G.O. Trevelyan, *Cawnpore*, 1865, republished by the Empire Book Association, Brentwood, 1986, p.115.
25. See Hibbert, *The Great Mutiny*, p.196.
26. See ibid., p.209.
27. Ibid., p.210.
28. Ibid., p.211.
29. Quoted in ibid., p.212.
30. Hibbert, *The Great Mutiny*, p.214.
31. Ibid., p.212.
32. Ibid., p.237.
33. Communication to Govt. of India from Forsyth quoted in Mukherjee, *Awadh in Revolt*, p.166.
34. Hibbert, *The Great Mutiny*, p.252.
35. Ibid., p.341.
36. Ibid., p.341.
37. Quoted in ibid., p.366.
38. Ibid.
39. Hibbert, *The Great Mutiny*, p.361.
40. Ibid., p.47.
41. Ibid., p.363.
42. Ibid., p.342.
43. Ibid., p.211.
44. Ibid., p.123.
45. Quoted in ibid., p.127.
46. Pemble John, *The Raj, the Indian Mutiny and the Kingdom of Oudh: 1801-1859*, Oxford, New Delhi, 1977, p.180.
47. Quoted in Wayne G. Broehl, Jr., *Crisis of the Raj: The Revolt of 1857 Through British Lieutenants' Eyes*, Published for Dartmouth College by University Press of New England, Hanover and London, 1986, p.283.
48. Quoted in Hibbert, *The Great Mutiny*, p.293.
49. See Hibbert, *The Great Mutiny*, pp.277-9.
50. Ibid., p.309.

51. Moon, *The British Conquest*, p.730.
52. Quoted in Wayne Broehl, *Crisis of the Raj*, p.113.
53. Quoted in Hibbert, *The Great Mutiny*, p.316.
54. Moon, *The British Conquest*, p.731.
55. Quoted in Hafeez Malik, *Sir Sayyid Ahmad Khan*, p.79.
56. Quoted in ibid., p.731
57. Ibid.
58. Mukherjee, *Awadh in Revolt*, p.174.
59. Hibbert, *The Great Mutiny*, p.372.
60. Trevelyan, *Cawnpore*, p.165.
61. See, e.g., Moon, *The British Conquest*, p.715.
62. Hibbert, *The Great Mutiny*, p.378.
63. Quoted in ibid, p.379.
64. Ibid.
65. Ibid., p.382.
66. Hibbert, *The Great Mutiny*, p.385.
67. Ibid., p.386.
68. Pemble, *The Raj, the Indian Mutiny and the Kingdom of Oudh*, p.248.
69. Quoted in Mukherjee, *Awadh in Revolt*, p.149.
70. Trevelyan, *Cawnpore*, p.14.
71. See S.N. Sen, *Eighteen Fiftyseven*, New Delhi, 1958, pp.410-11.
72. Ranajit Guha, *An Indian Historiography*, p.55.
73. See Wayne Broehl, *Crisis of the Raj*, p.159.
74. Ibid., p.47.
75. Trevelyan, *Cawnpore*, p.51.
76. See Trevelyan, *Cawnpore*, p.15, and Wayne Broehl, *Crisis of the Raj*, 159.
77. Mukherjee quotes in his *Awadh in Revolt*, p.172, from C. Ball, *History of the Indian Mutiny*, 2:550.
78. See Mukherjee, *Awadh in Revolt*, p.172.
79. Quoted in Wayne Broehl, *Crisis of the Raj*, p.215.
80. Hibbert, *The Great Mutiny*, p.390.
81. From H.G. Rawlinson, *A Concise History of India*, pp.336-37, and Hibbert, *The Great Mutiny*, p.390.
82. Pemble, *The Raj, the Indian Mutiny and the Kingdom of Oudh*, pp.247-48.
83. Ibid., p.248.
84. Quoted in Hibbert, *The Great Mutiny*, pp.389-91.
85. Malik, *Sir Sayyid Ahmad*, p.80.
86. Hibbert, *The Great Mutiny*, p.215.
87. Quoted in William Wedderburn, *Allan Octavian Hume: Father of the Indian National Congress*, T. Fisher Unwin, London, 1913, p.47.

8. Freedom and Reconciliation? Gandhi's Large Bid

1. See M.K. Gandhi, *Autobiography*, Navajivan, 1927, first edition, p.202.
2. *Indian Opinion* (Gujarati), 18.7.08, in *Collected Works*, 8:373-74; quoted in M.K. Gandhi, *Ruskin's Unto This Last: A Paraphrase*, reprinted, Navajivan, Ahmedabad, 1994, p.43.
3. See Shahid Amin, *Event, Metaphor, Memory*, Oxford, New Delhi, 1995, an instructive study focusing on Chauri Chaura and the character and legacy of the event.
4. Churchill quoted in Madhu Limaye, *Prime Movers*, Radiant, New Delhi, 1985, p.34.
5. Mahadev Desai, *Day-to-day with Gandhi*, Navajivan, Ahmedabad, 1:56-57.
6. Joseph J. Doke, *An Indian Patriot in South Africa*, Reprint, Publications Division, New Delhi, 1967, p.44.
7. See G.D. Birla, *A Talk on Bapu*, Sangeet Kala Mandir, Calcutta, 24.12.81.
8. In M.M. Juneja, *The Mahatma and the Millionaire*, Hissar, 1993, pp.201-03.
9. See Birla's contribution in Shukla (ed.), *Incidents in Gandhiji's Life*, Vora, Bombay, 1949, pp.26ff. and *Collected Works*, 76:63.
10. Lord Moran, *Winston Churchill*, Constable, London, 1966, p.52.
11. Moon (ed.), *Wavell: The Viceroy's Journal*, p.78.
12. Ibid., p.120 and p.168.
13. See Rajmohan Gandhi, *Patel: A Life*, Navajivan, Ahmedabad, 1990, p.232; and Rajmohan Gandhi, *Rajaji: A Life*, Penguin, New Delhi, 1997, p.66.
14. Entry dated 27.3.32 in Mahadev Desai, *The Diary of Mahadev Desai*, Navajivan, Ahmedabad.
15. Entry of 6.7.32, ibid.
16. Quoted in Mahadev Desai, *Day-to-day with Gandhi*, 2:323-36.
17. K.M. Munshi, *Pilgrimage to Freedom*, Bhavan, Bombay, 1967, pp.16-17.
18. Penderel Moon (ed.), *Wavell: A Viceroy's Journal*, Oxford, 1973, p.439 and p.314.
19. Quoted in Francis Watson, *Talking of Gandhiji*, Orient Longman, Calcutta, 1957, p.37.
20. Sumit Sarkar, *Modern India: 1885-1947*, Macmillan, New Delhi, 1996, p.178.
21. Mahadev Desai, *Day-to-day with Gandhi*, 1:56-57.
22. Manu Gandhi, *Ekla Chalo Re*, Navajivan, Ahmedabad, 1957, p.65.
23. Mahadev Desai, *The Diary of Mahadev Desai*, vol. 1, 1953.
24. Amiya Chakravarty quoted in Gene Sharp, *Gandhi Wields the Weapon of Moral Power*, pp.259-60.

25. See 89: 124-54, and Dalton, 'Gandhi During Partition,' in Philips and Wainwright, *The Partition of India*, pp.234-38.
26. Brij Krishna, *Gandhiji ki Dilli Diary*, Delhi, 1970, 3:287; and Nehru to Patel, 27.10.48, in SPC 7, p.672.
27. Jehangir Patel and Marjorie Sykes, *Gandhi: His Gift of the Fight*, Friends Rural Centre, Rasulia, 1987, p.188.
28. Account of fast from 90: 408-54 and Sharp, *Gandhi Wields the Weapon of Moral Power*.
29. Patel and Sykes, *Gandhi: His Gift of the Fight*, p.187.
30. Pyarelal, *The Epic Fast*, Navajivan, Ahmedabad, 1932.
31. [G. and C., p.155]
32. Omvedt, pp.151-52.
33. Entry of 12.3.33 in Mahadev Desai, *The Diary of Mahadev Desai*, vol. 1.
34. Entry of 16.2.33, ibid.
35. Quoted in Ambedkar, *Writings and Speeches*, Bombay, vol. 2.
36. Pyarelal, *The Epic Fast*, p.303.
37. Moon, *Wavell: A Viceroy's Journal*, p.425.
38. Quotes relating to the fast from Pyarelal, *The Epic Fast*.
39. Ibid.
40. In dedication to Mahatma Jotiba Phule in Ambedkar, '*Who Were the Shudras?*'
41. Tibor Mende, *Conversations with Nehru*, Wilco, Bombay, 1958, pp.24-27.
42. Gandhi's 1936 remark quoted in Dhananjay Keer, *Dr Ambedkar*, Popular, Bombay, 1954, p.255.
43. Ibid., p.259.
44. Ibid., p.498.
45. S. Ramakrishnan, who heard the remark, to author.
46. G. Ramachandran, *Thoughts and Talks*, Madurai, 1964, p.179.
47. Khairmode quoted in M.S. Gore, *The Social Context of an Ideology: Ambedkar's Political and Social Thought*, Sage, New Delhi, 1993, pp. 180-81.
48. Durga Das (ed.), *Sardar Patel's Correspondence*, Navajivan, Ahmedabad, 6:302.
49. From Kancha Ilaiah, *Why I am not a Hindu*, Samya, Calcutta, 1996.

9. *Why Partition Occurred and the Wounds of 1947*

1. H.V. Seshadri, *The Tragic Story of Partition*, Bangalore, 1982, p.115.
2. See, for instance, Mansergh and Lumby (ed.), *The Transfer of Power* (12 vols.), London, 1970-83; Pyarelal, *Mahatma Gandhi: The Last Phase*, (2 vols.), Ahmedabad, 1956; V.P. Menon, *The Transfer of Power in India*,

1957; Chaudhari Muhammad Ali, *The Emergence of Pakistan*, 1967; Khaliquzzaman, *Pathway to Pakistan*, Lahore, 1961; Bipan Chandra, *India's Struggle for Independence*, 1987; Philips and Wainwright, *The Partition of India*, London, 1970; Mushirul Hasan (ed.), *India's Partition*, 1995; and Rajmohan Gandhi, *The Good Boatman: A Portrait of Gandhi*, 1995, chapter nine.

3. From *Frontline*, Chennai, August 14, 1998.
4. Quoted in S.S. Pirzada, *Foundations of Pakistan: All-India Muslim League Documents*, National Publishing House, Karachi, 1:542-44.
5. Gopal Das Khosla, *Stern Reckoning: A Survey of the Events leading up to and following the Partition of India*, Oxford, New Delhi, 1989 Reprint, p.299.
6. Ibid., pp.289-90.
7. Ibid.
8. Such an episode, affecting a Muslim refugee column in East Punjab, is recorded in Khosla, *Stern Reckoning*, p.289.
9. The civil surgeon, who is not named, quoted in Khosla, *Stern Reckoning*, p.133.
10. Khosla, *Stern Reckoning*, p.133.
11. Ibid., p.127.
12. Account based on, and quotes taken from, Khushdeva Singh, *Love is Stronger than Hate*, Guru Nanak Mission, Patiala, 1973, as reproduced in Mushirul Hasan (ed.), *India Partitioned*, Roli, New Delhi, 1995, pp. 97-121
13. From 'Partition' by Suketu Mehta in *Communalism Combat*, Mumbai, April 1998.
14. Syeda Hameed, *Mainstream*, New Delhi, 4.4.98.

10. Two Cheerful Decades: India 1947-67

1. S. Gopal, *Nehru*, Oxford, New Delhi, 1979, 2:14.
2. Parekh's essay in D.R. Sardesai and Anand Mohan (ed.), *The Legacy of Nehru: A Centennial Assessment*, Promilla, New Delhi, 1992, pp.136-37.
3. G.M. Nandurkar (ed.), *Sardar Patel: Centenary Volumes*, Ahmedabad, 1974-78, 3:122-30.
4. Quoted in M.J. Akbar, *Nehru*, Viking, New Delhi, 1988, p.418.
5. Jinnah's remark to Eric Streiff of the *Neue Zurcher Zeitung* quoted in *Dawn*, Karachi, 12.3.48, and in S.M. Ikram, *Modern Muslim India and the Birth of Pakistan*, Lahore, p.499.
6. Quoted in Rafiq Zakaria (ed.), *A Study of Nehru*, Rupa, 1989, p.92.
7. Figures from Rafiq Zakaria, *The Widening Divide*, Viking, New Delhi, 1995, pp.135 and 163-64.

8. *Indian Express*, New Delhi, 7.2.98.

9. J.C. Heesterman in S.N. Eisenstadt (ed.), *Post-traditional Societies*, Norton, New York 1972, p.110.

10. Letter of 8.12.49 from Nehru to Rajendra Prasad, in Durga Das (ed.), *Sardar Patel's Correspondence*, Navajivan, Ahmedabad, 1973, 8:222.

11. Judith Brown, *Modern India: The Origins of an Asian Democracy*, Oxford, 1994, p.371.

12. Letter from Konda Venkatappayya to Gandhi in *Collected Works*, 90:410.

13. *Collected Works*, 90: 526-28.

14. Letter of 10.9.49 in Akbar, *Nehru*, p.456.

15. Zakaria, *A Study of Nehru*, Rupa, New Delhi, 1989, p.92.

16. For several of these statements see Rajmohan Gandhi, *The Good Boatman*, Viking, New Delhi, 1995, pp.364-88.

17. See S. Gopal, *Nehru*, Oxford, New Delhi, 1979, 2:66.

18. Broadcast of 14.2.48 in S. Gopal (ed.), *Selected Works of Jawaharlal Nehru*, 5:61.

19. Bhattacharjea, *Jayaprakash Narayan: A Political Biography*, Vikas, New Delhi, 1975, p.116.

20. Letter of 1.7.48 from Nehru to G.B. Pant in S. Gopal, *Nehru*, Oxford, New Delhi, 1979, 2:67.

21. Letter from Goray to Vinoba Bhave quoted in Bimal Prasad, *Gandhi, Nehru and JP*, Chanakya, New Delhi, 1985, p.219.

22. S. Gopal in *Nehru*, 2:66.

23. Akbar, *Nehru*, pp.525-26.

24. Ibid., p.532.

25. Letter of 20.1.31 in Nehru, *Glimpses of World History*, Asia, Bombay, 1965 edition, p.37

26. From *Digha Nikaya*, 3.180 ff., in Embree (ed.), *Sources of Indian Tradition*, Columbia, New York, 1:121.

27. This was the assessment of Hangen and of Nehru's biographer, Frank Moraes. See Akbar, *Nehru*, p.531.

28. See Akbar, *Nehru*, p.561, and J.P. Dalvi, *Himayalan Blunder*, Thacker, Bombay, 1969.

29. See Mohammad Ayub Khan, *Friends Not Masters*, Oxford, London, 1967, p.126.

30. Ibid., p.127.

31. Quoted in M.R. Masani, *Against the Tide*, Vikas, New Delhi, 1981, p.186.

32. Sheikh Abdullah, *Flames of the Chinar*, Viking, New Delhi, 1993, p.152.

33. In *Jawaharlal Nehru's Speeches*, Publications Division, New Delhi, 1968, 5:220.

34. Ibid., p.228.

35. L.P. Singh, *Portrait of Lal Bahadur Shastri*, Ravi Dayal, New Delhi, 1996, p.96.
36. Ibid., p.99.
37. Quoted in ibid., p.118.
38. See ibid., p.119.
39. Ibid., p.158.
40. Ibid., p.122.

11. The Unreasonable Other: South Asia After Independence

1. Ishtiaq Ahmed, *State, Nation and Ethnicity in Contemporary South Asia*, Pinter, London, 1996, pp.244-45.
2. Douglas Allen, 'Religious-Political Conflict in Sri Lanka,' in Allen (ed.), *Religion and Political Conflict in South Asia*, p.188
3. Quoted in ibid., p.188.
4. Ibid., pp.188-89.
5. Committee for Rational Development, *Sri Lanka: The Ethnic Conflict—Myths, Realities & Perspectives*, Navrang, New Delhi, 1984, p.45.
6. Ibid., p.44.
7. See chapter by Radhika Coomaraswamy in ibid., p.175.
8. Gananath Obeyesekere in *Sri Lanka: The Ethnic Conflict*, p.72.
9. Quoted by Reggie Siriwardene in his chapter in *Sri Lanka: The Ethnic Conflict*, p.219.
10. From V. Suryanarayan's chapter in N.N. Vohra and J.N. Dixit (ed.), *Religion, Politics and Society in South and Southeast Asia*, Konark, New Delhi, 1998, pp.131-32.
11. Quoted by Kumari Jayewardene in *Sri Lanka: The Ethnic Conflict*, p. 164
12. Gananath Obeyesekere in Allen (ed.), *Religion and Political Conflict in South Asia*, pp.152-53.
13. Committee for Rational Development, *Sri Lanka: The Ethnic Conflict*, p.47.
14. Allen (ed.), *Religion and Political Conflict*, fn. 21, p.20.
15. Kumari Jayewardene, in *Sri Lanka: The Ethnic Conflict*, pp.165-66.
16. Kumari Jayewardene, ibid., p.138.
17. Quoted by Kumari Jayewardene in ibid., p.156.
18. Ibid., p.161.
19. See chapter by Radhika Coomaraswamy in ibid., p.182.
20. Ibid., pp.177-79.
21. Perera in *Sri Lanka: The Ethnic Conflict*, p.99.
22. Ibid., p.98.
23. Quoted by Jehan Perera, ibid., p.104.

24. Quoted in chapter by Kumari Jayawardene, ibid., p.170.
25. Ibid., p.171
26. See Bruce Kapferer's chapter, 'State and Insurrectionary Violence in Sri Lanka' in David E. Apter (ed.), *The Legitimization of Violence*, pp.160-62.
27. Quoted by V. Suryanarayan in Vohra and Dixit (ed.), *Religion, Politics and Society in South and Southeast Asia*, p.129.
28. V. Suryanarayan in ibid., p.130.
29. Radhika Coomaraswamy, in *Sri Lanka: The Ethnic Conflict*, p.180.
30. *Sri Lanka: The Ethnic Conflict*, p.6.
31. Ibid., p.79.
32. Ishtiaq Ahmed, *State, Nation and Ethnicity in Contemporary South Asia*, p.32.
33. Bruce Kapferer in David E. Apter (ed.), *The Legitimization of Violence*, p.160.
34. Ibid., p.184.
35. Ibid., p.180
36. Kingsley de Silva in *Democratisation in South Asia: The First Fifty Years*, p.171.
37. Ishtiaq Ahmed, *State, Nation and Ethnicity in Contemporary South Asia*, p.264.
38. Ishtiaq Ahmed. citing P. Schalk, in ibid., p.264.
39. de Silva's chapter in *Democratisation in South Asia: The First Fifty Years*, p.182.
40. See Shahid Javed Burki's chapter in Craig Baxter and Charles Kennedy (ed.), *Pakistan 1997*, HarperCollins, New Delhi, 1998, p.21.
41. From Burki's chapter in *Pakistan 1997*, pp.19-22.
42. Shahid Javed Burki, *Pakistan: The Continuing Search for Nationhood*, Westview, 1991, p.38.
43. Lawrence Ziring, *Bangladesh From Mujib to Ershad: An Interpretive Study*, Oxford, Karachi, 1992, pp.14-15.
44. In C.M. Naim (ed.), *Iqbal, Jinnah and Pakistan*, Maxwell School of Public Affairs, Syracuse, 1979, pp.250-51.
45. Ziring, *Bangladesh*, p.15.
46. Quoted in Hector Bolitho, *Jinnah*, Greenwood Press, Westport, Connecticut, p.197, and Khaliquzzaman, *Pathway to Pakistan*, Pakistan Longman, Lahore, 1961, p.321.
47. Burki, *Pakistan*, p.51.
48. Ibid., pp.47-48.
49. Feroz Ahmed, *Ethnicity and Politics in Pakistan*, Oxford, Karachi, 1998, p.27.
50. Ziring, *Bangladesh*, p.6.
51. Ziring, *Bangladesh*, pp.16-7.
52. Ibid., p.25.

53. Ibid., p.26.
54. Ibid., p.30.
55. Ibid., p.35.
56. Ibid., p.36.
57. Ibid., p.49.
58. Ibid., p.55.
59. Burki, *Pakistan*, p.60.
60. Ziring, in his *Bangladesh*, p.69, states that Osmani told him this in a personal interview.
61. Ziring, *Bangladesh*, p.70.
62. Ibid., pp.60-61.
63. Ishtiaq Ahmed, *State, Nation, and Ethnicity in Contemporary South Asia*, p.223.
64. Speech of 15 December 1971 in Hamid Jalal and Khalid Hasan (ed.), *Politics of the People: Statements and Speeches by Zulfikar Ali Bhutto*, vol. 3, 1970-71, Pakistan Publications.
65. Ziring, *Bangladesh*, pp.72-3.
66. Ibid., p.72.
67. Burki, *Pakistan*, p.193.
68. Ibid., p.205.
69. Richardson and Herrmann in Richardson and Samarasinghe (ed.), *Democratisation in South Asia*, Kandy, 1998, p.318.
70. Burki, *Pakistan*, p.66.
71. Ibid., p.70.
72. Ibid., p.85.
73. Ibid., p.68.
74. Gardezi's chapter in Douglas Allen (ed.), *Religion and Politics in South Asia*, p.76.
75. Pasha's chapter in Douglas Allen (ed.), *Religion and Political Conflict in South Asia*, Westport, Conn., 1992, p.132, fn. 38, and pp.124-26.
76. Ibid., p.116.
77. Khursheed Kamal Aziz, *The Murder of History: A Critique of History Textbooks Used in Pakistan*, Vanguard, Lahore, 1993, pp.2-4.
78. From foreword by Mohammad A. Qadeer in Feroz Ahmed, *Ethnicity and Politics in Pakistan*, Oxford, Karachi, 1998, p.vii.
79. Richardson and Samarasinghe, *Democratisation in South Asia*, p.330.
80. Ishtiaq Ahmed, *State, Nation and Ethnicity in Contemporary South Asia*, pp.174-75.
81. Feroz Ahmed, *Ethnicity and Politics in Pakistan*, p.273.
82. Mumtaz Ahmad in Baxter and Kennedy (ed.), *Pakistan 1997*, pp.108-18.
83. Ibid., p.118.
84. More than one Pakistani observer to author in 1998-99.
85. See William Maley (ed.), *Fundamentalism Reborn? Afghanistan and the Taliban*, Hurst, London, 1998.

86. Ziring, *Bangladesh*, p.86.
87. Mujib's remark quoted in Muntassir Mamoon and Jayanta Kumar Ray, *Civil Society in Bangladesh: Resilience and Retreat*, Firma KLM, Calcutta, 1996, p.129.
88. Mamoon and Ray, *Civil Society in Bangladesh*, p.95.
89. See ibid., pp.107-29.
90. Ibid., p.98 and p.122.
91. Ziring, *Bangladesh*, p.92.
92. Mamoon and Ray, *Civil Society in Bangladesh*, p.109.
93. Ibid., pp.108-09.
94. Ziring, *Bangladesh*, p.112.
95. Mamoon and Ray, *Civil Society in Bangladesh*, p.127.
96. Ziring, *Bangladesh*, p.125.
97. Ibid., pp.136-37.
98. Mamoon and Ray, *Civil Society in Bangladesh*, p.127.
99. Zafarullah in Habib Zafarullah (ed.), *The Zia Episode in Bangladesh Politics*, South Asian Publishers, New Delhi, 1996, p.171.
100. S.M. Ali's chapter, 'The Demise of Zia,' in Habib Zafarullah (ed.), *The Zia Episode in Bangladesh Politics*, p.160.
101. Rehman Sobhan, *Bangladesh: Problems of Governance*, Konark, New Delhi, 1993, p.36.
102. Quoted in Mamoon and Ray, *Civil Society in Bangladesh*, p.179.
103. Ziring, *Bangladesh*, p.149.
104. Ibid., p.154.
105. Sobhan, *Bangladesh: Problems of Governance*, p.71.
106. Ziring, *Bangladesh*, p.165.
107. Ibid., p.205.
108. Sobhan, *Bangladesh: Problems of Governance*, pp.51-52.
109. Mamoon and Ray, *Civil Society in Bangladesh*, p.265.
110. Sobhan, *Bangladesh: Problems of Governance*, p.58.
111. Mamoon and Ray, *Civil Society in Bangladesh*, pp.287-88.
112. Ziring, *Bangladesh*, p.215.
113. Reproduced from *Mainstream*, 9.3.91, in Sobhan, *Bangladesh*, p.64.
114. *Daily Star*, Dhaka, 11.11.95.
115. Interview to Haroon Habib of *Frontline*, Chennai, Nov. 21-Dec. 4, 1998.
116. *Frontline*, Nov. 21-Dec. 4, 1998.
117. Quoted in Robert Hardgrave, Jr., *India: Government and Politics in a Developing Nation*, Harcourt Brace, 5th edition, 1994, p.245.
118. For a detailed account, see Mark Tully and Satish Jacob, *Amritsar: Mrs Gandhi's Last Battle*, Jonathan Cape, London, 1985, pp.192-217.
119. Hardgrave, *India*, p.156.
120. Ibid., p.157.

121. B.G. Verghese, *India's Northeast Resurgent*, Konark, 1996, p.44.
122. Based on interviews in 1966-69 with B.K. Nehru, Governor of Assam and Meghalaya, B.P. Chaliha, chief minister of Assam, and Stanley Nichols-Roy, minister for industries, Meghalaya.
123. Interview by Saeed Naqvi viewed by author, December 1992.
124. *Panchajanya*, New Delhi, 20.6.99, as translated in *Communalism Combat*, Mumbai, July 1999.
125. Quoted in *Communalism Combat*, Mumbai, July 1999.
126. Ibid.

12. The New Century: Strategies for Reconciliation

1. Quoted in Mira Behn, *The Spirit's Pilgrimage*, Longmans Green, London, 1960, p.143.
2. Quoted in David E. Apter (ed.), *The Legitimization of Violence*, p.1.
3. Edward Said in *The Nation*, May 31, 1999.
4. Major-General Vinod Saighal, *Third Millennium Equipoise*, Lancer, New Delhi, 1998.
5. Article by Balagopal in *Voices*, Bangalore, December 1998.
6. From T.N. Gopalan's review of *Scarred Minds: The Psychological Impact of War on Sri Lankan Tamils*, Sage, 1998, in *Indian Review of Books*, Chennai, March-April 1999.
7. David E. Apter (ed.), *The Legitimization of Violence*, p.1.
8. Quoted by Paul Arthur in Apter (ed.), *The Legitimization of Violence*, p.237.
9. Eliade, quoted by Paul Arthur in Apter (ed.), *The Legitimization of Violence*, p.262.
10. Quoted by Arthur in Apter (ed.), *The Legitimization of Violence*, pp.285-86.
11. Quoted by Arthur in Apter (ed.), *The Legitimization of Violence*, p.244.
12. Laure quoted in Michael Henderson, *The Forgiveness Factor*, Grosvenor, London, 1996, p.26.
13. Quotations from article by Mike Brown in *For A Change*, London, Aug./Sept. 1993.
14. Archbishop Tutu's comment in Simon Wiesenthal, *The Sunflower*, Schocken, New York, 1997, p.268
15. Mack quoted by Arthur in Apter (ed.), *The Legitimization of Violence*, p.284.
16. Romain Gary quoted by Tzevetan Todorov in Wiesenthal (ed.), *The Sunflower*, p.266.
17. Christopher Hollis in Wiesenthal (ed.), *The Sunflower*, p.180.

18. Quoted by Wendy Lambourne in 'ICAR Newsletter', Fall 1998 issue, Institute for Conflict Analysis and Resolution, George Mason University, Fairfax, Virginia.
19. Quoted in *Sunday*, 8-14 February 1998.
20. Ibid.
21. See *India Today*, 27.10.97.
22. Uma Chakravarti in the journal *Aman Panchayat*, New Delhi, May 1999.
23. Statement of 1.4.98, quoted in *Communalism Combat*, Mumbai, April 1998.
24. From 'Ramanuja's Last Discourse' by M.S. Rajajee, *New Swatantra Times*, Hyderabad, Oct. 1998.
25. From the Morning Prayer in *Ashram Bhajanavali*, Navajivan, Ahmedabad, 1987 edition, p.9. Translated from the Hindi by the author.

Bibliography

Abdullah, Sheikh *Flames of the Chinar: An Autobiography*, tr. Khushwant Singh, Viking, New Delhi, 1993.

Ahmad, Syed Nur *From Martial Law to Martial Law: Politics in the Punjab, 1919-58*, Vanguard, Lahore, 1985.

Ahmed, Feroz *Ethnicity and Politics in Pakistan*, Oxford, Karachi, 1998.

Ahmed, Ishtiaq *State, Nation and Ethnicity in Contemporary South Asia*, Pinter, London, 1996.

Akbar, Muhammad *The Punjab Under the Mughals*, Idarah-i-Adabiyat-i-Dilli, 1974.

Akbar, M.J. *Nehru: The Making of India*, Viking, New Delhi, 1988.

Akira, Hirakawa *A History of Indian Buddhism: From Sakyamuni to Early Mahayana*, University of Hawaii, 1990.

Ali, Chaudhari Muhammad *The Emergence of Pakistan*, Columbia, New York, 1967.

Aligarh Muslim University *Medieval India: A Miscellany*, vol.4, Asia, Bombay, 1977.

Allen, Charles *A Glimpse of the Burning Plain*, Michael Joseph, London, 1986.

Allen, Douglas (ed.), *Religion and Political Conflict in South Asia: India, Pakistan, and Sri Lanka*, Greenwood Press, Westport, Conn., 1992.

Ambedkar, B.R. *Thoughts on Pakistan*, Thacker, Bombay, 1941.

Ambedkar, B.R. *Ranade, Gandhi and Jinnah*, Bombay, 1943.

Ambedkar, B.R. *What Congress and Gandhi Have Done to the Untouchables*, Thacker, Bombay, 1945.

Amin, Shahid *Event, Metaphor, Memory: Chauri Chaura*, Oxford, New Delhi, 1995.

Ansari, Zoe (ed.), *Life, Times and Works of Amir Khusrau Dehlavi*, Seventh Centenary National Amir Khusrau Society, n.d.

Apter, David E. (ed.), *The Legitimization of Violence*, Macmillan, London, 1997.

Bakker, J.I. *Gandhi and the Gita*, Canadian Scholars' Press, Toronto, 1993.

Barua, B.N. *Asoka and his Inscriptions*, New Age, Calcutta, 1946.

Basham, A.L. *The Wonder that was India*, Rupa, New Delhi, 1982.

Baxter, Craig, and Kennedy, Charles (ed.), *Pakistan 1997*, HarperCollins, New Delhi, 1998.

Besant, Annie (tr.), *The Bhagavad Gita*, The Theosophical Society, Madras, 1977.

Besant, Annie *Mahabharata: The Story of the Great War*, The Theosophical Publishing House, Adyar, Madras, 1992.

Bhalla, Alok (ed.), *Stories About the Partition of India*, 3 vols., Indus, New Delhi, 1994.

Bharatiya Itihaas Sankalan Samiti, *Kurukshetra Through the Ages*, Haryana, 1988.

Bhattacharjea, Ajit *Jayaprakash Narayan: A Political Biography*, Vikas, New Delhi, 1975.

Ehattacharya, Sukumar *The East India Company and the Economy of Bengal*, Luzak, London, 1954.

Bhave, Vinoba *Moved by Love*, Sat Sahitya Sahayogi Sangh, Hyderabad, 1994.

Birla, G.D. *A Talk on Bapu*, Sangeet Kala Mandir, Calcutta, 1981.

Bjorkman, James Warner (ed.), *Fundamentalism, Revivalists and Violence in South Asia*, Manohar, New Delhi, 1988.

Bolitho, Hector *Jinnah*, Greenwood Press, Westport, Connecticut.

Bondurant, Joan *Conquest of Violence*, Princeton, 1988.

Bose, Buddhadeva *The Book of Yudhisthir*, tr. Sujit Mukherjee, Sangam, Hyderabad, 1986.

Broehl, Jr., Wayne G. *Crisis of the Raj: The Revolt of 1857 Through British Lieutenants' Eyes*, Published for Dartmouth College by University Press of New England, Hanover and London, 1986.

Brown, Judith M. *Modern India: The Origins of an Asian Democracy*, Oxford, New York, 1994.

Bryant, Arthur *The Story of England: Makers of the Realm*, Collins, London, 1953.

Burke, S.M. *The Greatest Mogul*, Munshiram Manoharlal, New Delhi, 1989.

Burke, S.M., & Quraishi, Salim Al-Din *The British Raj in India: An Historical Review*, Oxford, Karachi.

Campbell-Johnson, Alan, *Mission with Mountbatten*, Robert Hale, London, 1972.

Chaitanya, Krishna *The Mahabharata: A Literary Study*, Clarion, New Delhi, 1985.

Chakravarti, Uma *The Social Dimensions of Early Buddhism*, Oxford, New Delhi, 1987.

Chakravarti, Uma *Rewriting History: The Life and Times of Pandita Ramabai*, Kali for Women, New Delhi, 1998.

Chakravarty, S.R. (ed.), *Bangladesh Under Mujib, Zia and Ershad*, Har-Anand, New Delhi, 1995.

Chakravarty, S.R. (ed.), *Foreign Policy of Bangladesh*, Har-Anand, New Delhi, 1994.

Chandra, Bipan *Communalism in India*, Vikas, New Delhi, 1984.

Chandra, Bipan, and others *India's Struggle for Independence*, Viking, New Delhi, 1987.

Chandra, Satish *Mughal Religious Policies, the Rajputs and the Deccan*, Vikas, Delhi, 1993.

Chatterjee, Partha *The Nation and its Fragments: Colonial and Postcolonial Histories*, Oxford, Delhi, 1997.

Chattopadhyaya, Brajadulal *Representing the Other? Sanskrit Sources and the Muslims*, Manohar, Delhi, 1998.

Cole, Owen *Sikhism and its Indian Context: 1469-1708*, Darton, Longman and Todd, London, 1984.

Committee for Rational Development, *Sri Lanka: The Ethnic Conflict*, Navrang, New Delhi, 1984.

Dalrymple, William *City of Djinns*, Indus, New Delhi, 1993.

Das, Durga (ed.), *Sardar Patel's Correspondence*, 10 vols. Navajivan, Ahmedabad.

Das, Sukla, *Socio-Economic Life of Northern India: c. A.D. 550 to A.D. 650*, Abhinav, New Delhi, 1980.

Das, Veena (ed.), *Mirrors of Violence: Communities, Riots and Survivors in South Asia*, Oxford, Delhi, 1996.

Desai, Mahadev *The Diary of Mahadev Desai*, Navajivan, Ahmedabad.

Desai, Mahadev *Day-to-day with Gandhi*, Navajivan, Ahmedabad.

Doke, Joseph J. *An Indian Patriot in South Africa*, Reprint, Publications Division, New Delhi, 1967.

Edwardes, Michael *A History of India*, The New English Library, London, 1967.

Edwardes, Michael *A Season in Hell: The Defence of the Lucknow Residency*, Hamish Hamilton, London, 1973.

Eisenstadt, S.N. *Post-Traditional Societies*, Norton, New York, 1973.

Eisenstadt, S.N. (ed.), *Orthodoxy, Heterodoxy, and Dissent in India*, Norton, New York, 1984.

Embree, Ainslie (ed.), *Sources of Indian Tradition*, vol.1, Columbia, New York, 1988.

Engineer, Asghar Ali (ed.), *The Shah Bano Controversy*, Orient Longman, Bombay, 1987.

Friedmann, Yohann (ed.), *Islam in Asia*, vol. 1, The Magnus Press, The Hebrew University, Jerusalem, 1984.

Gandhi, Gopal *Dara Shukoh: A Play*, Banyan, New Delhi, 1993.

Gandhi, Manu *Ekla Chalo Re*, Navajivan, Ahmedabad, 1957.

Gandhi, Mohandas K. *Autobiography*, Navajivan, 1927, first edition.

Gandhi, Rajmohan *The Good Boatman*, Viking, New Delhi, 1995.

Gandhi, Rajmohan *Patel: A Life*, Navajivan, Ahmedabad, 1990.

Gandhi, Rajmohan *Rajaji: A Life*, Penguin, New Delhi, 1997.

Gandhi, Rajmohan *Understanding the Muslim Mind*, Penguin, New Delhi, 1987.

Gopal, S. *Nehru*, 3 vols., Oxford, New Delhi.

Gore, M.S. *Non-Brahmin Movement in Maharashtra*, Segment, New Delhi, 1989.

Gore, M.S. *The Social Context of an Ideology: Ambedkar's Political and Social Thought*, Sage, New Delhi, 1993.

Graham, G.F.I. *The Life and Work of Sir Syed Ahmed Khan*, London, 1885.

Grewal, J.S. *The New Cambridge History of India: The Sikhs of the Punjab*, Cambridge University Press, 1990.

Guha, Ranajit *An Indian Historiography of India: A Nineteenth-Century Agenda and its Implications*, K.P. Bagchi & Company for Centre for Studies in Social Sciences, Calcutta, 1988.

Gupta, Narayani *Delhi Between Two Empires: 1803-1931*, Oxford, New Delhi, 1981.

Halbfass, Wilhelm *India and Europe: An Essay in Understanding*, SUNY, Albany, New York, 1988.

Hamilton, Edith *Mythology: Timeless Tales of Gods and Heroes*, New American Library, New York, 1969.

Hardgrave, Robert L., Jr *India: Government and Politics in a Developing Nation*, Harcourt Brace, 5th edition, 1994.

Harvey, Peter *An Introduction to Buddhism: Teachings, History and Practices*, Cambridge, 1995.

Hasan, Mushirul (ed.), *India's Partition: Process, Strategy and Mobilization*, Oxford, New Delhi, 1993.

Hasan, Mushirul (ed.), *India Partitioned*, Roli, New Delhi, 1995.

Hay, Stephen (ed.), *Sources of Indian Tradition*, vol.2, Columbia, New York, 1988.

Henderson, Michael *The Forgiveness Factor*, Grosvenor, London, 1996.

Hibbert, Christopher *The Great Mutiny: India 1857*, Penguin, London, 1980.

Hiltebeitel, Alf *The Cult of Draupadi*, 2 vols., University of Chicago Press, Chicago, 1988.

Hoyland, John (tr.), *Village Songs of Western India*, Prinit Press, Dublin, 1992.

Ikram, S.M. *Modern Muslim India*, Institute of Islamic Culture, Lahore.

Ilaiah, Kancha *Why I Am Not a Hindu*, Samya, Calcutta, 1996.

Iqbal, Afzal *Mohamed Ali*, Idarah-i-Adabiyat-i-Dilli, 1978.

Iyer, Raghavan (ed.), *The Essential Writings of Mahatma Gandhi*, Oxford, Delhi, 1996.

Jalal, Ayesha *Democracy and Authoritarianism in South Asia: A Comparative and Historical Perspective*, Cambridge University Press, 1995.

Jalal, Hamid, and Hasan, Khalid (ed.), *Politics of the People: Statements and Speeches of Zulfikar Ali Bhutto*, several vols., n.d.

Joshi, Chand *Bhindranwale: Myth and Reality*, Vikas, New Delhi, 1984.

Juergensmeyer, Mark *Religious Nationalism Confronts the Secular State*, Oxford, New Delhi, 1994.

Kakar, Sudhir *Colours of Violence*, Viking, New Delhi, 1995.

Keer, Dhananjay *Dr Ambedkar*, Popular, Bombay, 1954.

Khan, The Aga *Memoirs*, Cassell, London, 1954.

Khaliquzzaman, Choudhary *Pathway to Pakistan*, Pakistan Longman, Lahore, 1961.

Khosla, G.D. *Stern Reckoning*, Oxford, New Delhi, 1989 (Reprint).

Krishna, Brij *Gandhiji-ki-Dilli Diary*, 3 vols., Delhi, 1970.

Krishnadas *Seven Months with Mahatma Gandhi*, Ganesan, Madras, 1928.

Lal, P. *The Mahabharata of Vyasa*, Vikas, New Delhi, 1980.

Latif, Syad Muhammad *History of the Panjab*, 1889. Reprinted 1989 by Kalyani, New Delhi.

Limaye, Madhu *Prime Movers*, Radiant, New Delhi, 1985.

Ludden, David (ed.), *Contesting the Nation: Religion, Community, and the Politics of Democracy in India*, University of Pennsylvania Press, Philadelphia, 1996.

Madan, T.N. *Modern Myths, Locked Minds*, Oxford, New Delhi, 1997.

Major, Andrew *Return to Empire: Punjab Under the Sikhs and British in the Mid-Nineteenth Century*, Sterling, New Delhi, 1996.

Malik, Hafeez *Moslem Nationalism in India and Pakistan*, Public Affairs Press, Washington D.C., 1963.

Malik, Hafeez *Sir Sayyid Ahmad Khan*, Columbia, New York, 1980.

Mamoon, Muntassir, and Ray, Jayanta Kumar, *Civil Society in Bangladesh: Resilience and Retreat*, Firma KLM, Calcutta, 1996.

Maniruzzaman, Talukdar *Politics and Security of Bangladesh*, University Press, Dhaka, 1994.

Mansergh, N., and Lumby E.W.R. (ed.), *The Transfer of Power* (12 vols.), HMSO, London, 1970-83.

Masani, M.R. *Against the Tide*, Vikas, New Delhi, 1981.

Matilal, Bimal Krishna (ed.), *Moral Dilemmas in the Mahabharata*, Indian Institute of Advanced Study in association with Motilal Banarsidass, Delhi, 1989.

Mazumdar, Subash *Who is Who in the Mahabharata*, Bhavan, Bombay, 1990.

McLeod, W.H. *The Evolution of the Sikh Community*, Oxford, New Delhi, 1994.

Mehta, Ashoka, and Nair, Kusum *The Simla Triangle*, Padma, Bombay, 1945.

Mende, Tibor *Conversations with Nehru*, Wilco, Bombay, 1958.

Menon, V.P. *The Transfer of Power in India*, Orient Longman, Calcutta, 1957.

Moon, Penderel (ed.), *Wavell: The Viceroy's Journal*, Oxford, London, 1973.

Moon, Sir Penderel *The British Conquest and Dominion of India*, Duckworth, London, 1989.

Moran, Lord *Winston Churchill*, Constable, London, 1966.

Mujeeb, Muhammad *Dr Zakir Husain*, National Book Trust, New Delhi, 1972.

Mukherjee, Rudrangshu *Awadh in Revolt: 1857-58*, Oxford, New Delhi, 1984.

Munshi, K.M. *Pilgrimage to Freedom*, Bhavan, Bombay, 1967.

Muztar, Balkrishna *Kurukshetra: Political and Cultural History*, B.R.Publishing, Delhi, 1978.

Nehru, Jawaharlal *Glimpses of World History*, Asia, Bombay, 1965 edition.

Nandy, Ashis *The Intimate Enemy: Loss and Recovery of Self under Colonialism*, Oxford, New Delhi, 1983.

Oberoi, Harjot *The Construction of Religious Boundaries: Culture, Identity & Diversity in the Sikh Tradition*, Oxford, Delhi, 1994.

Omvedt, Gail *Dalit Vision*, Orient Longman, New Delhi, 1995.

Pandit, R.S. (tr.), *Kalhana's Rajatarangini*, Sahitya Akademi, New Delhi, 1968.

Patel, Jehangir, and Sykes, Marjorie *Gandhi: His Gift of the Fight*, Friends Rural Centre, Rasulia, 1987.

Parikh, Narahari *Sardar Vallabhbhai Patel*, Navajivan, Ahmedabad, 1971.

Pemble, John *The Raj, the Indian Mutiny and the Kingdom of Oudh: 1801-1859*, Oxford, New Delhi, 1977.

Philips, C.H., and Wainwright, Mary D. *The Partition of India: Polices and Perspectives, 1935-1947*, Allen & Unwin, London, 1970.

Pirzada, S.S. (ed.), *Foundations of Pakistan: All-India Muslim League Documents*, National Publishing House, Karachi.

Pirzada, S.S. *Some Aspects of Quaid-i-Azam's Life*, National Commission on Historical and Cultural Research, Islamabad, 1978.

Pollock, Sheldon 'Ramayana and Political Imagination in India,' *The Journal of Asian Studies* 52, no. 2 (May 1993).

Prasad, Rajendra *Politico-Geographical Analysis of the Arthasastra*, Inter-India Publications, New Delhi, 1989.

Publications Division, Ministry of Information & Broadcasting, *Amir Khusrau: Memorial Volume*, New Delhi, 1975.

Publications Division, Ministry of Information & Broadcastsing, *The Gazetteer of India*, vol. 2, New Delhi, 1990.

Pyarelal *The Epic Fast*, Navajivan, Ahmedabad, 1932.

Pyarelal *Mahatma Gandhi: The Last Phase*, 2 vols., Navajivan, Ahmedabad, 1956.

Pyarelal *Mahatma Gandhi: The Early Phase*, Navajivan, Ahmedabad, 1965.

Radhakrishnan, S. *Indian Philosophy*, vol. 1, Oxford, New Delhi, 1994.

Rajagopalachari, C. *Mahabharata*, Bhavan, Bombay, 1968.

Ramachandran, G. *Thoughts and Talks*, Madurai, 1964.

Rawlinson, H.G. *A Concise History of the Indian People*, Oxford, Madras, 1958.

Raychaudhuri, Tapan *Three Views of Europe from Nineteenth-Century Bengal*, K.P. Bagchi & Company for Centre for Studies in Social Sciences, Calcutta, 1987.

Richardson Jr., John M., & Samarasinghe, S.W.R. de A. *Democratisation in South Asia: The First Fifty Years*, International Centre for Ethnic Studies, Kandy, 1998.

Ross, Nancy Wilson *Buddhism: A Way of Life and Thought*, Knopf, New York, 1980.

Rustin, Bayard *Down the Lane*, Quadrangle, Chicago, 1971.

Sardesai, D.R. and Mohan, Anand (ed.), *The Legacy of Nehru: A Centennial Assessment*, Promilla, New Delhi, 1992.

Sarkar, Sumit *Modern India: 1885-1947*, Macmillan, Madras, 1996.

Sastri, K.A. Nilakanta *A History of South India*, Oxford, New Delhi, 1955.

Sastry, R. Shama *Kautilya's Arthasastra*, Mysore, Reprinted 1967.

Sen, S.N. *Eighteen-Fiftyseven*, New Delhi, 1958.

Seshadri, H.V. *The Tragic Story of Partition*, Bangalore, 1982.

Sharp, Gene *Gandhi Wields the Weapon of Moral Power*, Navajivan, Ahmedabad, 1960.

Shriver, Donald W., Jr., *An Ethic for Enemies: Forgiveness in Politics*, Oxford, New York, 1995.

Shukla, C.S. (ed.), *Incidents in Gandhiji's Life*, Vora, Bombay, 1949.

Singh, Harbans, *Guru Tegh Bahadur*, Manohar, New Delhi, 1994.

Singh, Iqbal *Gautama Buddha*, Oxford, New Delhi, 1994

Singh, Gopal *Guru Gobind Singh*, National Book Trust, New Delhi, 1992.

Singh, Khushwant *A History of the Sikhs*, 2 vols., Princeton University Press, 1966.

Singh, Khushwant *How the Sikhs Lost their Kingdom*, UBS Publishers, New Delhi, 1996.

Singhvi, L.M. *The Jain Declaration of Nature*.

Smith, R. Bosworth *Life of Lord Lawrence*, 2 vols., Charles Scribner's Sons, New York, 1883.

Sobhan, Rehman *Bangladesh: Problems of Governance*, Konark, New Delhi, 1993.

Spear, Percival *Twilight of the Mughuls*, Oriental Books Reprint, New Delhi, 1969.

Subramaniam, Kamala *Mahabharata*, Bhavan, Bombay, 1988.

Sukthankar, V.S. *The Meaning of the Mahabharata*, Asiatic Society, Bombay, 1957.

Symonds, Richard *The Making of Pakistan*, Faber and Faber, London, 1950.

Talbot, Ian *Punjab and the Raj: 1849-1947*, Riverdale, Maryland, 1988.

Tambiah, S.J. *Sri Lanka: Ethnic Fratricide & the Dismantling of Democracy*, Oxford, Delhi, 1986.

Tendulkar, D.G. *Mahatma*, 8 vols., Bombay, 1951.

Thapar, Romila *Asoka and the Decline of the Mauryas*, Oxford, New Delhi, 1990.

Thapar, Romila *A History of India*, vol. 1, Pelican, U.K., 1986.

Thapar, Romila *Time as a Metaphor of History: Early India*, Oxford, New Delhi, 1996.

Tilak, Bal Gangadhar *Srimad Bhagavadgita-Rahasya*, English translation by B.S. Sukthankar, 2nd edition, Poona, 1965.

Trevaskis, Hugh *The Land of the Five Rivers: An Economic History of the Punjab*, Oxford University Press, London, 1928.

Trevelyan, G.O. *Cawnpore*, 1865, republished by the Empire Book Association, Brentwood, 1986.

Uberoi, J.P.S. *Religion, Civil Society and the State: A Study of Sikhism*, Oxford, Delhi, 1996.

Van Buitenen, J.A.B. (tr. & ed.), *The Bhagavadgita in the Mahabharata*, University of Chicago Press, Chicago, 1981.

Verghese, B.G. *India's Northeast Resurgent: Ethnicity, Insurgency, Governance, Development*, Konark, New Delhi, 1996.

Watson, Francis *Talking of Gandhiji*, Orient Longman, Calcutta, 1957.

Wedderburn, William *Allan Octavian Hume: Father of the Indian National Congress*, T. Fisher Unwin, London, 1913.

Wiesenthal, Simon, *The Sunflower: On the Possibilities and Limits of Forgiveness*, Schocken, New York, 1997.

Wilkinson, Theon *Two Monsoons*, Duckworth, London, 1976.

Wilson, A. Jeyaratnam, and Dalton, Dennis *The States of South Asia: Problems of National Integration*, Vikas, New Delhi, 1982.

Wolpert, Stanley *Jinnah*, Oxford, New York, 1984.

Wolpert, Stanley *A New History of India*, Oxford, New York, 1997.

Yagnik, Indulal *Gandhi As I Knew Him*, Danish Mahal, New Delhi, 1943.

Zafarullah, Habib (ed.), *The Zia Episode in Bangladesh Politics*, South Asian Publishers, New Delhi, 1996.

Zaheer, Hasan *The Separation of East Pakistan: The Rise and Realization of Bengali Muslim Nationalism*, Oxford, Karachi, 1994.

Zakaria, Rafiq (ed.), *A Study of Nehru*, Rupa, New Delhi, 1989.

Zakaria, Rafiq *The Widening Divide: An Insight into Hindu-Muslim Relations*, Viking, New Delhi, 1995.

Ziring, Lawrence *Bangladesh From Mujib to Ershad: An Interpretive Study*, Oxford, Karachi, 1992.

Index

PREFACE